Intelligence and Giftedness

Miles D. Storfer

Intelligence
and
Giftedness

*The Contributions of Heredity
and Early Environment*

Jossey-Bass Publishers

San Francisco   •   Oxford   •   1990

INTELLIGENCE AND GIFTEDNESS
The Contributions of Heredity and Early Environment
by Miles D. Storfer

Copyright © 1990 by: Jossey-Bass Inc., Publishers
350 Sansome Street
San Francisco, California 94104

Jossey-Bass Limited
Headington Hill Hall
Oxford OX3 0BW

Miles D. Storfer
350 Bayview Avenue
Manhasset, New York 11030

155
S 884 i
1990

Library of Congress Cataloging-in-Publication Data

Storfer, Miles D.
    Intelligence and giftedness : the contributions of heredity and
early environment / Miles D. Storfer.
        p.   cm. — (The Jossey-Bass social and behavioral science
series) (The Jossey-Bass education series)
    Includes bibliographical references.
    ISBN 1-55542-185-7
    1. Intellect—Genetic aspects.   2. Intellect—Social aspects.
3. Nature and nurture.   4. Gifted persons.   I. Title.   II. Series.
III. Series: The Jossey-Bass education series.
BF431.S755   1990
155—dc20 (alk. paper)   89-45593
                                                          CIP

Manufactured in the United States of America

JACKET DESIGN BY WILLI BAUM

FIRST EDITION

Code 9004

A joint publication in

The Jossey-Bass
Social and Behavioral Science Series

and

The Jossey-Bass Education Series

ꝏ Contents ꝏ

ᴚ *Preface* ᴚ

The "nature-nurture" controversy is, in essence, a debate about the basis of human intelligence. At one extreme are those who argue that a person's intelligence is determined almost exclusively by heredity—that is, by the genes that an individual inherits from his or her parents. At the other extreme are people convinced that a person's environment has much more to do with how well that person performs on an IQ test than does his or her heredity.

This controversy is of far more than academic interest, since a society's views concerning the extent to which lasting changes in intelligence can be stimulated, stunted, and shaped by the environment are likely to have a considerable impact on its educational and child-rearing philosophies. For example, people who believe that intelligence is almost entirely a function of one's genes would tend to view the basic responsibilities of parents during infancy and toddlerhood as taking care of their baby's physical and emotional needs and (except for providing a modest amount of sensory and verbal stimulation) allowing the child's intellectual development to proceed "naturally." Conversely, if one thinks that the "cognitive environment" during a child's initial years can exert a considerable and lasting influence on measured intelligence, then providing parents and

professional caregivers with information about child development, including the specifics of highly successful early cognitive
enrichment programs, becomes of vital importance in ensuring
that children come close to achieving their innate intellectual
potential.

Child-rearing practices have undergone a dramatic shift in
the past generation. Before that, mothers devoted most of their
time to caring for their young children, and this care was often
supplemented by extended family members who lived in close
geographical proximity. Now, however, a majority of mothers
reenter the work force while their children are still infants or
toddlers, and substantial involvement of grandparents or aunts
and uncles in child rearing is unusual. As a result, a portion of
the twentieth-century rise in IQ scores is in jeopardy, because
parents are unable to give their children the amount of "cognitive nurturing" that their own parents provided to them during the so-called critical periods of early brain development,
when key cell-network connections are being established and
are very responsive to environmental experience.

The Purposes of This Book

The primary objectives of *Intelligence and Giftedness* are:

- To demonstrate that—even though human intelligence
  is primarily a function of heredity—the quality of children's educational environments during infancy and
  toddlerhood can make a dramatic and lasting difference in their measured intelligence.
- To identify those features in the early home environment that affect intellectual development, with a particular emphasis on those that are of greatest importance
  in normal- and above-average-IQ populations.
- To detail the nature of highly successful IQ-raising
  programs begun in infancy and toddlerhood.
- To interrelate information about the major stages of
  brain and behavioral development and to use this

knowledge to suggest a rationale for effective stage-dependent "infant and toddler lessons."

- To provide organized, integrated, and well-documented summaries of the literature that relates human intelligence to familial, prenatal, and early environmental variables.
- To offer an alternative to certain widely held beliefs concerning the nature and pace of human intellectual evolution.

This book differs markedly from other works on the same general subject in several respects. To begin with, no previous book has attempted a comprehensive analysis of the factors that influence intelligence and giftedness. Second, it integrates findings from a number of behavioral and biological disciplines that have never before been brought together in a single volume. Third, in assessing relationships between IQ and those environmental factors thought to influence it, this volume focuses on findings from longitudinal studies of middle-class and upper-middle-class families rather than on findings about at-risk populations. Fourth, it establishes explicit standards for the quality of the IQ-test data to be included in the analysis of longitudinal studies; by applying these standards the incidence of conflicting data is considerably reduced. Fifth, it takes methodologies that have long been a mainstay of quantitative analysis in other social sciences and applies these to issues that have important implications for public policies — for example, the question of the IQ disparity between Blacks and Whites. Sixth, it advances several new theories that link neurobiology and behavior. These theories span such areas as the "stages" of infancy and toddlerhood (and their relationship to alternating hemispheric "growing seasons"), the biological foundations of intellectual giftedness, and the nature and pace of human intellectual evolution.

Intended Audience

Intelligence and Giftedness has been written for a number of diverse groups:

- For professionals and graduate students in the fields of child development, early childhood education, and educational testing, it provides an up-to-date assessment of factors in the early environment that influence the development of intelligence, an evaluation of the stages of early cognitive development, a discussion of several highly successful programs and strategies for increasing infants' and toddlers' IQ and language skills, and an extensive list of books, monographs, and articles that can serve as a ready reference for information about the factors that influence the development of intelligence.
- For professionals and graduate students in the fields of cognitive psychology, developmental neurobiology, and evolutionary biology and anthropology, it integrates the numerous findings that link early behavioral development with biological growth in those brain regions responsible for higher brain function; it provides a wealth of otherwise difficult-to-obtain information about the nature of intelligence and giftedness, as well as the nature of genes and the forces that govern their expression; and it advances several controversial and thought-provoking new theories.
- For practitioners in the fields of pediatric nursing and the care of homeless infants, it stresses the nature and extent of cognitive deficits that may result from low birth weight and/or the absence of maternal involvement, as well as the kinds of early sensory stimulation needed to avert or alleviate these deficits.
- For policymakers in governmental agencies and philanthropic foundations concerned with the field of education, it suggests various ways to provide early educational nourishment and to structure programs for the education of child-care workers and parents.

Because of its focus on the nature and development of intellectual giftedness and the characteristics of intellectually gifted people, *Intelligence and Giftedness* should also be of interest to organizations that advocate programs for, or deal with the problems and challenges of, gifted children. It should also appeal to all those who are curious about the nature of intelligence and giftedness, including college-educated parents and soon-to-be parents and grandparents, because it has a great deal of information about general approaches to, and specific techniques for, accelerating the cognitive development of infants and toddlers of above-average intelligence.

Although most well-educated people have a basic understanding of the nature and workings of such vital parts of the bodies as the heart, lungs, kidneys, and stomach, these same people may know next to nothing about the workings of those parts of the brain that govern mental function. In addition to providing such a basic understanding, this book also presents a detailed synopsis of recent research into the nature and function of our genes. Further, much of the information provided here about early postnatal brain development (and its links to behavioral development) would be otherwise almost impossible to obtain, short of undertaking an intense scrutiny of traditional sources.

Overview of the Contents

This book is organized into six parts. Part One assesses findings about IQ relationships within nuclear and adoptive families from a variety of perspectives. Thus, it (1) examines identical twins reared together and the effects of differences in twins' birth weights on their IQ scores; (2) quantifies the effects of family configuration (parental ages, birth order, family size, and child spacing) on intelligence; (3) presents the family configurations of intellectually gifted and/or eminent populations; (4) analyzes findings about within-family IQ correspondences; (5) presents the results of adoption studies, which are then used to suggest the magnitude of the "IQ uplift" likely to result when a child is reared in a highly nurturing home; and (6) integrates these findings into a model designed to depict the effects of early environmental nurture on intelligence.

Part Two begins by describing long-term trends in IQ scores across the developed world and presents evidence that links changes in IQ scores over time to the socioeconomic conditions prevalent during the test taker's early upbringing. It then examines trends in people's cognitive abilities across adulthood and suggests some of the ramifications of rising intelligence (in terms of increased twentieth-century living standards). The IQ disparity between Blacks and Whites is discussed in light of these trends, and the probable contributions of differences in family configuration, social class, and intrauterine environment to this disparity are assessed. The results demonstrate that this disparity is neither endemic nor immutable.

Part Three evaluates the effects of the early home environment on IQ through an analysis of the results of longitudinal studies of middle-class and upper-middle-class families. This is preceded by an assessment of various infant, preschool, and early-school-age cognitive tests in terms of their ability to prognosticate later IQ scores. This part of the book describes a number of maternal/infant interactive behaviors that seem to have a strong influence on later IQ performance, and it highlights differences in the extent to which parents engage in these behaviors with firstborn and laterborn children. It then presents information about effective behavioral control and educational practices during toddlerhood and supplements this information with findings from studies of the early educational environments of gifted and eminent populations.

Part Four begins by presenting information about highly successful educational enrichment programs begun in infancy and/or toddlerhood. There follows a detailed analysis of cognitive development during early infancy, with a view to structuring interactive behaviors and paradigms for "infant lessons" in ways that will promote cognitive development. Part Four then gives recommendations for furthering the development of language-comprehension abilities during infancy and toddlerhood. Finally, it compares and contrasts the traditional childrearing and early educational practices of two ethnic populations whose members display a tendency to score well above the norm in specific cognitive domains: the Japanese people, who tend to excel in those aspects of intelligence that involve a visuospatial, structural, and perceptual mode of analysis, and the Jewish people, whose tendency to excel encompasses the verbal, symbolic, and conceptual domains.

Part Five focuses on differentiating the various types of intellect and giftedness and on relating these to the biology of the brain. It summarizes the functions of our two brain hemispheres and describes the three relatively distinct memory systems that underlie intellect. It also makes some major distinctions among a number of highly valued domains of intellect and relates these domains to hemispheric functions and the three memory systems. Following that, it explores possible links between high IQ, on the one hand, and specific intellectual gifts, creativity, originality, and complex problem-solving skills, on the other. Part Five then discusses extraordinary intellectual giftedness in terms of some unusual biological characteristics that are disproportionately found in gifted populations (including myopia, immune disorders, left-handedness, high uric-acid levels, and differences in sleep cycles) and relates intelligence to the rate at which the brain processes information. It concludes by advancing some theories concerning possible relationships between intellectual giftedness and brain biology.

Part Six begins with an assessment of the contributions of improved health care and other environmental factors to the twentieth-century IQ increase. It then proposes the theory that much of this IQ rise is attributable to the ability of early environmental stimulation to alter the "developmental program" that governs genetic expression in the brain. Findings from a variety of disciplines are offered in support of this controversial theory, including the results of an evaluation of factors that affect the rates of evolution in animals as well as a discussion of recent findings from animal studies. Further support for this theory comes from studies of various human ethnogeographic populations — studies that reveal connections between cultural imperatives, early child-rearing practices, and those cognitive domains in which populations subjected to these practices tend to excel. The results suggest that intellect can in fact be shaped by child-rearing practices. Perhaps even more important, the high degree of cognitive skills possessed by some ethnographic groups suggests that a multigenerational process is at work—

rather than a process in which a single generation of training creates these abilities.

The appendix quantifies the relationship between intra-uterine problems and intelligence and suggests early intervention strategies.

Some people may feel that this book has an overly strong focus on IQ and on efforts to increase it and that IQ is not nearly the unidimensional, easily quantifiable, and "all-important" factor that they think this book makes it out to be. However, despite a number of shortcomings, comprehensive IQ tests are reasonably consistent indicators of the ability to solve the kinds of problems that the psychological testing community has judged to provide a balanced assessment of important cognitive skills. Second, considerable attention has been paid to the relative importance of the "factor loadings" of IQ tests and to differentiating among the various aspects of intelligence and giftedness. Finally, a person's IQ score is still the single most reliable and objective determinant of his or her employment status, job performance, and income—with each incremental IQ point being associated with more than $1,000 a year in income.

A Note on Format

Because of the variety of readers to whom this book is directed, considerable attention has been paid to balancing the technical needs of professionals in such fields as child development and cognitive neuroscience with the more general needs of educated laypeople, who may primarily want to know more about intellectual giftedness or find out how to enrich their children's learning environment. To this end, an extensive use has been made of various formats. For instance, the notes at the ends of chapters provide detailed information about the studies summarized, integrate neurobiological information with behavioral findings, provide technical neurobiological data and explanations, and provide interesting asides. In addition, some passages are set in smaller type to enable people with marginal interest in a particular topic to skim or skip over the detailed information provided. Liberal use is also made of italics, bold type, and combinations thereof to enable casual readers to locate the most salient information and conclusions quickly and easily. The detailed contents listings at the beginnings of chapters should also serve this purpose.

Acknowledgments

I wish to acknowledge the kind assistance of Adam Mathany, Jr., who supplied me with data on the IQ scores and birth weights of identical twins in the Louisville Twin Study, as well as Tom Su, who performed the correlations on these data. William Fowler provided me with a preview of his forthcoming book about the principles and practices underlying his highly successful educational enrichment programs, and Carolyn Rovee-Collier reviewed my initial efforts to summarize the foundations of infant lessons. To both of them I am very grateful.

I am also indebted to John Campbell for the clarity with which he has articulated recent understandings about genes, molecular biology, and the hereditary transmission of environmentally acquired tolerance, as well as for his review of my initial efforts to further simplify and clarify these complex subjects. In addition, I owe thanks to the many other researchers who supplied me with important information and insights, especially to Camilla Benbow, Victor Cicirelli, Michael Commons, Philip Drash, William Hahn, Ronald Lally, Marilyn Metzl, Meredith Olson, Raphael Patai, Kiki Roe, Julius Romanoff, Arnold Scheibel, and Robert Zenhausern. I would also like to thank Bernard Meisner for his helpful editorial comments concerning the initial drafts of several early chapters, Gracia Alkema (senior editor at Jossey-Bass) for her excellent advice concerning the organization of several chapters, and Angela Rolling and my daughter, Amy, for providing typing assistance under what were sometimes trying conditions.

A special note of thanks to Kristin Loomis is also in order. Her generous grant to the Foundation for Brain Research permitted the compilation and analysis of studies on the extent to which family configuration, birth weight, vestibular stimulation, and other maternal interactive behaviors affect IQ, of findings from adoption studies and highly successful IQ-raising programs, and of information related to the so-called critical periods of early development.

I would also like to express my gratitude to my parents for their having urged me to use my gifts of intellect to help make the world a better place and for the sacrifices they made that afforded me the opportunity to do so.

Manhasset, New York   Miles D. Storfer
February 1990

Intelligence and Giftedness

Part One

Factors Influencing
IQ Scores
Among Family Members

Four factors determine the measured intelligence of individuals: (1) their *heredity*, or the innate intellectual potential
conferred by their ancestors' genes; (2) the extent to which their
prenatal environment may have imposed limitations on this potential; (3) the ways in which their *postnatal environment* stimulated,
stunted, and shaped this potential; and (4) so-called *random
factors* related to the IQ test-taking situation.

Chapter One examines IQ correspondences among identical
twins reared together. Although identical genetically, the birth
weights of such twins often differ considerably, and the findings
in this area (although based on relatively small-sized samples)
suggest a clear tendency for the heavier twin in a pair to perform
better on cognitive tests than his or her co-twin. A large-scale
identical-twin birth-weight/IQ study would, by making it possible to evaluate how similar identical twins' IQ scores would be
with this "intrauterine factor" netted out, indicate how similar in
IQ genetically identical people reared in a nearly identical
environment are apt to be. Further, it would enable an estimate
to be made of the size of the random factor inherent in IQ test-
taking situations. To this end, raw data from the Louisville Twin
Study have been analyzed in detail. As set forth in Chapter One,
the results indicate that the magnitude of this random factor is

apt to be exceedingly small, which implies that comprehensive IQ tests such as the Stanford-Binet and the Wechsler provide a good approximation of most people's abilities in the cognitive skills that these tests are designed to measure.

A persuasively large body of studies amply demonstrates that intrauterine inadequacies (as reflected in such measurable surrogates as low birth weight, prematurity, and low "weight-for-date") will often affect IQ scores adversely and that a relatively long gestation and a relatively high birth weight are associated with above-average IQs. Presenting an organized, integrated, and detailed summary of this literature will serve several important purposes: (1) it will provide quantitative yardsticks for soon-to-be parents and health care professionals concerning the risks and consequences of several relatively widespread factors that (singly or in combination) often induce cognitive deficits; (2) it will help to distinguish those aspects of intelligence most prone to damage, which helps in suggesting effective early intervention strategies; and (3) it will serve as a "data base" for efforts to demark the contributions of the three other factors listed above to IQ differences in specific populations (for example, identical twins). However, because a detailed analysis of this subject is apt to be of considerable interest to only a small proportion of this book's readership, it is presented in the form of an appendix.

Chapter Two presents a detailed analysis of the effects on IQ of specific aspects of family configuration—including birth order, number and spacing of children, and parental ages when children are born—and this analysis makes it possible to assess the potency of these environmental factors, both individually and in combination. The significant effects on IQ of maternal age that appear across the entire age spectrum in all social classes provide a novel framework from which to view the much-discussed effects of birth order—effects that vary greatly in relation to economic class. This analysis, which incorporates the results of some extremely large studies, suggests that differences in early maternal nurturing have a good deal to do with these observed trends. These findings also suggest what—from an IQ perspective—are optimal family sizes and adequate child spacings.

An examination of the family configurations in which populations of gifted and/or eminent people were reared makes it clear that exceptionally favorable caretaker ratios during infancy and toddlerhood, older (more-mature) caregivers, and a special involvement of fathers or grandmothers in the gifted children's cognitive development are almost routine occurrences.

Chapter Three focuses on how within-family IQ correspondences vary in accordance with the degree of familial relatedness. Such findings tend to weigh heavily in researchers' assessments of the nature/nurture proportions — especially those findings that result from comparisons of identical twins with fraternal twins and fraternal twins with nontwin siblings. A detailed analysis of the extent to which certain types of "bias" inherent in the creation of within-family correlational data may have influenced the observed findings is thereby warranted. This is preceded by a simplified discussion of the meaning of the term *correlation*, with specific reference to IQ-point differences under the normal curve. This chapter also contains an assessment of the effects of family configuration and birth weight on siblings' IQ correlations. The results are then discussed in terms of their relationship both to a simple hereditary model of intelligence and to a heavily environmental model.

The primary question addressed in Chapter Four is, How much higher are the IQ scores of individuals reared in homes that are well above the norm in parental nurturing and cognitive stimulation, compared with the scores of individuals raised in homes that are somewhat below the norm? Because of the exceptionally high quality of the large majority of adoptive homes in several classic adoption studies, and because of the availability of IQ data for these adopted children's biological and adoptive parent(s) and/or siblings, it has been possible to assess the extent to which exposure to these adoptive homes caused the measured intelligence of these children to rise. The results of these studies indicate that nearly two-thirds of the gap between the IQs of the biological parents and the IQs of the adoptive parents and siblings was bridged — but not if the adoptive placement occurred after the middle of the second year (when the brain's speech strategy and speech execution cells are completing their "critical period" of rapid growth). These data also suggest that the quality of the parental nurture provided in an adoptive home is (except *in extremis*) of greater importance than the educational attainments or economic status of the adoptive parents.

Findings from adoption studies have, nonetheless, been frequently cited as providing strong evidence that heredity predominates over environment to a large extent — on the basis that, in most instances, a higher IQ correlation is found between an adopted child and its biological parent(s) than between that child and its adoptive parents. The appropriateness of using correlational data in this manner, however, will be seriously questioned.

Taken together, these findings suggest that, although heredity is usually more important than environment in determining intelligence, an exceptionally good or exceptionally deprived early upbringing can have a considerable and lasting effect on IQ. Chapter Four presents a model that suggests the likely shape of the "curvilinear function" depicting this proposed relationship between IQ and the cognitive quality of a child's early environment.

Contents

﹏ 1 ﹏

*What Studies
of Identical Twins
Tell Us About IQ*

1.0 Overview

As detailed in this chapter, the IQ scores of identical twins reared together are likely to be very similar, with existing differences averaging about one-third as large as those found among randomly selected people. Because identical twins are usually of differing birth weights and the lighter twin usually has a lower IQ score, evaluating this relationship between IQ and birth weight provides a unique opportunity to assess the effects of deficiencies in the intrauterine environment on IQ in people with identical genes and nearly identical postnatal environments.

This examination yields two important conclusions:

- When the average IQ disadvantage attributable to birth weight is subtracted from twins' IQ differences, the average within-pair IQ difference is reduced to about 4 IQ points. This strongly suggests that good-quality IQ tests do a realistic job of assessing individual differences in the particular skills that these tests are designed to measure.
- The slightly below average IQ scores registered by iden-

tical twins can be attributed to their less-than-adequate intrauterine environment; this is because the heavier twin in a pair is likely to have an IQ score equal to that of a nontwin of comparable birth weight and gestational age.

Because identical twins are much more alike in IQ than are fraternal twins — whose IQ correlations (as detailed in Chapter Three) barely exceed those of other siblings — this strongly implies that, for most people, IQ is determined more by heredity than by environment. The fact that identical twins' IQ scores show even greater similarity when the lighter-twin IQ disadvantage is factored out, further strengthens the hereditarian position in the nature-nurture debate.

1.1 Introduction

This chapter addresses the following questions: First, how similar are the IQs of people with identical genes and nearly identical environments (namely, monozygotic twins reared together)? Second, to what extent can differences in the intrauterine environment explain the within-pair IQ differences that are found? Third, how large is the remaining random factor, and what does the relative size of this factor tell us about the reliability of IQ tests?

As detailed in the appendix, a relatively low birth weight is likely to affect intelligence adversely, especially when accompanied by low weight-for-gestational-age (which is usually indicative of abnormally slow intrauterine growth). Twins are likely to be of low weight-for-date at birth, and they also have exceptionally high rates of prematurity. With respect to identical twins, a number of studies (detailed in this chapter) suggest that — in addition to the overall IQ disadvantage found in such twins — there is usually a within-pair difference favoring the heavier twin (whose birth-weight advantage averages about ten ounces). However, these studies suffer from a number of inadequacies: (1) the number of subjects per study has usually been very small; (2) comprehensive IQ measures have generally not been employed; (3) there has been some inconsistency between studies concerning the size of the heavier-twin advantage; (4) the published data usually do not provide sufficient detail to enable the testing of specific hypotheses; and (5) because most of these studies are older ones, they do not provide a sense of whether improvements in neonatal and infant care have reduced the IQ disadvantage of twins in general and the lighter-birth-weight disadvantage of identical twins in particular.

To clarify these issues, I have assembled and analyzed data from the Louisville Twin Study. This study constitutes what is by far the largest study containing information concerning birth weight and the results of periodic IQ testing of identical twins. It is also among the few that have employed a well-respected comprehensive IQ test (the Wechsler) that was administered after the twins reached an age when (as detailed in Chapter Seven) most children's scores are likely to resemble their IQ in adulthood (age six). These findings support the conclusion that differences in birth weight are an important factor in intrapair IQ differences, particularly when twin pairs in which both twins were of "normal" birth weight are excluded.

The appendix to this book (1) presents detailed findings that relate intelligence to birth weight, gestational age, and head circumference in nontwin populations; (2) describes the nature of the cognitive deficits that children who experience intra-uterine deficiencies are likely to demonstrate; and (3) discusses the effects of various early-intervention strategies designed to reduce or prevent cognitive impairments in these at-risk populations.

1.2 IQ Correspondence
Between Identical Twins Reared Together

There is general agreement that identical twins reared in the same household are likely to have very similar IQ scores. Three separate comprehensive surveys of the literature (Bouchard and McGue, 1981;[1] Scarr and Carter-Salzman, 1982;[2] and Erlenmeyer-Kimling and Jarvik, 1963[3]) each report IQ correlations among identical twin pairs of +.86—meaning that their

IQ-point differences will (on the average) be only one-third as large as those found between pairs of people selected randomly from a large heterogeneous population (for a general discussion of the terms *correlation* and *variance* as these terms apply to IQ scores, see Chapter Three, section 3).

The cognitive similarities of identical twins go well beyond the overall assessment of general intelligence that IQ scores reflect. For example, among 1,360 twin pairs taking the National Merit Scholarship Qualifying Test, the identical-twin correlation was also + .86 (Loehlin and Nichols, 1976; Nichols, 1965); and, in another study (Husen, 1960), correlations of + .89 in reading achievement and + .87 in arithmetic achievement were found among 134 identical twin pairs.

Despite these extremely close correlational proximities, the average difference in the IQ scores of identical twins is still about 6 points—compared with an average difference of about 18 points among randomly selected people. Because identical twins have identical genes and are exposed to a nearly identical postnatal environment, within-pair IQ differences may be thought of as a product of two factors: (1) differences in their intrauterine environment and (2) a random factor inherent in the IQ test-taking situation.

Numerous studies have been designed to identify and quantify the effects of a less-than-optimal intrauterine environment on intelligence, and these have concluded that *birth weight*, either singly or in combination with gestational age, does in fact influence IQ performance. A summary of the literature (contained in the appendix) confirms the validity of birth weight/weight-for-date as a mechanism for identifying those circumstances in which it is likely that IQ will be adversely affected, and suggests that certain aspects of cognitive functioning are more prone to substantial impairment than are others.

Identical-twin pairs often display a considerable birth-weight disparity—the average difference being nearly 10 percent of their total birth weight, or about 300 grams (Benirschke and Harper, 1977)—and findings from studies addressing this correspondence support the conclusion that an IQ advantage favoring the heavier twin does exist.

The size of this advantage is of more than passing interest in the nature-nurture debate, because the smaller the within-pair IQ differences, the greater the disparity between identical-twin and fraternal-twin correlations and the stronger the hereditarian position. Harry Munsinger (1977), for example, argues that IQ correlations among identical twins would be substantially higher (perhaps as high as +.95) were it not for the systematic variability accompanying this heavier-twin IQ advantage. He suggests that this heavier-twin advantage arises principally as a result of the so-called transfusion syndrome, but this hypothesis has been challenged by Leon Kamin (1978), a strong defender of the environmentalist position.

Unfortunately, there are few studies linking twins' IQs with their birth weights, and several of the available studies summarize results without including individual-twin birth weights, making it difficult or impossible to perform more-detailed data analyses. Further, most of these conclusions are based on studies of children born in the middle third of the twentieth century, and the considerable advances in neonatal and infant care since that time could have moderated the deleterious effects of low birth weight on IQ. Thus, I have undertaken to analyze information from a large, more recent twin study, namely, the Louisville Twin Study (these data were supplied through the courtesy of Adam Matheny, Jr., director of the project).

1.3 Birth Weight and Intelligence Among Twins: Aggregate Data

Twins, on average, have lower IQs and lower birth weights than do singletons. For example, a British study, which reported on "Verbal IQ" scores for 2,164 twins and more than 47,000 singletons (Record, McKeown, and Edwards, 1970), found an average IQ of 95.7 among twins—4.4 points below that found for singletons. This finding is consistent with other reports in the literature.

The comprehensive analysis of the relationship between intelligence and birth weight/weight-for-date in nontwin populations presented in the appendix makes it clear that (1) larger and more-frequent IQ deficits can be expected at progressively lower birth weights and that (2) among low-weight-for-gestational-age infants, the frequency and severity of such deficits increase markedly. Because twins' birth-weight and weight-for-date averages are substantially below those of singletons, the impact of these adverse effects on twins is magnified.

The lower birth-weight average found among twins is a product of three factors:

- A greater incidence of premature births. For example, data from the Louisville Twin Study (Wilson, 1986) indicate that a fifth of the (identical and fraternal) twins were born before the end of the thirty-fourth week of gestation and that another fourth were born between weeks thirty-five and thirty-seven.
- Lower birth weights among full-term twins. For example, the *median* birth weight of full-term twins (thirty-eight to forty weeks) in the Louisville study (Ramey and others, 1984) was only 2,638 grams (5.8 pounds), with only 10 percent weighing more than 3,250 grams; by comparison, only 7 percent of all U.S.-born children weighed less than 2,500 grams.
- The birth-weight decrement of the lighter twin in weight-discordant twin pairs.

Thus, lighter twins enter the world with a twofold disadvantage—being lighter by reason of being a twin and being lighter because they are not able to obtain as adequate a level of prenatal nutrition as their co-twins.

1.4 Historical Findings:
IQ and Birth Weight Among Identical Twins

Only two published studies provide individual birth-weight and IQ data for an appreciable number of school-age or older identical-twin pairs. One provides information for twenty-five sets of White, female, identical twins and triplets in the Boston area (Scarr, 1982), and the other contains data for twenty Caucasian and seven Black identical-twin pairs in Michigan (Willerman and Churchill, 1967). In analyzing the relationships between IQ and birth weight found in these studies, I will test two hypotheses: (1) if the lighter twin in a pair weighs at least 6.5 pounds (2,950 grams) at birth, the birth-weight deficit of the lighter twin

Table 1. Comparison of Heavier- and Lighter-Twin IQ Scores.

	IQ Average		Heavier-Twin Advantage
Study and Sample Size	Heavier Twin	Lighter Twin	
Scarr (18 families)	104.8	95.1	9.7
Willerman and Churchill (17 families)	102.8	95.0	7.8
Combined (35 families)	103.8	95.1	8.7

Note: Data shown are for those Caucasian families in which one or both twins (triplets) weighed less than 6.5 pounds and the birth-weight disparity was at least 20 grams.

will have little or no impact on measured intelligence; and (2) twins who are extremely similar in birth weight (defined as less than 20 grams apart in weight) will not be subject to an IQ differential favoring the heavier twin. In this analysis, data from the seven Black twin pairs are excluded because their birth weights were extremely low and their IQ scores averaged only 72.[4]

The aggregate results support the finding that lower birth weights "beget" lower IQs. In the Caucasian families, the eighteen children with birth weights below 2,000 grams had IQs averaging 91.2—compared with 97.8 for the twenty-five children who weighed between 2,000 and 2,490 grams at birth and with 103.9 for the forty-four children weighing above 2,500 grams.

After application of the "exclusion criteria" discussed above, a comparison of the lighter and heavier twins' IQs (presented in Table 1) shows a strong (8.7 point) average heavier-twin IQ advantage. For the six pairs in which both twins weighed above 6.5 pounds, however, the heavier-twin advantage was apt to be much smaller (averaging only 1.8 points) and more variable. Moreover, in two of the three pairs where birth-weight differences were negligible or nonexistent (20 grams or less), the twins' IQ scores were identical.

Somewhat surprisingly (in light of some of the other findings cited below), the ***extent*** of the difference in birth weight did not have a material impact on the IQ-point difference found; in the

sixteen twin pairs where there was more than a 300-gram difference, the heavier-twin advantage averaged 8.3 points — compared with 9.1 points for the nineteen twin pairs who were 30 to
300 grams apart at birth.

The following studies report only aggregate data comparing
IQs for "highly weight discordant" twin pairs or provide only
aggregate comparisons between "highly discordant" and "less
discordant" twin populations:

- A Polish study (St. Lis, 1974),[5] which compared the IQs of twin
  pairs "dissimilar" in birth weight. After excluding children tested
  prior to age three, the study found a heavier-twin advantage averaging 8.1 points in the fourteen pairs with the greatest weight
  discordance (101.2 vs. 93.1), compared with a 1.2-point average
  advantage in the thirteen "more similar" birth-weight pairs (100.7
  vs. 99.5). Unfortunately, actual birth weights were not provided.
- A study (Babson and others, 1964) containing data from nine
  identical-twin pairs varying in weight by at least 25 percent (with
  one or both twins weighing less than 2,000 grams), which reported
  a heavier-twin advantage averaging 6.6 points. Here, however, in
  five of the nine pairs, the twins' IQs were within 3 points of one
  another, with the majority of the IQ discordance being attributable to two extreme cases.
- A study of forty-four identical-twin pairs (Kaelber and Pugh, 1969),
  which found a 5.1-point heavier-twin advantage among the seventeen pairs with at least a 300-gram birth-weight difference but only
  a 0.5 IQ-point difference among the twenty-seven pairs whose birth
  weights were less far apart.

A study of preschool children, which included twenty-seven
White and forty-eight Black identical-twin pairs and excluded
twins who were extremely similar in birth weight (Fujikura and
Froelich, 1974) reported a 10-point between-pair IQ difference
on the Stanford-Binet test at age four. Among the Caucasian
twin pairs, however, the heavier-twin advantage averaged only
2.4 points — including 0.8 points for the sixteen twin pairs who
were weight discordant by less than 15 percent and 4.7 points for
the eleven "extremely weight-discordant" pairs.

Although clearly supportive of the existence of a heavier-twin
IQ advantage, this record is inconsistent, both with respect to
the size of the lighter-twin IQ decrement and in terms of whether
it validates a hypothesis (suggested by Babson and others, 1964)

that an especially significant IQ difference is likely to occur in so-called transfusion-syndrome cases. In this syndrome, which afflicts an estimated 22 percent of identical twins (Munsinger, 1977), one member of the twin pair is in effect a blood donor to the other and thus suffers impaired prenatal circulation (resulting in a markedly lower birth weight). Further, the results of Scarr's study are somewhat flawed by the nature of the IQ measure used (the Goodenough Draw-A-Person Test). Although scores on this test tend to correlate well (+ .75) with the "Performance" scale of the Wechsler (Scarr, 1982), they do not appear to be as good a measure of verbal IQ (Levinson and Block, 1977) and thus would be expected to produce a greater within-pair variability (in this study, 12.5 points) than would a full-scale IQ test. This is because (as suggested in the appendix) "Performance IQ" tends to be more affected by low birth weight than does verbal IQ.

Given these problems, there is a strong need to examine a large, more recent identical-twin population to help in resolving such issues as:

- To what extent do birth-weight differences inject a systematic source of variance into identical-twin IQ data, and how similar would identical twins' IQs be if this lighter-twin IQ disadvantage were factored out?
- To what extent are twins' IQs suppressed because of birth-weight/weight-for-date IQ effects, and how similar to singletons' IQs would twins' IQs be if their intrauterine environment were equivalent?
- Below what birth weights might relatively large IQ decrements be likely to occur?
- How do within-pair IQ differences in twins with extreme birth-weight discordance compare with the IQ differences of twins whose birth-weight differences are of more modest proportions?

1.5 Findings from the 1986 Louisville Twin Study

As noted earlier, data on the birth weight and six-year (full-scale Wechsler) IQ scores for 181 identical-twin pairs in this study

Table 2. Six-Year IQ Scores of Identical Twins Participating in the Louisville Twin Study, by Birth Weight.

		Birth Weight of Lighter Twin (Pounds)			
IQs of Twin Pairs in Weight Class	Total Sample	4.00 or Less	4.01– 5.00	5.01– 6.00	6.01 or More
IQ Average of Twin Pair	101.6	96.2	101.3	102.5	105.0
Average Within-Pair Difference	5.3	5.7	5.3	5.4	4.8
IQ-Point Differences (%)					
0–2 Points	33.2	42.4	27.7	28.6	39.5
3–5 Points	30.9	15.2	29.8	38.1	34.2
6 Points or More	35.9	42.4	42.5	33.3	26.3
Twin Pairs:					
Number	181	33	47	63	38
% of Total	100.0	18.2	26.0	34.8	21.0

Note: IQ scores are full-scale Wechsler (WPPSI); birth weights are reported in hundredths of a pound.

Source: Data extracted from the Louisville Twin Study.

have been made available. Table 2 provides information on the IQs of these pairs, grouped according to the birth weight of the **lighter** twin in each pair. These data indicate that:

- The IQs of these twins are highly responsive to their birth weights. When both twins weighed more than 6 pounds, their IQs averaged 105; when one or both twins weighed below 4 pounds, however, their IQs averaged 96.2, or almost 9 points lower. Moreover, at the extreme upper end of the birth-weight range (7.1 pounds or more), the fifteen twins (who constituted 4.4 percent of the sample) had IQs averaging 113.1.
- The average within-pair IQ difference was quite small, 5.3 points. Although this is somewhat less than the 6.3-point average difference suggested by the formula developed by Plomin and DeFries (1980) — see detailed discussion in Chapter Three, section 3 — the correlation coefficient for this sample (+ .854) is extremely consistent with correlations reported elsewhere in the literature, including those in a recently reported study (Segal, 1985).[6]
- *Approximately one-third of the twins scored within 2 points of their co-twin and nearly one-third more were only 3 to 5 points apart.*
- Among twins whose IQs were 6 or more points apart (36 percent of the total), the average IQ difference was only 10 points, and in only four pairs did IQ vary by more than one standard deviation (15 points). In these IQ-divergent pairs, the size of the IQ difference bore little or no relation to weight class (averaging 10.6 points

among the four-pound-and-under subsample, 8.7 points in the four- to five-pound class, 10.4 points in the five- to six-pound class, and 10.8 points in the over-six-pound class).

- The standard deviation of within-pair IQ differences in this study, at 5 points, is only one-third as large as found (on the Wechsler) in the normal population. Only 2 percent of the pairs had differences as large as the *average* difference found in randomly selected people.

Although the average IQ score of the 362 twins in this sample exceeded 100 (101.6), this was slightly below what might have been expected in a comparable population of nontwins. This is because there was a relatively small minority-group representation in this population (the IQs of Caucasians in the United States average more than 103) and because IQ scores in the United States have been gradually rising during the years following this test's standardization (see Chapter Five). But since the most recently normed versions of the Wechsler were used, this latter bias is very small. Consequently, these factors, taken together, suggest that the IQ average for a comparable population of single births would be about 104.

An in-depth analysis of the nature and extent of the lighter-twin IQ disadvantage (as shown in Table 3) suggests a magnitude of difference that averages just under 2 IQ points; approximately three-fourths of this difference can be attributed to twin pairs whose IQ scores diverged by 6 points or more. An analysis of these sixty-five IQ-discordant cases (shown in Table 4) reveals that only in the lower half of the birth-weight distribution is there a systematic pattern in the direction of a heavier-twin advantage. In the IQ-divergent pairs in which the lighter twin weighed over five pounds, the frequency of a substantial IQ advantage favoring the heavier twin was only slightly greater than the frequency of a lighter-twin advantage — averaging only one twin pair in twenty in these (combined) weight classes. By contrast, the (net) proportion showing a strong heavier-twin IQ advantage represented more than a fourth of the births in which one or both twins weighed under four pounds and a fifth of the births in which the lighter twin weighed four to five pounds.

A related issue — would there be *marked* IQ differences favor-

Table 3. Heavier-Twin IQ Advantage, by Weight Class,
in Louisville Twin Study.

Wechsler IQ Scores by Birth-Weight Status	Birth Weight of Lighter Twin (Pounds)				
	Total Sample	6.00 or More	5.01– 6.00	4.01– 5.00	4.00 or Less
IQ Scores: lighter twin	100.69	104.62	101.12	101.20	94.81
co-twin	102.67	106.49	103.24	102.32	97.94
Heavier-Twin IQ Advantage	1.98	1.87	2.12	1.08	3.13
Number of Twin Pairs[a]	35	58	44	32	169

Note: Includes identical twins for whom IQ tests at age six were administered through the close of 1986.
  [a] Data shown exclude twelve twin pairs whose birth weights were within one ounce of each other.
Source: Data extracted from Louisville Twin Study.

ing the heavier twin in those twin pairs that were ***extremely** weight discordant?* — was addressed by examining the relationships among twin pairs differing in birth weight by more than one and a half pounds. While eighteen pairs of twins, or a tenth of the sample, met this criterion, the pattern of IQ differences did not differ greatly from that found in the entire twin population:

Table 4. Comparison of Heavier and Lighter Twins' IQ Scores
in IQ-Discordant Twin Pairs, by Birth Weight of Lighter Twin.

Birth Weight of Lighter Twin (lbs.)	IQ Advantage Favoring			% of Cases Favoring	
	Heavier Twin	Lighter Twin	Twins of Equal Weight[a]	Heavier Twin	Lighter Twin
4.00 or less	11	2	1	33.3	6.1
4.01–5.00	14	5	1	29.9	10.6
5.01–6.00	11	8	2	17.5	12.7
6.01 or more	5	3	2	13.2	8.0
Total/Average	41	18	6	22.7	9.9

Note: Discordant twin pairs are defined as having IQ scores that differed by at least 6 points.
  [a] Defined as less than an ounce apart.
Source: Data extracted from Louisville Twin Study.

The IQs of five pairs varied by 2 points or less; six by 3 to 5 points; and only seven by 6 points or more. In this extremely weight-discordant subsample, the IQ difference averaged 5.8 points, or only slightly more than for the entire twin sample. Also supporting this conclusion is an analysis of those twin pairs with the greatest IQ divergence. Of thirty-four twin pairs whose IQs varied by 10 points or more, nineteen were less than 300 grams apart at birth, and only six were more than 500 grams apart. *Thus, these findings appear to dispel the transfusion-syndrome hypothesis as the major cause of the heavier-twin IQ advantage.*

Another important question to which these data suggest an answer is, Below what weight threshold is there a significant risk of a moderate to substantial reduction in IQ? The answer, at least in this sample, could depend on the birth weight of the twins *considered as a pair,* as well as individually:

- In the thirty-seven twin pairs where the *lighter twin weighed between four and five pounds* and the heavier twin more than five pounds, the lighter twins' IQs averaged 102.3, and the heavier twins' IQs averaged 103.0.
- In the thirteen pairs where *both the heavier and lighter twins weighed between four and five pounds*, the IQs of the heavier twins averaged 98.7, compared with 97.5 for the lighter twins.
- In the thirteen pairs where the *heavier twin weighed between four and five pounds and the lighter twin weighed under four pounds*, the IQs of the heavier twins averaged 94.5, and the lighter twins' IQs averaged 91.7.[7]

The relationships between IQ and birth weight found in this study suggest that (1) at birth weights of six pounds and above, twins' IQs are likely to be nearly equivalent to those of singletons; (2) at five to six pounds, twins' IQs will, on average, be slightly lower than those of singletons (perhaps 2.5 points below the IQs of twins weighing six pounds and over); (3) at four to five pounds, a somewhat larger (5- or 6-point) IQ deficit will appear (with both an increased risk and an increased extent of IQ reduction occurring when the co-twin is of progressively lighter birth weight); and (4) **at four pounds or less, a marked IQ reduction (averaging 9 points) will be likely** — *with the entire IQ distribution appearing to be affected adversely, not just a small number of extreme cases.*

On this basis, the impact on IQ of the less-than-normal birth weights of this twin sample is (conservatively) estimated to average 4.2 points.[8]

1.6 IQs of Twins and Nontwins of Equivalent Birth Weights

These findings that link birth weight and IQ receive broad support from studies of IQ and birth-weight relationships in nontwin populations (see appendix), including findings from the large study of English schoolchildren that links birth-weight and duration-of-gestation combinations with "Verbal IQ" scores (Record, McKeown, and Edwards, 1969b). In that study, *in the highest and lowest birth-weight classes assessed*—above 3,500 grams (7.7 pounds) and below 2,000 grams (4.4 pounds)—*the IQs of twins and singletons were equal* (even though they averaged 8 points lower in the lighter than in the heavier weight class). In the three 500-gram weight classes between 2,000 and 3,500 grams, however, twins' IQs averaged about 2 points below those of singletons of comparable weights. In these intermediate weight classes, a low *weight-for-date apparently compounds the IQ loss*. Findings from that study, however, might be expected to represent a slight understatement of the effect of low birth weight on *total* IQ, because "Verbal IQ" seems to be effected less by low birth weight than does "Performance IQ."

This suggests that *a large preponderance of the identical-twin IQ deficit can be accounted for by the generally lower birth weights and shorter gestational ages among twins rather than by postnatal influences.*

1.7 Conclusions and Implications

These findings suggest several provocative conclusions:

- Irrespective of whether they do a perfect job of capturing the essence of the *g* of general intelligence, high-quality IQ tests do an excellent job of measuring differences between individuals in the particular skills that these tests are designed to measure. For example, if the heavier-twin IQ advantage is factored out of the within-pair IQ variance, the average difference between heavier and lighter twins is reduced to approximately 4 points.

- The lower IQ average found among identical twins than among singletons appears to result primarily from a less-than-adequate prenatal environment; thus, the heavier twin is likely to have an IQ equal to or only slightly below that of a nontwin of comparable birth weight and gestational age.

- This finding implies that the shared maternal attention experienced by twins has only a minor long-term IQ consequence. Nevertheless, it would be incorrect to conclude that the amount of attention provided to children in their formative years has no lasting effect on their IQs (see especially Chapters Two, Five, Eight, and Eleven). This is because identical twins are, during infancy and toddlerhood, likely to receive considerable attention from other family members and strangers and learn by watching their mother attend to their co-twin.

- Just as deficiencies in the intrauterine environment have been shown to have a substantial adverse impact on *twins'* IQs, so too are the IQs of American Blacks lowered as a result of a high rate of intrauterine deficiency. Specific findings and their relationship to the Black-White IQ disparity in the United States are discussed in Chapter Six.

Notes

1. Correlations in this survey averaged +.86 in thirty-four studies encompassing 4,672 pairs of monozygotic twins. Bouchard and McGue excluded the studies of Sir Cyril Burt, most of which are now generally believed to have been falsified. They included only studies where the cognitive measures employed met their standards as widely accepted, standardized measures of intelligence.
2. The authors reported a +.857 correlation when they combined six older studies containing 526 pairs (from Jencks and others, 1972) and a +.86 correlation among newer studies of 1,300 twin pairs (cited in

Loehlin and Nichols, 1976). This survey also excluded the studies of Sir Cyril Burt.

3.   The correlation of .86 cited represents the median of fourteen studies containing 1,082 twin pairs.

4.   The birth-weight and IQ data for all the twins from both studies are contained in Scarr (1982). The case numbers meeting the specified criteria were: (1) Scarr study, #1, 3, 4, 6 (see note below), 9, 10, 11, 12, 13, 15, 17, 18, 21, 22, and 25; (2) Willerman and Churchill (1967) study, #1, 2, 3, 4, 5, 8, 9, 10, 12, 13, 22, 24, 25, and 27. For the set of triplets (Scarr #6), only one set of comparisons was made, the heaviest child being compared with the other two, who were equal in IQ.

5.   The Verbal and Performance scales of the Wechsler IQ test were used after age five and the Terman-Merrill Intelligence Scale (form L) was used for the seven children aged three to five. Six cases tested before age three on the Gesell Scales were excluded, because this measure bears no appreciable relationship to developing IQ (see Chapter Seven).

6.   The sixty-nine identical-twin pairs in this study had IQ scores averaging 110.8 on the full-scale Wechsler measured at ages five to thirteen. The reported correlation was + .85, and the mean intrapair difference was 6.43 points.

7.   These findings in the four- to five-pound weight class help explain an unusual result obtained when the data relating IQs of heavier and lighter twins are compared by weight class. Thus, the heavier-twin IQs averaged 113.0 at 7.10 pounds and above, 103.3 at 6.01 to 7.09 pounds, 102.3 at 5.01 to 6.00 pounds, and 96.5 at 4.01 to 5.00 pounds. Lighter twins averaged 103.5 at 6.01 to 7.09 pounds, 101.5 at 5.01 to 6.00 pounds, 100.9 at 4.01 to 5.00 pounds (which is more than the average for heavier twins in this birth-weight class), and 94.7 at 4 pounds or less.

8.   This estimate derives from the following analysis: (1) at six pounds or more, the 108 twins (29.8 percent of the sample) are conservatively assumed to have suffered a very slight IQ impairment relative to singletons, averaging 1.0 IQ point; (2) between five and six pounds (138 twins, or 38.1 percent), the impairment is assumed to average 3.5 points; (3) between four and five pounds (73 twins, or 20.2 percent), the impairment is assumed to average 6.5 points; and (4) below four pounds (43 twins, or 11.9 percent), the impairment is assumed to average 10.5 points.

Contents

⚭ 2 ⚭

Effects of Birth Order,
Parental Age,
and Number of Siblings
on IQ

2.1 Introduction

This chapter assesses the impact of family configuration — parental ages, birth order, and the number and spacing of children — on intelligence. By analyzing these factors, both individually and collectively, we can more easily:

- Discern which behavioral factors in the home environment contribute to IQ differences among individuals.
- Estimate the extent to which family configuration contributes to IQ differences between economic classes and between ethnic groups.
- Determine both the overall extent to which environment affects IQ and the extent to which a favorable early home environment contributes to the attainment of giftedness and eminence.

2.2 Parental Age and IQ

How old parents are when their children are born often has a considerable and lasting effect on the measured intelligence of these children. The older a person's parents, the higher that person's IQ score is likely to be — an effect shown to be independent of social class.

Children born to teenage mothers tend to perform especially poorly on tests of intellectual ability, and there is a tendency for children's IQ scores to rise with increasing maternal age up to age forty and quite possibly beyond (even though the risk of certain neurological impairments increases with maternal age). Further, an analysis of the characteristics of extremely gifted and eminent people reveals that they are usually the offspring of older parents, especially older fathers, even though it is also true that firstborns are substantially overrepresented among the gifted and eminent.

Most assessments of the effects of family configuration on IQ have focused on birth order and family size and have not undertaken a discrete analysis of the impact of parental age. *Because birth order exerts an effect opposite to that of parental age,* studies that fail to address this factor have tended to underestimate the effects of birth order, and studies that have not separated the effects of these variables from one another have understated the influence of each.

The Birmingham Study

Perhaps the strongest evidence that parental age has a considerable impact on intelligence comes from a 49,000-child British study (Record, McKeown, and Edwards, 1969a) that compared performance on a test of verbal reasoning given at age eleven[1] with information on birth order, maternal age, and social class.

These researchers report a pattern of rising scores with increasing maternal age for each of the three delineated social classes,[2] as follows:

- The scores of firstborns of teenage mothers averaged 8 points lower than those of firstborn children of mothers who were twenty-five or older when they gave birth — *irrespective of social class* (106 vs. 113 in social class A, 97 vs. 105 in class B, and 94 vs. 102 in class C).
- Secondborn children whose mothers were aged twenty to twenty-four scored 6 or 7 points lower than did secondborn children whose mothers were older (106 vs. 112 in class A, 97 vs. 103 in class

B, and 94 vs. 100 in class C), with a similar pattern found among thirdborns.

- Among secondborns and thirdborns, continuing increases were also evident beyond maternal age forty. For example, among thirdborns, the scores of children born to women age forty and over averaged 4 to 7 points higher than those born to women in the same social class aged twenty-five to twenty-nine, and 6 to 10 points higher than when the mother was twenty to twenty-four.
- Among fourthborn or later children, maternal-age effects were clearly displayed in the broad middle class, with scores rising from an average of 91 among the offspring of mothers aged twenty to twenty-four, to 97 among the offspring of mothers aged forty and over. In the lowest social class (where family size climbed rapidly with increasing maternal age), much less variation was seen.

Using the scores of children born to women between thirty and thirty-four as a yardstick, these data suggest that (1) a firstborn child's verbal IQ will be about 8 points lower if the mother was a teenager, 6 points lower if she was twenty to twenty-one, and 3 points lower if she was between twenty-two and twenty-four; and (2) a secondborn child's score will be 10 points lower if the mother was still a teenager, and nearly 7 points lower if she was twenty to twenty-four. Detailed findings by maternal age for each of the social classes are shown in Table 5.

Other Findings

A study of over 7,000 children, designed to be representative of all six- to eleven-year-old children in the United States in 1963 (Roberts and Engel, 1974), found that the IQ scores on the Wechsler Intelligence Scale for Children (WISC) of the offspring of teenage mothers averaged 6 points lower than the scores of those whose mothers were between twenty-five and thirty-nine. Further, the highest scores on the vocabulary subtest were attained by subjects born when their mothers were between thirty-five and thirty-nine. A further analysis of data from this Health Examination Survey (Belmont and others, 1981) revealed that the impact of teenage motherhood was far more pronounced in the Caucasian community than among Black families, a finding replicated in an analysis of the nearly 6,000 children aged twelve to seventeen who comprised cycle III of this survey. A com-

Table 5. Verbal IQ by Birth Order and Mother's Age at Birth of Child, by Social Class (Birmingham, England, 1961–1965).

	Test Score by Birth Order			
Mother's Age at Child's Birth	*1*	*2*	*3*	*4+*
Social Class A: Under age 20	106	NR	NR	NR
20–24	109	106	102	NR
25–29	113	111	107	104
30–34	113	111	109	103
35–39	113	112	108	103
40 plus	NR	115	112	103
Social Class B: Under age 20	97	94	NR	NR
20–24	101	97	95	91
25–29	104	101	97	93
30–34	106	103	100	94
35–39	107	104	100	95
40 plus	105	103	101	97
Social Class C: Under age 20	94	NR	NR	NR
20–24	97	94	92	92
25–29	101	99	95	91
30–34	103	100	97	93
35–39	103	100	100	93
40 plus	NR	NR	102	92

NR = Not Reported (sample size too small).
Source: Adapted from Record, McKeown, and Edwards, 1969a.

parison of findings on the Caucasian adolescents from this latter cycle indicates that there was an 8-point difference between the IQs of the offspring of mothers aged fourteen to seventeen and those of the offspring of mothers aged twenty and older. There was also a linear progression of IQ with increasing maternal age from twenty to forty (totaling 3 points), despite countervailing birth-order effects. These authors conclude that this maternal-age effect "was predominantly a direct effect, not mediated by social or demographic factors" (Belmont and others, 1981, p. 153).

In a study of two-child families, the offspring of parents who married at a relatively late age had considerably higher IQs than did those whose parents married at a relatively early age

(McKenna, Null, and Ventis, 1979). In an exceptionally large study of Dutch military recruits (Belmont and Marolla, 1973), scores of firstborn and secondborn children (on the Raven's test) were found to be significantly higher among those with older mothers.

It has recently been shown that the substantially lower IQs found among the offspring of adolescent mothers do not stem from inherent differences in these children's intrauterine environments, as a relatively large study of firstborn children found no significant differences in birth weight, gestational age, or neonatal competency (Apgar scores) between the offspring of adolescent mothers and the offspring of (married) nonadolescent mothers (Culp, Appelbaum, Osofsky, and Levy, 1988).

As already noted, most studies seeking to elicit links between family configuration and IQ have focused their attention on birth order and family size and ignored parental ages. Because parents are (necessarily) younger at the birth of their first child than at the birth of subsequent children and because firstborn children tend to have higher IQs than their siblings, **the perceived effects of birth order on IQ are reduced considerably when maternal age is not considered**.

2.3 Birth Order, Family Size, and IQ

A clear picture of the relationship between children's birth position (birth order), the number of children in a family, and measured intelligence emerges from a comprehensive review of the literature. The principal findings are as follows:

- Intellectual performance declines with increasing family size and later birth order, with the exception of only children—whose performance tends to be slightly poorer than that of children who occupy the most advantaged "sibship positions."
- Firstborns in families with two or three children tend to achieve the highest scores on IQ tests (as well as on tests of academic performance).
- The next highest scores tend to be attained by first-

borns in families of four or five children, followed closely by secondborns in families of two or three (whose scores tend to be slightly above or on a par with those of only children).

- The rate at which test performance declines with increasing birth order is more pronounced in the middle and lower social classes than in the upper-middle class and (especially) the upper class.

- Exceptions to these general findings seem to be limited to cultures in which the extended family or community provides considerable assistance in infant care or extraordinary attention is routinely paid to each new child—for example, among Quakers, Mormons, and Jews (Galbraith, 1983; Cicirelli, 1978)—or to backward cultures that are being rapidly transformed by exposure to modern society (Davis, Cahan, and Bashi, 1977).

The subsections that follow analyze data from three very large studies and several smaller studies of birth order, family size, and IQ.

Detailed Findings from Large Studies

In the first of these studies (Belmont and Marolla, 1973), the scores of almost 400,000 nineteen-year-old males in the Netherlands (born between 1944 and 1947) on a widely used nonverbal IQ measure (the Raven's Progressive Matrices test) were related to birth order, family size, and social class (the three classes—manual, nonmanual, and farm—being based on the father's most recent occupation). Scores on this test, which was given as part of the military fitness examination, were subdivided (by the Dutch military) into six classes, with these "class scores" (a score of one being the highest and six the lowest) forming the basis for subsequent analysis.[3] Table 6, which details these findings, reveals some fascinating conclusions:

- In the *manual* class (50 percent of the subjects), family size was of equal or greater influence than birth order in determining test

Table 6. Scores on the Raven's Progressive Matrices Test by Birth Rank, Family Size, and Social Class (The Netherlands, 19-Year-Olds Born 1944–1947).

| Birth Order/Family Size | Total | *Test Score (Class Averages) by Social Class* | | |
		Nonmanual	Manual	Farm
Firstborn: Family of Two	2.58	2.24	2.82	3.08
Firstborn: Family of Three	2.61	2.22	2.87	3.12
Firstborn: Family of Four	2.67	2.24	2.94	3.06
Secondborn: Family of Two	2.68	2.36	2.89	3.14
Secondborn: Family of Three	2.66	2.28	2.91	3.17
Only Child	2.69	2.38	2.87	3.25
Firstborn: Family of Five	2.74	2.28	2.99	3.07
Thirdborn: Family of Three	2.75	2.37	2.98	3.19
Firstborn: Family of Six to Eight	2.86	2.36	3.08	3.01
Thirdborn: Family of Four or More	2.92	2.43	3.16	3.27
Sixthborn	3.19	2.64	3.35	3.38
Families of Nine or More	3.26	2.72	3.43	3.34

Note: Lower numbers mean better scores.
Source: Adapted from Belmont and Marolla, 1973.

scores; only in this social class were the scores of children with no siblings nearly equal to those of children in the most advantaged sibship position.

- In the *nonmanual* class (38 percent of the subjects), birth order was somewhat more influential than family size in determining test performance. Thus, firstborns in families of three performed marginally better than firstborns in families of two, and secondborns in families of three also outperformed their counterparts in families of two. Only children, however, scored materially worse than children who had one or two siblings or firstborns in larger-sized families.
- In the *farm* class (12 percent of the subjects), scores were substantially poorer than those of children from more-urban families. However, firstborns — irrespective of family size — scored relatively well.

The principal author also examined the Raven's scores of 1,500 sibling pairs in two-child families living in the city of Amsterdam, comparing the relationship between test scores and maternal age at birth of child, and concluded, "Sons of older mothers had higher test scores whether they were firstborn

Table 7. National Merit Scholarship Examination Mean Scores
by Birth Order and Family Size Among 800,000 Examinees, 1965.

Birth Order	Mean Scores by Family Size					
	1	2	3	4	5	6+
Firstborn	103.8	106.2	106.2	105.6	104.4	NR
Secondborn	—	104.4	103.9	103.1	101.7	NR
Thirdborn	—	—	102.7	101.3	99.5	NR
Fourthborn	—	—	—	100.0	97.7	NR
Fifthborn	—	—	—	—	96.9	NR
Average[a]	103.8	105.3	104.3	102.5	100.0	96.4

NR = Not Reported; standard deviation = 20.

[a] These are unweighted averages of the mean values shown (and do not reflect the higher proportion of firstborns taking this exam), except for family size six plus; the scores of twins averaged 99.0.

Source: Derived from Breland, 1974.

or secondborn" (Zybert, Stein, and Belmont, 1978, p. 817). These authors also report that a "significant positive correlation [existed] for both birth orders in the Nonmanual social class and for firstborns in the Manual social class" (Belmont, Stein, and Zybert, 1978, p. 996).

The second large study, which encompassed 800,000 high school juniors in the United States, compared performance on the National Merit Scholarship Examination in 1965 with birth order, family size, and sibling spacing. The published material (Breland, 1974) also provides test-score averages for eighty-two sibship configurations, separately for males and females.[4]

The results on this test—which is to some extent more academically and verbally oriented than a comprehensive IQ test—are summarized in Table 7. The pattern closely resembles that found on the Raven's test in the Netherlands: (1) the highest scores were attained by firstborns in families of two or three children, (2) next in line were firstborns in somewhat larger-sized families and secondborns in two-child families, (3) secondborns in three-child families and only children scored slightly less well, and (4) progressively lower scores were registered as birth order and family size increased further.

Because of the exceptionally large size (800,000 students) of the National Merit Scholarship Examination, the detailed analysis of the specific data for the eighty-two sibship configurations provided by Breland offers a unique opportunity to examine the effects of differences in child spacing on test performance. For example, the enormous size of the subsamples that can be further differentiated (200,000 children in two-child families) gives an extraordinarily high reliability to relatively small IQ differences.

My own detailed analysis of the data indicates that child-spacing effects are quite profound and have important implications for family planning. Specific findings (based on Breland's twofold subdivision into a difference of three or more years in chronological age and a difference of two years or less) include the following:

- In three-child families, as long as there is a space of three or more years *either* between the first and second child *or* between the second and third child, the average test scores of the children will be quite high (as they are in two-child families).
- If, however, *all three children are closely spaced, test scores will be considerably lower* — particularly for the firstborns and lastborns, whose scores will each be approximately 7 points lower than those of their counterparts (averaging 100 for firstborns and 96.7 for lastborns).
- In two-child families, close spacing will not particularly affect the elder child's score, but it is associated with a slight (1.5 point) reduction in the average score of the younger child.

Thus, with adequate family spacing, a third child will not have a material effect on the IQ performance of the other children — the eldest child's score will tend to rise marginally, while the secondborn's score will decline by an average of less than a point.

Confirming these suggested sibling-spacing effects is a study of three-child families (Douglas, Ross, and Simpson, 1968) in which children "with narrow spacing had lower vocabulary and reading scores than the more widely spaced. For tests of nonverbal abilities, no differences were found between spacing interval subgroups" (Wagner, Schubert, and Schubert, 1985, p. 157). This

Table 8. Wechsler IQ Subtest Scores for Children Aged 6–11
(National Health Survey: 1963–1965).

Number of Children in the Household	Scores on the Wechsler IQ Subtests		
	Vocabulary	Block Design	Combined[a]
One	104.1	100.4	101.6
Two	105.4	101.8	103.0
Three	103.4	102.1	102.1
Four	100.2	100.5	99.8
Five	96.2	99.1	97.0
Six	93.7	96.9	94.7
Seven	91.4	95.2	92.7
Eight or More	88.4	93.7	90.5

[a] Correlations between scores on the full-scale Wechsler IQ test and the combined scores on these two subtests are reportedly + .88.
Source: Roberts and Engel, 1974.

latter finding also reinforces another aspect of the analysis of National Merit Examination scores (Breland, 1974)—namely, that birth-order differences were greatest on the most verbal subtest (word usage) and of minor influence on the least verbal subtest (math usage).

Further confirmation of this recurring theme—*that verbal aspects of intelligence seem to be more affected by the postnatal environment than do its nonverbal components*—comes from findings from the previously discussed National Health Examination Survey of 1963–1965 (Roberts and Engel, 1974). The results, displayed in Table 8, show that children in two-child families scored **17 points** higher on the vocabulary subtest of the WISC than did children in families with eight or more children in the home—compared with an **8-point** differential on the block-design subtest.

With respect to the National Merit Examination, these findings are apt to understate the effects of family configuration that would be found if high school dropouts and nonacademic-track high school students were part of the subject pool. Nonetheless, these data suggest that perhaps 40 percent of the National Merit examinees were in relatively advantaged sibship configurations, a fourth were in configurations that were neither advantaged nor disadvantaged, a sixth suffered a modest IQ decrement because of family structure (averaging perhaps 6 points in verbal IQ and 4 points in total IQ), and an additional sixth suffered a greater decrement (averaging perhaps 9 points in verbal IQ and 6 points in overall IQ).

The third extremely large study addressing birth order is the previously cited Eleven Plus examination given to the children of Birmingham, England (Record, McKeown, and Edwards, 1969a). Here, when the mother's age is held constant, the effects of birth order on verbal IQ scores are greatly magnified. An 11-point difference between firstborn and sixthborn or later children found without consideration of their mothers' age (103.0 versus 92.1) expands to 16 points among the offspring of mothers between thirty and thirty-four (106.7 for firstborns versus 90.6 for sixth or laterborns). It is also 16 points at age twenty-five to twenty-nine, and 15 points at age thirty-five to thirty-nine. By contrast, when the impact of birth order is examined in isolation, the larger proportion of younger mothers in the early birth orders (and in the lower social classes) reduces its perceived influence.

Family Size, Child Spacing, and IQ: Effects of Socioeconomic Status

A study of 11,000 high school graduates that relates IQ to family size and socioeconomic status (SES) found that (1) in the highest SES quartile, the number of children in the family had virtually no impact on test scores; (2) in the middle 50 percent, the relationship between family size and mental ability, although statistically significant, was quite modest; and (3) in the lowest quartile, performance declined considerably with successive increases in family size (Page and Grandon, 1979).

An analysis of the scores of 2,000 sixth-grade children and 800 of their older siblings who had taken the same verbal IQ test and the Raven's Progressive Matrices test when they were in sixth grade (Lancer and Rim, 1984), led to the following conclusions:

First, in the highest social class, children in family sizes one through four did equally well in verbal IQ, with scores of the children from the middle and lower classes showing the expected family-size effect. Second, only children did quite well on the nonverbal measure, which showed the usual family-size pattern. Finally, on both measures, sibling spacing was very important among laterborn children in *large* families. When the scores of children born after a one- to two-year spacing were compared with those born after a five- to six-year spacing, verbal IQ scores averaged 5.7 points lower for fourthborns and 7.3 points lower for fifthborns and sixthborns. On the Raven's test, the scores of widely spaced fifthborns and sixthborns *averaged 25 percent higher*.

Child spacing and the effects of SES also interact, both with each other and with maternal age; for example, very young mothers are more apt to have children relatively close together than are mothers in the median age range.

Taken together, these findings do much to explain why simplistic models designed to capture the effects of family configuration on IQ (Zajonc, 1976) do not replicate well across divergent populations.

2.4 Family Configurations of the Gifted and Eminent

This section discusses the results of studies that have reported on the nature of the families into which gifted and/or eminent people were born and received their early rearing, including the number and spacing of other children (if any), the gifted and/or eminent person's birth order, and the ages of that child's parents when he or she was born. If, as is suggested by findings from populations with normally distributed IQs, favorable family configurations in one's formative years have a strong influence on IQ, we would expect that an examination of the backgrounds of intellectually gifted and/or eminent people would reveal a *greatly magnified* incidence of these favorable situations.

As detailed in the studies that follow, this is indeed the case. The odds of becoming identified as a highly intelligent person and/or of attaining eminence are considerably enhanced (1) if one is the firstborn child in a small family; (2) if not a firstborn child, if one is born after an abnormally wide sibling spacing; and/or (3) if one's parents (in particular one's father) are considerably older than the norm—the high proportion of firstborn children notwithstanding.

Moreover, the higher up the IQ scale one looks, the more apt one is to find that an exceptionally favorable caretaker ratio existed in early childhood. Thus, a substantial majority of intellectually gifted people had the undivided or near-undivided attention of their mothers during the first few years of life. Most were firstborn children, including many who were only children. Furthermore, even among those with older siblings, favorable caretaker ratios were highly likely, because the older sibling(s) had frequently begun school by the time these children were born. Thus, an older sibling, rather than creating a dilution of the caretaker ratio, often served as a source of additional didactic support to the gifted child. Moreover, very often the fathers and/or grandparents of intellectually precocious children were also heavily involved in their early upbringing (see Chapter Nine).

Birth Order, Family Size, and Sibling Spacing

At the extreme upper end of the IQ spectrum, one finds an enormous overrepresentation of firstborn children, including only children. For example, of the eleven children identified by Hollingworth (1942) as having IQs of 180 and above, ten were firstborn, including five who were only children and four who had only one sibling. Among the twenty-eight New York area children identified by Sheldon (1954) as having IQs of 170 and above, twelve (of the twenty firstborns) were "onlyborns," eleven had one sibling, and five had two siblings. Similarly, in the Johns Hopkins study of extremely precocious seventh graders (see Chapter Seventeen), 62 percent were firstborns, while in a comparison group of high-achieving but less precocious youths 48 percent were firstborns (Benbow and Benbow, 1987).

In a study of sixty-four eminent American scientists, Roe (1953) found that thirty-nine (or 61 percent) were firstborn

children. Moreover, he reported that the average spacing between the laterborn scientists and their (next) older sibling was
five years. Additional support for the view that relatively wide
sibling spacing has a beneficial effect on intelligence comes
from an analysis of 229 Phi Beta Kappa members reared in two-
child families. Hayes and Bronzaft (1979) report that 38.4 percent of those studied were spaced five or more years apart and
fewer than a fifth were spaced less than three years apart.

Three analyses of the backgrounds of extremely large numbers of gifted and/or eminent people that reported on birth
order found exceptionally large proportions of firstborns in
these populations. The studies cited here include a sample of
more than 1,000 California schoolchildren with IQs above 135
(Terman, 1925), an analysis of (nonroyal) personages mentioned
in the English *Dictionary of National Biography* (Ellis, 1904), and an
analysis of 1,000 eminent American scientists (Cattell and
Brimhall, 1921). These findings take on even greater significance when it is noted that the average family size in the years
covered by these studies was far larger than it is today. In the
Cattell and Brimhall study, for example, the scientists had an
average of 3.6 siblings, which gave the firstborn child about a 22
percent chance of being the one to attain eminence. In fact,
however, more than 40 percent of the people achieving eminence were firstborns.

Schacter (1963) argues eloquently that the primary reason
that firstborns are greatly overrepresented among people attaining eminence as a result of scholarly pursuits is that they are
overrepresented among scholars in general. To support this view
he presents surveys indicating that firstborns are overrepresented, first of all, among college students. Thus, half the 4,000
freshmen who took introductory psychology at the University of
Minnesota between 1959 and 1961 were firstborns, compared
with a 30 percent "chance" expectation based on their family-
size distribution (Schacter, 1963), and half the college seniors
were firstborns (Osgood, personal communication, 1961). In
addition, firstborns made up 58 percent of the graduate students in psychology and child welfare at the University of Minnesota, compared with 38 percent based on "chance" distribu-

tion (Schacter, 1963). A national survey of students attending graduate schools in the arts and sciences found that 53 percent of these students were firstborns (Davis, 1962), and another study found that half of the 2,700 students in eight randomly selected medical schools were also firstborns (Coker and others, 1959). Moreover, Schacter's analysis of the grade point averages of Minneapolis high school students shows that, on average, firstborns get significantly better grades (2.25) than do secondborns (2.16) or laterborns (1.95) and that this tendency persists (albeit to a reduced degree) within family sizes.

Parental Ages

Despite the extraordinarily high proportion of firstborns reported in studies of eminent people, children's chances of achieving greatness are considerably heightened if, at the time of their birth, their parents are well beyond their youth. As shown below, the fathers of these eminent people were likely to be in their mid to late thirties, with their mothers approaching age thirty—the age spread between these parents averaging seven years:

- *Fifty great men (Yoder, 1897):* average parental ages—fathers thirty-eight and mothers thirty.
- *One hundred Englishmen of eminence (Galton, 1874):* average parental ages—thirty-six and twenty-nine.
- *Nine hundred and two top American scientists (Visher, 1948):* average parental ages—thirty-five and twenty-nine.

Although the number of studies providing information about the parental ages of gifted and eminent people is relatively small, the pervasiveness of the findings presented above is suggested by several other scholars (Fowler, 1983). For example, Goertzel and Goertzel (1978) conclude: "Like many other parents of the gifted, they were not in early youth when their 300 eminent children were born." Goertzel and Goertzel also note that many of these parents stayed intellectually and physically active well into their eighties and nineties.

2.5 Implications

Some important implications are suggested by these findings:

- The popular belief that the overall *quantity* of attention paid to children during their formative years is the critical variable in determining intelligence gains support from the findings of a firstborn IQ advantage, as well as from the extremely favorable caretaker ratios experienced by people later identified as intellectually gifted or who go on to attain eminence.
- The IQ disadvantage of the only child could be explained in several ways, including: (1) an above-average incidence of intra-uterine deficiency among women unable to bear more than one child; (2) a decision not to have more children by women who, after nurturing one child, consider themselves to be not especially well suited to mothering; and/or (3) only children not having the opportunity to learn by teaching their younger siblings. Nevertheless, the exceptionally high proportion of onlyborns found in gifted and eminent populations suggests no inherent disadvantage from the absence of siblings, particularly if the child receives considerable intellectual stimulation from its father or a grandparent.
- The extent of the adverse impact on firstborns' scores found among the offspring of teenage mothers (and, to a lesser extent, mothers in their early twenties) suggests that the *quality of maternal care* rather than its overall quantity may be of primary importance in determining cognitive performance — and that older, more mature parents are better able to subordinate their own needs and wants and supply more consistent, patient, and child-oriented maternal care.
- As detailed in Chapter Eight, substantial differences have been reported in *patterns of maternal behavior* toward the eldest and secondborn children during infancy — differences that are likely to heighten the cognitive development of firstborns. Nevertheless, the firstborn advantage may also relate to (1) the benefits of having opportunities for teaching younger siblings; (2) the greater maturity expected of the eldest child (for example, having to bear part of the responsibility for the caretaking of siblings); and (3) in cultures commonly practicing primogeniture, the greater amount of *paternal* intellectually stimulating attention.
- The finding that, in three-child families, the performance of firstborn children is no more dependent on the time span between their birth and the birth of the second child than it is on the time span between the birth of the second and third child further reinforces a conclusion that the undivided attention paid by mothers to their firstborn children during infancy is not the *sole* cause of these children's better performance.
- The finding that culture affects the relative importance of the

various components of family configuration supports a conclusion that these effects are primarily if not exclusively environmental and are not predicated on inherited aspects of IQ. For example:
(1) in middle- and lower-class nonfarm families, family size (and
secondarily parental age) has a greater impact on IQ than does
birth order; (2) in the upper and upper-middle classes, however,
parental age seems to be of far greater significance than family size
(with negligible birth-order effects found in cultures that provide
considerable extended-family support); and (3) among farm families, parental age and family size are secondary to birth order.

• The magnitude of the IQ differences imposed by sibship configuration and parental age is so large that these findings amply
demonstrate that *environment has a substantial influence on
intelligence.*

The matrix of family configurations faced by Black Americans has been particularly adverse and, when superimposed
upon a frequently poorer prenatal environment, appears to
account for a significant portion of what has come to be called
the Black/White IQ disparity. These factors are discussed in
Chapter Six.

Notes

1. The two subtests of this Eleven-Plus examination that have shown strong
    correlations with measures of verbal IQ were analyzed, but the mathe-
    matics and English subtest results were not analyzed. Children in pri-
    vate schools and schools for the handicapped, as well as children in
    ordinary schools who were classified as borderline retarded, were not
    given this examination.
2. Social-class data were determined from school records; the scores of the
    37,324 nontwin subjects whose fathers' occupations were known were
    virtually identical to the entire nontwin population (100.3 vs. 100.1). In
    the highest social class (12 percent of the children), scores averaged
    110.0 (based on a standard deviation of 15); in the broad middle class
    (74 percent of the children), 99.7; and in the lowest class (14 percent),
    96.4.
3. The overall average score was 2.76, with almost half the recruits scoring
    either one (19 percent) or two (30 percent); the proportions in classes 3
    to 6 were progressively lower. About 80 percent of the nineteen-year-olds
    took the exam (5 percent having been exempted from military service
    and 15 percent failing the medical exam).
4. The pattern of test results for males and females varied little from one
    sibship configuration to another (males scoring roughly 2 points higher
    than females).

Contents

☆ 3 ☆

Resemblances Among
Family Members' IQs

3.1 Introduction

Many researchers seeking to compare the contributions of nature and nurture to intelligence have focused their attention on IQ resemblances among siblings, between parents and their children, and so on. But despite the publication of numerous studies detailing within-family IQ relationships, these findings have done little to quell the considerable controversy over the nature-nurture issue. This is in part because the IQs of first-degree relatives are usually not very similar to one another, there being only a 25 percent smaller difference in their IQ scores than that found among randomly selected people. In addition, considerable study-to-study variation exists in the reported correlations. Nevertheless, these findings clearly support the view that *intelligence is both a hereditarily driven and an environmentally responsive phenomenon — with heredity usually having a considerably stronger influence than environment.*

This chapter presents (1) aggregate findings concerning within-family IQ resemblances and a comparison of these findings with expectations under a purely hereditary "model" of intelligence; (2) a discussion of the term *correlation* as it relates to IQ-point distances under the normal bell-shaped IQ curve; (3)

an analysis of how random and test-related factors associated with the IQ-examination process cause the scores of family members to diverge; (4) an evaluation of the effects of two sources of IQ-score divergence among siblings — family configuration and prenatal environment; and (5) an overall reassessment of the impact of heredity and environment on intelligence.

3.2 General Findings: IQ Correlations
Among First-Degree Relatives

A comprehensive analysis of the world literature concerning the correspondence between measured intelligence and familial relationships — which was limited to (111) studies that employed widely accepted standardized measures of intelligence (Bouchard and McGue, 1981) — reports the following positive IQ correlations:

- .47 among nontwin siblings reared together (based on 69 studies encompassing 26,473 sibling pairings).
- .60 among fraternal twins reared together (based on 41 studies encompassing 5,546 twin pairs).
- .42 between parent and child reared in the parental home (32 studies encompassing 8,433 pairings).
- .50 for child-midparent IQ comparisons (8 studies; 992 pairings of child's score with the average score of both parents).
- .72 for midparent-midoffspring IQ comparisons (3 studies; 410 families).
- .31 for half-siblings reared together (2 studies; 200 pairings).

These findings suggest that intelligence is primarily a hereditarily driven phenomenon and that the proportion of genes shared by family members is the principal factor governing the correspondence between their IQs. In a simple, purely genetic, and "additive" model of inheritance — meaning one in which (1) IQ is governed by a single gene (or group of genes that interact in an additive, rather than a multiplicative, manner); (2) there is no "assortive mating" (that is, no tendency for people to choose spouses similar to themselves in intelligence); and (3) environment has no influence — sibling correlations would be expected to average + .50, a value virtually identical to the + .47 average correlation reported by Bouchard and McGue. The sharply lower correlation found among half-siblings reared together corresponds with expectations under this model, and the moderately higher midparent-midoffspring correlations also conform with its general nature.

Perhaps the best evidence that *the genetic component of IQ is, on the average, significantly stronger than the environmental component* comes from studies comparing IQ correlations among identical twins, fraternal twins, and other siblings—in particular, the nearly universal findings that (1) fraternal twins (who are no more alike genetically than are nontwin siblings) differ in IQ to a considerably greater extent than do identical twins and (2) the average IQ difference between fraternal twins and nontwin siblings is far less than the difference between fraternal twins and identical twins.

Buttressing this argument is a study of language comprehension and syntactic ability among twins, in which blood tests revealed that several twin pairs thought to be identical were in fact fraternal—and vice versa (Munsinger and Douglass, 1976). The results showed that those fraternal twins who were treated by their parents as identical were no more alike in their language abilities than the other fraternal twins tested ($r = +.49$) and that the divergence in these fraternal twins' scores was far greater than that found among the thought-to-be-fraternal twins whose blood tests revealed them to be identical.

This review of the world literature on measured intelligence and family relationships also *eliminates any possibility that parent-child or sibling IQ correspondences vary by sex.* For example:

- Opposite-sex sibling pair correlations averaged +.49, and same-sex sibling pair correlations +.48 (+.47 for males and +.50 for females).
- Opposite-sex parent-child correlations averaged +.39, compared with +.40 for same-sex pairings (+.41 for mother-child correlations and +.41 for father-child correlations).

Figure 1. Normal Distribution of IQ Scores (Stanford-Binet IQ Test).

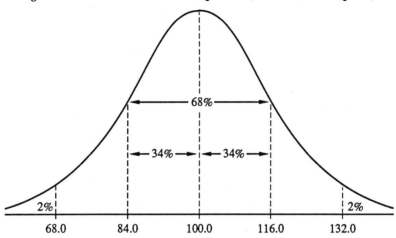

3.3 IQ Correlations and IQ-Point Distances
Under the Normal Curve

Intelligence-test norming is designed to produce an exact bell-shaped distribution of IQ scores so that (1) the average IQ is 100; (2) slightly more than two-thirds of the population falls within one standard deviation of this average (16 points on the Stanford-Binet test and 15 points on the Wechsler); and (3) all but the top and bottom 2 percent of the population falls within two standard deviations of the mean (32 points on the Stanford-Binet form L-M), as shown in Figure 1.

The term *correlation*, as used in assessing parent-child and sibling-pair IQ correspondences, is a measure of how alike these relatives' test scores are in relation to the pool of subjects studied. To develop such correlations, (1) subjects are ranked according to their IQ scores, (2) the rank order divergence of every pair of relatives is calculated, and (3) this divergence is compared with that found by comparing the scores of every nonrelated subject in the study with every other. The resulting correlation then reflects the likelihood that these relatives' IQ correspondences will be as similar as they are. For example, if a child's score was the 200th highest out of 1,000 children tested and its sibling's score was the 300th highest, this 100-rank divergence would result in a relatively high positive correlation, because comparatively few random comparisons would result in this small a rank order difference. Similarly, a rank order divergence greater than random chance would produce a negative correlation.

Plomin and DeFries (1980) have developed a formula for estimating the average difference in IQ scores associated with any given correlation. After testing this formula empirically, the authors reported a "close correspondence between expected average differences computed from correlations and empirically derived average differences for variables that were approximately normally distributed, such as IQ" (p. 23). When this formula is used (see Table 9), siblings reared together are likely to average 13 points apart (compared with an average of 18 among unrelated people whose correlation with one another was zero). Since *correlation* is a statistical concept designed to represent the square root of the variance, the rate at which IQ-point distances between people converge is in fact much slower than suggested by the numerical magnitude of the correlation — in this case, a correlation of $+.47$ theoretically explains 27 percent of the variance.

Yet, how can such low within-family IQ resemblances be possible? How is it that siblings, who have a considerable proportion of identical genes and are reared in a very similar home environment, have IQ scores that are so distant from one another, particularly since another factor — nonrandomness in the choice of one's spouse — creates an additional impetus for siblings' IQs to be somewhat more alike than would be expected under a simple Mendelian model?

One possible answer is that there are biases inherent in the IQ test-taking situation and that these cause within-family IQ correspondences to diverge. Thus, in addition to heredity and environment, so-called random factors generated by less-than-perfect mechanisms for evaluating intelligence can influence people's IQ scores. These factors may be internal to the person — for example, those caused by hour-to-hour, day-to-day, or longer cycles in that person's physical or emotional well-being,

Table 9. Effect on Within-Family IQ-Score Divergence of Adjusting for Estimated Variance Due to Randomness and IQ-Test Differences.

Familial Relationship	Average IQ Correlation Reported	Estimated IQ-Point Difference	Variance Caused by		IQ Score Divergence Due to		
			Random Factors	IQ-Test Factor	Random Factors	IQ-Test Factor	Both Factors
None	0.00	18.1[a]	4.4	0.0	0.0	0.0	0.0
Siblings	+.47	13.2	5.5	0.0	1.0	0.0	1.0
Parent-child	+.42	13.9	5.5	3.0	1.0	2.0	3.0
Midparent-child	+.50	12.8	4.0	2.8	0.8	1.8	2.6
Midparent-midoffspring	+.73	8.5	1.8	2.5	0.6	1.6	2.2
Half-siblings	+.31	15.0	5.5	0.0	0.2	0.0	0.2
Fraternal twins	+.60	11.4	4.4	0.0	1.0	0.0	1.0

[a] These estimates are derived by applying the following formula (Plomin and DeFries, 1980): the average numerical IQ point difference (z) equals 1.13 times the standard deviation found in the normal IQ distribution (16 on the Stanford-Binet) times the square root of (1 minus the correlation found).

or they may be the result of pure happenstance (for example, the person's luck in guessing). These factors are usually ignored, because in group-to-group comparisons (or comparisons of people with presumably random IQ relationships) they are as likely to increase IQ-point distances as to decrease them.

However, the more alike in IQ that two people are (a priori) expected to be, the less likely such biases are to be neutral in their effects. For example, if two people are in fact 3 points apart in intelligence, a 6-point random drop in the score of the person with the lower IQ (for example, because he or she has a cold) will markedly increase the variance (from 3 to 9 points), but a 6-point swing in the opposite direction will still leave their scores 3 points apart.

Likewise, the more dissimilar in age that two family members are when tested and *the more dissimilar the IQ-test content,* the greater the likelihood that nonrandom factors, as well as random test-related factors, will increase rather than decrease their reported distance. Moreover, because the importance of differences in test content is likely to be markedly greater in parent-child than in sibling IQ comparisons, the overall picture of familial IQ relationships is likely to be distorted.

3.4 Analysis of Biases Affecting IQ Correlations Among Family Members

The most frequently used method for estimating the impact of the random factors inherent in test-taking situations on people's IQ performance has been to look at changes in people's IQ scores over time, using the same (or equivalent) test instrument(s). Such studies have shown a test-to-test variation averaging about 6 points (over a time interval averaging fifteen months). These findings, however, have generally been based on changes in IQ during childhood, and—when the supportive data are analyzed in depth—it becomes evident that changes in children's IQ scores also contain an additional source of variation, namely, developmental trends. To differentiate between these two sources of test-to-test variation, a detailed analysis of IQ trends across childhood has been made among children who were part of the Fels Longitudinal Study (McCall, Appelbaum, and Hogarty, 1973). This analysis concluded that the large majority of children undergo *systematic changes* in their IQ-test performance over time, evidencing such patterns as a gradual increase in IQ as childhood progresses or several years of clearly increasing (or decreasing) scores followed by a period of stability (which may then be followed by a trend reversal). In this study, at least a fourth (and perhaps as much as a third) of the test-to-test variation seems to be attributable to these underlying trend factors.

A better but less often used approach has been to test subjects on two equivalent IQ tests after a relatively brief time interval, with half the sample given one test first and half the other test. Such an approach, employing the two versions of the Stanford-Binet then in general use, found an average correlation between test scores of + .94 among 619 children aged fourteen to eighteen (Breland, 1974). Under the previously referenced formula (Plomin and DeFries, 1980), this implies that their scores varied by an average of about 4.4 points. This finding is in close agreement with the results of the Fels study — as well as with the proximity of identical twins' IQ scores (after the divergence caused by birth-weight differences is factored out). Thus, this result can serve as the core (or minimum) random factor variance present in an otherwise identical test-taking situation.

Knowing the average size of this basic random factor is not, however, the same as knowing the magnitude of the divergence in IQ scores that it will cause among relatives (which grows larger the more alike the family members are in IQ). If we assume that the relationship between IQ-score proximity and the degree of divergence produced is reasonably well represented by a classically shaped curvilinear function, then this source of bias would account for roughly 1 point of the IQ-score divergence found in sibling or parent-child studies.

A more serious, and more systematic, source of test-related variance arises when the family members to be compared are far apart in age, especially when the factor loadings of the IQ tests used to compare their intelligence differ from one another to a considerable extent. The size of this induced bias is difficult to quantify, because it is in part dependent on the extent to which the tests differ, as well as on the age at which the children are tested. However, in contrast to the previously discussed random variance (which is intrinsically bidirectional in its effects on IQ scores), this test-related factor is far more likely to cause relatives' IQ scores to diverge than to converge. Based on the assumptions detailed in Note #1, and the discussion in section 3.5, *the extent of parent-child IQ-score divergence emanating from such test-related differences is estimated to average 2.0 points.*

When within-family IQ correspondences are derived by comparing the scores of more than two family members (for example, in midparent-midchild IQ correlations), the magnitude of the random variance (on their now-averaged scores) is reduced materially, but much of the bias related to the use of different IQ measures is likely to remain.

On the basis of the foregoing analyses, it seems appropriate to adjust the reported familial IQ resemblances in accordance with the figures shown in Table 9.

3.5 Impact of Family Configuration, Birth Weight, and Study Design on Siblings' IQs

Developing a reasonably good answer to the question — How much more alike would siblings' IQs be if the divergence in their scores caused by differences in their family configuration and prenatal environment could be quantified? — would make the respective roles of heredity and environment in intelligence much clearer.

Although the effects of within-family differences on some of the variables that collectively comprise family configuration — family size, child spacing, and maternal age — tend to be considerably less than those found in between-family comparisons, siblings are exposed to different-sized families during their initial years of development, and birth order is still of major significance.

To assess this birth-order impact, we will examine the results of two of the large studies detailed in Chapter Two: the National Merit Scholarship Examination (Breland, 1974) and the

Birmingham, England, Eleven-Plus Examination (Record, McKeown, and Edwards, 1969a). By extrapolating the National Merit Examination findings to the U.S. population at large, we can estimate that birth-order effects account for a between-sibling IQ-score divergence of 2.1 points.[2] Similarly, an analysis of the Birmingham data results in an estimated verbal IQ-point difference that averages 1.8 points per birth order, or a 2.6-point divergence between siblings.[3] Since these differences are reconcilable,[4] it seems appropriate to average these results and estimate that *family configuration creates a divergence in siblings' IQs averaging 2.3 points.*

The impact of birth weight and gestational age as a source of divergence in siblings' IQs is apt to be less than in the population at large, where it averages about 2.0 points (see Chapter Six). This is because (1) siblings show some birth-weight similarity, the + .50 correlation found in the Birmingham study being cited as paralleling general findings (Record, McKeown, and Edwards, 1969b); and (2) there is a diminished likelihood that a woman will bear additional children after serious intra-uterine problems with one. Consequently, the magnitude of intrauterine differences among siblings is likely to be about half that found among randomly selected people. On this basis, *the divergence in siblings' IQ scores caused by differences in their prenatal environment is estimated to average 1.0 point.*

The way in which studies used to generate IQ correlation among siblings are designed can also influence the size of the IQ correlations they produce. Examining only the *average* correlation reported in section 3.2 (+ .47) obscures a good deal of the between-study variability (for example, in only two-thirds of these studies did correlations range between + .33 and + .55). Moreover, at least one of the more commonly used methodologies appears to skew in a systematic manner the findings that it generates. When sibling pairs consist of a schoolchild who recently took an IQ test and an older sibling who previously took the same test in the same grade, the scores of these pairs are likely to be somewhat lower and more alike than those of other pairs of siblings living in the same community, for several reasons:

- These sibling pairs have a good likelihood of being of consecutive birth order, with the result that their IQ scores will be more alike than those of other siblings.
- These pairs are likely to be more closely spaced than average, which tends to depress the scores of both children.
- Larger families are likely to be overrepresented, which lowers both siblings' scores.
- The older sibling in a pair is likely to have been tested near the very beginning of the survey period and the younger sibling near its end; because of the gradual rise in IQ scores over time (discussed in Chapter Five), this is likely to cause their scores to converge slightly (compared with findings that use other methodologies).

To test whether such theoretical biases have indeed occurred, we will examine in detail the findings from a 5,000-pair survey of *consecutively born* siblings who were part of the 49,000-child Birmingham study. The sibling correlation in this study (+.55) is higher than the average (+.47) or the median (+.45) reported for siblings (Bouchard and McGue, 1981). This analysis[5] reveals that (1) the scores of these subjects were lower than those of the other children (2.0 points, $p \le .001$); (2) the family-size distribution of this sibling sample was exceedingly large; and (3) the limited duration of the survey (four years, nine months) very probably caused the scores of these siblings to converge.

However, another frequently used methodology, namely, obtaining IQ scores of siblings of varying ages at a single point in time, creates an opposite bias—one that tends to make their scores appear further apart than they really are. This is because—in addition to being a reflection of children's overall intellectual ability—IQ trends during childhood are a reflection of a child's "developmental timetables." Because such timetables are (like physical growth spurts) largely under genetic control, the scores of two brothers tested at the same age are likely to differ by less than they would if the subjects were tested at different ages.

Thus, even though some methodologies are apt to overstate

siblings' IQ similarities, alternative methodologies (such as those that test IQs at different ages) tend to understate such similarities. Without undertaking a thorough analysis of the methodologies used in each of the studies comprising the correlation reported in section 3.2, it is impossible to determine whether the impact of the "developmental-trend" effect is, on balance, larger than the bias produced by a primary or exclusive reliance on data from consecutive siblings.

Thus, the average difference in IQ scores of 13.4 points found between siblings (as suggested by the correlation of +.47) may be broken down as follows: (1) 2.3 points are attributable to family configuration (primarily birth order); (2) 1.0 point is attributable to birth weight; (3) 1.0 point is attributable to the "nonrandomness" of random variation discussed in section 3.4; and (4) there is a 9.1-point residual difference. These figures assume an offset between methodological biases engendered by testing siblings at different ages and by using the Birmingham approach.

3.6 Parent-Child IQ Correlations

Under a purely genetic model of intelligence, the IQ correlation between a child and either of its parents will average +.50 (meaning that the IQ variance ordinarily found between unrelated people will be reduced by about a fourth). Since each parent has two sets of genes, the chance of inheriting a given gene from any one parental set is one in four, hence a +.50 correlation. This is not far removed from the +.42 average correlation reported in section 3.1. Under this "additive" model of intelligence, midparent-child IQ correlations should, in theory, approximate +.71 (implying that the genetic similarity of parent and child should cut the IQ divergence normally found in half). However, the observed correlation is markedly lower: +.50. It is only when the average IQ of both parents is compared with the average IQs of all the children in a family that the reported correlations are able to explain half the random difference.

As previously suggested, biases inherent in the IQ-examination process cause the scores of parents and their children to diverge—with differences in the "factor loadings" of the IQ tests employed being of crucial importance in determining the extent of this divergence. For an illustration of how people's abilities differ from one aspect of "intelligence" to another, we can turn to the Wechsler Intelligence Test, which provides a "Verbal" score and a "Performance" score in addition to an overall IQ score. According to Kaufman (1976, p. 793), when the revised children's version of the Wechsler (WISC-R) was standardized in the 1970s, "about half of the children . . . had discrepancies [between their verbal and performance subtest scores] of 9 points or more, about one-third had discrepancies of 12 or more, and about a fourth had discrepancies of 15 or more IQ points." Moreover, these Verbal/Performance discrepancies do not always occur in a random manner, as Japanese people usually perform far better on spatial and perceptual reasoning tasks than on verbal tasks (see Chapter Thirteen), while Jewish people tend to perform far better on more verbally and conceptually oriented tests such as the Stanford-Binet (see Chapter Fourteen). A further complication is that the types of questions used to assess the intelligence (particularly the verbal intelligence) of very young children differ considerably from those used at a later age, and this difference may engender additional bias (Levinson, 1977). Consequently, even when the "same" IQ test is used in parent-child (or sibling) comparisons (such as the childhood and adult versions of the Wechsler), nonrandom test-related variance may still occur.

After an estimate is made of the effects of this test-related bias (see Table 9), the divergence in IQ scores between parents and their children lessens considerably—to about 11 points for parent-child differences and just over 6 points for midparent-midchild correlations.

Attempts to reconcile these adjusted adult-child findings with the expected results under a simple, purely genetic model and/or with the IQ correlations found between siblings are made extremely difficult by the intervention of several other factors, including these two:

- *Assortive mating.* The "simple" hereditary model assumes that spouses are genetically unrelated; however, spouses are likely to be somewhat similar in IQ (particularly on tests or subtests that measure verbally oriented IQ components, on which their scores are apt to average 3 or 4 points nearer to one another than would occur at random). The proportion of common genes between parent and child will therefore be higher than that suggested by the Mendelian model. But the average IQ correlation found between spouses (+ .33) is not necessarily an accurate reflection of their *genetic* similarity, because choice of marital partner is dependent on environmental as well as genetic factors.
- *Parental upbringing versus sibling upbringing.* On "environmental" grounds, it might be theorized that siblings will, on average, be more alike in IQ than a child is to either of its parents, because *the home environment provided to one sibling is likely to bear a closer resemblance to that provided to another sibling than to the home environment in which either parent was reared.* The intergenerational differences in family configuration thus remain as a potentially significant source of parent-child IQ divergence.

A further complication affecting within-family IQ comparisons is that the correlations found between family members are in part a reflection of the IQ characteristics *of the other families in the study*—which, if not randomly distributed, can bias the results and/or the analysis of the results. For example, if the IQs of siblings in an upper-middle-class suburban school system (or, conversely, a school in a poverty area) are being compared, their scores will usually be more narrowly dispersed than normal, making a high correlation somewhat more difficult to obtain than when the comparison group's scores are normally dispersed. Some researchers have developed statistical mechanisms to overcome this so-called attenuation factor. For example, they will adjust reported correlations to reflect the effects of smaller-than-normal standard deviations in a particular sample.

A number of other researchers, however, consider this approach as totally without merit.

3.7 Principal Conclusions

The most important conclusions of this analysis of IQ-score correspondences among family members include the following:

- Reported correlations among first-degree relatives indicate that their IQs are substantially more alike than those of unrelated people; the average IQ-point distance between siblings, or between parent and child, is about three-fourths as large as the 18-point difference found on average among randomly selected people.
- When certain biases associated with the IQ-examination process are factored out of the equation, however, the divergence in parent-child IQ scores narrows to about 11 points (see Table 9) — a finding that would correspond with a correlation of about +.63.
- Family configuration is an important factor in explaining IQ differences between siblings, and it also has an impact on parent-child resemblances. When reported IQ distances between siblings are adjusted to eliminate the effects of (1) family configuration, (2) differences in their prenatal environment, and (3) a minimum amount of bias from random factors inherent in the test-taking situation, the remaining IQ divergence is reduced to about 9 points.
- Midparent-midchild IQ distances average about half those found in the population at large. After the effects of bias arising from the IQ-examination process are factored out, the remaining divergence is about a third of that randomly found. Even in full-family comparisons, however, the effects of intergenerational differences in family configuration remain as a potentially important source of IQ variance.
- The relatively slow rate at which within-family IQ scores converge when additional family members are

added to the comparison implies that a purely genetic model of intelligence (whether additive or multiplicative) cannot adequately explain this pattern of results.

- The sharply higher IQ correlations found among identical twins than among fraternal twins — coupled with the finding that (when the effects of birth-weight differences are excluded) identical twins are almost as alike in IQ as the same individual tested twice — warrant the conclusion that *although environmental factors can and do have a substantial influence on the determination of intelligence, genetic factors are clearly predominant.*

Notes

1. This estimate assumes that (1) half of the parent-child studies used analogous test instruments (for example, WISC-WAIS, Binet-Binet) and a third used tests containing highly dissimilar verbal-spatial factor loadings; (2) highly dissimilar tests (for example, Binet or Otis vs. Raven's or Wechsler) will engender a nonrandom variance averaging 6 IQ points (of which three-fourths will represent a divergence in scores among family members); (3) moderately divergent tests will engender a variance averaging 3 points (and a 1.5-point divergence); and (4) seemingly analogous tests will cause a 1.0-point variance and a 0.3-point divergence; the addition of a second parent's score is assumed to reduce this test-related variance only slightly.

2. The birth-order-by-family-size distribution of the offspring of Caucasian women between forty and forty-four with two or more children (as derived from the 1980 U.S. Census Table 270) was chosen as representative of the population because it was the most recent cohort for which family formation is virtually complete (see Chapter Six). The score differences on the National Merit Examination (Breland, 1974) for the eighty-two family configurations were then combined as follows: (1) firstborn/secondborn: family of two, 1.7 points; (2) firstborn/secondborn: family of three, 2.3 points; (3) firstborn/thirdborn: family of three, 3.5 points; (4) secondborn/thirdborn: family of three, 1.2 points; (5) firstborn/secondborn: family of four, 2.5 points; (6) firstborn/thirdborn: family of four, 4.3 points; (7) firstborn/fourthborn: family of four, 5.6 points; (8) secondborn/thirdborn: family of four, 1.8 points; (9) secondborn/fourthborn: family of four, 3.1 points; (10) thirdborn/fourthborn: family of four, 1.3 points; (11) average difference, family of five, 3.8 points; and (12) average difference, families of six or more children, 4.5. These differences were then converted from a standard deviation of 20 to 16, and the results were cross multiplied by the

estimated proportions in each of the eleven cells noted above (31.78 percent for families of two, 10.28 percent for each of the family-of-three birth-order relationships, 3.25 percent for the six family-of-four cells, 9.52 percent for families of five, and 8.36 percent for larger families).

3. Since this study provides data by birth order and maternal age for three separate socioeconomic classes rather than holding maternal age constant, IQ changes are compared across two orders of birth and one five-year maternal age span. For example, the scores of firstborn children whose mothers were aged twenty-five to twenty-nine at their birth exceeded those of thirdborn children whose mothers were aged thirty to thirty-four by an average of 3.5 points in the highest social class, 4.0 points in the middle class, and 4.5 points in the lower class. The results of this analysis indicate that two orders of difference (across a five-year maternal-age span) produce a 3.6-point difference in IQ; thus, one order of difference (applicable to 68.4 percent of sibling comparisons) equals 1.8 points, three orders of difference (6.8 percent), 5.4 points, and four or more orders (3.5 percent), 7.0 points.

4. The Birmingham analysis is apt to overstate birth-order effects slightly, because child spacing across two orders of birth averages somewhat more than five years. Conversely, the National Merit Examination scores are likely to understate birth-order effects, because disproportionately large numbers of lower-class and lower-middle-class adolescents are excluded and birth-order effects lessen materially as SES rises.

5. *Family size:* even though only 11.1 percent of the schoolchildren in the full study had three or more older siblings, nearly a third of the comparisons in this "sibling" sample (31.3 percent) were between third and fourthborns, fourth and fifthborns, or even later orders of birth, implying that at least a third of these children were from families with four or more children. *Time clustering/child spacing:* for two siblings to have been included in the (four-year, nine-month) study period, (1) the older sibling in each pair had to have been tested in the very early part of the period, and/or (2) the spacing between the two siblings had to have been very narrow. On both counts, the average score found among these older siblings would tend to be lower than the average of all the firstborn subjects in the larger study. Conversely, younger siblings would be clustered toward the later portion of the survey period and (because of the "IQ-is-rising" effect) would tend to have higher scores than the average for all laterborn subjects of the same birth order. This is indeed what occurred, since (1) the average scores of the firstborns in the sibling subsample were lower than those of firstborns in the larger study; and (2) the scores of secondborn children in the birth-order one-two comparisons were (as predicted) higher than those of secondborns in birth-order two-three comparisons (the sample sizes amounted to 2,193 pairs of firstborn-secondborn comparisons and 1,278 pairs of secondborn-thirdborn comparisons, making the 1.5-point difference found very significant statistically). *Consecutively born sibling comparisons:* since consecutively born siblings are likely to be more alike in IQ than are nonconsecutive siblings, the divergence in IQ scores of all siblings is likely to average just under 1 IQ point greater than found in studies limited to consecutive siblings—as was this study.

Contents

✗ 4 ✗

How Adoption Influences IQ

4.0 Summary

Findings from adoption studies strongly support the view that being reared in a home that is well above the norm in parental nurture often results in a considerable increase in a child's measured intelligence. Whether one compares the IQ scores of adopted children with those of their natural parents, their non-adopted siblings, or other children from the same ethnic and geographical community in which their mothers resided, considerably higher-than-expected IQ scores are found to result from *early* adoptive placements.

Yet, as we shall see, this considerable "IQ responsiveness" to a cognitively enriched home environment neither negates nor even materially weakens the IQ correlations found between adopted children and their biological parents—correlations that are substantially higher than those with their adoptive parents.

These seemingly contradictory findings will be clarified in the next section, which details the results of a "classic" adoption study. This is followed by quantitive analyses of the influence on the IQ scores of adopted children of the occupational-class status of their adoptive fathers, their adoptive parents' education levels, and, wherever possible, their adoptive and biological parents' IQs. This review of adoption studies also suggests (1) the extent to which an early placement in a well-to-do adoptive home will raise the score of a child who would otherwise have been reared in poverty and (2) the size of the residual "IQ gap" that one is likely to find when comparisons are made between the scores of adopted children and those of the adoptive parents' biological offspring.

As detailed in Chapter Five, IQ has been rising; and, as it has risen, the magnitude of the "IQ-score boost" derived from being reared in an adoptive home appears to have lessened (this topic is discussed in depth in Chapter Eighteen). Among children whose adoptive placement was made after the middle of their second year, the IQ gains that they display during their early school years are apt to dissipate considerably when the hormonal surges of puberty are in ascendance (particularly among males). Among early adoptees, however, any such regression is apt to be smaller, and it would seem that it is, in the main, temporary.

This chapter also discusses how the sample selection process itself creates a statistical perception that the IQ scores of adopted children bear a greater resemblance to those of their biological parents than to those of their adoptive parents, and it critiques findings from studies of separately reared identical twins.

The theoretical framework for a general model designed to depict the interplay between measured intelligence and the intellectual quality of the home environment will then be developed, and its importance discussed.

4.1 The Iowa Adoption Study

Among the most striking examples of how children's IQs can be dramatically boosted by adoptive environments — yet remain correlated with the IQs of their parents to the usual extent — are found in a study of children in Iowa who were adopted during the 1930s (Skodak and Skeels, 1949).

The children's IQ scores averaged 116 on the Stanford-Binet,

Table 10. Iowa Adoption Study IQ Scores: Stanford-Binet Examination.

Child's IQ Range	Number of Children	Child's IQ (Avg.)	Natural Mother's IQ Score	Rise in Child's IQ
133 or more	9	139.1	97.1	+ 42.0
125–132	8	129.6	94.4	+ 35.2
117–124	13	120.5	83.5	+ 37.0
109–116	15	112.7	84.0	+ 28.7
101–108	10	104.7	82.6	+ 22.1
100 or below	8	87.4	75.0	+ 12.7
Total/average	63	115.7	85.7	+ 30.0

Source: Adapted from Skodak and Skeels, 1949.

which represented *a jump of 30 points* from the IQ scores of their natural mothers. When grouped by 8-point intervals (one-half a standard deviation), these children's scores formed an almost perfect bell-shaped curve centered on the mean value of 116, as shown in Table 10.

Yet, the IQ correlation between these children and their biological mothers (+ .44) was consistent with that usually found. How could this be? Because those children whose biological mothers had relatively high IQ scores performed far better than did those whose mothers had low scores. For example, the offspring of the eleven natural mothers with the lowest scores (averaging 63) had IQs averaging 104 (with none of these children having an IQ exceeding 120). By contrast, the eight children whose mothers' IQs were the highest (averaging 111) had scores averaging 129, *with only one of these children scoring below 120* (Scarr and Carter-Saltzman, 1982).

These adoptive homes were exceptional, since the exceedingly high demand for these children (all of whom were White and of Northern Euopean ancestry) resulted in the selection of families that were well regarded in their community, were above average in economic means and education, and had usually participated regularly in community and/or church activities. The children, in contrast, were not exceptional. They were very representative of all adopted infants relinquished into the care of either a large public agency or a statewide nonsectarian private agency between 1933 and 1937 *who were adopted prior to six months of age.*

One might ask, Couldn't such striking IQ correlations between mothers and adopted children result from a placement process that emphasized matching those children who were likely to be bright with the most intelligent adoptive parents? The answer is no. An analysis of the relationship between these children's IQs and their adoptive mothers' or adoptive fathers' educational level showed no correlation (Honzik, 1957); also, the IQs of the preadoptive parents were not known to the agency. Further, because the IQ test used (the 1937 Stanford-Binet) had been normed only nine years before this follow-up study, the finding that more than a fourth of these children were performing at or near what is generally considered the genius level is not seriously inflated by the gradual upward trend in IQ scores.

Nevertheless, the conclusion that these children's scores were 30 points higher than those of their natural mothers (which averaged 86) is apt to be overstated, because (1) the biological mothers usually took the test soon after the delivery of their child and/or its relinquishment (which could have affected their performance adversely), and (2) many of these largely rural Iowa mothers were culturally disadvantaged. By comparison, a slightly later study in neighboring Minnesota (Pearson and Amacher, 1956) of unmarried women who had relinquished their children for adoption found that these mothers' IQ scores were intellectually representative of the general population.

In conclusion, this study strongly suggests that a highly advantaged home environment considerably enhances children's IQs and that the resulting IQ gain is likely to be in direct relation to the natural (genetic) endowments of the child.

4.2 The "First" Minnesota Adoption Study

In this study, an average IQ of 110.5 was found among 193 children adopted in the late 1920s and early 1930s before they were six months old; again, all of these children were White and of Northern European parentage (Leahy, 1935; summarized in Scarr and Carter-Saltzman, 1982). This average is virtually identical to that found among children from a similar-sized sample of carefully matched intact families residing in the same communities — except that, in the adoptive families, there were fewer children in the highest and lowest IQ ranges. The IQ correlations between the biological parents and their children were in the normal range (+ .51 with mother's Otis IQ score, + .51 with father's Otis score, + .60 with midparent Otis score, and + .56 with midparent Stanford-Binet vocabulary score), but the correlation between these children and their adoptive parents was far lower (+ .21 with midadoptive parent's Otis score).

Normally, one expects to find a 15- to 20-point IQ difference between children whose fathers work in the professions and those whose fathers work in unskilled manual or service occupations (McNewar, 1942; Seashore, 1950; and Thorndike, Hagen, and Sattler, 1986). In the Minnesota study, such a relationship was observed in the control (that is, biologically intact) families studied: The average score was 118.6 for the offspring of professionals, compared with 101.1 for the offspring of semiskilled laborers and 102.1 for the category "slightly skilled and day labor." Nevertheless, only a small difference was found between the scores of adopted children reared in professional-class families (112.6) and those reared in families headed by semiskilled laborers (109.4) or by slightly skilled or day laborers (107.8) (Burks, 1938, summarized in Scarr and Carter-Saltzman, 1982). Moreover, in these unskilled and semiskilled labor-class families, the children reared in the adoptive families had significantly higher scores, even though the adoptive parents' IQs were virtually identical to those of the controls.

However, in those adoptive families where the father's occupational class was considerably higher, only a relatively small additional "boost" in the adoptive children's IQs was reported. For example, the scores of children adopted into families where the father was in the professions averaged 112.6 or only 3.2 points higher than those reared in families headed by semiskilled laborers, even though the Otis scores of the adoptive parents in the professional class were substantially higher than those of the parents in the laboring class (averaging 59.6 compared with 39.7).

Thus, these results strongly imply that the qualities that provide "IQ enhancement" to adoptive children are the superior *parenting skills* that people accepted as adoptive parents are apt to possess. It is not a matter of their having higher IQs or educational levels than the biological parents, since

- Children reared in adoptive homes where the adoptive father's occupational status was relatively low scored far higher than did children raised by their biological parents in families in the same paternal occupational class.
- Moreover, the additional IQ-enhancing benefits of being reared in an adoptive family where parental education and/or IQ were high were modest, compared with the overall IQ "boost" from being reared in an adoptive home per se. Although the IQs of adopted children were somewhat higher if they were placed with well-educated adoptive parents, they approached but did not attain equality with the IQs of children reared in nonadoptive homes of comparable socioeconomic status (SES).

4.3 Other Adoption Studies

How large an IQ gain is a Black or interracial child likely to attain when placed into a White adoptive home where both parents are college educated, have IQs averaging 120, and are in their mid to late thirties at the time of placement? The answer suggested by the Minnesota Transracial Adoption Study is that *it depends on the age at which the child was placed in the adoptive home.* The IQ scores for the ninety-nine Black and interracial children in this study who were *placed during their first year of life averaged 110.4* — or a full standard deviation higher than the average (93.2) reported (at ages five to nine) for the thirty-one later adoptees (Scarr and Weinberg, 1977). The IQs of the biological children in these highly advantaged families were, on average, quite similar to those of their parents — 118 (on WISC/WAIS) for the ninety-six biological children aged eight and older, compared with 119 for their parents (on the Wechsler Adult Intelligence Scale). Nevertheless, because these (1974) IQ scores were based on the 1947-normed version of the Wechsler, these averages are somewhat inflated (see Chapter Five).

A study of adopted children from families where one child had been given up for adoption but at least one other child had been kept (Schiff and others, 1978) found that the IQs of the adopted children averaged 16 points higher on the WISC than the IQs of their siblings (110.6 versus 94.7). In this 1970s French study, all the biological fathers were unskilled workers, and all the adoptive homes were of exceptionally high socioprofessional occupational status.

In the Texas Adoption Project (Horn, Loehlin, and Willerman, 1979)—which is unique in that the mothers placing their children for adoption were all relatively well off financially (and had IQ scores averaging 108.7)—the "usual" correlational relationship between the biological parents' and adopted children's IQ scores was again found. The scores of the 27 (of 300) children whose natural mothers had IQs of 95 or lower averaged 102.6 (a gain averaging 13 points), compared with a 118.3 average for the offspring of the 34 mothers whose IQs averaged 120 or higher. In this study, the effects of "assortive" (nonrandom) placement were examined by comparing the adoptive parents' IQ scores of the offspring of natural mothers having relatively high IQs with those having relatively low IQs. Although a difference was noted, it was relatively modest (averaging 4 points).

4.4 Adoptive Parent–Adoptive Child IQ Correlations

What does it signify when researchers report that the IQ correlations found between adoptive parents and their adoptees are much lower than the correlations found between these adopted children and their biological parents?

One might suppose that it implies that the IQs of these children are closer to those of their natural parents than to those of their adoptive parents—but, as we have seen, this is not the case. Instead, what these correlations signify is that it is easier to determine which child came from which biological parent than to determine which of these children was reared by which adoptive family.

A substantially more important question, however, might be posed as follows: Here are 500 children; 100 were placed in adoptive homes in infancy, and the other 400 were reared by biological mothers/parents whose demographic characteristics are similar to those of the 100 "relinquishing" parents. Based solely on these children's IQ scores, how good a guess can be made concerning which 100 were raised by adoptive parents and which by their natural parents? Obviously, it would be easy to come up with a good answer since the adopted children would be enormously overrepresented among the 100 children with the highest IQs.

With this in mind, the average IQ correlations found between adopted children and their adoptive parents can be summarized as follows:

- *Texas Adoption Study*: +.15, an unweighted average of 541 adoptive mother-child pairs and 454 adoptive father-child pairs, the correlations being +.18 and +.12, respectively (DeFries and Plomin, 1978). In a subsample taking the WISC, the correlations were +.19 for verbal IQ and +.05 for performance IQ (Horn, Loehlin, and Willerman, 1979).
- *Colorado Adoption Study*: +.15 for four-year Stanford-Binet scores, including +.18 for 161 adoptive mothers and +.12 for 157 adoptive fathers (Plomin and DeFries, 1985). A correlation of +.14 was reported for the verbal subtest, with negligible correlations for other subtests.
- *Transracial Adoption Study*: +.19 for the "early adoptees," including +.23 for 109 adoptive mothers and +.15 for 111 adoptive fathers (Scarr and Weinberg, 1977).
- *"First" Minnesota Study*: +.21 for (177) midadoptive parent IQ scores on the Otis test (including +.24 for adoptive mothers and +.19 for adoptive fathers). The midpoint Standford-Binet vocabulary test score correlation was +.29 (Leahy, 1935).
- *Stanford Adoption Study*: +.20 for (174) midpoint "mental age," including +.19 for adoptive mothers and +.07 for adoptive fathers (Burks, 1928).

A pattern emerges from a review of these studies: (1) *IQ correlations between adopted children and their adoptive parents are quite modest* (averaging perhaps +.16 with one adoptive parent's

IQ and + .19 for midadoptive parent scores); (2) in each of these studies, *the IQ correlations with adoptive mothers were higher than with adoptive fathers;* and (3) *substantially higher correlations were found with verbal than with nonverbal IQ measures.*

4.5 Adoptive Homes and Childhood IQ: Conclusions and Implications

Clearly, the environmental enrichment provided by adoptive homes has profound effects on the intellectual development of children receiving such care—provided they are exposed to these conditions from an extremely early age.

Although the occupational-class status of the adoptive father does make a difference in the extent to which an adopted child's IQ will be boosted by the adoptive experience, the socioeconomic status of the adoptive family is clearly not the primary determinant of whether an adoptive placement will result in an increased IQ. This is amply demonstrated by the previously cited findings from the "first" Minnesota study (Leahy, 1935)—a result strongly reinforced by findings from the Stanford Adoption Study (Burks, 1928), where a difference averaging only 4.5 points was reported when children adopted into professional-class families were compared with children adopted into families headed by skilled laborers. Only at the extremes of socioeducational class differences do the effects magnify considerably (Capron and Duyme, 1989).

These findings could be interpreted in two somewhat different ways:

- An excellent home life can raise the IQ of a child who otherwise would have scored in the average to slightly below-average range to perhaps half a standard deviation above the norm, but further gains are increasingly hard to achieve.
- An exceptionally good home environment is provided by adoptive parents of all occupational classes, and the further degree of intellectual stimulation that very bright, well-to-do adoptive parents provide is like "frost-

ing on a cake"—the cake being the high degree of
emotional and cognitive nurturing that almost all
adoptive families provide.

Both of these explanations have considerable merit. The IQ
gap between the biological and adopted children from
professional-class adoptive families reflects the lesser *innate* ability of the average adopted child (who is apt to come from lower-
middle-class parentage), yet the much higher than expected
scores attained by adopted children irrespective of the adoptive
parents' education also attest to the malleability of IQ during
children's formative years.

The rather low correlation found when the IQs of adopted
children are compared with those of their adoptive parents is
clearly an artifact of the approach used to generate this correlation. If, as seems likely, *almost all the adoptive homes that are being
compared offer cognitively enhancing qualities that are far above the
norm*, then a child adopted into almost **any** of these homes is
likely to have his or her IQ come much closer to its potential
than if he or she were reared in an average or below-average
environment. Thus, these adoptive-parent/adopted-child correlations are in essence answering the question, By how much will
a child's IQ differ if it is reared by an adoptive parent whose IQ is
105, compared with an adoptive home where the parent's IQ is
110, 115, or 120? The answer is, Not very much.

It is most unfortunate, however, that these same writers have
used these findings as evidence that heredity strongly predominates over environment simply because the adoptive child's
correlations with its biological parents are so much higher than
with its adoptive parents. If, instead, the correlation for each
adoptive family was calculated by comparing the proximity of
its IQ scores in relation to a large sample of *randomly selected*
homes—rather than a sample entirely comprised of adoptive
homes—*wouldn't the adopted children's IQ correlations with their
adoptive parents be higher than with their biological parents?* It would
certainly seem so, since these studies indicate that (in terms of
IQ points) adopted children's IQs are apt to be closer to those of
their adoptive parents than to those of their biological parents.

Consequently, such an approach would indicate that environment is a stronger influence than heredity.

More recently, Capron and Duyme (1989) undertook a full cross-fostering study designed to compare and contrast the IQ scores of four groups of adopted children: (1) children whose biological parents were of exceptionally high socioeconomic status (the biological father was a student, physician, or senior executive) who were adopted into families with a similar socioeconomic status (the adoptive father was a physician, senior executive, or professor); (2) children whose biological parents were of low socioeconomic status (neither parent had more than eight years of schooling and the father's job was in the lowest occupational classes) who were adopted into low SES homes; (3) children from low SES families who were adopted into exceptionally high SES homes; and (4) children from exceptionally high SES families adopted into low SES homes (the last category occurred only once per 600 adoption files examined). All the children selected were relinquished at birth and were adopted before they were six months old. There were no appreciable differences between the four groups in birth weight, perinatal health, or age at adoption.

When these 38 adopted children were tested at age fourteen on the French version of the WISC-R, their scores averaged as follows:

- Children born into and reared by exceptionally high SES families, 119.6.
- Children born into high SES families and reared by low SES families, 107.5.
- Children born into low SES families and reared by high SES families, 103.6.
- Children born into and reared by low SES families, 92.4.

Thus, being reared in low SES environments resulted in the IQ scores of children born into an exceptionally high SES home falling by an average of 12 points—while being reared in extremely high SES homes resulted in the scores of children from low SES homes rising by an average of 11 points. Irrespective of the socioeconomic status of the adoptive homes, however, the IQ scores of these adopted French children born into exceptionally high SES homes averaged 15 or 16 points higher than those of adoptees born into low SES homes.

4.6 Adoptive Children's IQ Gains: Temporary or Permanent?

Recent evidence calls into question whether the childhood IQ gains registered by adopted children are sustained into adulthood. For example, when two unrelated infants are adopted into the same home, they tend to show similarities in mental development during the early school years (correlations of +.34 being reported by Bouchard and McGue, 1981, who averaged together six studies). In contrast, it is often reported that little or no IQ correlation among unrelated children reared together exists (Willerman, 1987). In the Adolescent Adoption Study, the reported correlation between unrelated adopted children reared together was zero (Scarr and Weinberg, 1983). However, because the basis of comparison was again limited to adoptive homes, all that these results signify is that, during adolescence, the IQs of these adopted children would have been about the same almost irrespective of which of these (presumably highly nurturing) adoptive parents had reared them. Similarly, in the Texas Adoption Project (where most of the biological mothers of the adoptees were above the norm in income and IQ)—after comparing the early childhood and teenage IQ scores of adopted children with those of their biological and adoptive parents—the authors conclude that "Genes seem to continue actively contributing to intellectual variation at least into early adulthood, whereas the effect of shared family environment appears to be largely inertial after early childhood" (Loehlin, Horn, and Willerman, 1989, p. 1003).

Confirmation that puberty heralds a weakening of environmental influences on IQ also comes from studies of children reared by their biological parents. In the Louisville Twin Study (Wilson, 1983), the correlations for identical twins (seventy-eight pairs) reached their highest confluence at fifteen years of age (+.88), while the correlations among fraternal twins (sixty-four pairs) reached their lowest level at this age (+.54), a finding identical to that generally reported among consecutive siblings (see Chapter Three). Similarly, findings from the two largest (early) longitudinal studies (the Fels and Berkeley growth studies) support a conclusion that genetic influences are strengthened during adolescence. In the Berkeley Growth Study (Honzik, MacFarlane, and Allen, 1948), the children's average IQ score declined 5 points between the ages of fourteen and eighteen (from 123 to 118), with most of this decline attributable to children who registered large IQ gains between early and middle childhood. In the Fels Longitudinal Study (McCall, Appelbaum, and Hogarty, 1973), computer-generated patterns denoting similar trends in IQ scores across the frequent periodic childhood testing revealed that five-sixths of the children fell into one of five clusters. In the three clusters where significant IQ gains were achieved between early childhood and the ages of nine through eleven, there was a marked decrease in scores between the ages of fourteen and seventeen. In another cluster (where IQ scores had fallen markedly between the ages of three and six before becoming and remaining relatively stable through age fourteen), there was again a movement by age seventeen in the direction of the scores attained in early childhood.

There are several reasons for assuming that this apparent diminution in the environmental component of IQ is in large part temporary:

- Although visuospatial abilities reach an adult level of competence by mid adolescence, verbal IQ matures at a far slower pace. Because verbal IQ is more susceptible to environmental influence than is nonverbal IQ, the hereditary influence is temporarily magnified.
- Puberty is a period of relatively greater *right-hemisphere activation* than is preadolescence (see Part Five). Because the foundations of "right-brain" growth are laid in *early* infancy, adopted children may be at a cognitive disadvantage during this period, because many of them are likely to have received inadequate amounts of *vestibular* and *visual* stimulation during their initial weeks or months of infancy (see Chapter Eleven).
- A person's ancestral environment is likely to affect the nature and

strength of his or her hormonal surges during puberty. If the cultural and geographical imperatives of that ancestral environment favored the survival of ("high-testosterone") environmentally vigilant and responsive individuals, one might expect that the offspring of such a heritage would have a relatively difficult time paying attention (in a "left-brained" manner) to classroom lessons, when their body is urging them to be actively engaging in the rites of passage into adulthood (this seems to be especially the case among males).

4.7 Twins Reared Apart Versus Twins Reared Together

One of the strongest linchpins in the belief that heredity predominates over environment in the development of intelligence is that *the IQs of identical twins reared apart are more alike than are the IQs of fraternal twins reared together.*

The IQ resemblance of identical twins reared together has been firmly established, being represented by a correlation of + .86. Almost as widely accepted is the finding that the correlations of fraternal (dizygotic) twins reared together approximate + .60, a figure that Bouchard and McGue (1981) derived by combining forty-one studies totaling 5,546 pairings. Although fraternal twins are no more alike genetically than other siblings, their IQ scores resemble one another a little more than those of other siblings, presumably because they experience a greater similarity in their early environment and upbringing.

Unfortunately, opportunities for evaluating the IQ correspondences between identical twins reared apart are rare, and the few studies that exist suffer from more than the usual problems encountered in twin and adoption studies, in that their sample sizes are exceptionally small, the IQ measures used were sometimes not of the best caliber, and some of them are very old. Moreover, the environments in which the reared-apart twins in these studies were placed tended to be far from random, especially when both twins were reared by relatives. In those cases, common family values, personality traits, and so on would no doubt have caused these children to retain many of their culturally based ancestral similarities. Further, because separately reared twins often live in different communities, their IQs were sometimes assessed *at different times of the day.* It is known that significant time-of-day differences exist in cognitive abilities — for example, spatial ability is considerably better in the morning than in the afternoon or evening, immediate memory also peaks in the morning, while delayed recall shows a gradual improvement as the day progresses (Furnham and Rawles, 1988) — and these differences would tend to reduce the reported IQ correspondences of separately reared twins.

The IQ correlations reported in these studies tend to fall midway between those of identical and fraternal twins reared together. For example, Bouchard and McGue (1981) reported an average correlation of + .72 for three studies totaling 65 pairs that met their "quality" standards (see Chapter Three). Scarr and Carter-Saltzman (1982) reported an average correlation of + .74 for 65 (in part, different) pairs; and using less rigorous criteria, Erlenmeyer-Kimling and Jarvik (1963) reported + .75 for 107 pairs.

These data do, however, offer an opportunity to analyze two of the hypotheses set forth in this volume, namely: (1) maternal interactive behavior during the first several months of infancy will have a discernible and lasting impact on IQ (see Chapters Eight and Eleven), and (2) twins born in exceptionally good health will have closer IQ correspondences than those of low birth weight. To assess the first hypothesis, we can turn to Bouchard's (1983) analysis of IQ correspondences in relation to age of separation. Confirming an earlier analysis (Taylor, 1980), Bouchard's analysis showed *markedly higher correlations for twins separated after the age of six months than for those adopted prior to six months of age*, a finding that he "replicated" by assessing the correlations found when scores on alternative IQ measures were used and the investigators employed more than one measure of general ability. Thus, in the Newman study (Newman, Freeman, and Holzinger, 1937), where the Stanford-Binet correlation was + .67, the Otis IQ score correlation (+ .74 overall) was + .82 for late adoptees (after six months) and + .34 for early adoptees. In the Juel-Nielson (1980) study, where the Wechsler-Binet correlation was + .62, the Raven's raw score correlations (+ .77) were + .75 for late adoptees and + .58 for early adoptees. Only in Shields (1962), where correlations were + .77 for the

Dominoes and the synonyms part of the Raven's Mill Hill Vocabulary scale, were there no appreciable differences in correlations by age of separation.

To assess the hypothesis that twins in exceptionally good health at birth would have closer-than-average IQ correspondences, the children in Vandenberg and Johnson's (1968) analysis, which contains age-of-separation data for thirty-seven separated twin pairs, have been subdivided into those separated within their first month of life (eleven pairs), who differed by an average of only 3 IQ points (based primarily on the WAIS), and those separated after one month of age, who differed by an average of 9.2 points. Because of the high frequency of low birth weight among twins — and the additional risk that a twin having a markedly lower birth weight than its co-twin will have a cognitive impairment — twin pairs who were separated during their first thirty days of life are likely to be considerably stronger and more vigorous than the norm.

Unfortunately, as of this writing, the IQ results for reared-apart twins from the Minnesota Twin Study have not yet become available. When they do, it will be interesting to evaluate IQ correlations by age of separation (the average age of separation for this sample being only 3.6 months) and the relationship between IQ correlation and the age at which testing was done (which averaged 38.5 years) as this latter analysis may enable one to examine the long-term IQ effects of differential rearing on health. The Minnesota Study, however, does provide some fascinating anecdotal reports of behavioral correspondences among identical twins reared apart; for instance, the twins who built the same kind of semicircular table around a tree in their back yard, or the (unreunited) pair who married women with the same name and used the same names for some of their children and their dogs.

4.8 Constructing a Theoretical Model of the Effects of Environment on IQ

Before constructing a model designed to reflect the impact of environment on intelligence, we might introduce a number of simplifying assumptions:

1.   All children in the normal range of innate intelligence will re-
     spond to a similar extent intellectually to a given quality of educa-
     tional and emotional upbringing. Obviously, this assumption
     ignores those innate differences in children's temperaments that
     affect the types of behavioral approaches that will or will not be
     effective with them.
2.   It is possible to evaluate and to quantify precisely the impact on
     IQ of all aspects of the environment (such as love, encouragement,
     stimulation, and discipline) and create a weighted composite of
     intellectually stimulating and intellectually stifling environmen-
     tal features. Thus, by obtaining information about any given
     home, we can rank this home on a scale of zero to 100 — with zero
     being the educational and emotional milieu least conducive to
     intellectual growth and 99 or higher being the top percentile of all
     homes.
3.   The nearer one gets to the median or average home environment,
     the smaller will be the IQ impact of a 1-percentile change in a
     given home's intellectual quality — compared with the impact of a
     single-rank change as one gets nearer to the extremes. This means
     that the IQ difference that results from being reared in a 90th-
     percentile, as opposed to a 95th-percentile, home will be much
     larger than the difference between being reared in a 50th-
     percentile, as opposed to a 55th-percentile, home.
4.   For the sake of simplicity, it is assumed that (except near the two
     extremes) the shape of the "curved line" (representing the IQ
     effect of any rank order change) on one side of the median is the
     mirror image of its shape on the other side of the median. This
     signifies that the IQ increment produced by moving from a 50th-
     percentile to a 70th-percentile home is identical to the IQ decre-
     ment produced by moving from a 50th-percentile to a 30th-
     percentile home. A graphic display representative of this type of
     curvilinear function appears in Figure 2.

Within this framework, let us now consider where adoptive
homes are likely to rank (on the average) in relation to the
cognitive quality of all homes and use this analysis as an aid in
developing a real-world estimate of the effects of differential
environments on IQ. For purposes of this analysis, it is estimated that (1) the average environment provided by the adoptive homes in the classic studies reported on in this chapter is
equal to the 85th percentile of all home environments (with a
substantial majority of these homes clustered between the 70th
and 95th percentiles) and that (2) the IQ boost engendered in a
child in the normal range of innate intelligence from being
reared in such an adoptive home will average half a standard

deviation. This is a relatively conservative estimate of the IQ "enhancement" that seems to have occurred in the studies under consideration, since it takes into account the slight overstate-ment of adoptive-study IQ scores caused by the gradual rise in the general level of intelligence, as well as the possibility that this increase has, in part, reflected a gradual improvement in the average educational and psychological quality of home environ-ments. This development would of course cause the effects of being reared in a superior- rather than a standard-quality home to lessen (see Chapter Eighteen).

Table 11 depicts the impact of this model formulation on the IQ of a child whose innate intelligence is exactly 100 — under three varying degrees of assumed IQ sensitivity to environmen-tal influences. The middle column ("moderate sensitivity") is meant to be representative of the previously assumed 8-point boost from an 85th-percentile adoptive home. In addition, if the demographics of the "relinquishing" biological home (including maternal age) were such that the child would have been reared in

Figure 2. Impact of Different Home Environments on the Measured IQ of a Child of Average Innate Intelligence.

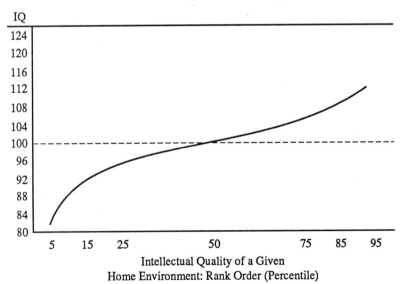

Table 11. Hypothecated Impact of the Environment on the Measured IQ of a Child of Average Innate Intelligence Under Various Sensitivity Assumptions.

	IQ Effect on Child of Average Intellect		
Quality of Home Environment[a]	Low Sensitivity[b]	Moderate Sensitivity[b]	High Sensitivity[b]
Lowest Percentile[c]	75	68	60
5th Percentile	85	76	70
10th Percentile	90	84	75
15th Percentile	95	92	84
25th Percentile	98	96	92
40th Percentile	99	98.5	97
50th Percentile	100	100	100
60th Percentile	101	101.5	103
75th Percentile	102	104	108
85th Percentile	103	108	112
90th Percentile	104	112	118
95th Percentile	106	118	124
99th Percentile	108	124	130
99.9th Percentile	110	132	145

[a] This quality assessment is predicated solely on the environment's ability to influence a child's IQ score and not on its humanistic, social, and/or emotional qualities.

[b] This is the assumed sensitivity of measured IQ to changes in environmental quality (introduced in early infancy).

[c] The likelihood that an extremely poor environment will produce children having IQs of 60 to 75 is well established (see, for example, the Tehran orphanage study in Chapter Eight).

a home that was far below the norm in cognitive quality (that is, the 15th percentile), the IQ boost from being reared in the adoptive home would be 16 points.

The value of constructing this type of theoretical model is that it provides a perspective from which to:

- Estimate the average IQ that might be attained by a physically and emotionally healthy normal-weight and -gestation neonate, reared in a "nonmalignant" family configuration by parents who provide an atmosphere that is both conductive to learning and devoid of major, intellectually stifling emotional problems.
- Assess the relative contribution of individual factors in the childhood home environment that might raise or lower IQ.

- Evaluate the effectiveness of efforts to engender a dramatic (and permanent) increase in measured intelligence by providing specific types of early environmental enrichment.

As detailed in Chapter Eighteen, this task is complicated by a realization that, in the more than fifty years since the children in the Iowa Adoption Study were placed in adoptive homes, IQ scores in the U.S. (and throughout the developed world) have risen substantially. As a consequence, early exposure to a cognitively enriched environment is now apt to have a somewhat less dramatic influence on IQ.

The debate between hereditarians and environmentalists is, in essence, a disagreement over the size of the lasting IQ increase that would be generated by early and continuing exposure to a very enriched cognitive environment, as depicted by the shape of the upper portion of the curvilinear function shown in Figure 2, there being little or no disagreement over the ability of a woefully inadequate environment to produce a major, permanent suppression of intellect.

Under the "moderate sensitivity" assumption (Table 11), a top-quality environment (that is, the 99.9th percentile) is assumed to be capable of transforming a neonate of normal intelligence into a borderline genius. Under the relatively "low sensitivity" assumption, the *best* that can be expected from being reared in a 95th-percentile home environment is an increase of 6 points in measured intelligence, and most strict hereditarians would consider this estimate to be far too generous and/or would view it as an IQ-test effect that is unrelated to real IQ. People holding this view might argue that efforts to boost cognitive development through preschool day care or other targeted intervention programs—although possibly able to produce a short-term IQ increase—cannot effectuate a significant long-term change in *innate* intelligence and would argue that once these special efforts cease, IQ scores will rapidly drift back toward their former levels. Under the "high sensitivity" assumption, an excellent (95th-percentile) environment is thought to be able to make a near genius out of a child with an average IQ and a "superenriched" environment to be capable of creating a genius mentality in most children.

Before we can give a good answer to the question of how much an excellent environment can raise IQ, we must first address the following areas: (1) what factors in the early home environment have been linked consistently with cognitive performance and how strong are these linkages, (2) what have been the results of the most successful efforts to boost IQ begun in infancy or toddlerhood, (3) what characteristics of the early home environments of gifted and eminent people appear to have facilitated their success, and (4) what aspects of the early nurturing and educational practices of those ethnic groups whose children (on the average) exhibit superior abilities in a particular cognitive domain are responsible for the development of these abilities?

These issues are the principal focus of Parts Three and Four.

~ Part Two ~

Changes in IQ Scores Over Time

A relatively steady and fairly rapid increase in IQ scores has occurred throughout the developed world over the course of the twentieth century—with scores on so-called culture-free tests rising even faster than those on more verbally oriented examinations. The analysis of trends in the rates of gain over time presented in Chapter Five indicates that these rates are affected by the economic and social conditions prevalent during people's infancy and toddlerhood.

Because IQ has been rising, studies comparing the IQ scores of adults of differing ages give the impression that IQ peaks at a considerably earlier age than is the case when people's performance is followed longitudinally. Further, longitudinal studies suggest that, with the exception of short-term memory, no significant erosion in people's cognitive ability is likely to occur until at least their mid sixties.

Although IQ is frequently a good predictor of academic performance, the two sometimes differ considerably, with academic performance in verbal areas being especially sensitive to the caretaker ratio present in a child's formative years. This provides an explanation for the period of declining Scholastic Aptitude Test (SAT) verbal scores of college-bound students, despite the general rise in IQ scores.

Chapter Six centers on the myths and realities that surround the IQ gap between Caucasian and Black Americans. Because the long-term rise in IQ scores has been so great, the large disparity in the average IQ scores of these two groups can be viewed as a measure of how long it took for Black Americans to achieve the Caucasian norms of an earlier era and how long it might take for them to achieve today's norms rather than as a gap representing an insurmountable barrier. Moreover, an evaluation of the contribution of two previously discussed factors that influence IQ—the intrauterine environment and family configuration—suggests that these two factors might account for about 40 percent of the disparity between Black and White IQ scores.

Contents

✄ 5 ✄

Evidence That IQ
Has Been Rising

5.1 Introduction

Throughout the developed world, IQ scores have been rising for practically the whole of the twentieth century. Although the growth rates have varied considerably from country to country, era to era, and test to test, certain patterns have emerged:

- Substantially larger gains are reported on nonverbal tests of the type heralded as culture-free measures of "fluid intelligence" (such as the Raven's Progressive Matrices test) with somewhat slower growth rates found on more verbally oriented tests.
- The fastest rates of gain tend to occur when the scores of people whose early upbringing coincided with an era of economic prosperity and social stability are compared with those of people whose formative years coincided with an era of severe economic and/or social upheaval.

How do we know that IQ is rising? The answer to that question is simple: Whenever a group of people are given two versions of an IQ test (with half of the subjects being given the new test first and half the old to eliminate any bias growing out of practice effects), they *always* score higher on the version developed and/or normed in the earlier period. Likewise, when an (unrevised) IQ test is renormed (by generating a more recent standardization sample), groups of subjects always perform significantly better against the earlier norms than against the more recent ones. Thus, it is reasoned that, because the norms predicated on the scores of earlier samples are consistently easier to exceed than those based on later samples, the average test taker's ability improved during the intervening years. An alternative approach (applicable to intelligence tests whose content has remained constant) is to compare the scores of a large number of subjects with those of an earlier population whose geographical and other demographic characteristics are nearly equivalent. Again, improved performance is almost universally reported.

Because IQ has been rising, studies that compare the intellectual ability of adults of different ages at a single point in time give the impression that intelligence peaks earlier in life than it actually does. An analysis of these so-called cross-sectional studies shows that over the past several decades, there has been a considerable increase in the age at which IQ stops rising, from people's late teens (in the early part of the century) to age thirty (as of 1978). Furthermore, longitudinal studies strongly suggest that most aspects of intellectual ability remain stable until age sixty or beyond, while other aspects do not reach their zenith until mid-life. As a consequence, the superior test performance registered by young adults seems to be attributable to the gradual rise in IQ, not to a decline in intellectual performance between young adulthood and mid-life.

Some additional good news is that, in relatively healthy people, the erosion in intellectual ability in later life is (with the exception of certain forms of short-term memory recall) considerably less rapid than is commonly believed, and improvements in health care are steadily pushing back the age at which serious declines in people's mental faculties become prevalent.

5.2 IQ Trends in the United States

Abundant evidence exists that IQ scores of Americans of all ages—when measured by the most respected comprehensive IQ tests (the Stanford-Binet and the Wechsler)—have been rising throughout the twentieth century.

Combining seventy-three studies between 1932 and 1978 led James Flynn, the most prolific assembler and analyzer of studies in this field, to conclude that IQ scores rose by an average of three-tenths of an IQ point per year over this forty-six-year period (Flynn, 1982, 1984b). A detailed review of these studies suggests that this estimate is slightly overstated because Flynn relied heavily on studies that used the scores of children whose early nurturing coincided with the Great Depression as the basis from which to calculate IQ gains, and these studies have tended to show higher rates of increase[1] than do comparisons using subjects born before or after this period. Recent (Stanford-Binet) data suggest the possibility that there has been some slowing in the rate of IQ increase in the past ten to fifteen years, but this may, in part, reflect the slightly slower long-term growth in IQ scores found on the more verbally factored Stanford-Binet than on the Wechsler.

IQ Trends Among American Children and Adolescents

This section summarizes studies that compared the performance of children on recently normed IQ tests with their scores on tests normed ten or more years earlier. By calculating the extent to which their scores on the earlier-normed test exceeded their performance on the more recently normed test and then dividing this increase by the number of years between the norming of the two tests, we can derive an estimate of the average IQ-point gain per year.

Rather than reflecting a rate of change in IQ between the two test years, I have reorganized these data to provide a comparison of the performance of children born during one time period with the performance of those born in another. My decision to relate IQ growth to the eras in which the subjects received their early upbringing is based on findings that, for a large majority of people, lifetime IQ is fairly well established by age six and that the early environment has an extremely important and lasting influence on IQ scores. The results of these analyses are summarized as follows:

Stanford-Binet (Form L-M): 1932–1972. The scores of 2,351 children on this test were calculated in two different ways — against this test's 1931–33 norms and against its 1972 norms (Terman and Merrill, 1973).[2] These children's scores averaged 9.9 points higher when the earlier norms were applied. Thus, over this forty-year period, *American children gained an average of 10 IQ points, or a quarter of a point per year.*

As shown in Table 12, an analysis of these data (Flynn, 1984a) indicates that the youngest and oldest age groups registered the most rapid IQ gains. The extraordinarily large increase displayed by the (514) children age two to four might be related to environmental factors, since (1) the 1931–33 norms for two- to four-year old children were established by testing subjects whose early upbringing coincided with the onset and initial years of the Great Depression (which might well have had an adverse affect on their performance), while (2) the later norms for young children were established on subjects conceived during the era of heavy U.S. involvement in the Vietnam War (when younger and less-well-educated men were somewhat more likely to be in military service). Similarly, many of the sixteen- to eighteen-year-olds tested as part of the 1931–33 sample may have been adversely affected by the absence of their fathers (who were serving in World War I) during their preschool years. By contrast, the slowest growth was found when scores of children whose early rearing was in a relatively prosperous, stable era (the 1920s) were compared with those of children born in later periods.

Wechsler: 1947 and 1972 Revisions. Flynn (1984b) has reported on a considerable number of studies that compared the IQ scores of children and young adults who took two different IQ tests (in randomized order),[3] at least one of which was the 1947 or 1972 Wechsler. The results of his analyses are as follows:

- *1932–1947:* Over 1,500 schoolchildren were given both the Stanford-Binet (form L) and the WISC; the combined results (of seventeen studies) showed an average gain of 4.7 IQ points, from 103.0 on the newer (1947-normed) test to 107.7 on the earlier test (normed in 1931–33). This translates into a gain of almost exactly *a third of a point per year* when the scores of children born between

Table 12. Stanford-Binet IQ Gains over Forty Years
(Form L-M, Normed Against 1932 and 1972 Standards).

| | Years of Children's Birth | | | |
Age of Children	Earlier Period	Later Period	Average IQ Gain[a]	Gain per Year (Rate)
All Ages	1913–30	1954–70	9.9	.25
2–4	1927–30	1967–70	14.9	.38
5–7	1924–26	1964–66	9.7	.24
8–15	1918–23	1958–63	7.3	.18
16–18	1913–17	1954–57	12.0	.30

Note: Flynn's analysis assumes that the scores of the all-White 1932 standardization sample would have been 2.8 points lower if Blacks and other minorities had been included (as they were in 1972); gains have been calculated on the basis of a standard deviation of 15 (Flynn, 1984a). The age ranges shown are close approximations, because the earlier norms were established over three years (1931–33) and the later norms in two years (1971–72).

[a] These are unweighted averages (each year's sample being counted equally, irrespective of sample size).

Source: Adapted from Flynn, 1984a.

1934 and 1943 are contrasted with the scores of those born between 1918 and 1928.

- *1947–1972:* This author found five studies covering 216 children who took both the WISC and the revised version (the WISC-R) normed in 1972; these children (who were somewhat above average in IQ) showed a gain of nearly 8 points — *a rate of increase almost exactly equal to that reported in the earlier period, namely, 0.32 points per year.* This suggests that the IQ scores of children born between 1956 and 1966 exceeded those of children born in the Depression and war years (1932 through 1942) to this extent.
- *1947–1972:* To increase the number of subjects upon whom to base 1947-1972 comparisons, Flynn merged all relevant studies of subjects taking various combinations of Wechsler and/or Wechsler–Stanford-Binet IQ tests normed in these two years, including the adult and early childhood versions — the WAIS and the Wechsler Preschool and Primary Scale of Intelligence (WPPSI). The rate of increase among the 1,077 subjects who were tested in this manner was *0.36 points per year.*

1985 Stanford-Binet Revision. In 1985, the Stanford-Binet Intelligence Test underwent a major revision. This fourth edition (called the SAS) (1) increased the number of tasks that appraised "quantitative reasoning," "abstract/visual reasoning," and "short-term memory" (which somewhat reduced the percentage of tasks focusing on verbal ability); and (2) reordered the presentation of test material to enable separate cognitive assessments to be made in these four categories, in addition to providing an overall IQ score.

The results of studies comparing scores on this new version of the Binet with those on earlier-normed tests (Thorndike, Hagen, and Sattler, 1986) are summarized as follows:

- *1972–1984 (Binet vs. Binet):* 139 children scored 2.3 points higher on the new version of the Stanford-Binet than they did on the (1972-normed) third edition (form L-M); this translates to a gain of 0.18 points per year.[4]
- *1972–1984 (WISC-R vs. Binet):* 205 children (average age 9.5) scored 2.8 points higher on the earlier-normed test (105.2 vs. 102.4), or an increase averaging 0.22 points per year. An analysis of the test components indicates that most of this increase was attributable to the (newly developed) "abstract/visual reasoning" area (6.5 points), when compared with scores on the "Performance" subtest of the WISC-R.
- *1965–66 to 1984 (WPPSI vs. Binet):* 75 younger children (average age 5.5) were given the SAS and the WPPSI; the 5.0-point increase (110.3 vs. 105.3) translates into a rate of increase of 0.28 points per year. Again, the "abstract/visual reasoning" area showed a far larger increase (9.4 points), or nearly half a point a year, than did the other components, which rose 2.7 points (0.15 points per year).[5]

IQ Trends Among American Adults

This section encapsulates the results of studies comparing the performance of adults on comprehensive IQ tests and/or other measures of learning ability. Here, in addition to a considerable growth in IQ over time, there is also evidence (elaborated in section 5.4) that the age at which IQ scores peak has risen over the past several decades. Moreover, people's cognitive ability remains at peak (or near-peak) levels until far later in life than had been commonly believed.

These data also suggest that faster annual rates of increase are found when the performance of people born in the 1920s is compared with those born between 1890 and 1910 than when the scores of adults born in relatively recent time periods are compared with those born ten to fifteen years earlier.

- *World War I and II Army Recruits:* A huge increase in performance on the Wells Alpha examination was reported when the scores of a representative sample of 768 men inducted in 1943 were compared with those of 48,000 enlisted soldiers in World War I on this measure of "general learning ability" (which emphasized verbal intelligence). More than three-fourths of the World War II sample scored above the World War I median, and a fourth scored at or above what had been the 95th percentile (Tuddenham, 1948).[6] In IQ-point terms, this is held to be the equivalent of an increase of 13 points, or a gain of one-half point per year (between the 1890s and 1910–25).

- *1932–1953:* 271 adults born between 1922 and 1938 scored *7.5 points higher* on the Stanford-Binet form L — normed on adults born between 1900 and 1917 — than they did on the recently normed WAIS. These results (which combine three studies) translate to a rate of gain of *0.35 points per year* (Flynn, 1984b). An almost identical growth rate was reported when other (smaller) studies covering this same test interval were combined (but using form L-M), except that the maximum age of these subjects was forty-eight (rather than thirty-two).

- *1936–1953:* A relatively elite group of 152 adults (aged sixteen to thirty-nine) scored 4.7 points higher on the 1936–37 normed Wechsler-Bellevue than on its successor (the 1953–54 normed WAIS) — 122.9 vs. 118.3 — *a gain of .28 points per year* (Flynn, 1984b). Subjects born between 1914 and 1937 were compared with those born seventeen years earlier (1897–1920).

- *1953–1978:* The scores of seventy-two adults aged thirty-five to forty-four (who were part of the 1978 WAIS-R standardization sample) were compared with their scores on the earlier (1953–54 normed) version of the WAIS (Wechsler, 1981). The 8-point IQ rise found implies that adult Americans born between 1934 and 1943 had a rate of gain averaging *0.33 points per year* when compared with those born twenty-five years earlier (1909 to 1918).

A Longitudinal Study of American Adults

Periodic intelligence testing of members of a Seattle, Washington, health maintenance organization has led researchers to speculate that intellectual ability (1) rose steadily from the early 1890s through the mid 1920s, (2) dipped slightly among children born during the depths of the Great Depression, (3) rose rapidly through the early postwar period, and (4) increased slightly from then until the early 1950s (Schaie, Labouvie, and Buech, 1973; Schaie, 1983, 1988).

By periodically testing the same individuals (clustered into groups born seven years apart) at seven-year intervals, these researchers (principally K. W.

Schaie) have been able to compare the performance of successive age groups at the same ages in a variety of cognitive dimensions. The test used—the most difficult form of the Primary Mental Abilities Test (PMA) (Thurstone and Thurstone, 1949)—has enabled the authors to observe trends in (1) *inductive reasoning*: the ability to identify "regularities" (principles or rules) and to infer and use them (as indicated by performance on a "letter series" task); (2) *verbal meaning*: choosing the correct synonym (with an increasing order of difficulty); (3) *number*: checking the addition of a column of numbers; (4) *spatial orientation*: indicating which letters are not mirror images of the example; and (5) *verbal fluency*: formulating words beginning with a given letter within a fixed time period (Schaie, 1983).

This periodic testing has permitted comparisons of one peer group against other peer groups at several different ages, as well as comparisons of people's performance against their own performance seven, fourteen, twenty-one, and twenty-eight years earlier—both individually and in groups (see section 5.4).

As detailed below, the two most "IQ-related" of the PMA subtests (namely, inductive reasoning and verbal meaning) evidenced the largest and most sustained increases (Schaie, 1988).

- *Inductive reasoning:* Steady increases at each successive seven-year period from the early 1890s through (preliminary data for) 1959[7] cumulate to produce *a rise in average performance equivalent to at least 20 IQ points.*
- *Verbal meaning:* Except for a dip among the children born during the early years of the Great Depression, performance *rose steadily and rapidly* from the 1890s through the mid 1940s, with apparent stability thereafter. Unfortunately, scores became so high that "ceiling effects" may well have severely limited significant further upward movement; consequently, recent trends (that is, after World War II or among peers who are still approaching their lifetime peak performance) are not necessarily valid.
- *Number:* Performance rose somewhat when comparing people born in the 1890s with those born in 1910, stabilized through the 1924 cohort, and then began a downward trend, *leaving it somewhat below the 1890s levels among the cohort of the 1950s* (perhaps reflecting an increased reliance on desk and pocket calculators).
- *Word fluency:* Scores rose moderately through the late 1930s and appear to have stabilized thereafter.
- *Spatial orientation:* Scores rose irregularly from the 1890s through the late 1930s, fell somewhat through the early 1950s, and recovered slightly among the latest (1959) cohort.

This study is discussed further in section 5.4.

5.3 International IQ Trends

In every country where high-quality studies of IQ trends over time have been undertaken, substantial gains have been reported throughout the twentieth century. The overall rate of increase has approximated a quarter of a point per year on comprehensive IQ tests, with the rate of increase from era to era tending to vary in relation to (1) the social and economic conditions prevalent in the years immediately following the birth of the subjects and (2) the type of test employed.

The period of slowest IQ growth was between the mid 1920s and the depths of the Great Depression. The most rapid growth is seen when the scores of the postwar generation are compared with those of "Depression babies" and when subjects born in the 1920s are compared with those born between 1890 and 1910.

Gains on verbally oriented measures have tended to be considerably slower than those on tests of problem-solving ability in the visual and "figural" dimension (shapes). Consequently, scores on the Stanford-Binet or the Otis IQ test have tended to show somewhat slower growth rates than have scores on the Wechsler IQ test, with the most rapid growth rates displayed by performance on the Raven's Progressive Matrices test and other totally nonverbal examinations.

This review of trends is divided into three subsections: Western Europe, British Commonwealth nations, and Japan (where an exceptionally large and very rapid growth in comprehensive IQ scores occurred after World War II).

Western Europe

Extremely large gains in the postwar period have been made on the Raven's Progressive Matrices test in virtually every country examined. Verbal IQ data show a somewhat slower growth rate — with the most rapid gains in verbal scores occurring when the baseline data measured the performance of subjects whose birth and/or early rearing coincided with the period of greatest World War II devastation.

Most of these studies have been summarized by Flynn (1987), who also evaluated the quality of the studies and then adjusted the results to reflect a standard deviation of 15:

- *West Germany (WISC vs. WISC-R):* 257 children (average age nine) took the West German version of the WISC, normed in 1954 (Priester, 1958), and the WISC-R, normed in 1981 (Schallberger, 1985); these children scored *20 points higher* on the earlier-normed test, including *11 points higher on the verbal subtest* (a gain of 0.41 points per year) and *25 points higher on the performance subtest* (0.93 points per year). The implication is that German children born between 1961 and 1974 are able to outperform German children born in the 1939–1947 period to this extent. Because considerably more than half the children in the earlier sample were, in 1954, between seven and nine years old, this comparison is heavily influenced by the scores of children who were born and/or spent their infancy and toddlerhood during the closing days of World War II and the period of devastation immediately following.[8]
- *France (1931–1956):* A gain of 9.1 points (or 0.36 points per year) was registered on a test of aptitude at manipulating verbal symbols, given as part of the French military examination in 1949 and again in 1974 (Girod and Allaume, 1976).[9] On the Raven's, the gains were enormous, with nearly two-thirds of the subjects exceeding what, in 1949, had been the 90th percentile, and only 5 percent scoring below the 1949 median, The magnitude of the Raven's gain, in IQ-point terms, can only be broadly estimated (most likely 20 to 25 points).
- *Norway (1935–late 1950s):* A verbal test (consisting of word-similarity items) administered as part of the Norwegian military examination showed an increase of 10.3 points between 1954 and the period from 1974 to 1980 (a rise of 0.41 points per year), with comparable gains made on the Raven's (Rist, 1982). This Raven's gain was at the slowest rate in Western Europe, apparently reflecting an above-average performance in the earlier period.[10]
- *Belgium (1940–1949):* A vocabulary test, given as part of military examinations, showed an annual rate of gain of 0.29 points for French-speaking recruits and 0.50 points for Dutch-speaking recruits (Bouvier, 1969); Raven's gains averaged 0.72 points and 0.87 points per year for the French- and Dutch-speaking recruits, respectively. On a test of "visualization of shapes" (a series of geometric designs), gains were slightly less (0.69 and 0.74 points per year).[11]
- *Belgium (WISC vs. WISC-R):* 220 French-speaking Belgian children were given the French versions of these two tests, which had been normed in France in 1940–48 and 1964–72, respectively (Hanet, 1984–85); on the verbal scale, a gain of only 2 points was registered, but Performance IQ jumped 15 points, yielding a 9-point total IQ gain.

- *The Netherlands (1934–1964):* Rapid, consistent gains were made by eighteen-year-olds on the Raven's across three decades (Leeuw and Meester, 1984).[12] The annual growth rates per decade were (1) 0.62 points, comparing recruits born in 1934 and 1944; (2) 0.59 points, comparing the 1944 and 1954 cohorts; and (3) 0.81 points, comparing the 1954 and 1964 cohorts. At the most recent testing, 82 percent performed at or above a level achieved by only 31 percent thirty years earlier.

The British Commonwealth

This section summarizes trends in IQ scores from Great Britain and Commonwealth countries. Because existing studies tend to provide either verbal or nonverbal IQ data, with studies of comprehensive IQ measures being virtually nonexistent, this summary is subdivided into trends in these two types of IQ measures.

Trends in Verbal IQ

- *Scotland (1921–1936):* Children born in the Depression year 1936 performed only slightly better on a seventy-six-item test of verbal reasoning (Moray House) than did children born in 1921, based on the scores of 158,000 eleven-year-old Scottish schoolchildren (Scottish Council for Research in Education, 1949, 1961). The annual rate of gain was 0.15 points (see summary in Lynn and Hampson, 1986c).
- *England (1927–1936):* No change in intelligence (as measured by the full 100-item Moray House Examination) was found among 60,000 eleven-year-old English schoolchildren, compared with the scores of children from these same geographical areas on this test nine years earlier (Emmett, 1950, summarized in Flynn, 1987). As in the United States, this is the only historical period for which some studies do not report IQ gains.
- *England (1937–1939 to 1944–1946):* Earlier and later versions of the Moray House Examination were administered in counterbalanced order to English schoolchildren; the scores of 1,084 children taking the 1955-57 standardized versions were 5.6 points lower compared with their scores on the versions normed seven years earlier (Pilliner, Sutherland, and Taylor, 1960, summarized in Lynn and Hampson, 1986c). *Thus, children born in postwar Britain showed a considerable rise in IQ scores over this short period.* These results, considered in tandem with the two studies cited above, highlight the negative effects of the Great Depression and the trauma and dislocations accompanying the bombing of Britain in the early years of World War II.

- *England (1948–1950 to 1966–1968):* The results of (unpublished) studies by the National Foundation for Educational Research (Lynn and Hampson, 1986c) indicate gains averaging 3.4 points on this NFER verbal test (among 14,766 English children aged nine to eleven and a half), or a rate of 0.19 points per year.
- *Canadian Prairie Provinces:* Scores on a (heavily verbal) comprehensive IQ test (the Otis/Otis Lennon) increased substantially when schoolchildren born in the mid to late 1940s were compared with those born twenty years later (Randhawa, 1980, summarized in Flynn, 1987); the average increase among these Saskatchewan children was at least 7 IQ points, or 0.35 points per year.[13]
- *New Zealand (1923–1926 to 1955–1958):* Verbal IQ gains of 0.24 points per year over thirty-two years were registered by New Zealand children (aged ten to thirteen) who took the unaltered (82 percent verbal items) form of the Otis test (Elley, 1969, summarized in Flynn, 1987). The later (1968) findings were based on an extremely representative sample of 4,000 children, and the earlier study included 26,000 children.
- *Australia (Otis A vs. Otis D):* A 5.5-point increase (0.42 points per year) was reported when the scores of ten- to fourteen-year-old children born between 1922 and 1926 were compared with the scores of those born between 1935 and 1939 (deLemos, 1984, summarized in Flynn, 1987). The reliability of this estimate is, however, lessened by (1) the exclusion of parochial and other private schools from the earlier (30,600-child) standardization sample, (2) a major change in test content, and (3) a lack of published information concerning the nature of the testing procedures employed.

Trends in Nonverbal IQ

- *England (1925–1927 to 1976–1978):* A so-called culture-reduced test of fluid intelligence was administered to 6,700 children in the city of Leicester in 1936 and 1949.[14] A negligible rise (1 point) in scores over this period (Cattell, 1950, summarized in Lynn and Hampson, 1986c, and in Flynn, 1987) seemingly reflects the effects on this later sample (born primarily in 1939) of the trauma caused by the bombing of Britain during their infancy and/or toddlerhood (Leicester being only sixty miles from London). In 1985, this test was administered to over 1,000 representatively selected English schoolchildren (Lynn, Hampson, and Mullineux, 1987) whose scores averaged 112.4, or a rise of 0.24 points per year compared with the 1925–27 sample (and 0.32 points per year compared with the 1939 cohorts).[15] Because Leicester was extremely representative of Britain in the earlier period (scores averaging 100.5), this gain might be a good reflection of trends in Britain as a whole.
- *English Raven's Data:* Several studies have compared the scores of British children on the Raven's Progressive Matrices test with the

test's norms (established in 1938). However, because these norms were based only on the scores of children from the city of Ipswich (who were not necessarily representative of British schoolchildren in general), exact growth rates cannot be accurately established (Flynn, 1987).

- *Canadian Prairie Provinces:* A gain of 8.4 points, or 0.40 points per year, was found (Clarke, Nyberg, and Worth, 1978a, 1978b, summarized in Flynn, 1987) comparing third-grade children from Edmonton, Alberta, born in 1946 with those born in 1967. Gains of 11 points (0.52 points per year) were also reported for these children on the California Test of Mental Maturity.

- *Australia (1935–1939 to 1967–1971):* On a test of fluid intelligence (Jenkins), a 15.7-point increase over thirty-two years (or 0.49 points per year) was reported among ten- to fourteen-year-olds (deLemos, 1984, summarized in Flynn, 1987).[16]

Japan

A dramatic increase in IQ scores has been registered by the postwar generation of Japanese children when their performance is compared with that of Japanese children born in the decade preceding the close of World War II.

These gains have taken place not only on tests of visuospatial and figural Performance, at which the Japanese, considered as a group, excel but also on verbal IQ measures. For example, a recent study of Japanese children who took both the WISC and WISC-R (Japanese versions) showed that these children scored **16 points higher** on the verbal subtests of the earlier-normed version and **17 points higher** on the performance subtests (Lynn, 1982; see also discussion by Flynn, 1982).[17] Combined, this produced a *20-point higher overall IQ score.* The implication is that the norms set by children born between 1936 and 1945 (who constituted the 1951 Japanese standardization sample) would be exceeded to this degree by the average Japanese child born in the 1960s. This amounts to a gain of five-sixths of a point per year in full-scale IQ.

On the Kyoto Intelligence Test,[18] a sample of 711 children born in the years 1961 and 1962 outperformed children from the same (stable) geographical area born in the years 1945 and 1946 (who were tested eighteen years earlier as part of the 1954 Japanese standardization sample) by **16.6 points**, or a rate of gain of nearly a full point per year (Sano, 1974, summarized in Lynn and Hampson, 1986c).[19]

Support for the hypothesis (Kirkwood, 1982) that most of this increase represented an extremely rapid upsurge in scores over a relatively short time span, rather than a slow and steady improvement over a longer period, comes from a study of two closely matched samples of nearly 1,400 children (aged nine to fifteen), one tested in 1963 and the other in 1970 (Ushijima, 1961, summarized in Lynn and Hampson, 1986c). Scores on the Ushijima Intelligence Test[20] rose 9.9 points over this seven-year period—with the scores of children born between 1948 and 1951 rising nearly twice as fast (compared with the 1941–44 cohort) as the scores of those born immediately after the war's end (compared with the 1938–40 cohort).

Direct comparisons between American and Japanese children on the subscales of the Wechsler that measure Performance IQ are possible because the test content for the two groups is virtually identical. When the WISC was standardized in Japan in 1951, the scores of Japanese children born between 1936 and 1944 (on these common subtests) averaged 103, which was virtually identical to the norm for Caucasian Americans. By 1975, the Japanese children comprising the WISC-R standardization sample were performing considerably better than American children (Lynn, 1982). In fact, *the Japanese children born in every year between 1961 and 1969 scored either 11 or 12 points higher than their U.S. counterparts!*[21] The implication (Flynn, 1983) is that because White American children's scores rose 8.3 points between the 1947 testing and the 1972 testing (WISC to WISC-R), the Japanese children must have gained an additional 7.2 points over this twenty-four-year period, or a total of 15.5 points, which translates into a rate of increase of 0.65 points per year.

On the common subtests of the Wechsler, Japanese children, considered as a group, dramatically outperform American children on "block design" (even though the most difficult item on this subscale is harder in the Japanese version) and also show considerable superiority on "object assembly," "picture arrangement," and "mazes" (Lynn, 1982). On the remaining component of Performance IQ, "coding," the Japanese children tested scored slightly lower than the American norm. On the one common verbal subtest, "digit span," the Japanese scores were slightly above U.S. norms. Thus, on visually presented problems in the figural domain, Japanese children appear to be particularly precocious but apparently show no special aptitude in the auditory and temporal memory domains.[22]

At the upper end of the IQ distribution, the Japanese gains have been less rapid than at the mean; this is in part a reflection of a somewhat lower standard deviation among Japanese subjects, compared with Americans (Vining, 1983).

Thus, Japanese children born in the postwar generation score about half a standard deviation higher than Caucasian Americans in visuospatial analytics and have improved their relative performance in the verbal reasoning domain. The nature and potential sources of this Japanese performance are explored in Chapters Thirteen and Twenty (see also Anderson, 1982).

5.4 Trends in Intelligence During Adulthood

Until recently, traditional wisdom held that IQ peaks in young adulthood and that cognitive ability thereafter erodes at a gradually increasing rate. Within this context, we can subdivide "intelligence" into two types:

- *Fluid intelligence*, or the ability to generate new insights and fresh concepts from novel experiences, is presumed to peak in late puberty. It is this kind of intelligence that IQ tests in the main attempt to evaluate.
- *Crystallized intelligence*, or the ability to make effective use of already existing problem-solving mechanisms, is thought of as peaking in mid-life. It can be improved by increased learning, the consolidation of knowledge in integrated concepts, and increased opportunities for applying, and generalizing from, known problem-solving techniques. For skills that continue to be practiced heavily, crystallized intelligence remains at a high level of competence until relatively late in life.

Table 13. Age at Which IQ Peaks: Cross-Sectional Studies.

Year of Data	Authors	Peak Age	Birth Year of Peak-IQ Group
1916	Terman (1916)	16.0	1900
1924	Willhoughby (1927)	20.0	1904
1926	Jones and Conrad (1933)	20.0	1906
1931	Miles and Miles (1932)	18.5	1912
1937	Wechsler (1939)	22.0	1915
1953	Howell (1955)	27.0	1926
1954	Wechsler (1955)	27.0	1927
1978	Wechsler (1981)	30.0	1948

Source: Adapted from Parker, 1986.

The view that IQ peaks in young adulthood was born of cross-sectional studies that show, for instance, that twenty-five-year-olds perform better on IQ tests than do fifty-year-olds. However, in light of (1) the body of data respecting IQ trends, (2) findings from recent cross-sectional studies, and especially (3) findings from longitudinal studies, this view requires some modification. To begin with, the results of cross-sectional studies (summarized in Table 13) clearly indicate that the age at which IQ peaks has been increasing over time.

Even though the number of good studies is small, these data provide support for the previously suggested links between socioeconomic conditions during the subjects' early childhood and subsequent IQ, as shown by the increasing peak ages when subjects were born in good economic times and the absence of increases during bad times (for example, the contraction following the financial panic of 1907, World War I and the sharp recession that followed it, and the Great Depression in the 1930s).

When the intellectual performance of people is examined longitudinally, the "peaks" in a number of important cognitive abilities appear even later. Moreover, even though certain aspects of cognitive performance often deteriorate with age, many important facets of intellect can, in otherwise healthy people, maintain youthful proficiency even in old age.

An important consequence of this progressively later peaking of IQ scores is that the performance of *young* adults tends to be lower than that of adults in general, and another is that the rate of gain over time is somewhat less than when the basis of comparison is older adults. Flynn's (1987) observation that during the thirty years following World War II the scores of American adults aged thirty-four and under rose far less (5.6 points) than did those of adults aged thirty-five to seventy-five (10.2 points) may reflect this phenomenon. Flynn's data might then suggest that the rate of increase in IQ has been slowing down.

Results from the Seattle Longitudinal Study indicate that certain cognitive abilities reach their heights far later than had been generally believed, will usually remain intact through age sixty or beyond, and (as shown in Table 14) decline at a relatively slow rate thereafter (Schaie, Labouvie, and Buech, 1973; Schaie, 1983). Between the ages of twenty-five and forty-six, the subjects in this study registered what (in IQ-point terms) would be equivalent to a 6-point rise in their comprehension of "verbal meanings" on the PMA tests, with considerably smaller or negligible increases from age twenty-five to peak in the other components of this test. Even though the PMA is not really a comprehensive test of general intelligence, it may be speculated that — if performance on this measure parallels trends in people's IQ — the IQ scores of these subjects would have risen about 4 points between their twenties and their late forties and early fifties.

The authors also constructed an index of "educational aptitude" (which is weighted two-thirds by "verbal meaning" and one-third by "inductive reasoning") from which they base their conclusion that peak performance occurs in the fourth and fifth decades of life. In addition, Schaie (1983) has recently added an "immediate recall" task to this testing, on which twenty-five-year-olds outperformed fifty-year-olds by the equivalent of about 10 IQ points, sixty-five-year-olds by about 15 points, and eighty-year-olds by more than 25 points (Schaie, 1983). The extent to which this decline represents a deterioration in performance with increasing age — as contrasted with a comparatively better short-term memory at age twenty-five among this later cohort of

Table 14. Age(s) of Expected Peak Performance and Subsequent Decline on the Primary Mental Abilities Test Parameters (Seattle Longitudinal Study).

Cognitive Ability	Age(s) of Peak Ability[b]	Last Age[a] Before Decline of:	
		A Half Std. Dev.[c]	A Full Std. Dev.
Inductive Reasoning	32–60	74	88
Verbal Meaning	46–60	67	81
Word Fluency	32–53	67	81
Number	32	74	88
Spatial Orientation	25–60	74	81
"Intellectual Ability"	46–60	74	81

[a] Data are available for seven-year age increments.

[b] "Peak" is defined as the group average score being within a tenth of a standard deviation of the highest average score registered by that cohort at any age on the subtest.

[c] Meaning that, at least until this age, scores on this subtest were, on a group basis, within the equivalent of 7.5 points (one-half standard deviation) or 15 points (one full standard deviation) of peak performance.

Source: Adapted from Schaie, 1983.

twenty-five-year-olds—cannot be determined, since these data are, at present, not available on a longitudinal basis.

Recent evidence from the animal kingdom supports the former view. For example, in one of our closest "relatives," the chimpanzee, no general decline in learning ability has been found to occur with aging, even among the two oldest chimps in captivity (who, in their mid-fifties, are believed to be pushing the limits of chimpanzee longevity). On a series of tests they had taken more than twenty years earlier, these chimps' overall level of intellectual function not only was intact but also was comparable to the ability of two teenage chimps on most measures (Aged Apes Show No Decline in Learning Ability, 1985). Moreover, on one test—the ability to "select an odd object from among three like ones"—*these aged chimps performed twice as well as their teenage counterparts.* In contrast, their performance on one test—which involved "delayed responding"—was worse, a finding analogous to the **loss in short-term recall ability** in human beings.

A debate has raged concerning the extent to which age-related changes in psychometric tests reflect a **slowing** in the rate of intellectual performance rather than a loss in thinking capacity per se. A recent cross-sectional evaluation of the effects of age-related changes in information-processing speed on scores on the kinds of tests employed by Schaie indicates that — after making adjustments for the effects of age on perceptual speed and on certain performance-related aspects of the PMA — *the decline in test scores with age was far less rapid, and on some components, "peak" performance occurred far later in life* (Hertzog, 1989).[23] Specifically: (1) on the inductive reasoning component, the "pre-adjusted" decline from "peak" to the late seventies was reduced by three-fourths; (2) on the spatial relations and spatial visualization components, two-thirds of the decline could be attributed to changes in processing speed; (3) on the numerical facility and verbal comprehension components, "speed-adjusted" scores rose until well past age seventy. These findings suggest that the large preponderance of the age-related declines in these tests are attributable to changes in perceptual and motor speed, rather than to a decline in underlying thinking ability.

A detailed dissection of the patterns of strength and decline in cognitive performance with age is beyond the scope of this present effort (the interested reader may wish to consult Birren and Schaie, 1985; Charness and Campbell, 1988; Salthouse, forthcoming; Light and Singh, 1987; McDowd and Craik, 1988; Salthouse and Somberg, 1982).

With respect to intellectual giftedness, the prognosis is quite optimistic, since it appears that among individuals who possess abilities that are highly prized by society, performance will often continue at exceedingly high levels until late senescence (Gardner, 1985). In addition, contrary to popular beliefs, there is little or no cell death between age sixty and eighty in such key areas of the brain as the frontal cortex (Hang, 1987). Thus, skills that a person has the greatest motivation to retain are apt to be well retained.

5.5 The Divergence Between IQs and SAT Scores

Among the most common ways of categorizing people's emotional outlook is to subdivide them into optimists and pessi-

Table 15. Average SAT Verbal Test Scores: Selected Years.

Year of Exam	Mid Year of Examinees' Birth	Average Score	Number of Test Takers (000)
1952	1935	476	81.6
1963	1946	478	924.8
1981	1963	424	1,600.0

mists. While optimists generally have no trouble accepting themselves as such, most people whom others would classify as pessimists reject this label and instead think of themselves as "realists."

Many such realists will not accept the proposition that IQ has been rising fairly steadily and relatively rapidly for several generations, as they are firmly convinced that things are getting worse and have been for some time. How can it be possible that intelligence is rising, they might ask, if academic competence — as reflected in scores on the Scholastic Aptitude Test (SAT) (taken by college-bound or potentially college-bound high school juniors and seniors in the United States) — fell between the mid 1960s and 1980?

The drop in SAT scores was particularly pronounced on the verbal subtest, where scores fell from an average of 478 in 1963 to 424 in 1981 (Flynn, 1984b) before increasing slightly through the mid 1980s (see Table 15).

To understand this phenomenon, we might consider three factors thought to contribute to the decline in SAT scores:

- Because the number of examinees increased, their average score is likely to fall, since expanding the pool of test takers adds a segment of the populace that is less elite scholastically. Consequently, the *stability* in scores between 1952 and 1963, in the face of this tenfold increase in test takers, implies that a considerable *increase* in the cognitive ability of children born in 1946, compared with those born in 1935, was masked by this enormous increase in the number of test takers.

- The 1946 cohort appears to have been an "environmentally elite" population, having benefited from exceptionally favorable caretaker ratios during infancy and toddlerhood.
- Certain societal trends have adversely affected the intellectual upbringing of children born in 1963, compared with those born in 1946.

With respect to changes in the size of the pool of SAT candidates, an advisory panel established by the College Entrance Examination Board (Wirtz, 1977) has estimated that half the SAT decline between 1963 and 1977 was due to a broadening of the candidate sample, with the balance of the decline probably reflecting a downward trend in the academic competence of the general population. If this conclusion is valid, then the huge increase in SAT test takers between 1952 and 1963 — all other things being equal — should have engendered a substantial decline in average test scores between these years. The fact that such a decline did not occur implies that there must have been intervening factors that improved the performance of the 1963 examinees (born in 1946) compared with the performance of those born eleven years earlier (in 1935).

In one extremely important respect, the cohort of children born in 1946 *was among the most advantaged in history*. Because of World War II, an unusually large proportion of children reaped the benefits of an extremely favorable caretaker ratio during infancy and toddlerhood — a fact shown (in Chapters Two, Ten, and Eleven) to be highly conducive to enhanced intellectual development (particularly in verbal skills). First, this initial crop of postwar baby boomers contained a disproportionate number of firstborn children; further, because many of the laterborn children were conceived after their fathers returned from the war, there was usually an exceptionally wide spacing between these children and their older sibling(s). Consequently, an exceptionally large proportion of these younger children had the undivided or nearly undivided attention of their mothers, with school-age siblings able to serve as educational helpmates (thereby improving, rather than diluting, the caretaker ratio).

Moreover, these returning veterans, once they made a commitment to marriage and family, tended to provide a relatively high level of paternal didactic support. In addition, the correspondence between maternal age and IQ (see Chapter Two) favored this cohort (since mature mothers are better able to subordinate their own needs to those of their children).

In addition, grandparents were often significantly involved in the early upbringing of these children since, during this era, families often tended to cluster within a small geographical area, and the acute housing shortage following World War II required married veterans to share housing with relatives.

By 1963, substantial societal changes had occurred—changes that probably reduced both the quality and quantity of verbal stimulation provided to children during certain critical periods for the acquisition of verbal skills. Factors likely to have contributed to these changes include:

- Two strong familial trends—marital breakup and working mothers—deprived many children of intellectually stimulating interaction with their parents, because of parental absence and/or because, after a full day's work, some mothers were too tired to respond to their children with freshness and enthusiasm.
- The decline in the role of the extended family (in particular, the declining influence of maternal grandmothers) has been a major social dynamic of the post–World War II era. Factors accentuating this trend include the considerable geographical mobility displayed by postwar American families, the huge rise in the proportion of older women in the labor force, and the retirement of many "senior" citizens to warm climates.
- Before ownership of television sets became widespread, *infants and toddlers received considerably more interactive verbal stimulation.*

In several other respects, the educational environment in the United States underwent changes in ways that probably impaired the transition from gains in underlying intelligence to improved academic competence. Chief among these was a reduction in the importance placed on self-discipline—and its corollary, good study habits. In essence, the prevailing sentiment among the parents of the 1946 cohort was that their children's success depended on how hard they worked at their studies. By the 1960s, however—after twenty years of rapidly rising economic affluence—many upper-middle-class children were made to feel that their economic future was secure, irrespective of whether they worked hard in school or not. In addition, in the 1960s and 1970s, the explosion of interesting (and inexpensive) entertainment enormously increased the *quantity* of stimulation available, but (many people feel) sharply decreased its overall quality. Moreover, this explosive jump in glittering but shallow entertainment made "highbrow" entertainment (such as classical books, films, and records) seem dull. At the same time, the proportion of children's stimulation derived from a highly verbal mode (reading, imagining) fell, while the proportion obtained in a passive, visual mode rose. Thus, it may well be that falling *academic* competence and aptitude occurred not because children came to *know less* but because they acquired less valuable knowledge. Some have speculated that "if teenagers only knew the plots of half the number of 'good' books as they do of 'sitcoms' and movies and could recall the meaning of words on vocabulary lists as easily as they do the lyrics of rock music. . . ."

Moreover, there are indications that the academic competence of younger schoolchildren rose substantially during the 1980s. In reading, for example, 67 percent of New York City's schoolchildren scored at or above grade level on the widely used Degrees of Reading Power Test, when the basis of comparison was the New York State norms established during the 1981–1982 school year. However, when their scores were instead measured against the then current (1987–88) norms, only 46 percent scored at or above grade level (Lewis, 1989).[24]

5.6 Rising IQ: Conclusions

The preceding analysis of IQ trends presents the following picture:

- Children's IQ scores are permanently lowered when adverse economic and social conditions are prevalent during the years of their early upbringing.
- The long-term increase in scores on tests of problem-solving ability in the spatial domain tends to overstate the rate of growth in the general level of intelligence.
- Conclusions by various authors that the long-term increase in IQ scores in the United States has been at a rate of about a third of a point per year slightly overstates the underlying trend. This overstatement results from an excessive reliance on (1) data that compared the scores of people born during the postwar era with those of people born during the Great Depression and (2) IQ tests whose factor loadings in the figural domain are relatively high. When these effects are discounted, the increase from the 1920s to the 1970s (as measured by the more verbally oriented Stanford-Binet) has been somewhere between a fifth and a quarter of a point per year; it is likely that IQ rose at a faster rate in the early part of the century.
- The conclusion by some authors that the rate of increase in IQ has been fairly steady over time is not supportable when the basis for this trend analysis is shifted from the date that the test was administered to the era of the subjects' birth and early upbringing. For example:
  - The Japanese trend data indicate that a *jump* in intellectual ability took place when the scores of children born after 1947 (that is, after the dislocation following World War II had subsided) are compared with the scores of those born ten years earlier. A similar jump is seen among West German children born after the postwar recovery was well under way, compared with those born near the war's end or in the years immediately following.
  - Conversely, when the scores of children born in the depths of the Great Depression are compared with those of children whose toddlerhood was completed before its onset, extremely slow growth (or occasional slightly negative trends) is reported.
  - This picture (of a slowdown in response to environmental trauma and a subsequent jump when it subsides) strongly suggests that there exists long-term impetus for IQ to increase, but it also suggests that the fruition of this underlying trend is sometimes held back for a time by adverse economic and social conditions.
- Some recent longitudinal studies that show the IQs of subjects declining between early and middle adolescence are somewhat biased by the progressively later peaking of IQ scores across adulthood; this is because adult versions of IQ tests such as the WAIS do not have age-related norms.
- The slowest rising aspects of IQ are reading comprehension and verbal problem-solving skills.[25]

If the twentieth-century rise in scores on comprehensive IQ tests in the United States has averaged one-fourth point per year, then the *average* child in the mid 1980s would—if compared with children born in 1890—score in the top 1 or 2 percent on tests of spatial problem-solving skills and in the top 5 or 10 percent in verbal ability. This would imply that, by 1890 standards, many of today's children would be thought to possess a near-genius level of ability in Performance IQ and verbal proficiency in the superior to very superior range.

Can this be true—is the average child of today almost as smart as the geniuses in the era of their great-great-grandparents, and is the above-average child of today the equivalent of a genius of that bygone era? At first blush, this seems unlikely. Although great pains are taken to design IQ tests to measure general ability across those mental dimensions that society considers indicative of intellectual competence, the term *genius* implies that a person has not only a high IQ but also an extremely high level of *originality*—an ability to tap into and use his or her cognitive skills *creatively*.

Possessing an exceptionally high IQ is by no means synonymous with being a genius. As detailed in Chapter Sixteen, certain forms of creative genius do not require a high IQ, and high IQ does not necessarily ensure creativity. What a high IQ does require is a superior degree of competence across a *breadth* of intellectual domains. Genius, conversely, requires extreme *depth of understanding* in one domain or in a combination of integrated domains. It is also heartening to realize that, despite the massive increase in IQ throughout the twentieth century, the depth of knowledge possessed and/or mental feats performed by some of history's greatest geniuses, both past and present, still leave us in awe.

One reason why the increase in IQ scores has not created wholesale geniuses is that an adult's IQ score reflects his or her *position* along the bell-shaped IQ distribution rather than a proportional representation of his or her intelligence in relation to someone else's (see Chapter Three). Thus, an IQ of 150 implies neither that its possessor is 50 percent smarter than average nor that a 25-point rise in a population's IQ during this century would bridge half this 50-point gap.

Moreover, the notion that one type of IQ point is as good as any other is fallacious on another count, since a 20-point rise in a person's verbal IQ is likely to be more valuable (in a great variety of ways) than a 20-point rise in his or her spatial IQ. Given this dichotomy between verbal and spatial intelligence, how might our overall progress be assessed? Surely spatial IQ is important in the tabulation of a total IQ score. Nevertheless, it would seem excessive to give greater weight to improvements in the ability to comprehend *structural* meaning than to linguistic comprehension and the related ability to infer causality. Admittedly, the social climate has for some time encouraged an emphasis on culture-free problems, and this has caused a relatively high factor loading to be given to nonverbal subtests. Consequently, the Stanford-Binet test may provide a better indicator of the upward movement in general intelligence than the Wechsler.

5.7 Past and Future Implications

What if this twentieth-century rise in IQ had not occurred— would the pace of technological progress have been far less rapid? Would the world's standard of living now be far lower? Would the prevalence of famine, disease, social unrest, and war have been, and still be, far higher? It would certainly seem so!

And what of the future? Is it possible for IQ scores to keep on rising, or have they been rapidly approaching a more or less permanent plateau? Although in some ways it may be impossible to replicate the advances of the past (such as the drop in family size and the eradication of some childhood diseases), it seems that a plateau is not being approached. If it were, a marked narrowing in the standard deviation of IQ scores would have been evident in the high-IQ or "matched" samples reviewed.[26]

Lest some people shudder at the thought that, if intelligence continues rising, those of us who are alive fifty years from now— or, given medical advances, even seventy-five years from now— will be at a considerable intellectual disadvantage compared with the successive generations of bright young minds, let us also recognize that the so-called health revolution is enabling human intellectual competency to peak later and later in life, to stay at or near peak levels far longer than in the past, and (in active, healthy people) to suffer far-less-rapid declines in later life. Moreover, the prospects for finding biochemical and/or nutritional mechanisms to enable the human race to better achieve, maintain, and possibly even *greatly enhance* its intellectual potential appear very favorable.

Notes

1. Of all (seventy-three) "usable" research studies cited by Flynn (1984b), only two small studies (totaling 110 subjects) showed even a slight decline in IQ scores across time. These compared the performance of ten- to fourteen-year-old children born between 1933 and 1937 on the 1947-normed WISC with their performance on its predecessor, the Wechsler Bellevue, which had been normed on children (of these ages) born between 1922 and 1925, whose infancy and toddlerhood coincided with the height of the affluent 1920s.

2. The Stanford-Binet form L-M was developed in 1960 from material contained in its two earlier versions (form L and form M), each of which was normed in 1931–33; as a consequence, it could be readily normed against the 1931–33 standardization sample's performance. These 2,351 children were selected as being racially and economically representative of the children who comprised the 1972 Stanford-Binet standardization sample.

3. This author discarded studies dealing with highly gifted or retarded groups and those that failed to allow for the possibility of "practice effects." All results have been standardized by being converted to a common scale (with the Caucasian mean set at 100 and a standard deviation set at 15).

4. This gain may be slightly overstated because of "practice effects" (86 percent of the subjects took the new test first); the inter-test interval averaged two weeks. The children, averaging seven years of age, were from small towns and small-sized cities in the South and Middle West.

5. The faster rate of gain among young children than among those over age seven parallels the results found in the 1932–1972 (form L-M) comparison; given the faster worldwide rise in nonverbal than in verbal IQ, the fact that IQ tests emphasize nonverbal tasks at younger ages may contribute to this finding. A comparison was also made for a sample of young adults, but an unduly small sample size (forty-seven) and a nonrandom order of test administration make these results unreliable.

6. The sample's representativeness was "prevalidated" in that the distribution of the Army General Classification Test (GCT) scores (with which

Wells Alpha scores correlated .90) closely paralleled that of all army inductees in 1943. Both samples were limited to Caucasians, and illiterate World War I recruits were tested in a different manner. Practice effects (from having recently taken the GCT) were quite small. The authors analyzed the minor revisions in the test's contents between the wars and concluded that, at the most, these caused an eighth of the increase. The authors conclude that educational attainment (which had risen from an average of eight years of schooling to ten) did not account for any substantial proportion of the increase. On the other hand, the exclusion of illiterates from the World War I examinees is likely to offset, in whole or in part, these biases.

7. The 1959 cohort is a small sample tested only once at age twenty-five. As of the 1983–85 testing, the total number of subjects studied had risen to 1,629; some data are extrapolations from figure (graph) 17 (Schaie, 1988).

8. The later sample were children who comprised the 1981 standardization sample. Flynn (1987, p. 182) notes that although "the West German WISC and WISC-R [standardization] samples were done with reasonable care, their quality is somewhat less than the American counterpart."

9. The later (1974) data are based on a representative sample of 200 recruits.

10. The latter-period results merge the data from the 1974 and 1980 full-population results (85 percent of Norwegian nineteen-year-olds) and a 1977 random sample.

11. The number of subjects tested in 1958 and 1967 totaled approximately 100,000; the gains are probably slightly understated because 83 percent of all eighteen-year-olds were tested in the earlier year (1958), compared with 77 percent in 1967.

12. Forty of the sixty items on the Raven's were used (the items judged in 1945 to be the "most discriminating"); data are based on the scores of approximately 80 percent of all Dutch eighteen-year-olds throughout the postwar era (5 percent having been exempt and 15 percent not passing the prescreening medical exam). The statistics cited include revisions provided to Flynn in 1986 by these authors.

13. The test content was altered from a purely verbal form (a mixture of verbal similarities and opposites, verbal comprehension and reasoning, vocabulary, information, and arithmetic) to a one-third nonverbal test (with the "transition" norms calculated on the basis of a sample of over 2,000 appropriately aged children given these two tests in counterbalanced order). Gains of 7 points each were registered by the fourth- and seventh-grade Saskatchewan samples. Because fourth graders in the later sample were slightly younger, their gain, if calculated on an age basis, was 2.5 points. Because the number of years between test norming and test administration was greater (by nine years) in the earlier sample, the "real" gain is likely to be slightly understated.

14. The test was the Cattell scale 1, form A; Flynn (1987) has rated this sample's quality "excellent."

15. The schoolchildren were attending fourteen "socially representative" schools in seven diverse districts.

16. The stratification procedures used in the later sample (1981) were assessed (by Flynn, 1987, pp. 180–181) as "at least as good as in American Wechsler-Binet samples"; the earlier 4,000-child sample was from one province (Victoria) "known not to have been elite." The Jenkins Non-Verbal Test is broader than the Raven's, in that it contains figural similarities and sequences as well as matrices.

17. The Japanese versions of the Wechsler Intelligence Scale for Children were normed (in Japan) in 1951 and 1975; these 112 children took the tests in counterbalanced order.

18. The Kyoto Test, which includes twelve subtests measuring verbal, numerical, and spatial ability for nine- to fifteen-year-olds, is thought to be similar to the PMA and the Differential Aptitude Test.

19. The ten- and eleven-year-olds who lived in the city proper had scores averaging 122.7 in 1972, compared with 104.5 for the 1954 test takers. In the surrounding towns within this prefecture, scores rose from an average of 99.7 to 114.8; an earlier small study of three city schools (whose catchment areas and "environment" remained stable) had suggested a gain of 10.4 points during the first half of this eighteen-year period (Kaneko, 1970, summarized in Lynn and Hampson, 1986c).

20. This test consisted of eight subtests covering verbal ability (two subtests), number, reasoning, spatial ability, perceptual ability, and memory (two subtests).

21. The U.S. sample was born three years earlier; the children born in 1959–60 performed slightly less well, but in another sample (of younger children) this cohort exhibited similar (WISC) scores. A sample of Japanese adults born in 1910 posted an average score of 105 on the common WAIS subtests.

22. On the recently revised Stanford-Binet, those Asian American subjects who were part of the standardization sample performed considerably better in the area of "abstract/visual reasoning" than they did in "verbal reasoning" (a difference that averaged 8.1 points). The average "short-term memory" score of these (107) subjects was not far removed from their performance on the verbal component (Thorndike, Hagen, and Sattler, 1986); similarly, Raven's Standard Progressive Matrices scores for several thousand ten-year-old children in Hong Kong (administered in the mid 1980s) averaged 108 in relation to the U.S. and British Caucasian mean (Linn, Pagliari, and Chan, 1988), and these children's scores on the spatial and perceptual speed primaries of the PMA (Thurstone and Thurstone, 1949) showed a similar difference. Nevertheless, they performed slightly below the norm on the word fluency primary.

23. The 342 subjects were college graduates ranging in age from forty-three to seventy-eight. Information-processing speed was measured in two ways: by a test of perceptual speed and by an answer sheet fill-in test, in which the correct answers (indicated by a visual code on a PMA-type test booklet) had to be transferred to an answer sheet. A control group of 210 university students confirmed that the "shape" of the cross-sectional PMA scores by age was consistent with Schaie's findings. In addition to the verbal meaning portion of the PMA, the verbal comprehension measure included advanced vocabulary.

24.   The extent to which the 1987–88 norms exceed those established six
       years earlier is exemplified by individual school-district comparisons
       of the percentages of children (in grades three to eight) scoring at or
       above grade level: 90.5 percent vs. 74.2 percent; 75.0 percent vs. 53.2
       percent; and 56.5 percent vs. 28.8 percent. The rise in the state norms
       has apparently paralleled national trends on this examination. In the
       1988–89 school year, a further (3.3 percentage point) rise in reading
       ability was registered; scores on the Metropolitan Reading Test in
       Mathematics also rose (from their 1985 national norms), albeit at a
       slower rate. The rapid decline in the birth rate among New York City's
       ethnic minority populations during the 1970s may have much to do
       with this improvement.

25.   In Japan, for example, the slowest rise (by far) on the Kyoto intelligence
       test was reported on the "jumbled sentences" subtest; for example, "rise
       does the sun which direction in the morning" ("west, below, south, east,
       north"). By contrast, the Japanese (on average) tend to excel in so-called
       nonsense syllogisms (such as "most elephants can fly; all pigs are
       elephants; most pigs can fly?"), where *structure* rather than *meaning*
       determines whether the third statement is true, false, or indetermi-
       nate. Flynn (1987) also notes that vocabulary subtest scores (on the
       Japanese WISC/WISC-R comparison studies) show a rate of gain only
       one-third as great as do full-scale IQ scores.

26.   See, for example, section 4.1 (the Iowa Adoption Study) and Lynn and
       Hampson, 1986c. The large postwar increase in the Japanese Wechsler
       IQ test performance was accompanied by a slight decrease in standard
       deviation to 12.8 (in contrast to 14 for Caucasian Americans). Never-
       theless, Vining (1983) has suggested that although the IQs of Japanese
       children as a whole have increased, there has not been a large jump in
       the number of those with exceptionally high IQs. But see Chapter
       Thirteen.

Contents

❧ 6 ❧

The Black/White
IQ Disparity:
Myth and Reality

6.0 Synopsis

Much of the difference in average IQ scores between Black and White people in America in the 1970s can be attributed to more frequent intrauterine problems and less-favorable family configurations among Black children.

The considerable increase in the IQ scores of Black Americans during the past fifty years dispels any thought that Black people are "genetically inferior" and strongly suggests that the "IQ gap" between Blacks and Whites is not an immutable barrier. Recent indications are that efforts to improve the health and early education of the lower and lower-middle classes are beginning to reduce the size of this gap.

6.1 Introduction

The average IQ score of Black Americans is considerably lower than that of Caucasian Americans. Because the size of this gap remained relatively constant between the late 1940s and mid 1970s, some people have concluded that the causes of this disparity must be essentially innate and that preschool programs and other efforts to increase the intellectual competency of young Black children have failed.

A closer examination, however, shows that both of these conclusions are clearly unwarranted. First, the IQ scores of Americans—Black as well as White—have been rising steadily and fairly rapidly throughout most of the twentieth century. Thus, this IQ disparity cannot be viewed as the consequence of an inherent inferiority, since *Black Americans today outperform their White counterparts of the 1930s.*

Second, as detailed elsewhere, deficiencies in the intrauterine environment and/or disadvantageous family configurations often severely depress IQ scores. The importance of these variables can be understood by considering, for example, that, in a middle-class White family, the elder of two children who was born to a thirty-four-year-old woman and weighed eight and one-half pounds at birth will have an IQ score averaging 15 points higher than that of the third of five children born to a twenty-two-year-old, when that neonate is of average birth weight and normal gestational age. Moreover, an additional 10-point drop in IQ would be expected if that infant instead weighed four pounds at term.

Black children are much more likely than White children to be members of those familial and intrauterine configurations associated with lower IQs and are much less likely to be members of the most advantaged configurations. Thus, a substantial portion of the IQ disparity between Blacks and Whites can be accounted for by, and attributed to, these factors. The question, How much lower would the IQ average of White children be if they were exposed to the same family configurations and had the same birth-weight and gestational-age characteristics as Black Children? is addressed in the sections that follow.

The conclusion that—because the size of the IQ gap between Blacks and Whites remained stable in the quarter century following World War II—the governmental programs to improve the health, early education, and general welfare of the lower-class and lower-middle-class populace in general and Black people in particular have failed is clearly erroneous. This is discussed in depth in the concluding section of Chapter Ten.

6.2 The Size of the Black/White IQ Disparity

The findings from the national standardization of the WISC-R are indicative of the average IQ difference found between Blacks and Whites in the United States in the early and middle 1970s (Jensen, 1985). In this study, the full-scale IQ of the (305) Black children tested averaged 15.8 points below that of comparably aged (1,870) White children, or a difference of slightly more than a full standard deviation (Kaufman and Doppelt, 1976). This study also found that Black children living in the north-eastern United States scored 9.6 points higher than those living in the South and 5.1 points higher than those living in the rest of the country.

Nearly identical results were found in the largest nationally representative study that provided separate IQ scores for Black and White children (the Health Examination Survey), where the 15.7-point differential at ages six to eleven paralleled the results found at ages twelve to seventeen (Cohen and others, 1980).[1] The recently (1985) revised and standardized version of the Stanford-Binet Intelligence Test (summarized in Table 16) shows a similar magnitude of difference among Black and White adolescents and young adults but suggests a somewhat narrower difference in childhood. As detailed in Chapter Ten, there is ample reason to believe that this reported improvement is not an artifact.

These IQ score differences between Blacks and Whites (1) cut across such distinctions as verbal and nonverbal IQ; (2) are somewhat larger on what are generally classified as culture-free types of IQ-test questions (Jensen, 1985); and (3) are somewhat smaller on such short-term memory tasks as the "digit span" and "tapping span" sections of the WISC and the "number recall" component of the Kaufman ABC, as well as on other tasks thought to have a relatively low factor loading on the g of general intelligence (Jensen, 1985) as defined by Spearman (1904).

6.3 Family Configuration and the Black/White IQ Difference

Because Black women tend to become mothers at earlier ages than do Caucasian American women and tend to have more children and more-closely spaced births, their children's IQ scores are likely to be affected adversely. Especially pernicious is the very young age at which a large proportion of Black women begin to have families, as suggested by findings that the offspring of teenage mothers had IQs averaging 7 points lower than children of comparable birth rank, family size, and social class whose mothers were in their middle to late twenties (Record, McKeown, and Edwards, 1969b).[2] Similarly, the greater the number of children, the lower their IQs will tend to be (especially if they are closely spaced). In the Birmingham, England, study (Record, McKeown, and Edwards, 1969b), the elder child in a family of two was likely to score 7 points higher than a thirdborn of five children born into a family of comparable social class.

Data from the 1980 U.S. Census provide a good basis for estimating the birth-order-by-family-size distributions of White and Black families in the United States, as well as the age dis-

**Table 16. Performance of American Blacks and Whites
on the Stanford-Binet IQ Test (Fourth Edition).**

| | IQ Scores by Race and Age | | | | | |
| | Age 12–Adult[a] | | Age 7–11 | | Age 2–6 | |
IQ Performance of the Standardization Sample	*White*	*Black*	*White*	*Black*	*White*	*Black*
Composite IQ	103.5	86.1	102.6	92.7	104.7	91.0
Verbal Reasoning	104.2	87.7	102.8	92.6	105.8	92.2
Abstract-Visual Reasoning	102.6	85.4	101.6	92.7	103.3	90.8
Quantitative Reasoning	103.1	86.4	102.3	94.6	103.6	93.1
Short-Term Memory	102.1	91.2	102.0	95.3	103.0	93.6
(Number of Examinees)	1,303	210	1,168	202	1,220	299

[a] "Adult" means aged eighteen to twenty-three. This (1,728-person) sample's scores averaged 99.3, including 99.9 for Asians, 94.9 for Hispanics, and 94.7 for Native Americans (American Indians, Eskimos, and so on).

Source: Thorndike, Hagen, and Sattler, 1986, pp. 35–36. Reprinted with permission of The Riverside Publishing Company from pages 35 and 36 of *Stanford-Binet Intelligence Scale Technical Manual: Fourth Edition* by R. L. Thorndike, E. P. Hagen, and J. M. Sattler. THE RIVERSIDE PUBLISHING COMPANY, 8420 W. Bryn Mawr Avenue, Chicago, IL 60631. Copyright 1986.

**Table 17. Estimated Age Distribution of Black and Caucasian Mothers
at the Birth of Their First, Second, and Third Children
(United States, 1980).[4]**

| | Percentage | | | | | |
| | Firstborn | | Secondborn | | Thirdborn | |
Mother's Age	White	Black	White	Black	White	Black
Prior to Age 20	12.0	30.7	2.2	8.9	1.8	7.4
20–21	12.7	18.5	5.5	12.0	4.5	10.3
22–24	17.0	17.7	12.2	17.3	13.0	19.1
25–29	24.1	16.8	24.2	24.0	24.1	24.8
30–34	21.8	10.6	30.2	20.5	29.3	23.6
35–39	9.3	4.5	18.3	12.3	22.2	14.4
40 plus	3.1	1.2	7.3	5.0	5.1	0.4
Totals	100.0	100.0	100.0	100.0	100.0	100.0

Source: 1980 U.S. Census, Table 270.

tributions of Black and White mothers at the birth of their
children (differentiated by order of birth). This section summarizes the methodology used in making these estimates and
presents the principal findings derived from this analysis of
census data. The impact of these differences in family configuration on IQ is then estimated. Because of its technical nature,
much of this analysis is presented in footnotes at the end of the
chapter, along with several of the more detailed tables.

Table 17 summarizes the results of the analysis of mother's age
at birth of child for first, second, and thirdborn children, based
on the childbearing characteristics of mothers born between
1935 and 1939.[3] It indicates that half of these Black mothers had
their first child before their twenty-second birthday, compared
with only a fourth of the White mothers, and that nearly 40
percent of the Black mothers who eventually bore two or more
children had their second child by age twenty-four, compared
with only a fifth of the White mothers.

An estimate of the impact on IQ of differences in Black and
White maternal ages has been developed, based on the findings
from the "social-class neutral" Birmingham, England, study

(Record, McKeown, and Edwards, 1969b). The results can be summarized as follows (see Table 23 for more detail):

- If all Black mothers had their first child between ages thirty and thirty-four, these children's IQs would average 4.45 points higher than at present; similarly, if all Caucasian mothers bore their first child at this age, these children's scores would average 2.61 points higher — a difference of 1.84 points.
- If all Black mothers had their second child at age thirty to thirty-four, these children's IQs would average 2.88 points higher; similarly, if all Caucasian mothers bore their first child at this age, these children's scores would average 1.30 points higher — a difference averaging 1.58 points.
- A similar analysis for thirdborn children yields 2.73 and 1.27 points, respectively — a difference averaging 1.46 points. For fourth and laterborn children, the difference narrows to 1.00 point.

This analysis suggests that the deleterious impact on IQ associated with the younger age distribution of Black mothers — holding family size, birth order, and social class constant — is approximately 1.5 IQ points.

To quantify the effects of birth order on the Black/White IQ differential, we can again use the verbal IQ data from the Birmingham study as a useful guidepost. Here, to avoid duplicating the impact of maternal age on IQ, only the scores of children whose mothers were between the ages of thirty and thirty-nine when they gave birth have been used in creating the comparative analysis of the Black and White birth-order distributions shown in Table 18.

A similar analysis performed on the National Merit Scholarship Examination data (Breland, 1974), displayed in Table 19, yields nearly the same estimate, 1.5 points.

Perhaps the best approach for assessing the impact on IQ of family-size differences in the Black and White populations — independently of birth order — is to compare the relative contributions of each to the successive declines found (in Raven's Progressive Matrices scores) with increasing family size and birth order among the 184,000 nineteen-year-old males whose fathers were in the manual socio-occupational class in the Netherlands (Belmont and Marolla, 1973). The results are as follows:

Table 18. Differential Impact of Birth Order on Black and White Verbal IQs
(Holding Mother's Age Constant).

Birth Order	Verbal IQ: Average	% in Birth Order		IQ(times)% in Birth Order	
		White	Black	White	Black
Firstborns (excludes only children)	108.0	30.6	24.2	33.05	26.14
Secondborns	104.4	30.6	24.2	31.95	25.26
Only Child	104.0	10.5	14.0	10.92	14.56
Thirdborns	100.9	16.4	15.0	16.55	15.14
Fourthborns	97.6	7.2	9.2	7.03	8.98
Fifthborns	94.8	2.8	5.4	2.65	5.12
Sixth/Laterborns	92.0	1.9	8.0	1.75	7.36
Totals	NA	100.0	100.0	103.90	102.56
Average Black/White Difference				1.34	

Source: Derived from Record, McKeown, and Edwards, 1969b.

- For each combination of family-size and birth-order increase, test results declined an average of a tenth of a "rank" (for example, from 2.89 for secondborns in a family of two children, to 2.98 for thirdborns in families with three children, to 3.08 for the fourth of four children, to 3.19 for the fifth of five children, to 3.31 for the sixth of six children, and so on).
- Successive family-size increases produced slightly smaller declines in test scores than did successive increases in birth order.

Applying this finding (that family-size effects are slightly less than those of birth order), we can then estimate that the combined IQ effects of the birth-order and family-size disparity between Black and White families will be slightly less than double the impact found for birth order alone — *or 2.5 IQ points.*

The final element in the cluster of variables that comprise family configuration is the spacing between children. As demonstrated in Chapter Two, three or more closely spaced children will result in a sharp reduction in the average IQ performance of

**Table 19. Differential Effect of Birth Order and Number of Children
on Black and White Intellectual Abilities
(as Measured by National Merit Scholarship Examination Scores, 1965).**

Birth Order/Number of Children	Test Score[a]	% of Children		Score(×)%	
		White	Black	White	Black
Firstborns: 2 children	106.2	14.21	9.16	15.09	9.73
Firstborns: 3 children	106.2	9.20	5.86	9.77	6.22
Firstborns: 4 children	105.6	4.36	3.73	4.60	3.94
Firstborns: 5 children	104.4	1.70	2.33	1.77	2.43
Secondborns: 2 children	104.4	14.21	9.16	14.84	9.56
Secondborns: 3 children	103.9	9.20	5.85	9.56	6.08
Only children	103.8	10.54	14.03	10.94	14.56
Secondborns: 4 children	103.1	4.36	3.73	4.50	3.84
Thirdborns: 3 children	102.7	9.20	5.86	9.45	6.02
Secondborns: 5 children	101.7	1.71	2.33	1.74	2.37
Thirdborns: 4 children	101.3	4.36	3.73	4.42	3.78
Fourthborns: 4 children	100.0	4.36	3.74	4.36	3.74
Third to Fifthborns: 5 children	98.0	5.10	7.00	5.00	6.86
Families of 6 or more	96.4	7.49	23.49	7.22	22.64
Totals (Percent/Total IQ)	100.0	100.00	—	103.26	101.77
White/Black difference: (standard deviation = 20)				1.5	
Difference adjusted to a standard deviation of 16				1.2	

[a] Derived from Breland, 1974.

all — and Black families tend to have significantly narrower child spacing than do White families (Suchindran and Lingner, 1977).[5] Much of the impact of this difficult-to-quantify factor has, however, already been taken into account, because (1) for second and laterborn children maternal age is necessarily dependent on child spacing and (2) there is a significant positive correlation between child spacing and family size. Whether the differences between Black and White families in sibling spacing are almost fully subsumed under these other family configuration variables, or whether the residual child-spacing effect is itself significant, cannot be determined. Consequently, except for recognizing that — when social class is not held constant — the additional effects on IQ of sibling spacing are likely to be relatively important, the "social-class neutral" analyses presented above will not be adjusted to incorporate this small "plus" factor.

An analysis of data concerning the more than 26,000 first-born children who were part of the Collaborative Perinatal Project suggests that in Black families the detrimental effects of extremely young maternal age on children's IQs are not as pronounced as in White families. In this study (Belmont and others, 1981), the IQs of the nearly 4,000 offspring of Black teenage mothers averaged only 1.7 points below those of the nearly 9,500 firstborn Black children whose mothers were aged twenty and older at the time of their birth, compared with a 3.7-point average difference in the Caucasian sample. Much of this difference, however, reflects the fact that Black women who bear their first child *after* age twenty still tend to be younger than their White counterparts; hence, the additional depressive effect of young motherhood is less. Nevertheless, it appears appropriate to make a slight downward adjustment to the estimate derived from the Birmingham study analysis, from 1.5 points to 1.0 point.

In conclusion, family configuration, in and of itself, is estimated to account for 3.5 points of the IQ disparity between Blacks and Whites in the United States — meaning that *if White mothers retained their social, educational, and economic status but bore the same number of children at the same ages as did Black mothers, their children's IQs would average about 3.5 points lower than at present.*

6.4 Birth Weight, Length of Gestation, and the Black/White IQ Disparity

A less-than-adequate intrauterine environment — as evidenced by prematurity, low birth weight, low weight-for-date, and (as discussed below) high birth weight coupled with an apparently erroneous presumption of prematurity — is demonstrated to have a very adverse impact on IQ.

As detailed below, Black children are much more likely to fall into those birth-weight and weight-for-date classifications where the risk of moderate to severe cognitive impairment is substantial and are less likely to fall into the most advantaged birth-weight/date combinations. Thus, a portion of the IQ disparity between Blacks and Whites can be attributed to differences in their prenatal growth environment. In the Collaborative Perinatal Project (Broman, Nichols, and Kennedy, 1975), a somewhat larger SES influence on racial differences was observed (on the short form of the Stanford-Binet) among four-year-old children, with mean IQ differences ranging from about 8 points in the lowest SES category to 13 points in the highest social class.

As part of the Johns Hopkins Study of Premature Infants, two samples of children (born in Baltimore in 1952) were followed and tested periodically—a low-birth-weight sample and a full-term sample—each matched according to race, birth order, and socioeconomic class. Within each of three weight classes (under 2,000 grams, 2,000 to 2,500 grams, and above 2,500 grams), an IQ difference of 11 points between Blacks and Whites was reported at six years of age on the Stanford-Binet examination (Wiener and others, 1965).

In a follow-up study (Wiener, 1970), the principal author interrelated data on birth weight and gestational length with full-scale Wechsler IQ test scores at ages eight to ten. The results (which were reported on a race-adjusted basis) have been combined (in this present analysis) with that author's findings on the distribution of birth weight by gestational age for nearly 100,000 births in Baltimore during the years 1961 to 1965 (approximately half of which were to Black women). The principal finding is that Baltimore's Black population was vastly overrepresented in those weight-for-date classifications where IQ deficits are most likely to occur and considerably underrepresented in those weight-for-date categories where IQ averages are the highest. Specific findings emerging from this analysis include:

- The rate of premature births to Black mothers was almost two and a half times higher than among White mothers—24.3 percent of the Black children having been born before the thirty-seventh week of gestation, compared with 10.3 percent of the White children.
- Among premature infants, the incidence of high weight-for-date babies (above 2,500 grams) was also two and a half times higher

among Black families — 15.4 percent, compared with 6.4 percent among White births. Paralleling the results of the Birmingham, England, study (Record, McKeown, and Edwards, 1969b), this short-gestational-age, normal-birth-weight group had markedly lower IQs; in the Baltimore sample, their scores averaged only 88.8 (on a race-adjusted basis), compared with 95.9 for children born after thirty-eight to forty weeks of gestation and 101.1 for children born after a forty-week or longer gestational period. This phenomenon is thought of as often reflecting "false prematurity," which results from bleeding early in pregnancy.

- The rate of full-term but low-birth-weight infants was also markedly higher among Black families — 5.7 percent vs. 3.8 percent. The race-adjusted IQs of this group were also extremely low, averaging 92 for children weighing 2,000 to 2,500 grams at birth and 84 for children weighing less than 2,000 grams.

- Conversely, the rate of forty-one-week or longer gestational-age infants of normal weight-for-age was far higher among the Caucasian population — 27.5 percent, compared with 17.6 percent. The IQ "advantage" of this group compared with normal-birth-weight infants born at term was 5.1 points (even though reported on a race-adjusted basis); again this finding is comparable to the results of the Birmingham, England, study.

The Collaborative Perinatal Project, a fourteen-hospital all-urban survey conducted primarily in the northeastern U.S. (Niswander and Gordon, 1972), found almost the same proportion of low-birth-weight infants (under 2,500 grams) among Black families (13.4 percent, compared with 14.6 percent in Baltimore) and among White families (7.1 percent versus 7.7 percent). Thus, given the similarity of findings from these studies, it seems appropriate to extrapolate from the Johns Hopkins data.

Examining weight classification statistics is apt to mask a small additional element unfavorable to Blacks, namely, differences *within* the weight categories used. At one extreme, in the Johns Hopkins study (Wiener and others, 1965), almost a third of the Black infants weighing under 2,500 grams also weighed less than 2,000 grams, compared with fewer than a fifth of the low-birth-weight Caucasian infants. At the other extreme, in the Collaborative Perinatal Project — *where over 45 percent of the Caucasian infants had a gestational period of forty-one weeks or more, compared with 30 percent among the Black infants* — the average birth weight of the long-gestation White infants exceeded that of their Black counterparts by 200 grams.

Table 20. Estimated IQ Impact of Various Weight/Gestational-Age Categories by the Proportion of Black and Caucasian Births in Each Category (Children Born in the 1950s).

Gestational-Age/Weight Class	Effect on IQ (Points)[a]	% of Births in Class[a] White	Black	Total IQ Impact White	Black
Premature: Normal birth weight	– 6.5	6.40	15.40	– 0.42	– 1.00
Full Term: Low birth weight	–	3.79	5.70	– 0.26	– 0.43
2,000–2,500 grams	(– 6.0)	(3.06)	(4.06)	(– 0.18)	(– 0.24)
below 2,000 grams	(– 11.5)	(0.73)	(1.64)	(– 0.08)	(– 0.19)
Premature: Low birth weight	–	3.87	8.44	– 0.24	– 0.58
2,000–2,500 grams	(– 5.5)	(3.00)	(5.12)	(– 0.16)	(– 0.28)
below 2,000 grams	(– 9.0)	(0.87)	(3.32)	(– 0.08)	(– 0.30)
Long Gestation: Appropriate weight					
White	+ 5.8	27.55	–	+ 1.60	–
Black	+ 4.3	–	17.10	–	+ 0.74
White Birth-Weight Advantage: Remaining births	+ 0.6	58.39	–	+ 0.35	–
Net IQ Impact				+ 1.03	– 1.28
Black-White Difference				2.31	

[a] Adapted from Wiener, 1970.

In Table 20, the IQ effects of these differences between Blacks and Whites (within and between birth-weight and weight-for-date classes) are estimated. This analysis yields an IQ impact favoring Caucasian children that averages 2.3 points.

More-recent data indicate that the incidence of less-than-adequate birth weights among Black babies is determined in large part by the adequacy of prenatal medical care. A study of births to members of a predominantly middle-class California prepaid health plan in 1978 (Murray and Bernfield, 1988) showed that those Black mothers who availed themselves of the plan's liberal maternity health benefits had only a 4.8 percent rate of low-birth-weight babies, including only a 1.2 percent rate of very low birth weight babies—compared with rates of 10.0 percent and 4.2 percent for Black mothers receiving an "inadequate" level of care. Moreover, prematurity occurred in a fifth of the (nearly 4,000) Black mothers receiving inadequate care, or three times as often as among those mothers who utilized the plan's benefits, and the incidence of low birth weight at term was nearly three and a half times as great among Black infants.[6] Several other recent studies support a continuing (if not increasing) disparity in the proportions of Black and Caucasian children suffering from low birth weight (Lieberman and others, 1987; Kleinman and Kessel, 1987; Shiono and others, 1986).

6.5 Family Configuration, the Intrauterine Environment, and SES

This section addresses two questions: First, do the 3.5-point IQ difference between Blacks and Whites attributable to family configuration variables and the 2.3-point difference attributable to birth-weight/date characteristics combine to produce a 5.8-point IQ disparity between the two groups, or do they interact to produce a larger or smaller disparity? Second, how do these variables interact with the IQ effects of socioeconomic differences between Black and White families?

Reynolds and Gutkin (1981) undertook an in-depth analysis of the effects of SES on IQ differences between Blacks and Whites, using children who were part of the renorming that accompanied the 1972 revision of the Wechsler Intelligence Scale for Children (the WISC-R standardization sample). The authors combed through the study to create a matched pair sample of Black and White children of equivalent SES, geographical area, and age. In this analysis, the IQ difference fell from 15.8 points (or slightly more than one standard deviation) to 12.3 points—a decrease of 3.5 points (or 22 percent).

On the surface, birth weight and/or date appears to be unrelated to family configuration, since (1) the average birth weight of firstborn children is 50 grams lighter than that of laterborns (Wiener and others, 1965), which implies that the so-called firstborn IQ advantage bears no relation to birth weight; (2) the birth weights of siblings correlate approximately + .50 (which is a somewhat greater confluence than found for their gestational ages); and (3) analyses of the relationship between child spacing and the levels of various sex hormones (measured in the umbilical cord) reveal minor or inconsistent results, with the possible exceptions of progesterone (which, after two years, returns to near-firstborn levels) and estrone (which may have a slightly higher level among firstborns). But testosterone, which has been strongly linked with the timing and strength of hemispheric growth patterns, shows no consistent relationship with birth order or child spacing (Maccoby and others, 1979).

However, the relation between family configuration and birth weight and/or date may become closer when the element of socioeconomic class is introduced. This is because the lower and lower-middle classes (into which a majority of Black children are reared) tend to have more "malignant" configurations in each of these variables.

There are reasons for assuming that family configuration and birth-weight/date characteristics interact with SES in a multiplicative manner. First, the effects of family configuration become more perverse at progressively lower social classes. Second, opportunities for overcoming the cognitive deficits associated with a less-than-adequate intrauterine environment are diminished with increasing family size and birth order, reduced child spacing, and other aspects of a progressively lower SES. Indeed, if the results of the comparisons made between twins and nontwins in the Collaborative Perinatal Project are indicative, the extent of the differential impact of prenatal inadequacies on Black and White IQs is considerable. At age seven, IQ scores for the 148 Caucasian twin pairs averaged 2.4 points below those of singletons, but the scores of the 186 Black twin pairs averaged 8.4 points below those of the Black singletons—84.0, compared with 92.4 (Brackbill and Nichols, 1982). But how much of this difference relates to the extent and severity of intrauterine deficiencies per se and how much to these deficiencies' interactive effects with family size and SES is not determinable.

There are some indications that the effects of birth weight/date and family configuration on IQ are not entirely independent of each other, especially in the lowest social classes. Thus, birth weight and/or date influences are apt to contribute to the IQ effects associated with family configuration (for example, the thirdborn in a family of five children born to a very young mother is likely to be of low birth weight). There may also be a so-called floor effect, in that additional environmental "malignancies" (such as teenage parenthood) will cause the adverse impact to be less in the lower third of the IQ range than in the above-average range. However, because family configuration tends to affect verbal IQ far more than nonverbal IQ—and a poor intra-uterine environment tends to affect spatial IQ more than verbal IQ—any "floor effects" in these somewhat separate intellectual spheres are likely to be relatively independent of one another.

Thus, it is estimated that approximately 5.5 points of the IQ disparity between Blacks and Whites are attributable to the combined effects of family configuration and the intrauterine environment. Further, because most of the effects of SES on IQ are probably caused by differences in family configuration and birth weight/date, the additional impact of SES is likely to account for an additional 1.5 to 2.0 points of this 15-point difference. This implies that *more than a third of the IQ gap between Blacks and Whites in the 1970s was caused by these prenatal and family configuration factors—with the proportion rising to nearly 50 percent when their interaction with SES is considered.*

6.6 The Black/White IQ Gap: Nurture Versus Nature

Many people will, without giving much thought to it, assume that the entire IQ effects of family configuration and birth weight/date should be attributed to the environmental side of the heredity-environment equation. The logic underlying this assumption is essentially as follows: Family configuration, by its very nature, affects the postnatal development of intelligence. Because the cognitive deficits attributable to the prenatal environment can (in large part) be reversed through an effective early-intervention regimen, deficiencies of this nature cannot be said to be innate. Moreover, in the foregoing analyses, many aspects of the effects of family configuration and intrauterine differences were calculated on a social-class-neutralized basis, on a race-adjusted basis, or on the basis of nearly all-White populations.

However, some people would argue that women who have too many children at too young an age are apt to be innately less intelligent than women (in the same social class) who are "more responsible" about parenthood. Hence, family configuration would affect multigenerational SES mobility by creating a downward migration of the less intelligent members of the middle and upper-middle classes and an upward migration of the more intelligent members of the lower class. As a consequence, family configuration can and does have a strong hereditary component. Further, certain aspects of the prenatal environment are apt to be influenced by heredity.

There is thus no simple answer to the question, How much of the observed IQ difference between American Blacks and Whites is inherited and how much is environmental? Moreover, there is considerable evidence suggesting that certain aspects of cognitive development are influenced by the "ancestral" environment and that these are highly malleable over the course of a few generations. Thus, the terms *hereditary, genetic, and innate* are not necessarily synonymous (see Part Four). If this hypothesis is valid, then the multigenerational effects of efforts to improve maternal and child health and to supply early remedial education will become increasingly manifest.

Notes

1. The sample sizes were 5,693 Caucasians and 879 Black children aged six to eleven and (for phase III) 5,125 Caucasians and 817 Black children aged twelve to seventeen (the median maternal birth year was 1928); scores are for the WISC vocabulary and block-design subtests, which in combination are estimated to show a +.88 correlation with full-scale WISC scores (Scarr, 1982).
2. For fifth and laterborns, it appears that (1) fewer children in the lower-class families took the examination and (2) the sample size of large-sized families in the "higher" social class was quite small; consequently, only the (broad) middle-class findings were used.
3. The data for mothers aged forty to forty-four (born between 1935 and 1939) have been assumed to be indicative of completed family size. This assumption takes cognizance of two offsetting factors. First, although some further childbearing will occur, the increase is marginal (women aged forty-five to forty-nine had borne only 6 percent more children than those aged forty to forty-four). Second, the number of "children

ever born" slightly overstates family size, because of neonatal and early childhood mortality.

4. The 1980 U.S. Census Table 270 displays information on the number of children ever born, by race and by age of mother. To accomplish this analysis, the census findings for the number of children ever born to mothers in successive age groupings were first "standardized," with the results then used to determine the increase from one age group to the next in the number of women who bear a child of a specific birth order — with the results expressed in relation to the number of women eventually bearing at least that number of children. The standardization process involved adjusting the data to equalize the total number of women in each age class; for example, there were 4,807,000 Caucasian women aged forty-five to forty-nine, and 7,984,000 Caucasian women aged twenty-five- to twenty-nine. Thus, to make direct comparisons between mothers in these two age groups, the numbers shown for twenty-five- to twenty-nine-year-olds would be reduced 40 percent, and the results of this procedure would be applied, for example, as follows: The total number of Caucasian women aged forty-five to forty-nine who had borne at least two children totaled 3,858,000; at age twenty-five to twenty-nine, there were 2,824,000 with two or more children; standardizing was accomplished by reducing the total for age twenty-five to twenty-nine 40 percent, which yielded 44 percent of the "eventual" (age forty-five to forty-nine) total. Then, by performing similar calculations for mothers aged twenty-two to twenty-four, we can make a good estimate concerning the number/percentage of women who bore their second child between these ages. Note: Table 17 also incorporates some within-category age interpolation, based on the weighted average of ages in the census categories listed.

5. Within the Caucasian population, socioeconomic status was not a major factor in determining child-spacing intervals between the first and second child or the second and third child (among women marrying between 1955 and 1959).

6. A third category, representing an intermediate level of maternal health care, produced rates of 17 percent prematurity and 8 percent low birth weight (including 2.5 percent very low birth weight) among the offspring of Black mothers. Twins were excluded from this analysis, prematurity was defined as giving birth before 260 days, and 90 percent of the Black mothers in this Kaiser-Permanente HMO had at least a high school education.

Table 21. Distribution of White U.S. Child Population by Birth Order and Family Size (Offspring of Mothers Born in the Years 1935–1939).

| | *Women Age 40–44 by Number of Children Ever Born* | | | | | | | |
	1	*2*	*3*	*4*	*5*	*6*	*7 +*	*Total*
Number (000)	469.0	1,265.4	1,228.1	776.0	379.1	178.8	154.4	4,450.8
Percent	10.54	28.43	27.59	17.44	8.52	4.02	3.47	100.00
Firstborns	10.54	14.21	9.20	4.36	1.70	0.67	0.44	41.12
Secondborns	—	14.22	9.20	4.36	1.70	0.67	0.44	30.60
Thirdborns		—	9.19	4.36	1.71	0.67	0.44	16.37
Fourthborns			—	4.36	1.70	0.67	0.43	7.16
Laterborns				—	1.71	1.34	1.72	4.77

Source: 1980 U.S. Census Table 270.

Table 22. Distribution of Black U.S. Child Population by Birth Order and Family Size (Offspring of Mothers Born in the Years 1935–1939).

| | *Women Age 40–44 by Number of Children Ever Born* | | | | | | | |
	1	*2*	*3*	*4*	*5*	*6*	*7 +*	*Total*
Number (000)	85.3	111.4	106.8	90.8	70.9	52.2	90.6	608.0
Percent	14.03	18.32	17.57	14.93	11.66	8.59	14.90	100.00
Firstborns	14.03	9.16	5.86	3.73	2.33	1.43	1.66	38.20
Secondborns	—	9.16	5.85	3.74	2.33	1.44	1.66	24.18
Thirdborns		—	5.86	3.73	2.33	1.43	1.66	15.01
Fourthborns			—	3.73	2.33	1.43	1.66	9.15
Laterborns				—	2.34	2.86	8.26	13.46

Source: 1980 U.S. Census Table 270.

Table 23. Impact of 1980 Maternal Age Distribution on Verbal IQ Compared with IQ Scores If All Children Were Born to Mothers Age 30–34.

Age of Mother at Child's Birth	Estimated IQ Impact[a]	% of Birth Order in Age Group		Total IQ Impact (Col. A × Col. B)	
		Black	White	Black	White
Firstborns					
Teenage	− 8.3	30.7	12.0	− 2.55	− 1.00
20–21	− 6.2	18.5	12.7	− 1.15	− 0.79
22–24	− 3.0	17.7	17.0	− 0.53	− 0.51
25–29	− 1.3	16.8	24.1	− 0.22	− 0.31
30–34 (parity)	0	10.6	21.8	0	0
35–39	0	4.5	9.3	0	0
40 plus	0	1.2	3.1	0	0
Total	—	100.0	100.0	− 4.45	− 2.61
Black/White difference				1.84	
Secondborns					
Teenage	− 10.0	8.9	2.2	− 0.89	− 0.22
20–21	− 8.5	12.0	5.5	− 1.02	− 0.47
22–24	− 5.2	17.3	12.2	− 0.90	− 0.63
25–29	− 1.0	24.0	24.2	− 0.24	− 0.24
30–34	0	20.5	30.2	0	0
35–39	+ 0.7	12.3	18.3	+ 0.09	+ 0.13
40 plus	+ 1.7	5.0	7.3	+ 0.08	+ 0.13
Total	—	100.0	100.0	− 2.88	− 1.30
Black/White difference				1.58	
Thirdborns					
Teenage	− 9.0	7.4	1.8	− 0.67	− 0.16
20–21	− 7.7	10.3	4.5	− 0.79	− 0.35
22–24	− 4.2	19.1	13.0	− 0.80	− 0.55
25–29	− 2.5	24.8	24.1	− 0.62	− 0.60
30–34	0	23.6	29.3	0	0
35–39	+ 1.0	14.4	22.2	+ 0.14	+ 0.22
40 plus	+ 3.3	0.4	5.1	+ 0.01	+ 0.17
Total	—	100.0	100.0	− 2.73	− 1.27
Black/White difference				1.46	
Fourth/Laterborns					
Teen–21	− 6.0	6.9	1.9	− 0.41	− 0.11
22–24	− 3.0	11.8	5.7	− 0.35	− 0.17
25–29	− 1.0	22.3	15.7	− 0.22	− 0.16
30–34 (parity)	0	30.0	29.6	0	0
35–39	+ 1.5	24.4	34.1	+ 0.37	+ 0.51
40 plus	+ 3.5	4.6	13.0	+ 0.16	+ 0.46
Total	—			− 0.45	+ 0.53
Black/White difference				1.00	

[a] Derived from the Birmingham Study (Record, McKeown, and Edwards, 1969b).

Effects of the
Early Home Environment
on IQ

Any person seeking an in-depth understanding of how children's early upbringing influences their intelligence is immediately confronted with a voluminous number of studies that
contain a seemingly endless array of findings. These findings
are themselves predicated on relationships between IQ scores
on a variety of standardized tests of intelligence and an assortment of home-assessment factors, evaluated at various ages and
among diverse populations. Not surprisingly, then, a wide range
of theories have arisen.

Consequently, before attempting to organize, summarize,
and integrate the diversity of findings bearing upon the question of IQ and the early home environment, we need to set forth
criteria for limiting the kinds of studies and data that will be
incorporated in our review. To this end, Chapter Seven indicates
which early childhood IQ measures appear to be reasonably
good predictors of school-age children's IQs and which do not. It
presents the rationale for emphasizing studies that

- Assess the home environment during the first two or
  three years of life.
- Provide longitudinal rather than concurrent assess-

ments of relationships between various aspects of the
early home environment and measured IQ.
- Stress findings from middle-class and upper-middle-
  class populations.

This last emphasis is necessary, first of all, because the environmental factors associated with differences in intellectual ability
among these children are usually quite distinct from those
factors that inhibit the cognitive development of children from
lower-class families. Second, despite the high degree of importance and widespread interest that an integrated analysis of
findings from these populations would seem to have, such an
analysis does not appear elsewhere in the literature.

Chapter Eight focuses on identifying those aspects of the
interactive relationship between mothers and their infants that
seem to have a significant impact on the infants' intellectual
development. These aspects include (1) using vocal imitation,
(2) using gaze behavior effectively, (3) applying contingent responsivity as a learning tool, and (4) encouraging an infant's
attention to objects and events and consistently labeling these
objects and events. Here, large differences between maternal
interactive behavior directed to firstborns and to laterborns
serve as a starting point for inquiring into the causes of the
"firstborn IQ advantage." Studies that report correlations between children's IQs and these environmental variables after the
influence of maternal IQ and education are factored out provide further evidence of the influence of these early environmental influences.

Chapter Nine focuses on several aspects of the home environment during toddlerhood and presents findings concerning (1)
the kinds of behavioral control strategies used to deal with the
"terrible twos" that, according to longitudinal studies, are detrimental to IQ development; (2) the need to alter the content and
structure of the educational program at about twenty-four
months of age to correspond with changes in brain biology;
and (3) whether it is more productive to let a toddler's intellectual development proceed "naturally," to provide a regimen of
academic stimulation, and/or to stimulate other types of

achievement-oriented behaviors. Findings concerning the early backgrounds of gifted and eminent people indicate an extremely high frequency of early environmental enrichment, as well as a special familial involvement in their cognitive development.

Contents

✕ 7 ✕

Evaluating Tests
That Measure IQ
in Infancy and Toddlerhood

7.1 Introduction

The past twenty years or so have witnessed an outpouring of studies designed to reveal meaningful associations between aspects of the preschool home environment and scores on IQ tests. As this body of data has expanded, so too have studies that examine (1) which early IQ assessment measures are reasonably good predictors of later IQ and which are not, (2) at what ages particular environmental factors seem to influence future IQ development, (3) at what ages these developing IQ correspondences will emerge or become strongest, and (4) how these findings are apt to vary in relation to the demographic, social, and economic characteristics of the families studied.

As a result, this analysis is limited to longitudinal studies that

- Determined cognitive ability at three years of age or older, using well-respected standardized IQ measures (the predictive validity of most of the widely used IQ tests prior to age three is poor).
- Examined relationships between factors in the home environment and IQ scores in terms of *subsequent* rather than *concurrent* test performance.

In addition, this chapter will stress the results of studies that reported on the environment provided by middle-class and upper-middle-class families. This will assist readers who wish to distinguish those features of the home environment where a well-above-average level of "stimulation" is apt to have positive effects on intelligence, from those most responsible for the deleterious effects on IQ seen in poverty populations.

This chapter also evaluates recent efforts to develop IQ predictors that can be assessed in infancy and provides an introductory look at the possibility that, by designing training programs to improve performance on one or more of these early IQ predictors, we may be able to generate lasting improvements in cognitive functioning.

7.2 The Primary Focus of This Inquiry

Much of the funding for longitudinal research has been allocated to studies of low-income (and other at-risk) populations. Government policy initiatives are usually aimed at distinguishing, from among the many types of inadequacy found in "deprived" environments, those that strongly contribute to impaired cognitive development—with a view toward developing remedial programs to normalize the IQs of these children. Therefore, reviews of the relationships between IQ and early home environments tend to rely heavily on findings from disadvantaged populations.

However, because the primary aim of Part Three is to identify factors associated with the development of *superior* intellectual abilities, this chapter focuses on associations between environmental factors and cognitive performance in families where parental education and/or children's IQs are above the norm.

The policy implications of the conclusions arising from studies of upper-middle-class populations are considerably different from those suggested by examinations of low-income populations. If, for example, the amount of a particular kind of cognitive stimulus is shown to have a strong positive correlation with IQ in a low-income population, it is likely that this outcome reflects *the differing effects of a normal and an abnormally low quantity of that stimulus.* As a consequence, it cannot be inferred that increased amounts of this stimulus—beyond that normally received by an average child—will enhance IQ. However, if a strong relationship between IQ and the frequency with which a specific type of stimulus is provided is found among groups of children whose IQs tend to be considerably above the norm, this would seem to imply that, for the large majority of children, more of this stimulus will be "better."

7.3 Subsequent Versus Concurrent IQ Assessments

There is a growing consensus among researchers who have undertaken longitudinal studies that compare the early home environment with IQ that measures designed to assess the home environment are much better at *predicting IQ* than at assessing *current* cognitive performance. For example, in a 1986 review of the longitudinal-study literature, Gottfried and Gottfried (1986, p. 4) cite eight longitudinal studies in support of this conclusion: "In studies where subjects were assessed from infancy through the preschool years,... correlations of greater magnitudes were found predictively (e.g., the one-year 'HOME' and three-year intellectual performance) than were found concurrently,... [with] correlations of greatest strength [found between] home assessments around two years of age or later, and measures of cognitive development during the preschool period."

Part of this stronger predictive (as opposed to concurrent) power represents the relatively poor ability of the most frequently used measure of IQ at age two, the Bayley Mental Development Index (Bayley, 1969), to predict later scores on Stanford-Binet or Wechsler IQ tests, even when this test is administered during the preschool years. Nevertheless, of at least equal importance are findings that the full effects of stimulation provided during one stage in the developmental process are usually not manifest until a subsequent stage in development. There are apparently peak periods of influence, and these are "peak" in two different respects: (1) the age or ages at which the quantity of a given variable that is received is crucial to the future course of cognitive development; and (2) the age at which IQ performance will be most affected by the quantity and quality of these antecedent environmental experiences. We can note two examples of this that involve factors in the HOME Infant Inventory (Bradley and Caldwell, 1984): First, the extent of "restrictiveness and punitiveness" present in the home at twenty-four months, but not twelve months, has a strong impact on subsequent IQ performance. Second, the impact on IQ-test performance of differences in the variety of stimulation provided to a child at fifteen months of age will tend to be far greater at or after the child's third birthday than at fifteen months.

7.4 Preschool IQ Predictors

The accumulated findings of the past generation have caused a major revaluation of certain test instruments once considered valid predictors of cognitive development. In one major respect, however, the picture has not changed. The two most widely used tests, the Stanford-Binet (Terman and Merrill, 1973) and the Wechsler (Wechsler, 1967), are still considered to be *excellent* predictors of adult IQ for about 85 percent of all children **by age six**. Moreover, **from age three onward**, these (as well as several other tests) are accurate enough predictors of later IQ to be used as reasonably reliable sources of information about associations between the early home environment and intelligence. Among the other preschool tests shown to be good evaluators of present and future intellectual performance are the Kaufman ABC Test (Kaufman and Kaufman, 1983) and the McCarthy Scales of Children's Abilities (McCarthy, 1972; see evaluation by Kaufman and Kaufman, 1977), except for the motor subtest.[1] For evaluating verbal IQ, the Zimmerman Language Scales (Zimmerman, Steiner, and Pond, 1979) and the language *comprehension* component of the Reynell Developmental Language Scales (Reynell, 1981) are useful (the *expressive* language component of the Reynell is less helpful).

The principal casualty of the new knowledge about IQ development during infancy and childhood has been the Bayley Scales of Infant Development (Bayley, 1969). Although these scales were long a standard measure of mental and motor development during the first three years of life, evidence now indicates that even when performance is assessed at twenty-four months (1) scores on the Bayley Motor Scales bear no correlation with later IQ scores (except at the extreme lower end), and (2) the gross score on the Bayley Mental Development Index (MDI) is only *weakly* correlated with subsequent IQ performance, even when such performance is assessed at three to six years of age (Bornstein and Sigman, 1986; Wilson, 1978b). Similarly, scores on the Gesell infant development scales show little correspondence with later IQ. Unfortunately, many longitudinal studies have relied on these measures to assess the effects of the early home environment on cognitive development. Often these studies were continued and were thus able to utilize subsequent, more reliable IQ assessment tools. Nevertheless, when these studies' conclusions relied heavily on these infant and toddler developmental scales, they must be viewed with considerable caution.

Researchers have been discovering fairly strong associations between performance on certain kinds of cognitive-response paradigms during the first year of life and IQ scores at three to six years of age and beyond. As discussed in the next section, chief among these are the so-called habituation and novelty paradigms (a tendency to gaze at a repeatedly shown stimulus for progressively shorter time periods and then, when a somewhat novel stimulus is shown, to gaze at it for a substantially longer time period).

7.5 Predicting Childhood IQ in Infancy

Recent developments in the quest for reasonably valid IQ predictors in infancy seem quite encouraging, both in terms of the direct benefits of having at one's disposal good yardsticks of early cognitive competence and as aids in (1) identifying those forms of maternal interactive behavior most closely associated with accelerated IQ development (and quite possibly conducive to it) and (2) designing "*infant lessons*" to strengthen those intellectual skills most likely to form the foundations for later cognitive competence.

Infants who encode visual or auditory stimuli more efficiently and/or recollect these stimuli better than other infants also tend to perform better on traditional tests of intelligence and language during childhood. Encoding and recall skills can be assessed through so-called decrement and recovery-of-attention tests (habituation behavior and response to novelty),[2] which can evaluate infants' information-processing abilities in ways that are relatively free of motor ability limitations.

Although not universally supported by research findings or accepted by all in the research community, an impressive body of evidence linking these infant behaviors with later cognitive competence has emerged from the published literature. With respect to habituation behavior, Bornstein and Sigman (1986) have summarized the results from eight research studies (incorporating ten separate samples of children) in which habituation efficiency, tested between the second and sixth months of life, was compared with performance on standardized tests of intelligence and/or language between three and eight years of age. The correlations found in these ten samples *averaged* + *.49*, with slightly higher correlations usually found among the more verbally oriented cognitive measures.

These relatively strong and consistent correlations are all the more remarkable when we consider that infants two to six months of age are apt to be quite inconsistent in their behavior (especially in terms of arousal and concentration). Moreover, unless researchers are able to design experiments suitable for capturing (at a variety of ages or stages) the "essence" of the common link between performance in infancy and later IQ scores, the reported correlations will tend to understate the de facto relationship between these behaviors.

Despite these constraints (Colombo, Mitchell, and Horowitz, 1988; Rose, Feldman, and Wallace, 1988), researchers have been able to design measures of infant habituation behavior that predict and account for a fourth of the IQ differences found between children.[3] It follows that, if effective habituation behavior can be taught in infancy (while the human brain is growing at an extremely rapid rate), this enhanced capacity might become part of the permanent infrastructure of an infant's intellect. Reported relationships: (1) between habituation behavior and the frequency with which a mother encourages her baby's attention to objects and events in the environment, and (2) between a mother's prompt, contingent, and appropriate responsiveness to her infant's nondistress activities, on the one hand, and habituation and novelty behavior, on the other hand (see sections 8.2 and 8.3) *suggest that these behaviors are often subject to environmental influence.*

Response to novelty, although somewhat related to habituation behavior, actually measures an entirely different aspect of cognitive functioning (Berg and Sternberg, 1985).[4] Novelty response requires successful visual or auditory retention and recognition (re-identification, based on effective discrimination at "encoding"), as well as a motivational interest in attending closely when a novel object or sound is presented. Some specific findings that show the relatively high correlation between novelty preference and subsequent IQ—and how these novelty scores are affected by various familial characteristics—follow:

- In a sample of ninety-three moderately high IQ children whose WISC scores averaged 113 (Fagan and McGrath, 1981), correlations between scores on a battery of infant novelty paradigms (at four to seven months) and verbal aspects of IQ at seven years of age (the WISC-R vocabulary subtest score) were +.57, while at four years of age, the correlation with Peabody Picture Vocabulary Test (PPVT) scores (a measure of visual and verbal IQ) was +.37. There was *no correlation between novelty response and parental education* in this primarily college-educated population, implying that (within a sample of relatively well-educated families) "novelty preference" measures some aspect of IQ unrelated to socioeducational-class status.
- Novelty preference at seven months correlated significantly with three-year PPVT scores, both among White (+.44) and Black (+.38) children (Fagan and Singer, 1983); in this sample, race, birth order, and mother's verbal IQ (and her vocabulary) all influenced PPVT scores. However, only novelty preference and birth order were independently (separately) predictive of IQ, meaning that knowing the mother's race, vocabulary test results, and education would not further improve the ability to predict a child's IQ score, in comparison with knowing only the child's birth order and novelty score in infancy. These authors then performed similar kinds of "multivariable" analyses on their earlier sample (the moderately high IQ sample cited above) and found comparable results,

with *novelty and birth order predicting four-year IQ almost as well* (+ .49) *as did novelty, birth order, parental education, and mother's vocabulary* (+ .51).

- In an ethnically mixed group of children (where only half the mothers were high school graduates), an extremely high correlation (+ .60) was found between response to *auditory novelty* at four months of age (measured by cardiac response) and Stanford-Binet scores at five years of age. Although mother's education was related to child's IQ, the relationship was no longer significant after novelty scores were factored out (O'Connor, Cohen, and Parmelee, 1984).

- In an ethnically mixed group of (average-IQ) New York City children (Rose and Wallace, 1985), novelty scores at six months (averaging the children's performance on three to four different types of problems) showed high correlations with six-year WISC-R IQ scores (+ .52 for the Wechsler's verbal-IQ subtests and + .56 for its performance-IQ components) and with earlier Stanford-Binet scores (+ .66 at thirty-four months and + .45 at forty months). In this sample (unlike some of the other findings cited), parental education, independent of novelty scores, contributed to these children's IQ differences.[5]

- In a recent sample of eighty-four New York City children (Rose, Feldman, and Wallace, 1988), novelty scores at six, seven, and eight months, taken together, were able to explain *almost half the total variance* in three-year IQ.[6] In a follow-up study (Rose, Feldman, Wallace, and McCarton, 1989), the correlations between these children's novelty preference scores at seven months and their (WISC) IQ scores at age five were + .54 for thirty-eight full-term infants and + .61 for thirty-nine preterm infants.

- In a sample of (primarily) firstborn children of White college-educated parents whose IQs averaged 119 (Caron, Caron, and Glass, 1983), scores on a "recovery to novel facial expressions" test at five to six months of age correlated + .42 with Stanford-Binet IQ scores at three (plus) years of age. Competency on this test (evidenced by treating new facial expressions as novel events, but not treating the faces of newly shown women as novel events when their facial expressions are the same as those shown in the immediately preceding photograph) is theorized (by these authors) to be indicative of advanced behavior at this age.[7]

Rapid habituation behavior appears to portend higher verbal IQ more than it does nonverbal IQ, with some studies suggesting that its correlations with performance IQ or discrimination learning are not substantial (Slater, Cooper, Rose, and Perry, 1985, summarized in Bornstein and Sigman, 1986; Rose, Slater, and Perry, 1986). However, among *newborn* infants, looking less at a constant stimulus (in other words, habituating rapidly to it) was, in a recent study, shown to correlate with persistence at a puzzle task at age two and with higher Stanford-Binet scores at age five (Sigman, Cohen, Beckwith, and Topinka, 1986). *Novelty preference, by contrast, appears to be related to full-scale IQ at least as much as it is related to verbal IQ.*

Test-retest habituation behavior (that is, a behavior to which a child was habituated then generates relatively greater initial interest when seen again after an intervening period) also showed good correlations (+ .54) between retest-sensitivity scores at four months of age and Wechsler IQ scores at age four (Bornstein, 1984). Those babies who were initially the most efficient habituators also tended to study the stimulus the most when it was re-presented (Bornstein and Sigman, 1986).

Another potential early prognosticator of cognitive development is the so-called differential vocal response (DVR) to mother and stranger. In this paradigm, the amount of vocalization infants make in response to maternal "encouragement-to-vocalize" at three months of age — in comparison with similar urgings by a stranger — is often found to be predictive of *verbal* but not performance IQ. In one study (of firstborn males from intact, White, English-speaking suburban one-wage-earner families), the infants who later tested as having the highest verbal IQs exhibited greatly contrasting amounts of vocal responses to mothers and strangers: *26 percent to mothers versus 3 percent to strangers* (compared with a baseline average of 11 percent), while infants whose vocal responses to both mother and stranger were near baseline tended to develop lower verbal IQs (Roe, 1978; Roe, McClure, and Roe, 1982).[8] Apparently, more-intelligent infants are better able and/or more willing to control their desire to engage in a familiar and rewarding social interaction game with strangers and, instead, sit quietly while attentively studying the features of this interesting, novel input.[9]

In a series of studies (discussed in section 8.6), Roe and her colleagues have explored relationships between DVR and maternal behavior. However, her initial efforts to raise DVR scores (by trying to induce the mothers of newborn infants to vocalize more to them) were not successful. Although the infants whose mothers followed this regimen exhibited relatively high levels of vocal response to maternal urgings, they also tended to show a high degree of responsiveness to strangers' urgings (Roe, forthcoming). These findings, however, do not necessarily imply that the program will prove ineffective in raising the infants' verbal IQ scores.

Infant memory was also shown to be an important prognosticator of preschool IQ among upper-middle-class suburban children whose IQs (on the Stanford-Binet) averaged 113 at thirty-nine months. In this study (Fagen and others, 1987), the correlations between long-term memory for previously conditioned experiences at three, seven, and eleven months[10] and IQ scores at age three were quite consistent across the three age groups: + .41, + .44, and + .43, respectively.

7.6 Major Factors Affecting Measurable Links Between IQ and Environment

Before proceeding to an evaluation of studies that attempt to discern links between intelligence and particular aspects of the early home environment, we must recognize that the effect of any one environmental factor on the IQ scores of a group of children is apt to be quite limited and that the discernible effect of any one factor will probably be somewhat less than the "real" relationship. We can note several reasons for this:

- The influence of heredity and prenatal environment on an individual's IQ performance is likely to be quite strong; hence, efforts to explain within- or between-family IQ differences in terms of any one aspect of the home environment would not (a priori) be expected to account for a major share of these differences — even if that aspect accounted for a majority of the entire environmental contribution to the IQ differences observed in the children studied.
- All children do not respond in the same manner to a given child-rearing approach; therefore, the most effective strategies for behavior control or teaching may differ considerably from child to child.
- The effects of environmental experiences on IQ will often not appear (or be maximized) until later; because major environmental changes may occur in the intervening period, the strength of linkages initially forged between the IQ outcome and antecedent

features of the home environment will sometimes be greatly attenuated.

- Although IQ-test performance, measured in early to mid childhood, is (for most children) a reasonably good predictor of adult IQ, these tests provide an evaluation of the pace of developmental progress rather than serving as direct indicators of the heights that IQ will reach in adulthood. This is evidenced by the somewhat greater variability of IQ scores between childhood and adulthood, compared with across-time adult IQ stability. Further, the cognitive performance of some children varies greatly by modality (visual versus auditory, verbal versus spatial, and so on).
- Evaluations of conditions in the home environment are at best "seminaturalistic" snapshots of what is sometimes a highly variable situation; consequently, observed assessments of home factors are not always reliable indicators of the usual nature of the home environment.

Given these constraints, the strength and relative consistency of many of the relationships reported between early home environment and later IQ seem truly impressive.

It might be argued, of course, that these relatively high correlations reflect the effects of heredity as well as the effects of environment. If mothers who are innately more intelligent tend to behave differently than do the less intelligent mothers studied, then the IQ outcome associated with an observed environmental behavior will result in part from the higher *native* intelligence of the offspring of those mothers, rather than entirely from the effects of cognitive enrichment on the child.

Fortunately, a number of studies indicate that the IQ effects of particular maternal behaviors (or other aspects of the home environment) are relatively independent of maternal IQ or parental education. In these instances, it was the cognitively enhancing aspects of the experience, not the innate IQ of the caregiver or the child, that caused the outcome. This conclusion—that, after socioeducational status or maternal IQ has been factored out, statistically significant correlations between home factors and cognitive development persist (although slightly reduced)—is well documented in a recent review of the longitudinal-study literature (Gottfried and Gottfried, 1986). This result is particularly noteworthy, because it is derived in large part from studies of middle-class (and higher) populations.

Moreover, even when the link between a given home factor and later IQ is positively correlated with parental IQ or socioeducational status, knowing the behavior of more-intelligent and better-educated parents may serve to illuminate the essential elements of effective teaching guides for people concerned with "making baby brighter."

Notes

1. However, a recent study suggests that the Kaufman K-ABC preschool test fails to distinguish a majority of children who have been identified as gifted by more traditional means (Roberson, 1988). Similarly, the new version of the Stanford-Binet (the fourth edition) appears to do a considerably less adequate job of identifying gifted children than its predecessor (Kitano and DeLeon, 1988).
2. "Decrement of attention" is frequently referred to as "habituation" and is usually gauged by the rate (or amount) of reduction in looking time. Greater decrements, quicker decays, or relatively lesser amounts of cumulative looking are generally interpreted as being more efficient styles of information processing. Recovery of attention, frequently referred to as "novelty preference" or "response to novelty," is measured by the excess amount of time that infants spend looking at novel compared with familiar stimuli. The term *novelty preference* is used when novel and familiar stimuli are compared simultaneously (after a familiarization period); the term *response to novelty* is generally used when novel and familiar stimuli are shown individually and successively after familiarization and habituation.
3. Recently, relatively consistent short-term habituation behavior has been demonstrated by an experiment in which five-month-old infants' "patterns of behavior" were compared with their behavior ten days earlier on the same paradigm (Bornstein and Benasich, 1986). At the second session, two-thirds of the infants were reported as exhibiting "the same pattern," and the rest were "close to their earlier pattern." In this middle-class to upper-class population, 60 percent were "quick habituators" to "social stimuli" (rapidly and enormously decreasing their looking time when a stimulus was repeated); 15 percent looked longer at the second showing and then rapidly habituated (using different stimuli, geometrical designs, there were none of these "increase-decreasers"); and 25 percent fluctuated in their responses. The rapid habituators were more likely to be consistent than were the "fluctuators."
4. In one study (of twenty four-month-olds), these two behaviors (habituation and response to novelty) showed a moderate (+.45) correlation (Bornstein and Ruddy, 1984; also see Ruddy and Bornstein, 1982). In another study (of forty-seven babies), their correlations (after a three-

month lag) were + .42 (O'Connor, Cohen, and Parmelee, 1984). Note: The "true" associations of these behaviors are likely to be somewhat higher than those reported.

5. Correlations with parental education were + .68 at thirty-four months, + .64 at forty months, and + .44 at six years; maternal age was also highly correlated with children's IQ, particularly at six years. The average IQ of these minority-group children was substantially above the norm for their ethnic groups.

6. This involved testing visual-recognition memory for abstract patterns and for faces (in paired comparison problems). Cross-modal transfer problems showed no correlation with later IQ, and a geometrical forms task showed more-modest correlations (beginning at seven months). Most of the infants were tested twice, with a one-month interval between tests, and about a third three times; both sets of problems (patterns and faces) contributed uniquely to the IQ correspondence, as did the multisession results. Similar findings were reported for a normal-birth-weight subsample (mean Stanford-Binet IQ 87.8) and very low birth weight infants (82.1); only 3 percent of these subjects were White non-Hispanic.

7. Advanced behavior means habituating to a "configurational dimension" rather than to the specific elements of the stimulus. For a second "nonoptimal" sample (low birth weight/weight-for-date), whose IQs averaged 8.5 points lower, a correlation of + .62 between Binet scores and "percent recovery to facial expression" was found when the face shown remained constant, and a negative correlation (− .51) to "percent recovery to persons" was found when the face was changed but the facial expression was held constant.

8. Three-year Stanford-Binet scores for the "high discriminators" averaged 10 points higher (108.4 vs. 98.5); five-year Illinois Test of Psycholinguistic Abilities (ITPA) scores averaged 136.2 vs. 122.3, with the difference concentrated in subtests measuring associative-symbolic and linguistic skills. Twelve-year WISC-R scores showed very strong (Spearman Rank Order) correlations with the WISC verbal subtests and other verbal measures but not with performance IQ; however, the sample size was only fourteen.

9. Somewhat later in infancy, children go through a stage in which they become fearful and fretful when strangers look at or talk to them. Japanese mothers tend to be quite proud if their infants attain this milestone at an earlier-than-normal age, since this is thought to be a sign of high intelligence.

10. Infant memory was assessed by operant conditioning tasks requiring a response. At three months, infants learned to produce movements in an overhead crib mobile by means of a ribbon that connected the infant's foot and the mobile stand. After two training sessions, the amount of kicking that the infant did in a "nonreinforced" reexposure seven to fourteen days later, compared with the amount of kicking it did in the (final) nonreinforced segment of the second training session, represented the "retention test ratio" score. At seven months, activating a musical toy and a bank of ten lights was linked to an arm-pulling response and, at eleven months, to a bar-press response.

Contents

156

❧ 8 ❧

Important Features
of Mother/Infant Interactions

8.1 Introduction

This chapter explores possible relationships between parental interaction with infants and toddlers and their later cognitive development. It begins with an analysis of studies that have examined the differences in parents' behavior toward firstborn and laterborn children, on the basis that these differences are likely to be a significant source of the firstborn IQ advantage (see Chapter Two).

Several aspects of maternal interactive behavior are then explored, including maternal encouragement of attention to objects and events in the environment, maternal imitation of infants' vocalizations, maternal gaze behavior patterns, and the use of contingent responsivity as a teaching tool.

An evaluation of several other important interactive behaviors (such as rocking) will be provided after findings related to successful accelerational attempts have been presented (Chapter Ten). Chapter Eleven provides a detailed assessment of the needs and cognitive limitations of young infants and how both of these change in the initial months of infancy, together with specific recommendations for using this knowledge to design effective "infant lessons."

8.2 Firstborn-Laterborn Differences in the
Early Home Environment

This search for clues to which aspects of the early home environment have special importance in cognitive development begins
by focusing on environmental factors that might form the basis
of the IQ advantage of firstborn children — a good place to start,
considering that there is no evidence suggesting any hereditary
or prenatal basis for this birth-order difference. We might therefore ask, Are there any systematic differences in the way mothers
attend to their oldest child during infancy and toddlerhood,
compared with their behavior toward laterborns?

A review of the literature strongly suggests that *there are
considerable differences in the nature and quality* — but not necessarily in the overall *quantity* — of stimulation received by firstborns and laterborns during infancy and early childhood.

One such study (Jacobs and Moss, 1976) compared the behavior of mothers toward their firstborn child at three months of
age with the behavior of these *same* mothers toward their secondborn child at a similar age[1] and found several important
differences: (1) virtually no mother *spoke* to her secondborn
child as frequently as the *average* mother in this study spoke to
her firstborn child; (2) virtually no mother *imitated the vocalizations* of her secondborn child as often as she did her firstborn's;
and (3) in each of the other measures of maternal interaction
described in Table 24, at least two-thirds of the secondborn
infants received less maternal attention than did the average
firstborn. In response to the higher frequency of maternal attention, these firstborn infants smiled more often than did their
younger siblings and vocalized more frequently.

Even though these firstborn infants received a greater overall
amount of **maternally initiated** visual and auditory stimulation
than did the secondborns, the overall amount of *visual and
auditory stimulation received by these secondborn children was considerably greater*. This is apparently because mothers made far
greater use of television as a source of stimulation for secondborns (H. A. Moss, personal communication, 1987).[2]

Lewis and Kreitzberg (1979) found the following substantial

Table 24. Comparison of Maternal Behavior Toward Firstborns and
Secondborns at Three Months of Age (Bethesda Longitudinal Study).

Maternal Behavior	Firstborn Advantage in Standard Scores[a]	Standard Deviation (Secondborns)[b]
Mother talks to infant	13.2	5.8
Mother imitates infant's vocalizations	6.0	3.4
Eye-to-eye contact between mother and infant	7.6	6.2
Mother smiles at infant	8.8	7.7
Mother initiates play activities	6.8	6.7
Mother bathes, changes, and dresses infant	8.7	6.1

[a] Firstborn scores were "standardized" for each of the three observers (mean = 50; standard deviation = 10) and then corrected for differences in raw score averages between observers. A firstborn advantage of 1 standard deviation implies that roughly two-thirds of the secondborns received a lesser amount of this type of maternal attention than did the average firstborn; a difference of 2 standard deviations implies that virtually no mother provided as much attention to her secondborn as was received by the average firstborn.

[b] The relatively low standard deviations for secondborns, compared with an average of (approximately) 10 for firstborns, implies that there was considerably less variability in maternal behavior toward secondborns than toward firstborns.

Source: Jacobs and Moss, 1976.

differences in maternal behavior toward firstborns and later-borns at three months of age in a rather large study (193 families):[3]

- The mothers of firstborns *vocalized* more frequently to their infants (58 percent) than did the mothers of later-borns (with secondborns receiving slightly more frequent maternal vocalizations than did third or laterborns).
- The mothers of firstborns *looked at* their infants 42 percent more frequently ($p < .00001$) and *smiled at and laughed with* them 40 percent more often than did the mothers of laterborns.
- Although there was little difference in the proportion

> of time that the mothers of firstborns and laterborns
> spent *holding* their children, the mothers of firstborns
> spent almost twice as much time **rocking** their children.
> - These firstborns were also *played with* more frequently
>   (70 percent) than the laterborns and were given toys
>   and pacifiers nearly twice as often.

In response, these firstborns spent 24 percent more time looking at their mothers, 33 percent more time smiling at and laughing with them, and 36 percent more time playing with objects. Although infant vocalizations to the mother showed only a slight diminution when first and secondborns were compared, they showed a much more substantial (25 percent) reduction when firstborns were compared to thirdborns or fourthborns. This implies that maternal "looking and vocalizing" behavior is to a considerable extent independent of a child's vocal responses.

In toddlerhood, firstborns appear to receive a greater variety of stimulation than do laterborns, and these differences are associated with IQ performance at a later age (Gottfried and Gottfried, 1984). This study is exceptionally noteworthy because of (1) the relatively high educational levels of the parents (nearly half of the fathers and a third of the mothers were college graduates, and another third of the parents had attended but not completed college); (2) its size (it included 130 California families); and (3) depth of analysis. At fifteen months of age, scores on the cluster of variables comprising the HOME Infant Inventory's "opportunities for variety in daily stimulation" factor were found to predict almost a fourth of the total variance in IQ (at thirty-six and forty-two months) found on the General Cognitive Index of the McCarthy Scale of Children's Abilities (McCarthy, 1972). This variety factor includes such elements as (1) the frequency of reading to the child (which averaged 18.3 minutes daily to firstborns and 5.7 minutes to laterborns); (2) whether the family visited, or received visits from, relatives; and (3) whether the father played a daily role in caretaking or ate at least one meal with the child. In this study, the firstborns' IQ advantage on the McCarthy test *averaged 5 points*.[4]

In another (unfortunately smaller) study, which contrasted maternal interactions with firstborn and laterborn toddlers (White, Kaban, and Attanucci, 1979), major differences were found in response[5] to the following questions:

- What percentage of the time do mothers *respond immediately* to their children's overtures? (firstborns, 90.3 percent; laterborns, 76.7 percent).
- When responding to their toddlers' questions, what percentage of the time do mothers *provide related ideas?* (firstborns, 68.8 percent; laterborns, 31.1 percent).
- What percentage of the observation time is spent in adult-initiated mother/toddler interactions? (firstborns, 24.0 percent; laterborns, 6.6 percent).
- What is the average duration of adult-mediated interactions? (firstborns, 7.1 seconds; laterborns, 4.3 seconds).
- What degree of language complexity do mothers use in responding to their toddlers? — (1) complex sentences: firstborns, 22.2 percent; laterborns, 5.5 percent; (2) one-word answers: firstborns, 4.3 percent; laterborns, 17.5 percent; (3) phrases: firstborns, 59.1 percent; laterborns, 64.6 percent; (4) no response: firstborns, 5.6 percent; laterborns, 12.4 percent.

These researchers also evaluated the frequency with which a mother responded verbally to her child's initiatives at what they thought to be an appropriate level and concluded that firstborns received appropriate responses 83 percent of the time, compared with only 35 percent for laterborns.

Some interesting contrasts are revealed by an examination of data from the individual case records of this study. The five firstborns with the highest IQs (their Stanford-Binet scores at age three averaged 142) had "appropriateness of response" ratings averaging 90 percent; by contrast, among the five firstborns with the lowest IQs (whose scores averaged 98), the mothers of four of the toddlers had ratings of less than 50 percent. "Related ideas" were provided to this high-IQ subsample 74 percent of the time, compared with less than 40 percent of the time for four of the five lowest-IQ firstborns. The mothers of the five high-IQ firstborns responded immediately to their children's overtures more than 90 percent of the time. Although the mothers of two of the five low-IQ firstborns also obtained high immediacy-of-response ratings, two were considerably "deficient" (scoring 65 percent and 74 percent).

In a recent study that compared maternal language directed toward firstborn children at twenty-one months with that directed by these same mothers toward their secondborn children at this age (McCartney, Robeson, Jordan, and Mouradin, 1989), the mean length of maternal utterances (MLU) to firstborns was significantly greater than to secondborns ($p < .001$). This tendency was evidenced in virtually all cases, as reflected in a correlation of $+ .76$ (an impressive statistic considering that the average interval between sessions was thirty-two months).

Two recent studies by Bornstein and Tamis-LeMonda (1989) lend additional support to the proposition that maternal responsiveness has a strong influence on cognitive development. One, of fifty-two firstborn five-month-old infants, found that mothers' prompt, contingent, and appropriate responsiveness to their infants' nondistress activities bore statistically significant correlations with these infants' habituation speed and with their "novelty preference" scores, even after the effects of these mothers' noncontingent stimulation were partialled out. The other study, of twenty firstborn four-month-olds, reported a correlation of $+ .60$ between maternal responsiveness to infants' nondistressful vocalizations, facial expressions, body movements, and the like and four-year IQ scores (WPPSI) — with no abatement in the strength of this correlation found after maternal noncontingent stimulation (which was also predictive of IQ) was partialled out.

8.3 Mother/Infant Interactive Behavior and IQ Development: Overview

The preceding analysis of differences in maternal behavior toward firstborns and laterborns during infancy suggests that (1) the *total* amount of environmental stimulation seems to be of

far less importance in determining a child's cognitive development than the amount of stimulation specifically directed *toward*
the child; (2) *effective maternal gaze behavior patterns*, as evidenced
by eye contact and the pleasure derived therefrom, promote
cognitive development; and (3) *imitating an infant's vocalizations* is
of special importance in early cognitive development.

Other aspects of early parental behavior that appear to contribute to children's emerging intellectual development include
(1) encouraging the child to attend to objects and events in the
environment; (2) naming specific objects (especially the parts of
an infant's body during activities such as bathing); (3) choosing
appropriate mechanisms for attaining and maintaining a state
of "quiet alertness" in early infancy and using this state to
provide appropriate visual and auditory stimulation; and
(4) providing opportunities for so-called contingent responsivity—by creating situations that enable infants to learn that,
through their actions, they can affect their surroundings in
particular ways.

8.4 Encouragement of Attention

Several studies indicate that the extent to which mothers encourage their infants and toddlers to attend to objects and events in
the environment has a strong relationship with subsequent IQ
performance, particularly in verbal areas.

In one of these studies, where the level of parental education
averaged a college degree (Ruddy and Bornstein, 1982; Bornstein, 1985), a strong association was found between (1) maternal encouragement assessed at four months and thirteen
months of age and (2) later intellectual performance. The correlation between "encouragement of attention" assessed at four
months and Wechsler IQ scores at four years was quite strong:
+.51. At this early age, the encouragement-assessment factor
included handing the baby a toy, pointing to a picture, or naming an object. At thirteen months of age, bringing a *new* prop-
erty, object, or event in the environment to a toddler's attention
(as opposed to elaborating on something that was already under
the child's purview) was highly correlated with an early develop-

ment of verbal *comprehension* (+ .67, as measured by the Reynell Developmental Language Scales at two years of age); a somewhat lower, but still substantial, relationship persisted with four-year Wechsler IQ scores (+ .36).

This study also found that (1) the extent to which an infant vocalized at four months was not at all predictive of the amount of maternal encouragement that he or she would receive at thirteen months. In addition, a high correlation was seen between such encouragement at four months and the speed at which these infants habituated to test stimuli at this age (+ .55). Nevertheless, in a follow-up study, it was determined that assessments of maternal encouragement at five and thirteen months and scores on infant habituation behavior measures—when evaluated independently—each bore statistically significant correlations with linguistic and representational competence in toddlerhood. The authors conclude that "maternal stimulation of young infants influences the development of children's representational competence over and above infants' own informational-processing abilities" (Tamis-LeMonda and Bornstein, 1989, p. 738).

In a study of 168 essentially middle-class families, Olson, Bates, and Bayles (1984) again found "encouragement of attention" at six and thirteen months to be predictive of cognitive competence. Two of these researchers' six-month variables, "verbal stimulation" and "mother object stimulation" ("offer toy to infant, offer and demonstrate toy, and return object to infant"), were modestly but persuasively predictive of "academic competence" at age six (Olson, Bayles, and Bates, 1986).[6] At thirteen months, the researchers' "maternal teaching" measure (which included drawing a toddler's attention to an object, offering the object, offering and demonstrating an object, questioning, naming, and accepting the toddler's actions) was strongly correlated (+ .49) with these authors' measures of cognitive competence[7] at twenty-four months.

A study that contrasted the behavior of high-IQ and low-IQ mothers in a play situation with their six-month-old infants is quite revealing (Ramey, Farran, and Campbell, 1979). When told that the researchers were interested in observing their children's play with toys and with them, the mothers from the upper-middle-class sample (in a semirural university-town atmosphere)—whose IQs averaged 117—spent 45 percent of the observation period demonstrating toys and 25 percent speaking to their infants. By contrast, mothers in the lower-class sample—whose IQs averaged 82—spent only a third of the observation period demonstrating toys and only 12 percent speaking to their infants.[8]

An understanding of the processes governing the ability of infants to attend to objects and events in their environments can enhance a mother's ability to isolate and highlight a wide range of environmental features. It appears that these efforts must either begin with an object on which an infant is already fixating, or else the object and the infant must be brought into proximity. To illustrate, in a series of well-conceived experiments, Butterworth and Cochran (1980) demonstrated that six-month-old infants will correctly focus their gaze in the direction in which their mother silently turns her head, provided that, first of all, the target is within the baby's "visual field." These infants would turn their heads approximately forty degrees and, if they could see the target within their peripheral vision at that point, they would continue to turn until they were looking at the target. Second, other physical aspects of the environment must be appropriate. For example, in one experiment, virtually all leftward turns were imitated correctly but only half of the rightward turns; it was then discovered (by transposing the positions of the mothers and their infants) that the presence of a room partition (at seventy degrees) caused the babies to focus on it rather than on the target.

Butterworth and Cochran concluded that the infants turned not because the adults' actions were interpreted as "referential" but because the infant learns that his or her own response leads to an interesting visual consequence. This is implied in the fact that infants do not merely turn in the *general* direction in which their mother is looking, since presenting an intermediate target in that line of vision (up to forty degrees) will not cause them to stop turning to focus on it. If, however, after they turn forty degrees, the target of their mother's focus is not in their field of vision, they will stop turning and will focus on the intermediate target.

At both five and a half and eleven months of age, when a mother observes that her baby is looking at a toy, she is likely to point to the toy and verbally label it or further comment on it (Sullivan and Horowitz, 1983b). Similarly, mothers of nine-month-old babies will often quickly adjust their line of vision to coincide with an object on which their infant is fixating and, when they do so, will almost always verbalize about the object, and name it about half the time (Murphy and Messer, 1977). These authors conclude that mothers also use pointing at the object as a means for stressing the event and, thereby, strengthening the impact of this opportunity to verbalize about objects of their joint attention focus.[9]

A word of advice to the parents of infants approaching their first birthday seems in order. Even though your baby may clearly understand the meaning of a word, it may still be unable to translate this knowledge into a simple action, such as turning its head to look at an object when it is verbally referenced. This became quite evident when the referential abilities of eleven- and thirteen-month-old children were contrasted (Thomas and others, 1981). At eleven months, when mothers made reference to familiar objects (using names that they were sure were well understood), half of the infants did not look at the referenced object any longer than they looked at three simultaneously shown toys. At thirteen months, however, these toddlers spent an average of twice as much time looking at a verbally referenced toy as they did the other toys.[10] These findings suggest that referential abilities are dependent on the maturation of a neurobiological pathway linking the sight of the object with its referent, and they suggest further that, until an infant evidences these abilities, its mother should either turn her head to look at, or should point to, objects on which she wishes her child to focus. Thus, mothers who are cognizant of the developmental limitations of their infants' gaze behavior and referential abilities and who pay due attention to environmental conditions are better able to elicit a joint attention toward objects.

8.5 Gaze Behavior and Vocal Imitation

It seems to be part of instinctive behavior for mothers to imitate their infants' facial expressions and vocalizations. At the same time, newborn infants themselves have a clearly demonstrated capacity to imitate facial expressions (Meltzoff and Moore, 1983) and also appear to possess an indigenous readiness to match vocal imitations (Papousek, Papousek, and Bornstein, 1985).

The extraordinary importance of imitating an infant's vocalizations to *normal* cognitive development has been aptly demonstrated. Further, several studies suggest that there are longitudinal linkages between effective gaze behavior in infancy and childhood IQ. Let us then turn at once to a discussion of these behaviors.

The Tehran Study (Hunt, Mohandessi, Ghodssi, and Akiyama, 1976)

In an orphanage in Tehran, where only routine custodial care was provided, virtually all the children reared there from infancy suffered a progressive decline in IQ until it tended to stabilize (most frequently at slightly above 60 points). When a regimen designed to foster imitative skills was introduced (Hunt, 1981), however, the effects were quite dramatic. Where previously the infants would have had little or no expressive speech at three years of age, *all the children* receiving this regimen had acquired vocabularies of fifty words or more by seventeen to twenty-two months of age.[11] The strategy employed was as follows:

Caretakers were instructed to initiate vocal games with their charges, either by imitating the spontaneous vocalizations of the infants in their care or by vocalizing sounds that they had heard an infant make repeatedly. The program began once an infant had been heard to repeatedly vocalize several different sounds. The caretaker began by uttering one of the sounds in the infant's repertoire and, when the infant repeated it, uttered it again. After several repetitions, the caretaker shifted to another of the sounds from the infant's repertoire to get a new vocal interchange going. After three different sounds were routinely repeated, the caretaker gradually reduced the number of times that each sound was repeated before shifting sounds, with the aim of getting the infant to immediately follow from one pattern to another, in effect playing a game of "follow the leader."

This vocal game was part of the caretaker-infant interaction during each stint of bathing, dressing, feeding, toileting, and so on. After the infant had acquired facility in this game, the caretaker introduced new vocal patterns from the native (Persian) language: new in the sense that the caretaker had never heard the infant make them. The caretaker uttered these unfamiliar sounds repeatedly as the infant, through successive approximations, came closer to repeating the sounds modeled for him.

Once the infant acquired the ability to copy novel sounds, the caretaker fostered the beginning of naming (or semantic mastery) by mentioning the names of the parts of the infant's body as they were touched by the washcloth during bathing (beginning with those body parts visible to the infant).[12]

In summary, caretakers (1) imitated the cooings and babblings of infants in their charge to get vocal games going; (2) expanded this game into a vocal "follow the leader" by using familiar vocal patterns; (3) modeled unfamiliar vocal patterns; and (4) sharpened the "game" conditions by teaching the infants to associate parts of their bodies with the sounds of the names of these parts as a means of teaching that sounds have meaning.

Smiling, Cooing, and Imitation: Timetables and Potential Importance

Several studies suggest that *the best way to sustain communication with an infant is to closely attend to and imitate the infant's behavior.* Maternal overactivity born of attempts to gain attention, however, appears to be adversive and causes the infant to gaze away. For example, in one study (Field, 1977) an inverse relationship between maternal activity and infant gaze was found in each of three interactive situations: "attention-getting," "spontaneous," and "imitative" situations. (The implication that, beyond a given level, additional [verbal and other] maternal activity can be deleterious is pursued in section 8.6 and Chapter Eleven.) Thus, infant gaze can be thought of as a signal indicating the readiness of the infant to engage in interaction, while gaze aversion appears to indicate a wish to terminate or temporarily suspend an interaction.

A mother's imitation of her infant's expressions and vocalizations appears to occur quite naturally, as evidenced by studies of mother-infant interactions when hospitals allow mothers to spend most of their time with their newborns (Hunt, Mohandessi, Ghodssi, and Akiyama, 1976).

Mothers and infants also enjoy cooing at each other. A pattern of alternate cooing and waiting has been observed in infant-mother interactions both at four and at eight weeks of age. *Infants appear to seek opportunities for such vocal dialogues and take great pleasure in these interactions.*

Vigorous smiling and cooing in response to the human face can be readily elicited in young infants. Increasing rapidly during the second and third months of life, these responses reach a peak at approximately fourteen weeks[13] and appear to be dependent on a proper alignment of the mother's face to the face of the infant (Watson, 1972). During the third and fourth months of life, "a face stimulus" can elicit *vigorous* smiling but only if it is aligned with the infant's face in a zero-degree orientation. Only half as much smiling will be elicited in response to either a 90-degree or a 180-degree facial orientation.

A series of experiments has demonstrated that this phenomenon of vigorous smiling and cooing also occurs in response to an inanimate object (for instance, a mobile) if the infant has learned that the object will behave in a manner *contingent* upon its behavior (Badger, 1977). For example, after three to five days of ten-minute-a-day exposure to a *contingently responsive* mobile, almost all infants are reported to respond with vigorous smiling and cooing, as follows:

- If the mobile's performance is clearly contingent on the infant's doing something (such as touching its head to a pillow or moving its leg), the infant will do considerably more of that activity.
- If the mobile moves, but its movement is not contingent on the infant's activity, the infant will alter its activity level back to baseline after several attempts to get the mobile to move.
- If, however, an ambiguous response occurs (the mobile sometimes moves contingently and sometimes doesn't) the infant's movements will fall well below baseline, as it tries to avoid the situation.

Badger suggests that these findings may explain an infant's vigorous response to the zero-degree facial orientation. Because most caretaking activities (such as feeding and diaper changing) are more commonly associated with a ninety-degree facial alignment, this response is clearly not related to primary rewards. Indeed, it is usually only when a mother begins *playing* with her baby that she aligns herself at zero degrees and that her facial and verbal behavior begins to respond to its actions and reactions. Therefore, one might conclude that infants greatly enjoy the process of assimilating response-contingent stimulation and are vigorously expressive of their pleasure in achieving control of their environment.

Thus, effective interactive behavior between mothers and infants apparently requires making use of opportunities for *contingent responsivity*. This can be done by designing interactive paradigms in which the responses of the mother and/or an inanimate object are made contingent upon the infant's actions. As shown in conditioning experiments (Rheingold, Gewirtz, and Ross, 1959), infants will vocalize more if maternal stimulation is contingent upon the infant's vocalizations. (The relationship between contingent responsivity and IQ is pursued in section 8.7).

Mothers who are initially frustrated by the early unresponsiveness of their infants and are then shown how to engage them in vocal games (which are begun by repeating their infants' spontaneous vocalizations) have generally been able to elicit smiles, laughter, and joy as a result of these efforts (Uzgiris, 1972).

In middle-class and upper-middle-class homes, so-called pseudoimitation (an infant's responding in kind to familiar vocalizations modeled by another person) is achieved at about eight weeks of age (Hunt, 1981; Uzgiris, 1972). "True" imitation (that is, imitation of vocal sounds generally unfamiliar to an infant) appears to occur at about eight to ten months of age. Once this latter capacity emerges, it seems to provide a basis for the acquisition of the names of objects.

Reciprocal vocal imitation provides the earliest opportunity for infants to compare both imitative and imitating products and discover similarities between them. Several prominent re-searchers (for example, Papousek, Papousek, and Bornstein, 1985) suggest that it might be highly productive for adults to imitate infants' first quiet vocalizations and to elaborate on them by repeating them several times and then varying the vocalization (such as the pitch) in some small measure. Mothers quite naturally use pitch contour to obtain and sustain their babies' attention and to encourage eye contact and smiling, and they also use exaggerated intonational contouring of utterances in face-to-face play (Stern, Spieker, and MacKain, 1982). Three-to six-month-old infants seem to very much enjoy opportunities to imitate pitch (tones) and, with sufficient practice, become reasonably good at it (Kessen, Levine, and Wendrich, 1979). Each of these topics is discussed further in Chapter Eleven.

8.6 Verbal Stimulation, "Informative Talk," and Affective Tone

The evidence that certain kinds of vocal stimulation (for in-stance, encouraging attention, providing related ideas [after saying "ball," adding "big ball"], and using vocal imitation) are beneficial to cognitive development would seem to imply that the greater the overall amount of child-directed vocal stimula-tion, the greater the likelihood of IQ enhancement.

Such a conclusion, however, is not necessarily warranted. Rather, there is evidence that—beyond a given amount of verbal stimulation—it is the *quality* of the verbally interactive rela-tionship between child and caretaker and not the *quantity of verbal stimulation* that matters. For example, in a study of long-term residential nurseries in London (Tizard, Cooperman, Joseph, and Tizard, 1972), a strong correlation was found (+ .51; $p < .001$) between language-comprehension scores on the Re-ynell Developmental Language Scales and the frequency with which **"informative talk"**[14] was directed toward these two- to five-year-old children. Nevertheless, only a modest correlation (+ .19) was found between these test scores and the overall fre-quency with which speech was directed toward the child. In fact, speech directed toward the child—other than "informative talk"—showed negative correlations with test performance. It is equally clear that when verbal stimulation is insensitive to the needs of the child, it can have adverse effects on cognitive development (Clarke-Stewart, 1973).

Support for the proposition that adjusting infant-directed parental speech to an infant's developmental level will foster its verbal comprehension comes from a recent study that compared developmental changes in mothers' speech behavior at three, six, and nine months with HOME Infant Inventory scores and with receptive and expressive language at eighteen months (Murray, Johnson, and Peters, 1989). In homes with relatively high HOME scores, the mothers reduced the average length of their child-directed utterances (MLU) from 3.8 words at three months, to 3.3 words at six months, to 2.8 words at nine months. By contrast, in homes receiving relatively low HOME scores, the mothers' MLU remained stable across these three periods (at 3.5 words). Further, the extent of a mother's MLU reduction between three and nine months—in combination with a relatively high frequency of maternal utterances at nine months—was much more predictive of a child's receptive (but not expressive) language development at eighteen months than was the overall HOME score.

If we are willing to accept the scores on the early infant IQ predictors discussed in section 7.4 as mechanisms for detecting and exploring potential causal links between maternal interactive behavior and later cognitive development, several conclusions might be drawn. One, discussed in section 8.4, is the high correspondence found between maternal encouragement of attention and scores on *habituation* paradigms. Another, if we accept the premise that a three-month-old's "mother-stranger vocal-discrimination" behavior is often a precursor of verbal IQ during childhood, is that we can use these three-month Differential Vocal Response (DVR) scores as a surrogate for childhood IQ[15] by comparing the behavior patterns of mothers whose children have relatively high and relatively low DVR scores. This type of analysis yields two important conclusions: First, a *moderate* amount of maternal vocalization to a three-month-old is associated with higher DVR scores than either a high or low amount, and, second, the degree to which a child is valued and desired by its caretakers seems to have an appreciable effect on DVR scores at this age.

This first conclusion has been replicated in a number of diverse populations by Roe and her colleagues. In one of these studies— of firstborn American children, subdivided into low-maternal-education and high-maternal-education subsamples (Roe and Bronstein, forthcoming)— infants in the "high-ed" group vocalized *twice as much* to their mothers as they did to the strangers, but the "low-ed" group responded equally to the mothers' and strangers' overtures. Nevertheless, over the course of the two observation periods, the total amount of infant vocal response was equal between the two groups. The primary difference was that *the "high-ed" group responded more to their mothers and less to the strangers,* but the infants from "low-ed" families responded equally to both. Within each of these educational strata, however, the highest DVR scores were associated with a *mid-level* amount of maternal vocal stimulation (recorded in a naturalistic setting), and the lowest scores were associated with high and low levels of such stimulation.[16]

The mother's affective tone also appears to have a substantial impact on DVR scores, as suggested by the following findings:

- In Greece, where (1) male children tend to be "more valued and desired by parents than female children" and (2) where males, both as children and adults, score "significantly higher than females on most cognitive tests, including verbal cognitive tests" (Roe, 1987, p. 2), the vocal response rates of the males to their mothers were two and a half times higher than to strangers. Among the females, however, the rates were nearly equal (Roe and others, 1985). In an additional study of twenty-five institutionally reared Greek children (Roe, 1987), DVR scores were negative for the males (they vocalized more to strangers than to caretakers) and neutral for the females. By contrast, in the American populations studied, no sex difference was observed.
- Whether or not a baby was "planned" has been shown to be related to DVR scores (Roe and Bronstein, forthcoming); even though this relationship is compounded by its interaction with educational level, it may in fact signify an important cause of SES differences.[17]

8.7 Contingent Responsivity

The term *contingent responsivity* refers to creating or using opportunities for the environment to respond quickly and predictably to an infant's actions (his or her movements or vocalizations). Teaching an infant that he or she can exercise control over the environment and exposure to early contingent action-outcome pairings lay the groundwork for subsequent learning and promote feelings of competence and a greater readiness to explore and master the environment (Brinker and Lewis, 1982).

Several studies suggest that providing infants with opportunities to control their environment can have a substantial impact on their intellectual development. For example, in a longitudinal study in which IQ scores at five years of age were compared with interactions between mothers and children during home visits at eight, twenty-one, and twenty-four months (Beckwith and Cohen, 1984), those toddlers who were evaluated as receiving *consistently responsive* care from their mothers *during each of the three home visits* had markedly higher Stanford-Binet IQ scores at age five, as follows:

- In the higher SES subsample, the scores of the children who received "consistently responsive" behavior averaged 114.5, compared with 104.0 for those where maternal behavior was not consistently responsive.
- In the lower SES subsample, the scores of the children who received "consistently responsive" behavior averaged 117.7, compared with 96.6 for those where maternal behavior was not consistently responsive.

This study also found that, after factoring out SES,[18] there were still significant relationships between IQ and (1) contingent maternal vocalization at one month of age and (2) maternal responsivity to distress at eight months of age.

In a follow-up evaluation at age twelve (Beckwith and Cohen, 1989), the offspring of those mothers who were adjudged at eight and twenty-four months to be more "verbally responsive" to the vocalizations of their children than the median scored 14 points higher (on the WISC-R) than did the children who "had been treated unresponsively" at both of these ages.[19]

A study of fifty infants adopted into well-educated families (Hardy-Brown, Plomin, and DeFries, 1981) showed highly significant correlations between a measure of infant communicative competency at one year of age and three variables — *the degree to which the adoptive mother imitated her infant's vocalizations* (+ .39), *the contingent vocal responsivity of the adoptive mother* (+ .30), and the natural mother's cognitive ability (+ .28).[20] Nevertheless, *the total amount of vocalization* to the infant by the adoptive mother bore little relationship to "communicative competence."

Another study, which sought to discern links between children's IQ scores at six years of age and maternal interactive behavior at three months of age (Coates and Lewis, 1984),[21] found strong associations between (1) Wechsler vocabulary subtest scores and the combination of the mother's vocal responsivity and her response to her infant's distress by holding, touching, and other "proximal" behavior (these two factors explained a fourth of the verbal IQ variance); and (2) Wechsler block-design subtest scores and vocal responsivity (this also explained a fourth of the variance).

8.8 Conclusions

The studies presented in this chapter strongly suggest that specific interactive behaviors between mothers and infants can have a considerable and seemingly lasting influence on childhood IQ scores. Behaviors of particular importance appear to include ample rocking, imitating infants' vocalizations, using gaze behavior effectively, encouraging attention to objects and events in the environment, seeking opportunities to use contingent responsivity as a teaching tool, responding immediately to an infant's or toddler's overtures and providing related ideas as part of verbal responses, and using an appropriate level of sentence complexity.

Specific recommendations for enhancing infants' cognitive awareness in the initial postnatal months are presented in Chapter Eleven, and recommendations for developing language skills in later infancy and toddlerhood are detailed in Chapter Twelve.

Notes

1. All the 32 (Caucasian) mothers had at least a high school education (median = 14.1 years of schooling); the range of the spacing between

siblings was restricted (from seventeen to thirty-five months). The 32 mothers, who lived in the Washington, D.C., area, were part of a 121-mother firstborn study, the Bethesda Longitudinal Study.

2.   The firstborns responded with 9.0 "standard points" more smiling and 7.3 points more vocalization; the secondborns received 9.8 "standard points" more overall visual stimulation and 8.5 points more overall auditory stimulation.

3.   The sample was comprised of 92 "high-status" SES families (Hollingshead occupational scales) and 101 "low-status" families.

4.   All of the families in this sample were Caucasian; two-thirds of the non-firstborn children were secondborns. At thirty-nine months, the Toys and Games cluster on the HOME Preschool Inventory was also highly correlated with IQ scores, but "ceiling" effects in this well-educated population (the average score being 8.8 out of a possible 10) muted differences between firstborns and laterborns.

5.   Median values were used throughout to reduce the effects of extremes.

6.   The sample was stratified to specifically include children whose temperaments were considered easy, average, and difficult. Half the sample were firstborns, and 71 percent were middle class. The sample size at the six-year follow-up was eighty. Academic Competence ratings were evaluated using the Achenbach assessment instrument (Achenbach, 1978).

7.   The cognitive assessment at age two was based on the Peabody Picture Vocabulary Test and the "mental index" portion of the Bayley Scales. At twenty-four months, even after "infant temperament" and infant cognitive competence at six months were controlled for, "mother object stimulation" still showed a correlation of +.31 ($p = .001$) with cognitive competence. Scores on a teacher-based Academic Competence assessment questionnaire scale administered at age six also correlated +.31 with "encouragement."

8.   The upper-middle-class mothers averaged twenty-eight years of age, compared with twenty for the at-risk group. Fifty-seven percent of the children in each group were firstborns, and many of the parents in this high-IQ sample were affiliated with the university.

9.   In a controlled setting with several toys, 86 percent of the observed maternal utterances to eleven-month-olds were references to the toys, and of these, nearly 90 percent occurred when the toys were being manipulated by the mother or the infant (Messer, 1978). The highest associations were found when a mother brought a toy near her baby and held it there (often to gain its attention), or when the infant picked up a toy. The use of pointing during the shared activity of looking at a picture book was also examined in nine-month-olds (Murphy, 1978); the development of social referencing is also discussed in Walden and Ogan (1988).

10.   The mothers (who were out of sight) repeated designated phrases to encourage their babies to attend to the toy. The experimental design also called for the mothers to sometimes use nonsense words to refer to objects and to refer to others using words they were convinced their baby did not know, thereby permitting comparisons with known and

unknown referents. At eleven months, only a fourth of the infants looked at the referenced toy twice as long as they did when a nonsense word was spoken; at thirteen months, all eight males and five of the eight females evidenced this referential capacity. The children were generally offspring of well-educated parents.

11.   These researchers also reported exceptionally high levels of "initiative" and "trust" in these children. In an earlier experimental "wave," reducing the infant-caretaker ratio from 10:1 to 10:3 did not produce an appreciable impact on expressive speech; this 10:3 ratio, in combination with the imitative regimen, resulted in the effects described.

12.   Hunt now recommends that caretakers also question infants. For example, they can ask, (1) "What is this?" as parts of the infant's body are touched; (2) which of two or three games the infant might want to play; or (3) which food he or she might want to eat first.

13.   Babbling develops at about eight weeks of age; it is not as dependent on "dialogue" as is cooing, and it often occurs even when the baby is alone. Babbling is apparently programmed in such a way that imitation of a model is not necessary. At about eight or nine months of age, babbling decreases or even stops completely for a time. Some researchers suggest that vocalization "reorganizes" itself at this point and begins again with what appear to be simple sounds.

14.   "Informative talk" included telling or asking a child something about present, past, or future activities, reading to a child, naming objects, or asking for or giving an opinion, an explanation, or a piece of information. Other categories included positive (or negative) control, expressions of pleasure and affection (or displeasure and anger), and "supervisory talk" (including repeating, confirming, or disconfirming what a child had said or making ritualistic remarks to accompany actions).

15.   Differential vocal response, or how much an infant is willing to vocalize in response to the urgings of his or her mother, minus the amount of vocalization in response to similar urgings by a stranger.

16.   Based on a thirty-minute observation period, during which the mothers were asked to "carry on routine activities." The mean maternal vocalization (as a percentage of the observation period) averaging four studies ($n = 135$) was (1) 14 percent for the low-level group (the lowest third), (2) 28 percent for the mid-level group, and (3) 48 percent for the high-level group. The mean educational level of the "low-ed" subsample was high school graduate (with a 0.8 year standard deviation); the "high-ed" mean was college graduate.

17.   This finding results from combining three of Roe's "samples" (including the "high-ed" and "low-ed" subsamples). Watching television was also negatively related to DVR, but whether this factor was a reflection of SES differences and planned-unplanned status, or an independent contributing agent, is not known.

18.   Of the fifty-three (English-speaking) mother-toddler dyads, fifteen of the twenty-nine mothers in the higher SES families were consistently responsive, compared with only three of the twenty-four in lower SES families.

19.   114.6 vs. 100.6; each of these "responsively stable" groups constituted 35 percent of the sample. The intellectual competence of these children at age twelve was unrelated to maternal responsiveness at one month, which parallels a recent finding (Bornstein and Tamis-LeMonda, 1989) that, even though maternal responsiveness at five months bore a strong relationship with the language and pretense-play competencies of toddlers, responsiveness assessed at two months did not.

20.   Gauged by such factors as "imitates words," "says two words," "uses gestures to make wants known," and the size of the infants' "productive vocabulary." The mean adoptive father's education was college graduation, while the mean adoptive mother's education was three years of college. The adopted children's *biological* grandparents were from relatively high occupational classes.

21.   Almost all (95 percent) the forty children were from middle-class and upper-middle-class families; one-third were Black. Most were second or thirdborns (the average order of birth was three), and 87 percent were from two-parent families.

Contents

ᴈ 9 ᴂ

Effective Behavioral Control and Educational Practices in Toddlerhood

9.1 Introduction

This chapter presents two sets of findings. First, certain approaches to behavioral control during toddlerhood are apt to have detrimental long-term effects on cognitive development. Second, at or about age two, toddlers undergo an important transition. Before this age, the frequency of *caretaker-initiated linguistic teaching experiences* is a strong predictor of preschool IQ scores. By age two and a half, however, the principal forerunners of cognitive and language development become (1) spatially or multisensory oriented experiences related to child-in-play situations and (2) *interactive language-mastery experiences*.

An examination of the familial backgrounds of intellectually gifted and/or eminent people reveals a very high frequency of extraordinarily enriched early home environments, including exceptionally favorable caretaker ratios during infancy and toddlerhood and a special involvement of one or more family members in the gifted child's development.

9.2 Behavior Control During Toddlerhood

Much has been written about the negative effects of an overly restrictive, overly punitive early upbringing on cognitive devel-

opment. Disciplinary methods that are thought to stifle intellectual development include enforcing rules in an inconsistent
way, exercising an immoderate degree of control, using negative
control techniques (criticism) rather than positive control techniques, and using judgmental (personalized) forms of criticism
(and praise) rather than non-ego-threatening forms. But studies
also indicate that only some of these caretaker behaviors are
likely to have significant adverse effects on IQ. Others seem to be
important only during specific stages of development, while
still others have effects that vary in relation to their child's
intelligence.

Parents usually make considerable changes in their control
strategies as their children approach and go through the "terrible twos" and "troublesome threes." Setting limits on the behavior of a two-year-old is often a taxing experience, as the child's
developing sense of autonomy and increasing resistance to
parental control can give rise to many exasperating confronta-
tions. Longitudinal studies examining this subject strongly suggest that how effectively parents and other caretakers handle the
task of exercising discipline and control at this critical age will
often have a considerable influence on IQ scores—as well as on
academic performance in adolescence.

Restrictiveness, Punitiveness, and Negative Control at Twenty-Four Months

The two-year-old child is an untamed explorer whose two
brain hemispheres are just beginning the process of working
together. By the age of three, children have attained somewhat
better control over their impulses and are better able to tell
themselves what (or what not) to do, although sometimes even
three-year-olds refuse to listen to their own (left hemisphere's)
verbal admonitions and perform a forbidden act anyway.

The extraordinary strength of the association between the
degree of restrictiveness and punishment found in the home at
twenty-four months and subsequent IQ performance was revealed by a study of 161 firstborn Seattle children and their
families (Barnard, Bee, and Hammond, 1984). When four-year

(Stanford-Binet) IQ scores were compared with the "restrictiveness and punishment" factor on the HOME Infant Inventory Scales (Caldwell and Bradley, 1984)[1] the results were as follows:

- For the ninety-nine children whose mothers had more than a high school education (averaging college graduate), the correlation between this factor and these children's IQs (which averaged 118.3) was +.60.
- For the sixty-six offspring of less well-educated mothers (whose IQs averaged 107.6), the correlation was lower (+.39) but still highly significant ($p < .01$).

In the Little Rock Longitudinal Study (Bradley and Caldwell, 1984), the correlation between the twenty-four-month HOME "restrictiveness" factor and three-year Stanford-Binet scores for the Caucasian children in this sample (whose IQs averaged 114.3) was +.44.[2]

A longitudinal study of predominantly middle-class families (Olson, Bates, and Bayles, 1984; Olson, Bayles, and Bates, 1986) found that the correlation between ratings of Academic Competence (Achenbach, 1978) at six years of age and the use of positive control techniques at twenty-four months was rather strong (+.46). By contrast, the use of negative control techniques at twenty-four months was negatively correlated with six-year Academic Competence ratings (−.35) and with earlier "receptive vocabulary" scores (−.31) on the Peabody Picture Vocabulary Test (PPVT).

A study that examined differences related to socioeconomic class in the control strategies used by parents at six different ages between eighteen months and four years (Kuczynski and Kochanska, 1987) found that (1) as SES declines, direct commands and physical enforcement are used more frequently ($p < .05$); and (2) as SES increases, so does the use of indirect commands ($p < .001$), explanations ($p < .01$), distractions ($p < .01$), and physical signaling from a distance ($p < .05$).

As the number of children in a family increases, discipline becomes more restrictive and punitive, rules become more authoritarian, and the incidence of corporal punishment in-creases (Nye, Carlson, and Garrett, 1970).

Further, Gottfried and Gottfried (1986), after averaging to-gether the results of five studies, concluded that the degree of restriction imposed prior to fifteen months of age showed little correlation with preschool IQ scores.

Mothers of firstborn children are also likely to be more consis-tent over time in the degree to which they apply restriction and punishment than are mothers of laterborns. In the study of firstborn middle-class Seattle children, the cross-time consis-tency of scores on this factor was among the highest for any of the HOME subscales, with similar results found in the "high-ed" and "low-ed" subsamples (Mitchell and Gray, 1981). Conversely, in the Little Rock study (Bradley and Caldwell, 1984), the cross-time correlation for the Caucasian families between twelve and twenty-four months was only + .30, which was far lower than that reported for any of the other five HOME clusters.

Findings from the Fels Study

In the Fels Longitudinal Study, of the many assessment factors in the early home environment examined, the one that bore the greatest relationship to subsequent IQ development was "clarity of the policy of regulation and consistency in its enforcement" (McCall, Appelbaum, and Hogarty, 1973, p. 52). In this evalua-tion, high ratings were given if the requirements were clearly formulated and consistently executed (so that children would know what was expected of them and what would happen if they failed to conform to the requirements), with low ratings as-signed to policies that were vague or fluctuating.

These researchers (McCall, Appelbaum, and Hogarty, 1973) grouped the eighty children from the Fels study who were tested at at least fourteen of seventeen data points into five separate computer-generated "clusters" based on their IQ trends during childhood. The mean IQ of these children was 119, or 15 points above their parents' (Otis) IQ average. Table 25 compares these children's IQs (at age fourteen to seventeen) with their scores on

Table 25. Comparison of Parental and Child IQ Scores with
"Clarity of Rules" in Early Childhood (Fels Longitudinal Study).

Cluster Designation(s)	Number of Children	Children's IQs	Parents' IQs	"Clarity" Scores
4 and 5	11	134	115	71.6
1	34	120	101	66.8
2 and 3	19	112	100	59.0

Source: Adapted from McCall, Appelbaum, and Hogarty, 1973.

this childhood clarity-of-rules factor and also with the IQ averages of their parents.

These five groups also differed greatly in the extent to which their parents strove to increase their rate of development. High ratings on a Parental Accelerational Attempts (PAA) scale were assigned "if the parents deliberately trained the child in various mental and motor skills that were not yet essential, whereas low ratings were given if the child was left to 'grow naturally' or was shielded from acceleration influences" (p. 52). In clusters two and three, PAA scores averaged 49, compared with an average of 57 for cluster one, 64 for cluster five, and 72 for cluster four. Interestingly, the children in cluster three, who were subjected to the greatest restrictiveness and severity of punishment and received (by far) the greatest amount of negative criticism, had IQ scores that averaged nearly 20 points higher than those of their parents.[3] By contrast, the children in cluster two, whose low "clarity-of-rules" and "accelerational-attempts" scores were coupled with little "restrictiveness" and an exceedingly mild "severity of punishment for rule breaking" (along with a high degree of "affection" and "babying") performed worse at ages sixteen to seventeen than they did in middle childhood (108 versus 120). *Moreover, this was the only group whose IQ scores in adolescence were below those of their parents.*

A review of the HOME Inventory (Stevens and Bakeman, 1985) found that parental responses to one of the questions comprising the "restrictiveness and punishment" factor, namely, whether the child had been spanked or slapped during the past week, bore little relationship to scores on the other parental behaviors comprising this factor. This suggests that *using physical means to discipline a two-year-old child is unlikely to have significant adverse effects on its cognitive development.*

Independence, Control, Cohesiveness, Expressiveness, and Later IQ

Among upper-middle-class adolescents, "independence" is often found to have strong positive correlations with IQ and academic performance. For example, in the Berkeley Growth Study, where the children's IQs averaged 120 over several testing points between ages six and fifteen (Bayley and Schaefer, 1964), the correlation between IQ and an evaluation of "independence" in adolescence was **+.66** for boys and **+.38** for girls.

Even though fraternal-identical twin comparative studies suggest that "independence" is in part under biological control, in most children it is also strongly influenced by the mechanisms used to effectuate "control" during their formative years. A home-assessment instrument called the Family Environment Scale (Moos and Moos, 1981) enables researchers to assess the relationship between IQ and a cluster of emotional and/or value-laden aspects of the early home environment, including independence and control. When this instrument was used, a moderately strong negative correlation was found between control and independence among participants in a large study of the environments of adoptive homes in Colorado in the early 1980s (Plomin and DeFries, 1985).[4] The authors' analysis of intercorrelations among these Family Environmental Scale variables has led them to conclude that the exercise of a high degree of control over children takes one of two forms:

- When a high degree of control is combined with cohesion, expressiveness, and/or a strong moral-religious emphasis, it interrelates positively with independence and does not adversely affect the "intellectual-cultural" atmosphere of the home.
- Nevertheless (and possibly more frequently), when a

high degree of control is accompanied by familial conflict and a low degree of expressiveness, it tends to
correlate with independence in a strongly negative
way; and, as a result, later IQ performance is likely to
suffer.

Confirmation for this type of dichotomy comes from two
recent studies. The first (Gottfried and Gottfried, 1986) found
that at age three, the FES clusters parental "cohesion" and "expressiveness" were each more important determinants of current IQ (among the offspring of generally well-educated California parents) than was the extent of parental "control" applied or
of parental "conflict" — each of which bore only a modest negative correlation with test performance.[5] The other study (Lin
and Fu, 1989), which compared the child-rearing practices of
middle-class Taiwanese families with those of immigrant Chinese American parents and non-Asian American families,
found that — contrary to common perceptions — six-year-old Taiwanese children (and, to a somewhat lesser extent, Chinese
American children) were accorded a significantly greater degree
of "encouragement of independence" by each of their parents
than were the non-Asian children.[6] This was true even though
both the Taiwanese and immigrant Chinese parents tended to
have higher ratings on "parental control" and "emphasis on
academic achievement" than did their American counterparts.
In addition, there were relatively strong positive correlations
between the "achievement" and "encouragement of independence" clusters (especially among the children's fathers), which
has led the authors to speculate that, although the Chinese value
family interdependence and minimize the development of individuality within the family, they tend to encourage their children to be independent in other domains. It also appears likely
that cultures that develop a deeply ingrained sense of respect for
family values and high academic aspirations can safely encourage independence in their children.

Thus, it seems that a relatively strict home — if accompanied
by clearly articulated and consistently enforced rules and consequences — will not be injurious to intellectual development but

that an overly restrictive environment at the crucial age of twenty-four months will frequently impede such development.

9.3 The Twenty-Four-Month Transition: The Studies of Jean Carew

Between one and a half and two and a half years of age, children go through a considerable biological and behavioral transition. As a consequence, the most effective methods for providing a child with "intellectually valuable" experiences prior to this transition differ considerably from those that are the most effective at age two and a half. Fortunately, two in-depth studies undertaken by Jean Carew provide considerable information about the nature and sources of activities associated with favorable IQ outcomes—and do so separately for time periods before, during, and after this transition (Carew, 1980).

The strength of these studies lies in (1) the considerable number of hours that were spent observing interactions between children and their caretakers;[7] (2) the detailed and well-conceived approach taken to distinguishing among various kinds of experiences and to delineating the source of their initiation (child, parent, or both) and (3) the characteristics of the children studied—a highly advantaged day-care sample, along with a "home sample" especially designed to highlight contrasts between children likely to be of relatively high and relatively low intellectual ability.[8]

Experiences in a naturalistic setting were coded in accordance with "type of experience" (ten types) and its situational source, which could be *interactive* (child initiated, caretaker initiated, or jointly initiated) or *solitary* (child playing alone, watching people, or watching television).

How frequently these children had engaged in two of these ten predefined activities during their second year of life was often highly predictive of their IQ at age three. These activities were defined as follows:

- *Intellectually valuable experiences:* The author subdivides these well-defined activities into four types—(1) language mastery; (2) concrete reasoning and problem solving; (3) spatial, perceptual, and fine-motor mastery; and (4) expressive/artistic-skill mastery — to enable clear contrasts to be made with so-called socioemotional experiences, "routine talk," and other defined activities.

- *Preparatory activities:* These are defined as activities performed in preparation for undertaking intellectually valuable activities (for example, when a child dumps out a set of blocks that he or she then uses to build something).

Carew's principal conclusion is that *intellectual development, and especially language development at three years of age, is strongly related to experiences during the **second** year of life in which caretakers interacted with children in specific types of "educational" activities — in particular, language-stimulating activities.*

Although the frequency with which these children engaged in these "intellectually valuable" and "preparatory" activities in each of the four time periods showed relatively strong correlations with their IQ scores at age three, the situational *sources* of these experiences shifted considerably with age. In the home sample, this shift occurred between the ages of two and two and a half, while in the (very high IQ) day-care sample it appears to have generally occurred by age two.

In the home sample, the strongest predictor of IQ was the frequency of language-mastery experiences between one and a half and slightly beyond age two *that were structured by an adult* after having been initiated by the adult or jointly initiated by the adult and child.[9] By contrast, no correlation was found between three-year IQ and the incidence of "intellectual experiences" between twelve and twenty-one months of age[10] *when these were generated by the child in solitary play*. Only after two years of age did this type of solitary experience begin to have modest predictive value.

By thirty months of age, however, the pattern changed markedly, as follows:

- Language-mastery experiences generated by the child—in either solitary or interactive situations—became a significant IQ correlate.
- Spatial-mastery experiences that, whatever their source, had not been predictive of three-year IQ became strongly predictive—irrespective of whether these experiences were structured by another person in a reciprocal interaction with the child or were "created" by the child (in solitary play or in a child-initiated interaction).

This basic conclusion—*of the need for a linguistic teaching emphasis in the middle of the second year and a more spatially centered (multisensory integrative) child-in-play approach by age two-and-a-half*—corresponds with some recent understandings of brain development. For example, a postmortem analysis of neurons in the so-called speech strategy and speech execution areas of the cerebral cortex indicates that their development occurs in stages, with the left hemisphere taking the lead during the second year of life and the right hemisphere during the third year.[11] Further, by age two and a half, the development of connections between the two cortical hemispheres[12] enables them to begin to work well together.

Moreover, in Carew's home sample, the best and most consistent early predictor of a child's disposition to create "intellectually valuable" experiences for himself or herself at age two and a half was the frequency of earlier intellectual experiences in which the caretaker provided the experience and the child, for the most part, simply looked and listened. The strength of this link between the actualized capacity for self-learning in the third year and earlier caretaker-created experiences is depicted in Table 26.

In the home-care sample, the results of multiple-regression analysis indicate that about 55 percent of the variance in IQ scores at age three could be predicted from earlier "intellectual experiences" unilaterally provided by other people, while only 15 percent could be predicted by knowing the frequency of earlier "intellectual experiences" that were generated by the

Table 26. Correlations Between Caretaker-Created Experiences
at 12–27 Months and Child-Generated "Intellectual" Experiences
at 30–33 Months (Home Sample).

| | Child-Generated Intellectual Experiences | |
| | Interactive | Solitary |
Caretaker-Created Intellectual Experiences	Situation	Situation
12–15 months	+ .62	+ .35
18–21 months	+ .53	+ .49
24–27 months	+ .48	+ .54

Source: Adapted from Carew, 1980.

child in solitary play. Similarly, in the day-care sample: "The first source explained 48 percent of the IQ variance, whereas the second accounted for only 4 percent" (Carew, 1980, p. 64).

In addition to predicting IQ, certain antecedent activities also predicted scores on tests of spatial abilities and receptive language abilities at age three. For example, in the day-care sample, slightly more than half the variance on the "spatial abilities" test could be predicted by knowing the extent of prior "intellectual experiences" jointly created by the child and his and her caretaker. Nevertheless, after evaluating the relationships between specific types of experiences and these children's performance on tests of spatial ability and receptive language, Carew (1980, p. 60) concludes: "We must not overlook the fact that *only one topic, language-mastery experiences, predicted IQ, and the context of these experiences always involved an interacter* [emphasis mine]. Other types of skill-mastery experiences, spatial, and expressive-artistic, seem to be of genuine intellectual value to the child in that they predicted performance on the Spatial Abilities and Receptive Language tests yet they bore no relationship to IQ."

This conclusion, that the direct teaching of language skills and "informative talk" during the second year leads children to become "self-stimulating in a verbal mode," with a heightened ability to conceptualize and to imagine, corresponds with findings by Clarke-Stewart (1973) that the amount of verbal stimulation provided to toddlers by their mothers and the amount of time that mothers spent playing with and stimulating their toddlers with play materials (in contrast to "purely social play") were each highly predictive of cognitive and language test scores, even though the amount of time spent by these toddlers using play materials independently of the mother was not predictive.

A recent study, examining the development of toddlers' competence in making taxonomic and thematic associations between twenty-six and thirty-four months of age (Fenson, Vella, and Kennedy, 1989), found that (1) both age groups were able to make thematic matches (for example, dog and dog house) but the older group was able to recognize a wider range of themes, and (2) the younger group was, for the most part, unable to make taxonomic associations (for example, dog and horse) when the pictures did not have strong *perceptual* features in common.

9.4 Early Cognitive Stimulation: Findings from Gifted and Eminent Populations

Associations between certain forms of intense parent-child interaction and intellectual precocity appear in the literature with marked regularity, despite the bias of early researchers toward a purely hereditary theory of genius (Fowler, 1983). Following are some of the in-depth analyses that have arrived at this conclusion:

- *Cox (1926)*: This painstaking collection of nearly 300 of the best-documented instances of historical brilliance, taken from Cattell's (1903) review of 1,000 great geniuses, is replete with instances of unusual attention to the individual's intellectual development beginning early in life. Cox's conclusions emphasize the frequency with which early stimulation (along with special later educational and social opportunities) contributed to the development of these geniuses.
- *McCurdy (1957)*: An intense examination of the biographical records of twenty members of Cox's sample led McCurdy to conclude that all twenty received in childhood "a high degree of attention from their parents as well as others". . . "expressed in [the applica-

tion of] intensive educational measures" (summarized in Fowler, 1983, p. 362).

- *Root (1921)*: Reporting in detail on twenty-three of his "supernormal" children (140 IQ or higher), Root demonstrated that twenty had experienced a "highly superior" early home education (receiving a rating of *A* or *A +* on Root's scale).

- *Terman (1919)*: A detailed analysis of the twenty-three highest-IQ children from Terman's 1919 collection of forty-one case records led Fowler (1983) to conclude that "in this set of children, early stimulation, beginning between early infancy and age five, is directly linked to accelerated skill development in the area stimulated" (p. 363). Fowler continues, "Although these children were often competent in more than one category, of course, the association between types of stimulation and types of competence was well delineated in the twenty-three case descriptions" (p. 364).

- *Sheldon (1954)*: This analysis of the families of twenty-eight exceptionally high IQ (170 plus) New York area children (largely the grandchildren of Jewish immigrants from Eastern Europe) revealed that in sixteen of the twenty-four full-study cases, the maternal grandmother was depicted as "the most dynamic factor in the family life" (p. 60) and exerted an unusual degree of control in five others. The value systems of these grandmothers stressed the achievement of academic honors, with a strong emphasis on verbal and dramatic performance.

William Fowler is a strong (and highly successful) proponent of the use of early educational enrichment to enhance intellectual ability (see section 10.2). Fowler states (1975, p. 22) "Among the countless great minds who benefited from the intensive tutorial efforts in a one-to-one ratio beginning in infancy" were Francis Galton, Frank Lloyd Wright, and Mozart. Frequently, Fowler concludes, it was the child's father who provided the early intensive stimulation. For example, the backgrounds of two great mathematicians, Leibnitz and Pascal, show intense early paternal involvement (Fowler, 1971, 1975). Leibnitz's father taught the boy to read and then to absorb historical and biblical concepts in his preschool years, while Pascal's father devoted all his time to his son's education beginning at age three. In the realm of music, similar examples abound of conscious attempts to create environments in which extraordinary musical talent could develop very early (Maazel, 1950). For example, Yehudi Menuhin was, as a baby, regularly taken to symphony concerts, and he began violin lessons with a skilled musician before he reached the age of three; Yasha Heifitz enjoyed a similar background, and it is well known that Mozart's musical education began at age two (Fowler, 1983).

Fowler (1983) also holds that the regularity of associations found between specific manifestations of ability or talent, on the one hand, and a milieu in which the corresponding types of competence are highly valued and fostered, on the other, suggests that some, if not all, of the inherited components of ability are general rather than specific and that "high-potential" abilities that are stimulated early on may be malleable in almost any direction in which stimulation is applied. Fowler further emphasizes that "a one-to-one relationship over many hours of the infant's day is integral to a single intensive attachment to a highly caring and competent adult who stimulated the development" (Fowler, 1975, p. 22).

Recent studies of world-famous individuals by Benjamin Bloom (Bloom, 1982a, 1982b; Bloom and Sosniak, 1981) revealed that primary educational variables that contributed to outstanding intellect — earliness, duration, and intensity of stimulation — included a high frequency of one-to-one relationships with mentors and models and/or small group interactions that stress communication and analysis. Bloom concluded that there was an intense interest by the families of these gifted individuals to "live the life of the intellect, to strive and create, sometimes expressed in direct demands to learn and achieve, but sometimes intrinsic to the process of everyday involvement in the activities and concerns of the adult's scientific, literary, musical, sports, or artistic life from early childhood on." Bloom's detailed analysis of the strategies and techniques used by such parents suggests that, in 48 percent of the subjects studied, the parents "deliberately and planfully" instructed their children during their early years in the specific areas in which their exceptional talents ultimately emerged.

9.5 Parental Achievement Orientation Versus Stimulation of Academic Behavior

There are substantial differences in several parental behaviors and attitudes toward firstborns and laterborns at three years of

age, and these differences are linked with subsequent IQ performance. In a large study of California families in which most of
the parents had college educations (Gottfried and Gottfried,
1984), large birth-order differences were found in three of the
assessment factors included in the HOME Preschool Inventory
(Caldwell and Bradley, 1978), and each of these differences
showed significant correlations with the children's IQs. The
three factors were "variety of stimulation," "language stimulation," and "stimulation of academic behavior."[13] This last factor,
stimulation of academic behavior, had been shown to be quite
different from a parental achievement orientation. This distinction becomes clearer when the IQ scores of these children are
compared with their scores on two variables gauged by another
home-assessment instrument used in this study, the Family Environment Scale (Moos and Moos, 1981). Although scores on
this scale's *"provision of an intellectual-cultural environment"* factor
bore a statistically significant correlation with IQ scores
($p < .05$), scores on the *achievement orientation* factor showed **absolutely no correlation** with emerging intelligence. This finding—of a lack of correlation between parents' achievement orientation and their provision of an academic environment—has
also been reported in a recent study of adoptive homes in
Colorado (Plomin and DeFries, 1985).

Thus, simply "pushing" one's child to *achieve* is not the key to
his or her intellectual development, unless this achievement
orientation is coupled with opportunities for academic and
cultural stimulation.

Before proceeding to specific recommendations for developing toddlers' language skills (see Chapter Twelve), it is appropriate to present information concerning the nature of highly
successful IQ-enhancing programs (see Chapter Ten). Then,
information concerning the nature of the environments provided during toddlerhood by two ethnic groups that have produced children whose competences in (somewhat contrasting)
cognitive domains tend to be well above the norm is presented
in Chapters Thirteen and Fourteen.

Notes

1. The items comprising this "avoidance of restriction and punishment" factor include: (1) Mother does not shout at child during the visit; (2) mother does not express overt annoyance with or hostility toward the child (for example, mother does not call the child "bad," does not complain that the child is hard to take care of or is wearing her out); (3) mother does not scold or run down the child during the visit; (4) mother does not interfere with or restrict the child's actions or movements more than three times during the visit unless a clear instance of safety is involved; (5) mother neither slaps nor spanks the child during visit; (6) mother reports no more than one instance of physical punishment during the preceding week (using mother's definition of physical punishment); (7) at least ten books are present and visible; and (8) the family has a pet.

2. Among the Black children in this sample (whose IQs averaged 85), every major factor in the HOME Inventory "contributed" significantly to IQ differences. In the Caucasian sample, "restrictiveness" scores averaged 6.6 and 4.9 for middle-class and lower-middle-class mothers, respectively.

3. The scores of the children in cluster three (mainly females) barely exceeded 100 from the ages of six through fourteen and then rose to above 110 by mid adolescence (ages sixteen to seventeen); their parents' IQs averaged only 92.

4. This adoption study is highly unusual in that the occupational-class status of the children's biological grandparents was somewhat higher than that of their adoptive parents.

5. Their correlations with IQ (averaging together the thirty-six- and forty-two-month McCarthy GCI correlations) were + .31 for cohesion, + .24 for expressiveness, − .13 for control, and − .10 for conflict. Extremely large differences between firstborns and laterborns in degree of control and conflict at this age were reported; the firstborns had an IQ advantage (averaged across three test ages) of 5 points.

6. Factors from the Child-Rearing Practice Report (CRPR) (Block, 1986) were used to assess these variables. To facilitate data collection, parental responses were rated on a 5-point Likert-type scale (strongly disagree = 1; strongly agree = 5). The CPRP measures encouragement of the development of independence, but not family interdependence; the three samples totaled 138 families.

7. In the home sample, there were an average of seventeen one-hour observation periods for each child, clustered into four time spans (twelve to fifteen months, eighteen to twenty-one months, twenty-four to twenty-seven months, and thirty to thirty-three months). In the day-care sample, there was one forty-minute period per month, with the data analysis grouped into three clusters (eighteen to twenty-three months, twenty-four to twenty-nine months, and thirty to thirty-four months).

8. In the day-care sample, over 90 percent of the children's fathers and

more than half of their mothers had, or were pursuing, advanced degrees, and only three of twenty-two mothers had not completed college. The average IQ (Stanford-Binet) of the day-care group (who attended five very high quality day-care centers) was 125. The home sample was composed almost entirely of younger siblings of elementary school children who had either a high IQ score or were given a high intellectual-competence rating by their teachers or a low teacher rating; these children's IQs averaged 110.

9. In the day-care sample, the percentage of time spent in "intellectual" experiences was 22 percent at eighteen to twenty-three months, 26 percent at twenty-four to twenty-nine months, and 32 percent at thirty to thirty-four months; in the home sample, it was 8 percent at twelve to fifteen months, 16 percent at eighteen to twenty-one months, 21 percent at twenty-four to twenty-seven months, and 31 percent at thirty to thirty-three months.

10. These include situations in which the child and the other person (generally an adult) jointly fashioned the experience and also ones in which the other person essentially created the experience unilaterally for an attentive but otherwise noncontributing child.

11. Comparisons of the left hemisphere's "speech-strategy formation" area (Broca's area) and the analogous right-hemisphere area (Simonds and Scheibel, forthcoming) suggest that at twenty-four to thirty-six months, the right hemisphere is undergoing a massive development relative to the left, as the "outer-branch" development of these cells (fourth to sixth orders of branching) greatly exceeds that of their inner-branch development, in contrast to adult brains, where more than two-thirds of the dendritic length is concentrated in the inner branches (Scheibel and others, 1985). By contrast, outer-branch growth is far greater in the left hemisphere at twelve to fifteen months and forty-two to seventy-two months. This study also found that in the orifacial motor zone ("speech execution" area) outer-branch growth was far greater in the right hemisphere than in the left at five to six months and twenty-four to thirty-six months, but left-hemisphere growth was substantially greater at twelve to fifteen months and forty-two to seventy-two months. Moreover, at fifteen months, *new primary dendrites are emerging from the cell body of the left hemisphere's "speech strategy" cells.*

12. As reflected in the myelination of the corpus callosum linking the two cortical hemispheres, as well as by recent PET-scan findings that show a rapidly increasing rate of glucose utilization in the cerebral cortex through age four (at which time a lifetime peak is reached). This linkage between the hemispheres corresponds with the emergence (at about eighteen to twenty-one months) of an ability to evoke an object, person, or event that is not present (Fischer, 1987).

13. These (thirty-nine-month) HOME correlations with the McCarthy General Cognitive Index at forty-two months were + .39, + .25, and + .39, respectively; the components of variety measured on the Preschool HOME Assessment Inventory differ from those on the Infant Inventory.

✂ Part Four ✌

The Foundations
of Intellectual Giftedness

Chapter Ten provides detailed information about several highly successful educational enrichment programs that were initiated in the first or second year of life. These are subdivided into (1) programs that produced dramatic increases in the IQs of children who, on the basis of their parents' income and education, would have been likely to achieve somewhat above-average IQ scores even without these programs; and (2) highly successful programs that served children from lower-class and/or lower-middle-class families. The chapter then analyzes the child-rearing practices of Israeli kibbutzim and provides data about the impact that being reared in these communal settings had on the IQs of children from disparate cultural backgrounds. Data from the consortium that evaluated the long-term impact of the Head Start Program are then evaluated in terms of the effects of the IQ trends discussed in Chapter Five.

Using findings which suggest that maternal interactive behavior during the initial months of infancy can have a considerable impact on emerging intelligence, Chapter Eleven (1) details the development of visual and auditory competence in early infancy; (2) stresses the need to induce a state of quiet alertness to promote infant learning and indicates mechanisms for doing so; (3) presents findings suggesting that long-term memory for visual stimuli and the ability to create "categorical representations" develop earlier than are commonly believed; (4) details the nature of early face-to-face interactions between mother and infant, including gaze behavior, smiling, turn taking, vocal imitation, and the need for periodic pauses; and (5) suggests how infants' emerging preferences for visual stimuli of various sizes, shapes, levels of complexity, and viewing distances and angles can be used to accelerate the development of visual and auditory learning. The chapter also presents theories concerning the stages of early infancy and the relationship of these stages to the developmental timetables of brain growth, and makes recommendations for altering the nature of visual and auditory stimulation in response to these changing capabilities.

Chapter Twelve presents some detailed recommendations for the development of language comprehension and expression in infancy and toddlerhood, including details of the approach employed by William Fowler (the developer of an enormously successful "IQ-raising" program). It also gives the ingredients of a language-stimulation program that engendered a dramatic acceleration in the language development of toddlers from upper-middle-class families.

Chapters Thirteen and Fourteen then explore the relationship between a child's early environment and the development of exceptional cognitive ability by comparing the child-rearing and educational practices of two ethnic groups. The members of one of these groups tend to score well above the norm on tests involving a visual/structural/perceptual mode of analysis (the Japanese people), while the members of the other tend to demonstrate exceptional aptitude in solving verbal/symbolic/conceptually oriented problems (the Ashkenazi Jews). This analysis strongly suggests that the traditional parenting and educational customs of these groups foster the kinds of brain development related directly to the areas of heightened ability found in their children. These results, however, also suggest that the magnitude of the "domain-specific" population advantage is too large and is fully manifest too early in childhood to have been the result of a *single generation* of training—especially since (as detailed in Chapter Twenty) this acumen does not dissipate markedly when modern American child-rearing approaches are substituted for many of these traditional customs.

Contents

ℵ 10 ℵ

Successful Early Educational Enrichment Programs

10.1 Introduction

This chapter contains information on early childhood educational enrichment programs that have generated substantial IQ gains, with an emphasis on those in which participants attained well-above-average or exceptionally high IQ scores. The intention is to serve the needs of readers interested in developing educational enrichment programs either for their own children or for the larger community.

The results of these programs are presented in terms of scores on IQ and language-comprehension tests and are accompanied by information about the length of time since the IQ test used was normed, to enable an estimate to be made of the bias generated by the gradual rise in IQ scores over time (see Chapter Five). Where possible, the chapter also provides information to enable readers to estimate how high the participants' IQs would have been without the enrichment.

Although the primary emphasis of this chapter is on programs serving children who would, even in the absence of enrichment, be expected to have above-average IQs, it also provides considerable information about programs begun in infancy or toddlerhood that have substantially increased the

cognitive competence of children from disadvantaged populations. The principal conclusions of this examination are as
follows:

- *Substantial and long-lasting increases* in measured intelligence have been attained by children who (on the
  basis of their family's SES) would be expected to possess
  an adequate set of information-processing skills without the enrichment; participants in the most successful
  programs (such as those of William Fowler and Philip
  Drash) had IQs **averaging in** *the top 1 to 2 percent* of the
  population (130 and above).
- Programs that educate parents in effective child development principles and procedures are most effective
  if they are begun in infancy, contain well-defined
  language-development programs, and limit participation to first-time parents.
- Center-based programs are most successful when they
  are begun early (in infancy or during the second year
  of life), provide extremely favorable caretaker ratios,
  and emphasize language training.
- Efforts begun in infancy to "normalize" the IQs of at-
  risk children are more successful in raising IQ scores
  and in sustaining these gains than are traditional preschool programs; again, those programs that stress
  language enrichment and parental education are the
  most successful.
- The environment provided in Israeli kibbutzim (in the
  1960s) produced *near-genius IQ averages* among the offspring of reasonably well educated parents and *dramatically* increased the IQs of the children of immigrants
  from Middle Eastern and North African Arab lands.
- In terms of IQ points, the gains registered by participants from upper-middle-class families tend to be
  slightly smaller than those made by at-risk children but
  also tend to dissipate less after program completion.

To help readers assess the scores attained by participants in
these programs, two tables have been prepared that relate IQ

**Table 27. Approximate Test Scores (or Ranges) Associated with Defined
IQ Nomenclature or with Selected Demographic-Group Averages
(Upper Portion of the IQ Distribution).**

IQ Range or Average	Defined Nomenclature/Demographic Group
176 and above	one in a million IQ; eligibility for the Mega Society
140 and above	generally considered to be genius-level IQ (top 1% of the population)[a]
130 and above	borderline genius; eligibility for Mensa (top 2%)
120 and above	potentially gifted (top 10%)
115 and above	superior or higher IQ (top sixth)
110 and above	top third of the population
107.5	approximate IQ average of firstborn Caucasian children[b]
103.7	approximate IQ average of all U.S. Caucasian children
100.0	theoretical median and average IQ score[c]
90-to-110	middle half of the IQ distribution
85-to-115	middle two-thirds of the IQ distribution

[a] In certain cognitive domains, exceptional ability need not be accompanied by an unusually high IQ.

[b] Firstborns in families with two or three children.

[c] Applicable to the year in which the IQ test was normed; because IQ scores have been gradually rising, more people will score above these averages than below.

scores and ranges to given percentiles along the bell-shaped IQ curve. The first (Table 27) concentrates on the upper portion of the IQ distribution, and the second (Table 28) concentrates on the lower portion.

10.2 Programs That Have Successfully Raised the IQs of Normal and Above-Average Children

This section presents the results of highly successful early childhood development programs geared toward middle-class and upper-middle-class children. It includes programs that stressed direct child training, as well as those that stressed teaching parents how to be effective child educators.

Enrichment Programs of William Fowler

For more than two decades, William Fowler has been successfully raising the IQs of infants and toddlers by exposing them to

**Table 28. Estimated IQ Averages and Ranges Associated
with Various Sociodemographic Groups and Occupations
Considered in Relation to the Normal IQ Curve.**

IQ Range or Average	Defined Nomenclature/Demographic Group Averages
114	estimated IQ average of people in the professions
110 and above	top fourth of the IQ distribution
103.7	average IQ of U.S. Caucasian population (early 1970s)
100.0	theoretical mean and median IQ
95	estimated IQ average of semiskilled workers
93	estimated IQ average of northeastern U.S. Blacks (early 1970s)
88	estimated IQ average of all U.S. Blacks (early 1970s)
84	estimated IQ average of southern U.S. Blacks (early 1970s)
84	estimated IQ average of offspring of teenage minority-group mothers
83 or below	bottom sixth of the IQ distribution
68 or below	mentally defective: bottom 2% of the IQ distribution

Note: Averages and ranges are applicable to the year in which the IQ test was normed; because IQ scores have been gradually rising, more people will score above these averages than below them.

a carefully constructed program of language stimulation. In one of these programs, where guided learning was coupled with an intensive caretaker ratio, a group of thirty children (who were primarily firstborn children from middle-class and upper-middle-class families) *posted IQ scores that averaged 135.* Significantly, these scores were recorded three years after the children left the program and were attained on the just-renormed (1972) Stanford-Binet examination (Fowler, 1975). Although most of these children began the program prior to the age of seven months, seven of them were first enrolled at seventeen to twenty-two months of age. Nevertheless, the younger the child was when he or she entered the program and the longer the program's duration, the greater the benefits were likely to be (Fowler, 1972, 1975).[1]

In a further series of smaller-scale projects, Fowler's efforts again produced extraordinarily high intellectual performance. For example, IQ averages ranging between 133 and 140 from ages three through eight were reported for three firstborn off-spring of college-educated parents after the children partici-pated in a program that lasted from their fifth through their twelfth month of infancy and stressed language stimulation (Fowler and Swensen, 1979). Evaluations of specific areas of cognitive competency at thirty-six to forty-two months (using the Griffiths Language and Cognitive Development Scales) showed extraordinarily precocious scores in the areas of "hearing and speech," which averaged 183 (a level not normally reached until age six), and "practical reasoning" (this included counting and measurement), which averaged 160. Importantly, scores averag-ing 128 were registered on the "personal-social competency" subtest and 122 on the "performance" subtest.

In a later study of six firstborn children whose parents were generally well educated, similar results were attained at thirty-two months of age, except for a somewhat lower "hearing and speech" quotient (149), which could be attributed to external events that affected three of the six children adversely.[2]

These programs focused on language labeling in six common caregiving and play activities. This approach looked upon lan-guage development as a series of interactions between the child and a linguistic environment in which models and guidance (corrective feedback) gradually enable the child to master, in sequence, the hierarchy of rules with which language is struc-tured. Parents were presented with written guides (which in-cluded vocabulary lists), and, in weekly home visits, they re-ceived further instruction through demonstrations, comments on the techniques they used, and discussions of the program's goals and methods.

A key aspect of these programs was guided learning in inter-active play, provided individually and in small groups of two or more children. These sessions were interspersed throughout each day to each child in three or more five- to fifteen-minute specialized learning activities. These sessions were typically car-ried out in a tutorial mode (alone with the child or in small groups) and focused on integrating the use of language with various types of play activities.

Fowler's center-based programs also included specific projects designed "to teach information concepts (such as the names, characteristics, functions, groupings, and so on of common objects), problem solving (learning to use objects as tools or learning to get around barriers), and language syntax (for instance, how subjects and predicates can describe people performing actions)" (Fowler and Swenson, 1979, p. 153). "A variety of routine sessions setting up play and guidance with sensory motor toys (form boards, stacking toys, puzzles) and teacher-initiated lesson plans on information concepts, similarities and differences, spatial relations, object features, and sensory qualities (such as texture and odor) were typical of other more-or-less regular offerings in the program" (p. 80).

Fowler has recently completed a book entitled *Talking in Infancy: How to Nurture and Cultivate Early Language Development* (forthcoming). A description of the approach taken in Fowler's book and a summary of his specific recommendations for structuring language-stimulation activities during infancy and toddlerhood are presented later in this book (see Chapter Twelve).

Operant Conditioning: The Work of Philip Drash

Extraordinarily high intellectual competence, speech development, and emotional maturity were attained as a result of a program designed to modify the behavior of parents in specific ways during the first year of their child's life (Drash and Stolberg, 1972). The Stanford-Binet scores for the four children reached (1) 170 at forty-three months, (2) 141 at forty-four months, (3) 160 at forty-nine months, and (4) 150 at twenty-five months (Drash and Stollberg, 1979).[3] *Thus, the mean IQ of these program participants was 155.*

On the Vineland Test of Social Development, administered two years after program participation (at forty-one to forty-four months of age), **scores ranged from 149 to 256** and averaged 207—indicating that, at three and a half years of age, these children had achieved a "social maturity" equal to a child of seven.[4]

The program employed the parent as a so-called intervention agent and concentrated on teaching behavior modification procedures and child development principles to the parent. In a weekly three-hour format, the program included (1) the mother's review and demonstration of observed changes in her child's motor, intellectual, and linguistic behaviors; (2) the staff's modeling of behavioral and stimulation procedures; (3) lectures and discussions on aspects of infant development; and (4) supervised play for the infants. After two months of weekly application of this seven-month regimen, the frequency of the three-hour sessions was reduced to a biweekly basis and, after four months, to one session per month.

The intervention program consisted of the operant conditioning of linguistic, social, self-help, and motor skills and the training of parents in child management and child development topics. Operant conditioning of speech included the labeling of objects and rewards. Also stressed were social skills (both self-help and interpersonal), compliance with verbal commands, and motor skill development (including an exercise regimen).[5]

The effectiveness of this operant conditioning approach is based on (1) the development of a language-training curriculum that ensures that a child has mastered all skills below the level at which new skills are being taught and (2) the use of contingent reinforcement as the primary mechanism for controlling learning. The conditioning begins by *imitating the infants' sounds*, after a period of rewarding (reinforcing) any sound made by the infant. The child is then rewarded if he or she repeats the sound made by the conditioner. Gradually, over a period of days or weeks, the conditioner assumes the lead role and determines which sounds to present to the infant. Correct sounds are reinforced immediately and errors are not.

As the infants' imitative repertoire expands to fifteen or twenty basic sounds, these are then grouped to form words. When about 20 words can be imitated, environmental objects become the stimuli for labeling. When 20 objects are reliably named, pictures of objects become the new stimuli. When the names of 100 words are remembered, the next step is 2-word phrases (Drash and Liebowitz, 1973).

At twenty-five months of age, two of the four children were using 6- to 7-word sentences and had expressive speech vocabularies of approximately 700 words; a third child was using 3- to 4-word sentences and had a 500-word vocabulary.[6] The principal author attributes the program's success to its employing parents as intervention agents and its focus on teaching these parents behavior modification procedures as well as important child development principles.[7]

The Missouri Project: The Work of Burton White

A program of instructing first-time (primarily upper-middle-class) mothers how to teach their children resulted in substantial

IQ gains. At their third birthday, the language abilities of first-born children whose parents had received this training were between 130 and 140 on each of the subscales of the Zimmerman Language Scales, or 14 points higher than the scores of controls (White, 1985).[8]

On the highly respected Kaufman Achievement Scales (Kaufman and Kaufman, 1983), the children's *overall score was 123, or 13 points higher than that of the controls.* These gains (to a level of 3.7 years) occurred even though there was no difference between the experimental group and controls on two subtests: (1) "faces and places" (the only heavily culturally based subtest on the Kaufman) and (2) the replication of hand movements, which is easier for children who have the ability to evoke concrete visual imagery rather than a heavily auditory "cognitive style" (see Chapter Sixteen).[9]

The program was designed to provide educational guidance to parents and soon-to-be-parents by preparing them for the developmental stages that their babies would soon be going through (Meyerhoff and White, 1986; White, 1977, 1981). In the early months, there were regular group get-togethers at a child-care center, along with individual visits to the home. At five months, the frequency of contact was reduced to a monthly one-and-a-half-hour session.[10]

A Brief Parent-Teaching Program: The Work of Marilyn Metzl

Can training first-time parents how to provide language stimulation to their newborn infants engender higher IQs in these infants? If the results found in a longitudinal study by Marilyn Metzl are indicative, it certainly can!

The training (Metzl, 1980) emphasized language enrichment in six specific interactional situations: (1) imitating and responding to an infant's vocalizations (which Metzl dubbed "back talk"); (2) verbalizing during routine caregiving activities (so that verbal learning accompanied repetitive sensory-motor activities); (3) setting aside a special time of day for quiet rocking, holding, and talking (called "quiet talk"); (4) verbalizing what the baby is doing, especially such actions as laughing, crying, and smiling, (called "parallel talk"); and (5) taking the baby from place to place while performing routine chores and talking about these chores (behavior was not materially altered in the sixth situation).

The training was brief: only three one-and-a-half-hour home visits were made (at six, twelve, and eighteen weeks of age). In twenty families both parents received training, in thirty families only the mother was trained, and in twenty other cases carefully matched families received no training and thus acted as controls. The Stanford-Binet IQ scores of the children in the group in which both parents were trained *averaged 124.6 at age six* or 10.5 points higher than the average score of the controls (Metzl, personal communication, 1988), while the scores of the group where only the mother was trained averaged 7.1 points higher that those of the controls.

Scores on the Zimmerman Language Scales, measured at the same ages (five to six), showed a similar pattern of results — the scores of the eighteen children in families where both parents received training averaging between 121 and 131 on the three Zimmerman scales, or 9 to 15 points higher than those of the controls, with the scores of children in those families where only the mother had been trained falling midway between.

The Frank Porter Graham Project: The Work of the Robinsons

A carefully structured, center-based intensive educational program resulted in extraordinarily high IQ scores both among children entering the program in early infancy and among those who started at about age two (Robinson and Robinson, 1971).

The seven Black children (for whom Stanford-Binet IQ scores were available) averaged 119.7, **or 33.6 points higher than their controls,** while the nine Caucasian children averaged 129.7, or 12.8 points above their controls. The IQ scores of these children also varied in relation to the child's age at program entry and the age at which the child's IQ was tested. In the authors' final report, the IQs of those children who had entered the program at age two and received two and a half years of enrichment averaged

127.2, while the scores of the three-year-olds (who had been in the training program for only one year) averaged 123.8. Among children who had entered the program as infants, only a few were old enough to take the Stanford-Binet test (thirty months), and the scores of these children averaged 117.3. As with several other enrichment programs reviewed in this chapter, the children achieved higher scores on verbally oriented cognitive measures than on nonverbal measures. Greater differences between the experimental and control groups were also found on verbal than on nonverbal measures.

This full-day program also required the cooperation of the parents (virtually all of whom were employed). There were daily conversations between parents and staff, as well as home visits by public health nurses (Robinson, 1969). The center had cottages for eating, sleeping, and free play, and it also had specialized areas for instruction (in small homogeneous groups).

10.3 Programs That Have Substantially Raised the IQs of Children from Disadvantaged Families

This section presents the results of early childhood development programs that substantially increased the performance of children who would otherwise be expected to have IQ scores materially below average. Table 28 provides a perspective on the heightened IQ averages achieved by participants in these programs, considered in relation both to the "normal" IQ distribution and to estimates of the average IQs reported for various occupational and socioeconomic groups.

Residential Nurseries of London

The success of the long-stay residential nurseries of London in normalizing the cognitive development of children expected to have below-normal IQs has generally been attributed to the quantity and quality of their staffs and, in particular, to their high concern with the psychological and intellectual development of these children.

In a study of eighty-five children aged two to five years old from thirteen nurseries (Tizard, Cooperman, Joseph, and Tizard, 1972), the average score on the Reynell Language Comprehension Test was 104.6, while scores on the nonverbal subtests of the Minnesota Preschool Scale averaged 104.9. These scores are approximately 12 to 15 points higher than those attained by children of similar backgrounds reared by their mothers.[11] Moreover, among children reared in nurseries rated considerably above average,[12] Reynell comprehension scores averaged 10 points higher than the "all-nursery" average, placing these children almost among the top 10 percent of all children.[13]

There was some preselection of the nurseries chosen for the study to highlight differences in staff autonomy. London's long-stay nurseries were generally thought to have high standards of physical care and to be concerned for the psychological well-being of the children as well. In theory, but not always in practice, a nurse and assistant nurse cared for groups of six children.[14] Staff turnover was low, and there was always a long list of applicants. The job of nurse in a residential nursery, which required both college and practical training, had a relatively high status in England, and each student on entering had to agree to remain for three years. The nurseries were plentifully supplied with toys and books, and children were read to at least once a day.

The only cognitive area tested in which the quality of the above-average nursery made a considerable difference (compared with the average nursery) was in language comprehension. Virtually no effect was visible on measures of expressive language[15] or "nonverbal intellect," where the children in the best-rated nurseries scored only 1.8 points above the all-nursery average. The children reared in the poorly rated nurseries, however, scored half a standard deviation below the all-nursery average on each of these cognitive measures. Thus, favorable caretaker ratios and significant staff autonomy produced *superior language comprehension skills* among children who would otherwise be expected to have below-average abilities.

Tizard, Cooperman, Joseph, and Tizard (1972) then evaluated differences between nurseries in specific aspects of caretaker-child interactions and found:

- The frequency with which "informative staff talk" was provided by the caretakers[16] was somewhat strongly correlated (+ .51) with children's Reynell Language Comprehension scores; nevertheless, the overall frequency of **all other speech** directed to the child had *no correlation with this score.* When the nursery's "informative-staff-talk" observations were compared with the average Reynell Language Comprehension score for all sampled children from that nursery, a + .83 correlation was found ($p < .001$).
- Other staff-child interactive behaviors bearing strong correlations with group Reynell Language Comprehension scores included *the amount of active play with staff,* which averaged 3 percent of the total observation time (+ .68), *"staff answer children"* (+ .77), and *"social activity by staff"* directed toward the children (+ .62).

Early Intense Caretaking: The Milwaukee Project

When children at severe risk of developing low IQs were given direct, early, and intensive family intervention, they were able to acquire and sustain normal to well-above-average cognitive ability.

Forty children from families in the most poverty-stricken areas of Milwaukee, Wisconsin, were selected on the basis that their mothers' IQ scores were 75 or below (on the WAIS). The program—begun when a child was three to four months of age and lasting until age six—had group-to-staff ratios of one to one during the first year and two to two in the middle of the second year. It then gradually changed to two to one and (by twenty-four months of age) was three to one and then changed to twelve to four.[17]

The children receiving this enrichment attained IQ scores averaging 121 at age six (on the Stanford-Binet), compared with 87 for controls (Garber and Heber, 1973).[18] On the somewhat less verbally oriented Wechsler tests (WPPSI and WISC), the experimental group's IQs averaged only 110 between the ages of four and six, compared with 84 for controls. Follow-up WISC scores at ages nine to ten (based on scores for three-fourths of the initial group) showed a slight decline to an average of 106 — which was still 23 points above the controls, or one and a half standard deviations higher (Garber and Heber, 1977, 1981).

The children participated in an eight-hour-a-day, five-day-a-week, year-round center-based educational program (after a two- to eight-week in-home "acquaintanceship period" to establish rapport and trust), while their mothers were given a vocational and social education program. The caretaker-teachers were paraprofessionals, generally living in the same community, who had been chosen because they were both extremely affectionate and language-facile people. Their education ranged from eighth grade to a maximum of one year of college.

The language development program employed *imitation* as the primary mechanism for teaching children the meaning and structure of speech, including (1) imitation with reduction, where the toddler reduces adult language to its essentials; (2) imitation with expansion, where the adult repeats the tod-dler's utterance but adds certain missing words, in essence mod-eling the way that the thought should have been phrased; and (3) teaching the rules of language structure.

The maternal rehabilitation program was quite successful, as a substantially greater proportion of the mothers in the experi-mental group found and kept jobs than did mothers in the control group, and they also earned considerably higher wages.[19] This may have reduced the reported IQ gains for the experimental children somewhat, as several of the more suc-cessful mothers moved and could not be included in the follow-up study.

Despite the massive group IQ increase, risk factors still con-tinued to be important in determining an individual child's IQ score. At follow-up, those experimental children in the authors' highest-risk group (based on maternal literacy, the number and spacing of children in the family, maternal age, and an assess-ment of the quality of the home environment) had scores averag-ing 8 points below those of children in their lesser-risk group; among controls, the difference between these groups averaged 11 points.

Champaign-Urbana Study: The Work of Genevieve Painter

Ten racially mixed, culturally disadvantaged children from Champaign and Urbana, Illinois, who received intellectual stimulation in their homes for one year beginning at an average age of fifteen and a half months (ranging from eight to twenty-four months) attained scores on the Stanford-Binet averaging 108.1, *or 15.1 points higher than their older siblings, who had attended a nursery school for culturally disadvantaged children* (Painter, 1969). Taking into account the deprived cultural background of these children, as well as the recent (1960) norming of the test used, this average is exceptionally noteworthy.[20]

This one-hour-a-day, five-days-a-week training program emphasized language development, symbolic representation, concept formation, and, to a lesser extent, fine-motor development. Language development was encouraged in all activities. For example, when the child was given manipulative materials, the tutor[21] emphasized words pertinent to the activity, as well as words that naturally evolved during the activity. In addition, a structured language program was presented for each child. The program consisted of (1) beginning language, (2) elaborative language, (3) the breaking down of "giant" words into units, and (4) the encouragement of internal dialogue.

Language instruction for the children who did little babbling or spoke few words was begun by teaching the infant to *imitate* the tutor's vocal sounds, which at first were *sounds that the infant had made spontaneously* and later were sounds devised by the tutor. The child was also encouraged to repeat the names of objects found in his or her environment. In addition, there was a highly structured activity that stressed the identification, differentiation, labeling, and use of objects and pictures. Gesturing in lieu of words was discouraged once the child was able to talk. Elaborative language was encouraged through (1) the use of dramatic play, rhymes, and songs; (2) the use and modeling of adjectives, adverbs, and prepositions by the tutor; and (3) the use of antonyms and analogous words (for example, milk and juice, water and ice). Overly simplified phrases were enlarged upon to make simple but complete sentences.

When problem-solving activities (involving the manipulation of objects) were undertaken, the tutor verbalized the appropriate words used in planning while the infant observed the problem and planned for its solution. The child was then asked to repeat these "planning" phrases aloud (as they were whispered by the tutor). Later, the child was told to say the words to himself.

Conceptual training was also stressed. The techniques here included (1) using a mirror to point to parts of the child's body or to parts of a doll or puppet; (2) introducing the child to form, size, space, and shape conceptualization and seriation; (3) categorizing objects in one or several ways; (4) engaging in number-concept activities; and (5) promoting temporal awareness, primarily by means of associating certain activities (for example, puzzle time) with certain times of day.

As a result of this program, younger siblings from socially disadvantaged families—whose IQs would be expected to average somewhat less than those of their older siblings—increased their IQs by at least a full standard deviation.

Syracuse Project: The Work of Dr. J. Ronald Lally

IQ scores averaging 111.1 were attained by a group of sixty-nine three-year-old children from "low-income, multiproblemed" families who participated in a Family Development Intervention Program (Lally, 1973).

Five-point-higher scores (on the Stanford-Binet) were reported for the forty-four children whose parents began the training three to six months before their birth than for the children who entered the program at six months of age. A subgroup of thirty-one children for whom carefully matched controls were selected and followed outperformed the controls by an average of 13.4 points.[22] Stanford-Binet scores at age four (for the thirty-seven children who reached this age when this report was due) also averaged 111.0.

The prenatal and early infancy component of this program featured weekly home visits by paraprofessionals who provided information on prenatal and child nutrition, demonstrated ways of nurturing child development, and assisted parents in coping with their problems. Both the in-home program and the half-day center-based program (begun at six months) emphasized the use of routine caregiving activities (such as diapering) as opportunities for joyful emotional encounters, language experiences, and the building of positive self-concepts.

By twenty-four months, a full-day, multiage group experience (modeled after the curriculum of the British infant schools) was begun. This program allows children to choose their activities from among listening and looking experiences, expressive play, small-muscle games, and large-muscle games—with different areas of the center and different teachers set aside for each activity.

In addition, weekly in-service training sessions were held for all teachers and for family members who wanted to attend them. Frequent (center-based) meetings between mothers and staff members were also encouraged.

Some Other Successful Early Intervention Programs

A program of parental education, begun when children were three months old and continued until age three, "normalized" the IQ performance of a group of children from indigent Black families in northern Florida. In this program, paraprofessionals were used to demonstrate specifically designed home learning activities. The purpose of these activities was to teach parents how to engage in instructional interactions with their children. The home visits averaged only *twice every three weeks* until age two, at which time most of the children received twice-weekly two-hour sessions at a backyard "center," where a "parent-educator" worked with five children and one mother. The project was terminated at age three. The six-year Stanford-Binet IQ scores for this group averaged 98. In a follow-up study, these researchers (Guinagh and Gordon, 1976) found that in the third grade only 10 percent of these children were in special education classes, compared with 30 percent among controls.

A program that administered care for ten hours a day from five months to two years of age "normalized" the IQ scores of the children of teenage, minority-group mothers whose IQs would otherwise be expected to average a full standard deviation below the norm (Lewis and others, 1975). Six of the seven children whose IQs were assessed at three to three and a half years of age or later (on the just-normed 1972 Stanford-Binet) had scores between 91 and 116.[23] This program provided a one-to-four caretaker ratio, emphasized individualized stimulation, and allowed for maternal involvement in the center on a weekly basis (including counseling, education, and training for parents).

Retarded Women as Caretakers: The Skeels Study

What would happen if children, aged seven months to three years, who had suffered severe delays in cognitive development (from an almost total lack of nurturing and stimulation) were to be placed in the care of a group of severely retarded women?

In a landmark study (Skeels, 1966), thirteen children who had been reared in an Iowa orphanage (where virtually the only care they received was feeding and changing) were transferred to an institution for the retarded. The IQs of these children underwent a rapid "rebound" to the normal range, which was then sustained into adulthood.

This "experiment" grew out of the serendipitous finding that two orphaned girls who had been placed in a ward of retarded women whose mental ages ranged from five to nine had experienced a dramatic increase, rather than the "usual" continuing fall, in their IQ scores. Each of the two girls was, in a sense, adopted by an older woman in the ward, with the other women acting as "adoring aunts." Attendants and nurses also showered affection on the infants, spending time with them, taking them on trips, and supplying them with an abundance of toys, picture books, and play materials. This led to a trial with eleven additional children, with similar results. Once again, the residents became very fond of these infants and took great pride in them. In almost every case, one adult (either an older girl or an attendant) became particularly attached to an infant. The eleven children spent an average of nineteen months in the wards before returning to the orphanage, after which most were quickly adopted.

The earlier these children were transferred to the wards, the better was their IQ prognosis. When IQ was assessed three years after they returned to the orphanage (at an average of six years of age), eight children who had transferred to the institution before eighteen months of age had IQ scores averaging 107, compared with an average score of 92 for five children who were not transferred until twenty-two to thirty-six months of age (and with an average score of 66 at age eight for a control group that remained in the orphanage).[24]

In a follow-up study, the IQs of the twenty-eight offspring of these children were found to be quite normally distributed (Skeels, 1966).

10.4 The Kibbutz Experience

Perhaps the best evidence that a good early environment can routinely engender superior intellectual abilities comes from a 1968 study of nearly 1,600 kibbutz-reared children (from 125 kibbutzim) whose parents had migrated to Israel from a variety of foreign countries (Smilansky and Smilansky, 1968). This study was specifically designed to compare and contrast the IQ scores of children whose parents had migrated from Middle Eastern or North African counties with (1) families in which one parent was of European (Ashkenazi) extraction and (2) matched controls[25] in which both parents were of European origin.

In Israel, the IQs of the offspring of immigrants from under-developed Sephardic lands tended to be far lower than the IQs of children of European immigrants, probably averaging between 92 and 95 and when the father's education had not gone beyond elementary school only 90 (Smilansky, 1964). By contrast, the offspring of poorly educated European immigrants were found to have IQs averaging 105, while those whose fathers had more than a high school education averaged 125 (Smilansky and Smilansky, 1968).

The IQs (Stanford-Binet and WISC) of kibbutz-born children were found to be exceptionally high, irrespective of their fathers' education, even though parental education persisted as an

Table 29. Percentages of Kibbutz-Born Children Aged Six to Fourteen with IQs in the "High," "Superior," or "Very Superior" Ranges, by Father's Education and Parents' Place of Birth.

	Cumulative Percent with IQ Above		
Father's Education and Place of Birth	*128*	*120*	*110*
High School Graduate			
Both Parents European	26.1	47.0	71.2
One Parent European	19.7	42.3	74.6
Both Parents Middle Eastern/North African	0.4	40.8	65.2
Elementary School or Less			
Both Parents European	11.2	28.0	46.4
One Parent European	8.4	31.3	48.2
Both Parents Middle Eastern/North African	5.0	12.5	27.6
Normal (U.S.) Population	(2.2)	(8.9)	(25.0)

Note: IQs were measured on the WISC (1947). The sample included 401 children whose fathers were high school graduates and 268 whose fathers had an elementary school education (or less). It excludes 309 whose fathers had some high school education (the scores of these children were midway between the scores of the other two groups).
Source: Adapted from Smilansky and Smilansky, 1968.

important determinant of IQ differences among these children (see Tables 29 and 30):

- The average IQ of the (400) children tested at age four to five (on the Stanford-Binet) was 123, including 119 for children with two Sephardic parents and 125 for children one or both of whose parents were European.
- The 1,150 children tested at age six to fourteen whose fathers had completed high school were **ten times more likely to be in the "very superior" range** (128 or higher on the WISC) and five times more likely to be in the "superior" or higher ranges than the norm. However, the proportions of children in these upper ranges declined as their fathers' education decreased, particu-

Table 30. Mean IQ of Kibbutz-Born Children Aged Four to Five,
by Father's Education and Place of Birth (Stanford Binet, Form M).

| | Parental Background | | |
Paternal Education	Two Sephardic Parents	One European Parent	Two European Parents
Elementary school or less	114.2	119.6	118.7
Some high school	119.5	125.1	124.6
High school or more	123.5	128.7	128.1
Average	119.0	125.8	124.1

Source: Smilansky and Smilansky, 1968.

larly among the offspring of immigrants from Arab lands.

The subsections that follow describe the nature of the home and educational environments provided by kibbutzim, detail and analyze the IQ scores of children raised in these settings, and assess the possible reasons for and implications of these findings. Some broader issues—intelligence and giftedness among the Jewish people and the potential contribution of the Jewish home life and Jewish mothering to the development of these characteristics—are addressed in Chapter Fourteen.

10.5 The Early Home and Educational Environments in Israeli Kibbutzim

The educational environment that these kibbutzim provided during the children's formative years appears to have been exceptional. Even though there was not a heavy emphasis in the early years on academic learning or competitive accomplishment, many elements of these kibbutzim appear to have fostered a favorable rate of cognitive development. These included outstanding child-caretaker ratios, the excellent quality of the caretaking staff, and avoidance of certain behaviors known to be deleterious to cognitive performance.

The living arrangements of young kibbutz-reared children are (with some variability) as follows: (1) "infants' homes" (from five to seven days after birth through twelve to eighteen months of age); (2) "toddlers' homes" (until about age three); and (3) the "kindergarten house" (from ages three to five or four to six).

The actual caretaker-child ratios reported by these researchers were, in most kibbutzim, far superior to their "prescribed" standards.[26] In the infants' homes, "the average number of children per nurse in one [kibbutz] movement was 3.1 and in another 3.6" (Smilansky and Smilansky, 1968, p. 24). In the toddlers' homes studied, there was an average of 6.8 children to 3.0 caretakers in one movement, and a 7.1 to 3.1 ratio in another.[27] Every kindergarten group (excepting small kibbutzim in isolated areas) had four or five nursery teachers/attendants, with ratios averaging 13.4 to 4.4 in one movement and 15.7 to 4.8 in another.

Parental involvement is also considerable. The mother and nurse are "jointly responsible for the infant's care" up to the age of nine months. For the first six weeks, the mother is relieved of all work duties, and until the child is four months old she is on a half-day work schedule.[28] During this period, the mother is responsible for the afternoon washing and changing and play period with the infant. Other family members visit at this time (while the nurse has her time off). At six months of age, a child's early evening hours are spent in its parents' quarters, where it is an object of attention and play for family and friends. The mother may continue to visit the child several times a day after the weaning period.[29]

During toddlerhood, the nursery teacher is totally in charge of the child's development and education. The daily schedule includes group visits to various parts of the kibbutz, storytelling, singing, and physical exercises. At age two, children get two long periods of *unrestricted* free play in a (spacious, well-equipped) courtyard, one in the morning and another, indoors or outdoors (as the child pleases), in the afternoon. Two hours in the evening are spent with the family, and bedtime includes a story or a lullaby.

Kindergarten stresses (1) "opportunities for rich, varied and directed experiences" both within the kindergarten and all about the kibbutz (including frequent guided tours of kibbutz installations)(Smilansky and Smilansky, 1968, p. 30); (2) freedom to select activities, with encouragement to do so;[30] (3) directed group learning, including gym and rhythmic motion lessons, the teaching of stories and songs (in part, tied in with holiday celebrations), and, during the final transition stages, the rudiments of reading and arithmetic. At about age seven, formal schooling begins with what is the equivalent of second grade.

The most frequent elementary school class size is fourteen, with one teacher and one attendant. If the class is as large as twenty, there will generally be two teachers and two attendants; this is in part because classes (in the smaller kibbutzim) may encompass an age span of two or three years (which also necessitates some individualized instruction). In elementary school, tasks are frequently assigned to groups and/or individuals within a group in such a way that children can contribute according to their abilities. The ideological emphasis is on the project (as an integrated, thematic teaching tool and method). Children read material, discuss it, carry out experiments, and write their own reports and summaries. The climate is one of cooperation and tolerance rather than competition, and the gifted are encouraged to help the less talented. There are generally three to five hours of formal study, covering four to six lesson areas.

This entire educational experience takes place against a backdrop of two additional psychocultural dimensions: (1) a strong desire to develop interdependence among kibbutz members, so that an individual comes to consider himself or herself as part of a "we"; and (2) a cultural milieu whose social and cognitive norms were, for the most part, determined by those kibbutz members who (before the Nazi era) had been part of the upper educational strata of Europe.

The strong influence that these highly educated European Jews had on the decisions of the strictly democratic kibbutz government helped ensure that candidates for child-care responsibility were well selected, that superior training programs were organized at the kibbutz and university levels, and that most kibbutzim acquired ample and high-quality play and learning equipment.

IQ Scores: Findings and Analysis

As shown in Table 29, somewhere between 20 and 25 percent of the kibbutz-born offspring of immigrants who were high school graduates scored in the borderline genius or higher ranges (on the WISC), compared with the 2.2 percent rate expected in a normal population. Moreover, there was five times the normal rate of superior or higher-IQ children (45 percent compared with an expected rate of 9 percent). Conversely, only 1.4 percent of these children scored below 90, compared with the 25 percent in a normal population who would do so.

Despite these high averages and smaller-than-usual disparities in the distribution of the IQ scores, the environmental equality provided to children belonging to the same educational unit in a kibbutz did not eliminate the IQ gap between children from well-educated families and children from poorly educated ones, nor did it eliminate the effects of geographical ancestry—even though it reduced both of these effects considerably. For example, although children from Sephardic families where the father's education did not exceed elementary school performed considerably above average, they scored substantially lower than did the children from better-educated and/or European families. Even among this poorly educated Sephardic group, however, gains on the order of 15 points occurred (compared with the average score reported for this group in the Israeli community at large).

These Wechsler IQ test scores are likely to both overstate and understate the IQ distribution of this population. On the one hand, although performance was measured on what was the most recent (1947) version of the WISC, IQ scores in general increased considerably during the twenty years between this test norming and the study—by perhaps 4 or 5 points (see Chapter Five). On the other hand, the Wechsler— even though considered superior to the Stanford-Binet in quantifying and delineating the parameters of cognitive *deficits*—seems to do a poorer job of discerning differences among people whose IQs are near the upper end of the intelligence scale. Moreover, because Jewish people are more likely to excel in the verbal and symbolic analytical domains, and the Stanford-Binet has a markedly higher verbal factor loading, there is a quite pervasive tendency for Jewish people to perform somewhat better on the Stanford-Binet than on the Wechsler (see Chapter Fourteen).

Table 30 presents the average Stanford-Binet scores for 400 kibbutz-born children aged four and five. Although this test (the Stanford-Binet form M) was normed considerably earlier than the WISC, the annual "rate of inflation" in IQ scores has been slower than on the Wechsler, so scores may be overstated by 5 to 7 points. However, because of this study's selection criteria, the IQs of kibbutz-born children in general are apt to be **much higher** than those of the children selected for inclusion in the study. Three reasons can be singled out:

- The large majority of kibbutz children had parents who migrated from Westernized nations.
- One of the criteria for the selection of the European kibbutz children who served as controls was that their fathers' educational level closely approximate that of the Middle Eastern or North African children selected. Consequently, a greater proportion of the heads of all the Ashkenazi families living in kibbutzim would have a high school education—in other words, a better education than those selected for the study.[31]
- Many of the kibbutzim with the highest concentrations of well-educated Ashkenazi families were likely to be underrepresented in this survey or not represented at all.

Thus, despite the somewhat dated nature of the IQ instruments used, certain conclusions can be drawn from these data:

First, the IQ scores of children whose parents migrated to Israel from (semifeudal) Arab lands, can be increased quite dramatically as a result of the kibbutz experience. Second, *for the offspring of well-educated European families, growing up in a kibbutz is likely to engender an extraordinarily high IQ.* Third, parental education nonetheless continues to be an important determinant of individual IQ differences.

These findings, however, need not imply that the kibbutz environment also engendered a large increase in the rate of giftedness among the offspring of well-educated European Jews. This is because (as documented in Chapter Fourteen) the proportion of extremely high IQ children of European Jewish ancestry found in this study was not dramatically higher than that regularly found among the offspring of reasonably well-educated Jewish parents (Ashkenazi or Sephardic) living in highly cultured lands throughout the world (for example, the United States, South Africa, Hong Kong, and Canada). But neither can it be said that this environment inhibited their intellectual development materially.

Another question of more than passing interest can also be addressed by analyzing data from this study, namely, Will the IQ gains achieved by the children of these Sephardic immigrants dissipate to some degree when these children reach adolescence? To address this question, the Wechsler scores of Sephardic children aged six to eleven were compared with the scores of those aged twelve to thirteen. The results show only a slight attenuation in the IQ performance of this group, particularly when these scores are related to the "expected" performance of nonkibbutz offspring of Sephardic immigrants:

- When the father's education was elementary school or less, scores averaged 106.3 at ages six to eleven and 104.7 at ages twelve to thirteen.
- When the father had some secondary school education but was not a graduate, scores averaged 116.4 at ages six to eleven and 109.3 at ages twelve to thirteen.
- When the father was a high school graduate, scores

averaged 116.5 at ages six to eleven and 112.8 at ages twelve to thirteen.

However, the slightly lower IQ performance of these older children can also be attributed to other factors. The parents of these older children migrated to Israel during an era when large numbers of new immigrants had to be housed, fed, and acclimated to Israeli life. By contrast, the younger children surveyed had parents who were likely to have been in Israel for a somewhat longer time and were also likely to have been reared in more firmly established kibbutz educational systems. Thus, by all appearances, the IQ gains of these children either did not dissipate at all in early adolescence or declined only to a small extent.

Implications of the Kibbutz Experience

These results suggest that, in the late 1960s, about **a fourth** of all kibbutz-born children would score at the level of **borderline genius or above** on well-respected, comprehensive (although somewhat dated) IQ tests and that an additional fourth would perform at the level often referred to as "potentially gifted."

Upon further analysis, these results appear to reflect three factors: (1) the environmentally enriching aspects of the educational programs in these kibbutzim, (2) the level of competency of the caretakers, and (3) the effect of those kibbutz children of innately high intelligence on other kibbutz children.

Clearly, the environment provided by these kibbutzim contains numerous elements that foster cognitive development:

- *Avoidance of restriction and punitiveness at age two*: A great deal of free play is allowed in spacious, well-equipped courtyards. Clear rules are enforced by "professionals," who are themselves supervised by the governing committee of the kibbutz.
- *Variety of stimulation*: There is a heavy emphasis on daily group visits during toddlerhood, and the child is ex-

posed daily to several caretakers, including his or her mother, other family members, and teachers.

- *Responsivity*: The child-care staff is of professional quality, there are low caretaker ratios, and mothers feel less beleaguered. This, together with the *ingrained* responsivity associated with "the Jewish mother," combine to ensure a high degree of immediate and adequate response to the child's initiatives.

- *Provision of an intellectual and cultural environment*: The kibbutz emphasizes verbal stimulation, the use of "contingent responsivity" as an educational tool, the verbal encouragement of attention to novelty, and the labeling of objects and events.

Additionally, the IQ gains of the Middle Eastern and North African children in part reflect their heavy exposure to "housemates" whose well-educated Ashkenazi parents would score in the top 10 percent on intelligence tests. The atmosphere was one in which brighter and older children were greatly encouraged to help their classmates who were less well endowed intellectually. Further, the IQ gains made by the "kibbutz" children of poorly educated immigrants from Arab regions compared with their "nonkibbutz" counterparts suggest that most children could benefit intellectually from being reared in such an environment.

10.6 Sustainability of IQ Gains Generated by Environmental Enrichment Programs

It is clear, then, that environmental enrichment programs begun in infancy and toddlerhood are capable of generating substantial and long-lasting increases in IQ. The extent of the IQ gains achieved and the degree to which these can be sustained in the years following completion of such programs appear to depend on several factors:

- The overall quality of the enrichment program in terms of program content, staff quality, caretaker ratio, and intensity and duration of training.
- The child's age when introduced to the program.
- The extent to which the postprogram environment offers opportunities to use and expand upon the program's cognitively enriching features—opportunities that, in part, depend on the success of efforts to train parents to be effective child educators.

Taken together, these studies also indicate that the IQ-point gains registered by children who—even in the absence of enrichment—would be expected to have above-average IQs tend to be somewhat smaller but also somewhat easier to sustain than those registered by children reared in families from the lower third of the socioeconomic-class distribution.

These may be several explanations for the relatively mixed long-term results reported in evaluations of preschool programs serving lower-SES populations (Lazar and Darlington, 1982), as well as for the indications that the IQ gains made by disadvantaged populations reported in this chapter are somewhat less sustainable than are those of above-average SES populations. The most plausible of these explanations is that the postprogram environment of families living in above-average SES neighborhoods is more conducive to applying and enlarging on the cognitive skills taught. Another consideration is that children from above-average SES families are more likely to possess a better set of information-processing skills at program entry. Conversely, because of the somewhat greater likelihood that children from lower economic strata will have deficiencies in these basic skills, it may be difficult for them to extend the knowledge that they acquire to advanced analytical contexts.

However, it appears that the basis used by many researchers to conclude that preschool compensatory programs are of little lasting value is highly flawed. This is because a major portion of the IQ losses reported for minority-group populations in the years following participation in these programs appears to be **an artifact of the test measures used and thus does not repre-**

sent an actual IQ decline. For example, in the report of the Consortium for Longitudinal Studies (Lazar and Darlington, 1982), the IQ scores of the children served by these programs were considerably lower when they were retested on the revised and renormed (1972) Wechsler IQ tests. What should be emphasized, however, is that **the IQs reported for controls fell by the same amount** as did the scores of program participants.

Thus, the findings of the long-term evaluations of Preschool Compensatory Education Programs (Head Start) appear to have been **seriously biased by outside factors that negatively affected the *relative* position of low-income Black families on IQ tests** between 1947 and 1972. The findings do not, in other words, mean that the IQs of these children fell as they matured.

If the WISC-R and the (mid-1980s) Stanford-Binet standardization samples are indicative of real-world trends in IQ performance (see, for example, section 6.2), *the relative position of low-income Black children first worsened between 1947 and 1972 **and then registered a considerable improvement in the following decade.***

Several good reasons exist for concluding that the differential trends observed over these two time periods did in fact occur. Among these are events that affected (1) trends in child health; (2) the nature and timing of the enormous changes that occurred in the demographics of these populations; (3) the cumulative effects of what, in 1972, had been recently instituted governmental antipoverty programs on maternal health and education and child development; and (4) the cumulative effects of the breaking down of racial barriers to employment and education.

In 1947, illness was of far greater importance as a cause of low IQ than in 1972, as the benefits of modern medicine began to be felt throughout mainstream America. This health revolution, however, did not deeply permeate the lower-income Black community until the establishment and expansion of major governmental child health programs (including Medicaid) in the 1960s and 1970s.

A massive decline in the number of families below or near the poverty level occurred between 1947 and 1972 (with little change since). This decline took place almost entirely among intact families, being especially helped by a sharp drop in the number of very large families. Because the rate of single-parent families in the Black community in 1972 was three to four times that of Caucasian families,[32] the decline in the rate of poor and marginally poor Black families was proportionately less. In addition, the "post-pill baby bust" had, to a large extent, run its course in the White community—in contrast to the Black community, where birthrates continued to decline sharply for another decade. Moreover, the huge migration of Blacks from the rural South to the urban Northeast and Midwest had the effect of depriving Black children of the family support networks that, in earlier generations, had provided favorable caretaker ratios (which helped to offset some of the deleterious effects of single parentage on cognitive development).

The average level of educational attainment of new parents soared in the generation following World War II, particularly among Caucasian women. But again, it was not until the 1970s and 1980s that any significant proportion of Black women began to achieve the kinds of gains that their Caucasian counterparts had achieved a generation earlier. The cumulative effects of *Brown* v. *Board of Education*, the development of widespread higher education tuition assistance programs, and the breaking down of entry barriers to universities and jobs gradually combined to improve the abilities of Black parents as child educators.

The considerable (10-point) IQ advantage of northeastern Blacks (on the WISC-R) compared to southern Blacks (see Chapter Six) strongly suggests that IQ gains occurred in those areas of the country where comprehensive health and social service programs substantially predated national legislation. This hypothesis gains support from the studies noted in Table 31. In the two rural area studies (Gordon, in northern Florida, and Gray, in Tennessee), large IQ losses were associated with the WISC revision and renorming, compared with the results reported in urban areas (Miller, in Louisville, Kentucky, and Palmer, in Harlem). This urban-rural differential (examining only the IQ score decline among the controls) averaged nearly 7 points, and implies that *governmental antipoverty programs have been effective in raising the IQs of minority-group children.*

Test-Retest Incompatibilities

In addition to the IQ losses caused by the shift to later-normed tests, it is also apparent that the reported scores of children benefiting from early enrichment programs suffered considerably in those instances where the basis of determining IQ was shifted from the Stanford-Binet (the most frequently used preschool IQ measure) to the Wechsler (the most frequently used school-age measure).

It is clear from the correspondences between IQ and the

Table 31. Change in IQ Scores over the Age Spans Indicated Among Participants in Preschool Compensatory Education Programs and Their Controls.[33]

Project and Ages at Which IQ Was Measured	Change in Average IQ	
	Program Participants	Controls
Projects Using the Revised and Renormed Wechsler Scales		
Gordon: 6 and 10	− 10.9	− 9.8
Gray: 10 and 17	− 9.7	− 8.5
Miller: 8 and 13	− 4.8	− 3.0
Palmer: 5 and 12	− 4.0	− 2.3
Projects Using the Unrevised Wechsler Examinations		
Levenstein: 7 and 10	− 0.6	− 6.3
Weikert: 10 and 14	− 4.0	− 3.9
Unweighted Averages: six programs	− 5.7	− 5.7

Source: Adapted from Lazar and Darlington, 1982.

home environment presented throughout this volume that the verbal and symbolic aspects of IQ are influenced to a considerably greater degree by the early environment than is the visuospatial-figural dimension. Thus, the somewhat greater verbal factor loadings of the Stanford-Binet favor a higher IQ outcome among children who have received early (verbally oriented) educational stimulation of the kinds discussed in this chapter. Consequently, there is likely to be a considerable difference in performance on the Wechsler and the Stanford-Binet among such children. In a practical sense, since success in academic endeavors and employment is, in most fields, more heavily dependent on verbal skills than on performance IQ, the Stanford-Binet approach to assessing cognitive ability seems preferable.

Consequently, it may be concluded that IQ gains generated by these early environmental enrichment programs are more sustainable than they appear initially,[33] particularly in the areas of greatest practicality.

Why Programs Begun Early Are More Effective in Enhancing IQ

Data concerning the so-called critical periods of brain growth (elaborated on in Chapter Nineteen) suggest that programs begun after the age of two or three—even though capable of inducing considerable short-term increases in cell-to-cell communication—have little effect on the biological *foundations* that underlie the ability of these cells (neurons) to sustain this communication in the absence of continued nurturing. By contrast, efforts begun in infancy and/or early toddlerhood are able to modify the primary (inner) branches of the "dendritic trees" of these brain cells (that is, the message-receiving extensions that sprout from these cell bodies) and thus are better able to create lifelong changes in the **capacity** to generate and sustain cellular and biochemical responses to cognitive stimulation.

Thus, it is appropriate to undertake a detailed analysis of the behavioral and neurobiological stage of infancy and toddlerhood, with a view toward discerning stage-dependent intervention strategies. Although this review is presented in the next chapter, readers who prefer to first acquaint themselves with the biological underpinnings of intellect and giftedness may wish to examine Chapters Fifteen, Sixteen, and Seventeen.

Notes

1. The program (which employed a child-caretaker ratio of less than two to one) was continued for five to seven months for eighteen children (including the group of toddlers); the remaining infants were enrolled for an average of sixteen months. Three-fourths of the children were firstborn, and five were Black. The scores of a group of nine disadvantaged infants (from single-parent welfare families) who were also enrolled in this program reached a high of 125 at program's end (for those old enough to take the Stanford-Binet). At age six, however, their scores fell to 109.5 (on the renormed Binet), although this was still considerably above the norm.

2. The mean paternal education was 15.6 years and the mean maternal education was 14.1 years. At fifteen months, their "REEL" scores averaged 168 for "receptive" and 151 for "expressive" language. The adverse circumstances included (1) marital breakup, (2) maternal employment

and placement of the child in a bilingual day-care program, (3) fever-related seizures that necessitated the long-term use of phenobarbital.

3. These children were White, from middle-class and upper-middle-class families; all were firstborns whose mothers had been enrolled in La Lèche classes. The last child started at a younger age (at three rather than six months of age) and participated for a shorter duration (five versus seven months); these scores were the last available, until (at my request) Drash was able to locate two of the participants and ascertain their recent IQ-test scores; at age thirteen, one scored 139 on the WISC-R and the other (who took only the verbal portion of the test) also scored 139.

4. "An analysis of the items on the Vineland indicated that this assessment tool primarily measures self-help skills. The Behar Preschool Behavior Questionnaire was used to evaluate those social skills required in interpersonal interactions" (Drash and Stollberg, 1979, p. 4).

5. Reports of noncompliance with verbal commands at seven months (when the children learned a means of self-locomotion) were averted through the demonstration of behavior control techniques and the early identification of one parent as an effective disciplinarian.

6. This infant, who was in the program for the shortest period, was considerably less advanced at the twenty-month testing but subsequently developed an exceptionally high IQ (160 at forty-one months).

7. This program of operant conditioning of speech, which is modeled after the Kennedy Program, has also been proven effective as a facilitator of mental development in Down's syndrome children, the principal focus of Drash's efforts in recent years. An almost year-for-year growth in cognitive development among Down's syndrome children has recently been reported by Drash and Tutor (forthcoming).

8. This difference was significant at $p < .001$; the highest average score was achieved on the "auditory comprehension" subscale (the other components being "language age" and "verbal ability"). White limited this program to first-time parents because his earlier work indicated substantially greater success in altering their behavior patterns.

9. The Kaufman provides scores on two subscales, "sequential processing" (an essentially left-hemisphere domain that includes the "faces and places" subtest) and "simultaneous processing" (or essentially right-hemisphere functions, which includes the hand movements subtest). The children's scores on each of these scales averaged 117, despite their mediocre performances on the two subtests.

10. The average family attended thirteen group meetings and had twenty-three private (principally in-home) visits; child-care problems not related to the educational regimen (such as child health, feeding problems, or parental discord) were not addressed by this program.

11. Background factors included (1) the average social-class standing of the biological parent(s) was well below average; (2) almost half were of mixed or West Indian parentage; (3) only a fourth were visited regularly by their mothers and two-thirds had no family contacts; (4) many of the White children had not been adopted because of a family history of "psychopathy" or epilepsy; and (5) although 70 percent had been

placed in these nurseries before their first birthday, 15 percent were placed after age two.

12. At least one standard deviation above the average measured in terms of staff autonomy, the length of time that the staff had worked with the same group of children, and the staff ratio. The sample was stratified to ensure that nurseries with exceedingly high and low staff autonomy were included.

13. The Reynell scores had been converted to a standard deviation of ten; the Minnesota test was only given to the children aged three and older, excluding the children aged two to two and a half. The Reynell Comprehension scores averaged slightly higher, 106.7.

14. In the best-staffed nurseries, there were at least two staff members for every six children; in the worst-staffed facilities, a six-to-one ratio existed for "much of the day."

15. Reynell "expressive language" scores (which, in the middle area of the IQ distribution, tend to show a relatively lower correlation with IQ than does language comprehension) were not materially affected by this qualitative variable; the all-nursery average for expressive language was 98.5.

16. Provided by the staff on a group basis, not an individual-child basis (measured over four half-day observation periods); see section 8.6 for a definition of "informative talk."

17. When a child was fifteen to twenty months old (depending on his or her progress), he or she was grouped with two other children and brought into contact with three different teachers for specific instructional areas. Schedules for children under twenty-four months were varied in accordance with their moods and attention spans.

18. The mothers of the controls had IQs of 80 or below (rather than 75); thus, the average IQs of controls would be expected to be slightly higher than those of the experimental group. The Stanford-Binet scores of this experimental group averaged 123 between the ages of three and six.

19. The rehabilitation program concentrated primarily on developing job skills and thereafter on reading skills and home management abilities. The wage differential (converted to mid-1980s purchasing power) averaged well over $100 a week; nevertheless, the program itself was extremely expensive (in part, because of proven financial mismanagement).

20. Their scores (at age four) were also 9.3 points above those of matched controls (who were also the younger siblings of attendees of the same nursery school).

21. The tutors were college graduates (of differing undergraduate disciplines) with experience and interest in working with very young children.

22. Near-optimal test-taking conditions increased the reported IQs of a number of children, especially among controls. Because thirty-month-old children are not consistent in their ability to be attentive, postponements were common; a considerable effort was also made to establish a comfortable relationship between child and test giver be-

fore testing. The average score of the controls (many of whom could not complete the testing until the third scheduled session) was 98.6, among the highest in the literature for children of this background.

23. Their scores (as part of a slightly larger sample) averaged 10 points higher on an earlier-normed Stanford-Binet (1960), but this average included some younger children (aged two and a half); greater gains were also suggested by a twenty-four-month assessment (the Merrill-Palmer Mental-Age and the Bayley MDI). Unfortunately, no follow-up IQ testing was undertaken.

24. Excludes one (low-IQ) "outlier" in each group; inclusion of these outliers would lower the scores of each of these groups by 6 points. When these children returned to the orphanage the average score of the early "transferees" was 99, and the scores of those who transferred after twenty-two months averaged 88.

25. Children of the same sex reared in the same educational group, matched according to their fathers' educational background, length of time in Israel, and so on. Some stratification was undertaken to ensure adequate representation of kibbutzim from each of the major kibbutz movements.

26. This was because parents insisted on more intensive care or because fewer babies were born.

27. Theoretical ratios were one nursery teacher and one assistant for six children, or nine children with two nursery teachers plus part-time help, or two groups of four children with two nurses.

28. In most kibbutzim (in the 1960s), parents were encouraged to visit their babies at all hours.

29. After which, if she is nursing, she gets one hour off for each feeding (which she must "repay" at a later date); otherwise, the child is weaned at four to five months.

30. "In many kibbutzim, children may go on playing or drawing during mealtimes, and may leave the table as soon as they have finished, even when others are still eating" (Smilansky and Smilansky, 1968, p. 31).

31. Nevertheless, this bias is somewhat confounded by the deleterious effects of the Nazi era on educational attainment, which affected European Jews to a greater extent than it did Sephardim.

32. Before the dramatic rise in marital breakup in the Caucasian community reduced this disadvantage.

33. For example, in the Milwaukee Project, only a 4-point decline in the Wechsler IQ score average occurred when test results at ages four to six were compared with those at ages nine to ten.

Contents

ᴚ *11* ᴙ

Accelerating an Infant's Cognitive Development

11.1 Introduction: Early Infancy as a Window of Opportunity

Because the cognitive abilities of young infants are extremely limited, very few infant-care specialists have advocated teaching babies in any formal way before the sixth postnatal month. However, as techniques for assessing cognitive abilities in early infancy have improved, an awareness has grown that newborn infants possess some rather remarkable visual, auditory, and sensory-integrative competencies. This suggests that structured efforts to provide appropriate auditory and visual stimuli *during the first several months of infancy* can accelerate cognitive development and, by so doing, enhance lifelong problem-solving abilities.

Therefore, to aid parents and child educators who want to structure a regimen of stimulation suitable to an infant's physical needs, attentional limitations, and motivational interests, this chapter presents an overview of the newborn infant's cognitive abilities and how these change during the initial months of life.

Many early nurturing behaviors ordinarily carried out by parents promote cognitive development. The most important of these (1) help a baby arrive at and maintain a state conducive to learning; (2) elicit its attention to sights and sounds in the environment; (3) match the visual and verbal stimuli presented and the manner of their presentation to the individual infant's abilities and motivational interests; and, perhaps most importantly, (4) provide an infant with the self-esteem that grows out of the sense that it is highly valued.

Fortunately, the human brain's information-processing systems seem to possess an intrinsic need for stimulation. If given appropriate opportunities, therefore, the infant will tend to take great pleasure from solving the kinds of problems that its brain is "programmed" to analyze. This sort of problem-solving compulsion is also found in monkeys. For example, in a landmark study, after working at repeatedly disassembling a six-device puzzle for ten consecutive hours, with no reward other than the privilege of taking it apart, monkeys still demonstrated great enthusiasm for this task (Harlow, Harlow, and Meyer, 1950; Harlow, 1950). It would seem to follow that providing an infant with a regimen of effectively constructed learning tasks will—in addition to laying the basis for what society considers highly valued skills—also promote an avid interest in mentally challenging pursuits. Moreover, if such an interest on the part of the infant can be coupled with the growing self-esteem that it derives from achieving desirable consequences from its actions, these early experiences should culminate in a lifelong love of learning.

How might child educators tap into the newborn's innate capacities for sensory analysis? There would seem to be four prerequisites for a successful early infant education program: (1) helping the baby achieve and maintain a "cognitive state" conducive to learning; (2) attracting the baby's attention to stimuli appropriate to its limited abilities; (3) using the kinds of "educational paradigms" that will enable infants to become skilled at categorizing objects and sounds; and (4) making these educational games enjoyable, so as to generate a positive motivation for infants to engage in them. To these ends, it would seem appropriate that early "infant lessons" do the following:

- Stress those nurturing behaviors used by caretakers in cultures that rear disproportionately large numbers of very intelligent children. One example is the heavy regimen of rocking and other soothing behaviors routinely employed by mothers in traditional Japanese and Jewish families (discussed in Chapters Thirteen and Fourteen).

- Adapt lesson plan motifs such as "repetition with patterned novelty" to the infants' developing visual and auditory discrimination skills.
- Expose infants to learning situations that enable them, by their actions, to affect their surroundings in a consistent manner.

11.2 The Three Cognitive Stages of Early Infancy

As experimental techniques for assessing infants' abilities have improved, so too has the research community's awareness that very young infants are, in several important respects, far more advanced than had been commonly believed.

Two factors—one behavioral and one biological—had made it difficult for researchers to appreciate the neonate's innate abilities. Behaviorally, the inability of ten-week-old infants to localize sounds in space and their lack of preference for three-dimensional objects over two-dimensional ones created the assumption that these infants *had simply not yet developed* certain cognitive abilities. Biologically, it was known that those portions of the cerebral cortex that perform "higher" visual and auditory analytics in adults are functionally immature until about the fourth month of infancy.

More recent findings, however, suggest a rather different picture, namely, that early infancy consists of three fairly distinct cognitive stages: (1) an initial period of integrated auditory, visual, and motor competence (somewhat analogous to the imprint period in many animals); (2) a transitory period of reduced three-dimensional perception (occurring at about ten weeks of age and associated with the development of specific auditory and visual pathways in the infant's brain); and (3) the emergence at about four months of age of more-advanced biological mechanisms for encoding and retaining cognitive information.

In the auditory domain, both day-old and month-old infants are capable of locating the source of sounds. For example, in one experiment, calm, well-fed, and swaddled neonates turned their heads correctly in response to sounds 87 percent of the time (Muir and Field, 1979). In another (Clarkson, Morrongiello, and Clifton, 1982), a 91 percent correct head-turn rate was reported (in the absence of "no head-turn" trials).[1] Although two- to three-month-old infants performed poorly on this task (Sullivan and Horowitz, 1983a; 1983b), with performance reaching its lowest point around eighty days of age, near-perfect performance is restored by four months (Muir and others, 1979; Muir, 1985). Correspondingly, in the visual domain, an early preference for gazing at three-dimensional objects (compared with two-dimensional views of the same stimulus) all but disappears by about eight weeks of age and then reappears more strongly a few weeks later.[2] Ten-day-old infants will reach out and touch a ball without hesitation, thereby demonstrating a remarkable degree of eye-hand coordination (Bower, 1971); yet, by the age of four weeks, this ability disappears and does not begin to reappear for another four months.

Neonates are also "programmed" to encode speech in a different manner than they do other environmental sounds — they use their left hemisphere to encode speech, their right to process other sounds — and by the time an infant is two or three days old, it can usually distinguish its own mother's voice from the voices of other mothers in the nursery. Further, after being with its mother three or four times, an infant is likely to prefer its mother's voice to all other stimuli (Mehler and others, 1978) and "will actively work to produce it" (DeCasper and Fifer, 1980, p. 1175), perhaps because the infant has become attuned to its mother's voice in the womb (DeCasper and Spence, 1986).[3] Moreover, newborns demonstrate a remarkable capacity for facial mimicry, including the ability to imitate expressions such as happiness, sadness, and surprise (Field, Woodson, Greenburg, and Cohen, 1982), orifacial stimuli such as tongue protrusions and mouth openings (Meltzoff and Moore, 1983), and sequential finger movements (Jacobson, 1979). Clearly, such an ability points to the existence of an instinctive matching process that enables newborns to perceive equivalences between body transformations that they see and body transformations of their own.

Thus, infants are very sensitive to the temporal and spatial information that characterizes human expressions and utterances and seem to possess an innate readiness to encode correspondences between the auditory and visual events that accompany this information, as well as the emotional aspects of the message. Moreover, a microanalysis of correspondences between changes in the sound elements of human speech and points of change in neonatal movement configurations indicates the existence of an exact synchrony, which is sometimes sustained over more than a 100-word spoken sequence (Condon and Sander, 1974), with other auditory stimuli evoking no such responses.[4] This has led several researchers to speculate that there is a "unity" of the senses of sight and hearing at birth (Sullivan and Horowitz, 1983a; 1983b) and to suggest that the infant's primary developmental task is to discover the distinctive features of each sight and sound present in the environment and to work out a set of flexible strategies for discovering the multimodal properties of objects/events (Spelke, 1979)[5] — goals that are achieved by active search and exploration, by looking and listening. Infants are also able to recognize whether visual patterns have been shown to them in the recent past, as evidenced by their behavior on "habituation and novelty" paradigms (described in section 7.4).[6]

Early infant memory has also been found to be more proficient than had previously been thought, now that techniques for optimizing the retrieval of learned information have improved. For example, researchers have demonstrated that even very young infants can learn to recognize a complex stimulus (a mobile) and retain this knowledge over long intervals (Rovee-Collier and Fagen, 1981). In these experiments, after two identical fifteen-minute training sessions on successive days, followed by a test of retention administered between two and fourteen days later, infants as young as eight weeks of age displayed a clear remembrance of mobiles that they had been shown. Rovee-Collier and Fagen's additional finding that a brief reexposure to the training stimulus prior to testing improves the accessibility of infant memory[7] is confirmed by other studies (for example, Cornell, 1979). The keys to creating such long-term retention are that (1) the stimulus presentation be associated with a "contingently responsive" event during which the infant, by its actions, is able to create a predictable and interesting consequence (such as making a mobile move or a music box play); (2) the training session be repeated or be fairly long; and (3) the surroundings at the time of retrieval be similar to those in which the experience was encoded.

The relatively short period during which infants' auditory and visual three dimensionality is reduced (which will be referred to as the GAP) is linked to the development of visual and auditory pathways that lead to and from a key midbrain area (the thalamus), especially those leading to and from the so-called auditory and occipital regions of the cerebral cortex. Once these regions become "hooked up" to the midbrain, they assume the primary responsibility for higher-order associative functions.[8] Thus, the interruption in the neonate's sensory-integrative capacities must mean that midbrain areas are performing functions that in older infants are undertaken in the cerebral cortex — the implication being that this transitory period constitutes a stage during which these functions are in the process of being "deeded over" from the thalamus and adjacent areas to the maturing cortex.[9]

The onset of this GAP is accompanied by the beginnings of strong, positive emotional responsiveness on the part of the infant. The infant begins to smile and coo quite vigorously in response not only to the human face but also to other objects whose behavior is contingently responsive to its own behavior (see section 8.4). As we have seen, the neonatal "imprint period" has an important survival value in that it endows the infant with the ability to respond to maternal nurturing. By eight or ten weeks of age, however — when the three-dimensional sensitivity and responsiveness have waned — the infant's ability to engage in vigorous smiling and cooing provides it with an alternative mechanism for strongly reinforcing this mutual bonding.

11.3 Infant Lessons During the First Few Months of Life

In the initial months of life, when a baby's motor control is very limited, its primary sources of cognitive awareness are its eyes and ears. Thus, attempts to promote awareness of distant categories should concentrate on matching visual and auditory stimuli to the infant's changing attention preferences and cognitive limitations.

Careful attention to stimulus presentation is especially important in the visual domain, where it might take the form of displaying an object at an optimal distance and angle, using preferred shapes, colors, and levels of complexity, and reinforcing the "lesson" at intervals conducive to the formation of a retrievable memory.

The development of auditory comprehension can be aided by using the following kinds of "interactive designs":

- *Slow repetition*, which helps a baby to apprehend the exact correspondence between a sound and the shape of the speaker's mouth.
- *Repetition with "patterned" novelty*, which evokes attention to the changing feature(s) of the sound, while ingraining its repeated aspects.
- *Vocal imitation*, which enables an infant to compare the products of its own vocalizations with an adult's perceptions and imitations.

As infants become familiar with the patterns governing the introduction, repetition, and disappearance of novel stimulus features, they begin to learn how to discern patterns, which permits them to assimilate more-complex patterns and strengthens their basic problem-solving mechanisms. In addition, a parent's impulsive inclination to imitate its baby's vocal sounds provides the infant with a biological mirror and echo, which allows it to compare auditory products on both sides and to learn which motor schema correspond to the sounds produced (Papousek and Papousek, 1981).

By creating learning situations that enable an infant, by its actions, to affect its surroundings, parents can help their baby to develop feelings of competence and effectiveness — which strengthen its motivation to learn — and also help it to integrate cognitive and kinesthetic functions. To this end, an infant's motor abilities (although limited) have often been employed effectively. For example, connecting a mobile to a baby's leg by a thread will usually result in its keeping the mobile moving for long periods of time (the importance of consistency in the use of contingent responsivity is discussed in sections 8.5 and 8.7).[10]

11.4 Evoking and Maintaining a Cognitive State Conducive to Learning

Newborn infants are best able to register and categorize things that they see and hear when they are in a state of "quiet alertness." In fact, during the first several weeks of life, quiet alertness appears to be the only state in which a baby is capable of assimilating new information; by contrast, in an "active alert state," young infants seem to be capable of practicing familiar tasks but not of assimilating new information (Wolff, 1965).[11]

During the initial weeks after birth, this quiet alert state usually begins after a feeding and bowel movement. During the first week, an infant is likely to be in this state for about ten minutes at a time (Clifton and Nelson, 1976), but the proportion may increase to 20 percent of its waking hours by the third or fourth week. How much time infants spend in this state is likely to be heavily influenced by the actions of its caregivers. By three months, nonfeeding alert periods average ninety minutes. An infant's alertness depends in part on its innate capacity, in part on the mother's ability to elicit "quiet alertness," and in part on the cultural norms that influence her willingness to do so (Bennett, 1971). Papousek, Papousek, and Bornstein (1985) suggest that the state of wakefulness can be lengthened by periodically altering the type of vocal stimulation and holding the baby in an upright position.

A significant impediment to attaining and remaining in this state is an infant's tendency toward becoming overaroused —

which explains the effectiveness of such soothing behaviors as rocking and swaddling in promoting quiet alertness. The calming effects of rocking come from the stimulation it provides to the infant's vestibular system. The immaturity of this system at birth requires it to obtain heavy stimulation, and insufficient vestibular stimulation is a major cause of crying. Aside from its calming effects, rocking also stimulates the developing infants' "ability to learn" in other ways—one of these being that it engages a reflexive tracking of moving objects[12] and another that it enables infants to practice their ability to join auditory and visual events intermodally, which in turn hones their ability to analyze movement across time.[13]

How effective rocking will be in calming an infant is a function of its frequency and displacement—but not of its direction (head-to-toe, side-to-side, and up-and-down rocking being equally effective). Apparently, relatively sharp change-of-direction movements best fulfill a baby's needs. In a series of studies with two-month-old infants (Ter Vrugt and Pederson, 1973; Pederson and Ter Vrugt, 1973; Pederson, 1975), frequencies of 70 to 90 cycles per minute, and a displacement of 1.5 Hz, were found to have the greatest efficacy, particularly among the most highly aroused infants. Thus, when their baby is over-aroused, parents should consider experimenting with greater rocking frequencies and velocities than they would ordinarily employ.

Swaddling—or binding an infant's arms and legs with soft cloths—is not a restriction of its otherwise naturally free condition; rather, it is a logical extension of the warmth and security of the womb. When infants are swaddled soon after birth, they not only accept this restraint but seem to welcome it as comfortable and familiar (Moss and Solomons, 1979).[14] A major benefit of swaddling is that it reduces the reflexive movements of the arms and legs to which newborns are often subjected. These seemingly purposeless movements tend to startle infants and cause insecurity, confusion, and overarousal.[15]

Several other studies have confirmed the soothing effects of swaddling (for example, Lipton, Steinschneider, and Richmond, 1965; Bloch, 1966; Giacoman, 1971; Brackbill, 1971; Romanko and Brost, 1982; Riccillo and Watterson, 1984). One of these (Brackbill, 1971) reports that when recently fed babies were swaddled, crying time was cut a remarkable 60 percent.[16] The swaddled infants slept more, *but not at the expense of quiet alert time, which increased 15 percent*. Further, in a study of hungry six-week-old infants, although the unswaddled babies cried for three-fourths of the observation period, the swaddled infants cried an average of only one-fifth of the time (Giacoman, 1971). Swaddled babies are also more apt to engage in long, quiet, peaceful sleep and tend to be calmer, as evidenced by lower cardiac and respiration rates (Lipton, Steinschneider, and Richmond, 1965; Whiting, 1981). "Extra" rocking also leads to the appearance of distinct sleep cycles at an earlier age (Restak, 1984), which implies that the maturational development of long-term memory is being accelerated.

Swaddling practices differ from culture to culture, varying in how tightly a baby is bundled, whether or not a rocking cradle is used, and how often free movement of the arms and legs (an unswaddled state) is allowed. If swaddling is undertaken, the swaddling practices of traditional Jewish families are strongly recommended. These practices include applying bindings to the baby's arms and legs softly, firmly, and caringly (using thin strips of linen or flannel), with only the head (which is laid upon a soft pillow) exposed.[17] After the first few weeks, the arms are freed and the wrappings relaxed, so that the restraint is made cozy. The swaddling is removed several times a day, during which time the baby's limbs are massaged and it is permitted to move freely, and it is preferable that verbal encouragement accompany these movements (see section 14.4).

Placing a baby on a lambskin rug instead of its usual bedding is also helpful in reducing overarousal. The lambskin keeps the baby warmer and drier and thereby induces longer, more restful periods of sleep (Montague, 1983).[18]

Another effective soothing mechanism is establishing eye contact and heightening this contact with vivid facial expressions such as widely opened eyes, raised eyebrows, an open mouth, and/or a smile of delight (Lewis and Goldberg, 1969).

The highly animated face elicits strong interest in infants and may lead them to attempt to communicate (Trevarthan, 1977).[19]

11.5 The Development of Visual Competence

Infants like to look at objects that contain a particular degree of contour density, they prefer certain shapes and colors to others, and, in early infancy, they have significant visual limitations. Because these limitations and preferences undergo considerable change during the first several months after birth, understanding these early visual preferences and how they change developmentally can enable parents and other infant caregivers to highlight visual stimuli more effectively.

One such early limitation relates to distance. The newborn infant can focus excellently at about seven and a half inches but considerably less well at much greater or lesser distances (Haynes, White, and Held, 1965). Even though there is a fairly rapid developmental progression of focusing abilities during the first month of infancy, an adult level of competency is not attained until six months of age (Banks and Salapetek, 1981; Banks, 1980; Olson and Sherman, 1983). Nevertheless, infants younger than three months of age still show significant focusing errors at viewing distances of less than two and a half feet (Braddick and others, 1979). Another limitation is that infants are initially unable to focus well on objects placed directly in front of them while objects introduced peripherally (ideally at about 40 degrees) tend to capture their attention.[20]

The motion of rocking helps young infants to follow and focus on moving objects. In fact, many aspects of infant perception depend on information that is given to them while they are in motion (Gibson, 1987), especially detecting the structure of three-dimensional objects.[21] During the first several months of life, a major portion of an infant's time is spent looking at things that change, or move, or have highly contrasting edges (Rheingold, Gewirtz, and Ross, 1959; Rheingold, 1961). Some early visual preferences include curved lines as opposed to wavy ones, regular/symmetrical/concentric patterns over irregular/asymmetrical/nonconcentric ones (Olson, 1979, 1981; Olson and Sherman, 1983), and patterns with a medium-high contour density.[22] Infants also tend to have distinct color preferences; for example, they tend to prefer blues and reds to yellows and greens (Peeples and Teller, 1975), presumably (at least in part) because they are less able to distinguish some wavelengths from white.

In the early weeks of life, infants display a marked preference for looking at objects containing a high brightness contrast (Fantz and Nevis, 1967b), with differences in black-and-white patterns being strongly preferred to differences in other attributes (including color, overall brightness, complexity, form, depth, or movement). This is apparently because infants require great amounts of contrast to distinguish differences spanning even moderate spacial frequencies (Aslin, 1986).

As early as two weeks after birth, infants show a strong preference for inspecting three-dimensional versions of objects, compared with analogous two-dimensional representations, but this preference for three-dimensionality all but disappears during the GAP.[23] During the initial weeks of infancy, larger versions of pictures (for example, a caricature of a face) are preferred to smaller ones (Fantz and Nevis, 1967a). With the onset of the GAP, however, this preference ends.[24]

One-month-old infants evidence an ability to discriminate shapes,[25] and the subject of changing shape and complexity preferences has been studied extensively. The studies summarized below and in the research literature[26] should help to acquaint parents and child educators with the type of information they are likely to encounter in the research literature. For example, Greenberg (Greenberg and O'Donnell, 1972) reports these findings:

- At six weeks of age, a 36-square black-and-white checkerboard pattern evokes far greater interest than either a 4-square or a 121-square version, and a 12-stripe black-and-white array is looked at far more than are 3-stripe or 25-stripe versions. With respect to concentric circles, however, very little difference is seen between responses to 2-circle, 16-circle, and 100-circle arrays. Of the three shapes, the checkerboard squares evoked, by far, the greatest interest, and the stripes the least.

- At eleven weeks, infants prefer to look at patterns containing more "contour per unit area" than at six weeks, and concentric circles evoke greater interest than do the black-and-white contrast edges of the checkerboard squares.

Three-month-old infants have some understanding of mechanical causality. For example, in one study, a red cube was moved along a track until it disappeared behind a screen and a white cube then emerged (in tempo) at the other side. Three-month-old infants showed substantially greater attention when, on subsequent trials, a raised screen revealed no collision between the objects, compared with trials in which the raised screen showed that the objects had collided (Borton, 1979, summarized in Golinkoff and others, 1986; Ball and Tronick, 1971). Borton's demonstration that three-month-old infants possess the concept of mechanical causality means that (1) during the initial weeks of life infants have acquired this concept from things they have seen and heard or that (2) the neonate's brain is not the tabula rasa that some eminent evolutionary theorists and neurobiologists conceive it to be but is instead *"preprogrammed" to encode certain shapes, sounds,* **and complex events** *in a particular manner*. In either case, early infant lessons would seem to be of substantial value. Under the first assumption, these experiences would be able to teach infants more complex concepts than they are generally thought capable of learning. Under the second, if infants innately possess the ability to register and retain the salience of forms and speech sounds, providing opportunities to broaden and deepen these "categorical registers" would certainly contribute to neonatal development.

Three-month-olds are able to perceive the constancy of a shape when it is rotated and, by four months, can discriminate very small changes in the orientation of shapes,[27] and they can also discern invariant configurations across stimuli whose elements differ in shape, color, or density. Four-month-olds also rapidly become habituated to patterns containing vertical, but not horizontal, symmetry.[28] Five-month-olds can recognize information common to objects and pictures of these objects and can encode either the invariant form or the invariant color of target objects as a basis for later recognition (Fagan and Singer, 1983; Fagan and McGrath, 1981). Further, they will increase their fixation substantially if the size of a high-contrast interior portion of an object is enlarged, but not if the shape of this interior segment is changed (Linn, Reznick, Kagan, and Hans, 1982).[29]

The distinction between an infant's ability to apprehend the *external* configuration of an object and its being cognizant of the object's *internal* details is fundamental to determining when infants become capable of absorbing the details of relatively complex objects.[30] Newborns and one-month-olds tend to focus on a single peripheral feature and will seldom look at the internal elements of compound figures (Banks and Salapetek, 1981). One-month-olds (but not neonates) attend to the central elements of a compound stimulus if these are moved in relation to the outer contour or if their patterns are highly attractive.[31] Six-week-olds prefer to look at items that are noncomplex and convey little information, but two-month-olds regularly inspect the internal components of objects. Four-month-olds can discriminate changes in either the internal or external shape of compound stimuli (Milewski, 1976, 1978, 1979).

By five weeks of age, infants can discriminate between photographs of different faces (Bushnell, 1982) and, by ten weeks of age, can differentiate among facial expressions by the emotions they display (Haviland and Lelwica, 1987; Barrera and Maurer, 1981). The preference of two-month-olds for looking at facelike patterns is related to the fact that these patterns look like faces rather than to their "stimulus energy" (Kleiner and Banks, 1987). At five to six months, "exceptionally advantaged" infants (primarily firstborn children whose parents both had college degrees) were examined to determine if they would be more responsive to changes in the configuration of a face or to changes in the nature of its elements (Caron, Caron, and Glass, 1983). This was accomplished by assessing whether the infants would habituate more to changes in facial expression or to the same expression seen on a number of women's faces. As a group, these infants, especially the girls, were highly responsive to the changes in expression (configurational changes) but not to the changes in people. A later comparison with childhood IQs showed strong positive correlations between responsiveness to configurational changes and Stanford-Binet scores (+ .68 for the girls and + .20 for the boys) but a strong negative IQ correlation (– .57) among girls who were responsive to a change in person when the facial expression was held constant. In a less advantaged sample of infants (whose IQs averaged 110.9, compared with 119.4 for the previously referenced sample), similar results were seen (+ .62 for the female babies who displayed a "configurational concept" sensitivity and – .51 for those who concentrated on the elements of the woman's face).[32] In a more recent study of facial-expression recognition (Caron, Caron, and Maclean, 1988), (1) five-month-olds discriminated between happy and sad expressions when these were accompanied by a voice (or by voice alone) but could only discriminate a one-way shift (from sad to happy) in a "face-alone" presentation; (2) four-month-olds could discriminate a sad-to-happy shift but not a happy-to-sad shift; and (3) by seven months, babies could discriminate between angry and happy emotions when these were presented as face-voice combinations or voice-alone stimuli, but not face-alone presentations.

Some aspects of the stimulus-viewing conditions—for example, whether infants are in a familiar or a novel environment—will affect their response. In this regard, there is some suggestion that male and female babies differ in their preferences for familiar versus unfamiliar surroundings, at least in early infancy. In a study of eight- to nine-week-olds, when the female babies were in familiar bassinets, they gazed at a very familiar stabile hung above their bassinet far longer than they did at an unfamiliar one.[33] When they were placed in novel bassinets, however, novel stabiles held their attention longer than did familiar ones. For males, the situation was reversed, as they looked at novel stabiles longer than they did at familiar ones when they were in a familiar bassinet (Weizmann, Cohen, and Pratt, 1971).[34]

The presence of an interesting sound will often cause infants to look more intently at a visual display, even infants younger than six weeks of age (Mendelson, 1979), as sound automatically increases attention to visual stimuli by engaging a scanning routine that is apparently spatially biased. Increased attention to unchanging visual stimuli also occurs with the addition of the mother's voice (Culp, 1973).

Greenberg (1971) has demonstrated that the developmental progression of infants' "complexity preferences" can be accelerated by presenting appropriate visual stimulation and that providing infants with dangling visual targets (to invite fixation at various distances) accelerates the maturation of a process that had previously been thought to be relatively independent of environmental influence.[35] Greenberg argues convincingly that such preferences must result from considerably more complex cognitive processes than basic sensory responses to maturational aspects of visual acuity.

Similarly, arranging crib conditions to elicit the reaching and touching of visual targets has been shown to reduce the median age for achieving the top level in a visually directed reaching scale from 145 days (in controls) to 89 days (White, 1967, discussed in Bower, 1974). Using operant conditioning techniques, researchers have found that six- to twelve-week-old infants can be taught visual pattern discrimination, *when the stimuli are interesting* (McKenzie and Day, 1971). These techniques consisted of reinforcing head turns in the direction of some stimuli, but not others, with the reinforcement consisting of smiling, praising, presenting a brightly colored toy, shaking a rattle, or ringing a bell.[36]

Thus, if babies are exposed to the kinds of visual stimuli they find attractive and those categorical distinctions that seem to be the forerunners to highly desirable skills are presented in appropriate ways, such as using the conjoint movement of a three-dimensional object and the infant's rocking motion (see Note #21), it is likely that an infant's overall cognitive development will be materially accelerated.

11.6 The Development of Auditory Competence

Since infants are in many ways auditorily competent at birth and auditory-discrimination skills (even when they are assessed

as young as four months of age) are usually good prognostica-
tors of children's verbal IQs,[37] it is possible that (1) such skills can
be enhanced in infancy and that (2) such enhancement will
facilitate development of the crucial foundations of language
comprehension.

From birth onward, an adult human voice has a special salience — speech, for the most part, is analyzed in the left hemisphere, in contrast to most other environmental sounds, which
are processed in the right hemisphere.[38] As a consequence, the
specific speech discrimination contrasts that children learn are
governed by experience. This is because parental behavior
shapes the individual sound elements (and their constructs) to
which babies pay attention by stressing the sounds and patterns
of the family's cultural traditions.[39] Thus, introducing a regimen
designed to teach auditory- and speech-discrimination skills in
infancy might be perceived as providing structure to a task that
parents routinely undertake anyway.

Most speech perception abilities are evident within the first
few months. Young infants are particularly sensitive to the pitch
of adult speech, and they can discern variations in intensity,
duration, and the temporal or spatial patterning of sounds
(Eisenberg, 1976; Eisenberg, Coursin, and Rupp, 1966; Stratton
and Connolly, 1973), as well as in rhythmicity (Condon and
Sander, 1974) and certain culturally related phonetic components of speech (Butterfield and Cairns, 1974). Initially, infants
are unable to hear extremely low tones or to discriminate between consonants that differ in only a single feature (such as
fricatives that differ only in voicing). For effective encoding,
sounds also need to be presented somewhat more slowly to
infants than to adults, and infants have an easier time decoding
speech when it has a rising-falling pitch contour, as in baby talk.
Five-month-olds will, after a fifteen-second delay, discriminate
between various kinds of changes in a six-note melody but will
not detect a transposition to an adjacent key when each component tone is changed (Chang and Trehub, 1977).

By three months of age (when orientating toward sounds is
virtually nonexistent), infants can already make categorical distinctions between most phonemes (Eimas, Siqueland, Jusczyk,

and Vigorito, 1971; Eimas, 1975). At this age, the baby's especially strong interest in the elements of musical sounds makes
the use of vocal games by adults very enjoyable (Stern, Beebe,
Jaffee, and Bennett, 1975; Stern, Jaffee, Beebe, and Bennett,
1977; Trevarthen, 1974, 1977). At three to four months of age,
infants can group together English syllables that share a common consonant and can remember these across daily test sessions (Fodor, Garrett, and Brill, 1975). Findings of this nature
(such as how "vowel environments" affect an infant's ability to
distinguish changes in consonants) establish useful guidelines
for determining which specific words and individual letter
changes to incorporate into "repetition with patterned novelty"
paradigms at particular ages. There is now compelling evidence
that, even in early infancy, the syllable, and in particular the
vowel, is a very salient unit for speech categorization (Bertoncini
and others, 1988).

In light of these early abilities, a number of specific findings
concerning the development of auditory discrimination skills
are worth noting:

- The rises and falls of speech contour (which represent part of what
  is called the "power envelope" of speech) are an early mechanism
  for the formation of a system of phonemic contrasts for perceiving
  and remembering a phonetic inventory (Eilers and Oller, 1985).
- Two-month-old babies are able to detect changes in the component tones of a sequence of sounds (Trehub, 1985) and can detect
  the time-spanning structure of the rhythm or rhyme contained in
  speech sequences (Horowitz, 1974). Whether these facilities require the ability to encode relatively precise interval information,
  or whether they can be predicated solely on an ability to track the
  ups and downs of contour information, is apparently still unre-
  solved; nevertheless, familiar melodic patterns are still recognized
  by two-month-olds when the "key" is changed.
- Seven-week-olds have the capacity to segregate two simultaneously
  presented auditory "streams," seemingly by detecting the similarity in frequency of each stream (Morrongiello, Kulig, and
  Clifton, 1984, summarized in Rovee-Collier and Lipsitt, 1980; and
  Demany, Mackenzie, and Vurpillot, 1977, summarized in Demany,
  1982). At this age, infants can also discriminate intonation and
  "place of articulation" (Morse, 1972).
- At one and four months of age, infants can discriminate between
  certain consonants (such as "va" and "pa") and have an easier time
  discriminating consonants from different adult phonemic catego-

ries than when they are from the same category (Eimas, Siqueland, Jusczyk, and Vigorito, 1971).

- Two-month-olds are sensitive to subtle differences between two-syllable utterances (Jusczyk and Thompson, 1978; Jusczyk and others, 1977; Levitt and others, 1988), irrespective of whether the so-called stop consonant that changes is stressed or unstressed, or is in the initial or third position of a four-letter sound. They are equally facile (for example) in detecting a change from "Bada" to "Gada," "daBa" to "daGa," or "Daba" to "Daga."

- Four-month-olds' ability to appreciate the perceptual identity of stop consonants must stem from a segmental analysis of the syllables they form, because the mechanisms that they use in making these differentiations vary in relation to the accompanying vowel (Fodor, Garrett, and Brill, 1975).[40] By this age, infants can discriminate among many fricative consonants but have difficulty with those that differ only in "voicing" (Eilers and Oller, 1985).[41]

- It is also possible to change the "pitch contour" of the vowel portion of a speech sound and still have an infant react to changes in other dimensions (such as altering the first or third letter of a syllable from d to p). Thus (in the environment of an emotionally positive educational training session), changing what is a well-understood and "irrelevant" dimension (pitch) does not affect an infant's ability to detect changes in these other features (Kuhl and Meltzoff, 1982).

A series of well-designed experiments examined the question of whether six-month-olds can discriminate changes in the auditory and visual components of a compound stimulus equally well (Lewkowicz, 1988a, 1988b); the results strongly suggest that, at this age, *auditory discrimination dominates over visual discrimination*.[42]

11.7 The Early Development of Categorical Representations

The information on the development of auditory and visual discrimination abilities presented in the preceding sections does not address the question of when infants develop "categorical representations" that go beyond the specific stimuli presented and are able to abstract a "prototype" that can then serve as a summary representation of all members of that category. For unless infants possess a perceptual apprehension of (for example) the concepts of "squareness" and/or "triangularity" as discrete categories, exposing them to examples of squares and triangles provides little assurance that this exposure will enable them to become aware that these forms have a special salience.

Recent studies have clearly demonstrated that three-month-old infants are able to abstract such prototypes and to use these prototypes, rather than the specific exemplars presented, as the basis for determining whether a newly shown form is a member of a category. In one of these studies (Bomba and Siqueland, 1983), infants demonstrated that they perceived a previously unseen prototype of a familiar category as more familiar than previously seen but somewhat distorted members of the same category. This effect was observed when a three-minute delay was interjected between the category-familiarization phase and the recognition test, and when the number of exemplars during the familiarization phase was increased from six to twelve. Enlarging on this experiment, other researchers (Younger and Gotlieb, 1988) have demonstrated that, by three months of age, infants will attend more to (that is, show less recognition of) a recently seen distorted version of a simple form than they will to the previously unseen and undistorted version of that form, even when the extent of distortion is relatively minor $(p < .001)$.[43]

By six months of age, infants have already organized adult vowel sounds into distinct categories, as evidenced by their heightened ability to perceive adult-defined prototypes as belonging to the same category, compared with infants who were habituated to relatively poor representations of these vowels (Grieser and Kuhl, 1989).

Another more general finding that emerges from these studies of auditory and visual development is that an infant's perceptual abilities often appear well in advance of its ability to convey these perceptions to those portions of its brain that govern its actions and reactions. The most important implication here is that the introduction of certain aspects of "infant lessons" need not always await conclusive evidence that the infant is able to absorb and retain the material presented (a conclusion not meant to endorse those infant-stimulation programs that would expose young infants to very complex visual configurations, such as famous paintings). This seems to be especially true in the verbal domain, where it is certainly appropriate to expose infants to information that will one day be used to comprehend and articulate speech, long before speech, or evidence of language comprehension, begins. Moreover, the visual attention paid by infants to maternal speech (Collis, 1977; Collis and Schaffer, 1975), especially when accompanied by a rocking motion (Carpenter, 1974), suggests that the active synchronization of speech and facial movements constitutes an early "encoding" experience.

It is therefore especially important to provide parents and other child educators with information about these developmental timetables, for a keen appreciation of an infant's strengths and weaknesses during certain critical stages of cognitive development cannot help but improve his or her capacity to exploit these improved learning opportunities.

11.8 Smiling, Cooing, Turn Taking, Vocal Imitation, and Gaze Behavior

Between four and eight weeks of age, children begin to engage their mothers in an alternating pattern of cooing and waiting. Almost all infants seem to seek opportunities for such vocal dialogues and to take great pleasure in them (Wolff, 1969). Toward the end of the second month, when more-frequent and more-vigorous smiling occurs and infant "babbling" starts,[44] mothers begin to spend a great deal of time trying to elicit smiling and vocalizations during interactions with their babies (Richards, 1971). At three months, positive affective facial expressiveness on the part of the mother (such as smiling or exaggerated expressions) almost always precedes a positive affective response by the infant but usually does not precede the infant's attending to its mother's face (Cohn and Tronick, 1987, 1988; Fogel, 1988).

When an infant engages its mother in social interaction, it usually does not gaze at her steadily. Rather, it will look at her, smile, vocalize, and begin to show signs of mounting arousal and positive affect (including increased motor activity). The intensity of this aroused state continues to build, until the infant begins to show signs of displeasure, at which point there may be a momentary sobering. Then, all of a sudden, the infant may sharply avert its gaze, which enables its level of excitement to decline. Eventually, its gaze returns, and it may burst into a smile, as its level of arousal again begins to build (Stern, 1974).[45]

The facial expressions made by mothers to their three- to four-month-old babies during play are quite extraordinary by adult standards, especially in their degree of exaggeration, slowed tempo of formation, and long duration (the often seen "mock surprise" expression being a good example). The imitation by mothers of their babies' facial expressions occurs with an especially high frequency at about three months of age.

At three months, mother-infant vocal "dialogues" tend to employ the alternating (or turn-taking) mode when the mother's intentions are serious or tutorial (Anderson, Vietze, and Dokecki, 1977) and/or are applied to task-oriented situations (Rosenthal, 1982). Nevertheless, simultaneous (or coactional) vocalizations predominate at this age (Freedle and Lewis, 1977), and occur when mother and infant are simply having fun (Stern, Beebe, Jaffee, and Bennett, 1975; Stern, Jaffee, Beebe, and Bennett, 1977). These vocalizations are thought to be principally efforts to maintain an infant's attention and positive affective state. Whispered vocalizations and vowel-like sounds are also frequently used by the mothers of one- to three-month-olds (Ling and Ling, 1974).[46]

Mothers who subject their infants to a constant barrage of stimulation without pausing to let the infants "reply" seem to overwhelm them, but mothers who are able to establish a synchrony in this interactive relationship with their babies are able to engage in this mutually satisfying activity for prolonged periods (Osofsky and Commons, 1979).[47]

Mothers tend to use specific pitch contours to obtain and sustain their babies' attention and to encourage eye contact and smiling. When an infant is not visually attending and its mother wants to make eye contact, rising contours are used (Stern, Spieker, and MacKain, 1982; Stern, 1985). When an infant is gazing and smiling at its mother and she wants to maintain its positive affect and gaze, she tends to use sinusoidal contours (up-down-up or down-up-down) or bell-shaped contours. Substantial mother-to-mother variation is reported in the contours used to elicit smiling, and little use of the terminal (end-of-sentence) fall is found—declarative sentences having sinusoidal rather than bell-shaped contours.[48]

A large upward increase in the pitch contour of "white noise" caused four-month-old infants to attend (as measured by visual fixation time), whereas smaller increases or relatively large decreases did not (Colombo, Mitchell, Horowitz, and Rash, 1989). These authors speculate that the exaggerated intonation patterns of adult-to-infant speech patterns result from deficits in infants' abilities to detect low frequencies.

Imitating her baby's vocalizations is clearly a part of a mother's intuitive behavior, and several researchers assert that not only are attempts by infants to match adult vocalizations part of their natural behavior[49] but that it is also "natural" for a mother to make her imitations contingent on her baby's behavior (Papousek and Papousek, 1981). Papousek, Papousek, and Bornstein (1985) suggest using imitative behavior as a tool for developing an infant's cognitive skills. They specifically recommend that "[t]he first portions of didactic support should be small, simple, delivered patiently and repeated many times during infants' short periods of attention. Correct proportions between repetition and variation should be sought and applied to increasing and maintaining infants' attention" (p. 273). They further recommend that these initial "language lessons" start with the most universal and categorical features of social messages, namely, the "prosodic envelope" that gives a message the character of meaning (for example, a statement, question, warning, or invitation to dialogue). They then suggest, "Only when repetitive syllables appear in infant vocalizations can parents interpret them as meaningful words or 'protowords.' Until this time, parents' interventions should reinforce infants' motivation for vocal modulation, [and concentrate on] teaching turn-taking and emphasizing prosodic contours" (p. 273).

The exceptional importance of vocal imitation to language development is discussed in detail in sections 8.5 and 10.2 in reference to the work of Fowler (1972, 1975) and Hunt (1981). A number of other researchers have concluded that vocal imitation plays a crucial role in the development of language and speech (Kuhl and Meltzoff, 1988; Speidel and Nelson, 1989; Snow, 1981; Meltzoff, 1988a, 1988b).

With sufficient patience, babies can be taught to imitate sounds, and they seem to especially enjoy playing pitch-imitation games (Kessen, Levine, and Wendrich, 1979). In this study, mothers were instructed to initiate specific pitch-imitative games with their three- to five-month-old infants for at least five minutes a day, matching their babies' pitch, inflections, and vowel sounds as closely as possible.[50] Commenting on these sessions, the authors report, "The babies worked hard at their assignment. They watched the experimenter closely and they vocalized to her often and energetically. . . . Pitch imitation seems natural to young infants who are happily engaged in the task" (p. 96).

Operant conditioning techniques have recently been used to foster vocal imitation in nine- to twelve-month-old infants from upper-middle-class families (Poulson and others, 1989). With contingent parental praise (for the imitation of sounds such as "geh," "ah," "mm," and "ee") serving as the sole inducement, all the infants registered a large increase in the proportion of the time that they imitated the reinforced sounds (from a 15 percent baseline rate to a 38 percent rate over the entire course of the twenty-minute training sessions conducted three to four times a week). Moreover, within a few sessions, the proportion of the time that these infants imitated nonreinforced sounds also jumped dramatically, from a 6 percent baseline rate to 23 percent over the entire course of the (twelve- to thirty-five-session) training regimen, with somewhat higher rates registered after the first several sessions.

Aside from auditory and facial imitation, other sensory modes in which mother-infant imitative behavior occurs include body movements and bodily-kinesthetic interactions (Stern, Beebe, Jaffee, and Bennett, 1975; Stern, Jaffee, Beebe, and Bennett, 1977).[51]

11.9 Encouragement of Attention and Labeling

As detailed in Chapter Eight, studies indicate that infants who received a relatively high frequency of maternal encouragement of attention to objects and events in their environment are likely to have higher childhood IQ scores than infants who received less of such encouragement. Moreover, the strength of these reported correlations abates only slightly when certain other, usually explanatory variables (such as the mother's education) are factored out.

Prior to the fourth month of life, mother-infant interactions strongly emphasize face-to-face "social games" and maternal references to the baby's feelings and experiences. At around four or five months of age, however, a major shift occurs (Trevarthen, 1974; Snow, 1976). As infants begin to show an increasing interest in the surrounding environment, "maternal monitoring of the infant's direction of gaze and her response to the infant's current focus of attention become an important part of their interaction" (Sullivan and Horowitz, 1983b, p. 526). Further, because some two- to four-month-old infants display an ability to follow the gaze of another person (Scaife and Bruner, 1975), some parents can use their infants' emerging referential skills at this earlier age as mechanisms for encouraging them to attend to objects and events in their environment.

Parents should thus seek out opportunities to label words that have considerable significance for their infants. Hunt (1981, 1986) advocates mentioning the names of parts of the baby's body as they are touched by the washcloth during bathing, beginning with those body parts visible to the baby, as this enables the infant to make associations between the spoken word, the touch of the washcloth on a specific part of its body, and the sight of the washcloth touching its body. A detailed discussion of effective labeling techniques is presented in Chapter Twelve.

11.10 Paradigms for Early Infant Lessons

When a single feature of a stimulus is changed and its remaining features are held constant—and this novel element is introduced, withdrawn, and varied according to a prescribed pattern—infants exposed to this "game" of repetition with patterned novelty will tend to gain a growing familiarity with (1) the attributes of the stimulus that changed, (2) those aspects of the stimulus class that did not change, and (3) the repetitive aspects of the pattern(s) used.

There are several reasons for presupposing that the efficacious use of such "habituation-with-patterned-novelty" paradigms can enhance intellectual competence. One is that these paradigms provide practice in developing "mental representations," a facility that influences a person's general problem-solving skills.[52] Another is that when infants are provided with interesting opportunities to focus their attention, they may gain an enhanced capacity to regulate their state of arousal (Bornstein and Sigman, 1986). Moreover, because an ability to focus attention in infancy is usually a forerunner to task persistence in childhood (Sigman, Cohen, Beckwith, and Topinka, 1986, summarized in Bornstein and Sigman, 1986), such practice would seemingly make it easier for infants to overcome obstacles to learning. Thus, they will be more likely to seek opportunities to learn, get more out of their environment, and (in the process) strengthen their concentration skills and build better analytical reasoning processes (Sophian, 1980).

Further, the presentation of patterned verbal stimuli can provide infants with opportunities to detect the nature of the orifacial movements that accompany shifts in a sound, as well as to highlight those orifacial movements that underlie the sound's invariant features. In this regard, it has recently been demonstrated that one-month-old infants will look longer at an object constructed from what is to them a "novel" substance, irrespective of which of two similarly shaped substances (hard or spongy) had been presented to them during a sixty-second oral-familiarization period (Gibson and Walker-Andrews, 1986).[53]

In the auditory domain, the parent should introduce this "game" by slowly and repetitively "singing" a word and occasionally varying its contour (its pitch, duration, or intensity). As the baby matures, the parent would progress to varying one aspect of the sound (a consonant), choosing a variant from a different phonemic class, and shortening the number of repetitions before a variation is introduced. He or she would next introduce a third variant (such as changing the word presented from "sound" to "round" to "pound") and follow that by varying both a single letter and the contour. Last, the parent would use letters in the same phonemic class that differ by only a single feature.

Familiarity alone can become boring. If it is counterbalanced with an adequate proportion of novelty, however, it elicits maximum attention (McCall and Kagan, 1967, discussed in Kinney and Kagan, 1976). Consequently, matching the nature of the novel stimuli presented (and the frequency of their interjection) to the preferences, developmental timetable, and temperament of the individual infant would seem to be the key to avoiding a negative reaction to such learning situations. Here, coupling patterned novelty with a consistent, contingently responsive environment provides a way of maintaining and enhancing the "innate" human preference for novelty.

The so-called discrepancy hypothesis provides one explanation for the particular novelty preferences of infants. This theory postulates that infants attend to stimuli that are moderately discrepant from their internal cognitive standards as a means of developing such standards in an orderly way. It would follow that exposure to visual and auditory stimuli that are moderately discrepant from a baby's internal standards will cause both these standards and the baby's preferences to change.

Researchers seeking to assess the capabilities of young infants have created a variety of interesting techniques and equipment, including mechanisms that permit an infant to produce its own contingent responsivity by controlling the rate at which novelty is introduced into otherwise repeated sounds and sights. For example, researchers have designed equipment that responds automatically to changes in the rate and strength at which an infant sucks on a pacifier. Originally developed to assess visual capabilities, this pacifier-sucking paradigm has also been adapted to the auditory domain.[54]

The issue of the age at which a single session of training can be productive—either in a cognitive or a motivational sense—has been addressed in a study (Lewis, Sullivan, and Brooks-Gunn, 1985) where a contingency learning task was presented to infants who were ten, sixteen, and twenty-four weeks old. At each of these ages, the infants who were exposed to a contingently responsive audiovisual stimulus (children's voices singing the theme song to "Sesame Street," plus a color slide of an infant's happy face, whose continued presence was contingent upon an arm pull) evidenced substantially less fussiness than did controls and, as a consequence, were able to stay "on task" far longer. The session's length was controlled by the infant and ended when the infant got and remained fussy.

The ten-week-old infants spent considerably more seconds per minute attending to the stimulus than did the two older age groups.[55] Although they were cognizant that the stimulus presentation occurred in response to their arm pulls, *a majority* of the ten-week-olds in the contingently responsive group were unable to translate this association into an action that would increase the frequency of this desirable response; nevertheless, *some* of these infants clearly exercised such control over their environment.[56]

These results confirm that infants between sixteen and twenty-four weeks of age will pay attention to contingent paradigms for long periods without distress and also indicate that at these ages most, but not all, infants respond in a manner that induces the presentation of these stimuli. These researchers conclude, "Although it is not known whether more contingency experience results in greater competence or the competent child elicits more contingent behavior from its parents, the present study suggests that it is the contingent stimulation itself which results in a child who is more involved and interested in its environment, factors which should promote subsequent competence" (Lewis, Sullivan, and Brooks-Gunn, 1985, p. 314).

The work of Carolyn Rovee-Collier and her colleagues is especially instructive in understanding the processes of long-term memory formation and retrieval in early infancy, as well as in discerning the rules that govern the circumstances under which infants will and will not retain the information presented in a training session. For example, in recalling a specific training stimulus after a re-cuing, a young infant's memory is likely to return very slowly, with those aspects of the stimulus that were forgotten last—the jist—recalled first, and the details last. Three-month-olds do not begin to recover the "forgotten" memory until at least eight hours have passed, with memory continuing to improve over a period of forty-eight to seventy-two hours. By six months of age, however, recovery begins within the first hour (Rovee-Collier and Fagen, 1981).[57]

These studies portray categorical memory development in infancy as a growing ability to successfully retrieve categorical information in the context of increasingly remote clues. This suggests that young infants can retain categorical information if there are sufficient opportunities for repeated exposure to the target category.

Moreover, these studies (for example, Davis and Rovee-Collier, 1985) also seem to answer with a firm yes the question of whether — prior to the maturation of the visual and occipital cortex at about sixteen weeks — infants can retain what they learn as a result of repeated exposure to a contingently responsive stimulus.

Further experiments by Rovee-Collier and her colleagues reveal that the surroundings in which memory training and retrieval are attempted during early infancy are especially important (Rovee-Collier, personal communication, 1988). This is because, at this age, learning appears to be context bound.[58] For instance, changing a liner draped around an infant's playpen or crib (from one with squares, to one with straight lines or circles) will frequently result in the infant treating an otherwise familiar mobile as unfamiliar. Thus, thought needs to be given to maintaining the constancy of the surroundings in which training experiences for very young infants are embedded.

One of these experiments explored the question of cross-paradigm learning in six-month-olds (Timmons, forthcoming), and the results indicate that learning that an arm pull (or a leg kick) will cause a mobile to move (or a music box to play) will not facilitate more rapid acquisition of the concept that the same action will cause another toy to respond. For example, if infants have learned that a leg kick will make the mobile move, it will take them just as long to learn that a leg kick will make the music box play. However, when infants have had prior training with both types of toys and both target responses, acquisition of a new toy-response pairing is greatly facilitated.[59] These results imply that as infants achieve a growing familiarity with a training paradigm, they will tend to acquire new information about an exemplar class more rapidly.[60]

Lastly, in designing a regimen for the early teaching of auditory and visual salience, parents and child educators would be well advised to tailor both the substance of the information presented and the mode and frequency of its presentation to the *temperament* of the baby (and its caregiver). Unless such lessons are enjoyable to an infant,[61] there is no assurance that they will accomplish the most important task of all—fomenting the kind of satisfaction that will mature into a lifelong love of learning.

Notes

1. In an unswaddled state, however, a correct rate barely greater than chance was reported (Castillo and Butterworth, 1981): in a recent study, two-thirds of the 89 percent of the infants who turned correctly to a repeated sound then turned in the opposite direction in response to a change in the sound's location (Swain, Clifton, and Clarkson, 1989).
2. The reappearance of this preference began at about twelve weeks of age among institutionalized children awaiting foster or adoptive placement and at about ten weeks of age among the offspring of highly educated parents (Fantz and Nevis, 1967a, 1967b). This study contains considerable week-to-week information about shifting visual preferences during the first six months of life.
3. They also show a preference for a prenatally experienced melody (Panneton and DeCasper, 1986). Recordings in humans and sheep reveal that low-frequency sounds are heard by a fetus with very little attenuation and that a high-pitched mother's voice in conversation is likely to stand out (Vince and Billing, 1986; Armitage, Baldwin, and Vince, 1980).
4. Since infants encode the repetitions of linguistic forms kinesthetically long before they are used in communication and speech, it appears that the form and structure of the language system are ready to be encoded long before speech begins.
5. The presence of an "invariant detection mechanism" for the confluence of sight and sound at fourteen weeks of age has recently been clearly demonstrated (Bahrick, 1988).
6. In one experiment (Friedman, 1972), forty of fifty-three neonates evidenced habituation to a two-by-two checkerboard target (shown for sixty seconds at a time). Of these forty, two-thirds evidenced "recovery" (they gazed at somewhat similar novel targets for considerably longer than they did at familiar targets). It has also been shown ($p < .002$) that neonates are "capable of remembering simple, high-controlled visual targets for at least three minutes with little forgetting" (Gotlieb and

Sloane, 1989, n.p.). Habituation has also been demonstrated at five weeks, and the addition of either music or a tape-recorded maternal voice helped elicit recovery to habituated visual stimuli (Horowitz, 1974).

7. These infants learned to produce movements in an overhead crib mobile by means of foot kicks. A length of ribbon connected from the infant's ankle to a suspension hook from which the mobile hangs permits it to draw and release the suspension bar, thereby moving the mobile in a manner commensurate with the vigor and rate of foot kicking (Rovee-Collier and Fagen, 1981; Rovee-Collier and others, 1980; Sullivan, Rovee-Collier, and Tynes, 1979). Little or no forgetting was seen after eight days, but there was some forgetting after fourteen days when no additional "reinforcement" was provided. When infants received a brief reexposure forty-eight to seventy-two hours before testing, recognition of mobiles used in the training sessions persisted for two weeks (Rovee-Collier and Fagen, 1981). The results reinforce these authors' hypothesis that a forty-eight- to seventy-two-hour period after training is of special importance at this age, in the sense that this is the length of time that it takes for "abstractions of prototypic cues [to] become the principal memory attributes that become aroused and noticed" (p. 248). These findings also suggest that a failure to elicit evidence of retention in young infants constitutes retrieval failure, instead of any intrinsic inability on the part of infants to encode and retain information.

8. The thalamus is a pair of walnut-sized "organs" in the center of the brain; the rear portion of the thalamus receives visual and auditory analytical inputs from adjacent "bulbs." By the fourth month after birth, the thalamus transmits the products of these analyses to the occipital and auditory cortex. The periods of greatest cognitive impairment are apparently coterminous with the rapid formation of myelin sheaths around bundles of axons that lead to the thalamus from the auditory canal, the primary visual areas, and the axonal tracts connecting the thalamus with these cortical regions. Once these myelin sheaths form, the routing of nerve fibers connecting these areas is "hard wired."

9. During this neonatal imprint period, neurons in these thalamic regions contain large numbers of dendritic "spines." However, these spines begin to disappear at the same time as spines begin to appear on the dendrites of neurons in the "receptive" layer of the auditory and occipital cortex — areas that receive direct inputs from these thalamic regions. This suggests the existence of a mechanism that allows "imprint-stage" experiences to have lasting effects; that is, information encoded on these spines is able to be transferred to the developing cortex. For a discussion of the extraordinary degree of lifelong "plasticity" associated with neurons containing "spiny" synapses, see Chapter Fifteen.

10. Contingently responsive maternal behavior has also been linked with habituation behavior (Lewis and Coates, 1980; Bornstein and Tamis, 1986, summarized in Bornstein and Sigman, 1986), which, in turn, is positively correlated with (the verbal aspects of) childhood IQ scores

(Rose, 1981; Rose and Wallace, 1985). Even in newborns, contingently responsive events can be detected and responded to (Papousek and Papousek, 1981).

11. In a quiet alert state, infants have a bright look, seem to focus their attention on something, and show a minimum of motor activity (Brazelton, 1973).

12. This process (known as "smooth visual pursuit") is markedly improved by the rocking motion, which enhances visual attentiveness (Schaffer, 1977) and helps maintain a state of visual alertness (Gregg, Haffner, and Korner, 1976; Korner and Thoman, 1970); using a pacifier further increases visual attentiveness (Wolff, 1966). *Extra rocking is extremely important to the cognitive development of premature and small-for-date babies* (see the appendix at back of this book, especially the discussion of Rose (1980), who found that habituation and novelty behavior at six months of age improved dramatically from a regimen of rocking and exposure to visual stimuli).

13. Our cerebellum (the brain's balance center) also serves another major cognitive function — that of being the brain's "time-motion" analyst. An acquisition of the rules governing the confluence of time and space is essential to the cognitive competence (and indeed the survival) of virtually every animal.

14. Infants rarely protest swaddling, and such instances usually involve its introduction after several weeks or months of relative freedom. "Some infants are quite tolerant of swaddling for many months and . . . may even demand to continue being swaddled when weaning is attempted. Others, however, rapidly give up their restraints and may demand early freedom" (Lipton, Steinschneider, and Richmond, 1965).

15. These "startle" movements include a sudden splaying out of the fingers, or feet or legs shooting straight up and out (Brazelton, 1974). The supportive control supplied by placing one's hand on a baby's abdomen or by holding its arms so that it cannot startle itself may also help reduce the overreactions of a hyperactive neonate. Patting an infant three times a minute is considered soothing, but five or six times a minute is considered to be an alerting procedure.

16. Neither a tape-recorded heartbeat nor bright lights significantly reduced the duration of these infants' crying episodes (which averaged a third of the observation period).

17. Extra care should be taken to keep the back and hips straight to prevent hip injury (Owen, 1983).

18. The resilience and springiness of the wool also prevent the baby's head from being flattened in the back; one type of lambskin considered especially suitable for babies' use comes from New Zealand (unshorn Southern Romney crossbred lambs). The use of wool should possibly be avoided in families where there is a history of nasal allergy.

19. Eye contact has been shown to be a two-way process of communication that leads to stronger bonding with the mother (Moss and Robeson, 1967) and to advanced social and cognitive development (Wolff, 1969). From birth onward, some infants characteristically and vigorously seek out their mothers' eyes, while others avoid them. As young as two

months of age, *some* infants (a third in the 1975 Scaife and Bruner study) exhibit referential head turning, meaning they will turn in the same general direction that a researcher, who had previously made eye contact with them, turns to look.

20. This is because the foveal area (a small retinal region in the center of the visual field with enhanced powers of spatial resolution) matures slowly (for a review, see Aslin, 1986).

21. Being moved around an object can enable sixteen-week-old infants to perceive its three-dimensional form, but multiple static views of the object cannot, even at twenty-four weeks (Kellman and Short, 1987); spatiotemporal continuity (rather than the summation of two-dimensional views) seems to underlie this process. Conjoint motion of the object and the infant elicits considerably greater attention than either object or observer motion alone (Kellman, Gleitman, and Spelke, 1987).

22. Olson (1979) tested the recognition memory of a group of four-month-olds of relatively bright parentage using a variety of briefly presented visual stimuli, and his findings suggest the kinds of visual stimuli such children are capable of assimilating and retaining.

23. For example, newborns who were habituated to a color or shape under monocular viewing conditions demonstrated an interocular transfer of this information when tested in the other eye (Slater, Earle, Morison, and Rose, 1985). Although one- to three-month-olds do not discriminate between "depth" and "no depth" displays (Fox, Aslin, Shea, and Dumais, 1980), their "stereoacuity" improves very rapidly between sixteen and twenty weeks of age (Held, Birch, and Gwiazda, 1980).

24. Among the offspring of the college faculty, this switchover (from a strong, consistent preference for looking at a larger caricature of a face to a moderate preference for looking at a smaller one) occurred in only one week's time (the ninth week). Among a sample of institutionalized infants, the shift occurred over several weeks, with only a slight preference for the smaller face. Shortly after the return of three-dimensional cognition, size was no longer a factor in the preferences of either group. Bronson (1974) reports a similar u-shaped developmental cycle in the visual system in this age range.

25. In one experiment (Treiber and Wilcox, 1980), one-month-olds evidenced an ability to perceive a "contourless" figure (the Kanizsa triangle) specified by the relationship of three figures external to the triangle. Thus, they were responsive to form, not to properties specific to contour.

26. See, for example, Hershenson, 1967; Greenberg, Uzgiris, and Hunt, 1970; Greenberg, Hillman, and Grice, 1975; and Schwartz and Day, 1979. For neonatal preferences, see Slater, Earle, Morison, and Rose, 1985.

27. Changes of as little as 5 degrees could be detected (Bornstein, Krinsky, and Benasich, 1986); these infants (from upper-middle/upper-class families) were first habituated to multiple orientations of a given shape and then tested on new orientations of that same shape. Three-month-olds respond to the angular relations of lines rather than to their orientations (Cohen and Younger, 1984; Owsley, 1983).

28. At this age, the primacy of vertical symmetry over horizontal or no symmetry (Bornstein, Ferdinandsen, and Gross, 1981) or vertical non-symmetry (Bornstein and Krinsky, 1985) is reported. Diagonal symmetry is also encoded (Humphrey, Humphrey, Muir, and Dodwell, 1986), but horizontal symmetry/nonsymmetry is not distinguished (Fisher, Ferdinandsen, and Bornstein, 1981). Differences in complex shapes (cartoon representations of similar-sized rabbit and bear heads) were readily apparent to twenty-week-olds when such differences were accompanied by a cross-categorizational change in hue (from blue to green), but not when they were accompanied by an equivalent-wavelength change within the same hue category (Catherwood, Crassini, and Freiberg, 1989).

29. The stimulus was two black dots placed within a larger white circle. Little or no dishabituation was seen when the dots were changed to triangles or squares or their position was changed within or above the circle; moderate dishabituation occurred when the position of the dots was lowered, their size was decreased, or their number increased; and strong dishabituation was seen when their size was increased or their position was changed from horizontal to vertical. Strong responses to "looming" visual displays are also seen in week-old infants (see Aslin, 1986).

30. Because the right hemisphere bears the primary responsibility for apprehending the overall configuration and the left for assessing internal details (see Chapter Fifteen), findings such as these may help elucidate changing gradations of hemispheric dominance during infancy and toddlerhood (see, for example, Gibson and Walker, 1984, who note that a shift in preference from the novel to the familiar appears to portend a period of rapid left-hemisphere growth and increased involvement in cognition).

31. For example, these elements will be attractive if they have markedly higher contour density than background elements (Ganon and Swartz, 1980; Bushnell, Gerry, and Burt, 1983). At three months (but not one month), "element rearrangement" configurations operate on established Gestalt principles (Van Giffen and Haith, 1984).

32. For the boys in these samples, prolonged attentiveness was a reasonably good predictor of IQ; this is compatible with the findings (in Chapter Seventeen) of a relationship between exceptionally high intelligence in females and a more "right-brained" dominance (and/or a "bilateralized" condition).

33. The subjects were the full-term offspring of very well educated parents; familiarization episodes lasted thirty minutes a day for four weeks. At four to six weeks of age, infants will tend to gaze longer at familiar stabiles, but by eight weeks their interest in familiar stabiles wanes and their interest in unfamiliar ones grows.

34. The mean looking times (in seconds) at novel vs. familiarized stabiles were as follows: (1) in a familiar bassinet, males 98 vs. 79 seconds and females 67 vs. 79 seconds; (2) in a novel bassinet, females 96 vs. 72 seconds and males 81 vs. 87 seconds. Thus, the averages for female infants ranged from 67 to 96 seconds. The possibility of sex differences

in the extent of "right-brain"/"left-brain" activation in familiar/unfamiliar surroundings is not at variance with the greater (visual and motor) exploratory behavior found in males in most species of animals (and the more auditory and "social" behavior in females). Fathers of infant girls tend to engage in more frequent verbal interactions with their babies than do fathers of infant boys; Rebelsky and Hanks (1971) report twice as many father-daughter as father-son interactions during the first three months.

35. A three- to four-week acceleration in the "blink response"; the training was begun at five weeks of age.

36. A sixty-four-square checkerboard pattern evoked the highest proportion of correct responses; the reinforced head-turn direction was altered during the six training sessions. Although an infant's ability to orient its head and eyes toward a sound source is readily elicited by the fourth month, "conditioning" usually could not be accomplished until infants were five to six months of age (Moore, Wilson, and Thompson, 1977).

37. In one of the several studies cited in section 7.4 (O'Connor, Cohen, and Parmelee, 1984), little difference was found in the abilities of premature and full-term infants, implying that conceptional age and the commensurate biological timetable are not a major determinant of an infant's ability to perform this relatively difficult novelty-discrimination task at four months of age.

38. For instance, operant conditioning tasks demonstrate that newborn infants overwhelmingly prefer to listen to heartbeat sounds in their left ear (right hemisphere) and female speech in their right ear (Prescott and DeCasper, forthcoming; Davis and DeCasper, 1989).

39. For example, when Japanese adults are asked to discriminate between the speech syllables "ra" and "la," on the one hand, and nonspeech signal equivalents, on the other, they are unable to do so when these contrasts are incorporated in a speech discrimination test, even though they perform as accurately as English-speaking adults when this discrimination task is presented in a nonspeech format (Miyawaki and others, 1975). English-learning infants discriminate English-voicing contrasts but do not demonstrate discrimination of Spanish-like contrasts (Butterfield and Cairns, 1974). Infants lose the ability to discriminate foreign-language contrasts during the second six months of life (Werker and Tees, 1983, 1984). Some of these can be reactivated by exposure to a nonnative language, while others are resistant to reactivation despite extensive training (see Aslin, 1986).

40. The kinds of acoustical cues that infants use to distinguish "stop consonants" that differ in place of articulation (such as a sound pushed out from in front of the teeth) include "burst frequency," "aspiration," and "format transitions." These first two are of great importance in the "i" and "u" vowel environments, and the last is of greatest importance when the vowel sound is "ah."

41. For example, they can distinguish between "ah" and "sa," "sa" and "va," or "ba" and "fa" but have difficulty with fricatives cued solely by voicing (for example, "sa" vs. "za"), where the "onset time" is the primary clue (Eilers and Minifie, 1975).

42.   Changing the rate at which a visual stimulus flashes and an auditory
        stimulus pulses on and off demonstrates that infants recognize that a
        previously habituated-to auditory-visual compound stimulus has
        changed. Altering the auditory stimulus alone also induces such recog-
        nition, but altering the visual aspect while leaving the auditory aspect
        intact does not. In the absence of any auditory stimuli, the infants
        evidenced discrimination of these visual alterations. At ten months
        (the middle of a major visuomotor development period), the degree of
        auditory dominance had waned considerably but was still evident,
        particularly when slightly less bright visual contrast conditions were
        employed.

43.   The prototypes recognized by the three-month-olds consisted of dots
        arranged into simple forms (for example, a square or a triangle); the
        set of exemplars were spatial distortions of these forms. The extremely
        well designed and analyzed Younger and Gotlieb study varied the
        exemplars by the extent of their spatial distortion, as well as by how
        "good" the prototype was (measured in terms of its "regularity/asymme-
        try" and the simplicity/complexity of the information to be cate-
        gorized). Studying 108 (predominantly lower-SES) infants who were
        three, five, and seven months old made it possible to discern a progres-
        sive ability to develop a "mind's eye" picture of forms that were of less-
        than-good quality.

44.   Babbling develops by two months of age; it is not as dependent on
        social interaction as cooing and often occurs when a baby is alone.
        Listening to human speech encourages infants to babble, but a pure
        tone stimulus does not (Kuhl and Meltzoff, 1982). The amount of
        babbling a baby does, however, bears little relationship to later intel-
        ligence. Three-month-olds will also often interrupt their own vocaliza-
        tions (including crying) to listen for the response of their caretaker
        (Bruner, 1977).

45.   If the mother's facial expression does not react to the infant's gaze, a
        brief positive display by the infant will usually be followed by negative
        affective behavior; the joint positive state is rarely terminated by the
        mother.

46.   These authors made comparisons at twelve ages, ranging from one
        month to three years.

47.   Two-month-olds anticipate that a visible person will communicate with
        them and become disturbed by an immobile face, a person who
        suddenly becomes unresponsive, a lack of synchrony between facial
        movements and speech, or a spatial displacement of a face and voice
        (Spelke and Cortelyou, 1981). Beginning at about seven weeks, infants
        tend to focus their gaze at or near a person's eyes, as — during their
        third month — only 6 percent of the time that they spend looking at a
        human face is directed at the mouth (Haith, Bergman, and Moore,
        1977, discussed in Haith, 1980).

48.   Four-month-olds generally prefer hearing baby talk to adult speech
        (Fernald, 1987). Its enhanced melodic contours are especially attrac-
        tive, an attractiveness that transcends its temporal structure and inten-
        sity characteristics. The vocal selectivity accompanying baby talk helps

infants more easily comprehend information about their caretaker's emotional state (including acceptable infant behavior), as well as discern significant "vocal information" (Papousek, Papousek, and Bornstein, 1985). Using baby talk to toddlers, however, is considered detrimental to development (see section 12.2). Elongated vowels are discriminated in a continuous rather than a categorical manner, while brief presentations of the same sounds (0.06 vs. 0.24 seconds) are discriminated categorically (Swoboda, Kass, Morse, and Leavitt, 1978).

49.   For example, when infants were thirteen to sixteen weeks of age, the imitation of infants' facial gestures and vocalizations by mothers was found to be a pervasive characteristic of unconstrained episodes of social interaction (Moran, Krupka, Tutton, and Symons, 1987), with infants at this age also displaying patterns of matching behavior; infants eighteen to twenty weeks old attempt to mimic the rise-fall contours of an adult female's vowels and produce pitch patterns that (although higher in frequency) are clearly attempts to direct their articulated responses toward the auditory "targets" they hear (Kuhl and Meltzoff, 1982). With infants between four and ten months of age, weekly observational sessions revealed an average of between five and eight vocal imitative sequences per ten-minute period, with four-fifths of these being maternal imitations (Pawlby, 1977). Pitch imitation far outdistanced more complex types; infants' attempts at imitation are seen as young as two months of age (Papousek and Papousek, 1982).

50.   With pitchpipes provided to mothers who could not easily match pitch. The results were assessed an average of fifteen and forty days later in thirty-minute sessions with the experimenter.

51.   Because bodily-kinesthetic interactions between infants and their mothers in traditional Japanese families are so frequent (see Chapter Thirteen), the possible contribution of this little understood sense of "perception" to intelligence (and especially to the performance aspects of IQ) should not be underestimated. This interrelationship might be related to the ability of these interactions to promote (1) soothing, (2) a sense of oneself as part of a "we," and/or (3) an emotional passivity that might make it easier to master "concentration training" in toddlerhood.

52.   Generating mental representations is common to both decrement (habituation) and recovery of attention (a strong response to novelty). Mental representations may assume analog forms (such as pictures, holograms, tape recordings, or three-dimensional models), symbolic forms (such as linked-list-structures, conceptual graphs, or verbal codes), or propositional forms (such as abstract concepts, networks, or associative structures); see Bornstein and Sigman, 1986.

53.   Whether such encoding abilities exist during the GAP is questionable, since studies indicate that at this age only a very small proportion of the time that an infant spends attending to its mother's face is directed toward her mouth (Haith, Bergman, and Moore, 1977). Nevertheless, recent findings indicate that, at fourteen weeks of age, an "invariant detection" mechanism for the confluence of sight and sound does exist (Bahrick, 1988; Bower, 1979), which could suggest that the nine- to

eleven-week finding (Haith, Bergman, and Moore, 1977) is specific to this period.

54.   See Kuhl, 1976; Kuhl and Miller, 1975. Infants usually respond quite well to these opportunities to control contingently responsive sound presentations (after an initial period of acclimation). By sucking relatively hard on the nipple, they obtain repeated opportunities to experience sights and sounds they find interesting, and when their interest wanes (and the rate and amplitude of their sucking declines to a specified criterion), the stimulus changes automatically.

55.   During the initial four minutes, the time spent looking at the face did not differ materially between the two conditions; this was true at each of the ages. Thereafter, the inability of controls to manipulate their environment caused many to get fussy; such fussiness increased with age among the controls but decreased markedly with age in the subjects exposed to the contingent condition.

56.   Both groups of ten-week-olds (contingent and control) substantially increased their arm pulls per minute from baseline and showed the same pattern of changes in arm pulls over time. However, several infants in the contingently responsive group exhibited a fivefold or greater increase in their base rate ($p < .01$). The authors hold that the markedly longer period of interest displayed by these subjects is evidence of their appreciation of control over their environment. Brinker and Lewis (1982) have employed such contingently responsive consequences as tape-recorded music, a tape recording of the mother talking to her baby, a light, a vibrating pad, and photographic slides to encourage such infant behaviors as learning to kick a panel, raising their head, vocalizing, or pulling a string attached to their wrist. Microcomputers were used to analyze the infant's learning and to communicate to parents, via graphic displays on home television, the progress made.

57.   A recent study of the development of long-term memory for events occurring at fifteen weeks of age suggests that it occurs very slowly (Bahrick and Pickens, 1989). When infants' recall of specific objects undergoing one of two particular motions (shown during four forty-second familiarization periods) was tested after one day, two weeks, and one month, only the group retested after one month displayed a "familiarity preference" for the previously seen object and motion ($p < .02$).

58.   This is somewhat akin to the experiences of divers who remember things learned under water better when they are under water and points to (1) the exceptionally important role of the cerebellum in early learning and memory and (2) the role of contingent responsivity in engaging these how-to memory processes and ensuring long-term retention.

59.   For example, in the first training session, leg kicks might make the mobile move, and in the second session (three days later), arm pulls might make the music box play; the results would then be assessed in a third session (seven days after the first). When a given toy had been used in one of the previous sessions and the contingent action in the

other, the time needed to reach criterion in the third session averaged 2.7 minutes (after reinforcement was begun). This compared with 1.8 minutes for reacquisition of a previously experienced pairing and with 4.5 minutes when a novel element (activity or toy) was introduced (for example, when the arm pull had been used in both previous sessions, once with each toy, and the leg kick was introduced in the third). It made little difference whether the previous exposure to the toy had been in the first or second session. All training sessions began with a two-minute nonreinforced familiarization period (which provided baseline activity rates), followed by six minutes of reinforcement and a further two-minute nonreinforced period (extinction).

60.   At nine months, "categorical" information can be recalled (after ten minutes) but only if a brief re-cuing with new exemplars in the class precedes the testing (Roberts, 1987, 1988). In these experiments, habituation to line drawings of three types of birds was followed by testing ten minutes later. When there was no re-cuing prior to testing, or a brief re-cuing confined to the birds previously habituated to, the infants did not evidence generalization to other exemplars in this category. After a brief re-cuing (one-eighth as long as the original habituation) that contained new exemplars, however, they did generalize to other within-category stimuli and "recovered" to out-of-category stimuli. Thus, they had formed a categorical representation of a prototype of a bird rather than arriving at a strict identification of specific exemplars; this implies that early word learning is preceded by an ability to detect the structural similarity of nonlinguistic categorical information.

61.   However, seemingly unsuccessful studies can also generate useful information; for instance, when too much is demanded of infants, their limitations are learned (Morse, 1985). Again, a given set of variations — in the case of the Morse and Suomi (1979) experiment (summarized in Morse, 1985), vowels — proved so interesting to the infants that they failed to habituate during the familiarization phase. In another instance, five-month-olds demonstrated such a strong preference for gazing at rotating objects compared with nonrotating ones that their novelty preferences could not be evaluated (Ruff, 1987).

Contents

ꝗ 12 ꝗ

Stimulating
Language Comprehension
and Expression
in the Early Years

12.1 Introduction

The information presented in Part Three makes it abundantly clear that early environmental stimulation can make a substantial and lasting difference in a child's cognitive development— particularly its language development.

Certain common themes appear in all the successful early stimulation programs, such as the early imitation of infant vocalizations and the labeling of familiar objects by caretakers— while other themes seem to use one of several possible approaches to advancing cognitive development.

This chapter (1) discusses the language-stimulation regimen advocated by William Fowler, one of the most successful developers of IQ-enhancing programs (see section 10.2); (2) describes findings from a recent study indicating that the effective use of "picture-book reading time" during toddlerhood can, with relatively little effort, greatly promote the development of language skills; and (3) presents empirical and theoretical information concerning the major developmental stages of toddlerhood and how knowledge of these stages might help in planning "toddler lessons" to take advantage of periods of right- and left-hemisphere brain dominance. This will set the stage for a presentation of the cognitive and behavioral approaches used by traditional Japanese and Jewish families.

12.2 How to Nurture Language Development: The Approach of William Fowler

This section summarizes Fowler's extremely successful language-stimulation program, which is detailed in his forthcoming book entitled *Talking in Infancy: How to Nurture and Cultivate Early Language Development.*

Fowler's approach to teaching language to young infants requires that parents be taught how to effectively label the objects and actions with which their babies are most familiar. He postulates that infants learn language when, as a concomitant part of drawing their attention to objects, actions, and events in their environment, parents provide them with clear and precise word labels for these objects and events. If a sufficient number of labels are provided in ways that make it easy for the infants to learn the individual rules of language, they will then develop a precocious understanding and use of language.

Fowler holds that the keys to the successful teaching of word labels are (1) timing the labeling action to coincide with the infant's attending to the object or action so that the connection between the language label and the referent can be discerned; (2) stressing the word used to label the object or action (for example, "Here is your *bottle*"); (3) using the same word consistently to designate an object; and (4) treating the task of labeling as a form of wordplay rather than as a chore. Fowler (p. VII–3) postulates that, although caregivers normally do a certain amount of labeling, "[f]ew are sufficiently precise and consistent, and rarely does any one start early enough."

With respect to the labeling of familiar objects, Fowler advocates that, after a relatively brief period of using single words in isolation, caregivers should incorporate labels into short, simple sentences, as this helps infants become aware of and familiar with the normal contextual basis of speech.

To achieve consistency in the use of labels, Fowler recommends that caregivers should train themselves to avoid using

(1) those tenses or or "persons" that require a change in the sound of the label (such as the past tense or third person); (2) multiple labels for the same object (such as "carrot," "vegetable," and "food"), preferring instead the most precise label (particularly in the early stages of language development); and (3) baby talk, except for affectionate names for the baby or pet animals and toys. Nevertheless, multiple words should be used for an object when the exemplar class that the word is used to designate is altered (for example, dog versus puppy), because this enables infants to learn categorical distinctions (the labels serve as examples to make it easy for infants to figure out both the relevant categories and the language rules).

The play aspects of these word-labeling experiences involve (1) turn taking, which makes the activity both involving and satisfying for infant and adult (and helps the caretaker avoid overdirection), and timing the introduction of adult initiatives to natural pauses in the infant's attention and play cycles; (2) being responsive to a child's initiatives, which includes making a concerted effort to label things that the child uses and does at least as often as labels are applied to caretaker initiatives; (3) encouraging the infant to manipulate toys and other small objects while the caretaker is talking about and labeling them; (4) among older infants, using "social play" (for example, manipulating miniature animals and dolls while pretending that they are alive or using labels for concrete actions, such as walking, rather than abstract movements, such as going); and (5) pacing these sessions to the infant's attention span, which usually means limiting "language play" to frequent two- to five-minute sessions, and its cognitive "style" (fast versus slow, playful versus task centered).

Fowler advises that "[w]ordplay can profitably begin as early as three or four months of age, leading infants to begin understanding words by six to eight months and saying their first real words by seven to nine months (sometimes earlier)" (p. III–2). He recommends that the emphasis in labeling should be on frequently seen small objects and on action verbs. Routine caregiving activities such as feeding, bathing, and dressing provide important opportunities to label, because the same set of objects and movements are involved day after day. These activities are also ideal ones for teaching an infant a basic set of words.

Fowler has composed specific lists of words for parents to use as labels during various caregiving activities. He stresses that, after a baby's understanding develops, asking very specific questions (as opposed to asking abstract questions or making general statements) encourages the infant's active participation in language learning. He recommends that, during bottle feedings and nap and bedtime routines, language should be used to quiet rather than stimulate the infant. Nevertheless, lullabies and gentle songs and poems (used repetitively to maximize familiarity) can also serve to heighten an infant's skill with and esthetic appreciation of language.

Fowler stresses that the mastery of each successive language concept depends on the child's first understanding the simpler concepts that lead up to it.[1] He advises caretakers not to expect either instant progress or consistent gains in language skills from week to week; rather, he indicates that it usually takes time at each stage for notable advances in language skills to develop, with persistent efforts often resulting in an infant making a sudden advance, sometimes after weeks with no apparent progress at all.

When this program is begun in infancy, "vocalization play" (or interactive play with sounds) should precede the introduction of labeling. In vocalization play, the caregiver first imitates the vocal sounds made by the infant. Before long, most infants will begin to repeat the sounds the caretaker has just imitated, and then imitate other sounds often made by the caretaker. Fowler suggests that during this form of play, the baby should be held in the caregiver's lap (with the baby's and caregiver's faces no more than a foot or so apart). If the caregiver engages the baby in this kind of sound play several times a day, it will usually not take long for both baby and adult to become "sophisticated players, vocalizing, smiling, and sometimes laughing in an ongoing cycle of pleasure" (p. IV–2)[2] The next step in this "sound play" is to introduce new sounds (new in the sense that the baby has never or seldom made them). The caregiver should choose sounds that bear a resemblance to the sounds and syllables of real words and prefer those that the infant displays a facility in acquiring. As these play sessions continue, infants will gradually get the idea that all new sounds are to be imitated and will imitate an increasing number of sounds, as well as learn to imitate them with greater accuracy. Fowler recommends that "imitative play" should be continued in the same form (but with decreased frequency) for a few weeks after "language play" is introduced.

Fowler also recommends that picture books be introduced at a very early age, even though it will usually take one to two weeks of daily sessions before a baby will become willing to look at even a specially designed book for as long as a few minutes, particularly when this activity is begun at three to six months of age.[3] With experience, however, most infants will display a definite interest in books, especially if parents are relaxed about it.[4] The same interactive labeling techniques that parents use with toys and other objects are helpful here, especially such techniques as showing an immediate interest in and labeling a picture when the baby points to it first. Similarly, verse and song should be used as vehicles for sound and word learning, particularly those songs and poems rooted in sensory-motor activity (and physical interactive play), since these provide repetitive links between parts of the body (and/or facial expressions) and actions. Fowler provides examples such as playing "This little pig went to market" while wiggling the baby's toes.

Fowler's book also gives detailed information about the mechanisms for expanding language comprehension during the second year of life. These include:

- Extending "word play" and simple "sentence play" into more complex forms (with special emphasis on combining nouns with action verbs).
- Stressing prepositions when they are used as part of an action ("Let's put the car *in* the box").
- Teaching adjectives by contrasting opposites (such as saying, "Here is a *big ball*, and here is a *small ball*," and pointing to each in turn at the moment these key words are stressed).
- Using dramatic and/or manipulative play (with miniature animals, dolls, and other objects) to highlight constancy and "patterned novelty" (for example, "The doll *pets* the *dog*; now the doll *pets* the *ball*").

- Teaching pronouns by taking turns saying and acting out opera-tions (for example, "*I* give the apple to *you*. *You* give the apple to *me*"; or "*I* walk to the door. *You* walk to the door").
- Substituting nonsense words for real words to increase sensitivity to sound patterns, provided that the alterations are silly, obvious, and based on words that the child knows thoroughly; for instance, calling a cat a "scat" or a cup a "mup" will usually evoke a response that indicates that the toddler considers the "misexpected" sound funny and the "game" an exciting challenge.[5]

Aside from facilitating an understanding of the individual rules of language, these approaches also constitute mechanisms for teaching toddlers **how to learn**. Moreover, the linguistically competent toddler's success is apt to be rewarded by adults with attention and praise, leading to greater feelings of competence and to the sorts of interactions with adults that can result in further developmental advances.

Fowler indicates that it is usually not very difficult for toddlers to advance from labeling objects seen in pictures to understanding more complex scenes, provided that the process moves forward one step at a time. The first step is to introduce books that depict the actions of a single animal or child over a series of pictures, with each picture depicting a single, familiar action. This will enable toddlers to "progress quite easily from understanding individual scenes to connecting the familiar actions from picture to picture, and thereby recognize them as a series of events happening to the same creature" (p. IX–5). Parents are advised to examine each new book before introducing it and to think about those features that may pose new challenges to their child's understanding. Then, if unfamiliar settings are introduced, they may consider making connections to things with which the child is familiar. If the narrative is too difficult, they can formulate a highly simplified version (focusing on concrete action statements) and then expand on the story line with subsequent repetitions.

Little by little toddlers will develop the ability to talk about recent events. When this facility develops, Fowler advises parents to set aside a few minutes once or twice a day to induce their child to talk about his or her experiences. Often, they will need to stimulate their toddler's consciousness by providing specific reminders of recent events (stressing achievements, activities the child enjoyed, or things he or she found interesting or funny). The more specific the questions asked of the child and the more relaxed the atmosphere is for these three- or four-minute "guided narrative" sessions, the more easily will parents be able to motivate the child to participate in expressive language experiences.

Fowler indicates that using the curricula laid out in his book is likely to produce an acceleration in language skills on the following order of magnitude:

- *Repeats two-syllable sounds*: from six to seven months in a normal cognitive environment to five to six months in a language-enriched environment.
- *Recognizes the names of some objects*: from eight to nine months to six to eight months.
- *Imitates words*: from ten to eleven months to seven to nine months.
- *Says first real words*: from ten to twelve months to seven to nine months.
- *Develops ten- to twenty-word vocabulary*: from eighteen to twenty months to nine to eleven months.
- *Says two- or three-word combinations*: from twenty to twenty-four months to twelve to fifteen months.
- *Talks in sentences*: from twenty-four to twenty-seven months to sixteen to eighteen months.
- *Relates experiences*: from thirty-three to thirty-six months to twenty-one to twenty-four months.
- *Uses basic rules of grammar*: from forty-eight months to twenty-four months.

12.3 Effective Use of Story Time for Language Development

An examination of parental behavior during "picture-book reading time" reveals that nearly all parents use this activity as an opportunity to teach language to their toddlers. To accomplish this, they ask questions (which they adjust to the developmental level of their child) and, as detailed below, give feedback to their toddlers' speech.

How adept parents are in this tutorial behavior has recently been shown to make a considerable difference in the pace at which toddlers' language skills develop (Whitehurst and others, 1988). This study of upper-middle-class suburban families demonstrates that the "reading behavior" of parents is far from optimal—even among motivated, affluent families—and strongly suggests that relatively simple changes in this behavior are very likely to accelerate language development.

The parents were taught certain experimental techniques, with the training (which was limited to two forty-five-minute sessions spaced two weeks apart) consisting of (1) a verbal explanation of the experimental techniques; (2) a "role play" demonstration of the techniques (by the experimenter and an assistant); and (3) participation by the parent in a role-playing session, with feedback about his or her performance then provided. The parents were also given a handout describing the techniques.

Even though the parents in the experimental group read to their toddlers with the same frequency as did the controls and used similar picture books,[6] the language development of the experimental group surged ahead dramatically within a month, and most of the differential was retained at a follow-up testing nine months later.[7]

The training sessions instructed parents how to alter the frequency, timing, and form of their child-directed speech during joint picture-book reading time.[8] According to Whitehurst and others (1988, p. 553), the principles governing this intervention strategy were:

- "The use of *evocative* techniques by the parent that encourage their child to talk about the pictured material is preferable to techniques that place the child in a more passive role; for example, asking children 'what' questions is preferable to reading to them without asking questions or to asking them yes-no questions."
- "The mother's use of *feedback* to the child should be maximally informative, for example, by incorporating expansions, corrective modeling, and other forms that highlight differences between what the child has said and what he might have said."
- "The mother's mastery standards for the child should show *progressive* change that is sensitive to the child's

developing abilities; for example, a child should indicate knowledge of the names of objects in books before the mother attempts to evoke talk about object attributes and relations."

Comparisons of the behavior of the parents and children in the experimental and control groups[9] during the fourth (and final) week of the program revealed that substantially greater frequencies of the following types of child-directed speech were uttered by parents in the experimental group: First, open-ended questions (nonspecific requests for descriptions, such as "What's happening to Oscar?" or "Tell me more") were posed on the average of once every thirty seconds, while virtually no open-ended questions were posed by the controls. Second, "expansions" (for example, the child says, "Dog," and the parent responds, "Big dog") were at the rate of once a minute, compared with once every three minutes in the control group. Third, praise or confirmation of the correctness of their toddlers' speech occurred two and a half times a minute, or twice as often as among controls. Fourth, repetition of a toddler's utterance (or a shortened version of it) occurred nearly twice a minute, or two and a half times as often as among controls. Fifth, labeling, coupled with a request to imitate (such as, "Doggie, you say please!"), occurred nearly once a minute, or eight times as often as among controls. Finally, complex "what" questions (where the expected answer is a function, attribute, or action) occurred twice a minute among the experimental group, or one-third more often than in the control group. By contrast, reading without requiring a response occurred with nearly two and a half times the frequency in the control group (nine phrases a minute versus four), and simple yes-no questions were posed 50 percent more often.

By the end of the four-week program, the children in the experimental group spoke in multiword phrases twice as often as controls, and the average length of their utterances was 2.55 words, compared with 2.04 words among controls.[10]

Thus, by inducing parents to (1) encourage their toddlers to think and to speak more during these reading sessions through their use of open-ended and wh— questions (that is, who, what, why, when questions); (2) repeat, expand upon, and recast their children's speech; and (3) provide praise and corrective feedback contingent on their child's speech, this program was able to accelerate language development.

Whitehurst and his colleagues then set about the task of developing a manual to train parents in the use of these techniques on their own. This manual contained specific age-appropriate reading materials with scripts designed to ensure adherence to the regimen used in the face-to-face training sessions. Nevertheless, use of these manuals generated only a slight increase in language skills (Whitehurst and others, 1989). The principal author suggests that the substantially greater benefits of the hands-on training were probably attributable to (1) the use of parent-selected reading materials (which were apt to be better attuned to the individual child's interests than the scripted material and (2) the maternal spontaneity associated with use of "novel" rather than prescribed reading materials. Mothers had a better opportunity to follow up on a child's responses with expansions and other feedback, and there was also better timing of open-ended questions. In addition, it would seem that *the parents' ability to absorb, retain, and apply the program's general principles was better when they witnessed live modeling and received feedback and reinforcement from their own behaviors than when they had to rely solely on a written training manual.*

A study that compared the form and function of maternal questions to twenty-one-month-old firstborns with the growth of these toddlers' language skills between twenty-one and twenty-eight months (Robeson, 1989)[11] found that a mother's use of "what is" questions and questions that were "topically and semantically related to her child's previous utterances" was associated with her child's increased use of syntactically advanced expressive language (such as verb phrases) and negatively correlated with the increased use of simple language (such as single nouns). Conversely, a mother's use of "huh tag" questions (to which the toddlers tended not to respond) was positively correlated with the toddler's later reliance on simple language and negatively correlated with more complex language forms. In addition, "mothers who initiated and kept to the same self-initiated topics through their questions when the children were twenty-one months of age had less linguistically able children at twenty-eight months of age" (n.p.) than those who made more frequent use of questions related to their child's utterances.

12.4 Understanding and Using the Transitions During Infancy and Toddlerhood

An infant's ability to register and retain auditory and visual information and to perceive that certain aspects of these stimuli have special salience sometimes appears well in advance of its ability to convey this knowledge to those parts of the brain that govern its actions. *Thus, knowledge that a baby acquires during a particular stage in its development may not show up in effective behavior until one—or even several—stages later.*

However, studies that reveal disparities between the **perceptual** acquisition of categorical knowledge in isolation and the translation of this knowledge into action make it possible to distinguish major cognitive transitions. Then, by examining findings about particular aspects of brain development during and just before these cognitive transitions, we can delineate the links between biology and behavior. Some of these stage-related anomalies between the perceptual or cognitive acquisition of knowledge and control over response behavior include:

- A two-and-a-half-year-old child does something that it is not supposed to do, even though it has just finished (or is in the process of) verbalizing aloud why this action is wrong.
- Most sixteen-month-old toddlers display an almost total disregard for a gross violation of the rules governing mechanical causality, even though three-month-old infants evidence a cognitive awareness that a "misexpected" event has occurred.
- Most eleven-month-olds are unable to make the connection between a well-known word for a familiar object

and the presence of that object in front of them, while most thirteen-month-olds can make such connections.

The behavior of the two-and-a-half-year-old gives some clues to the independent workings of the two brain hemispheres and to the circumstances in which one or the other tends to be "dominant." In the first instance described above, the left hemisphere — which is associated with language and tends to be *dominant during periods of quiet concentration* — is unsuccessfully trying to control the right hemisphere's "exploratory" behavior. The right hemisphere, which attends more to visuospatial and motor responses, is, in this situation, in firm control. Since this hemisphere tends to be *dominant during states of relatively high arousal*, trying to restore control over the child's behavior by shouting or physical punishment is unlikely to work. Rather, distraction (finding an activity that will engross the right hemisphere or will induce the left hemisphere to reassume control) or isolation would seem to be the preferred forms of discipline when the toddler's activities seem to indicate lack of control (see section 9.2).

Postmortem examinations of children's brains reveal that there are periods when the right hemisphere is growing at a considerably faster rate than the left, as well as periods when the left hemisphere's growth is considerably faster (Simonds and Scheibel, forthcoming). If these biological findings and their behavioral linkages are correct, the ages at which people are most heavily "right brained" are eight months, three years, and fifteen years, while the ages of four and sixteen months represent periods of greater left-brain development.[12] Thus, because right-hemisphere growth tends to predominate during the third year, "toddler lessons" should, at this age, stress the involvement of several of the child's senses (including motor activity).

When a chair at which a sixteen-month-old infant is looking appears to move of its own accord, there is a good likelihood that the toddler will not appreciate the bizarre nature of this event (Golinkoff and others, 1986),[13] even though (as indicated in Chapter Eleven) three-month-olds do possess a basic perceptual recognition of mechanical causality (Borton, 1979).[14] At sixteen months of age, the left hemisphere's speech areas are growing at a prodigious rate, with new primary dendrites emerging from the cell bodies of the so-called speech strategy and speech execution cells (Scheibel, 1985; Simonds and Scheibel, forthcoming). These changes are preparing for the emergence (at about eighteen to twenty-one months) of an ability to "represent" or to "symbolize" concrete objects and past events in one's mind and to "cognitively" evoke objects, people, or events that are not present, such as pretending that a doll is walking across the table or talking about what their uncle did several days earlier (Watson and Fischer, 1977).

The studies of Jean Carew (cited in section 9.3) indicate that the best predictor of a child's disposition to create "intellectually valuable" experiences at age two and a half is the frequency of experiences in the second year of life in which the caretaker provided the child with the experience and the child (for the most part) looked, listened, and imagined. Thus, during this era of heavily left-brained growth and dominance, children are, in a sense, paying more attention to their internal thoughts and visions than to the "holistic" aspects of visuospatial analytics (described in Chapters Fifteen and Sixteen), compared with their behavior at age two and a half.

At around twelve or thirteen months, the emergence of a verbally based referential capacity marks the onset of a stage in which toddlers become able to acquire more-abstract verbal concepts, to anticipate the consequences of sensorimotor actions, to undertake experiments, and to carry out simple pretending, and it also marks the end of a sensorimotor period during which spatial-skill development predominates (Campos and Bertenthal, 1989). This sensorimotor stage begins at about eight months and appears to be preceded by a period of extremely rapid brain growth (Fischer, 1987).[15]

With this as background, some salient stages of cognitive development and their implications for "infant and toddler lessons" are suggested in Table 32.

Notes

1.   Each of the stages of language stimulation involves a "characteristic set of processes for interacting with the baby to teach about that dimen-

Table 32. Cognitive Stages of Infancy and Toddlerhood.

Time Period	Principal Feature(s)	Keys to Effective Lessons
Birth to 6–8 weeks (the "imprint" period)	Sights and sounds are encoded holistically; right hemisphere is dominant	Promote quiet alertness; be aware of infant's limitations; use slow, exact repetition
8–13 weeks (the GAP)	Reduced importance of three-dimensionality; social behavior dominates	Use vocal imitation with patterned novelty; stress effective gaze behavior and pitch; use contingent responsivity
4–7 months	Many key cortical areas now connected to midbrain; three-dimensional acuity returns	Stress "encouragement of attention," visual habituation and novelty, and verbal patterning of imitative games
8–11 months	"Right-brain" dominance; motor skill development paramount	Present, label, and elaborate on objects; imitate baby's early words
Second year	Exceedingly rapid linguistic growth; left hemisphere is dominant; at 18–21 months "imagination" blossoms	Promote linguistic learning; use "quiet concentration" and elaborative reading style
Third year	Right hemisphere again dominant; the hemispheres are better able to communicate with and teach each other	Promote "interactive" multisensory learning, interactive reading, and holistic visualization; avoid punitive, inconsistent, and restrictive actions

sion of language," and each of these processes is capable of being broken down into a series of detailed steps. Fowler (forthcoming, p. III–4) indicates that, although infants should always be stimulated in language according to the skills they have mastered (not simply according to age), a somewhat flexible course (that is, "one which moves back and forth between adjacent steps more or less within the same level") is frequently advisable.

2. Nevertheless, in the early months, some babies will vocalize very little, and it will take several sessions before a child begins to vocalize, and even longer before imitation of parental sounds begins. In such cases, Fowler urges parents to talk to their infant gently, naturally, and not too rapidly and to emphasize pausing to give their baby a chance to respond.

3.   He recommends that, initially, pictures should be shown side by side with the objects photographed (to make it easier for infants to learn the rules about how pictures represent objects) and that these first books should show only a single object per page. Further, the photographs or drawings should be simple, clear, and realistic, with more-complex pictures (for example, scenes of people and things in action) post-poned until the infant has become an inveterate looker at picture books and shows stable signs of recognizing a variety of different objects. Fowler gives specific suggestions for the content and design of these homemade picture books.

4.   That is, they will want to look at more pictures, will smile and/or show excitement as the parent turns a page, and (depending on their age) will want to turn the pages themselves and/or respond when asked to point to a familiar object (such as an animal or a car). By the end of the first year, many babies will have a favorite book, wanting to look at it again and again.

5.   As the infant's language progresses, multisyllable nonsense variations are used (such as "nable" for table). Fowler presents several useful strategies for nonsense wordplay and indicates that this game is es-pecially helpful in promoting later reading and spelling skills, as well as poetry appreciation.

6.   Books with many vivid and easily described pictures (from among those brought by the parents during the first visit) were selected as examples of the type of books that should be used for reading sessions. The parents read to their twenty-one to thirty-five-month-old toddlers slightly more than seven times a week.

7.   After one month, their scores on the "verbal expressive" subtest of the Illinois Test of Psycholinguistic Abilities (ITPA) for the toddlers in the experimental group (Kirk, McCarthy, and Kirk, 1968) averaged 13.6 (compared with 5.1 for controls); their scores on the Expressive One-Word Picture Vocabulary Test (EOWPVT) (Gardner, 1981) averaged 14.5 (vs. 8.5 for controls); and their scores on the Peabody Picture Vocabulary Test (PPVT) (Dunn and Dunn, 1981) averaged 11.1 (vs. 7.9), meaning that, on average, they were nine months ahead of controls. At the nine-month follow-up, their average EOWPVT scores rose from 14.5 to 22.0, well above that of the control group (16.1). Although their ITPA scores remained stable (13.7), this was still far higher than that of the control group (7.8); on the PPVT, however, their slight increase (to 11.7) was on a par with that of controls. The PPVT (a measure of "receptive language") requires the child to point to the picture of the object referenced; by contrast, the EOWPVT requires the child to name the common object pictured, and the ITPA asks the child to tell about objects presented to him or her.

8.   During the first session, the mothers were urged to concentrate on (1) asking wh— questions, (2) modeling answers, (3) emphasizing "turn taking," and (4) encouraging their toddlers to use noun labels, at-tributes, and functions. In the event that a toddler's attention was not focused on the situation, parents were instructed to close the book and wait for a better opportunity. In the second session, the mothers were

encouraged to generate open-ended questions and expansions and to try to evoke multiword responses from their toddlers.

9. The parents in both groups audiotaped their reading sessions three to four times a week.

10. Interestingly, the frequency of several types of vocalizations did not vary between these groups. These vocalizations included "simple labeling" by the parent, single-word utterances by the child, and nonword vocalizations by the child (for example, "wheee").

11. The sample consisted of thirty-seven (primarily upper-middle-class) Caucasian families.

12. Cortical activity reaches its lifetime peak at age four and continues at this nearly double adult level until age eleven; this suggests that both hemispheres are processing virtually all information simultaneously. However, because certain (within-hemisphere) cell-network connections have not yet been established, some interesting behavioral anomalies persist (Joseph and others, 1984; Joseph, 1982).

13. In the study, the chair was moved three feet by a hidden person pulling clear plastic wires attached to its legs; a combination of affective and motor responses were used to distinguish children who perceived interesting vs. "misexpected" events. Sixty-one percent of the sixteen-month-olds did not perceive this event as a "gross violation," compared with only 22 percent at twenty-four months.

14. A red cube moves along a track until it disappears behind a screen, and a white cube then emerges (in tempo) at the other side. Three-month-old infants show a substantial increase in attention when, on subsequent trials, a raised screen reveals no collision between the objects, compared with trials in which the raised screen shows that the objects had collided (Borton, 1979, summarized in Golinkoff and others, 1986; Ball and Tronick, 1971).

15. This study of over 1,000 infants found that, following a growth spurt in mean head circumference the month before, there was virtually no growth in head circumference between eight and nine months of age; the mean growth rates were: eight to nine months, 0.1 percent; seven to eight months, 2.7 percent; six to seven months, 1.5 percent. Similarly, a rapid growth spurt of 3.1 percent occurred between the third and fourth months (focused between the fifteenth and seventeenth weeks), just when many key cortical and subcortical pathways' myelination cycles are heaviest and nearing completion; this was the largest percentage increase found for any month of infancy. Fischer and Silvern (1985) conclude that empirical evidence supports the existence of at least three further periods of rapid behavioral change: at six to seven years, ten to twelve years, and fourteen to sixteen years. They also consider the age at which a child begins to relate "mental representations" to one another (three and a half to four and a half years) as delineating the onset of a major developmental stage.

Contents

✗ 13 ✗

How
Japanese Mothering Practices
Heighten Spatial/Structural
Reasoning Ability

13.0 Synopsis

The exceptional performance of the Japanese people in some cognitive areas but not in others can be traced to the nature of traditional Japanese child-rearing and educational practices. These may be summarized as follows:

- *In infancy,* maternal behavior emphasizes visual stimulation, along with emotional communication through physical contact, and deemphasizes verbal stimulation and communication; this fosters the development of spatially and bodily oriented modes of perception and analysis, skills that are associated with the right hemisphere of the human brain.
- *In children's initial educational experiences,* there is an emphasis on motivational arousal, the training of "concentration skills," and — through painstaking practice — the development of visual-motor integrative skills.
- *In school,* the emphasis is on group learning and achievement, perseverance, a heavy regimen of home-

work, testing as a requirement of advancement, and the importance of having a good education.

13.1 Introduction

The Japanese people, considered as a group, excel on those segments of IQ tests that measure spatial intelligence (in particular, those segments that assess three-dimensional analytical skills),[1] and they also evidence a superior ability in solving those types of logical-mathematical problems for which a "structural reasoning" approach can be utilized.[2] This heightened spatial and structural acumen has enabled Japanese children to do particularly well on international tests of mathematics and science (Husen, 1967; Comber and Keeves, 1973). Nevertheless, in verbally oriented areas, the Japanese people do not display significantly above average ability.

Because specific aspects of the early home environment can induce profound and lasting changes in people's cognitive abilities, we will examine, first, whether there are features in traditional Japanese child-rearing practices that are especially conducive to the development of spatial and structural competence and, second, whether there are aspects of these practices that do not favor the development of exceptional verbal abilities.

13.2 The Traditional Japanese Child-Rearing Philosophy

To develop an understanding of traditional Japanese maternal nurturing behaviors and how these are transformed into Japanese educational practices, let us begin with a description of the traits of character that Japanese culture seeks to implant in a growing child. We will then examine how these aspirations are reflected in the Japanese mother's perceptions of her newborn infant and of her role in that infant's development. Fortunately, the studies and analyses of the late William Caudill present a clear and comprehensive picture of the "philosophical imperatives" that underlie these early nurturing practices.

Caudill's (1973) delineation of behavioral traits that are highly regarded in traditional Japanese culture incorporates the following themes: There is, first of all, a strong sense that the group or community is of central importance, particularly with reference to one's family but also extending outward to other groups (such as one's school and place of employment). This feeling includes a strong sense of "we," since for most Japanese self-esteem derives largely from membership in and contributions to various groups. Next comes devotion to parents, including an especially strong and long-enduring tie (in almost childhood form) to one's mother, who "appears in the minds of a majority of Japanese [as] a self-sacrificing, succoring, and enveloping being" (p. 245). The Japanese also have a strong sense of obligation and gratitude (which is especially acute in respect to the need to repay personal obligations) just as they are given to strong feelings of sympathy and compassion. Their willingness to work hard to achieve long-range goals has become legendary, and this is combined with an attitude of deference and politeness, especially toward their superiors. For our purposes, it is especially noteworthy that the Japanese exhibit a tendency "to rely on emotional feeling and intuition as much as on reason" (p. 245). Just as important, they are also highly sensitive to various forms of nonverbal communication in human relations, such as body motion—including gestures, facial expressions, and eye movements (Morsbach, 1973)—and physical proximity, "in comparison with Americans who predominantly use verbal communication within a context of physical separateness" (Caudill, 1973, p. 246). A discussion of the possible origins of several of these "cultural imperatives" is contained in Chapter Twenty.

Caudill's comparative study of maternal-infant behavior in Japan and America (Caudill and Weinstein, 1969) led him to conclude that in America infants tend to be seen as dependent biological organisms who, in order to develop, need to become increasingly independent of others. By contrast, in traditional Japanese society, infants tend to be viewed as separate biological organisms who, in order to develop, need to be drawn into increasingly interdependent relations with others.

This philosophical distinction underlies a number of fundamental differences in child-rearing practices—differences that, in American children, foster the development of a verbally oriented, independent style of thinking and, in Japanese children, result in a more visually oriented, more structurally denominated, and more disciplined style of perception and analysis.

13.3 Maternal Care in Infancy: The Work of William Caudill

The initial portion of Caudill's study provided a detailed analysis of the patterns of behavior displayed by Japanese and American mothers toward their three- to four-month-old firstborn children (Caudill and Weinstein, 1969). This study of college-educated Japanese families in the early 1960s, along with their carefully matched American counterparts,[3] revealed a number of striking differences in maternal behavior, even though, in several important respects, there was considerable similarity.[4] The following were among the largest differences reported:

- The Japanese mother spent more than twice as much time *rocking her infant* as the American mother.
- The American mother *chatted with her infant* one and a half times as often as the Japanese mother.
- The Japanese mother *held her infant* for a substantially greater proportion of the time (24.6 percent versus 17.4 percent), especially when the infant was sleeping.

These (and other) observed differences led Caudill and Weinstein (1969) to comment, "The mothers in the two cultures engage in different styles of caretaking: The American mother seems to encourage her baby to be active and vocally responsive, while the Japanese mother acts in ways which she believes will soothe and quiet her baby" (p. 23). Caudill (1972) then concludes, "The mother's perception of her infant and of her relation to him would seem to be different in the two cultures. In America the mother views her baby as a *potentially separate and autonomous being* who should learn to act and think for himself. For her, the baby is from birth a distinct personality with his own needs and desires which she must learn to recognize and care for. She helps him to learn to express these needs and desires through her emphasis on vocal communication so that he can 'tell' her what he wants" (p. 43). By way of contrast, the Japanese mother "views her baby more as *an extension of herself*, and psychologically the boundaries between the two of them are blurred. The mother feels that she knows what is best for her baby, and there is no particular need for him to tell her what he wants because, after all, they are virtually one" (p. 43).

Thus, in Japan, there is a greater emphasis on the interdependence of mother and child, an interdependence that extends throughout childhood (for example, Japanese children will ordinarily sleep in the same room with their parents until the age of ten) and on into adulthood.

The American mother responded more rapidly to her infant's vocalizations—particularly to unhappy vocalizations. By contrast, the Japanese mother did not differentiate between happy and unhappy vocalizations in determining the speed of her response. The American mother also engaged in considerably more verbal interaction with her baby, "especially by chatting to him at the same time that he is happily vocalizing" (Caudill and Schooler, 1973, p. 325). Thus, by these behaviors, American mothers are apparently seeking to encourage their infants' happy vocalizations and discourage their unhappy vocalizations, while at the same time emphasizing the overall importance of vocal communication and teaching their infants to make a more discriminating use of their voices.

The Japanese mother's behavior appears to reflect a desire to produce a passive, compliant baby who will rely on her to fulfill its needs. She does this in part by offering little encouragement to her infant's efforts to express its needs through an auditory mode and in part through a reliance on physical contact—on holding, carrying, rocking, and other activities designed to produce a quiet, content infant. However, despite this more abundant provision of soothing and quieting behavior, the Japanese infants slept no more during the morning and afternoon observation periods than did their American counterparts. There are apparently two causes for this seeming anomaly—one related to differences in the behavior of the Japanese and American mothers while their children were asleep, and the other to an outgrowth of the Japanese infants' increasing reliance on being held and rocked.

The American mother was far more likely to use her baby's nap time to fulfill other aspects of her (busy) life than was her Japanese counterpart, and when she remained in her baby's room, she was likely to spend considerable time watching her baby sleeping peacefully. The Japanese mother, by contrast, spent much more time holding her sleeping baby, and—presumably because he or she had come to depend on this rocking and holding—the infant would often awaken when put down. Further, the Japanese mother often engaged in a pattern of behavior that would, by Western standards, seem strange: After pacifying her baby and getting it to fall asleep, she would then reawaken it by adjusting its covers, wiping its forehead, and so on, after which she would return to her regimen of holding and rocking. Moreover, this behavior would continue even though the infant often registered unhappiness at being awakened. This suggests that the object of this pattern of behavior had more to do with a desire to create a relaxed, passive, dependent baby than to induce sleep (Caudill and Schooler, 1973).[6]

13.4 Rocking, Soothing, and Intelligence Building in Infancy

During the first several weeks and months of life, infants already possess a considerable capacity to learn, particularly when they are in a state of *quiet alertness*. The greatest impediment to entering and remaining in this state is an innate tendency toward overarousal—a tendency that relates, in large part, to the needs of the baby's immature vestibular system. The sharp changes of direction that are a concomitant part of rocking help to satisfy this vestibular need and thereby reduce overarousal. Thus, by supplying her baby with more rocking than her American counterpart, as well as engaging in greater amounts of other activities designed to soothe her infant, the Japanese mother is likely to induce more-frequent and longer-lasting periods of quiet alertness. When accompanied by the motion of rocking, this state of quiet alertness stimulates an infant's visual-tracking reflexes and focuses its attention on visual and auditory stimuli.

Since the act of holding and quietly rocking an infant is likely to heavily engage the right hemisphere of the brain (see Chapter Fifteen), Japanese infants would seem to receive relatively more "right-brain" stimulation than do American infants. Moreover, the tendency of Japanese mothers to provide physical rather than verbal interaction adds to this reliance on the right hemisphere's mode of encoding and analysis. Why this result? Because, even in day-old infants, speech is "processed" in the left hemisphere, in contrast to other environmental sounds, which are processed primarily in the right hemisphere (Condon and Sander, 1974; Prescott and DeCasper, forthcoming). Further, the Japanese mother's emphasis on the expression of feeling through nonverbal communication (that is, through physical contact and lulling), in contrast to expressing feeling through the tone of voice accompanying speech, also enhances the right hemisphere's involvement. Consequently, this emphasis appears to be a precursor to the Japanese child's developing skill in, and reliance on, nonverbal communication (Morsbach, 1973) as well as his or her use of "intuition," rather than logic, which are considered to be integral parts of the Japanese character (Caudill, 1973).

If one subscribes to the increasingly prevalent view that the nature and amount of environmental stimulation received during the formative stages of postnatal brain development can have considerable and lasting effects on that development, then the relative amounts of visual, verbal, tactile, and motor stimulation received during these initial weeks and months of life will alter *the capacity of the analytical mechanism of each of these sensory systems by strengthening or attenuating the (preprogrammed) biological endowment of the structural architecture of these cell networks*. Thus, by inducing a greater degree of "right-brain" activity during early infancy, the Japanese mother appears to strengthen the biological foundations that underlie those cognitive domains in which her child will one day be likely to excel.

13.5 Initial Educational Experiences of the Japanese Child

Another fundamental difference between the early upbringing of Japanese and American children involves their introduction to the educational process, including preschool learning situations and the initial school experience. Because Japanese children experience an extraordinary sense of accomplishment upon gaining entry to high-prestige "learning" groups, the Japanese educational system is thus able to use these feelings as an opportunity to teach novice learners basic learning skills and appropriate attitudes, by making acquisition of these skills and attitudes a prerequisite to joining an elite group of learners. Peak (1986, pp. 113–114) has summed up this process beautifully as follows: "Both traditional and contemporary Japanese education place an extremely high priority on careful structuring of novice students' introduction to learning situations. Typically, the period of transition from initial application to fully accepted beginning student is considerably protracted, encompassing several months or more. During this period the new student undergoes systematic training in the basic attitudes and cognitive support skills fundamental to the medium to be learned. This preliminary training requires a long period of diligent study and thorough mastery of precisely defined basic routines before the student is allowed to engage in the medium itself."

The initiation period usually begins with the time-honored practice of learning through watching, which has two different objectives: First, it helps the child to acquire an ability to sit quietly and attentively (which Peak refers to as the development of "concentration skills"). Second, it creates an atmosphere in which the child can develop an increasingly aroused motivation as the child gets closer to the day when he or she will attain membership in a new elite social group.

This "concentration-skill" training usually entails a diligent regimen of practice in a motor skill. (Gardner, 1985, instances the teaching of the Suzuki method of learning to play the violin as an extreme example of the successful application of this method to very young children [see Suzuki, 1969]). In first grade, the class will generally spend the first several days practicing how to stand, bow, and say, "Good morning, teacher," in unison — with every move of the routine broken down into a series of tiny steps that are painstakingly practiced until the task becomes an automatic, smoothly executed skill.

This sense of pride in becoming a part of the "we" of a prestigious learning group is then transformed into a spirit of cooperation in the schoolroom. Challenging problems may be posed to entire classes, whose members will work together to develop a solution (Gardner, 1985), sometimes over the course of several days. Children are encouraged to help one another, and sometimes older children visit the classrooms of younger ones and assist them in their tasks. The common effort to understand difficult problems—accompanied by the feeling that it is acceptable not to be able to come up with a correct answer right away as long as one keeps plugging away at a problem—is a hallmark of this type of group learning (Easley and Easley, 1982).

In instructing their children in a task that has both conceptual and procedural aspects, Japanese mothers will usually employ the *procedural* approach and American mothers the *conceptual* approach. For example, in teaching their children a sorting task, the Japanese mothers were observed to "consistently emphasize the procedural aspects of the task, while [their] U.S. counterparts emphasize[d] a conceptual grasp of the sorting principles . . . recycling the instruction [they received] sometimes verbatim [and] pressing the child for a verbal response to [determine if] the child had mastered the concept of the exercise" (Hess and Azuma, 1986, p. 4). These behavioral differences imply that the Japanese mother expects her child to infer the correct principle or concept by repeating the correct procedure. This use of "procedural" rather than "conceptual" learning as the primary approach to solving visual-analysis and visual-motor integration problems[7] is a logical extension of the Japanese mothers' early emphasis on providing visual and physical—rather than verbal—forms of stimulation.

In languages such as Chinese and Japanese, reading is heavily dependent on the right hemisphere's holistic mode of perception and analysis. Thus, words whose characters are ideographic or pictographic representations are read holistically (as complete templates), in contrast to words whose characters consist exclusively of vowels and consonants that frequently need to be sounded out phonetically (sequentially).[8] Therefore, it should come as no surprise that Japanese children become capable of distinguishing which of several drawings is identical to the original at a substantially earlier age than American children. In one study, the competence of the average eight-year-old Japanese child had already surpassed that of the average ten-year-old American child (Salkind, Kogima, and Zelniker, 1978). These authors conclude that, because the Japanese language "is characterized by symbolic as well as phonetic alphabet characters, stresses attention to detail and to the formation of images involved in learning complex symbolic characters, [and] requires accurate processing of pictorial information" (p. 1026), the process of language acquisition enables the Japanese child to develop an accelerated and more accurate performance in processing pictorial information.

The mathematical superiority of Japanese schoolchildren (compared with Americans) is already apparent in the first grade. In a comparative study of first- and fifth-grade children in Japan, Taiwan, and Minneapolis (Stigler and others, 1982; see analysis by Fiske, 1987),[9] the Japanese children outperformed the American children by 18 and 20 percent, respectively, even though the testing modality included "word problems" (at which American children are thought to be at a "lesser disadvantage").[10] Other differences noted in this study include: (1) the average class size in first grade was twenty-one in Minneapolis, thirty-nine in Sendai (Japan), and forty-seven in Taipei (Taiwan); (2) in the first grade, homework per week averaged 79 minutes in Minneapolis, 233 minutes in Japan, and 496 minutes in Taiwan; and in the fifth grade, 256 minutes, 368 minutes, and 771 minutes, respectively; and (3) the proportion of classroom time spent in mathematics was 14 percent in America, 25 percent in Japan, and 17 percent in Taiwan. Nevertheless, these authors judged that curriculum was not a major factor in the better performance of the Asian children.

In contrast to their scores on mathematics, the scores of these first-grade American children on tests of their knowledge of general information were well above those of their Japanese and Taiwanese counterparts. Stigler and others attribute this to an apparently greater amount of intellectual stimulation provided by American parents in the preschool period, and reinforce this conclusion with a finding that, in kindergarten, 98 percent of these American parents had read to their children, compared with 84 percent in Sendai and 76 percent in Taipei. The authors further speculate that after their children enter first grade, American parents "tend to turn education over to the schools, while Chinese and Japanese parents become heavily involved in their children's schoolwork, encouraging homework and financing tutoring" (Stigler and others, 1982, p. 320).

13.6 Conclusions

In early infancy, Japanese child-rearing practices foster the development of the human brain's visual skills, along with nonverbal mechanisms for the expression of emotion, while somewhat suppressing verbal communication. This is followed by an approach to initial educational experiences that demands that children pay close attention to the physical aspects of their environment and use their developing powers of concentration to hone their perceptual and visual-motor integrative skills. They are then taught to use these skills as a basis for conceptual learning.

These practices foster the use of spatially oriented, externally focused, and holistically based perceptual skills, as well as of emotionally intuitive skills, all of which are considered to lie primarily within the province of the human brain's right hemisphere. They also reduce the use of the brain's verbally based and internally focused mode of thinking, which is dominated by the analytical skills of the left hemisphere. This approach has apparently facilitated the development of those cognitive abilities that rely heavily on the right hemisphere — namely, spatial intelligence and a structural approach to logical and mathematical reasoning.

Perhaps this is why, after a twelve-year investigation into the factors underlying the Japanese proficiency in math and science, Hess and Azuma (1986, p. 4) have concluded that "the close bonding between the Japanese mother and child is at least as important as the extra hours of study put in by Japanese children." They also note that a young Japanese child's maturity is generally gauged on the basis of "the politeness, compliance, and self-control shown in relationships with adults," while in the United States, "the 'good' child is assertive, socially competent with peers, and courteous." Given these basic differences, it is unlikely that applying Japanese educational practices in America will produce equivalent effects.

Despite their outstanding achievements in mathematics and science, many Japanese people greatly admire one aspect of what they see as the "intellectual character" of the American people—namely, the strong sense of individuality displayed in their verbally oriented creativity and originality. This is particularly evident in university courses such as economics in which the underlying principles and their applications can be understood and/or expressed verbally, mathematically, or in both ways. Here, again, the distinction apparently relates to the alternative use of structural or conceptual approaches to understanding the confluence of and interrelationship between variables. Moreover, just as those American students who are unable to maintain a lasting grasp of calculus are often envious of the ease with which Oriental students seem to master its intricacies, so too are many structurally oriented students painfully aware that they will never attain the depth of understanding demonstrated by verbally gifted people in areas where the shades and nuances of verbal meaning are all-important.

Notes

1. The ability to make direct comparisons between Japanese and American subjects on verbal subtests is limited to those areas that do not require the specific use of language (for example, "digit span"). Exceptional Japanese performance is noted on the WISC "block design" subtest, with less exceptional but still significantly above average performance found on the "object assembly," "picture arrangement," and "mazes" subtests (for detailed findings, see Chapters Five and Twenty).

2. For example, the performance of Japanese children on tests known as "nonsense syllogisms" tends to be exceptional, relative to their scores on syllogisms where meaning, rather than structure, determines the validity of the statement to be evaluated.

3. The matched sample of thirty intact middle-class Caucasian American families from large urban areas was also (to the extent feasible)

matched on the nature of the father's employment, including type of employer.

4. For example, the infants in both cultures spent approximately the same proportion of these morning and afternoon observation periods eating and sleeping, and the Japanese and American mothers in this study spent, on the average, the same proportion of their time (42 percent) in caregiving activities. These findings are based on 800 coded observation points for each child over a two-day span.

5. Chatting (exclusive of "lulling") accompanied 39 percent of the American mothers' "awake-child" caregiving activity time, compared with 28 percent (of a slightly lower "awake-child" caregiving total) among the Japanese mothers. Lulling an infant to sleep averaged 2.7 percent of the observation time among the Japanese mothers, compared with 0.4 percent in the American sample.

6. At age two and a half, these Japanese children showed significantly less vocal activity than their American counterparts ($p < .003$), with this difference widening even further at age six ($p < .001$). At age two and a half, the Japanese children were also more likely to seek reassurance from their mothers, and these mothers were far more likely to carry and hold their children. Nevertheless, a recent Japanese study (Bornstein, Miyake, and Tamis-LeMonda, 1989; Bornstein and Tamis-LeMonda, 1989) found a correlation of $+.44$ between prompt, contingent, and appropriate maternal (verbal or physical) responsiveness to four- to five-month-old infants' nondistress initiatives, on the one hand, and these infants' PPVT scores at age two and a half, on the other.

7. This involves attaining a conceptual grasp of categorizational skills by paying primary attention to visually observable aspects of physical structure, as opposed to having the "structural" aspects of a task flow from an understanding of its "conceptual" aspects.

8. The Chinese language contains approximately 5,000 pictographs (a picture of a sun, a moon, or a tree, with two trees denoting a forest); nevertheless, the large majority of Chinese words are written as ideographs (the concept of "goodness" being depicted by a woman leading a child by the hand, and the concept of family by a roof overhanging a pig). Although beyond the scope of these present writings, certain commonalities between Chinese and Japanese cultural values, child-rearing practices, and written language are worthy of note, including a heavy maternal regimen of carrying, rocking, and other soothing behaviors, a strong sense of "we" in respect to one's family, and a reverence for one's elders—as well as their apparent cognitive effects (exceptional ability in math and in specific areas of the sciences). The traditional use of an abacus for mathematical calculation also induces a reliance on a visuospatial approach (rather than a "left-brained" approach) to basic math.

9. Two hundred and forty randomly selected first graders and 240 fifth graders were tested in each country, and common elements from each country's curricula formed the basis for selecting the questions used. Socioeconomically, Minneapolis is well above the U.S. average and is now ranked as the most desirable U.S. city in which to raise children.

10. For example, 55 percent of the American first graders could not determine how many pencils were purchased by three boys who bought two pencils each, and 36 percent could not determine the sum of seven and five when presented as a word problem. The Taiwanese children had a slight advantage over their Japanese counterparts in first grade, but the fifth-grade Japanese children demonstrated a slight advantage. These Japanese and Taiwanese students have a five-and-a-half-day school week and a longer school year than in America.

Contents

❧ 14 ❧

The Nurturing of Verbal/Conceptual Reasoning Abilities in Jewish Families

14.1 Introduction

Numbering only seventeen million people, the Jewish people represent about 1 percent of the population of the developed world. Yet their contributions to human progress have been so great and have encompassed so many vital areas that if causal connections exist between traditional Jewish child-rearing and educational practices and the types of intellectual abilities at which the Jewish people frequently excel, then elaborating on this early Jewish home life would surely provide information of considerable value in efforts to design and implement effective child education programs.

Although the range of exceptional Jewish intellectual accomplishment is extremely broad, it is far from all-encompassing. Like the Japanese, the Jewish people, considered as a group, display heightened ability in some cognitive areas, but not in others. In contrast to the visuospatially based, structurally oriented giftedness of the Japanese, the "Jewish intellect" appears to be centered on

- An ability to manipulate and integrate chains of reasoning, especially those related to "causality," coupled

313

with a faculty otherwise known as verbal and/or symbolic analytics to interrelate and explain derived
meanings.

- An ability to integrate emotional context with such
analytical frameworks as the skills needed to attain
proficiency in conducting and playing classical music,
acting, selling, and practicing psychotherapy.

The review of the traditional Jewish home presented in this
chapter suggests that close correspondences exist between
(1) the nature of the environment provided in the Jewish home,
(2) the types of cognitively enriching early experiences that are
associated with higher IQ outcomes, and (3) the areas in which
Jewish people tend to display markedly above-average ability.
Nevertheless, it would be inappropriate to conclude that a single
generation of exposure to such an environment is sufficient to
produce the extent of giftedness displayed among the "people of
the Book," just as it would be wrong to conclude that one or two
generations of rearing in an environment lacking in these "enrichments" will cause the complete disappearance of this
giftedness.

14.2 The "Shape" of Jewish Intelligence

Jewish people, considered as a group, tend to excel in some
cognitive domains—for example, verbal and numerical ability—but not in others, as witness their unexceptional performance on certain types of spatial or perceptual problems
(where their scores sometimes average slightly below test
norms). As a consequence, the scores of Jewish subjects on tests
that have high verbal, numerical, and conceptual factor loadings (such as the Stanford-Binet) will usually exceed their scores
on tests that have a greater or exclusive emphasis on nonverbal
and/or perceptual skills.

To evaluate the possible effect of a traditional, religiously
orthodox Jewish environment on IQ performance, we can subdivide our review of findings from postwar American studies
into those that tested public school students and those that

tested only students attending full-day religiously oriented, private schools.

Jewish Students Attending Public Schools in Postwar America

A nationwide survey of American high school students in the late 1960s — called Project Talent — provides an excellent basis for comparing the ability of Jewish and non-Jewish children in several academic and nonacademic cognitive areas (Backman, 1972). Because the non-Jewish Caucasian sample's performance was exactly in accordance with expectations[1] and the number of Jewish students sampled (1,236) was relatively large, the results provide an excellent portrayal of the Jewish students' "pattern" of abilities:

- *Mathematics:* The scores of the Jewish boys averaged almost a full standard deviation above those of the non-Jewish boys, and the Jewish girls' scores exceeded those of their non-Jewish counterparts by a nearly equivalent degree (0.75 standard deviations); because boys substantially outperform girls on this test, the *average score of the Jewish boys was in the top 1 percent of all test takers.*[2]
- *Verbal knowledge:* The Jewish boys' scores averaged 0.7 standard deviations higher than those of the non-Jewish boys, and the Jewish girls outperformed their non-Jewish Caucasian counterparts by slightly more than half a standard deviation.
- *Perceptual speed and accuracy:* The non-Jewish students' scores were on a par with the Jewish students in this test of visual-motor coordination under speeded conditions, as well as on a test of grammar and language usage.
- *Reasoning with spatial forms:* The Jewish students scored significantly less well on this test (half a standard deviation lower than the non-Jewish sample) and also performed poorly on a measure of short-term recall of sequences of nonword letter strings (scoring 0.3 standard deviations below the non-Jewish sample).[3]

Following are some other postwar American studies of Jewish children who attended public schools:

- *Suburban Detroit* (1972): The scores of 88 sixth-grade Jewish children averaged 119.2 on the California Test of Mental Maturity (short form), or 7 points higher than their 425 non-Jewish classmates (Cicirelli, 1978, 1976; personal communication, 1988); part of this difference was due to the excellent performance of those

Jewish subjects who were the youngest children in their families. Among the non-Jewish subjects, the usual birth-order effects were found, but in the Jewish families — where being a youngest child usually meant a very favorable (rather than an unfavorable) care-taker ratio — the scores of the youngest children *exceeded those* of earlier birth orders.

- *Philadelphia* (early 1970s): Seven hundred and seventy Jewish adolescents attending public high schools (who were seen at a career counseling center) had scores averaging 115 on the Otis IQ test (Romanoff, 1976);[4] again, the usual birth-order effects were absent.[5]

- *New York City* (early 1960s): Eighty Jewish children aged six and seven (forty upper-middle-class; forty lower- and lower-middle-class) were tested on a battery of "culture-reduced" tests, and their scores were then compared with those of similar samples of Chinese, Black, and Puerto Rican students. The Jewish students scored exceptionally well on the verbal test — the upper-middle-class Jewish students averaging 96.8 and the lower-middle-class Jewish students 84.0 (compared with 76.8 for the upper-middle-class Chinese, 65.4 for the lower-middle-class Chinese, and 74.3 for the Black sample). In space conceptualization, however, the Chinese scored the highest, and on tests of numerical ability and reasoning with spatial forms the Jewish and Chinese scores were roughly comparable (Lesser, Fifer, and Clark, 1965).

- *College students*: A comparison of Jewish and non-Jewish college freshmen on a ten-test battery of *perceptual skill* abilities found that (after equating these students on the basis of their scores on the SAT) the Jewish students' performance was significantly below that of their classmates (Adevai, Silverman, and McGough, 1970).

IQ Scores of Orthodox Jewish Students in Postwar America

In postwar America, a considerable majority of Jewish families belonged to either the Conservative or the Reformed movement (or had entirely given up the practice of Judaism), and only a relatively small proportion maintained the rigorous life-style of Orthodox Judaism. Nevertheless, the importance of a good education was stressed in virtually all Jewish families. The major studies of IQ scores among children from Orthodox families can be summarized as follows:

- *Hebrew day school applicants (Stanford-Binet)*. The scores of 2,083 four- to six year-old applicants to sixteen New York yeshivas averaged 114.9 (Levinson, 1957b);[6] 9 percent scored 132 and above and only 13 percent scored below 100.

- *Hebrew day school students (Stanford-Binet).* The scores of 1,210 students attending nine all-day Hebrew schools averaged 118.6, including 121.3 for the 320 students in the less religious "modern Hebrew academy" schools and 117.2 for students of the more traditional type of yeshivas (Nardi, 1948).[7]
- *Stanford-Binet vs. Wechsler.* The Stanford-Binet scores of 117 Hebrew day school applicants exceeded their scores on the Wechsler Intelligence test for Children (WISC) by 12 points.[8] The scores of the fifty-seven applicants who spoke only English at home averaged 120.5 on the Stanford-Binet (with boys and girls doing equally well), and bilinguals averaged 113.0. The monolingual and bilingual groups registered similar Binet-WISC discrepancies (Levinson, 1959).
- *Wechsler IQ score changes among yeshiva students.* Because of the perception that exposure to the rigorous verbal and analytical training of the yeshiva might engender IQ-score increases, and because of several findings that Jewish children and adults often score substantially higher on the verbal than the performance subscales of the Wechsler (Dershowitz, 1971; Dershowitz and Frankel, 1975; Wendt and Burwell, 1964; Witkin, 1962), a three-year follow-up study of Wechsler IQ scores among Hebrew day school first graders was undertaken (Levinson, 1962). A large increase was found, but it was essentially confined to the verbal subtests of the WISC.[9] However, because WISC verbal-subtest scores of Jewish children attending public schools also appear to rise significantly, this rules out a conclusion that the participation of these children in the intense, verbally stimulating yeshiva environment was responsible for the entire increase (Levinson, 1977) and instead suggests the existence of a maturational (genetic?) process at work, in addition to the effects of environment.[10]
- *The Wechsler verbal-performance disparity among Yeshiva University students.* When students attending Yeshiva University were tested on the adult version of the Wechsler IQ test, *their verbal scores averaged 125.6 — or 20.3 points higher than their scores on the performance-IQ subtests* (Levinson, 1958, 1960).
- *Stanford-Binet vs. Goodenough.* Four hundred kindergarten and first-grade students attending suburban New York City Hebrew day schools scored an average of 112.2 on the just-normed (1972) Stanford-Binet (Levinson and Block, 1977); nonetheless, these children scored significantly below the test norms ($p < .01$) on the Goodenough Draw-A-Person Test (which has been thought to be a good reflection of performance IQ). Because this sample was limited to children from second- and third-generation American ("modern orthodox") homes, where (in addition to traditional academic pursuits) representational art, music, and dance were likely to have been heavily emphasized, these remarkably poor Goodenough test scores cannot be due to an environment that emphasized verbal skills and denigrated the performing arts. Consequently, the efficacy of this test as a discriminator of intelligence

must be called into serious question, at least among children who tend to favor a verbal, rather than a spatial, "cognitive style."

Parallel Findings in British Commonwealth Countries

Three studies from Great Britain and Canada confirm the pattern of Jewish cognitive performance found in the United States, as follows:

- *London:* A 9-point IQ differential favoring Jewish schoolchildren was found when the scores of 1,894 eight- to fourteen-year-old Jewish and non-Jewish children were compared in relation to their fathers' occupational backgrounds (Hughes, 1928). In each of the three socioeconomically diverse schools examined, the Jewish students substantially outperformed their classmates on the recently standardized Northcumberland IQ test, with the greatest advantages found in the schools serving lower-middle-class and lower-class areas, particularly among the boys (Davies and Hughes, 1927).
- *Scotland:* "In one of the largest and best controlled studies of its type, carried out in Glasgow on a very representative sample of Jewish and Gentile children, [the Jewish children] emerged with a mean IQ of 118, boys and girls having very similar scores" (Eysenck and Kamin, 1981, p. 2).[11]
- *Canada:* One hundred eleven-year-old Jewish boys were tested on the SRA Primary Mental Abilities Test, and their scores compared with like-sized samples of Protestant, French Canadian, Southern Italian, and Canadian Indian eleven-year-old boys. The scores of these Jewish children averaged one and a half standard deviations above those of the other four groups on the verbal and number tests. Nevertheless, on the spatial subtest, their scores averaged only 0.2 standard deviations above the average for the other four groups—and on the (nonverbal) reasoning test were half a standard deviation above the average (Marjoribanks, 1972).

Evidence from Israeli Studies

Two rather substantial IQ studies—one of children reared in "mainstream" Israeli society and the other a representative survey of kibbutzim—indicate that children whose ancestors migrated to Israel from Eastern Europe had IQ scores that averaged well above the norm. These studies are summarized as follows:

- *Israeli schoolchildren:* This study (Ortar,1967) found a 14-point differential between scores of 11,000 children of Ashkenazi heritage and scores of 7,000 children of Middle Eastern and North African heritage. The 1,500 children whose fathers were Israeli born scored midway between.
- *Israeli kibbutzim:* Four hundred children aged four and five from a large number of Israeli kibbutzim were tested on the Stanford-Binet (see section 10.4); the scores of the Ashkenazi children averaged 124, including 128 among those children whose (immigrant) fathers were high school graduates. If we subtract perhaps 7 points from these averages because of the gradual increase in Stanford-Binet scores between the test's norming and the study, these scores imply an IQ average of more than a full standard deviation above the norm (Smilansky and Smilansky, 1968).
- *Israeli kibbutzim:* Twelve hundred six- to fourteen-year-old children from a large number of Israeli kibbutzim were tested on the WISC (Smilansky and Smilansky, 1968); the IQ scores of the offspring of Ashkenazi fathers with more than an elementary school education (who comprised the large majority of Ashkenazi fathers living on kibbutzim) averaged 117 (see section 10.4).

Conclusions

The "shape" of Jewish intelligence is clearly one that favors the use of verbal and/or numerical (conceptually based) mechanisms for analyzing and integrating knowledge — in contrast to the more structurally analytical and perceptually based mode of analysis at which many Japanese people excel. This causes Jewish subjects to perform less well on tests that give equal or greater weight to assessing the so-called perceptual and performance aspects of IQ than on tests that stress the ability to comprehend and apply conceptual understandings to problems that are either presented in (or transferred into) a verbal or symbolic mode. This explains why Jewish children's scores on the Wechsler IQ test are usually well below their scores on the Stanford-Binet (Krugman, 1951; Smilansky, 1964). As childhood progresses, Jewish subjects' scores on the Wechsler, but not on the Stanford-Binet, are likely to improve (Levinson, 1977), since the Wechsler's mechanisms for measuring verbal skills become somewhat more like those used with adults. On the adult version of the Wechsler, the verbal subtest scores of Jewish subjects are usually markedly higher than their scores on performance subtests.

Jewish children's scores on the Stanford-Binet will average about a full standard deviation above test norms. When Jewish children are compared with non-Jewish Caucasian children born in the same year (which adjusts for the effects of rising IQ), this difference is reduced to about three-fourths of a standard deviation, or an average of about 112. The standard deviation of Jewish subjects' IQ scores is likely to be slightly smaller than average (a finding comparable to that for other culturally homogeneous groups). This is due primarily to the very low percentage of Jewish subjects with below-average scores rather than to a truncation of scores at the upper extreme.

The exceptionally large percentage of Jewish people who score at or near the genius level on the Stanford-Binet can be inferred from the average scores reported, as well as from the findings of specific studies, such as the huge Terman sample in California in the early 1920s, Sheldon's study of New York City children with IQs above 170 in the late 1940s, and the IQ scores of the 800 offspring of Ashkenazi immigrants reared in 125 Israeli kibbutzim (detailed in section 10.4). The Terman study (Terman, 1925), which identified 1,444 exceptionally gifted children from among 160,000 California schoolchildren in grades one through nine, reported that 10.5 percent were Jewish, compared with a Jewish population in the cities selected for study of about 4 percent. This finding, however, has been acknowledged to represent a substantial underenumeration of the Jewish proportion of gifted children, since (1) for a child to have been classified as Jewish, both parents and all four grandparents had to have been Jewish; (2) in that era, many Jewish families hid the fact of their Judaism (Terman and Oden, 1947); and (3) in a large proportion of these Jewish homes, Yiddish was the primary spoken language, which several studies suggest often depressed children's Stanford-Binet scores, especially in the early school grades.

The study by Sheldon (1954) identified twenty-eight children in New York City with Stanford-Binet scores of 170 or higher—*twenty-four of whom were Jewish*. These families had several things in common (see section 2.3), including in almost every instance (1) few if any siblings, (2) grandparents who had migrated from

Eastern Europe, and (3) a maternal grandmother who was deeply involved in the child's upbringing. These factors imply an exceptionally favorable caretaker ratio, as well as the use of traditional child-rearing approaches.

The IQ scores of American children of Jewish ancestry appear to have risen somewhat faster than those of non-Jewish Caucasians, when the scores of Jewish children tested in the 1920s (most of whose parents had immigrated between 1890 and 1910) are compared with those of children born after the early 1930s. Greater familiarity with English, along with a generation of living in a free society, appear to be major factors underlying this increase.

The overall intellectual proficiency of American Jewish children does not appear to depend on whether or not their families adhered to the Orthodox Jewish traditions. However, the below-average IQ scores registered by Jewish children whose forefathers lived in backward Arab lands for ten or twenty generations *and assimilated to the Arab child-rearing customs* suggests that after several generations of "intellectual neglect," the verbal precocity of the Jewish people will dissipate. Nevertheless, as detailed in section 10.4, exposure to a cognitively enriched (primarily Ashkenazi) kibbutz environment may be able to restore as much as two-thirds of this loss in a single generation.

14.3 Areas of Exceptional Jewish Accomplishment

Although they represent only a handful of the earth's peoples — just 3 percent of the American population and less than 1 percent in the remainder of the developed world — the contribution of the Jewish people to human progress has been, and is now, so considerable — and has encompassed so many important areas — that much may be learned by (1) delineating the areas in which the achievements of the Jewish people have been most notable; (2) contrasting these with areas in which their accomplishments have been quite ordinary; (3) evaluating whether correspondences exist between the areas of exceptional Jewish acumen, on the one hand, and traditional Jewish maternal nurture and educational practices and priorities, on the other; (4) evaluating whether correspondences exist between areas that were not stressed in infancy and toddlerhood and areas of unexceptional Jewish performance; and (5) relating the "shape" of the "Jewish intellect" to the functions of (and relationships between) the two hemispheres of the human brain.

In examining the overall record of Jewish accomplishment, one cannot help but be struck by the extraordinary degree to which the Jewish people have been drawn to occupations in which the emphasis is on improving the human condition, whether in physical, emotional, intellectual, economic, or legal terms. For example, few could argue with the statement that the Jewish contribution to progress in the field of *science and medicine* has been immense. Whether one wishes to recount the accomplishments of individual Jewish theoreticians (for example, Albert Einstein or Sigmund Freud) or to examine anthologies that summarize Jewish contributions to various scientific fields, the end result is the same. For example, *nearly a fourth of the Nobel Prizes in physiology and medicine have been awarded to people of the Jewish faith or heritage* (Patai, 1977; Koppman and Postal, 1979; Patai, personal communication, 1988). Furthermore, *the Jewish Nobel achievement* in the more recently created award *in economics is no less impressive, and more than a fifth of the prizes in physics have been won by people of Jewish descent*. Only in chemistry is the Jewish accomplishment a "mere" 10 percent of the total, which is still almost ten times the proportion that the Jews represent of the developed world's population.

The outstanding scientific achievements of the Hebrew people have not been confined to the twentieth century. Whenever Jews have been given the freedom to attend universities and engage in scientific pursuits, their accomplishments have been extraordinary. For example, in his *Introduction to the History of Science*, Sarton (1927–1948) identified 626 "outstanding" scientists living between 1150 and 1300 A.D.—of whom 95, or more than 15 percent, were Jewish. Patai (1977) estimates this figure to be "thirty times as many Jewish scientists as would be expected on the basis of the proportion of Jews in the countries in which scientific work was pursued" (p. 318).

The Hebraic contribution to uplifting the human spirit

through music has also been immense. For example, if con-noisseurs of classical music were asked to compose a list of the top twenty-five violinists, pianists, and symphony orchestra conductors of the past generation, almost everyone's list would contain the names Vladimir Ashkenazy, Leonard Bernstein, Jasha Heifetz, Yehudi Menuhin, Itzhak Perlman, Artur Rubenstein, and Isaac Stern (and most lists would contain several other Jewish notables, such as Vladamir Horowitz, Serge Koussezitsky, Lauren Maisel, Nathan Milstein, Artur Schnabel, George Solti, and Bruno Walter). Moreover, the Jewish contribution to music goes well beyond the classical domain, as witness the accomplishments of Irving Berlin and Benny Goodman.

The many intellectual pastimes at which Jewish people have excelled include chess and bridge. "Of the fifteen world [chess] champions since 1851, seven (Steinitz, Botvinnik, Smyslov, Tal, Spassky, Fischer, and Kasparov) can claim Jewish ancestry" (Cranberg and Albert, 1988, p. 158). These authors further note, "In the famous U.S.-U.S.S.R. radio match after World War II, the Soviet team of ten included five Jews and the U.S. team seven. And in a later match, the British team included five Jews." Similarly, it is estimated that more than half of the great American bridge players and theoreticians of the past fifty years have been Jewish.

The record of outstanding Jewish accomplishment does not, however, pervade every cognitive domain. Among the fields in which Jews represent a relatively insignificant proportion of historically great people are painting, architecture, and the more observational sciences. For example, the proportional representation of Jews appearing in *American Men and Women of Science* in such fields as earth science, botany, zoology, and plant physiology and pathology falls behind that of non-Jewish Whites (Eysenck and Kamin, 1981).

From the information presented in the preceding chapters, it can be inferred that the Hebrew people perform well in areas that depend (1) on the ability to comprehend and skillfully manipulate long chains of verbally coded reasoning and/or (2) on the ability to integrate emotional or other behaviorally coded information into a temporally coded, meaning-oriented framework. By the same token, they perform less well in areas where the visuospatial and emotional perceptions of the brain's right hemisphere are directly available to the "mind's eye" and are integrated into a pictorial or structural framework.

Because many of the key channels for interhemispheric communication are established very early in life—and because person-to-person differences in the size of these pathways are so great—it is appropriate to examine the nature of traditional Jewish child-rearing practices and their possible effects on brain development in infancy and toddlerhood.

14.4 Infant Care in Traditional Jewish Households[12]

Traditional Jewish infant caretaking practices incorporate many features that seem to be highly conducive to cognitive development in general and to the development of verbal skills in particular. We might single out the following:

- Rocking, holding, singing to, and especially talking to infants, along with the encouragement of verbal responses.
- The traditional Jewish swaddling practices.
- An exceptionally favorable caretaker ratio.

An excellent description of traditional Ashkenazi child-rearing practices is contained in the book *Life Is with People* (Zborowski and Herzog, 1952), from which several passages have been extracted:

> The first months of the baby's life are a constant bath of warmth, attention, and affection. At first it sleeps with the mother, then it is placed in its own cradle or swinging crib near her bed. She may hold a string attached to the baby's cradle, which she rocks incessantly, even in her sleep. If the baby wakens and cries, then it must be picked up, carried about, and crooned to until it falls asleep again [p. 323].
> The mother talks to the baby constantly, telling it about its future as it lies in the crib, "talking out her heart" to it. It is sung to, petted, addressed with endearments. . . . The father sings to it, visitors coo over it, speaking in . . . a special singsong voice. [Everyone tries to] say all kinds of funny things to try to make the baby laugh. . . . From the

outset of life, the shtetl child associates verbal expression with warmth and security, and silence... with rejection and coldness [p. 325].

He is treasured as a potential adult, and the admiration of his audience is most evident when he shows signs of precocity. Early sitting,... standing, walking, and above all early talking give tremendous satisfaction to parents and family. A smile, an unexpected gesture, an imitation of an adult's expression will be taken as a sign of exceptional intelligence. Everything the child says is a bright saying, and everyone likes to hear the baby say and do things [p. 328].

Thus, the Jewish infant is provided with an abundance of three kinds of stimulation: verbal, visual, and vestibular (the heavy regimen of rocking providing the vestibular stimulation).

In marked contrast to this outpouring of visual and auditory stimulation, however, traditional Jewish caretaking practices actively suppress motor activity during the first several months of life, through *swaddling* (wrapping the baby's arms and legs and binding them to the body, which prevents their movement). Swaddling is not thought of as an unnecessary restriction on an infant's naturally free condition; rather, it is considered a logical extension of the warmth and security of the womb. Traditional Jewish swaddling practices differ somewhat from those of other cultures in which swaddling was or still is a tradition. The chief differences include the nature of the swaddling cloths, the gentleness employed in swaddling, and the planned periods in which the infant is given freedom of movement. As described in *Life Is with People:*

The swaddling... is also warm, for [the infant] is laid on a pillow and wrapped with firm, soft cloths [p. 328].

During the first few weeks the wrappings are snug and the baby is literally "like a mummy" [with] the coverings drawn up over the neck... its back and legs must be kept straight.... Several times a day the swaddling is removed and the baby is massaged and allowed to move freely, always with an obbligato of loving coos and murmurs.... Later the arms are freed and the wrappings are relaxed, so that the restraint is almost cozy against the soft pillow.

Wrapped and pillowed, the baby is carried around a great deal by grown-ups and by older brothers and sisters [and] is almost never allowed to remain still or unattended.... If it is not being carried, then it is rocked endlessly, hour after hour. The combination of rocking, swaying, and singsong will be familiar from the cradle on. In the kheyder [schoolroom], the yeshiva, the shul, one rocks and chants as he studies. . . or thinks [p. 324].

As detailed in Chapter Eleven, infants apparently possess a considerable capacity to learn during the first few weeks of life, provided that they are in a state of quiet alertness (Wolff, 1965). In this state, infants are highly attentive and are maximally capable of absorbing perceptual information (Berg and Berg, 1979). In an "active alert" state, an infant between one and three months of age appears to be capable of practicing familiar tasks but not of learning new material (Wolff, 1965). An infant's ability to enter and remain in an alert state is in large part "dependent on its mother's ability to elicit such a state and on the cultural norms that influence the attainment and maintenance of this state" (Bennett, 1971, p. 326). Because a major impediment to "quiet alertness" is an infant's tendency to become over-aroused — and because swaddling dramatically reduces periods of overarousal and crying[13] — swaddling (especially in combination with a heavy regimen of rocking and carrying) induces more frequent and more sustainable periods of quiet alertness. Reducing unnecessary motor movements also sharply increases the relative importance of visual and auditory stimulation during the initial weeks and months of life. For example, swaddled infants show a remarkable ability to turn toward and follow sounds (Clarkson, Morrongiello, and Clifton, 1982). Moreover, rocking automatically engages an alert infant's visual and auditory tracking responses (Korner and Thoman, 1970). Thus, both visual and auditory tracking and *audiovisual integration* are strongly promoted by this regimen of maternal behavior. As a consequence, the Jewish infant tends to have considerably greater opportunities to encode visual and auditory stimuli during this initial "imprint period" (see section 11.3) than a child who does not receive this early caretaking regimen.

14.5 Language Comprehension and Reading in the Early Years of Life

It is part of a mother's intuitive behavior to imitate her infant's behavior. Nevertheless, substantial cross-cultural differences exist in the extent to which mothers engage in facial and vocal imitation. As detailed in Chapters Eight and Ten, *reciprocal vocal imitation plays a crucial role in infant development*, since it provides a child with the opportunity to mirror and echo the visual and auditory products on both sides of the interaction, discover similarities, and learn which motor schema corresponds to the speech sound just heard or uttered. Further, the realization that objects have names (and that objects with common properties have common names) provides infants and toddlers who receive heightened maternal encouragement of attention to objects and events in the environment with early experiences in learning *conceptual* similarities.

Thus, in actively seeking opportunities to engage her baby in two-way verbal interactions, the Jewish mother provides her infant or toddler with considerable feedback — both imitatively and, during toddlerhood, by means of the didactic communication mechanisms highlighted in section 12.2 as crucial to linguistic development. Perhaps this is why — despite the significantly greater religious responsibilities of the male in traditional Judaism and the patriarchal nature of the traditional Jewish family — a person is considered as having been born Jewish if he or she had a Jewish mother.

The environmental situations most favorable to the teaching of words and ideas are ones in which words and phrases (1) are repeated often, (2) are uttered with the same inflection (as when they form part of a song or are spoken with a strong ethnic flavor), and/or (3) are accompanied by strong emotion.

Traditional Jewish family and religious practices contain many such opportunities for learning meaningful linguistic information at a very early age. This results from

- The highly repetitive use of specific words and phrases as part of prayer rituals — words and phrases that are enunciated with invarying singsong inflections and often accompanied by strong emotion.
- Attitudes toward (and mechanisms for) the expression of emotions.

The Jewish child's initial exposure to the written word begins with the development of a familiarity with the (Hebrew) words of commonly said prayers, for example, those recited at the dinner table (as soon as a boy was able, he would be taught how to recite portions of these blessings). Then, in the synagogue,[14] the toddler would hear the familiar dinner-table words sung by the cantor and possibly the entire congregation, and his father would simultaneously point to the words in the prayer book, thereby imprinting the physical "shape" of the word or phrase used into the sound heard and the emotion experienced by the child.

This linking of words, melody, and *strong emotions* was embedded in the liturgy of the Jewish rituals. Whether praying for a restoration of the homeland in Israel and a rebuilding of the temple in Jerusalem, or remembering the enslavement in Egypt, or crying out for relief from current afflictions, the tight-throated singing of the cantor would often sound like weeping as the congregation joined in this unified outpouring of emotion.[15] Thus, long before entering a classroom, the Orthodox Jewish child could sight-read a number of relatively complex words and phrases—with each of these words recognized as a complete template, which implies that the right hemisphere's holistic abilities were being utilized.

The method of teaching the alphabet to the Jewish child differed greatly from that used in most Western cultures. Teachers "created dozens of descriptions, riddles, and and puns to help their students remember and recognize the letters" (Roskies and Roskies, 1975, p. 154), which were often combined with a moral saying almost identical in pronunciation with the names of the letters (Fishman, 1944).[16] Once the child became able to recognize and pronounce the letters, instruction in reading was begun—with the first Hebrew text, the book of Leviticus, usually introduced at the age of five or six (Herschel, 1946).[17] *To the Ashkenazi child of Eastern Europe, Hebrew represented a foreign language*—one used for praying, as well as for reading and discussing the Torah—in contrast to Yiddish, the language spoken in the home.

Once the entire Torah had been read through and discussed,

the boy could then progress to what was considered the real task — studying the massive compendium of biblical commentary and moral and religious proscriptions called the Talmud, which was written in Aramaic. It was not unusual for four students to be seated around a small table sharing one copy of the Talmud, and students often remarked later that they "learned the Talmud upside down." Consequently, when a previously discussed portion of the Talmud was reviewed, the sight of a word or phrase might evoke the memory of the discussion of meaning that accompanied its previous presentation(s).

Many Jews view the study of the Talmud as the epitome of learning how to think. A Talmudic discussion between a rabbi and his students revolves around the meaning of biblical words and phrases and how their messages could serve as guides to decision making in the realm of human behavior — for instance, which of two *mitzvahs* (good deeds) is the more important to perform or which of two competing obligations is the more important to fulfill.[18]

In Orthodox Judaism, the ultimate degree of prestige, respect, authority, and status is shown to anyone (even a prepubescent boy) who has mastered the Talmud and has the "gift of Talmudic reasoning." But in every branch of Judaism, "intellectual achievement is the universal goal. Lifelong study is considered to be commanded directly by God and highest social status goes to him who can give evidence of prolonged and fruitful study" (Zborowski, 1949, p. 87).

14.6 Conclusions and Implications

The areas of cognitive strength exhibited by the Jewish people conform closely with the maternal and educational emphases provided in traditional Jewish homes. This strongly suggests that it is these practices that have been responsible for the considerably above-average intelligence displayed by the Jewish people — and, even more importantly, for its useful application.

Nevertheless, several considerations work against the conclusion that a single generation of exposure to such an environment could have enabled children to attain these heightened abilities. These include (1) the large percentage of Jewish people that test at a genius or near-genius level and the exceedingly small proportion scoring below the norm, both of which suggest that the entire IQ distribution has risen; (2) the early age at which high IQ scores are routinely displayed; (3) the marvelous accomplishments of the Jewish people, which amply demonstrate that the forms that the Jewish intellect has taken are exceedingly favorable for meaningful achievements; and (4) as suggested in section 10.4 and elaborated in Chapter Twenty, evidence that this heightened ability neither develops nor dissipates in a single generation.

What an optimistic scenario this Jewish model offers the human race! If the child development principles employed by the Jewish family can generate such a **multifold increase in the rate of productive genius,** then understanding and utilizing this knowledge for the betterment of all mankind could and should be viewed as a golden opportunity — not just an opportunity to develop a future population of highly intelligent people but, most importantly, an opportunity to use these heightened gifts of intellect to promote the kinds of achievements exemplified by the Jewish mission.[19]

Notes

1.   On each of the tests, the non-Jewish Caucasian children's scores were within one- or two-tenths of a standard deviation of the norm established three years earlier on 100,000 high school seniors participating in the original Project Talent study. The 1,051 non-Jewish subjects constituted a 5 percent sample of ninth-grade students who participated in the original study and who were included in the follow-up study in twelfth grade. Because the norms included the scores of Black and Hispanic students, the non-Jewish Caucasian sample's performance (which averaged one-tenth of a standard deviation above the norm) was unexceptional, implying that the follow-up population's scores were quite comparable to the original participants, and that the sample was representative (unbiased).
2.   The mathematics scores of a sample of 150 Asian students were on a par with the scores of Jewish students.
3.   On the short-term recall measure, all three non-Jewish groups surveyed (Black, Asian, and White children) outperformed the Jewish students

by an approximately equal amount. Children from upper-middle-class and lower-middle-class families performed equally well, suggesting a low correlation between performance of this task and IQ.

4.   The Otis has traditionally had a high verbal factor loading. This eighty-item "quick-version" (Gamma) includes word meaning, verbal analogies, scrambled sentences, interpretation of proverbs, logical reasoning, number series, arithmetical reasoning, and "design analogies" (nonsense syllogisms); the standard deviation was 10.5. Thanks are due to Julius S. Romanoff for providing a copy of his dissertation.

5.   Thirdborn males and firstborn females performed the best for their respective sexes (there were only fourteen fourthborns in the sample). On the School and College Ability Test, these high school seniors and juniors scored at the 66th percentile in the verbal section and at the 64th percentile in math (where a similar pattern of birth-order differences was observed). A note about sample biases is in order: Although parental education exceeded that of the community at large (half the fathers and a fourth of the mothers being college graduates), these proportions are not exceptional among Jewish families. Most of the subjects sought counseling because they were unsure of whether to go on to college after graduation, and some were experiencing problems in school. Consequently, the average Jewish child would seem likely to outperform this sample (although only intact families were included in the study).

6.   This average both overstates and understates these children's IQs. On the one hand, the gradual increase in IQ scores in the years following the norming of the Stanford-Binet implies that, in relation to their birth cohorts, their advantage would be slightly less. On the other hand, the scores of foreign-born children or first-generation American Jewish children from bilingual homes are (as shown in other studies) likely to be lower than those of American-born children from monolingual homes (bilingualism was not an advantage in these Hebrew-language day schools, because the other language spoken in the home was generally Yiddish). The standard deviation was 12.9.

7.   The version of the Stanford-Binet test used had been normed thirteen years earlier, implying an IQ-score inflation of 3 or 4 points.

8.   Perhaps 4 points of this discrepancy can be accounted for by the general rise in IQ between the years in which these tests were normed; the Stanford-Binet was standardized in 1933 and the WISC in 1947 (see section 5.2). By the time of this study, the average WISC score in America was likely to have risen about 3 points.

9.   The twenty-seven boys gained 11.8 verbal IQ points (from 107.5 to 119.3) and the twenty-seven girls gained 10.4 points. The nineteen students from monolingual homes gained 13 points, and the thirty-five students from bilingual homes 10 points; nevertheless, WISC Performance-IQ subtest scores rose only 1.3 points, an increase attributable solely to the "coding" subtest.

10. If one believes that verbal and/or conceptual IQ points are usually of greater value than spatial and/or perceptual IQ points (once a reasonable level of competency in each domain has been reached), then the

Stanford-Binet approach to IQ testing is clearly better at discriminating overall intelligence near the upper end of the scale (in contrast to the Wechsler's oft-cited superiority in discerning and diagnosing specific deficits), particularly during the early and middle childhood years. Alternatively, it might be suggested that, at younger ages, the WISC does not do an adequate job of discriminating verbal IQ in the high and moderately high range but improves as childhood progresses.

11. In reporting on this prewar study, Eysenck suggests that this figure is likely to have understated the mean IQ of the Jewish children in this city, because fee-paying schools (which a substantial proportion of the Jewish children attended) were not included in the study, and the mean IQ in these fee-paying schools tended to be higher.

12. Although the sources cited in this section portray the traditions employed among the Ashkenazic (Eastern European) Jews, similar practices were also employed in those Sephardic lands where the Orthodox Judaic teachings were maintained (see section 20.5); in modern Orthodox Judaism, some of these traditions have undergone change.

13. So-called reflexive motor movements are one of the chief causes of overarousal during the first several weeks of life; another is the immaturity of the vestibular system, which cries out for rocking every bit as much as the body does for food. When a child is one week of age, most motor movements seem purposeless and often result in "startles" (fingers splay out and feet and legs shoot straight out or up). Unswaddled neonates spend much of their time in a tightly constricted position (Brazelton, 1974), and swaddling is thought of as protecting the infant from causing long-term harm to itself from such constrictions, by keeping the spine straight.

14. "The synagogue was a place where children were normally brought and treated in a way that would encourage their attendance . . . the father would pay great attention to them and display his love for the child . . . and would pray with a small child in his lap (or shoulders)" (Kanarfogel, 1985, p. 8).

15. To talk out or cry out one's problems and verbalize one's emotions were for the most part, considered to be healthy means of emotional cleansing—ones that helped lighten the heart, bring a renewal of energy, and make the rest of the world more bearable. The community placed no value on the suppression of tears (nor were they considered essentially the mark of or prerogative of childhood). On the contrary, weeping was accepted as a normal means of expression, available to a child to express grief or pain, joy, or even rebellion, when a child dared not talk back to its parents (Zborowski and Herzog, 1952).

16. For example, giml (the third letter of the alphabet) looks like a man with a pocket of money at his side, ready to help the poor, and dalled (the fourth letter) may be combined with it to form the expression *gemol dallim*, which means deal bountifully with the poor. The child might be asked, "Why is the foot of the giml stretched toward the dalled?" The answer is, "Because it is the way of the bountiful person to run after the poor." "And why is the foot of the dalled stretched toward the giml?" "To

allow himself to be found" (Fishman, 1944, p. 62). Thus, a poor person should let the charitable person assist him.

17. The "ritual" for a child's first day of school includes a recitation by the child of the letters of the alphabet in regular and then reversed order while on the lap of the teacher, who then recites the first verse of Leviticus. Honey is then smeared on the letters of the verse, to be licked by the child. At home, the child gets a hard-boiled egg whose shell has been inscribed with biblical verse, and he eats the egg after the inscriptions have been read to him. In the evening, a festive meal or a party (to which the poor are invited) is held. Thus, the child's five senses are utilized in imprinting the experience.

18. Such a Talmudic discussion might sound something like this:

Rabbi: Why do we reach out for God in this manner? [calls on beginning student]

Student: Because when Abraham...[the student recites from the book of Genesis]

Rabbi: How do we know that this didn't mean...? [calls on second-year student]

Student: Because Rabbi Y—— said...[provides an interpretation of this passage]

Rabbi: But didn't Rabbi S—— say J...? [calls on third student]

Student: Yes, but that was only meant to apply when....

Rabbi: Then may we conclude...? [he calls on an advanced student]

Student: No, Rabbi G—— suggested another exception, to apply when....

Rabbi: Any other exceptions—anyone? [hearing no answer, he calls on his best student]

Student: Rabbi H—— suggested that..., but Rabbi Akiva explained that....

Rabbi: What about when..., shouldn't this take precedence over...?

19. In virtually every one of the so-called helping professions—medicine, psychology, the shaping of legal and ethical standards, the education of young minds, or the shaping of public opinion, the "people of the Book" have made their presence keenly felt. It is almost as though (irrespective of whether the researcher/practitioner was a devout practitioner of the Hebraic faith) his or her efforts have been dedicated to the fulfillment of the "Jewish mission": "To help make the world a better place to live, in the hope that God will finally say 'You have done well my children,' and will cast down his countenance to shine upon the human race and reveal himself anew."

✕ *Part Five* ✕

Intellectual Giftedness
and Connections to Biology

Before tackling the complex task of differentiating among the several major types of extraordinary intellectual ability, we must first have a good understanding of the cognitive responsibilties "normally" undertaken by our brain's left and right hemispheres, as well as of the three rather distinct memory systems that (singly or in combination) underlie exceptional performance in one or several related cognitive "domains." To accomplish this, Chapter Fifteen describes the roles of the left and right hemispheres in a variety of cognitive functions, articulates the differences between the three memory systems, and suggests a developmental theory concerning the "sharing and shielding" of hemispheric functions.

With this as background, Chapter Sixteen articulates and distinguishes among the major forms that giftedness might take. The chapter (1) discusses the relationship between the three memory systems elaborated in Chapter Fifteen and the seven "domains" of intellectual giftedness developed by Howard Gardner; (2) delineates the different types of "spatial-mathematical" intelligence; and (3) sets forth the difference between mental imagery and concrete visual imagery and the importance of each to different types of exceptional cognitive ability. There follows an elaboration of several types of exceptional ability that are independent of IQ (or are considerably more likely to be displayed by people who exhibit cognitive deficits in other domains). The chapter discusses possible relationships between intelligence and such concepts as creativity and originality, and it then articulates the recent contribution of Robert Sternberg to understanding the skills needed for problem-solving competence.

Chapter Seventeen discusses (1) unusual biological traits commonly found among people who evidence extraordinary intellectual ability (especially childhood myopia, immune disorders, and high uric-acid levels); (2) findings from postmortem studies of the cerebral cortexes of Albert Einstein and other people who possessed extraordinary gifts; (3) how the sleep cycles of gifted children differ from those of people with average and below-average IQs; and (4) the relationship between high IQ and the rapidity with which the brain processes information. The chapter presents hypotheses concerning possible links between biology and behavior including a cholinergic theory of why allergies and myopia may represent the "price" of giftedness, and discusses the relationship between IQ and the speed at which the brain processes information. It also explores the concept that some forms of giftedness may be predicated on an ability to perform functions adroitly in either hemisphere — functions that, in people of average ability, can be performed by (or performed well by) only one hemisphere. Finally, the chapter raises the prospect that verbal and other conceptual types of giftedness represent a bilateralized capacity for humankind's greatest gift of intellect: its gift of speech.

Contents

❧ 15 ❧

One Brain,
Two Hemispheres,
Three Memory Systems

15.1 Introduction

This chapter discusses in detail the roles of the two markedly different types of human "computers" inside our brain—our left hemisphere's "analytical-sequential" mode of processing information and our right hemisphere's "analog-parallel" information processor—and suggests how their combined efforts enable us to perform the wondrous feats of integrative analysis needed to comprehend language, create music, or construct a bridge. It also explores the three virtually distinct memory systems that underlie intellectual function—episodic (or event-related) memory, semantic (or thematic) memory, and procedural learning (or how-to memory). Table 33 summarizes the different roles of our brain's hemispheres in human intelligence.

15.2 Hemispheric Specialization by Cognitive Function

This section delineates the differential roles of our two brain hemispheres for a variety of cognitive areas. It contains separate discussions of (1) our (nonlinguistic) visuospatial skills, in which the right hemisphere predominates; (2) the different roles of our hemispheres in emotions; (3) how visual and emotional capaci-

Table 33. A Simplified Summary of the Contributions of Our Brain's Hemispheres to Intellectual Function.

Dimension	Right Hemisphere	Left Hemisphere
Mode of Analysis	Excels at visualizing a whole (forming an entire picture out of its component parts)	Excels in performing an analytical, serial, or segmental breakdown of a whole into its component parts
Integration of Inputs	Better at integrating inputs from several modalities (for example, vision and hearing); better at "parallel processing"	Better at unimodal processing (that is, processing stimuli from one sensory mode); better at serial (sequential) processing
Novelty-Practice	More adept at coping with novel stimuli, particularly if no familiar contextual mechanisms are readily discernible	Contains a store of familiar contexts within which to analyze a task (see crystallized intelligence)
Judgmental Mode	Better at purely physical judgments (structural similarities)	Better at categorical judgments (for example, conceptual or functional similarities)
Emotional	Recognizes emotional content; contains most of our emotional reactivity; contains mostly pessimistic emotions	Cannot recognize the emotional content of stories, despite understanding the literal meaning; contains many of our optimistic feelings
Facial Recognition	Predominates due to its visuospatial and emotional processing superiorities	Involved in very difficult or categorical judgments or recognizing very familiar faces
Attention	Better at sustained attention and at paying attention to environmental stimuli; engaged by high arousal	Better at focused attention to analytical processes than to surroundings; better at "quiet concentration"
Arithmetic	Responsible for initial arrangement and alignment of columns and for "global conceptualizations" of methodology	Calculation involves primarily the left hemisphere
Music	Better at perceiving pitch, timbre (melodic contour), and unfamiliar melodies; used more by untrained listeners	Better at sequential, time-dependent aspects of music comprehension and at recognizing familiar melodies; used more by trained musicians
Verbal Skills (nonspeech)	Possesses considerable comprehensive abilities; organizes information at the paragraph level; understands the metaphorical meaning and the emotional content of words	Undertakes most aspects of language comprehension; understands the literal meaning of words
Speech	Can utter expletives (curses) and possibly "sing" words	Performs virtually all facets of language expression (in almost all people)

ties combine to allow us to recognize faces; (4) how music is perceived and appreciated; and (5) how these spatial, auditory, temporal, and emotional "divisions of labor" are brought together to form an understanding of the most complex of human cognitive gifts — the ability to comprehend and use language.

The Analytical-Holistic Distinction

Our left hemisphere employs an analytical strategy to recognize and compare information (words, pictures, sounds), while the right hemisphere is able to immediately apprehend complex configurations as an entirety (a gestalt).

In this context, the term *analytical* implies an attempt to break down a complex input (for example, a visual array or an auditory grouping) into separate components, features, or elements by means of a serial (time-dependent) mode of information processing, much like that used by a standard computer.

Conversely, the term *holistic* (or *gestalt*) implies an immediate mode of recognition, that which places emphasis on a whole configuration and on the patterns of interrelations between the inputs that form the whole. This apperceptive recognition occurs without any analysis of its component features or elements, like an "analog" computer or "parallel" processor. Holistically processed inputs are visualized as is, with the emergent whole being more than the sum of its component elements.

Visuospatial Analysis

Although both sides of our brain possess considerable ability to comprehend and process visuospatial information, they do so in entirely different ways and, consequently, tend to be specialized for different aspects of understanding visually presented information.

As summarized in Table 34, our right hemisphere undertakes the preponderance of visuospatial tasks because it is better suited to:

Table 34. Contrasting Patterns of Left- and Right-Hemisphere Skills for Processing (Nonlinguistic) Visual Stimuli.

Processing Function	Left Hemisphere	Right Hemisphere
Visual Matching	Matches pictures (into similar categories) using a conceptual or functional approach (associative matching)	Uses a structural approach (similarity of shape) to match pictures (apperceptive matching)
Types of Information Processed	Better at processing (1) information where previously developed mechanisms can be used and (2) temporal aspects of visual stimuli (temporal order)	Better at processing (1) novel stimuli and (2) spatial aspects of visual stimuli
Mode of Information Processing	Serial: one step at a time; slower, analytical processing of visual stimuli	Parallel: simultaneously processing different stimuli
Sensory Integration	Better at unimodal processing	Better at multimodal processing (such as integrating information from vision and hearing)
Control of Attention	Less adequate than right hemisphere in maintaining extended attention; better at paying attention to internal analytical processes	Greater ability for sustained attention; engaged by emotional arousal
Drawing Ability	Ability to produce detailed pictures containing inaccurate overall configuration	Ability to produce pictures with good overall outline and spatial relationships but with deficient detail

- Recognizing such spatial attributes as size, location, orientation, rotation, reflection, and distortion.
- Making dynamic transformations (moving maps of our environment) that are essential to finding our way in our environment.
- Integrating cues from a variety of sensory inputs (such as vision and hearing), since it has a better capacity for the simultaneous perception and integration of multimodal information; conversely, the left hemisphere appears to have a better capacity for unimodal processing.
- Matching structural similarities (similarity of shape), in contrast to

categorical similarities (for example, matching a capital O and a small o vs. a capital E and a small e).
- Comprehending and storing visual information *holistically* rather than segmentally; the "right brain" processes sensory information simultaneously (in parallels), whereas the "left brain" processes information serially, in a slower and more systematized manner.[1]

The Laterality of Emotions

Although each of our hemispheres plays an important part in the shaping of our emotional states and personalities, the right hemisphere clearly predominates.

Findings from a variety of studies indicate that the right hemisphere tends to be "responsible" for negative feelings and their expression and the left for optimistic feelings (Kinsbourne, 1981). For example, damage to certain areas of the *right* hemisphere (leaving the left hemisphere predominant in emotional matters) will often have these results:

- Patients feel cheerful about, joke about, or express indifference to their condition, despite its severity; for example, they may deny that it is of any importance (Bradshaw and Nettleton, 1983).
- Following right-hemisphere removal, patients experience a flattening of "affect"[2] accompanied by a loss of interpersonal relationships, and dependent, regressive, and ineffective behavior frequently occurs. Following a left hemispherectomy, however, affect and "personality" are usually preserved (Gardner and others, 1985).
- Patients may suffer from an inability to recognize the emotional content of sentences despite being able to understand their literal meaning (Heilman and others, 1975), and they may have a diminished perception of other people's affective tones and facial expressions as well as the emotional content of musical passages.

Conversely, damage to certain portions of the left hemisphere often has different results:

- Patients cry, swear, or express anger or guilt.
- Patients enter a state of severe depression. In one large study, 60 percent of stroke victims with damage to their left frontal region experienced "major" depression within two years of their stroke, whereas none of the patients studied with only right-frontal

damage experienced these symptoms (Depression Linked to Stroke Damage, 1982).
- Shock therapy to the left side tends to make patients morose.

Studies on "split-brain" patients, using psychological test pictures, indicate that the right hemisphere tends to "possess" considerable altruism, sharing, and cooperativeness (Zaidel, 1983).

Memory for Faces

People have an enormous capacity to recognize faces, almost irrespective of the emotions that the faces may display or the viewing conditions. Tachistoscopic tests[3] demonstrate the superiority (speed and accuracy) of the right hemisphere at facial recognition under most conditions, presumably because of its capacity for holistic visualization and emotional encoding. Nevertheless, the left hemisphere appears to be better at facial recognition if very difficult recognitions are required (for example, where distinctions between faces involve only a single feature or detail), if very familiar faces are shown, or if simple categorical distinctions are required (Bradshaw and Nettleton, 1983; Benowitz and others, 1983).

The Processing of Music

The ability to appreciate music or to play an instrument is a complex skill, and our two hemispheres must work together to integrate a sound's rhythm, pitch, and emotional aspects into a cohesive whole:

- The left hemisphere is more responsible for temporal order, duration, simultaneity (Gates and Bradshaw, 1977), and the temporal sequence of rhythm (Carmon, 1978); conversely, the right hemisphere is more responsible for pitch, timbre, harmony, emotionality, intonational contour, distinguishing sounds from different instruments, and distinguishing locational sources of sounds.
- The left hemisphere is generally superior in recognizing familiar melodies, while the right hemisphere specializes in recognizing unfamiliar melodies (Gates and Bradshaw, 1977).
- The left hemisphere can sing in a rhythmically correct but terribly

off-key manner or in a monotone, and the right hemisphere can sing with clearly recognizable pitch.

PET-scan studies indicate that the left hemisphere is used in sophisticated sound recognition. For example, experienced musicians, who perceive melody as an articulated set of elements, use the left hemisphere for music recognition, while novice musicians primarily use their right hemisphere when they listen to music. This probably reflects the distinction between the left hemisphere's superiority in discriminating between rapidly changing acoustical sounds and the right hemisphere's attention to the emotional aspects of sound.

The Laterality of Language Comprehension and Expression

Because damage to certain portions of the left hemisphere will, in the large majority of people, cause a loss of the ability to speak, while damage to the right hemisphere will rarely cause such an inability, language came to be seen as an exclusive function of the left hemisphere. Many recent studies, however, have demonstrated that our capacity for visual and auditory language *comprehension* involves a complex interaction between the holistic processing of our right hemisphere and the analytical, time-dependent processing of our left hemisphere. This is in contrast to *expressive* language, which in 98 to 99 percent of right-handed people and nearly 70 percent of left-handed people is essentially confined to the left hemisphere.

The roles of the two hemispheres in language can be summarized as follows:

- The left hemisphere matches letters by name; the right, by physical appearance (Sergent, 1984).
- The left hemisphere reads words phonetically (the word is sounded out); the right hemisphere reads words ideographically (the word is seen or recognized as a whole).[4]
- The left hemisphere is faster at processing pronounceable letter strings; the right is faster at processing unpronounceable nonword letter strings (Young, Ellis, and Bion, 1984).
- The left hemisphere understands the literal meaning of words; the right has a better understanding of metaphors.
- The left hemisphere has a better comprehension for dry textual

material and a better understanding of complex analytical sentences; conversely, there is more "right-" than "left-brain" activity for comprehension of fiction that contains a great deal of imagery (Wapner, Hamby, and Gardner, 1981);[5] the right hemisphere also possesses simple, but not complex, syntactic abilities.

- The left hemisphere is better at grammatical and semantic use of language; the right has the primary responsibility for organizing language at the paragraph level, as demonstrated by the inability of patients with certain types of right-hemisphere damage to organize paragraph narratives from unorganized component sentences (Delis and others, 1983).
- The left hemisphere is better at digit and letter recognition, word recall, lexical decisions, and phonological discrimination. The right hemisphere is able to make "concrete" but not abstract judgments based on use; for example, in a word association task, it could associate "spoon" with "fork," "soup," "silverware," and "cook" but not with "nutrition."
- The left hemisphere is better at discriminating rapidly changing phonological aspects of speech, and the right is faster at recognizing steady-state vowels (Sergent, 1984).
- The left hemisphere possesses the ability to articulate language; in the large majority of people, the right hemisphere has no expressive abilities except noises, "expletives," and possibly words of very familiar songs (Gazzaniga and others, 1984).

Our left-hemisphere (right-ear) advantage for speech perception may result from its ability to adjust to the rate of acoustic change rather than to the linguistic nature of the stimuli (Schwartz and Tallal, 1980). The ability to preserve the temporal order of speech while some of its components are processed "in parallel" may, in a sense, present a "template" upon which to rejoin segments after they are processed. The right hemisphere (when disconnected from the left) is poorer at reading than at auditory comprehension, but its auditory comprehension also degenerates when it is asked to decode inputs containing three or more critical items. This suggests the absence of a constructive "phonemic rehearsal mechanism," as well as the absence of "grapheme-to-phoneme translation rules" (Zaidel, 1983). Speech is also shown to be disrupted when the left hemisphere is temporarily incapacitated either by Sodium Amytal or by electrical stimulation (Ojemann, 1983; Fried and others, 1982).[6]

To summarize, even though the right hemisphere possesses little ability for speech, it does play a substantial role in the more global and holistic aspects of organizing verbal information (such as organizing paragraphs) — in contrast to the left hemisphere, which plays the role of a "workhorse" in organizing (and providing temporal order to) the task of constructing sentences.

15.3 One Brain: Three Memory Systems

Three virtually distinct, but often interrelated, memory systems underlie human intelligence. The first two, which together comprise our "declarative" or fact-based memory systems, are called *episodic* or event-related memory and semantic or thematic memory. The third memory system is often called how-to memory but also goes by the name of procedural memory. The major characteristics of these memory systems may be summarized as follows:

- *Episodic memory:* (1) It represents the confluence of sensory and emotional inputs that accompany an event; (2) its emotional aspects are "imprinted" directly and immediately into long-term memory, forming a "template" upon which the factual elements of the event are "written";[7] (3) it can be re-cued most easily by events that evoke similar feelings; and (4) the primary determinant of the future accessibility of an episodic memory is the strength of the emotions contained in the template (the strength of emotions being based in part on how prior events have sensitized the area).
- *Thematic memory:* (1) It represents fact-based knowledge capable of being retained independently of the events accompanying its encoding; (2) it is organized into themes (schemata); (3) it is first encoded into "working" memory (postdistractional memory) and thereafter is embedded in long-term memory, generally during the rapid-eye-movement (REM) phase of our sleep cycles,[8] where it is "crosshatched" with episodic memory to form an "associative store" of declarative memory;[9] and (4) its accessibility is generally dependent on the number of directly retrievable files into which an element of knowledge is placed and the number of times these files containing this knowledge are subsequently accessed.[10]
- *How-to memory:* (1) It builds up with practice; (2) it is immune to the kinds of brain damage affecting "fact" memory;[11, 12] (3) it requires body movement (or visual tracking) for its encoding; (4) it is, in a sense, "state" dependent;[13] and (5) its full accessibility following a period of disuse necessitates a (relatively brief) "relearning curve."[14]

Memory can also be subdivided into three distinct memory *durations*: immediate or short-term memory (which has a capacity for about seven "chunks" of information and lasts from seconds to one or two minutes); intermediate memory (which is also called postdistractional or working memory);[15] and long-term memory (or postconsolidational memory).[16] The difference between immediate and postdistractional memory may be exemplified by what happens while you are dialing a telephone number that you do not expect to call again. After it is dialed, it is retained in immediate memory (in case the line is busy), but the instant the phone begins to ring, it is forgotten.

15.4 Novelty and Task Transference

Because our right hemisphere bears the primary responsibility for recognizing and interrelating diffuse sensory inputs to form a single "supramodal" space, its attention is triggered when the situation calls for coping with the novel and unknown, especially when the need for acute attention is aroused. This enables these sensory inputs to converge into an "experience," which then can be embedded into a familiar context. This is the source of the popular belief that one's instincts are associated with the right brain.

By contrast, when a familiar context exists or is developed for dealing with a problem the left hemisphere's involvement is likely to grow, and it may take the lead in a task initially performed by the right. This offers an explanation of why the PET-scan studies previously cited indicate that, in contrast to novice musicians, accomplished musicians have considerably more "left-brain" than "right-brain" activity when listening to music.

The right hemisphere takes the lead in the formation of procedural learning mechanisms, as well as being a storehouse for the bulk of the sensory aspects of episodic memory (see section 15.3), while the linguistically coded and time-dependent aspects of thematic memory are the province of the left hemisphere. It also follows that peak performance in addressing problems in a "right-brained" manner is likely to be attained under conditions of high arousal, while optimal "left-brained" performance is generally associated with quiet concentration.

Thus, the right hemisphere is, in many ways, a jack-of-all-trades, a generalist that addresses new problems and tries different approaches until it finds one that fits the situation. Conversely, the left hemisphere is more of a specialist, solving familiar problems quickly and effectively by using established methods.

15.5 Hemispheric Sharing and Shielding

The emergence of the human race as a highly intelligent species has, as its foundation, the development of a "specialization of labor" between the two hemispheres of our brain. It has been the evolutionary development of our left hemisphere's analytical-sequential mode of thinking—which complements our right hemisphere's holistic perceptions and parallel-processing capabilities—that has established the base for the integrated storehouses of the two fact-based memory systems that underlie higher intelligence.

There are some species of animals that—despite having tiny brains—exhibit an extremely well-developed "spatial map" memory. The Clark's nutcracker's food-finding habits are a good example of this. This small bird may stash as many as 30,000 pinyon seeds (four or five to a spot) on the south slopes of mountains (in the American Southwest), and it then returns throughout the winter and easily locates and uncovers its hidden food supplies, even when they are covered by snow.

Clearly, the Clark's nutcracker's food-finding habits demonstrate that event-related memory—centered on a survival theme—has not sprung up miraculously in human beings. (Neither do we possess an enormous advantage over the animal kingdom in our ability to move gracefully through space.) Rather, the principal impetus behind the accelerated growth of human intelligence has been the development of a wide-ranging and integrated thematic memory system.

Considerable variability exists in the extent to which our brain hemispheres are involved in what we are doing, depending on the nature of the task, the degree to which we are emotionally aroused, and whether other demands on our cognitive resources are being made simultaneously.

Numerous studies have shown the nature and extent of functional impairments that accompany damage to one side of the brain but not the other, and these findings provide what is becoming an increasingly detailed functional "road map" of the nature and extent of hemispheric *lateralization*. These studies indicate that there are functions that can be performed well by either hemisphere, tasks that require the cooperation of both hemispheres, and capacities that in almost all people are possessed by only one hemisphere. Effective task management might then be viewed in terms of an optimal *sharing and shielding* of both information and functional responsibility between the hemispheres.

For the most part, neither hemisphere exhibits the full spectrum of functional abilities. Nevertheless, if neurological damage occurs quite early in childhood, the hemisphere that would normally be incapable of undertaking a particular task is usually able to develop the capability, often with little or no discernible loss in performance (Zaidel, Zaidel, and Sperry, 1981). These findings suggest that, even though both hemispheres innately possess the capacity to perform almost every function, either (1) certain capacities do not become actualized in one hemisphere, or (2) initially present capabilities become "deactivated" during childhood.

Recent evidence strongly supports the view that, by the time a child is three or four years of age, both hemispheres are separately and simultaneously receiving and acting upon almost every cognitive input (hemispheric sharing), even if the fruits of only one hemisphere's analysis are used. In adolescence, however, "gatekeeping" mechanisms become established that determine which hemisphere will be assigned the primary or the full responsibility for certain tasks at any particular moment (with the opposite hemisphere *shielded* from access to the information needed to undertake the task).

Recent PET-scan findings provide the primary evidence for this first conclusion. These studies indicate that between the ages of three and eight the rate of "energy use" in the cerebral cortex *is twice as great* as the rate in adults aged twenty to thirty (Chugani, Phelps, and Mazziotta, 1987).[17]

Support for the conclusion that a full hemispheric sharing of function during childhood is followed by an adolescent onset of hemispheric shielding comes from an analysis of age-related changes in how children perform a task that can be either projected to one hemisphere or divided between the two (Liederman, Merola, and Hoffman, 1986). At age ten, almost all the children tested were unable to use their hemispheres as "relatively insulated independent work stations" (p. 194) when the particular task conditions made it much more efficient for them to do so. By the age of twelve, however, this capacity was clearly evidenced by the large majority of the subjects.[18]

Assuming that this scenario is accurate, then the maturational development of functions that can be performed by *either* hemisphere in adulthood may be thought of as consisting of three elements: First, one hemisphere learns how to perform the function (or components thereof) using its unique mode of perception and analysis. Second, a similar learning experience occurs in the other hemisphere, using its sensory-associative analytical areas and mechanisms.[19] Finally, as "automatization" mechanisms are developed in the more efficient hemisphere (the *dominant* hemisphere), a biological replica is constructed in the opposite hemisphere,[20] and this increases its effectiveness in performing the function without the involvement of the dominant hemisphere. What is being suggested is that, in effect, **not only do our brain's two halves have the capacity to exchange information with one another but they are also able to teach each other about the mechanisms that they have developed to deal with similar situations**—the result being that either hemisphere can then effectively perform the task when called upon by the "gatekeeper." *The maturational and evolutionary development of human intelligence may then be viewed as resulting from an improved **specialization and integration** of labor between the hemispheres.*

Thus, extraordinary intellectual giftedness might derive from having the capacity to perform—**in either hemisphere**—tasks (or portions of tasks) that for most people can be performed only in one hemisphere. A detailed discussion of this thesis that **bilateralized** function underlies intellectual giftedness is presented in the last section of Chapter Seventeen.

Notes

1. For example, if you were asked to "picture your living room," your right hemisphere would "see" the room as a single entity; if you were then asked to count the number of items in the room with four legs, your left hemisphere would undertake this task, drawing upon the right hemisphere's "vision" for information.

2. "Affect" being defined as a liveliness of expression, a manifestation of feelings through tone of voice, gesture, and/or facial expression.

3. In which visual stimuli are presented briefly to either the right or left "visual field" of each eye, while a "mask" is presented simultaneously to the opposite visual field (Galper and Costa, 1980).

4. This has been aptly demonstrated by teaching a person with "left-brain" damage who was totally alexic (that is, was completely unable to read and/or use words) to read close to a thousand words, by recognizing each as a complete template (Carmon, 1981).

5. As evidenced by the inability of some patients with "right-brain" damage to decontextualize verbal material in stories and jokes.

6. Electrical stimulation mapping studies in humans indicate that the shifting of focus from what is going on around us to what is going on inside our heads is governed by a "switch" in the thalamus (Ojemann, 1983; Fried and others, 1982). The attention "trigger" appears to be in the form of an increased flow of (the neurotransmitter) norepinephrine to one or the other hemisphere. The thalamus is a principal source of biological inputs to functionally corresponding areas of the cortex, and such stimulation is performed on surgical patients to alleviate intractable epilepsy. Touching a very weak current to a section of the living brain temporarily incapacitates its function (which returns immediately when the current is removed).

7. The path followed by a strongly emotional event takes it through a midbrain area called the amygdala, which directly connects with and "imprints" the cerebral cortex; a "flight or fight" situation typifies such a strongly imprinted event.

8. Long-term thematic memory encoding occurs primarily (or exclusively) during the so-called consolidation phase of our sleep cycles, during which time considerable "reverse learning" of relatively unimportant or "inappropriate" memories apparently also occurs, as cortical neuronal connections are disconnected (Crick and Mitcheson, 1983; Hopfield, Feinstein, and Palmer, 1983; Melnechuk, 1983). REM sleep totals perhaps one and one-half to two hours a night, in periods of ten to thirty minutes each, the longer periods occurring during later sleep cycles. Long-term thematic memory encoding may also be possible under conditions of quiet concentration.

9. During REM sleep, it is likely that a major part of the memory-building process involves the "crosshatching" of our two fact-based memory systems into an "associative memory store" (Broadbent, 1984; Martin, 1984). This is apparently a primary reason for the long-term memory-encoding problems associated with conditions that interfere with REM

sleep, such as the manic phase of a manic-depressive cycle, heavy alcohol use, and high-stress forms of "unipolar" depression.

10. When a frequently used concrete noun (for example, chair) is conceptualized, many more cells will fire than when a particular exemplar of that word is thought of (Weingartner and others, 1983). A frequently used word will be located nearest to our left hemisphere's "naming" areas (Ojemann, 1983).

11. It involves an entirely different brain structure, the cerebellum, which serves as the brain's "time-motion study analyst"; thus, the cerebellum is essential to the development of two "gateways" to our sense of time — one auditory and the other visuospatial. One might also consider the confluence of episodic memories related to the acquisition of food to be a fourth memory system, since it is under the control of an entirely different region of the brain (the hypothalamus); however, these writings focus on memory systems associated with "higher" brain function.

12. The famous case of H. M. is illustrative. After his hippocampus and amygdala were sliced (to arrest intractable epilepsy), he could no longer transfer new fact-based memories from immediate to post-distractional memory, even though his earlier memories were well-preserved. Although he was taught to "mirror-read," he could not remember having learned how to do it.

13. For example, procedures learned by divers while under water can be remembered better under water. Cannabis also interferes with "state" learning. Users report that they had to carefully relearn tasks they could do well "straight" before feeling comfortable performing them "stoned."

14. How-to memory is often best accessed if performance is not accompanied by thinking about what one is doing; for example, verbally explaining to someone how to tie a shoelace while performing the act may make it difficult to perform well.

15. Our "working memory" is located primarily in the brain's hippocampus (Olton, Becker, and Handelmann, 1979); its duration may be hours, days, or weeks. The hippocampus has various discretely identified cell populations, including "counting cells," which exhibit repeated bursts of identical patterns of firing (Vinogradova, 1970); "place" cells, which fire when (for example) a rat is at a particular place in a maze and no other, with other "place" cells firing at other locations (O'Keefe and Nadel, 1978, 1979); and "novelty" cells, which (in monkeys) fire in response to stimuli that had not been previously seen but not in response to recently seen stimuli (Rolls and others, 1982).

16. The cerebral cortex contains our storehouse of long-term episodic and thematic memories. While an "individual memory" does not occupy a single location (Hebb, 1949), stimulating a particular cortical location may evoke a memory, or sometimes a false perception of a memory, that turns out to consist of elements of several related memories. "Analogous" parts of a memory may be stored somewhat differently in the two brain hemispheres; the "peaks" and "valleys" of short- and long-term memory ability follow separate daily cycles. Knowledge retained after six years (for example, foreign-language words learned in high

school) will still be retained after twenty-five years or more, even in the absence of opportunities for further use (Bahrick, 1984).

17. PET-scan values reflect the use of glucose, the brain's source of energy, which varies in relation to brain activity. These values approach their childhood peak by the age of four; at this age, glucose use in the thalamus is 150 percent greater than adult values.

18. The task involved the decoding of upright and inverted print; a significant advantage of the two hemispheres' working in parallel on separate tasks occurs when upright letters are projected to one visual hemifield, while inverted letters are projected simultaneously to the other. A follow-up study of these ten-year-olds (undertaken eighteen months later) showed that the large majority had made this transition to "hemispheric shielding"; there was no recidivism.

19. The individual learning experiences of the two hemispheres do not necessarily occur at the same time(s) or produce equal or near-equal proficiency.

20. And vice versa. Such a biological "template" might consist of dendritic branches and spines whose synapses contain a similar biochemical mix, along with equivalent cell-network connections.

Contents

ℵ *16* ℵ

Types of Giftedness

16.1 Introduction

Human intelligence is often thought to resemble a diamond, that is, it has so many facets that it cannot be comprehended fully, even when viewed from a multiplicity of angles. As a result, it is not possible to compose a universally accepted definition of intelligence.

Efforts to distinguish the variety of aspects, components, features, or domains of intelligence from one another usually begin by contrasting people's performance on tasks that require markedly different types of ability. The distinction between verbal and spatial intelligence is one such dichotomy—a dichotomy based on differences in the ways that the brain's two hemispheres perceive and analyze information.

Of the major approaches to subdividing intelligence, the most detailed is the so-called structure-of-intellect approach (Guilford, 1967). This approach envisions intellect as a three-sided cube encompassing 128 separate abilities (Meeker, 1969). The three sides, or axes, distinguish the following categories and subcategories:

- Four "classes of information" across which a given individual may possess highly divergent levels of ability for what are otherwise "analogous" problems — analogous in terms of the "operations" required for their solution and the "products" generated. These include (1) *figural* classes of information — in which the shape of the object (a triangle, a tree, or a concrete object) is comprehended as a totality; (2) *semantic* classes — in which words, pictures, or abstract ideas are given meaning by the individual's repertoire of knowledge; (3) *symbolic* classes — in which a stimulus is "seen" in the form of a numeral, a single letter, a note of music, or a code symbol; and (4) *behavioral* classes — in which comprehension relates to emotional context (for example, facial expression).

- Five "operations" (the activities or *processes* required to solve a problem). These include (1) *cognition*: the immediate discovery, awareness, rediscovery, or recognition of information; (2) *memory*: retention of information in the same form it was committed to "storage," and availability of that information in response to the same cues that attended the encoding of the information; (3) *evaluation*: the ability to reach the decisions or to make the judgments needed to satisfy the criteria presented (for example, correctness, suitability, adequacy, or desirability); this "implies a kind of sensitivity to error or discrepancy on the one hand, and [on the other] the ability to make judgments in relationship to known or understood standards"; (4) *convergent production*: the "process of finding the answer where 'finding' is something more than mere retrieval, and 'the answer' suggests that [the] domain is so systematic, ordered, and determinant that there are rules or principles for converging on the solution"; the "emphasis is on achieving unique or conventionally accepted best outcomes"; and (5) *divergent production*: the ability to generate information "from given information, where the emphasis is upon variety and quality of output" (Meeker, 1969, pp. 35–38).
- Six ways ("structural organizations") in which information may be presented. These six ways determine the *products* that the operations performed will engender, and they assess functional abilities in such skill areas as (1) determining *relationships* between items of information presented, (2) distinguishing between *classes* of information, (3) discerning the *implications* of information, (4) performing (or discerning) *transformations* on information (for example, block design), (5) discerning the *information systems* contained in the material and using them to solve problems, and (6) handling individual (unrelated) *units* of information.

Even this level of specificity, however, is insufficient to capture all the distinctions between major aspects of intelligence, as evidenced, for example, by people's divergent performance on different types of spatial problems and the fact that "behavioral" intelligence can be subdivided into two distinct forms: "intrapersonal" and "interpersonal" skills.

The structure-of-intellect concept can be useful in identifying people with specific forms of intellectual giftedness and/or distinguishing the parameters of giftedness (Guilford, 1977, 1979). For example, many psychometricians associate a high level of competence in the intellectual abilities based on *divergent production* with creativity. These abilities are seen as incorporating fluency, flexibility, and individuality, on the one hand, and quality, reverence, and discipline, on the other. The first set of characteristics contrasts sharply with *convergent production*, and the second set suggests a "parallel mechanism" that is similar to or identical with that displayed in convergent production.

Further, because it provides a detailed picture of the areas of intellectual strength and weakness that an intellectually gifted individual displays, a structure-of-intelligence evaluation could be used to develop an individually tailored regimen designed to broaden, enhance, or integrate that individual's areas of greatest cognitive strength.

Another approach to examining extraordinary gifts of intellect is to identify those domains of intelligence in which exceptional competence is highly valued by society. To this end, Howard Gardner has distinguished seven highly valued cognitive **domains**. These are detailed in the next section, and — after a discussion of spatial intelligence and mathematical reasoning ability — are further discussed in relation to the three memory systems delineated in Chapter Fifteen.

Not all extraordinary gifts of intellect require an exceptional or even a normal level of overall intelligence, although many obviously do. Concrete "pictorial" imagery is a necessary component to several valued cognitive skills, but it is apparently unrelated to IQ scores. In fact, people who possess little or no concrete visual imagery seem to be overrepresented in several professions that require graduate school training and an excellent command of "mental" imagery.

As suggested in this chapter and in Chapters Thirteen and Fourteen, which contrasted the abilities of the Japanese and Jewish peoples, extraordinary competence in the "symbolic" domain can be achieved in two different ways — through a visuospatial-procedural (right-hemisphere) approach, in which the *structural* relationship between variables determines the "access coding" of integrated meanings, or through an auditory-conceptual (left-hemisphere) mechanism, in which *meaning* determines how concepts are organized and integrated.

This chapter goes on to explore the processes that make it possible to develop "creative insights" — processes that appear to be predicated on the ability to generate insights in three separate, but related, aspects of problem solving (selective encoding, selective combination, and selective comparison). It also presents some measures for identifying people who possess high levels of creativity and/or insight, and it discusses the relationship between insight, perseverance, and the age at which great theoretical works tend to be completed.

16.2 Highly Valued Domains of Intelligence:
The Work of Howard Gardner

In his well-written book *Frames of Mind*, Howard Gardner (1985) sets forth seven relatively autonomous intellectual competencies, defined as skills that meet two basic standards: (1) they are used in finding or creating problems to solve and in resolving genuine problems; and (2) they are deemed extremely useful to, and are highly valued by, society.[1] Within this framework, the intelligence of individuals can be viewed in terms of their competency in seven *domains*:

- *Linguistic intelligence*, which is based on a sensitivity to the meaning of words and an effective verbal memory.
- *Logical-mathematical intelligence*, which focuses on the ability to create, retain, and use long chains of reasoning.
- *Spatial intelligence* (defined in section 16.3).
- *Bodily-kinesthetic intelligence*, which includes athletics and dancing.
- *Musical intelligence*, which requires a sensitivity both to the characteristic qualities of a tone (including its pitch, timbre, and rhythm) and to the affective aspects of music (mood and emotion).
- *Intrapersonal intelligence*, which is the ability to examine and comprehend one's own feelings.
- *Interpersonal intelligence*, or the ability to notice and make distinctions among other people's moods, temperaments, motivations, and intentions.

Even though each of these "intelligences" is semiautonomous, they may work in tandem to produce a particular competency. For example, spatial intelligence and bodily kinesthetic intelligence often combine to produce competence in the so-called mechanical realm, which is one of the two forms of intelligence invoked when people are referred to as having common sense, the other being competence in the kinds of social skills that underlie *interpersonal* intelligence.

Although proficiency in a particular domain is essential to a high level of achievement in some occupations (for example, certain aspects of spatial intelligence are a necessary component of competence in painting or architecture), there may be several pathways to success in many fields. As an example, Gardner cites the legal profession, in which (1) an individual who has outstanding *linguistic* skills—who excels in the writing of briefs, the phrasing of convincing arguments, the recall of facts from hundreds of cases, and the like—may rise to the top; alternatively; (2) an individual with highly developed *interpersonal* skills—who displays an engaging personality, can skillfully interview prospective jurors and witnesses, and can speak to the hearts of the jury—may also excel; and (3) an individual who is able to analyze a highly complex situation—by isolating its underlying factors and following a tortuous chain of reasoning to its ultimate conclusion—may also be highly successful.

16.3 Spatial Intelligence and Insight in Mathematics

Spatial intelligence appears to consist of not one but a number of loosely related capacities. Among the several types of spatial ability that have been differentiated are (1) a facility in performing three-dimensional spatial transformations and in using structural approaches to comprehending symbolic relationships (whether these relationships are presented in spatial or in verbal form), (2) a facility in solving two-dimensional spatially oriented perceptual matching problems (such as jigsaw puzzles), and (3) a facility in comprehending and adjusting to situations in which the observer's body orientation is an essential ingredient. Distinctions such as these, however, are further complicated by the recognition that two- and three-dimensional spatial aptitudes can each have both static and dynamic aspects, that the ability to conjure up and transform a mental image is not analogous to the ability to draw it, and that it is frequently possible to solve various types of supposedly spatial problems through the exclusive use of nonspatial (logical-mathematical and/or verbal) mechanisms (Gardner, 1985). Part of the problem in isolating spatial factors is that the approach taken by a given individual to solving a given type of spatial problem may undergo considerable change as the difficulty of the problem is increased. As a consequence, for some types of spatial problems, the more difficult the question, the higher the factor loading on the so-called g of general intelligence, and the more difficult it is to isolate specific spatial factors (Lohman and Kyllonen, 1983).

Some aspects of spatial ability appear to be essential to an aptitude for certain types of mathematics or science, while proficiency in other spatial areas is more a reflection of general intelligence. The relationship between insightfulness in mathematics and facility in solving various types of spatial problems was explored in a group of fifty-nine students in grades four to seven attending a school whose admission standards favored high scores on the WISC block-design subtest (Olson, 1984, 1985). Because those students who exhibited creative insights in math[2] substantially outperformed their classmates on several, but not all, components of this battery of spatial tests, an analysis of these results should help in identifying which aspects of spatial ability form the underpinnings to mathematical insightfulness, as well as disclosing areas of spatial acumen in which performance is a manifestation of general intelligence.

Most striking was the performance of the mathematically insightful students on a test called "nonsense syllogisms," on which they achieved an average of 14.5 correct answers, compared with 4.5 for their "noninsightful" classmates. This test measures the ability to reason logically when structure—rather than meaning—determines the correct answer.[3] These students also showed considerably greater aptitude on each of three tests measuring ability in spatial restructuring ("surface development," "form board," and "paper folding") and also outperformed their classmates on other tests requiring three-dimensional visualization (for instance, "cube comparison," where they averaged 40 percent more correct answers).[4] Nevertheless, they scored no better than their peers on five different tests designed to measure the ability to distinguish (or match) objects or words from backgrounds. On two of these two-dimensional tests ("identical pictures" and "hidden pictures"), a group of twenty-two of their noninsightful, "socially focused" classmates[5] outperformed the insightful students.

Even though the ability to visualize spatially appears to be an essential ingredient in the kind of mathematical genius displayed by Albert Einstein[6] — and spatial visualization is carried out in the human brain's right hemisphere — the autopsied portions of Einstein's brain revealed that the primary "biological template" upon which his genius lay was in the so-called association area of his *left* hemisphere's cerebral cortex (see Chapter Seventeen), implying that his gift of insight was dependent on the integrated efforts of each of his hemispheres — the right to *see* and the left to *analyze* (Diamond, 1985; Zweig, 1985). The linkage between the right hemisphere's spatial visualization skills and mathematical aptitude has led some cognitive biologists to suggest a possible biological explanation for the 13:1 ratio of male to female junior high school students scoring 700 or higher on the mathematics portion of the SAT and for the fact that all the top forty scorers in the Johns Hopkins Talent Search project were male (Marjoram and Nelson, 1985). Because a high level of brain testosterone apparently fosters longer and more vigorous right-hemisphere growth cycles,[7] the generally higher levels of this hormone in the brains of males are said to explain their superior performance on mathematics tests (Geschwind and Behan, 1982) as well as certain gender-based behavioral differences described by anthropologists, both in primitive human populations and animal species. The question of the existence of a gene for "spatial giftedness" has been explored in two large and ethnically different populations by means of a computer simulation of the distribution of scores on a mental-rotations task (Vandenberg and Kuse, 1978), and the results indicate that because there are two partially overlapping distributions, exceptional ability on this task is based on the presence of a (relatively rare) "major gene" that is "autosomal" rather than sex linked.

Although most people think that rapid computational skills automatically accompany competency in higher mathematics, this perception is apparently not accurate. For instance, Gardner (1985, p. 155) suggests, "The ability to calculate rapidly is at best an accidental advantage for mathematicians." It is considered "far from central to their talent, which must be of a more general and abstract variety. At the core of this talent is the ability to handle skillfully long chains of reasoning." Gardner concludes that an ability to discover an analogy and then to integrate this analogy into an archive of analogies, thereby creating new ones, constitutes the essence of mathematical insight.

The rising tide of IQ scores has apparently had a dramatic effect on the field of mathematics. Because structural organization is key to the development of meaning in higher mathematics, the rapidly improving body of mathematical knowledge can be absorbed by young mathematicians with considerably greater ease than it was by their predecessors. Gardner postulates that the major creative work of most mathematicians is over by the age of twenty-five or thirty, with productivity dropping off in each decade, as "what is known with difficulty by the teacher is picked up easily, sometimes even effortlessly, by the student" (p. 154). This situation is in marked contrast to that found in many humanistic areas of scholarship, where (as detailed in section 16.8) major works typically appear during the fifth, the sixth, or even the seventh decade of life. In these later-peaking occupations, where verbal-symbolic analytical thinking predominates, symbolic structures tend to be organized and integrated around the *conceptual* rather than the perceptual aspects of meaning, with causality being the principal driving force, rather than a derived dimension.

Irrespective of which approach is used for building this "symbolic" dimension, the ability to solve complex analytical problems appears to require a kind of cross-dimensional viewing capability, in which the ability to conceive, hold in memory, and compare and contrast divergent (and even opposite) concepts is critical. Two mechanisms for assessing people's ability to engage in this type of integrative "insightful thinking" are presented in section 16.8.

16.4 The Domains of Intellect and Our Three Memory Systems

A discussion of the relation between the memory systems outlined in Chapter Fifteen and the various *domains* of intellect now seems in order. We might summarize this relationship as follows:

First, *bodily kinesthetic* intelligence falls squarely in the domain of how-to memory, requires a substantial involvement of the right hemisphere in the processes of learning, and (in some people but not all) is stimulated by a high state of arousal.[8] Second, because *interpersonal* intelligence is based on adeptness in comprehending the emotional nuances of a situation, which apparently derive from *episodic* memory, this implies a substantially heavier involvement of the right hemisphere than the left in this kind of thinking (at least during the perceptual stages of knowledge building). Third—and conversely—the building of *intrapersonal* intelligence is thought to be effectuated under conditions of reflective analysis (for example, being in touch with your own emotions during a highly stressful situation differs from having a clear retrospective understanding of your motivations and intentions). Fourth, although *musical* intelligence contains features that involve the functional abilities of both hemispheres, accomplished musicians use their left hemisphere far more than their right. If more than music appreciation is involved, musical intelligence must be integrated with bodily kinesthetic intelligence as well. Fifth, even though the left hemisphere clearly predominates in *linguistic* intelligence, the right hemisphere's ability to read holistically, to decipher the emotional content of language, and to organize thoughts at the paragraph level implies that verbal giftedness must also be predicated on the integrated efforts of both hemispheres.[9] Moreover, many linguistically gifted individuals appear to possess a bilateralized ability for speech (see Chapter Seventeen). Finally, although the spatial aspects of *logical-mathematical* intelligence derive from the right hemisphere's visual perceptions, the *integrated analysis* of these inputs is clearly a left-hemisphere, thematically coded function, as witness the size and complexity of the neurons in Albert Einstein's left, but not right, association cortex (see Chapter Seventeen).

If Gardner's concept of acumen in the logical-mathematical *domain* is accurate, then this adeptness at handling long chains of reasoning suggests that competence in this domain can be built either on a "structure-determines-meaning" basis or on a "meaning-determines-structure" basis. Further, these two divergent mechanisms for "symbolic" dimension building may also be viewed as two separate doorways to the development of our comprehension of the dimension of time: one being a visuospatial ("right-brained") mechanism[10] and the other an auditory ("left-brained") approach.[11] As a consequence, one of the primary tasks involved in constructing effective early childhood education programs is to facilitate the development of each of these biological mechanisms.

16.5 Mental Versus Visual Imagery

The capacity to envision that which is not immediately present is a hallmark of higher intelligence. Such visualization may be concrete—in the sense that people experience the sensation of actually *seeing* an object, scene, or person thought about—or it may be abstract—in the sense that only a *perception* of what is "cognized" is available to the "mind's eye." This abstract or mental imagery is thought of as being conceptual and proportional, rather than sensory or pictorial (Pylyshyn, 1973, 1980).

Although most people possess considerable concrete visual imagery, there are wide individual differences, with many people reporting either exceedingly little imagery or none at all (Gardner, 1985).[12] For "nonimagers," it is as if the "visions" of the brain's right hemisphere, rather than being directed outward, are instead routinely directed across the brain to the left hemisphere for further mental processing.[13]

Concrete visual imagery (in the sense of visual retention or recall) is quite distinct from visual recognition memory or spatial orientation. Even though its absence may result in certain cognitive handicaps—for example, such imagery is needed for describing things or people and for perfecting certain mechanical skills—there is no reason to believe that it impedes IQ-test performance. In fact, it appears that people of well-above-average intelligence are more likely to have poor or absent concrete imagery than are people of average intelligence. In his book *Image and Mind*, Kosslyn (1980) concludes that many very bright individuals cannot be used as subjects in studies of visual imagery, because they report absent or very poor visual imagery. Further, in his analysis of eminent scientists, Galton (1907) found that a large proportion of the scientists he examined typically reported little or no visual imagery, while individuals of apparently modest intellectual powers often reported detailed concrete imagery. Concrete imagery does not even seem to be a precondition for writing novels. For example, Aldous Huxley confessed to being a poor visualizer and conceded that words did not evoke pictures in his mind (Huxley, 1970). Other professions in which a high proportion of workers reputedly have poor or absent concrete imagery include law and psychology (Zenhausern, personal communication, 1987)—fields where linguistic, logical, and/or interpersonal skills are of considerable importance. Roe (1953) notes that among her sample of sixty-four eminent scientists, only two of nineteen psychologists and cultural anthropologists had concrete imagery, compared with slightly more than half of the biologists and physicists, and Gardner (1985) indicates that concrete imagery occurs more often in the observational sciences (such as botany, zoology, or geology) than in the behavioral or social sciences.

The possible impact of having little or no visual imagery on a person's IQ score may depend on the IQ test used and the age at which IQ is tested. It may be of particular relevance in the years immediately following the replacement of pictorial with mental imagery (see section 16.6) for IQ tests that require some facility in visual recall. Moreover, even though relatively bright "non-imagers" construct alternative ways of solving spatially factored IQ-test problems, they probably solve these problems in slower or less reliable ways than do individuals who have the ability to "see" an exemplar as it is being manipulated in their minds. This is particularly evident when it is a question of difficult structural-transformation problems. Nevertheless, "vividness of visual imagery" appears unrelated to overall spatial ability (Poltrock and Agnoli, 1986; Lohman, 1987).

People with poor or absent pictorial imagery will usually display strong "auditory conservation" skills. In a study of children with above-average IQs, the nine children identified as auditory conservers had IQ scores (WISC-R) averaging 120, compared with 114 for the thirty-two children who were not so identified (Norton, 1980). Only three of these nine children were also visual conservers. In this sample, significant positive correlations were found between auditory conservation and the verbal, but not the performance, portion of the WISC-R, as well as on tests of musical aptitude and ability.[14] To understand what they are reading, people who lack visual imagery recite the words to themselves. Thus, attempts to teach "speed reading" to people who can only encode in an auditory mode will not work.

Concrete visual imagery would seem to be essential for proficiency in chess, since the ability to anticipate moves and their consequences would appear to require extraordinary pictorial imagery. However, even though chessmasters generally possess what in their words is an outstanding visual imagination, closer examination shows that this capacity is not dependent on visual imagery per se, since in "blindfold chess"[15] the sight of the chessboard sometimes upsets a chessmaster's calculations (Binet, 1966). Rather, chess seems to require a superb memory for meaningful configurations.[16]

16.6 Forms of Giftedness Not Requiring a High Level of General Intelligence

The possession of extraordinary talent in certain cognitive domains does not necessarily require a high overall IQ. For example, several forms of artistic giftedness—such as painting and sculpture, which require strong concrete imagery as well as excellent eye-hand coordination—do not necessarily require a high IQ or even an average IQ. In fact, at least one noted sculptor is also a resident of an institution for the mentally retarded.

Eidetic imagery (or, as it is more commonly called, photographic memory) is another gift that—although occasionally present among people with exceptionally high IQs—is also frequently found among people with well-below-average verbal ability, since, in most people, it is apparently the antithesis of verbally encoded short-term memory. About a fourth of all young children and an equivalent portion of the very old possess it. The incidence of eidetic imagery falls off between the ages of five and eight (Giray and others, 1976),[17] as initial pathways linking specific cell networks in the human brain mature and verbal skills sharpen. Among adults in their mid twenties, the incidence of eidetic imagery is perhaps 3 percent (Giray and others, 1976), and among college students, it is reported to be about 7 percent (Giray and others, 1978). This u-shaped age-related curve implies that (1) in children, a preexisting "pictorial" memory becomes inaccessible to the consciousness, because of the development of a more mature (verbal) mode of short-term information storage; and (2) among those elderly people who suffer a severe decline in verbal ability, the return of eidetic imagery is essentially a reflection of the erosion of a pathway that transmits pictorial information to the verbal hemisphere. Supporting this construct is the finding that, in a sample of college students who reported having eidetic imagery as children, hypnotically induced age regression was frequently able to generate its temporary reemergence (Wallace, 1978). Further, eidetic imagers generally block the formation (or retention) of an unwanted image by "verbally rehearsing" what they see (Haber, 1979).

Both the brilliant and the retarded are very overrepresented in the ranks of people possessing an ability to perform complex arithmetical calculations in their heads (Smith, 1988). When found among retarded or autistic people, this "gift" is usually narrowly focused and is associated with a fixation on one kind of tangible item (most frequently, a calendar).[18] The most dra-

matic instance of what has come to be called "calendar calculation" appears highly instructive in several ways:

George Finn, a resident of an institution for the mentally retarded, is
unable to do simple addition, beyond that which he can accomplish by
counting slowly on his fingers; nevertheless, he can (with nearly 100 percent
accuracy) rapidly and easily answer such questions as "What was the date of
the third Friday in May in the year 1246?" or "During which months of the
year 23,198 will the seventh be on a Thursday?" The mathematical calculations required to correct for leap years (and the shift, in 1752, to the
Gregorian calendar) are exceedingly complex, and efforts to develop a
formula that is easy to learn and/or not time consuming to apply have failed
dismally. Rather, in George's case, the skill appears to have been an outgrowth
of his ability to maintain nearly total concentration for prolonged periods
(poring over an almanac containing a perpetual calendar at age six), plus an
outstanding event-related memory (George can also provide a detailed description of the weather conditions every day of his life since early childhood). His (now deceased) twin brother had similar skills (but limited to the
twentieth century) (Hill, 1978).[19]

The two separate abilities possessed by George Finn seem to
suggest that, in him, the normal processes by which people use
episodically encoded memories to construct their thematically
associated memory system are impaired but that he possesses an
intact, separately developing (and perhaps self-rewarding) cognitive "summarizer" that seeks out and utilizes an episodic vehicle for expressing its analytical skills.[20]

Almost all "calculating prodigies" are male, and there is no
evidence that an ability for mental calculation is inherited.[21]
People with exceptional proficiency in mental calculation have
also been classified by the way in which they imagine numbers:
those who see them in their "mind's eye" and those who hear
them.[22]

Another extraordinary talent that may be possessed in isolation is hyperlexia, which is defined as an individual's ability to
recognize and read words at a far higher level than he or she can
understand their meaning. Children with hyperlexia usually
teach themselves to read without comprehension (usually between two and a half and three and a half years of age), will tend
to display a compulsive preoccupation with reading, and will
quite often begin to read before they begin to speak. These
children will generally perform considerably better on tests of
auditory memory and verbal fluency, tests that require categorizational skills, and block-design tests than on tests requiring

comprehension, problem-solving skills, or the ability to follow a route (Aram and Healy, 1988).[23]

16.7 High IQ, Creativity, and Originality

Although exceptional intelligence and creativity are usually thought to go hand in hand, most tests designed to measure creativity show very low correlations between it and intelligence among people having IQs above 120 (Simonton, 1976).[24] For example, a study of 100 Oxford University students (Cantor, 1973) found that at IQs above 120, creativity bore little relationship to IQ — at least when creativity was assessed by the kind of open-ended questions designed to measure divergent thinking.[25]

A study of fifty prepubescent British children whose verbal IQ scores (on the WISC) were at least 140 (Lovell, 1986) may shed some light on the difference between the type of creativity assessed by tests of divergent thinking, on the one hand, and exceptional problem-solving ability, on the other. By comparing these children's scores on traditional tests of creativity with the responses of their teachers to various items on a teacher-assessment questionnaire, the researcher discovered that — although high teacher ratings for "originality" and "logical thinking" were strongly related to scores on the general IQ component of the cognitive measures employed — the teachers' evaluation of *these students' originality bore absolutely no relationship to their scores on these creativity measures*.[26] Thus, these teachers conceived of originality more in terms of *reasoning ability* than in terms of "inventiveness" or "unusual" ideas.[27]

Because these creativity assessment measures emphasize divergent thinking — and logical thinking processes strongly emphasize convergent thinking — there is a strong inference that abnormally large differences between divergent and convergent thinking abilities exist among people having exceptionally high IQs. Support for this hypothesis comes from a comparative assessment of the "crystallized" and "fluid" intelligence levels of children who scored in the top 1 percent on a test of fluid intelligence. Even though the crystallized intelligence of these children tended to be considerably above the norm, the correlation found between these two types of intelligence was only + .26, or far lower than the "typical average of around + .6 found in British or American populations" (Freeman, 1983, p. 308).

The early home environment can exert a strong influence on scores on tests of divergent thinking in young adulthood. A strong firstborn advantage ($p < .001$) was found among male college students (Eisenman and Schussel, 1970) on each of the three measures of creativity employed: (1) "unusual uses for common objects" (scored for fluency and originality); (2) preferences among symmetrical polygons of varying complexity (creativity being associated with a preference for complexity); and (3) a thirty-item true-false personal opinion survey.[28] Additional support for a strong birth-order effect comes from a study of 380 "gifted and talented" high school students, based on their scores on the Terman Concept Master Test[29] — with the notable exception of children from two-child families (Pulvino and Lupton, 1978).

As a result of these and similar studies, a number of researchers have concluded that divergent thinking should not be equated with creativity and have challenged the proposition that scores on traditional tests of creativity actually correlate with creative performance. Instead, creativity is increasingly thought to be domain-specific talent rather than a general ability.

Nevertheless, such diverse talents as mathematical inventiveness and exceptional verbal and general problem-solving skills do appear to share a common denominator — the ability to generate and use insights.

16.8 Problem-Solving Skills and Analytical Insight

The ability to generate insights is considered by most cognitive psychologists to be central to intellectual giftedness. Consequently, researchers have sought to gain a better understanding of this insight-generating process. They have focused on the question of insight from two different perspectives: (1) working out theoretical constructs of the processes that people use to generate creative insights and (2) developing tests to assess whether a person has a high potential for generating such insights. In this latter area, two mechanisms will be presented for evaluating whether people possess extraordinary competence in the ability to solve complex analytical reasoning problems. The first involves the so-called Janusian thinking processes (named after the two-faced Roman god Janus), and the other measures people's ability to generate the kind of "simultaneous vision" needed to solve complex causality problems.

Janusian thinking involves an ability to actively conceive of two opposites simultaneously and thereby process two disparate views on a subject in parallel. This type of thinking is believed to be "a key step in the processes of the creation of the kind of scientific theories and/or discoveries of such people as Einstein, Darwin, Watson, Pasteur, and Fermi" and to be essential to the creative thinking processes of literary critics, poets, and philosophers (Rothenberg, 1979, p. 38).

A test designed to assess the extent to which people routinely engage in Janusian thinking (J T)[30] has been shown to be an excellent indicator of productive insightfulness in the arts and sciences. After it was tested favorably in two controlled studies, it was administered to three groups of people: (1) high-IQ college students who had been categorized as "highly creative" (on the basis of a "quantitatively designed and cross-validated assessment of their documented creative achievements in the arts and sciences" and on the strength of their "creative" interests); (2) similarly high-IQ college students who did not evidence this "productive creativity); and (3) nine Nobel laureates in science (spanning physics, medicine, and chemistry). As expected, the highly creative college students had a markedly higher "J T quotient" than did their less creative high-IQ peers, and exceptionally high J T scores were reported among the Nobel laureates.[31] Moreover, as the creativity level of respondents rose, there was a significantly faster response time associated with J T answers (Rothenberg, 1982).

The second psychometric approach assesses people's ability to generate the kinds of insights associated with superlative "general" problem-solving skills. It involves difficult versions of so-called formal-operational causality problems. These problems are designed to test people's ability to detect (from among a number of possible choices) which variable or combination of variables is responsible for the outcomes shown and, thereafter, to apply this knowledge in the solution of additional problems containing these same variables. To solve such problems, the subjects must be able to discern and test potential relationships between the variables, which first requires them to convert the "semantically presented" information into a "symbolically coded" mode and then to hold in memory (1) the sets of relations, (2) the outcomes (implications) associated with these variables, and (3) the "causality" evidence. At the same time, they must test combinations of variables as potential solutions (Commons, 1985).[32]

The ability to generate insights in the problem-solving domain appears to require more than the possession of an exceptionally high IQ and superior analytical reasoning skills. Robert Sternberg and Janet Davidson have identified three separate kinds of insight that combine to form "creative intelligence" (Sternberg and Davidson, 1982; Sternberg and Powell, 1983). These are:

- *Selective encoding*, or the ability to discern what pieces of information are relevant to the solution of a problem (from among considerable irrelevant information) and to discern in what way(s) they are relevant.
- *Selective combination*, or the ability to discern how to combine what might originally be seen as isolated (or at least not obviously related) pieces of information into a unified whole.
- *Selective comparison*, or the ability to compare newly acquired information to that acquired in the past and to discover unexpected or unusual relationships between the new and the old information.

These authors believe that it has been difficult to isolate "creative insight" because this kind of insight involves the ability to successfully employ **all three of these separate but related processes** rather than depending on only one of them. Sternberg and Davidson have demonstrated that high-IQ people do possess a markedly greater ability to generate insights in all three of these areas, in that they need less information to solve "insight problems" than people of more modest intellect, who benefit incrementally as progressively more information is supplied (Sternberg, 1985). Nevertheless, Sternberg (1986) holds that, in addition to an ability to generate insights, intellectual giftedness requires a passion for employing these skills in new and imaginative ways in response to novel tasks and situations.

The distinction is often made between people who are geniuses in an analytical mode and people whose extraordinary intelligence is of the "synthetic" variety. The analytical mode has been defined as "a preference for processing information by decomposing a situation into its component parts, examining the relationship among these, and, ideally, resynthesizing the parts into a whole that reflects the new understanding gained from this decomposition process. [The analytical person] is often described as intelligent, reasonable, and understandable,. . . because his reasoning proceeds in a linear fashion, so that others can follow the pattern of his thoughts" (Powell, 1987, p. 97). By contrast, the synthetic mode of intelligence involves the capacity to discover new relationships — new in the sense that they are novel to the person engaged in thinking them through. Although the synthetic process apparently originates with analytical reasoning, there comes a point at which the synthetic genius "constructs a product so novel and involving so many leaps in levels of thought that a linear chain of reasoning can never be demonstrated adequately, not even by the synthetic genius herself" (p. 98). This is not to say that the analytical genius does not have "the capacity to be synthetic — it is what is done with the newly synthesized [thought] that makes this type of genius analytic. Such a person, after years of analysis and occasional leaps of thought, analyzes each of these leaps for their implications to explicate all meanings from them" (p. 98). Powell contrasts the "impeccable logic" of Immanuel Kant's philosophical writings (which he cites as the work of an analytical genius) with Einstein's theory of relativity, in which almost every sentence Einstein "uttered was packed with layers of meaning which reflected considerable integration of many different levels of information." Powell concludes by asserting that the kind of "integrated genius" that allowed Leonardo da Vinci to excel in many different areas of intellectual endeavor is extremely rare.

In fact, achieving the heights of productive creativity usually requires more than an intellectual capacity to pursue creative endeavors and a passion to investigate the novel. It usually also requires an extraordinarily high level of motivation and mental energy, the ability to bracket parts of a problem too complex to solve in its entirety, and—most of all—perseverance. Gruber (1986) cites the following examples: Even though Isaac Newton wrote and published *Principia Mathematica* over a two-year period (when he was in his mid forties), modern studies of his manuscripts show that it really took him twenty years to move from his preliminary sketches to the actual writing of his great treatise. Charles Darwin fashioned the outline of his theory of evolution in about one and a half years of work, but it was not until twenty years later (at age fifty) that he wrote and published *On the Origin of Species.* John Milton first began to contemplate an epic poem at the age of thirty-three, started work on *Paradise Lost* some sixteen years later, and completed it eight years thereafter (at age fifty-seven).

Thus, the transformation of a creative insight into a monumental literary, mathematical, or scientific achievement often represents the culmination of years or decades of dedicated effort.

Notes

1. Thus, in this construct, extraordinary adeptness at facial recognition (although it is a relatively autonomous ability and is governed by a specific region of the brain) does not achieve the status of an "intelligence," because it provides few opportunities for problem solving and (except in unusual circumstances) the value placed on it by society is not especially high. Nevertheless, it may form an important component of another "intelligence" (for example, interpersonal skills).

2. Based on their ability to make "original discoveries" on open-ended problems of the type presented in *Scientific American* in the early 1980s (in Martin Gardner's column)—for example, "magic squares," "Pascal's triangle," and "color cubes."

3. Nonsense syllogisms require the application of structural reasoning to nonsensical information. For example, if all fish can fly, and most fish

are elephants, is the conclusion that most elephants can fly true, false, or indeterminate? Consequently, if a person had markedly divergent scores on tests of "meaning-laden" and "nonsense" syllogisms, this would be indicative of a differential use of structural or semantic approaches to "symbolic" encoding.

4. They generally achieved (or slightly exceeded) an adult level of performance on these subtests. "Cube comparison" falls under the cluster of spatial abilities dubbed (Lohman, 1987) "speeded rotation" (spatial relations), in contrast to the surface restructuring problems that assess "visualization."

5. Students were defined as "puzzle focused" or "socially focused" by whether they showed an interest (on any of fifty days) in a variety of puzzles (such as Rubic's Cube) that were made available to them when they entered the classroom.

6. Einstein reputedly had a very visual mind and was drawn to visual and spatial forms of Euclid's writings. It is said that he thought in terms of images and drew insights from spatial models rather than from purely mathematical lines of reasoning (McKim, 1972).

7. Particularly during specific stages of prenatal, infant, and preschool brain development and again during puberty. In a college sample, sex differences on the math portion of the SAT were not significant, after controlling for spatial ability (Burnett, Lane, and Dratt, 1979). Other authors (for example, McGee, 1979) conclude that sex-observed differences in perceptual and cognitive functioning are secondary consequences of differences in visualization and spatial orientation abilities.

8. For example, Larry Bird, of the Celtics basketball team, who plays at his best when maximally aroused. Nonetheless, "quiet concentration" may be more conducive to maximal performance in other sports or for other basketball players (who perform erratically when overaroused emotionally).

9. In addition to the type of verbal intelligence usually evaluated by IQ tests—which centers around verbal *comprehension*—another highly correlated but relatively distinct "form" of verbal intelligence exists—one centered on verbal *fluency*. A discussion of verbal fluency and how to test for it is found in Sincoff and Sternberg (1987). A further distinction may be made between exceptional verbal fluency in an analytical mode and fluency (in speech and/or writing) in a conversational mode (which is often an important component of interpersonal intelligence).

10. Which is developed from knowledge derived from the visual tracking of objects across space, over time, and from visual-motor integration (which, in turn, is derived from our body movements across space, over time).

11. Using this approach, learning the structure and meaning of repetitively used sounds forms the (initial) basis for the sequencing of meaningful analysis.

12. For example, when asked to "picture your favorite animal," a "poor" imager (in contrast to a person with no imagery whatsoever) may report experiencing a momentary flash of cognition, possibly followed by an extremely short-lasting "semiwhite" outline of its shape. Some

"nonimagers" report being able to evoke faint images by an "effort of will."

13. Rather than taking place in a single part of the brain, visual imagery is thought to be dependent on three processing modules: (1) a "picture activator," (2) a "foundation finder," and (3) an "assembler" that looks up and interprets information concerning how the parts are to be arranged (Kosslyn and others, 1985); in the process of creating a mental image, the left hemisphere is better at arranging shapes when categorical information is needed and the right when coordinated information is required (Kosslyn, 1988).

14. The correlations were +.36 ($p < .05$) for musical aptitude and +.44 ($p < .01$) for musical ability. For the arithmetic and similarity subtests of the performance portion of the WISC, the correlations were +.35. The children averaged 6.6 years of age.

15. Where a chess player plays a number of different opponents simultaneously, with his only cue to the positions on each board being a recitation of the last move made by an opponent.

16. Pattern recognition and forward planning are seen as the keys to success in chess; memory for random arrangements of chess pieces is no better among chessmasters than less expert players, although it is for structured arrays (deGroot, 1978). There are very few instances of great chess skill running in families (Cranberg and Albert, 1988).

17. Eidetic imagery generally occurs as an all-or-nothing phenomenon rather than existing on a continuum. In this study, all "eidetikers" scored a perfect 20, meaning all five primary criteria (Haber and Haber, 1964) were satisfied on each of four test stimuli shown for thirty seconds. Among the exceptionally high-IQ people possessing a photographic memory is Jerry Lucas, the former basketball player, who can "memorize" an entire page of a telephone directory.

18. The frequency of savantism of various types is estimated to be 0.6 percent among the mentally retarded (Hill, 1978) and 9 percent among people suffering from "classical early infant autism" (Rimland, 1978); calendar-calculating ability is the most common type.

19. Another set of retarded twins had an outstanding ability to generate very complex prime numbers; one would relate a newly generated prime to his co-twin, who would induce a prime in response, usually within thirty seconds (Sachs, 1985).

20. By examining the lateral eye movements of a moderately retarded (right-handed) calendar calculator who "was capable of identifying the correct day of the week for any given date into the remote past or future," the researchers found "the strongest left-hemisphere specialization for the perceptual calendar task, moderate left-hemisphere specialization for mathematical questions, and no specialization for musical and spatial questions" (Burling, Sappington, and Mead, 1983, p. 327).

21. In the few cases where there was more than one mental calculator in the same family, they lived in the same household, with one the instigator and the other "an inferior emulator" (Smith, 1988).

22. The latter are often given to muttering while calculating and may also

have exaggerated motor movements, while visual calculators tend to be placid. Auditory calculators are usually self-taught and use left-to-right multiplication, whereas visual calculators tend to use cross multiplication. Some visual calculators need to see the numbers in their own handwriting (Smith, 1988).

23. Most hyperlexics (perhaps 85 percent) are male and most are right-handed. Familial language-learning and/or reading disorders are a frequent occurrence.

24. Although tests usually do show moderate correlations between intelligence and creativity up to this IQ level. Simonton cites nine studies supportive of this hypothesis.

25. In this test, the evaluation criteria consisted of the total number of responses, along with the number of "unique" responses. The questions were designed to measure "inventiveness" and "unusual ideas" (for example, "pattern meaning" or "unusual uses for things"). The students were both undergraduate and graduate students and were majoring in a wide variety of areas.

26. It "had a zero loading on the rotated axis which reflected the ability to answer the tests of virgin thinking on which creativity-summed scores had a [factor] loading of .82" (Lovell, 1986, p. 125).

27. The author notes that the teacher ratings for these children (which were based on the teacher questionnaire originally developed for the Terman study) were very similar to those reported among the Terman gifted population (despite a gap of forty years and one continent).

28. The firstborn males scored 29 percent higher on the fluency aspect of the unusual uses task and 26 percent higher on the survey. On the originality aspect, their scores averaged 2.50, compared with 1.05 for the laterborn men. On the complexity measure, their scores averaged $+13$, compared with -30 for the laterborns. Less significant birth-order differences were found among a smaller sample of young women. The total sample size was 450.

29. This test is designed to measure the ability to deal with abstract ideas at a high level. Firstborns were also greatly overrepresented in this population, particularly among subjects from larger families.

30. This test (an offshoot of the Kent-Rosanoff test) involves having subjects respond to ninety-nine (orally presented) words with the first word that comes into their heads. Responses to these very common words are then divided into three categories: (1) response words that mean the opposite of the stimulus word; (2) "primary" nonopposite responses ("primary" meaning that the response word is the most common answer); and (3) all other responses.

31. The Nobel scientists responded with an opposite more than 60 percent of the time, compared with 50 percent and 40 percent for the "more creative" and "less creative" groups of (63 and 50) Yale University students, respectively. Nevertheless, in all three groups, the number of "primary" nonopposite responses was virtually identical, constituting a fourth of the total. Because the primary response words were also opposites in thirty-four of the ninety-nine cases, the Nobel scientists may be said to have averaged 76 percent more than the "expected"

number of opposites, compared with 48 percent for the "creative" and 19 percent for the less creative students. For the test criteria, see Carroll, Kjeldegaard, and Carton (1962).

32.   An example is the so-called washing machine problem (which is an extension and transformation of the classic Inhelder and Piaget's pendulum and bending rod tasks). Developed by Michael Commons, this problem presents a series of washing operations — with variables such as (different) soaps, bleaches, water temperatures, and boosters resulting in one of two outcomes, a clean or a dirty wash. Using these examples, the solver must determine the sets of relationships causing the outcomes shown and then determine the outcomes under additional sets of conditions (Commons, 1985).

Contents

๙ 17 ๖

Unusual Biological Traits
in Intellectually Gifted People

17.0 Synopsis

This chapter (1) delineates several relatively unusual biological traits commonly or disproportionately found among people with extraordinary intellectual ability; (2) presents hypotheses concerning causal relationships between intellectual giftedness and several of these traits; (3) presents findings concerning the relationship between high intelligence and the speed with which gifted people's brains process and respond to information; (4) discusses findings of some dramatic differences in gifted people's sleep cycles; (5) presents evidence that the IQs of the offspring of high-IQ people do not regress toward the norm; and (6) discusses findings suggesting that specific forms of intellectual giftedness are accompanied by a "bilateralized" capacity to perform tasks that in nongifted people are either specific to, or performed far better by, one hemisphere.

17.1 Childhood Myopia, Allergies, Handedness, and Testosterone

Even though studies generally indicate that gifted people tend to be above the average in physical and emotional health (Free-

man, 1983), the commonly held perception that most intellectually gifted persons wear glasses and/or have asthma or allergies is not a myth. Indeed, studies indicate that exceedingly
large proportions of gifted persons are afflicted with myopia or
immune disorders. Further, a relatively high incidence of left-
handedness and/or familial sinistrality is also found in these
populations.

To examine these questions in depth, the National Talent
Search Program of John Hopkins University seeks out children
who are extremely precocious in their mathematical or verbal
reasoning ability. For a child to qualify, his or her score on the
verbal or mathematics portion of the SAT must be at or above
the 1-in-10,000 level for his or her age (a score of 700 or higher in
math and/or 630 in English prior to age thirteen).[1]

Biological information concerning over 350 of these exceptionally precocious children, their parents, and nearly 200 of
their high-achieving but less precocious peers has enabled researchers to examine:

- Whether, as has been suggested, certain biological conditions — although relatively uncommon in the general
  population — will be found with considerably greater
  frequency among these extremely precocious children.
- Whether the frequency of any biological commonalities found will vary in relation to the type of
  precociousness displayed by the child (verbal, mathematical, or both) and/or the sex of the child.
- Whether the prevalence of these unusual conditions
  will be materially greater among the extremely precocious children than among their high-achieving but
  less precocious peers.

The principal findings concerning these mathematically and/
or verbally precocious children (Benbow and Benbow, 1986;
Benbow, 1985) may be summarized as follows: First, a majority
wore glasses. Second, a majority had allergies or other immune
disorders. Third, although the frequency of left-handedness,
ambidexterity, and familial left-handedness was in each case

considerably above the norm, the large majority of these children were right-handed with no history of familial sinistrality. Fourth, there was no relationship between blood type and giftedness. *Overall, 80 percent of these precocious children were myopic, allergic, and/or left-handed.*

Higher rates of childhood myopia were found among the verbally precocious (74 percent) than among the mathematically, but not verbally, gifted (53 percent). Allergy rates did not vary by type of precocity, and the pattern of occurrence of myopia and allergy led Benbow and Benbow to suggest that *the two conditions are independent of one another.* Left-handedness was, however, linked with allergy.

Childhood Myopia

To virtually no one's surprise, an unusually large proportion of gifted children wear glasses. Although many people assume that this is primarily a result of eyestrain caused by peering into books for hours on end, the prevailing medical wisdom—supported by studies of twins (Sorsby and Fraser, 1964; Lin and Chen, 1988), including studies of identical twins reared apart (Knobloch and others, 1985)—is that childhood myopia is primarily, if not exclusively, a hereditary condition.

Associations between IQ and the incidence of myopia in the general population have often been reported (Rosner and Belkin, 1987; Grosvenor, 1970; Heron and Zytkoskee, 1981; Hirsch, 1959), but these associations do not seem to relate to its severity (Teasdale, Fuchs, and Goldschmidt, 1988).

In the John Hopkins sample, the incidence of childhood myopia was *75 percent among the 115 verbally precocious children, 53 percent among the 218 mathematically precocious youths, and 72 percent among the 34 children who were exceptionally precocious in both areas.* This compared with a 20 percent incidence of myopia among a sample of 191 preadolescents who scored in the top 3 percent on an academic achievement test but whose SAT performance was not appreciably above "chance" (Benbow and Benbow, 1986). By comparison, only about 15 percent of American high school students wear glasses (Karlsson, 1973, 1975). The prevalence of myopia among the parents of these precocious children was slightly more than 50 percent (equivalent percentages were found among fathers and mothers), but the age-equivalent rates of myopia in these parents were probably considerably lower.[2]

Allergies and Other Immune Disorders

The frequency of allergy and/or other immune disorders among this select Johns Hopkins population was 55 percent,[3] with virtually no difference found between the mathematically precocious and the verbally precocious groups. This compares with a rate of about 10 percent in the general population (Stites and others, 1982). About a third of these precocious children had at least one parent with allergies, but, as with myopia, there was little variation by sex of parent.

Left-Handedness and Giftedness

Slightly more than 90 percent of the population at large is primarily or exclusively right-handed. The proportion of left-handed people seems to vary by age and sex, with a considerably greater incidence of left-handedness found among males than among females (Beale and Corballis, 1983; Hardyck, Petrinovich, and Goldman, 1976), and among young people than among middle-aged people (Flemington, Dalton, and Standage, 1977; Porac, Coren, and Duncan, 1980; Tan, 1983).[4] Aside from man, there is apparently only one other type of animal whose paw preferences are not "random" or task specific, namely, *talking birds*. Thus, in animals possessing the gift of speech, the left hemisphere's (near-universal) dominance for speech is almost always accompanied by its control over "motor output."

Although some children undergo shifting hand preferences on the way to establishing permanent preferences, handedness appears to be preordained biologically. For example, a recent study that compared the head-turning habits of newborn infants with the handedness that they displayed in mid childhood found that eighteen of the twenty children classified as left-handed had a strong leftward head-turning preference in their initial days of life.

A substantial *minority* of left-handed people are the victims of neurological impairments (occurring prenatally or through injury) that prevent the *"left brain"* from assuming its usually dominant role in "motor-output" chores. Most of these instances apparently constitute "hemispheric-reversal cases," in which speech is also centered in the right hemisphere. But a substantially different form of brain organization appears to accompany the confluence of left-handedness and giftedness (or, at least, verbal giftedness)—namely, one in which the capacity for speech is "bilateralized"—that is, it exists in both hemispheres.

The prevalent view—based in part on historical analyses of hand preferences among people who attain eminence in fields requiring extraordinary intellectual abilities—is that there is a far higher rate of sinistrality among gifted people than in the population at large. The (non-Asian) Johns Hopkins sample contained these findings:[5]

- A fourth of the verbally precocious males were left-handed, which is approximately twice the rate normally found in the comparison group (the high-achieving seventh graders who were not sufficiently advanced to comprehend the concepts contained on the SATs), among which the overall rate of left-handedness was 9.7 percent.
- Fifteen percent of the mathematically precocious children were left-handed, with a slightly higher rate found among the small number of mathematically precocious females than among the males.
- Eighteen and a half percent of the verbally precocious females were either left-handed or exactly ambidextrous.[6]
- Almost a third of the immediate families of these children had one or more left-handed members. The precocious children who were right-handed were almost as likely to have a left-handed family member as those who were themselves left-handed.[7]

Thus, in this sample, left-handedness was associated with increased verbal precocity among males, and left-handedness or ambidexterity was associated with verbal or mathematical precocity among females. Left-handedness has also long been associated with increased rates of allergy and other immune disorders, both in the population at large and among gifted people. For example, in the Johns Hopkins sample, *82.4 percent of the verbally precocious left-handed children also had moderate to severe allergies.*

Giftedness and Intrauterine Hormone Levels: The Geschwind Hypothesis

Norman Geschwind has advanced the theory that a major cause of both immune disorders and sinistrality is a relatively high prenatal level of brain testosterone (or possibly a sensitivity to it), leading to an acceleration of growth in the right hemisphere and a delay in the growth of the left hemisphere. Geschwind has postulated that—when the time arrives for determining which side of the brain will assume the primary responsibility for those "motor-output chores" performed by one's hands—people with high testosterone become left-handed because their right hemisphere's development is more advanced, making it better able to undertake these functions (Geschwind and Behan, 1982, summarized in Durden-Smith and DeSimone, 1984). Geschwind has buttressed this hypothesis with evidence that the left thymus of people with immune disorders is often of below-average weight, a condition that could have resulted from abnormally high testosterone levels in utero and that could in turn affect the immune system's function adversely (Geschwind and Behan, 1984).

Since males generally have higher brain testosterone levels than females, this hypothesis offers a biological rationale for the finding that, in most mammals, males tend to have better spatial skills and females better auditory skills. Extreme mathematical precociousness is almost entirely a male phenomenon—the top forty scorers on the math portion of the SAT in the National Talent Search Program were all males.

Geschwind also predicted that an analysis of the birth months of extraordinarily gifted people would reveal that a proportionately greater number were conceived in the summer, when daylight is maximized (and melatonin has an inhibitory effect on certain sex hormones),[8] and that a proportionately low number were conceived in the winter. An investigation of this hypothesis was undertaken in the Johns Hopkins population (Benbow and Benbow, 1987), and the results clearly bear out the existence of such a seasonal influence—as 10 percent of the children were born in each of the spring months (April, May, and June), compared with an average of 7 percent in each of the fall and winter months of September, October, November, and December.

These findings also lend support to the hypothesis (discussed below) that early right-hemisphere growth facilitates the "imprinting" of audiovisual templates upon which subsequent experiences can be encoded and related and that this early "right-brain" growth will produce a longer and more vigorous period of left-hemisphere catch-up. The end result will be a more optimal "specialization and integration of labor" between the hemispheres.

17.2 Allergies, Myopia, and Handedness: The Mensa Samples

Mensa is an international society open to persons who have scored in the top 2 percent on a standardized test of intelligence. American Mensa has about 50,000 members. Over the past several years, I have lectured at a number of its national and regional gatherings in the United States and Canada, and at several of these meetings I have undertaken polls concerning allergies or other immune disorders, childhood myopia, and handedness. Although the 506 respondents in these polls are not extremely representative of very high IQ people in general or even of all Mensans,[9] the results—a 28 percent incidence of childhood myopia, a 31 percent rate of "severe or multiple allergies," and a 14.4 percent rate of left-handedness—are likely to be fairly representative of the high-IQ population at large.

In a study of the 2,100 British members of Mensa (Sofaer and Emery, 1981), the results of a survey questionnaire that drew a 65 percent response rate revealed a 19.9 percent incidence of wearing glasses for myopia before age ten, which was nearly twice the incidence reported for the siblings and children of members and four times that of their parents. The incidence of gout, 1.7 percent, was more than three times that of the members' siblings and the British "norm" (see section 17.5), while the rate of infantile autism among their first-degree relatives was 6.3 times that found in the general population.

17.3 Intellectual Giftedness and the Cerebral Cortex

Postmortem examinations of people who possessed extraordinary cognitive abilities demonstrate a link between the nature of their specific gifts and brain biology, as evidenced by the size of the neurons in the so-called receptive layer of their cerebral cortexes. For instance, in the "auditory cortex" of a great musician who reputedly had perfect pitch from infancy onward, as well as in the "visual cortex" of an artist who demonstrated an outstanding photographic memory, the receptive layer (layer four) was approximately twice as thick as normal. This was the result not of having more neurons but of having larger neurons, with longer and more numerous message-receiving branches (Scheibel, 1985). This observed linkage has recently been reinforced by an analysis of Albert Einstein's brain (Diamond, 1985, summarized in Zweig, 1985), which showed that in the exact cortical region where one would expect to find it—his left hemisphere's so-called association cortex[10]—the receptive layer was approximately twice as thick as normal, and there were many more "support" cells (glia) to serve the structural and metabolic needs of these larger neurons (in Einstein's case, 73 percent more glial cells).

Despite the lack of controlled studies, the observed differences in the size of these gifted people's neurons are highly persuasive because they appeared in the exact areas of cortex associated with their gifts. Moreover, neurons examined in three other portions of Einstein's cortex were of normal size. Although there seems to be little association between overall brain size and extremely high intelligence (for example, Einstein's overall brain size and weight were below average), it is also true that the brain regions most involved in higher cognitive functions constitute a relatively small percentage of total brain weight.

The receptive-layer neurons of the cerebral cortex have an especially high lifelong "plasticity" — a plasticity attributable to the continued presence of the so-called nerve growth factor (NGF) that, in the brain, is extremely active in those neurons that use the neurotransmitter acetylcholine. This NGF confers an ability to create and modify synapses in response to use or disuse, especially in neurons in which synaptic connections are found on "spines" rather than on wirelike dendrites (Scheibel and Paul, 1985; Lund, 1984).

The receptive-layer in sensory-analytical areas of the cerebral cortex — and of the other neurons to which they directly connect[11] — constitute the innermost workings of higher intelligence, and it is within this cholinergic system that the "price" of giftedness appears to be exacted, in the form of myopia and allergies.

17.4 A "Cholinergic Recruitment" Theory

Extraordinarily gifted people make considerable demands on the cell networks most involved in carrying out those tasks at which they excel. This would seem to imply (1) a high rate of utilization of the various enzymes and neuropeptides needed to execute mental skills, and/or (2) a redirection of these proteins from one kind of sensory-analytical function to another, and/or (3) a redirection from sensory-analytical to associative-integrative functions.

Much of the brain's supply of a key acetylcholine-making enzyme (ChAT) is produced in a single brain region (Alzheimer's disease being the consequence of the destruction of the cells in this region). This suggests that there are limitations on the overall supply of this neurotransmitter and that a well-above-average level of *cholinergic* activity by some cell networks results in a somewhat smaller allocation of ChAT to the remainder of the cholinergic system, especially to those "smart-cell" networks whose abilities have diminished considerably as modern man has evolved.

Although human beings are, by a human definition of "higher intelligence," vastly superior to other animals, many other mammals are, in several respects, far more intelligent than human beings. For example, many species possess a very keen sense of smell—a form of "intelligence" or a "skill" on which their survival has depended. Because the olfactory-analytical system is an exceptionally heavy user of acetylcholine (as well as other neuropeptides needed for abstract learning and memory),[12] the evolution of extraordinary competence in one form of human higher intelligence was likely to have been accompanied by—and may well have depended upon—a *redirection* of our brain's cholinergic energies (1) away from the analysis of scents and from a reliance on holistic mechanisms for analyzing and responding to the external world and (2) toward the capacity to visualize internally constructed spatial designs and to integrate linguistically and symbolically coded meanings.

Allergies and Giftedness

Allergies and myopia are associated with deficits in the workings of the cells responsible for the analysis of incoming sensory stimuli. The most common type of allergy (to pollens) represents an erroneous conclusion on the part of these cells that the air entering our nasal passages contains unfriendly invaders whose destruction necessitates the activation of our immune system's antigens.

The ability of many mammals to recognize and react to scents is quite remarkable, especially when compared with our own. In modern society, the need for skill in analyzing olfactory stimuli is far less that it was at the beginning of human evolution, and the demands placed on other (cholinergic) "smart-cell" networks has increased dramatically between then and now. By extension, in people with exceptional cognitive talents, the cognitive demands placed on some cell networks *increases the likelihood of analytical deficits in the olfactory-analysis system.*

Myopia and Giftedness

Because the prevalence of childhood myopia approaches 75 percent among extremely precocious *verbally gifted* children—

and is considerably greater in this group than among mathematically precocious children — it seems possible that the exceptional demands placed on the cells responsible for encoding and analyzing the written word cause a redistribution of functional responsibilities among the cell networks directly connected to those cells along the cognitive chain. Significantly, it is the malfunction of one of these cell networks that causes the visual defect represented by myopia.

Reading, or the rapid analysis of linguistically coded "figural forms," is a very recently developed cognitive function, and (in the developed world) is also among the most heavily taxed. Analysis of the written word contrasts with the analysis of most other visual inputs in that the products of both hemispheres' envisionings and analyses[13] *are directed to the left hemisphere's "language center" for further processing.*

Although verbal giftedness requires a very high degree of temporal and acoustical acumen in the left hemisphere, it must also entail a superb holistic encoding ability. The competence displayed by the left-hemisphere areas that govern these highly stressed functions suggests that cells in analogous areas of the right hemisphere would also be enlarged. This supposition, however, is not valid if the tissue samples from Einstein's right hemisphere's association cortex are any indication because — in contrast with the neurons in his left hemisphere — his right-hemisphere neurons were of normal size.

As human speech evolved, portions of the left hemisphere were "deeded over" to language functions. This leads one to wonder how the cells in geographically analogous areas of the right hemisphere carried on their earlier responsibilities (after losing all or part of the services of their left-hemisphere "helpmates"). In particular, one may question how, in verbally gifted people, the cells in the right hemisphere that recognize the shape of letters and words are able to do such an effective job. One possible answer is that they are able to enlist the support of cells in other cell clusters and networks to perform functions for which they now take less responsibility or have surrendered entirely. Since "thinking" represents both a chain of events and a set of parallel processes, the neuronal networks "recruited" to perform undermanned or very highly stressed functions will be those that have the *structural and biochemical* ability to under-take such assignments—hence, they will be other cholinergic neurons.

One may then speculate that the cells responsible for encod-ing and/or transmitting images in the portion of the visual field disrupted in myopia *have been recruited to perform linguistically related shape analysis—or to perform essential services to those cells that do.*[14] This explanation is consistent with the finding that people who are the most likely to make an extraordinarily heavy use of this capacity (such as children in the verbally precocious Johns Hopkins sample) evidence extraordinarily high rates of myopia.

Heritability of Changes in the Cholinergic Blueprint

As amply demonstrated by findings from the environmental enrichment studies of extremely aged rats (Diamond and others, 1985),[15] and by the ability of eighty-year-old symphony orchestra conductors to learn new musical pieces, considerable lifelong plasticity pervades cholinergic neurons. Nevertheless, almost universal agreement now exists that how much a particular cognitive system is challenged during the so-called *critical* or *sensitive* period(s) of postnatal development will have a consider-able and permanent impact on cell structure and associative cognitive ability. These critical-period experiences may then be thought of as expanding or limiting the lifelong capacity of a given cognitive system and thereby determining how much effort will be needed to master a new cognitive skill.

There are also some indications that such critical-period experiences also affect the so-called developmental program of one's progeny, in the sense that they can *alter the blueprint that governs how the brain's limited cholinergic energy will be apportioned (for example, to linguistic rather than to olfactory analysis).* This sug-gests that the overall **shape** of human intelligence can adapt to ancestrally stressed experience. In support of this thesis, we can note that the medical community regards allergies and myopia as hereditary conditions. If these indications are correct—that the extent of the use or disuse of various cholinergic cell populations during their critical periods does have heritable consequences — then the environment provided to our children during these early windows of opportunity may affect the nature of our grandchildren's intelligence.

17.5 IQ and Uric-Acid Levels

A rather strong correspondence has been found between uric-acid levels (measured in the blood) and occupational class. In one large study (Dunn and others, 1963), the average uric-acid level of 339 male executives was 5.73, compared with an average of 4.77 for 532 male blue-collar workers.[16] Other studies by these authors produced these findings:

- Ten medical students had uric-acid levels that averaged an extremely consistent 5.75.[17]
- Thirty-one high school students who engaged in extracurricular activities of a scholastic nature had levels averaging 5.7, compared with 5.1 for 104 of their classmates whose extracurricular activities were of other types.
- The levels of seventy-six scientists (physicists and chemists) averaged somewhat lower than the other professional and academic groups examined (5.34) but were still well above the average found among the blue-collar workers.

Uric-acid levels among these executives appeared to form a bimodal pattern, with one "peak" in the same range as the blue-collar workers and another at about 6.0. A substantial proportion of these executives (and virtually none of the blue-collar workers) had readings in the range of 7.0 to 9.0 (a reading of about 10.0 indicating borderline gout). Despite the relative rarity of gout in the general population, "[a]n impressive list of people prominent in science, letters, diplomacy, and war who purportedly had gout has been assembled" (Stetton, 1958, p. 73).

It has recently been demonstrated that uric-acid levels tend to have strong hereditary linkages. A Japanese study of the families of adult identical twins (Inouye, Park, and Asaka, 1984) found that the uric-acid-level correlation between these identical twins and their spouses was quite low (+ 0.1), which indicates that diet is of relatively minor consequence. In this study, other within-family correlations bore an exceptionally close resemblance to those usually found for hereditarily transmitted traits (+.51 for parent-child, +.75 for midparent-child, and +.84 for identical-twin correlations).[18] These authors also studied Japanese children who performed well enough on an academic achievement test to be admitted to junior high school (where IQs are likely to average about 120), and they report a significant correlation (+.3; p_1.03) between their uric-acid levels and their scores on achievement tests.

In the previously mentioned British Mensa survey (Sofaer and Emery, 1981), the incidence of gout at an average age of thirty-six was more than twice that reported in a somewhat older British population.

In mammals, significant levels of serum uric acid are found only among higher apes and man. It has been suggested that uric acid, like other purines (such as caffeine), stimulate the cerebral cortex and that people with high intellectual energy are likely to have either a high rate of purine use (Gutman and Yu, 1965) or a below-average use of enzymes that break down these brain-stimulating substances (Orowan, 1955).

17.6 Sleep Cycles

The sleep cycles of extraordinarily gifted children are reported to differ markedly from those of normal and mentally deficient children of the same age (Grubar, 1985). In this study, each of the five gifted children tested, whose IQs averaged 149, had either *six or seven sleep cycles*—compared with an average of 4.2 for seventeen children of normal intelligence (all of whom ranged between three and six cycles) and with an average of 2.7 among fifty-four mentally deficient children. The sleep cycles of these gifted children were also considerably more regular—a regularity that was particularly evident during the fifth and sixth sleep cycles (when normal-IQ children tended not to reach the deepest phases of sleep) and did not enter into or remain in so-called stage-four or REM (rapid-eye-movement) sleep as often.[19] This finding confirms an earlier report on adults with IQs above 140 (Huron, 1981).

During REM sleep—when vivid visual dreaming is accompanied by a shutdown of body (but not eye) movements and by an extraordinarily high degree of mental processing—these gifted children experienced nearly twice as many high-frequency eye movements as did the normal-IQ children (283 versus 168), but low-frequency eye movements were found to occur somewhat less often in the gifted children than in the normal children (200 versus 240). Because certain aspects of the transfer of new memories into "long-term storage" are thought to occur primarily during REM sleep (in particular, the effective organization of retrieval cues),[20] the greater amount of REM sleep experienced by gifted children, along with the presumably better information-processing mechanisms available to gifted people during these "memory consolidation" periods, is likely to enable a more effective organization of the cell connections needed to encode and interrelate prior events and thematically coded knowledge.

17.7 Intellectual Giftedness and Speed of Information Processing

This section explores the relationship between high IQ and the speed with which people can process information. The findings suggest that (1) a unitary set of information-processing mechanisms underlies the so-called g of general intelligence rather than that a person's relative "processing speed" varies in relation to his or her domain-specific skills; and (2) a well-developed information-processing capability is often a necessary, but not a sufficient, prerequisite for giftedness.

In addition to being associated with the ability to perceive, comprehend, reason, and/or fashion new insights at an extraordinarily high level, intellectual giftedness also usually implies a basic underlying quickness—an ability to comprehend and analyze incoming problems rapidly and efficiently.

Researchers have long sought to determine whether intellectual giftedness is dependent on a single "universalized" high-speed information-processing mechanism or on separate mechanisms that underlie performance in specific cognitive domains and to quantify the relative "speed advantage" of high-IQ people on stimulus-response tasks during particular stages of the cognitive process. One highly productive approach to addressing these issues has been to compare the response times of intellectually gifted people and controls on an assortment of diverse yet simple tasks, and another is based on determining the relationship between IQ and the shortest "inspection time" needed to encode relevant information. The principal conclusions growing out of the studies discussed below are as follows:

- People with exceptionally high IQs display extremely rapid encoding and response times on simple stimulus-response tasks encompassing a variety of cognitive areas. *Their greatest speed advantage appears in the middle stages of these tasks (the "thinking" part)*[21] rather than in the earlier or later portions.[22]
- The correlation between IQ and "mental intake speed" ("inspection time")[23] is fairly strong up to IQs of about 115.[24] Several studies indicate that above this level, higher IQs engender only modest reductions in the time needed to register salient information (Brand, 1984; see also Deary, Caryl, Egan, and Wight, 1989).
- Because the comparative "thinking-time" advantage of people with high IQs is not related to the domains in which gifted subjects are precocious, this strongly suggests that they apply a generalized set of information-processing mechanisms to the solution of problems rather than use separate (spatial or verbal) mechanisms, depending on the nature of the task.

In what is probably the best study of information-processing times among highly intelligent people (Cohn, Carlson, and Jensen, 1985), precocious junior high school students displayed considerably faster "thinking times" than did their above-average-IQ schoolmates, an advantage that generally averaged 50 to 70 percent on a variety of diverse but simple stimulus-response tasks.[25] Because the average response times of this group of precocious students *on each of these tasks* were extremely close to those recorded for a group of Berkeley undergraduates,[26] it seems possible to draw two important inferences from these data. First, extremely bright young adolescents are able to *achieve but not surpass* the information-processing competency attained by adults who are in the superior IQ range. Second, because these junior high school students were especially precocious in math and science — yet did not demonstrate proportionately faster response times on the nonverbal tasks than on the verbal tasks (compared with their peers)—their performance was based on the functioning of a generalized information-processing mechanism rather than on domain-specific mechanisms.[27]

The extent of the "thinking-time" advantage displayed by these precocious seventh graders[28] is approximately equal to that displayed by people with IQs in the normal range (85 to 115), when their times are compared with those of people having subnormal IQs (Brand, 1984).[29]

Confirmation for a basic processing-speed advantage among gifted children comes from a recent study that compared the postdistractional memory of forty-five gifted elementary and junior high school students with that of forty-two less gifted children who nevertheless possessed considerably above average IQs.[30] Because the gifted children did not display a greater use of "categorical clustering" in remembering words from word lists, these researchers (Muir and others, 1989; Muir and Bjorklund, forthcoming) concluded that the gifted group's ability to recall more words was not dependent on a superior processing strategy. The use of categorical clustering did, however, bear a significant relationship to the rate at which they recalled words.[31]

There are several possible consequences of viewing the capacity for rapid inspection and analysis as a single (integrated) set of mechanisms. First, the mechanisms used to perform these relatively simple tasks[32] are likely to be the same as those employed in the analysis of complex problems. Second, if some or all of these basic information-processing skills are "teachable" during a child's formative years, then facilitating the development of an "adequate" or "superior" set of skills may well engender lasting cognitive gains among children who receive such instruction. Third, because the precocious development of an optimal (or near-optimal) set of basic information-processing skills does not indicate an ability exceeding that of competent adults, such skills appear to be a necessary (but not a sufficient) precondition for the emergence of an exceptionally high level of general intelligence. Fourth, given the strength of the correlations between IQ and processing speed found across the normal IQ range (85 to 115), at least a fourth of the measured IQ differences among individuals within this range *might be attributable to* the relative adequacy of these basic information-processing mechanisms.

Psychometricians have also attempted to measure the relationship between IQ scores and the complexity of the brain waves induced by the presentation of simple stimuli, and these efforts have produced some exceptionally high correlations. Specifically, the length of the trace made by "evoked potential" waveforms[33] induced by the presentation of auditory stimuli (tones) has been reported by at least two sets of investigators to show *correlations with Wechsler IQ scores*[34] *in the range of +.70* (Blinkhorn and Hendrickson, 1982; Haier and others, 1983). One of the principal authors suggests that this correspondence might relate to the need to reduce error before responses are generated (Hendrickson, 1982). In this view, the existence of longer waveforms in high-IQ people suggests that, in response to the brain's need for information to rapidly and reliably solve problems, these waveforms generate a larger "fan of activation." This implies that (1) more information-gathering apparatus is employed; (2) more information upon which to predicate a decision becomes rapidly available; and, as a consequence (3) the length of time it takes to generate sufficient confidence in an answer to be willing to risk registering it is reduced.

The link between IQ scores and information-processing speed and complexity is thought by Sternberg to revolve around the ability to rapidly delegate the repetitive aspects of novel situations to "automatization" programs especially constructed for such purposes. As he aptly puts it:

> The more intelligent person will be able to more rapidly and fully cope with novel demands being made on him or her by devoting fewer resources to processing the novelty of a given task or situation and using available resources to automatize performance; conversely, more efficient automatization leaves over additional processing resources for dealing with novel tasks and situations. As a result, novelty and automatization trade off with one another. As experience with the kind of task or situation increases, novelty decreases and the task or situation will become less apt in its measurement of intelligence from the

standpoint of the processing of novelty. However, with practice, automatization skills may come into play, in which case the task will start
to become more an apt measure of automatization skills [Sternberg,
1986, p. 233].

If these evoked potential waves are indeed measuring the
effectiveness of the brain's automatization mechanisms, then the
existence of more-effective mechanisms will result in a greater
amount of cell firing in the cerebral cortex. This suggests one of
two possibilities: Either there is more communication between
the cortical hemispheres,[35] and/or this increased cortical cell-
network involvement indicates that deeper brain regions (such
as our hippocampus) have been freed up, enabling their "mental
energies" to be directed elsewhere or to remain "at rest,"
while mundane stimuli are responded to in a nearly effortless
manner.

Nevertheless, there is increasing evidence that the more intelligent a person is *the less energy his or her brain uses to solve complex
problems*. For example, a recent PET-scan study of healthy young
adults taking the Raven's Advanced Progressive Matrices test
(RAPM) showed that there was a strong negative correlation
between test scores and glucose metabolism in the brain (Haier
and others, 1988).[36] In combination with other findings,[37] this
suggests that, rather than being a function of more brain activity, intelligence is dependent on the efficiency of the brain
processes relevant to a particular task.

17.8 IQ Scores Among the Offspring of
Intellectually Gifted People

The term *regression to the mean* refers to the tendency for the
offspring of individuals having extreme values in any given
characteristic to have less extreme values. It is believed that this
tendency "can be seen in any organism which reproduces sexu-
ally and any trait which is less than 100 percent inherited"
(Eysenck and Kamin, 1981, p. 62), and studies of people with
normally distributed IQs suggest that this concept also applies
to human intelligence. Nevertheless, it appears that there is little

or no regression to the mean in the IQ scores of the offspring of people with extremely high IQs.

The IQ scores of 1,571 offspring of the Terman gifted sample averaged 133.2 (Oden, 1968), which was only marginally different from the average IQs of their Terman-study parents (152) and those parents' spouses (125). Rather than these children's Stanford-Binet scores averaging at the 98.8th percentile of the established norms, their average score was at the 98.2nd percentile. Given the enormous societal changes that occurred between 1922 (when the Terman sample was selected) and the early 1960s (when the IQs of these offspring were measured), the consistency of these findings indicates that, at worst, only a marginal reduction in their "expected" IQ occurred. Because evidence of a regression toward the mean would tend to support a primarily genetic model of high intelligence rather than a primarily environmental model, these findings from the Terman study suggest that there is a stronger environmental contribution to the intellectual development of people scoring in the extremely high IQ range than is found in the normal IQ range.

17.9 Intellectual Giftedness and Bilaterality

As suggested in section 15.5, the maturational development of functions that can be performed by *either* hemisphere in adulthood may be thought of as consisting of three elements: First, one hemisphere learns how to perform the function (or components thereof) using its unique mode of perception and analysis. Second, a similar learning experience occurs in the other hemisphere using its sensory-associative analytical areas and mechanisms. Third, as "automatization" mechanisms are developed in the more efficient hemisphere, a replica of the biological structure needed to perform the task is constructed in the opposite hemisphere. Thus, *our brain's two halves have evolved the capacity to exchange information with one another and to teach each other about the mechanisms they have developed to deal with similar situations. The maturational and evolutionary development of human intelligence may then be viewed as resulting from an improved **specialization and integration** of labor between the hemispheres.*

Consequently, a high level of verbal and symbolic analytical ability could derive from the capacity to establish and maintain an effective division of labor between the two hemispheres. Under this construct, the better the mechanisms for performing tasks (or portions of tasks) in the nondominant hemisphere, the better able a person will be to (1) think about many things simultaneously; (2) apply more resources to whatever area of thought is of greatest interest, while "automatization" programs handle more mundane matters (such as driving a car while planning a speech); and/or (3) being able to (simultaneously) envision, compare, and contrast dichotomous aspects of complex problems such as those described in section 16.8.

The validity of this hypothesis (that high intelligence is predicated on efficient **bilateralized** function) gains support from findings that many extremely precocious teenagers do not seem to display the usual hemispheric advantage in areas where such an advantage would ordinarily be expected. For example, a sample of seventy-two children identified by the Johns Hopkins Talent Search program as scoring above the 1-in-10,000 level for their age in mathematical and/or verbal reasoning were tested on two types of problems: (1) a letter-matching task (Do the two vowels shown have the same name or a different name?) and (2) a rotation task (Is the second letter R shown, in one of four rotated orientations, in a normal or a mirror-image position relative to the first?). By means of a computer simulation of a tachistoscope, these tasks can be shown to either the left or the right visual field in each eye while a blank screen is shown to the other visual field, thereby enabling the reaction time of each hemisphere to be measured precisely, with the number of errors made by each hemisphere providing a further basis for comparing them.

In contrast to the expected left-hemisphere speed advantage for letter matches and the right-hemisphere advantage on the spatial task, these subjects showed the following pattern of results: On the letter-matching task, the right hemisphere was faster and more accurate for all subjects (verbally gifted or mathematically gifted or both; male or female), especially for males and for subjects of both genders who were left-handed and/or had a family history of sinistrality. On the rotation task, there was virtually no difference between the hemispheres in reaction time, and somewhat fewer errors were made by the left hemisphere (Benbow and Benbow, 1987).[38]

There is also evidence that, with respect to our most lateralized brain function, speech, some people—especially left-handed and intellectually gifted people—possess a *bilateralized* ability. Almost all (98 to 99 percent) of right-handed people have speech confined essentially to their left hemispheres, meaning that damage to specific areas of their left hemispheres, but not their right hemispheres, will cause them to lose the ability to speak (except that they may be able to utter expletives when angry and/or sing the words of exceptionally familiar songs). Nonetheless, *an estimated 15 to 20 percent of the left-handed population* appears to be **bilateralized** for speech. This has been amply demonstrated by so-called Wada tests that are used to temporarily incapacitate one hemisphere prior to surgery in order to determine which hemisphere or areas not to slice into when seeking access to deeper regions of the brain. Bilateralized people do not lose their ability to speak when either their left hemisphere's or their right hemisphere's speech areas are thus incapacitated (Rasmussen and Milner, 1977; McManus, 1979, summarized in Bradshaw and Nettleton, 1983).

There is some strong (albeit inferential) evidence suggesting that, as a group, bilateralized left-handed people possess above-average IQs. The analysis proceeds as follows: First, a large body of evidence demonstrates that there is no overall difference in IQ between the left- and right-handed population, including one study (Hardyck, Petrinovich, and Goldman, 1976) that compared the scores of 541 left-handed children in elementary school with 5,192 of their right-handed classmates. Second, approximately 15 percent of left-handed people are so-called hemispheric reversal cases, in which the right hemisphere is dominant for both speech and "motor-output" tasks. In most (if not all) cases, this "reversal" is associated with prenatal neurological damage that prevents the left hemisphere from assuming its usual roles. Third, because hemispheric reversal tends to be accompanied by a significant degree of cognitive impairment, and left-handed people are significantly more prone to certain disorders that result in cognitive impairment, this creates a strong presumption that the remaining population of left-handed people (especially those who are bilateralized for speech) must have IQs that, on the average, are above the norm (which compensates for the lower-than-average scores of other left-handed people). In addition, several studies of gifted children indicate that they are less likely to be strongly right-handed than are nongifted children living in the same community (Hicks and Dusek, 1980).

Moreover, the substantially higher rate of left-handedness reported among laterborn cohorts (Flemington, Dalton, and Standage, 1977; Porac, Coren, and Duncan, 1980; Tan, 1983) is in the direction suggested by the gradual increase in scores on IQ tests. For example, Tan (1983), reporting on the handedness of 508 (Australian) parents and their 917 offspring, found an 11.8 percent rate of sinistrality in the younger generation compared with a 5.9 percent rate among the parents. Tan also determined that although the effects of cultural pressures on hand preferences in writing and holding a fork were far more prevalent among forty- to sixty-year-olds than among their offspring, large differences between the generations were still observed in tasks for which there was little or no social pressure.

Further, an analysis of biological and psychometric studies on extremely gifted multiple-language learners has led Schneiderman and Desmarais (1988) to conclude that "the right hemisphere plays a major role in the acquisition of various skills and knowledge, including language, which are then organized into left-hemisphere-based descriptive systems" (p. 115). They argue that extremely talented second-language learners are less left-lateralized for language, because the additional portions of their cortex devoted to language skills are primarily in the right hemisphere (in contrast to nongifted people, whose right hemispheres do not retain this early open-ended acquisitive ability). This analysis dovetails with a finding based on open-brain operations, namely, that the verbal-analytical centers of people with above-average verbal IQs are apt to occupy more compact portions of their left hemispheres than is the case with people who have below-average verbal IQs (Ojemann, 1983; Wood, 1983).

There is some reason to believe that the extent of cell connections across the two halves of the cerebral cortex is a major determinant of the nature and extent of these bilateralized abilities. If so, the initial months of infancy constitute a unique opportunity for affecting the extent of communication pathways that link the halves of the frontal cortex (the "seat" of thinking and judgment), although linguistic experiences during the second year (and, secondarily, during the third year) can still affect the size of the corpus callosum (see Chapter Nineteen).

To summarize, these findings suggest that, for functions that are usually lateralized, bilaterality represents an advanced stage in human intellectual development. Further, the existence of people possessing bilateralized speech implies that their "speech-gifted" left hemisphere has successfully *taught* their right hemisphere how to talk.

Notes

1. The mathematics portion of the SAT is viewed as a test of mathematical reasoning rather than of knowledge of higher mathematics, since only rudimentary knowledge of algebra or geometry is needed to solve the multiple-choice questions. Similarly, the verbal portion of the SAT (which stresses reading comprehension, analogical reasoning, and understanding difficult words) is seen as largely a test of verbal reasoning (Benbow and Benbow, 1984; Benbow, 1987). The Johns Hopkins population had only slightly more course work in mathematics than did the comparison group.

2. Myopia increases with age, and so does the likelihood of an environmental cause. Consequently, the parental statistics include many instances where myopia began well after the onset of puberty (the average parental age of onset was sixteen, compared with 8.5 for the precocious youths). This implies that rates of myopia among these precocious children will further increase. Less than 2 percent of the general population is diagnosed as myopic before the age of eight.

3. This finding is based on the use of a sophisticated allergy and immune disorder questionnaire that included allergies (and/or asthma) and autoimmune disorders such as rheumatoid arthritis, myasthenia gravis, ulcerative colitis, celiac disease, and lupus; migraine headaches are also thought to be an autoimmune disorder.

4. The rate of left-handedness found among males tends to be about 75

percent higher than that found among females. Handedness is usually measured by the Edinburgh Handedness Inventory (Oldfield, 1971), which consists of ascertaining people's hand preferences on ten tasks (writing, throwing, drawing, opening a jar lid, using a broom [upper hand], using scissors, using a toothbrush, using a knife, holding a spoon, and holding a match when striking it), with a score assigned for each task (plus or minus 5 or 10), depending on whether the preference is so strong that "you would never try to use the other hand unless forced to." A score of -5 to -100 is considered to mean that the person is left-handed. In many cultures, social pressures in an earlier era discouraged people from performing certain skilled manual tasks (such as writing and holding a fork) with the hand they would naturally prefer to use; nevertheless, in tasks for which there was little or no social pressure (such as swinging a hammer or holding a toothbrush), substantial differences were still found in hand preferences between the generations (Tan, 1983).

5. Many left-handed students of Asian ancestry are taught to eat and write with their right hand. Asians constituted 22 percent of the mathematically precocious group and less than 2 percent of the high-achieving but low-SAT-score comparison group.

6. A score of exactly zero on the Edinburgh Handedness Inventory was considered ambidextrous. About 5 percent of the precocious children (including 11 percent in this "cell") were exactly ambidextrous compared with perhaps 2 or 3 percent of the nonprecocious children studied and less than 1 percent of all adults (including the parents of these precocious children).

7. Eleven percent of this "nonprecocious" sample's fathers and 7.5 percent of its mothers were left-handed. These proportions are slightly higher than expected.

8. For a discussion of these hormonal relationships, see Lewy (1983) or Lewy and others (1980).

9. Members of Mensa represent a somewhat skewed sample of the high-IQ population; for example, Mensa's greatest appeal is in geographical areas where stimulating intellectual activities and opportunities for social contacts with highly intelligent people are relatively rare. Mensans who attended these talks (on topics such as human intelligence and giftedness, memory, hemispheric functions, and progress in brain research) might possess unusual physical and mental characteristics to a greater extent than other Mensans, since these characteristics might stimulate their interest in discussions about giftedness and/or the brain. The number of Mensans polled is perhaps 25 percent smaller than the sample size reported because some people were polled at more than one gathering.

10. This area (lying above the ear) is also known as the "association area of association areas," in that it receives sensory inputs after they have finished undergoing "associative" processing by primary and secondary sensory analysis areas (auditory, visual, linguistic, and occipital).

11. These include, first, adjacent layers of the cortex. Second, they include the *hippocampus*, a midbrain area that has come to be known as the "seat

of our working memory." It has (discrete) cell populations that have been given such functional names as (self-in-space) "place" cells, "counting" cells, and "novelty" cells. Third is the *frontal cortex*, which lies an inch above the hairline and is thought of as the "decision center" for nonroutine problem solving. Finally, there is the *pulvinar*, which is the name given to the rear portion of our brain's thalamus (a pair of walnut-shaped organs in the center of our brain). The pulvinar is the major "sorting station" for visual and auditory inputs (after they have undergone primary and secondary analysis). It has two-way connections with the frontal and association areas of the cerebral cortex (through two immediately adjacent areas of the thalamus), as well as with its language areas. Thalamic mechanisms also govern our "focus of attention" (paying attention to environmental stimuli, in contrast to paying attention to our internal thoughts) by stimulating activity in the right or the left sides of the cortex. The human pulvinar is "remarkable for its large size" (Heimer, 1983). Although it has cholinergic "spines" during early infancy, it loses these by the fourth postnatal month.

12.   The primary cause of hay-fever symptoms is apparently the immune system's belief that ragweed spores entering the nose constitute a menace that must be destroyed. Information about the contents of the air we breathe is processed by the so-called entorhinal cortex ("rhinal" meaning nose), which is adjacent to and directly connects with the hippocampus and which (in an emotionally charged situation) can directly imprint the frontal cortex (Perl and Good, 1987). The only area of the brain where new neurons and glia continue to be created throughout childhood into adulthood (namely, the hippocampal dentate gyrus) interconnects with the entorhinal cortex. This area evidences high plasticity in rodents (based on studies of enriched environments and lesions).

13.   Although both of the brain's hemispheres are deeply involved in reading, they perform rather different roles. The right hemisphere encodes words as complete templates, and the left hemisphere performs a segmental-sequential processing, with their combined products enabling us to comprehend what we have read. The right hemisphere comprehends meaning at a more global, more emotional level and the left in a more detailed, analytical manner. Language analysis is, nevertheless, essentially a left-hemisphere function, because the cell networks governing speech strategy and execution are (in almost all people) confined to the left hemisphere. Images of the written words (and phrases) go through the left hemisphere's "auditory" and "sequential" information-processing mode, before a "mental" judgment and physical reaction are evoked.

14.   This general principle—of functional recruitment within the cholinergic system—might imply that in gifted people with allergies there has been a reassignment of certain highly stressed hippocampal functions to a portion (or a larger portion) of the entorhinal cortex and/or its afferents, leaving it with insufficient resources to do an effective job in analyzing the components of scents.

15.   The rats were in the human equivalent of their mid-seventies when the

environmental enrichment was begun. By the time they were sacrificed (at 927 days of age, or the human equivalent of their early nineties), an appreciable increase in the thickness of the occipital portion of their cerebral cortex had occurred.

16. They were all production workers, factory-maintenance men, or coal miners in the same geographical area as the executives and often worked for the same companies. In this "craftsmen" sample, the average uric-acid level of the small number of college graduates was equal to that of the executives.

17. This value represents the average found over a two-month period. The extreme consistency of the levels found is evidenced by the fact that (1) the standard deviation averaged only 2.8 percent of the mean value; and (2) when multiple readings were taken over an eight-hour period, the average was 5.76.

18. After being corrected for recently standardized uric-acid norms by age and sex. The executives over the age of sixty had somewhat lower levels. There is a slight increase of uric-acid levels with weight and a larger increase with relative overweight; nevertheless, the thin executives in the sample had higher levels than the stout blue-collar workers.

19. For those having five or six cycles. In the first four cycles, the normal children also had more irregularity (more ups and downs across levels of sleep before reaching the deepest sleep phase).

20. Along with a reorganization of existing memory connections. Crick and Mitcheson (1983) espouse the view that forgetting irrelevancies is the primary function of REM sleep.

21. Beginning after perception has occurred, continuing through the point at which a decision has been reached, and then terminating when the decision has been transformed into instructions for a "motor-output" response.

22. These earlier and later stages are referred to as "inspection time" (or the time it takes to discern relevant features of the environment) and "motor-output" time (registering the decision by, for example, pushing a button).

23. In these inspection-time paradigms, the objective is to determine the shortest time that a stimulus (for example, a figure) needs to be visible for a person to successfully make the kinds of perceptual discriminations being tested (without regard to the length of time it takes the person to make these discriminations). Although these tasks are intrinsically simple (such as determining which of two lines is longer, when their "length ratios" are 1.4:1), they are made more difficult by the introduction of an intervening stimulus ("masking") before the request for a response to ensure that an "iconic picture" of what was just seen (heard) does not remain in visual (or auditory) memory.

24. Correlations of $-.4$ to $-.5$ are reported for visual inspection-time tests. Auditory inspection times (after discounting data from people who could not discriminate between fairly narrow tonal differences) were found to correlate even higher, for example, $-.60$ with (Air Force QT) scores across the normal IQ range (90 to 115). Several studies show that longer inspection times are needed by older people; among

children aged 6 to 12, they follow the development of fluid intelligence, correlations of − .6 being found with Cattell test scores (Brand, 1984).

25. The nongifted students were 50 to 70 percent slower on most of the twelve tasks. In this study, motor-output time was excluded by stopping the timer the instant that the response was initiated (that is, when the finger was removed from "home base" to press one or another of the answer buttons). The actual "thinking-time" advantage is likely to be slightly greater than that reported, because inspection time was included, and only a slight inspection-time advantage can be presumed.

26. Their average response times were within 5 percent or so of those of the Berkeley students on each of these twelve tasks; their scores on the Raven's Progressive Matrices were also equivalent to those of the Berkeley students.

27. These students were seventh graders taking college-level courses in math and science; therefore, if domain-specific processing mechanisms had been employed, their relative advantage (compared with their classmates) would have been considerably greater on the number and ideographic tasks than on the word tasks and/or on the literal tasks. In a further study comparing exceptionally precocious seventh graders with their less gifted nearest-in-age siblings, these researchers (Jensen, Cohn, and Cohn, 1989) demonstrated that reaction-time differences are influenced by cultural and socioeconomic variables to the same extent as these factors influence IQ (Raven's Advanced Progressive Matrices scores). The processing-speed advantage of the precocious group (on a simple semantic verification task) averaged 30 percent compared with their siblings, who showed almost 50 percent greater "internal variability in their reaction times."

28. The "processing-time" advantage (or the time span between stimulus recognition and cognitive decision) is apt to be even greater, not just because inspection time was included at the front end but also because "premotor"-output time (or the time needed to reformulate a decision into motor-output form) was included as well. A person's premotor-response time is apt to depend, in part, on factors extraneous to "general" intelligence.

29. With differences expressed in terms of standard deviation (for example, averaging 1.34 standard deviations in the cited study).

30. The gifted children in grades 4 and 5 and 7 and 8 scored above 132 on the Stanford-Binet or 130 on the Wechsler, and met other explicit criteria; the less gifted controls had IQs averaging 116.

31. Each randomly ordered list of twenty words contained five words from each of four categories (for example, fruits, animals, body parts, and furniture). A brief Matching Familiar Figures task was interjected before the subjects were asked to recall as many words as possible. Children were categorized as using a "clustering strategy" if (1) the order in which they remembered the words on a list included a string of three or more consecutive words from a single category and (2) they showed faster within-category than between-category recall speeds. Even though the number of words recalled was highly correlated with the use of clustering within each of these groups (+ .73 for the non-

gifted group and + .56 for the gifted group), the gifted children (who recalled an average of 11 percent more words per list) made no greater use of clustering than did their nongifted peers. The speed advantage of the gifted children was significant only when the consecutively remembered words came from different categories.

32. Examples include: (1) was the number 7 included in the (short) string of numbers just seen? (2) a "same/opposite" task (using simple, third-grade words); and (3) a "same/same/opposite" task in which the words might look the same, have the same meaning, or be different.

33. A tracing that signifies changes in the magnetic polarity of cells as they "fire" and "recharge." The so-called N140 and P200 waves (which reach their maximum strength 140 and 200 milliseconds after stimulus presentation) were the primary components responsible for the correlation (Haier and others, 1983). Evoked potentials are averaged across a large number of trials; consequently, they are more a measure of cortical activity in "automatization" programs than of initial responses to novel classes of stimuli.

34. The correlations with the Wechsler were higher than on the Raven's test, implying that comprehensive IQ measures (such as the Wechsler) have closer links with activity in the analytical (left) hemisphere in response to auditory inputs.

35. In which case the increase in waveform length would relate primarily to an incrementally greater activation of the nondominant hemisphere as IQ rises. This certainly appears testable.

36. The strong negative correlations found were not confined to a particular brain region or hemisphere but pervaded all the areas heavily involved in this cognitive processing. Even though the Raven's generated more right-hemisphere than left-hemisphere activity, the incremental use of glucose (comparing subjects who took the Raven's with those who performed a visual vigilance task) occurred primarily in the left hemisphere and was almost exclusively in the rear half of the brain (especially in the occipital cortex). The abstract reasoning aspects of the Raven's appear to generate increased glucose use in the left hemisphere (especially the parieto-temporo-occipital junction) with the visuospatial reasoning aspects entailing use of the corresponding area of the right hemisphere. Nevertheless, because the sample size was small (only nine of the thirty subjects having been given the Raven's), a replication is needed to ensure that these findings are not an artifact of the subjects chosen. A recent study of 133 normal subjects (Corballis and Sergent, 1989) confirms the existence of a significant right-hemisphere advantage on an equivalent letter-rotations task.

37. For example, the finding that pupillary dilation during mental activity (which is considered to be a rough index of mental capacity) is smaller in more intelligent people (Ahern and Beatty, 1979).

38. These authors report a personal communication from Jerre Levy to the effect that a co-worker obtained similar results on this computer-generated letter-matching task in a "group of extremely intellectually talented students," in contrast to nongifted controls who showed a clear left-hemisphere advantage.

⚡ Part Six ⚡

The Recent Evolution
in Intelligence and Giftedness

Chapter Eighteen assesses the probable contribution of environmental factors to the twentieth-century rise in IQ scores in
the United States, based on models that incorporate improvements in health and nutrition, as well as in a variety of other
factors (such as trends in family size) that influence children's
early educational environment. The results strongly suggest
that environmental factors cannot account for the entirety of
this secular increase.

   Chapter Nineteen examines the hypothesis that stressing
particular cognitive domains during certain critical periods of
postnatal brain growth induces a greater "biological preparedness" for similar experiences at similar ages in the offspring of
parents who, as children, were exposed to these experiences.
The suggestion is not that postnatal experiences induce changes
in the genes but that changes are induced in the "developmental
blueprint" that governs gene expression — a blueprint that may
determine the duration of particular developmental stages and
hemispheric "growing seasons" and/or the supply of neuro-
chemicals that will be apportioned to particular sensory and
analytical cell networks. A possible mechanism by which such
changes could be transmitted from a parent to its offspring is
suggested, and support for this conceptual framework is pro-

vided in the form of findings from a statistical analysis of familial and adoptive study correlations, as well as from an analysis of evolutionary rates in animals.

Chapter Twenty examines the development of exceptional intellectual ability by looking at ethnogeographic populations that display exceedingly high rates of domain-specific intellectual giftedness. The results are consistent with a multigenerational interaction between heredity and environment, in that these exceptional abilities neither develop nor dissipate over a single generation of "training," and yet they seem to develop over the course of what classical theories of population genetics would view as an impossibly small number of generations.

Contents

✻ 18 ✻

The Twentieth-Century
Rise in IQ:
A Discussion of Causes

18.0 Synopsis

This chapter explores the potential contribution of environmental factors to the extremely large rise in measured human intelligence during the twentieth century, including advances in health and nutrition and improvements in children's early educational environments. Although these factors account for a large part of the increase in IQ, it does not seem possible that they can explain it completely. Rather, an interaction between environment and "hereditary biology" is proposed as the primary cause of this growth in measured intelligence.

18.1 Introduction

There are, in effect, three possible causes for the rapid, sustained increase in scores on comprehensive IQ tests during the twentieth century:

- Environmental factors (principally advances in health and nutrition and improvements in children's early educational environment) may have had a truly enormous impact on actualized intelligence.

- Changes over time in IQ test scores may simply not be valid indicators of changes in intelligence.
- The pace at which human intelligence is evolving biologically may be far more rapid than would seem possible if the processes by which brain evolution occurs were limited to those specified in the neo-Darwinian principles of genetic evolution.

This chapter explores the likely contribution of each of these elements to the long-term IQ increase. There are two principal conclusions to this analysis. First, although environmental factors have certainly contributed to this upswing, the magnitude of the overall IQ increase — at least a quarter point per year from the 1890s to the mid 1970s — is far larger than what these factors seem capable of explaining. Second, although there are no empirical methods for resolving the question of the equivalence between what IQ tests attempt to measure and "underlying intelligence," both logic and prevailing evidence strongly favor a conclusion that comprehensive IQ tests are, for the most part, able to capture the essence of what has come to be known as the g of general intelligence.

18.2 Health and Nutrition

The considerable improvement in the overall health of people in the developed world during the twentieth century has undoubtedly had a material impact on intellectual performance. This is particularly true of the cognitive functioning of people who, in an earlier era, would have suffered significant mental deficits. For example, medical advances have enormously reduced the incidence and severity of many childhood diseases that were the scourges of past eras, just as they have substantially reduced the incidence of seriously adverse cognitive effects that result from intrauterine deficiencies and/or neonatal problems.

In addition, the *general* improvement in health and nutrition has undoubtedly had positive effects on both mental development and physical stature (height, weight, and proportions). Fortunately, a number of relatively consistent findings linking

IQ outcomes with birth weight and weight-for-date permit the use of secular trends in birth weight as a basis for accurately estimating the impact of the overall improvement in general health on childhood IQ. These effects (subdivided into their impact on verbal and spatial reasoning) are summarized in Table 35, which also incorporates an estimate of the impact of advances in treating and preventing childhood illnesses and diseases on the IQ of the population as a whole.

Physical stature, as an indicator of the effects of nutrition on intelligence, does show a positive, albeit small, relationship with IQ—one apparently linked to socioeconomic status (SES). For example, a recent study of 14,000 "representative" American youths born in the mid and late 1960s shows a correlation between IQ and height of +.18 among preteens and +.20 among adolescents—implying that slightly less than a tenth of the IQ variation between these subjects disappeared when height was factored out (Wilson and others, 1986). Moreover, only 2 percent of the IQ variance could be associated with height when SES (and race) were factored out first. Nevertheless, there is some evidence that periods of rapid physical growth in a population correspond with rapid rates of IQ growth. For example, the Japanese born in 1960 were 2.1 inches taller than those born in 1940 (Anderson, 1982), and a similar increase was observed in Western Europe in the late nineteenth and early twentieth centuries (Vogel and Matulsky, 1979). However, the existence of ethnic groups of relatively short stature (such as the Ashkenazi Jews and the Japanese) whose members, on the average, perform well above the norm on IQ tests strongly argues against any inherent relationship between height and IQ. Thus, within an ethnic group (or a family), height differences do bear a modest statistical relationship with IQ, but between ethnic groups they do not. Even though height reflects postnatal factors (nutrition, sunlight, and exercise), it also bears a significant relationship to birth weight. Consequently, a substantial portion of this (relatively modest) influence has apparently already been subsumed under the estimate of the effects of the secular increase in average birth weight on intelligence.

Also arguing against the conclusion that the general improve-

Table 35. Estimated Effects of Improved Prenatal, Neonatal, and Child Health on IQ Scores of Children in Developed Countries (1900–1980).

Area of Improvement	% of Population Affected	Impact on Measured Intelligence					
		On People Affected (avg.)			On Population at Large		
		Total	Spatial	Verbal	Total	Spatial	Verbal
Prenatal/Neonatal Care							
Reduction in low birth weight/date							
Severely affected[a]	5	10	13	7	0.5	0.7	0.3
Mildly affected[a]	10	4	5	3	0.4	0.5	0.3
Increase in: optimal weight/date[b]	10	5	5	5	0.5	0.5	0.5
Remaining births (increased weight)[b]	75	2	2	2	1.5	1.5	1.5
Other health problems	3	10	?	?	0.3	0.3	0.3
Reduced Incidence of Childhood Illness/Disorder							
Severely debilitating illnesses	5	14	?	?	0.7	0.7	0.7
Illnesses with mild cognitive effects	15	2	?	?	0.3	0.3	0.3
Vision and hearing	2	10	13	7	0.2	0.3	0.1
Total: Impact of improved neonatal and child health						4.4	
Less: Duplication contained in above categories						− 0.4	
Estimated effect on total IQ distribution					4.0	4.5	3.5
Lower half of IQ distribution					(5.5)	(6.2)	(4.8)
Upper half of IQ distribution					(2.5)	(2.8)	(2.2)

[a] Includes both a reduced incidence of prematurity and low weight-for-date and improved treatment thereof (see appendix). Note: Societal mores concerning whether "heroic" and/or other efforts should be made to maintain the life of extremely premature and/or malformed neonates have, in recent years, created a countervailing force.

[b] See especially Record, McKeown, and Edwards, 1969b, and Neligan and Prudham, 1976.[1]

ment in health and nutrition has been the major impetus for rising IQ is the absence of a close correspondence in timing between health trends and IQ trends.[2] For example, had this factor been paramount, American children born in the mid to late 1970s — when compared with those born thirty years earlier — should have shown an extraordinarily rapid rate of IQ growth, given the advances in neonatal care and the advent and increasingly widespread use of vaccines and antibiotics during these years. This period, however, appears to have been one in which IQ growth was somewhat below the twentieth-century average.

In summary, it does not seem possible to attribute more than a fifth of the total twentieth-century IQ increase to health and nutritional factors per se, even when the correspondence between increases in height and/or birth weight and gains in IQ is fully attributed to these factors.[3]

18.3 Impact of the Early Home Environment on IQ

As detailed in Parts Three and Four, there is clear and convincing evidence that a very favorable or unfavorable cognitive environment in one's formative years can have a substantial and lasting impact on cognitive development.[4] Such factors as the so-called caretaker ratio, maternal interactive behavior (especially the degree and nature of verbal attention directed toward a child), the quality of toys and other playthings, the degree of consistency in discipline, and the "academic" and emotional atmosphere of the home all combine to determine whether a child's innate cognitive abilities will be nurtured, left to grow naturally, modified, or stifled.

However, for changes in the average quality of the early educational environment to have produced large enough changes in IQ to account for the preponderance of the twentieth-century IQ increase, one or both of the following must be true (1) relatively modest improvements in particular environmental factors (or combinations of factors) have the capacity to generate substantial IQ gains, and/or (2) a considerable long-term increase in the overall quality of these cognitively enriching variables (considered collectively) has in fact occurred.

There are two basic approaches to evaluating the effects of environmental differences on IQ scores. One—the macro approach—looks at differences in the aggregate, either by comparing the *average* contribution that environment makes to the *total* variation in people's IQ scores or by contrasting the effects of relatively "good" or "bad" cognitive environments on a group of people. The other approach—the micro view—requires the development of detailed assessments of the effects on IQ of changes in individual components of the cognitive environment. This micro approach consists of (1) a delineation of those features of the early home environment that significantly affect cognitive development, (2) a description of the forces providing the impetus for change in these aspects, (3) an assessment (quantification) of the relative importance of these various features and the degree of change that has taken place in each, (4) an integration of these individual results into major environmental factors, and (5) an integration of these dimensions into an overall "conduciveness-to-cognitive-development" index.

The Macro View

Before undertaking these analyses, it is important to note that *findings in two areas create a strong predisposition to assume that improvements in the overall quality of home environments could not have accounted for the preponderance of the twentieth-century IQ increase.* For one thing, since environmental factors in the aggregate constitute a significantly smaller source of IQ variation between individuals than does heredity, we can assume that the impact of upward movement along the "environmental spectrum" will be correspondingly small. Moreover, there has not been a substantial reduction in the standard deviation of IQ scores accompanying the rise in IQs. This holds true, for example, when children's scores are compared on two tests normed in different eras or when one test is scored against two intergenerational norms. This outcome is at variance with what would have been expected had the major impetus for the IQ increase come from a reduc-

tion in the frequency with which poor environments had pre-
vented the attainment of normal IQ scores.

The results of familial studies suggest that, of the 17- to 18-
point difference in IQ that will be found on average among
randomly selected individuals (Plomin and DeFries, 1980), perhaps 4 to 6 points can be attributed to *the average environmental
difference* existing between them. This analysis leads to the presumption that modest improvements in the average quality of
environments over time are not capable of generating more
than a modest change in a population's IQ performance. Thus,
to generate a 5- to 7-point increase in a population's IQ, parents
would have to improve the quality of the home environment to
such an extent that two-thirds of all homes in more recent eras
would surpass the top third of all homes in earlier eras.[5]

Nevertheless, the finding that home environments of exceptional quality can generate exceptional IQ increases has been
well documented. In particular, the adoption-study literature
(reviewed in Chapter Four) demonstrates that substantial IQ
effects do occur when infants are moved from below-average
environments to significantly above-average environments. This
suggests that, if the cognitive quality of today's homes could be
shown to be far superior to those of the past, we might be correct
in concluding that environmental factors produced a major
share of the long-term IQ increase.

Adoption studies provide an excellent mechanism for contrasting the effects of being reared in a high-quality versus an
average or below-average cognitive environment. The IQ performance of children adopted in infancy can first be compared to
standard IQ norms. It can then be compared to the IQs of their
biological parent(s), of controls living in the same community in
which the biological mother resided, or of biological siblings or
half-siblings who were not adopted. Last, it can be compared to
the IQs and/or occupational class status of their adoptive parents. By following this procedure, we can make reasonable estimates of the differential effects of environments of diverse quality[6] on measured IQ. To summarize some of the most pertinent
findings:

- Children adopted as infants into "exceptional quality" midwestern homes and families in the early 1930s attained IQ scores 10 to 16 points above average (Skodak and Skeels, 1949; Leahy, 1935, summarized in Scarr and Carter-Saltzman, 1982). By the 1970s, however, the cognitive advantage of having been reared in an adoptive home appears to have lessened somewhat, to perhaps 3 to 8 points above the norm.[7]
- These gains appear to be due more to the superior "emotional quality" of these adoptive homes than to improved socioeconomic status. In the Minnesota study, for example, those children adopted into homes where the father was in the professions scored only 4 to 5 points higher than those reared in semiskilled and unskilled working-class adoptive homes (Leahy, 1935), paralleling an earlier finding in California (Burks, 1938, summarized in Scarr and Carter-Saltzman, 1982).
- When the IQs of the adoptees' biological parents were well below those of their adoptive parents and siblings, approximately two-thirds to three-fourths of this IQ difference was neutralized as a result of exposure to the adoptive environment, a finding similar to the gains reported among kibbutz-reared offspring of immigrants from (relatively backward) Asian or African lands (see section 10.4). A loving, intense caretaker ratio has also been shown to be capable of normalizing the IQs of at-risk children, even when the caretakers were themselves of extremely low intelligence (see section 10.3).
- Nevertheless, *biology*, as represented by the IQs of the adoptive child's biological parent(s), remains a critical variable—far more critical, on the average, than the particular adoptive home (from among those studied) in which the child was reared.[8]

The Micro View

In several important respects, there have been considerable and widespread improvements in the overall quality of early home environments over the course of the twentieth century when these environments are measured in terms of "conduciveness to cognitive development." Factors creating these improvements include (1) the long-term downward trend in the number of children in families (and the corresponding increase in child spacing); (2) the effects of the development and increasing use of age-appropriate educational playthings; and (3) other effects of the long-term rise in the economic and educational status of parents, which—together with their improved knowledge of child development principles and their increasing intelligence—has made them better child educators and psychologists.

In several important respects, however, the overall rate of improvement in early home environments has not kept pace with what studies show to be the influence of declining family size on IQ—differences that may be attributed to increases in the amount of specific early maternal caregiving behaviors (rocking, holding, vocal imitation, effective gaze behavior, and other mechanisms for inducing and making effective use of quiet concentration as a learning tool), as well as the quantity of verbal stimulation directed toward infants and toddlers. This is because the considerable postwar decline in the availability of the extended family as a source of caregiving has certainly dissipated at least part of the improvement in caretaker ratios that has accompanied the decline in the number of children per family. On balance, however, few would disagree that there has been a very significant long-term improvement in those aspects of the home environment that contribute to cognitive growth.

18.4 Factors Influencing the Cognitive Quality of the Early Home Environment

This section delineates eight major criteria for evaluating the cognitive quality of the early home environment. At the same time, it describes a number of factors that have a strong influence on a home's "quality rating" and provides some mechanisms for measuring changes in these factors (see Table 36).

There follows an analysis of the probable influence of these factors—number and spacing of children, educational play ma-

Table 36. Evaluative Criteria for Measuring the Effects of Early Environment on Cognitive Development.

Major Evaluative Criteria	*Factors Influencing or Mechanisms for Measuring These Criteria*
Quantity of Early Caregiver Attention	
A — Caretaker ratio	Number and spacing of children; involvement of grandparents and father; day care
B — Other influences	Maternal age/maturity; societal mores (ethnic mothering techniques)
Quality of Caregiver's Attention	
A — Early mother-infant interaction	Inducing and using "quiet concentration"; effective gaze behavior; use of vocal imitation; encouragement of attention to objects and events
B — Avoidance of cognitively destructive behavior	Consistency in responsivity and discipline; avoidance of ego-deprecating and -threatening behavior; avoidance of restriction (at 24 months)
C — General encouragement	Encouragement of efforts; effective task development; treatment of child as highly valued and special (includes "grandparent spoiling")
Quantity/Quality of Enrichments	
A — Educational materials	Age-appropriate educational play materials: spatial toys (that teach shape and size conceptualization and/or visual-motor integrative skills); children's books; opportunities for contingent responsivity in early infancy (for example, mobiles)
B — Educational methods	Rising maternal education, intelligence, and vocabulary; specific knowledge; substitution of passive, heavily visual stimuli (TV) for interactive auditory (imagination-inducing) stimuli; group learning experiences
C — Stimulation of academic behavior	Exposure to and/or parental attitude toward academic activities; expectation of obedience, self-discipline, and regimen of study; repetitious inculcation of difficult value-laden (biblical) prose and song

terials, rising maternal education, and so on — on six of these criteria during the course of the twentieth century (the other two criteria are discussed in the model presented in the next section). It seemed appropriate to subdivide the educational and other factors into those of greatest significance during the first half of the century and those of greatest significance during the postwar era.

Early Caretaker Attention

1900–1946: Gains primarily in relation to birth order and family size; less housework; more paternal presence (shorter work hours).

1947–1972: Greatest gains primarily limited to largest and poorest families; little change in inducing and using periods of quiet concentration in infancy (through rocking, holding, swaddling, singing to) or in using vocal imitation, consistency of responsiveness, or encouragement of attention to objects and events in the environment (in part because of the reduced availability of caregiving by members of the extended family).

Avoidance of Cognitively Destructive Behavior

1947–1972: Considerable improvement in the quality of criticism (avoidance of ego-destructive behavior) as a result of greater knowledge of basic psychology (rising education, talk shows, family television shows such as "Father Knows Best," word of mouth, and "help" groups);[9] some improvement in consistency of discipline; little improvement in avoidance of restriction at age two, in part, because of the effects of urbanization (see section 9.2).

General Encouragement

1900–1946: Increased frequency of children being "valued" (in other than a future economic sense); also gains related to reduced family size, less housework.

1947–1972: Some continuing gains from fewer children and less housework—in part offset by lesser availability of extended family members and of the primary caregiver (maternal employment); improved knowledge of psychology (for example, how to praise in a non-ego-threatening manner) and effective task structuring (with a large post-1972 change); reduced feelings of "specialness" (because of the waning of strong religious and ethnic mores and less grandparental attention).

Stimulation of Academic Behavior

1900–1972: Improvements due to rising parental educational levels and SES, the belief that education leads to financial security, reduced family size, availability of cultural activities (including educational television), better books, and more reading to children.

1947–1972: Reduced expectation of obedience and self-discipline; reduced frequency of prescribed study (such as a repetitious inculcation of difficult, value-laden, biblical, or "classical" material); societal proclivity for "lowbrow" as opposed to "highbrow" entertainment; reduced influence of grandparents; but major increase in availability of, and (to a lesser extent) interest in, academic activities.

Educational Materials

1900–1947: Improved SES; greater parental interest in providing toys; general improvement in quality of play materials.

1947–1972: Enormous progress born of rising SES and development of age-appropriate educational playthings—especially in the spatial domain (for example, toys that teach shape and size conceptualization skills and/or visual-motor integration), as well as contingently responsive toys; improved quality of baby books.

Educational Methods

1900–1972:   Rising (maternal) education levels (primarily postwar) and vocabulary; rising parental IQ; improved knowledge of child development principles and basic teaching skills; however, in the posttelevision era, increased input from passive, heavily visual stimuli and a decrease in toddler-directed, interactive (heavily auditory) stimuli (books, radio), which reduces imaginative thinking.

18.5 Modeling the IQ Effects of Secular Improvements in Environmental Quality

The model of environmental influences on twentieth-century IQ scores that is presented in Table 37 represents an integration of estimates for two factors:

- Changes in the proportions of children reared in homes that meet particular standards of cognitive quality at specified points in time — with these standards based on a defined amalgam of the cognitively important aspects of the early home environment.
- The impact on IQ of being reared in homes in these defined quality classifications.

The presentation and discussion of this model will proceed in the following order: (1) a statement of the purposes for which the model has been designed; (2) a presentation of the nomenclature used to define the "quality" classes of the home environments found in the model, along with a description of the hypothetical effect of being reared in homes of one or another class; (3) a description of the major components used in constructing the model (and some indication of how they are combined to form selected classes; (4) a presentation of the results, including the assumed percentages of children reared in homes of each of these quality classes in the years 1900, 1947, and 1975

Table 37. Effects of Improvements in the Cognitive Quality of Home Environments on IQ (United States: 1900–1947 and 1947–1975).

| | Effects of Qualitative Differences Between Environments on IQ | | | | | | |
| | Unfavorable Effects | | Neutral Effects | Favorable Effects | | | Totals/ Effects |
Impacts/Time Periods	Profound[a]	Moderate	Effects	Moderate	High	Exceptional	
Percentage of children in each class:							
1900	30%	20%	25%	15%	7%	3%	100%
1947	20%	15%	25%	20%	15%	5%	100%
1975	10%	10%	25%	25%	20%	10%	100%
Average impact: IQ points	−12	−6	0	+6	+12	+25	—
Overall IQ effect by year:							
1900	−3.60	−1.20	0	+0.90	+0.85	+0.75	−2.30
1947	−2.40	−0.90	0	+1.20	+1.80	+1.25	+0.95
1975	−1.20	−0.60	0	+1.50	+2.40	+2.50	+4.60
Increase from 1900 to:							
1947							+3.25
1975							+6.90

Note: The standard against which IQ scores and early home cognitive quality are compared is the average score and quality for all years from 1900 to 1975. This model excludes (and, as a consequence, assumes no change in the proportion of) homes where significant cognitive deficits occur as a result of the severe emotional illness of the principal caregiver(s).

[a] The quantitative effects of the "profoundly unfavorable" classification could have been related either to the mean IQ score or to a "standard of normalcy" developed by excluding the scores of people in this class. The former measure was selected in the main because of a recognition that baseline IQ samples were somewhat elite (for example, prewar American IQ standardization samples were all-White and overrepresented urban subjects, and the World War I Army Alpha Test excluded illiterates).

and the effects that the assumed extent of upward mobility would have on the IQ of the entire population; and (5) a brief discussion of the implications of these results, in terms of the extent to which this improvement in environmental quality is able to explain the twentieth-century IQ increase. The model is summarized as follows:

Purposes

This model has two primary purposes. The first is to illustrate the impact that rather significant improvements in the cognitive quality of early home environments over the course of the twentieth century would have had on the measured intelligence of Americans, based on the assumption that IQ development is highly sensitive to the cognitive quality of the home environment during infancy and toddlerhood. The other is to serve as a methodological and empirical basis for other researchers to use to develop their own estimates of past and future environmental contributions to IQ.

Quality Classifications and the Size of Their IQ Effects

Consistent with the primary purpose of this analysis, six basic classes of home environmental quality (measured along a "conduciveness-to-cognitive-development" axis) are proposed: profoundly unfavorable, moderately unfavorable, neutral, moderately favorable, highly favorable, and exceptionally favorable.

The next task is to determine what magnitude of IQ effect to assign to "membership" in each of these classifications. Here, studies of the kind delineated in Part Three quite clearly support the general finding that both poor- and excellent-quality home environments frequently engender considerable and lasting IQ effects. Nevertheless, not all writers who have examined this question share this opinion, primarily because of the large hereditary contribution to IQ. Deference to these contrasting views might suggest a conservative approach to estimating the magnitude of the IQ effects incorporated in this model, but the principal purpose for which this model is designed dictates use of the full measure of the IQ-point effects suggested by the studies in Part Three.

The relationship between environmental quality and IQ outcome is clearly a "curvilinear function," meaning that there are small IQ effects for large percentile changes along the middle portions of the environmental quality spectrum, and increasingly large effects for small percentile movements as one approaches the environmental extremes.

These findings lead to the conclusion that exposure to the types of environmental conditions used to formulate the classification "profoundly unfavorable" would result in an average IQ score of 88 among a group of newborn infants possessing the biological "hardware" and "software" needed to score 100 — or a loss of 12 IQ points compared with children reared in cognitively neutral environments. Conversely, these same children would achieve considerably above-average IQ scores as a result of exposure to very favorable cognitive environments, attaining an average IQ score of 112 when reared in a highly favorable environment and 120 and above when the environment has been exceptionally favorable. IQ outcomes are assumed to average 6 points above and below the mean when the environment has been moderately favorable or unfavorable, or half the effect estimated for the next most extreme category. A neutral rating implies less than a 2-point IQ effect.

The validity of such a model then becomes dependent on our definitions of the component features that form the "mold" of a given quality classification and our judgments concerning the proportion of each era's children reared in each class. In making such judgments, our viewpoint may differ depending on whether we are looking forward from the year 1900 and classifying homes on the basis of the degree of improvement since that era — or whether we are looking backward from the present and assessing the degree of cognitive impoverishment present in homes in earlier periods. This dilemma is resolved by employing a mechanism for simultaneously reviewing progress and regress from both ends of the time horizon. This is accomplished by using as one baseline our conceptualization of the average quality of all homes combining all the years of the twentieth century and then comparing this with a second baseline developed by an IQ-score average calculating the average IQ score for this seventy-two-year period.[10]

Components

This model can be approached in two different ways. One is to detail the necessary conditions (including qualifications and exceptions) that comprise the basis of a given quality rating. The other, which is the approach employed here, is to trace through the steps involved in its construction, including the nature of its foundation and its "building blocks," and thereby form a picture of how various demographic and educational factors combine to produce a given classification. In either event, some of these environmental features may be envisioned (and quantified) most easily along an inhibitory/permissive axis. But for others (enrichments), the degree to which they are provided to the child represents the sole viewing dimension.

Two of the four cornerstones of this model foundation involve the demographic characteristics of the family, as expressed in the care-taker ratio present in a child's formative years. One of these corner-stones is predicated on the results of extremely large studies that indicate that being a non-firstborn child in a family with many chil-dren carries with it a high likelihood of developing a significantly below-average IQ. The cornerstone diagonally opposite rests on find-ings that (1) there is a massive overrepresentation of very favorable early caretaker ratios among populations of gifted and eminent people, and that (2) cognitive outcomes well above those expected occur in response to an extremely favorable quantity of caregiver attention, even in an institutional setting. Thus, we can conclude that—although an extremely unfavorable ratio is very likely to *inhibit* IQ development—the most we can say about an extremely favorable ratio is that even though it may be highly *permissive of* a cognitively stimulating environment, it can furnish no assurance that such an environment will be provided.

Family size and birth order are the statistical yardsticks by which the relationship between family configuration and IQ has been crudely but—because of the huge number of subjects contained in several studies—quite effectively measured. Nevertheless, two adjustments (one positive and one negative) are needed in order to take account of secular changes in the degree of caregiving by relatives other than the mother. The first of these involves the twentieth-century trend toward a greater involvement of fathers in children's early development. The sharp decline in the workweek (particularly in the first half of the century) materially increased opportunities for early paternal involvement.[11] Conversely, the geographical dispersion of families in the postwar era and the rising rate of participation in the labor force among middle-aged women have combined to deprive many infants and toddlers of a cognitive asset that, in an earlier era, would have been available, namely, the adoring love and attention of grandparents and other mature relatives.

Across this foundation is laid a segment of the IQ effects associated with SES. Major portions of the relationship between SES and IQ are, however, attributable to two factors already considered—birth weight and family size. Moreover, correlations between IQ and SES reflect innate IQ differences, as well as environmentally induced effects (see especially the Iowa Adoption Study). Consequently, it is appropriate to incorporate only a small portion of this statistical relationship in the model.

At the extremes, however, the impact of SES on IQ is often considerable. In combination with a poor caretaker ratio, low SES ensures that relatively few laterborn children from large families will escape significant cognitively debilitating effects from receiving insufficient attention and inconsistent parental behavior. Thus, these two elements—large family size and low SES—combine to form the nucleus for the "profoundly unfavorable" classification. Conversely, as one approaches the upper economic tiers, opportunities for providing a highly favorable caretaker ratio through the use of well-trained paid caregivers are substantially greater.

The next component of the model is *parental age*, which has substantial IQ effects that are independent of SES and, to a lesser degree, of birth order and family size. The magnitude of this effect—which has been well quantified (see Chapter Two)—clearly indicts young motherhood as a primary "cause" of considerably lower than expected (SES-adjusted) IQ outcomes. In contrast, the positive IQ effects of increasing parental age continue to age forty and beyond. The likely reason for this result is that — independently of SES — more-mature, more-patient caregiving contains important elements of the kinds of behavior that are conducive to cognitive development.[12]

Two other, less easily quantifiable building blocks incorporated into this model are the advent of cognitively enhancing toys and playthings and increasing caregiver knowledge of and use of child development principles.

The (primarily postwar) explosion in the quality and use of educational playthings is difficult to assess. This is because quantitative measures of environmental differences in the provision of age-appropriate play materials are of relatively recent vintage and are ill fitted for measuring differences between good-, excellent-, and superb-quality homes, since these measures were designed to expose the cognitive deficits associated with homes that do not provide *basic* cognitive enrichments.[13]

Despite the absence of data, one cannot dismiss the possibility that exposure to educational playthings, in and of itself, may be capable of raising measured IQ by more effectively teaching specific "categorizational" skills, especially those involving the size and shape of objects. As a result (and in keeping with the primary purpose for which this model is designed), the advent of educational playthings is hypothesized to have had a considerable impact on overall IQ — in particular by enlarging the proportion of the 1972 population judged to be reared in what (by twentieth-century standards) are highly favorable or exceptionally favorable homes.

The remaining component of the model — parents as child educators — has several subcomponents that are likewise difficult to quantify. These include trends in parental education, in parental intelligence, and in parental and societal knowledge of how to provide a cognitively conducive educational and psychological environment. The impact of parental educational levels on IQ scores is — after parental age, family size, and economic status are factored out — extremely modest (and, in part, a reflection of parental IQ).

Assessing the impact of rising parental IQ poses a dilemma. If, as seems likely, there is a compound effect of rising IQ, to what extent is this effect biological, environmental, or both? Clearly, the fairly strong statistical linkage between the IQs of parents and those of their offspring is related more to hereditary (and prenatal biological) factors than to environmental factors, but this need not imply that the cause of *rising* parental IQ is more biological than environmental (since, for example, the adoption-study literature shows that being reared by brighter, better-educated parents has an effect on IQ outcome).[14] Moreover, studies indicate that such early evaluative measures as "effectiveness of mother as a toy demonstrator" and "maternal vocabulary as a predictor of a child's acquisition of verbal skills" (especially near the lower end of the IQ spectrum, where a paucity of maternal vocabulary is often associated with a considerable linguistic handicap) display IQ correlations that are independent of maternal IQ (see Chapter Eight). It is also impossible to discern the extent to which children's interests and responsiveness guide parental behavior, particularly as brighter children are also able to extract more from any given environment. Nevertheless, the hypothesis that brighter parents beget brighter children partly because they provide a more cognitively conducive environment certainly appears to be valid.

The third subcomponent—the advent and dissemination of specific knowledge about educational and psychological child development principles (including the ill effects of certain types of negative parental behavior)—has been detailed in this section. It is hypothesized that the benefits of this knowledge have been greatest in the upper quadrant of the IQ distribution (although near the lower extreme, a reduced incidence of cognitively destructive behavior as a result of parent education may also be important). This is because high IQ scores often result from the cumulative effects of high-quality parental didactic skills, along with a willingness (and ability) to devote considerable effort to provide cognitively enriching experiences. This is a major reason that the percentage of homes assigned to the highly and exceptionally favorable classifications in the most recent era shown in Table 37 is markedly higher than in the earlier periods.

The last subcomponent—a negative factor in the postwar era—relates to the decline in the use of traditional child-rearing practices—a decline that is associated with the reduced availability of members of the extended family as early caregivers. Although certain ethnically based traditional approaches to child rearing are best discarded in favor of the advice provided by "how-to-parent" books, this familial trend has apparently also resulted in a reduction in the *quantity* of early caregiving provided by mothers (on a birth-order-adjusted basis). A decline in the amount of holding, rocking, singing to, looking and smiling at, and vocalizing in response to infants—along with the tendency for mothers to spend more time watching television than interacting with their toddlers—has paralleled the decline in obedience to traditional maternal role models. In earlier generations, such a model had been ingrained in young girls through their exposure to and interaction with members of their extended family and reinforced by the families of young mothers through approval and disapproval. In this earlier era, when a woman derived most of her self-esteem from her role as wife and mother, the pressure to conform was far stronger than after the growth in educational levels and employment opportunities for women began to accelerate.

Results

The model assumes that in the year 1900 half of all infants and toddlers were subjected to cognitively unfavorable home environments—including 30 percent in profoundly unfavorable and 20 percent in moderately unfavorable environments. It further assumes that in 1900 only a fourth of these young children were being reared in moderately favorable or superior environments.

By 1975, the model assumes that the situation had changed radically, with only 20 percent of all infants and toddlers in profoundly and moderately unfavorable cognitive environments (10 percent in each) and nearly a third receiving the benefits of highly favorable or exceptionally favorable environments (see Table 37).

If this model accurately reflects (1) the factors important to cognitive development, (2) the magnitude of quality changes in these factors, and (3) the effects of these changes on IQ, then *environmental improvements are able to account for approximately 7 points of this twentieth-century IQ increase — or only one-third of the total.*

Summary: Impact of the Early Cognitive Environment on IQ

The principal conclusions growing out of these micro and macro analyses are as follows:

- Exceptionally good and exceptionally bad early home environments (measured along a "conduciveness-to-cognitive-development" axis) are capable of engendering substantial and lasting increases and decreases in expected IQ scores.
- There has been a considerable improvement in the overall cognitive quality of early home environments in the United States over the course of the twentieth century.
- Nevertheless, both the micro and macro approaches suggest that it is highly unlikely that this environmental improvement can account for as much as a *majority* of the impetus for this twentieth-century IQ increase.

18.6 Validity of IQ-Test Scores as a Measure of Rising Intelligence

Several researchers, after being unable to find an environmental cause for the phenomenon of rising IQ, have concluded that

IQ tests must bear only a "weak causal link to intelligence" (Flynn, 1987). Flynn reinforces this conclusion by his estimate that only 3 points of the 20-point increase in scores on the Raven's Progressive Matrices test in the Netherlands over a thirty-year period can be attributed to rising SES.

Attacks on the validity of changes in IQ-test results over time are based on two hypotheses: (1) IQ tests do not measure the fundamental nature of "general intelligence";[15] and/or (2) repeated exposure to IQ tests (or similar types of questions) has enabled later generations of test takers to outperform earlier cohorts. It is of course true that there are no empirical means for resolving the question of the equivalence between what IQ tests are designed to measure and underlying intelligence. Nevertheless, logic and prevailing evidence strongly favor the position that comprehensive IQ tests are, in large part, able to capture the essence of what has come to be known as the *g* of general intelligence (Spearman, 1904).

The basis for this conclusion may be summed up as follows:

- Comprehensive IQ tests are designed to measure *general problem-solving ability* across a variety of cognitive domains chosen, after protracted study and continuing review, as representative of important aspects of intellectual ability. Equally significant, success on these tests does not require knowledge of specific subjects.[16]
- Scores on nonverbal tests of so-called fluid intelligence—heralded even by detractors of intelligence testing as coming closest to capturing the essence of *g*—have risen at far faster rates than have scores on more verbally oriented IQ-test components.
- So-called practice effects are relatively small, even when the time span between taking tests of a similar nature is weeks rather than years; moreover, the rates of gain reported among subjects who were naive test takers have not differed materially from those in school districts that had previously given children IQ (or wide-range achievement) tests.
- Irrespective of one's views on the relationship between IQ-test scores, intelligence, and real-world perfor-

mance, empirical evidence refutes any conclusion that IQ is unimportant (Brand, 1987). For example, IQ is reported "to be the major predictor of occupational success in the United States, despite occupational psychologists having labored for decades to stress the importance of other factors" (Hunter and Hunter, 1984, p. 110).[17] Certainly, 10 IQ points translates (on the average) to more than $10,000 in annual earnings.

In effect, the issue is not whether these tests capture the essence of g perfectly—the important thing is that we can, with certainty, conclude that today's young people are vastly superior to their great-great-grandparents on tests painstakingly designed to be indicative of intelligence in a conglomerate of mental dimensions thought to be of high cognitive value.

But the conclusion that highly regarded IQ tests are generally valid indicators of what they are designed to measure—namely, cognitive capacity in the so-called semantic, symbolic, and/or figural domains (as exemplified by such contrasting problems as antonyms, number and letter series, and figural transformations)—does not address the issue of what is the appropriate weight to assign to each of these domains in the development of a total IQ score. If scores on every IQ-test component rose at the same rate, this would not be a problem. However, the considerably faster rise in scores on tests of spatial IQ[18] requires that, if a reasonably good estimate of the magnitude of the twentieth-century (American) IQ increase is to be developed, we must try to judge the relative importance of each of these domains. My own view is that (1) the emphasis given each of these domains on the pre-1985 Stanford-Binet is appropriate; (2) an unduly large emphasis is given to the nonverbal (spatial) subtests in computing aggregate IQ scores on the Wechsler Intelligence Test;[19] (3) spatial IQ is underemphasized in certain primarily verbal tests used heavily in the prewar period; and (4) totally nonverbal tests, such as the Raven's, grossly exaggerate IQ increases, given the nearly uniform finding of exceedingly rapid growth in scores on this nonverbal measure. Unfortunately, it is not possible to make a reasonable inference concerning the extent of a population's verbal IQ growth from knowing how fast its performance IQ or Raven's test scores rose during a given period.

This qualitative assessment makes it possible to formulate answers to two questions about the twentieth-century IQ increase, namely:

- Are there any countries for which there are sufficient data to estimate, with reasonable accuracy, the extent of their population's twentieth-century IQ growth? Yes, the United States, and only the United States.
- How many IQ points did Americans gain over this period? Approximately 22, or slightly more than a quarter point per year.

This growth-rate estimate (derived from data presented in Chapter Five) is as follows: (1) one-fourth of a point per year from the mid 1920s through the mid 1960s when scores on two equivalent versions of the Stanford-Binet normed forty years apart are compared, (2) three-eighths of a point per year during the first quarter of the century (based on data comparing the performance of World War I and II army recruits and on results from the Seattle Longitudinal Study, and (3) slightly slower rates of growth after the mid 1960s.

18.7 Causes of the Twentieth-Century American IQ Increase: Conclusions

The principal conclusions of this analysis are as follows:

- Americans gained roughly 22 IQ points over the course of the twentieth century.[20]
- Roughly 4 points of this total appear to be attributable to improvements in health and nutrition.
- Only a third of the increase in children's IQs over this period (which rose at the same rate as adults' IQs) can be attributed to improvements in the cognitive quality of their early home environments — even when we assume that (1) there was a considerable decrease over

time in the proportion of homes that provided cognitively poor environments; (2) there was a considerable increase in the proportion of homes that provided excellent- or outstanding-quality cognitive environments; and (3) there are considerable IQ effects (negative and positive) that result from being reared in poor- or excellent-quality homes.

- Arguments that IQ tests are not valid indicators of IQ or that they otherwise overstate underlying IQ changes appear to be without merit, with one exception: trends in spatial-figural IQ considerably overstate the rise in scores on comprehensive IQ tests. Thus, the most appropriate mixture of spatial, verbal, and symbolic test questions appears to be one in which the weight given to the spatial-figural domain is about a third of the total IQ score.

It appears, therefore, that only half of this twentieth-century IQ rise can be attributed to environmental factors, including prenatal health factors, and that half remains of unknown origin. This analysis suggests that if, at the moment of conception each successive generation began life with the same biological "hardware" and "software" as preceding generations, an IQ increase of this magnitude could not have occurred.

18.8 Implications

The fact that only half of the twentieth-century American IQ increase can be attributed to environmental factors requires us to examine the potential role of heredity in this "intellectual evolution."

Most modern scientists have summarily dismissed heredity as a potential source for rapid changes in a population's characteristics. This is because the commonly understood mechanism by which evolutionary adaptations are generated and eventually become dominant in large populations precludes rapid changes.[21]

Evidence from the animal kingdom strongly supports this

aspect of the Darwinian view of evolution—there now being near-universal acceptance that the primary reason why giraffes have long necks is that the longest-necked giraffes survived when the trees from which they obtained food grew taller. Little cre-dence is now given to the Lamarckian view that the offspring of giraffes that continually stretched their necks to obtain food grew longer necks as a result of parental neck stretching.

The lack of (or at best minuscule importance of) adaptive evolution with respect to the evolution of giraffes' necks is, however, not absolute proof of its lack of importance in the *evolution of human intelligence.* On the contrary, there is enough evidence—both experimental and statistical—to suggest that not only can such adaptive evolution occur but that it could be the primary source of the twentieth-century increase in IQ.

There is a basic difference between giraffes' necks and the brain centers responsible for higher intelligence that could enable evolutionary forces to have a strong impact on the latter but not on the former. To put it briefly, the developmental program governing the anatomy and biochemical activity of neurons in these brain centers unfolds postnatally and is subject to considerable "adaptive plasticity" in response to early en-vironmental exposure. Consequently, teaching young children (during the critical periods of postnatal brain development) that specific concepts have special significance not only may endow these children with basic skills for lifelong learning but may also make it easier for *their* children and/or grandchildren to learn these same concepts. This approach, in other words, could engender an increased biological *preparedness* for similar stimuli at the same stage of development.

This theory of adaptive plasticity may explain the huge rise in scores on the Raven's Progressive Matrices test in the Nether-lands over a single generation. For example, a major increase in early exposure to shape-conceptualization toys (such as those in which toddlers insert pieces into openings in a sphere) might cause certain shapes to be assigned special salience, which, in turn, might cause the brain cells "responsible" for spatial recog-nition and categorization to pass on this "experience-expectant" knowledge to subsequent generations in the form of a slightly altered "genetic blueprint."[22] Or, more generally, the act of putting a great deal of stress on these shape-conceptualization cells may induce in the next generation an increase in the amount of growth factors that are "preassigned" to these cells during their period(s) of rapid dendritic growth. Thus, the act of strengthening the biological underpinnings of these cells may engender in one's offspring an ability to cope more effectively with the demands that their ancestors' adaptive processes have prepared them to expect. In short, each new generation is not doomed to begin life with the same set of biological equipment as the generations immediately preceding it but instead receives some biological benefit from the cognitively enriching early environmental experiences of its forefathers.

Notes

1. In Neligan and Prudham, the children whose birth weight was over 4,000 grams scored 0.28 standard deviations higher on the Good-enough Draw-A-Person Test at age five (4,524 subjects) than children weighing 2,500 to 4,000 grams and 0.60 standard deviations higher than those under 2,500 grams. At age ten ($n = 3,788$) the differences on a nonverbal test were comparable (0.25 and 0.47 standard deviations). The population examined constituted 98 percent of all surviving births in Newcastle, England, from 1960 to 1962.

2. As measured in childhood and young adulthood. As one approaches midlife, however, era-to-era IQ comparisons reflect an additional impetus from the health domain — namely, the cumulative effects of better health and nutrition across a lifetime, which are primarily manifest in the maintenance of effective cognitive functioning until later in life (see section 5.4).

3. Some correlates of increasing birth weight — namely, increasing head circumference (as indicative of the thickness of people's cerebral cortex) may reflect biological factors that are independent of general health and nutrition.

4. Because (1) the "foundations" of lifelong intelligence tend to be firmly established (both statistically and biologically) before the age of six (and to almost as large an extent by age three) and (2) the IQ gains registered by six-year-old children do not differ markedly from those exhibited by other age groups, conclusions about the strength of the association between IQ and environmental variables that use IQ evaluations undertaken at, for example, the age of six are likely to have substantial validity. This is true at least with respect to trends in

people's IQ scores until the age at which population IQ scores peak—
after which the import of health factors is likely to grow.

5. A one standard deviation increase in "quality" would, in theory, engender a 5- to 7-point IQ gain (rather than a 4- to 6-point gain) because
the size of the average deviation of IQ scores is slightly larger than a
standard deviation.

6. Measured along a theoretical axis labeled "conduciveness to cognitive
development." This, in turn, can enable an estimate to be made of the
potential effects of secular movements along this axis by the average
home.

7. For example, in the Texas Adoption Project (Horn, Loehlin, and
Willerman, 1979), the scores of the 405 children tested on the WISC
averaged 111.9. Because this test was normed twenty-five to twenty-nine
years earlier, these children's "true" scores are likely to be only slightly
above the race-adjusted average (given the average improvement in
American children's performance over this period). The biological
mothers of these children also scored above average (on the Beta Test).

8. Meaning, if you knew the IQ scores of all the adopted children in a
study, as well as the scores of all their adoptive parents and their
biological parents—but did not know which child "belonged" with
which sets of parents—you could make a more accurate estimate by
knowing the *biological* mother's IQ than you could by knowing the
adoptive mother's IQ.

9. The improvement occurred in mainstream homes, with no change in
the "best" and "worst" homes.

10. With each year's "mind's eye" average being summed and the total
averaged (a procedure designed to give each year's data a weight of
one).

11. Nevertheless, in the United States, the "ideological" expectation of
considerable paternal involvement in an infancy is of such recent
vintage that IQ data through the mid 1970s would not capture much of
the effects of this phenomenon.

12. For second and laterborn children, the impact of parental age on IQ
follows the firstborn pattern, even though another effect, wider spacing between children, becomes more important; nevertheless, as discussed in section 19.10, older parents might also beget brighter children for biological reasons.

13. An example of one yes-no question from the HOME Infant Inventory
is, Does mother provide stacking or nesting toys, blocks or building
toys, or other eye-hand coordination toys that permit combinations?
Almost all upper-middle-class homes get very high scores on this entire
cluster of yes-no questions.

14. Four to five points in the Minnesota Study, contrasting professional-
class and semiskilled working-class homes (which were apt to differ by
15 to 20 points in paternal IQ and 6 to 8 points in maternal IQ).

15. Following this logic, performance on those aspects of IQ tests that bear
the weakest relationship to underlying intelligence must be expanding
quite rapidly in order for those aspects that come closer to capturing
the essence of g to be either inching upward or not rising at all.

16.   In the verbal domain, specific knowledge (such as word meaning) is
       necessarily more of a factor; nevertheless, political pressure for IQ tests
       to be "culture fair" and "culture free" has kept this influence to rela-
       tively minimal levels.

17.   Hunter's analysis of hundreds of studies that evaluated the relationship
       between intelligence and job performance (in manual as well as mental
       jobs) has led him to conclude that general cognitive ability is an
       excellent predictor of supervisor ratings and training success and an
       even better predictor of empirically measured job knowledge and job
       performance (Hunter, 1986). Further, it is general cognitive ability, not
       specific cognitive aptitudes, that predicts performance.

18.   Such as the Raven's Progressive Matrices test, in which each item
       consists of nine elements arrayed as a three-by-three matrix; the ele-
       ments form a pattern, but one element is always missing, and the task is
       to infer the pattern and select the missing element from among the (six
       to eight) choices presented. The scores of university students on the
       most difficult (adult) version of this test (the Raven's Advanced Progres-
       sive Matrices) have been shown to be highly correlated with scores on
       the WAIS and with Spearman's g (Paul, 1985). The Raven's was most
       recently restandardized in 1979 (Raven, 1981), with norms published
       for ages six to sixty-five.

19.   On this test, arithmetic is considered part of the subtest cluster called
       verbal IQ; so-called performance IQ is given equal weight with verbal
       IQ in computing the overall Wechsler score.

20.   On comprehensive IQ tests, where the weighting of the spatial domain
       is moderate. This figure includes 10 points between 1932 and 1972,
       slightly less than 10 points in the preceding quarter century (a some-
       what conservative estimate), and slightly more than 2 points over the
       remaining thirteen years.

21.   A gene mutates (in a more or less random manner), and the mutant
       variety—through better survivability and/or more-propitious mating
       and breeding—becomes dominant. This process necessarily takes a
       very considerable number of procreations (generations) to occur (bar-
       ring some catastrophic environmental event that wipes out one variety
       of a species but not another).

22.   The obverse of this critical-period enrichment is seen in the Nobel
       Prize–winning work of Hubel and Wiesel (1970), in which cats de-
       prived of the opportunity to see vertical lines during a specific stage of
       brain development permanently lose the power to give "verticalness"
       the special salience upon which cats depend.

Contents

19

Toward a New Theory
of Human Intellectual
"Evolution"

19.1 Introduction

The classical theory of evolution is unable to provide an adequate explanation for the extreme rapidity with which the human brain has been evolving. Neither can it explain what appears to be a dramatic acceleration in the rate of higher cognitive development, including the functional divergence of the brain's hemispheres the closer one gets to the modern era. Moreover, it is difficult to account for the magnitude of the increase in IQ scores that has occurred over the past several generations, particularly when studies indicate that, for most people, heredity has a considerably stronger influence on IQ than does environment.

This chapter proposes that an interaction between "adaptive plasticity" and heredity has been responsible for this biological and cognitive advance, and it suggests possible mechanisms for the transmission of adaptive changes in the "developmental blueprint" of the brain through the germ line to one's offspring.

19.2 Fundamental Differences Between
the Human Brain and Body

As scientists have learned more about the human brain, there has been an increasing realization that vast differences exist

447

between those segments of DNA that are active in the brain and those active in the remainder of the body. For example:

- There appear to be at least 20,000 different genes expressed in the human brain—most of which are thought to be active **only** in the brain.[1]
- The human brain is evolving at a rate at least ten times as fast as the most rapidly evolving part of any other animal's body—horses' hooves (Young, 1971).
- Brain-active genes tend to have "evolved" much further than those expressed elsewhere, in the sense that a large proportion of their DNA sequence length is transcribed into messenger RNA and then transported to a "protein-manufacturing plant" (a ribosome). Recent estimates are that three to four times the proportion of the brain-active DNA in these genes is so utilized, compared with the rate of such activity in genes expressed outside the central nervous system.[2]
- The rate of protein-making activity in areas of the brain responsible for higher cognitive functions is especially rapid; Thomas and Thompson (1977) report that the activity level in neurons in the cerebral cortex is an average of four times greater than that of cells from organs external to the central nervous system and also that of glial cells.
- In contrast to the rest of the body where every gene is expressed prior to birth,[3] only half of the total "sequence complexity" of the adult brain's active genome is present in a cell's "protein-manufacturing plants" (its ribosomes) at birth,[4] with several RNA "species" not appearing until near the end of childhood. Therefore, the genes they encode are not expressed until then.

Thus, in contrast to the remainder of the body, the unfolding of the brain's developmental blueprint extends well into the postnatal era. This in part reflects the fact that the functional development of neurons does not end when their cell bodies form. Instead, it continues until channels of communication are established with: (1) other neurons within the same cell network, (2) neurons in many key cell networks, and (3) neurons in the analogous area of the opposite hemisphere.

From the time that a neuron's "interior message-receiving apparatus"[5] begins to develop and its initial connections with other neurons are established until its inner branches have become fully developed and communication pathways with other cell networks have been firmly entrenched,[6] environmental experiences can considerably modify the developmental blueprint of these neurons and neuronal networks. Because the large majority of the brain's postnatal growth is completed before the age of three—with most of that growth occurring by age two—much of this functional plasticity diminishes by the end of infancy or toddlerhood.[7] This pattern dovetails with the emerging mountain of integrated behavioral and biological knowledge that points to the existence of what have come to be called **critical** or sensitive periods of postnatal development.[8] Once this critical period has passed, the amount of effort needed to generate and sustain a given level of outer-branch dendritic growth has been determined. This is analogous to providing ample water to a young tree; once its inner root and branch systems are formed, the extent to which it can adapt to changing environmental conditions is firmly established.

The neurons of the receptive layer of the cerebral cortex and those of the adjacent cortical layers,[9] however, have an especially high lifelong plasticity—a plasticity attributable to the continued presence of the so-called nerve growth factor (NGF), which, in the brain, is active in cells that use the neurotransmitter acetylcholine (see section 19.9).[10] This plasticity confers an ability to create, destroy, and modify dendrites, dendritic spines, and synapses in response to use or disuse.

19.3 The Biological Effects of Providing Rodents with Environmental Enrichments

Researchers seeking to understand the biological changes engendered in the human brain by exposure to environmental enrichments have focused much of their attention on the effects of such enrichments on the brains of rodents.[11] However, because the human brain is so much more advanced than that of other animals—particularly those portions of the brain that govern complex associative thinking and memory—the human brain's biological response to environmental enrichment cannot be extrapolated from these studies with any certainty.[12] Nevertheless, these studies give us some valuable insights into those portions of the human brain that are likely to respond to enrichment and the kinds of results we might expect from enrichment.

The normal laboratory environment of rats or mice contains far less visual stimulation than they would encounter in "the wild." Consequently, these rodents possess an innate capacity to assimilate a more complex visual environment than is normally present under laboratory conditions—meaning one that contains a variety of toys and "complex social living conditions" (for example, twelve rats housed in a large cage rather than three rats in a small cage). This has made the portion of the rodents' cerebral cortex responsible for the secondary analysis of visual inputs (the occipital cortex) into the focus of a considerable number of enrichment studies.[13] Some of the results of this research can be summarized as follows:

- Irrespective of the age at which environmental enrichment is begun, it induces a significant increase in the depth of the occipital cortex;[14] nevertheless, the age at which the exposure begins does affect the nature and extent of biological changes, as well as the rapidity of their occurrence.[15]
- Rats raised in enriched environments tend to perform better on complex mazes than do rats raised in standard laboratory environments. But enriched social conditions, in the absence of other visual enrichments (toys), do not produce an improvement compared with standard conditions. Further, if a single set of toys remains in the group cage throughout the enrichment experience, maze performance tends not to improve (Greenough, 1976).
- Exposure to a "super-enriched" environment produced larger effects, in terms of thicker, heavier occipital cortexes, than did exposure to standard enrichment conditions.[16]
- Accompanying these structural effects are changes in brain metabolism, but these latter changes are transitory for the most part and appear to be related to the construction of new (outer) dendritic branches. For example, exposure to an enriched environment

results in an increase in RNA synthesis that peaks about thirty days after enrichment is begun and returns to a near-baseline level after sixty days.[17] PET-scan findings suggest that, during this period, overall cortical glucose use rises only slightly (far less than the change in cortical volume), with the increased use in the occipital cortex accompanied by a reduction of use in frontal and association areas.

Thus, it is apparently natural and easy for rats to somewhat deplete the outer branches of some neurons and transport the energy to other neurons where new connections are constructed. Under conditions of stress (caused by increased cognitive demands) previously inactive genes are expressed and/or the production of biochemicals necessary to these genes is greatly increased.

Insofar as the question of whether *multigenerational exposure to normal laboratory conditions or multigenerational exposure to enriched environments engenders discernible multigenerational biological effects — such as a heightened biological preparedness to benefit from environmental enrichments or a faster-than-expected pace of genetic evolution — the answer seems to be* **yes, on both counts**.

First as detailed in the next section, the rate of genetic divergence of inbred strains of laboratory mice from their ancestors has, over the past half century, been **ten to twenty times that expected** — with this *adaptive versatility* apparently emanating from or being spread by mechanisms entirely different from those proposed in classical evolutionary theory. In addition, an experiment undertaken by Marian Diamond at the University of California, Berkeley, suggests that toys galore (changed frequently) and "optimal" social living conditions may well have effects on brain growth in subsequent generations.

Diamond began this experiment by placing sixty-day-old rats in enriched conditions, where (except for a short break for mating) they remained until the females delivered their litters. The offspring were then reared in normal laboratory conditions until they were sixty days old, at which time half were sacrificed for purposes of measuring the thickness of their occipital cortexes. The remaining rats were then housed in the same enriched conditions for the second round of the experiment, which was continued in the same manner for four generations. With each successive generation, the thickness of the occipital cortexes of the baby rats became measurably greater, *even though these rats had not been exposed postnatally to these enriched environments* (Diamond and others, 1984).

Can this be possible? Can the environment of a rodent's forebears really engender an increased biological preparedness for a similar environment at a similar stage of development? Unfortunately, this study did not employ a large enough sample size to ensure that the results could not have occurred by chance. Therefore, these findings must, for now, be considered speculative.

19.4 The Spread of Adaptive Plasticity Among Laboratory Mice

The evolutionary mechanisms described in neoclassical Darwinian theory fail to explain the extremely rapid rate of genetic divergence among inbred strains of mice reported several years ago by Fitch and Atchley (1985). Specifically, these observations call into question several of the major neo-Darwinian precepts, including the nature of the genetic changes that initiate this evolutionary divergence and the manner in which they are spread through a population (Nei, 1987).

Specifically, this extreme divergence from their ancestors (1) was not accompanied by a high rate of "point mutations" in these species,[18] (2) has primarily affected loci that encode proteins, although sites related to immune function have an intrinsically greater potential for genetic diversity; (3) has often involved a "maximal divergence" from the ancestral genome; and (4) has been coupled with an exceptionally high frequency of exactly two alleles (or forms of a gene) appearing at these sites. More specific findings include:

- The degree of genetic divergence at the ninety-seven chromosomal locations examined was approximately 45 percent (in ten inbred strains of mice over an average of fifty-eight years), compared with an estimated ancestral heterozygosity of 9 percent—or a fivefold increase. If the estimate of heterozygosity found in wild mice

(Racine and Langley, 1980) is applied to the ancestors of these mice, the rate of genetic diversification found would be twenty times faster than expected rather than five.

- Exactly two alleles were found at 80 percent of the fifty-nine sites where variations appeared; this included more than 90 percent of the sites for protein-coding genes.[19]

- The large majority of the gene substitutions required to explain the divergence found represent the appearance of *nonunique forms of genes*;[20] further, an analysis of fifty-two "cladistically informative" two-allele sites revealed that the divergence from the ancestral strain required 113 gene substitutions. Had these variations been caused by random mutations, a much higher prevalence of three or more variants per site would be expected, especially at protein-coding loci.

- For several strains of mice, the degree of divergence from other strains approached the maximum possible.[21] This finding strongly suggests a high frequency of simultaneously generated (and, therefore, adaptively generated) alterations in the position and/or state of the regulatory sequences of DNA that govern gene expression. It also gives further support for the conclusion that this diversification is not a reflection of the allopatric mechanisms (described in the next section), based on findings that the rate of *mutation* in these species is "two orders of magnitude slower" than the rate of "genetic diversification" found in this analysis (Johnson and others, 1981). In addition, the literature lends no support to the proposition that mutant varieties are occurring in these inbred strains of laboratory mice.

These findings suggest that this exceptionally rapid divergence of inbred mice from their ancestors must have been predicated on (1) the presence of a preexisting switching mechanism that generally restricts variability to only two alternatives (even when rearrangements of several DNA sequences are required to create the second variant); (2) a sensitivity of this mechanism to specific features of the environment; and, it would appear, (3) a "preadaptive" capacity to express alternative forms of a gene.

19.5 Factors Influencing Evolutionary Rates in Mammals and Birds

Even though mammals do not undergo a greater rate of so-called point mutations than nonmammals,[22] placental mammals in particular evidence considerably higher overall rates of evolutionary change. This is because these mammals' genomes tend to undergo sharply higher rates of regulatory-sequence rearrangements (Wilson, Carlson, and White, 1977).[23]

The most rapid rates of evolution in the animal kingdom occur among horses, songbirds, and certain kinds of barn mice. As already noted, however, *the rate of evolution of the human brain is at least ten times faster* than the most rapidly evolving part of the most rapidly evolving animals' body—horses' hooves.

An analysis of the rate of evolutionary change among over 200 genera of vertebrates (Wilson, Bush, Case, and King, 1975) reveals some discernible patterns of environmental influences—with the fastest rates of evolution generally being associated with the *social isolation* of a *deme* (that is a group, troop, or clan of animals), especially of demes having *a single reproductive male*. In contrast, the slowest rates are associated with social structures that evidence considerable sexual intermingling (Bush, Case, Wilson, and Patton, 1977). The authors present numerous examples, including these:

- *Primates*. The vervet monkeys, which generally travel in small troops with a single adult male and several females, have the fastest evolutionary (speciation) rate, while baboons (which travel in large troops and, although male-female friendships usually precede mating, tend to engage in considerable sexual commingling) have an almost zero rate of chromosomal change.
- *Horses*. Excluding man, horses appear to have the fastest rate of evolution in the animal kingdom. Here, family groups generally consist of "a stallion, several mares (which remain with the group their entire lives), and their young. The young leave the family group at 2-4 years of age to join a bachelor group or, in the case of females, to join or form a new family group. When an adult member dies, it is usually replaced by a younger individual either from the same or a neighboring group" (Wilson, Bush, Case, and King, 1975, p. 5064).
- *Mice vs. "cats."* Many rodents have sociability patterns similar to the harem formation of horses; for example, certain barn mice "are subdivided into small family groups of 4-7 reproductively active individuals with one dominant male. Group territories are defended and, when young individuals disperse from these social groups, there is little interchange between them" (Bush, Case, Wilson, and Patton, 1977, p. 3945). Considerable chromosomal variation is found both within and between demes of mice having this social organization. The authors note, "Even within the con-

fines of a single barn, genetically distinct demes of mice have been recognized." By contrast, lion prides are organized around a group of reproductive females and, even though one or two males are usually associated with a pride at any one time, "[t]here is a constant turnover in males, with few remaining for more than two years in any pride. Virtually all other cat species spend their lives alone except at the time of mating or while rearing young" (p. 3945). These authors attribute the low rate of chromosomal evolution found among felines to this behavior.

By comparing evolutionary rates among species with (other-wise) similar social structures, Wilson, Bush, Case, and King have arrived at the conclusion that a slow rate of chromosomal evolution is associated with a high rate of juvenile dispersal and individual wandering (as in cats).

Of particular note is the finding that demes of *barn* mice have markedly higher evolutionary rates than do those of field mice. When this is considered in conjunction with the previously discussed findings about rodents raised in *laboratories*, one may wonder whether rearing animals in a physical and social en-vironment that closely resembles that encountered by their immediate ancestors and/or rearing them in an environment that differs considerably from that encountered in the wild would cause alternative forms of gene expression to sweep through a population.

The rate of anatomical evolution among birds—particularly songbirds—has recently been shown to have been extremely rapid (Wyles, Kunkel, and Wilson, 1983),[24] a finding that sup-ports the theory that high brain weight—considered in relation to body weight—is often (but not always) an excellent determin-ant of a species' rate of anatomical evolution.[25] Songbirds also appear to be unique in that neurons in their frontal cortex die out in the fall, and new neurons are generated in the spring when these birds learn a new repertoire of songs (Nottebohm, 1981; Alvarez-Baylla and Nottebohm, 1988). Thus, a songbird's cerebral cortex possesses extraordinary lifelong plasticity.

19.6 Evolutionary Theory Confronts the Realities of Molecular Biology

The rapid expansion of knowledge about the mechanics of evolutionary processes has revealed that evolutionary progress is generated through a variety of mechanisms that tend to vary in importance according to the genetic complexity and "evolutionary status" of an organism.

The most well-understood evolutionary mechanism—allelic substitution—occurs when a mutation affecting that portion of a gene's DNA message that is transcribed into protein results in the creation of an altered gene product. Allelic substitution generally results from an imperfect replication of DNA, usually consists of a "single-genetic-character" change from the normal sequence (an inversion, a translocation, or a "frame shift"), and is considered to be an entirely random occurrence.

Alternatively, changes in the *position* of the so-called regulatory sequences of DNA or of the regulatory genes in relation to a gene's structural elements may also have evolutionary consequences.[26] These regulators provide the instructions for the transcription and transportation of the gene's protein-coding segments and thereby *control the nature and pattern of gene expression.* Not only can these regulators affect the *amount* of a given protein into which a gene will be transcribed in any given cell population at any given stage of development,[27] but—because the position of a regulatory gene is not always stationary[28]— changes in this positioning can also alter the *nature* of proteins "manufactured" by combinations of genes.[29] Further, because some DNA sequences are able to transverse chromosomal boundaries, the rate at which an organism's individual genes are evolving and the rate at which its chromosomes are evolving are not necessarily linked.

An increasingly understood (and frequently occurring) process called *gene duplication* is often an essential first step in creating and maintaining the kinds of variation necessary for advanced species to evolve (Ohta, 1988). When redundant copies of a gene exist, changes in the structure of these copies,[30] including nucleotide substitutions[31] and gene conversions (discussed below), along with geographical transpositions of gene sequences, are often a continual occurrence. Gene duplication and subsequent divergence have been the dominating processes for evolving new proteins, and the development of "multigene families" is an outgrowth of these processes (Ohno, 1970).[32] This is seen as a highly efficient way of attaining functional diversity and of accumulating genetic information (Hood, Campbell, and Elgin, 1975; Ohta, 1987).[33]

If only one vital function is assigned to a single gene locus within the genome, natural selection remains the dominant force behind evolution. If, however, alternative but passive gene loci are permitted (as they are at some but not all sites), mutations at these passive points (whether advantageous, deleterious, or neutral) can be tolerated (in other words, a "house cleaning" process does not destroy them). Because there may be a large number of tandemly arranged copies of the DNA sequence, the original function can be preserved, while some copies are unhindered in acquiring new functions. A rapid rate of unequal-exchange crossovers might then enable a single aberrant copy to propagate. Thus, this process can create a particularly favorable environment for the development of "preadaptations," which then become available resources for an organism to utilize when environmental conditions warrant.[34] Further, because most related genes have related functions, it may be argued that, when genes necessary for a particular function begin to proliferate, the preadaptive potential for further advances in that general direction is also apt to increase.

The interested reader is urged to consult the writings of John Campbell (especially Campbell, 1982, 1985, 1987) for clearly articulated overviews of these complex subjects.

The rapidly expanding body of findings from the so-called "molecular revolution" cannot be reconciled with the neo-Darwinian theory's view that *natural selection* (coupled sometimes with neutral drift) *is the only mechanism for the spread of variation through a population*, particularly with respect to evolution in the most highly evolved organisms and genes. Instead, analyses of variations (between individuals and between populations) in multigene families and so-called (noncoding) repetitive DNA families have led to the development of a concept called *molecular drive*. Proposed by Gabriel Dover (Dover, 1982; Dover and Flavell, 1984), this theory holds that once the connection between gene and chromosome behavior is broken, internal turnover mechanisms such as the unequal exchange of chromosomal information by cells during cell division, DNA transpositions, and gene conversions (processes that have been collectively dubbed *concerted evolution*) are occurring with sufficient frequency (Ohta, 1983) for a population's genome to move toward a stabilized homogeneity under its own power without any involvement of selective forces.[35] It is argued that these processes, by acting in a concerted manner, become reflected in swift transformations that occur in a cohesive and quite possibly synchronous manner.

One of these mechanisms, gene conversion,[36] contravenes the normal Mendelian rules. It often occurs immediately preceding meiosis (the creation of the sperm or egg)[37] and involves the substitution of one parental allele for another. Recently, researchers have isolated one of the crucial factors that determine whether a DNA sequence will be expressed, namely, the methylation state of regulatory sequences adjacent to the gene's structural parts,[38] and, as indicated below, gene conversion also appears to contravene these Mendelian rules. This is because, when foreign genes are inserted at these sites, *the active form of the allele is often transmitted to the offspring by only one sex* — males. In a series of recent experiments in which foreign genes were injected into the DNA of developing mouse embryos, when researchers followed the transmission of these "transgenes" from the carrier mice to their offspring, they reported that *the sex of the parent contributing the gene* has far more to do with whether the gene is expressed than does the dominant or recessive nature of the gene itself.[39] At sites where the implanted gene was active only if inherited from the father and dormant if inherited from the mother, male mice inheriting such dormant genes from their mothers were, nevertheless, able to convert them to their active form and transmit them to their offspring. This was because the methylation state of the genes **in their sperm cells had changed.**[40] By contrast, no differences in methylation states between a female carrier's egg cells and her soma have been reported (Swain, Stewart, and Leder, 1987; Reik and others, 1987; Sapienza and others, 1987; Solter, 1988).[41] Thus, as a transgene is passed from one generation to another, its methylation is reversed again and again, depending on the sex of the parent that transmits it.

These findings dovetail with an emerging theory of differential parental imprinting, *which holds that some genes are differentially expressed when contributed by the maternal and paternal genomes and that the timing of their expression and/or repression is also affected by the gamete-of-origin*. This theory has gained support from a number of recent findings about human diseases:

- *Tumors.* Susceptibility to several different tumor-causing mutations (such as mutations at tumor-suppressor loci) occur at far higher rates in paternally derived genes (Wilkins, 1988; Schroeder, 1987; Solomon and others, 1987; Naylor and others, 1987; Toguchida and others, 1989).
- *Huntington's disease.* Even though the familial penetrance of this disease is nearly 100 percent, approximately 90 percent of the juvenile-onset cases are inherited from the father (Farrer and Conneally, 1985).[42]

Findings such as these do much to explain why both parental genomes are needed for an embryo to develop to term, as the differential expression of some parental alleles gives rise to functional differences between parental genomes (Surani and others, 1988). Because stage- and tissue-specific demethylation and remethylation occur during embryonic development, the maternal genome is able to bear a greater responsibility for the early growth of the embryo and the paternal genome for the development of the extraembryonic tissue (Monk, Boubelik, and Lehnert, 1987).

Differential parental imprinting is of particular importance for genes whose **developmental** activation and inactivation enable them to function as "gene dosage compensation" mechanisms. "Then, whenever a gene must change expression levels during development, its activation by specific parental imprinting might well be a mechanism of choice" (Solter, 1988, p. 142).

If—as is suggested in sections 17.5 and 19.9—the "shape" of a person's intelligence is (in part) determined by the length and strength of the "growing seasons" of various neuronal networks, then these parental imprinting processes are apt to be a major impetus in providing human intelligence with the adaptive plasticity that it obviously possesses. Because most of the development of the brain regions that govern higher brain functions occurs postnatally and a considerable number of brain-active genes do not begin to be expressed until childhood, it would seem that the paternal genome makes a greater contribution to the development of human intelligence than the maternal genome. The veracity of this assumption would presumably be indicated by a shift in the extent to which person's male and female parents have contributed biologically to his or her intelligence—from a fifty-fifty balance to a ratio favoring the father. This is certainly testable, and the results of studies bearing on this issue are presented in the next section.

19.7 Evidence for a Strong Paternal Role in the Transmission of Human Intelligence

Some people believe that the underlying g of people's intelligence is so strongly governed by heredity that environment (except under conditions of extreme deprivation) is of little or no consequence. Proponents of this position have cited the equal correlations found between children's IQs and those of *either* of their parents as presumptive evidence of an equal parental contribution to intelligence. Moreover, because this equality was found in the face of what—in the middle third of twentieth-century America—was usually a very unequal parental contribution to the early upbringing of these children, hereditarians contend that these results demonstrate that the biological contribution to intelligence overwhelms that of environment. However, the burgeoning evidence that specifically defined factors in the early home environment strongly influence IQ scores—and that these influences transcend such quantifiable factors as parental IQ, parental education, and the family's social class—reduces the salience of the hereditarian argument.

Since mothers are typically far more involved in their children's early upbringing than are fathers, it would seem logical to conclude that, *if environment is of **any** consequence*, a child's IQ score will bear a closer resemblance to its mother's IQ than to its father's. Moreover, the effects of the intrauterine environment on the cognitive well-being of the developing fetus also favor a closer IQ relationship between mother and child than between father and child. For example, environmental interference with certain neuroendocrine hormones has been shown—in animals, as well as in pregnant women who abuse drugs or medications—to produce pronounced effects on their immediate offspring, as well as on subsequent generations. These hormones include the catecholamines—neurotransmitter systems responsible for concentration, arousal, and the ability to cope with stress—that can, in turn, influence IQ-test performance. This finding provides a further rationale for presupposing a greater maternal than paternal influence on IQ.

As it turns out, however, maternal influence is not greater. In reporting on IQ correlations found between parents and their reared-together offspring, a comprehensive and high-quality review of the world literature (Bouchard and McGue, 1981)[43] concludes that *father-offspring correlations and mother-offspring correlation are* **identical.**[44]

Thus, the equal correlations between children's IQs and the IQs of both of their biological parents—in the face of strong evidence of a substantially greater maternal role in determining both *the environmental contribution* to actualized IQ and the prenatal environment—is presumptive evidence that one of three conditions exists: (1) **neither prenatal nor postnatal environments have any impact on intelligence**; or (2) *despite the relatively small amount of time that they spend with their young children, fathers have a greater postnatal impact on their children's cognitive development than mothers*;[45] or (3) **fathers must be able to make a greater genetic contribution to their children's IQs than do mothers**—and do so to an extent sufficient to offset the mother's greater environmental contribution.

Any possibility that fathers—despite their more limited role in early child rearing—might be able to make a greater *environmental* contribution to their children's "intellectual upbringing" than their mothers would seem to be dispelled by the findings from the adoption studies presented in Table 38. These

Table 38. Correlations Between Adopted Children's IQs
and Those of Their Adoptive Parents.

	Correlations of Children's IQs with	
Adoption Study[a]	Adoptive Mother	Adoptive Father
Burks (Stanford Study)	.19	.07
Colorado Adoption Study	.18	.12
Leahy Adoption Study	.24	.19
Texas Adoption Study	.18	.12
Transracial (early adoptees)	.23	.15

[a] Chapter Four describes, and gives references for, these studies.

adoption-study findings take on even greater significance when we recognize that, because of the special characteristics of the adoptive families in the earlier adoption studies cited in Chapter Four (including Burks, 1928, 1938, and Leahy, 1935), *the average adoptive father was likely to be considerably more involved in parenting than the average biological father of the 1920s and 1930s.*[46] Thus, at least in theory, these children's IQs should evidence a greater similarity to the caretaker providing the preponderance of the nurturing in the case of biological—rather than adoptive—families particularly when the effects of the intrauterine environment are added into the equation.

Consequently, *the existence of biological factors strong enough to overcome these maternal biases must be assumed.*

19.8 The "Isolation" of the Germ Line in Males

The findings detailed in the previous sections challenge a major tenet of mainstream evolutionary theory, namely, that environmentally induced changes in gene expression cannot alter what parents pass on to their offspring. This belief—that the germ line is isolated from other cells (the soma)—grows out of the knowledge that immunity to disease is generally not transmitted to one's offspring (for example, children remain susceptible to chicken pox even if both their parents had it), coupled with the conviction that once the germ line develops, its genetic program cannot be altered by changes that occur in other cells. Adherents of this position maintain that, because the germ line of females develops prenatally and the mechanisms for the hereditary transmission of genetic information are presumed to be identical or equivalent for both sexes,[47] the postnatal experiences of either parent cannot alter the genetic blueprint of their as-yet unconceived offspring[48] — there being no (known) mechanism by which the knowledge of environmentally induced alterations in the blueprint governing (for example) the growth of neurons in the cerebral cortex could reach and permeate their sperm or eggs and induce corresponding changes in the genetic blueprint of these germ cells.

Neo-Darwinian theory no longer argues that there are **inherent** properties in genes or the forces acting upon them that preclude the heritability of acquired characteristics, because many organisms that do not possess a germ-line/somatic-cell barrier are able to transmit environmentally adaptive changes to their progeny.[49] Rather, the isolating agent is thought of as being contained in these barriers themselves — the so-called blood-testes barrier in males and the egg and placental barriers in females. Consequently, it is appropriate to examine the nature of any "holes" in these barriers through which "blueprint-altering" instructions might pass, as well as whether the characteristics of these two barriers are identical.

With respect to the immune system, the blood-testes barrier is virtually impenetrable, there being only three sets of experiments in which induced viral tolerance or susceptibility were shown to have permeated this barrier. In one study (Brackett, Baranska, Sawicki, and Koprowski, 1971), a green-monkey virus (SV40) (which is not normally transmittable to rabbits) was transmitted to rabbit embryos when the virus was placed in the proximity of rabbit sperm prior to fertilization. In another study (Gorczynski and Steele, 1981), when young male mice were made genetically tolerant to two transplanted antigens, they passed this acquired immunity to their offspring — with the transmission of tolerance to each antigen independent of the other — and the hereditary path for each closely followed predicted (Mendelian) norms.[50] Difficulties in replicating these results, however, support the position that, with respect to the immune system, this barrier is indeed formidable (but see Mullbacher, Ashman, and Blanden, 1983).[51]

However, many of the so-called neuroendocrines are able to transverse the blood-testes barrier with little difficulty.[52] Following are some of the more notable studies that have assessed the transgenerational effects of altering neuroendocrine levels in animals and humans of both sexes:

- *Removal of the thyroid.* This resulted in enlarged pituitaries and thyroids in the offspring of young male rats that were then mated with normal females; despite these compensatory enlargements, TSH levels were reduced and other manifestations of thyroid deficiency were evident.[53]
- *Insulin impairment.* Injecting preweanling male rats with alloxan,[54] mating them with normal females, and then inbreeding the offspring (with no further treatment) caused a progressive deterioration in glucose tolerance, leading to overt diabetes in most of the rats by the sixth generation.
- *Thalidomide deformity.* This was induced in the progeny of young male rabbits (Lutwak-Mann, 1964).
- *Methadone.* Administering this to male rats before mating resulted in the death of nearly three-fourths of their live offspring by twenty-one days of age (Soyka and Joffe, 1980; Joffe, 1979).
- *Caffeine.* The offspring of males treated with high doses of caffeine for four days before mating had high rates of neonatal mortality, particularly between eight and fourteen days of age (the same age range as peak mortality among the offspring of methadone-treated males) (Joffe, 1979).
- *Anesthesia.* The wives of dentists and anesthetists have high rates of spontaneous abortions, and their offspring have a high incidence of "congenital anomalies" (American Society of Anesthesiology, 1974).
- *Opiates.* Deleterious effects are seen in the offspring of male mice who were given opiates and then mated with normal females; continuing effects in subsequent generations indicate that the effects (less pain sensitivity and reduced juvenile body weight) are "in the genes" (Friedler, 1974; Sonderegger, O'Shea, and Zimmermann, 1979); "weak" intergenerational effects have also been reported when conception follows cannabis use (Fried and Charlebois, 1979).

There is a fundamental difference between the sexes that might make it possible for a child's intelligence to be affected by aspects of its father's, but not its mother's, **environmentally** modulated developmental blueprint, namely, that its mother's lifetime supply of eggs is fully formed prior to her birth, but its father's sperm do not begin to be created until puberty and are thereafter "manufactured" on a continuous basis. Consequently, if some aspects of the developmental blueprint are not incorporated initially into the genetic archives of immature sperm cells, *but are instead added during their maturation process*, then the process governing the incorporation of environmentally induced changes into the developmental blueprint of the male might be less constraining than those that govern access to the genetic blueprint of an already fully formed egg.

Support for this construct comes from a **new** report that shows that *when the mature sperm of mice are placed in close proximity to a particular foreign gene* — in this case an easy to detect bacterial gene involved in the synthesis of the principal acetylcholine precursor, CAT — *relatively large quantities of this genetic material are captured by specific sites within the sperm head, where they are incorporated tightly within the sperm's own genome* (Lavitrano and others, 1989). About 30 percent of the 250 progeny of these sperm inherited this foreign gene. And when mated with untreated mice, most of the progeny carrying this gene transmitted it functionally to their own offspring.

The fact that foreign cholinergic DNA has been implanted successfully in sea urchins (Arezzo, 1989) and toads, which involves a nonrandom rearrangement of this DNA of the sperm during the integration process (Birnstiel and Busslinger, 1989), suggests that sperm possess an intrinsic ability to assimilate certain DNA molecules when these are present in their prefertilization environment. Thus, if molecules encoding environmentally induced changes in the brain could be transmitted to the site of sperm development and/or maintenance, it seems there would be no innate obstacle to such alterations being incorporated into the sperm's genome.

Because many brain-active genes do not begin to be expressed until well into the postnatal period[55] and almost all cortical cell networks develop postnatally, this ability to incorporate environmentally induced alteration in the developmental blueprint into the germ line does not imply that this responsiveness can be applied to cell populations whose *developmental blueprint unfolds prenatally.* This would explain why virtually all efforts to validate a Lamarckian point of view based on morphological differences in the body have failed—and yet, with respect to the rapid evolution of higher brain function, remain possible.[56]

It has also become evident that, *during embryonic development, the roles of the paternal and maternal genomes differ considerably* (McGrath and Solter, 1984), with each being required for the successful maturation of the fetus. As a result, the **mechanisms** by which the maternal and paternal genomes *supply developmental information to the fetus* could differ.[57] There is no intrinsic necessity that the developing fetus receive an equivalent *amount* of developmental information from each of its parents—either in the aggregate or with respect to the particular neuropeptides that underlie exceptional problem-solving skills.[58]

The addition of the developmental blueprint to the sperm during their maturation process (beginning at puberty) *could explain the recent PET-scan findings that glucose use in the cerebral cortex begins to fall dramatically between the ages of eleven and a half and thirteen* (Chugani, Phelps, and Mazziotta, 1987), decreasing almost 50 percent by adulthood.[59] What happens to all the biochemical receptor sites whose activity had previously used this mental energy? Could it be that the biochemical messages contained in "redundant copies" of neuropeptides encoding, for example, the special salience of vertical or horizontal lines[60] are "transported" to the germ line, where they are used to alter the amount and nature of gene expression that the corresponding cell networks in their offspring will be predisposed to display during development?

Although *these findings suggest that the preponderance of this **transfer of developmental information*** *is likely to occur at puberty,* this rules out neither a far earlier end to the ability to engender major structural changes in a given cell network's dendritic ensemble, particularly since cortical metabolic activity peaks at age four (at nearly twice the adult level) and remains at this very high level through age eleven, nor the possibility that some transfer of developmental information continues beyond puberty. This subject is discussed further in section 19.10.

First, however, certain unique properties of the brain's cholinergic system warrant elaboration. In addition, to promote a better understanding of how a male-denominated transfer of adaptive plasticity to the germ line might occur, I will discuss the nature and functions of the Sertoli cells of the testes.

19.9 Unique Properties of Cholinergic Neurons and the Evolution of Higher Intellect

In this section, it is proposed that cholinergic neurons possess properties that could enable postnatally induced alterations in their developmental blueprint to be conveyed to, permeate, and make corresponding changes in the germ line of males and thereby alter the nature of the intellectual abilities of their progeny.

What are these properties? First, the cell networks most associated with higher intelligence are cholinergic, develop postnatally, and are highly responsive to critical-period experiences. Second, despite the blood-brain and blood-testes barriers, substantial biochemical communication between the testes and the brain does occur. Third, acetylcholine receptors have been found in germinal cells,[61] and, last, the peptides active in these "smart cells" have access to the only area of the brain where a reservoir of new neurons and glia continues to be generated at least through the end of childhood.

In contrast to the neurotransmitters that comprise the catecholamine system, "[t]he cholinergic system does not adapt to pharmacological alterations in the availability of acetylcholine during prenatal development" (Miller and Friedhoff, 1988, p. 514). The catecholamines,[62] which can influence cognitive performance by affecting arousal, concentration, and the ability to handle stress, are able to cross the placenta and influence fetal brain development.[63] Thus, the *amine* system's influence on IQ is apt to contain a maternal bias — in contrast to the neurotransmitter acting in opposition to the *amines*, acetylcholine,[64] which would have no such bias.[65]

The production of new nerve cells in the brain ceases at birth or soon after, except in a small (cholinergic) region called the dentate gyrus.[66] Thus, adaptation to the environment generates the formation of new or enlarged dendritic branches (or spines) and synapses, rather than the formation of new neurons.

The evolution of intellect in modern man might be conceived as having been predicated on three developments: (1) an increasing specialization of labor between the brain's hemispheres (lateralization), (2) the ability to integrate the products of each hemisphere's analyses, and (3) a shift in cortical activity away from such decreasingly important functions as smell and toward internally generated associative and linguistic functions. Because intellectual giftedness is usually associated with cognitive deficits in other sensory-analytical areas (see Chapter Seventeen), a gifted person's intellectual prowess is likely to be less a function of the *overall* use of proteins active in cholinergic neurons than of the distribution of this "cholinergic energy." For instance, enlarged neurons in the left hemisphere's "auditory-linguistic" areas and/or the right hemisphere's "visual-linguistic deciphering" areas might mean that less cholinergic energy is distributed to the entorhinal cortex and/or to the primary visual encoders. This would result in a verbally gifted individual whose olfactory-analytical and/or primary visual functions are impaired.

As mentioned previously, the exceptional plasticity of cholinergic neurons in the cerebral cortex stems in part from nerve growth factor (NGF), which enables these neurons to grow dendrites and/or dendritic spines with extreme rapidity. Thus, an ability to incorporate environmentally induced changes in NGF distribution (within or between the cortical hemispheres) into the germ line might, in and of itself, be sufficient to induce transgenerational changes in intelligence.[67]

Consequently, it is hypothesized that, although the **"hardware"** of the genetic message—the *structural* composition of every gene's segments—is encoded in the nucleus of the germ cells of both sexes as an integral part of their *initial* development,[68] the **"software"**—the *developmental* program containing the instructions that govern the when, where, and how much of gene product expression in the brain's cholinergic neurons—is, in the male, transported to the testes, where it is affixed to the sperm during their maturation process.

The **Sertoli** cells in the testes, which provide a "nurturing womb" for sperm during their development, are apt to be essential to this process—particularly as these cells' tight junctions constitute the basis of the blood-testes barrier. The slow process by which immature sperm (spermatogonia) mature into spermatozoa begins when a large number of them enter and form a ring around the basement membrane of the Sertoli cell. After receiving relatively prolonged base-level nurturing, they are pushed along an upward path to higher levels, where different functional processes are undertaken (Bardin and others, 1988).[69] A Sertoli cell may be called on to provide for the differing needs of several generations of germ cells simultaneously (Fawcett, 1975).

These cells, whose nature and function are still not well understood, are in many respects like the neurons of the brain. First, new Sertoli cells cease being generated at birth, or just after (Nistal, Abaurrea, and Paniagua, 1982). Second, several of the features that usually characterize the nuclei of most somatic cell types are largely lacking (Fawcett, 1975). Third, the nucleus of the Sertoli cell has a large proportion of euchromatin, which strongly implies that a large proportion of its genome is actively expressed.[70] Sertoli cells also have numerous and uniquely shaped mitochondria, in comparison with those found in other organs.[71]

The well-demonstrated effects of the male sex hormone testosterone on brain lateralization indicate the extent to which the sex glands are capable of influencing brain biology and suggest that, at puberty, paternal influence on hemispheric specialization may be far greater than maternal influence.[72] Other evidence of testes-to-brain communication includes a recent finding that a protein (sulfated glycoprotein) that is believed to originate only in Sertoli cells is expressed in the brain.[73] Thus, the intercommunication between the brain and the testes may be a two-way process, with information concerning the distribution patterns of certain neuropeptides (such as those active in cholinergic neurons) being transported from the brain to the testes. Further, because spermatogonia lie outside the blood-testes barrier before they become attached to the Sertoli cells and the Sertoli cells afterwards "govern" what passes through this barrier, ample opportunities exist for messages from the brain to imbue these sperm precursors. In addition, since neither the blood-brain barrier nor the blood-testes barrier is fully mature at birth,[74] experiences during the initial months of infancy might be passed through these immature barriers to the (already mature) Sertoli cells during this limited period of time.[75]

19.10 Until What Age Might Adaptive Changes in Human Intellect Be Heritable?

For adaptively generated changes in a major aspect of human intelligence to be heritable, environmental exposure must be able to engender significant, lasting changes in the neurobiological underpinnings to that aspect of intelligence, and these changes must be transmittable to one's progeny. Thus, adaptive evolution faces two kinds of constraints: (1) adaptive plasticity is constrained by an increasing rigidity in the information-processing systems that underlie a cognitive skill, and (2) whatever mechanism enables adaptive changes to be incorporated into the genome of germ cells may not be able to incorporate newly generated changes across the entire reproductive lifetime of the individual.

The distance between directly connected cholinergic cell populations in the brain is often relatively large, and after their communication channels have been firmly established, the intervening territory may become "hostile" biochemically. To protect the integrity of these connections and the strength of the electrical impulses they convey, the (message-sending) axons of these neurons become encased in myelin sheaths. The timing of the formation of "tracts" of myelin sheaths that link specific cell networks can then serve to mark the beginning, middle, and ending points in the establishment of permanent communication channels between these "smart-cell" networks. Formation of these sheaths indicates that "canalization" has limited the functional flexibility of a cell network, and its developmental blueprint may be said to have finished unfolding.

Such functional abilities may be thought of in terms of the cognitive activities that cells can be programmed to perform; thus, the development of adult competence in a given cognitive domain incorporates three elements:

- *Genetic endowment.* This is set by one's genes, together with the blueprint governing the pattern for their expression that is inherited from one's ancestors (genetic endowment is also called *innate* capacity).
- *Developed capacity.* This reflects a person's genetic endowment after it has been modified by environmental experiences during critical periods of brain infrastructural development.
- *Capability.* This refers to a person's *momentary* ability to make effective use of an established capacity; this is modifiable throughout life by recent practice, within the limits set by developed capacity, and it has come to be called *plasticity.*

Some of these "smart-cell" network intercommunication channels form between birth and six months of age — for example, the auditory and visual connections through the thalamus to the sensory-analytical areas of the cortex that finish myelinating at about four months. Thus, there is a brief period during which environmentally induced changes can be incorporated into the germ line through what is still an immature blood-brain barrier.

Most of the cognitively important cell-network connections are "hard wired" very early in a child's life, including the interhemispheric connections between the two halves of the frontal cortex (which finish myelinating at about one year), the corpus callosum (by age two), the left hemisphere's speech-strategy and speech-execution areas — where, at fifteen months of age, new first-order dendrites are sprouting from the cell bodies and toddlers' receptive language skills are expanding explosively (Simonds and Scheibel, forthcoming; Scheibel and others,

1985). Lastly, by age four, the posterior commissure, the thalamic connections to the temporal lobe, and the initial speech and association cortical tracts have all been "wired." Many others, however, are formed during later childhood,[76] and some continue myelinating into adolescence.[77] The final stages of the last-to-mature area, the association cortex (where Albert Einstein's giftedness was highly evident), are not completed until the early or mid forties (Yakolev and Lecours, 1967; Dobbing and Sands, 1973; Martinez, 1982; Holland, 1986) when (perhaps not coincidentally) longitudinal studies indicate that verbal skills reach their lifetime peak (see section 5.4).

If the *existing* developmental blueprint of cholinergic neurons is transmitted to sperm cells during these cells' maturation process, then the continuing development of the association cortex until people reach their mid forties could be related to the progressively higher IQ scores found with increasing paternal age. For instance (as detailed in Chapter Two), several studies have shown that the *average* **paternal** age when gifted and eminent people were born was thirty-seven, *even though a majority of these people were firstborns*. Furthermore, the continuing upslope in children's IQ scores with increasing maternal age (such as reported in Chapter Two for the mothers of 37,000 English schoolchildren adjusted for social class and birth order)[78] might in part or in the main be a reflection of increasing paternal age.[79]

To summarize, the potential for the transmission of adaptive changes to one's progeny is constrained by (1) the nature and developmental timetables of the brain/germ-line barrier, and (2) the reduction in adaptive plasticity of cell networks that accompanies the completion of their infrastructure growth. The principal positions concerning the possible transmission of adaptive changes are as follows:

- *The neo-Darwinian position* asserts that the principles of random mutation and survival of the fittest (plus genetic drift) are fully responsible for the rapid pace of human *brain* evolution.
- *The minimalist position* is that, because the blood-brain barrier does not approach adult competency until perhaps six months of age, biological responses to increasingly competent early parenting

may enable biologically advantageous changes to permeate the germ line and alter hormonal balances in succeeding generations. Because the auditory and visual analysis areas of the cortex become "hooked up" to their midbrain source of sensory inputs by the fourth month of infancy, the experiences of the first several postnatal weeks or months could be analogous to what, in certain animals, has come to be called the "imprint" period (see Chapter Eleven). Thus, the full impetus for rapid intellectual evolution can be explained in terms of these early experiences (such as teaching an infant that particular shapes and sounds have a special salience).

- *A male-oriented pubescent transfer of the developmental blueprint* implies that until a male reaches puberty, changes in his developmental blueprint can affect his contribution to his offspring's developmental blueprint. By contrast, the developmental blueprint that a female will pass on to her offspring is, in the main, determined before she is born, but with some alterations possible from her hormonal inputs to her growing embryo and neonate through the placenta and milk until the blood-brain barrier forms. Thus, in the male, limits on the transmission of adaptive changes are set by prepubescent constraints on plasticity and by the nature of the proteins permitted passage through the blood-testes barrier.

- *A male-oriented transfer beginning at puberty* implies that newly maturing sperm cells contain the developmental blueprint of the male as he is during their maturation. Because myelin tract formation continues in some areas until one's early forties (such as the tracts connecting cholinergic neurons in the frontal and association cortex), the positive correlation between children's IQ and paternal age could be attributable to the biological manifestations of continued IQ gains rather than being entirely a product of greater emotional maturity.

Under any of the last three constructs, the extent to which environment will alter the heritability of a person's *developed capacity* in a given "aspect" of human intellect is then theorized to be dependent on the following:

- The timetables for the development of the inner dendritic branches of the neurons performing the functions that underlie the cognitive abilities in question.
- The extent to which the *developmental blueprint* of each of these cell networks is susceptible to environmental influence (which, in part, depends on whether they go through a transitory prenatal cholinergic period, a transitory postnatal cholinergic period, or remain cholinergic throughout life).
- The extent to which the physical and cultural environments (1) influence cognitive behavior in ways that foster growth in particu-

lar portions of the postnatally developing brain and detract from growth in others and (2) restrict the choice of one's mate to people sharing similar cognitive backgrounds.

19.11 Altering "Experience-Expectant" Brain Organization

Although some eminent researchers still conceive of a newborn baby's brain as a blank slate or tabula rasa (Hellerstein, 1988), it has become increasingly evident that much of the human brain's neuronal circuitry is "preprogrammed" to recognize and respond to stimuli in ways that are specifically related to ancestral experience. For example, newborn infants possess an innate preference for the principal features of the human face over comparable patterns[80] and encode speech sounds very differently from the way in which they encode other auditory stimuli.

This strongly suggests that genetically prescribed biological processes direct how the brain's neuronal circuitry is assembled and that these processes include "sensory filters" through which stimuli are screened, as well as schemata for classifying and storing these perceptions.[81] Much of the neuronal circuitry responsible for higher brain function can then be conceived of as "developmentally probabilistic," in that its final form is governed by fuzzy sorts of rules that specify neuronal form, location, and connectivity. Then, given even a modest amount of reinforcement, the unfolding biological system will be sensitive to and organize itself around experiences that have occurred reliably in an individual's "ancestral history." In this respect, the genome's developmental blueprint can be viewed as a specifier of tissue structure—with these "selectional guidelines" possessing sufficient critical-period plasticity to incorporate unique aspects of the environment into the circuitry governing these prototypical "knowledge structures."[82]

This concept is aptly demonstrated by John Kovach's detailed studies (Kovach, 1983, 1985, 1986), which show that strong genetic proclivities are able to inhibit the expression of conflicting learning and to facilitate the expression of congruent learning. In addition, "[a] genetic trait that is not subject to selective identification and genetic selection under one set of developmental circumstances may become identifiable and naturally or artificially selectable under another set of conditions" (Kovach, 1986, p. 114).[83] Kovach's studies and analyses lead him to the further conclusion that—before such a routine expression of a preexisting but rarely expressed genetic trait can be achieved— the environmental exposure must first induce the trait to breach a "threshold of penetrance."[84]

Thus, "unusual" early environmental experiences may be able to induce a switch from what is "the usual experience-expectant" neuronal organization to a previously existing alternative organization— and, in the process, facilitate the continued expression of this "preadaptive" organization.

A key question then becomes, Given a preadaptive potential, how many generations might it take for an adaptively advantageous cognitive ability to become prevalent in a population? As suggested below, when environmental exposure *is coupled with selective mating*, the answer could be, Very few. For example, a massive study of maze learning in rats found that seven generations of experience coupled with selective mating produced a strain of rats that were exceptionally proficient in what is now recognized as a specific cognitive domain: self-in-space learning and memory.[85] These rats seldom entered blind alleys and showed less hesitation at choice points.[86]

With respect to recent evolution in humans, once decisions respecting mates become increasingly governed by cultural practices and restrictions, these practices make possible a rapid spread (fixation) of newly expressed preadaptive abilities. In conjunction with an increasing specialization of labor and a proclivity to protect physically weak members of a clan, these culturally determined survival and procreation criteria have now superseded environmentally based selection processes in defining the attributes that constitute "fitness."

Some social anthropologists have suggested that the combination of (1) innovation and (2) the social transmission of learned behavior is able to generate selection pressures that favor complementary anatomical evolution (Wyles, Kunkel, and Wilson, 1983).[87] E. O. Wilson and Charles Lumsden, for instance, suggest that these factors might make it possible for substantial genetic evolution of cognitive traits in humans to occur over a 1,000-year gene-culture "coevolutionary cycle" (Lumsden and Wilson, 1981; Wilson, 1975).

The findings presented in Chapter Twenty, however, strongly suggest that the speed at which domain-specific intellectual giftedness has permeated large populations **is considerably faster** —*particularly when (1) the culture has a strong impact on behavior, (2) the cultural practices are nearly uniform, (3) the society has been isolated reproductively, and (4) the possession of exceptional aptitude in the cognitive domain has been and still is highly valued and has been "trained for."*

Although neo-Darwinianists may be able to use survival-of-the-fittest doctrines to explain certain of the culturally linked domain-specific "population superiorities" delineated in Chapter Twenty (such as the exceptional spatial skills possessed by many Eskimos), other examples of the proposed human model that depict **the hereditary transmission of newly utilized adaptive versatility** are less receptive to explanation by this "survival" principle.[88]

Whether this intergenerational transmission of biological *proclivities* meets the classic definition of evolution is apt to depend on three factors: (1) the nature of the processes that govern the creation of new adaptive plasticity, (2) whether the generation of "potential" giftedness is a single stage or a multistage and multigeneration process, and (3) whether the creation of new forms of a gene is an essential part of this process. If, on the one hand, environmental pressures favoring the use of existing plasticity in a particular direction *generate* movements in people's *adaptive potential* in the same direction—and close off potential "plasticities" in other directions—then this process would seem to meet the formal definition of evolution. But if, on the other hand, the process of generating new adaptive potentials is separate from, and not affected by, the extent to which existing potentials are being used, then this process could fall short of meeting such a formal definition.

Although the transition from an "ungifted" to a "gifted" state might, in some domains or instances, be predicated on the existence of a simple single-stage process, the evidence seems to favor a multistage, multigeneration interpretation of the process at work.[89] In such a model, the "activation" of a normally present but generally unexpressed form of a gene in one generation would be a necessary precedent to the establishment of the potential for giftedness in the next. The switch to the "giftedness-facilitating" form of the gene would be induced by environmental stress, which would then enable those offspring who already possess a particular gene (or combination of genes) to acquire the *potential* for giftedness—a potential whose fulfillment would then depend on the early environment. In such instances, the penchant for giftedness might be conceived of as "evolving," but the processes governing its evolution might still not satisfy the classical definition of evolution.[90] If the effects of environment on the developmental blueprint do lead to the activation of a preexisting alternative form of gene expression (see Technical Note One), *and this makes it either **easier** or routine for a subsequent generation to express this alternative form*, then the question of whether this process constitutes an evolutionary phenomenon would appear to depend on whether new gene products result from this change. If the biological processes leading to the attainment of an exceptional ability do not engender the production or use of proteins that differ from those found in the brains of nongifted people, but are predicated solely on *changes in the **amounts** of various proteins produced and/or used in particular brain regions*, would not such adaptive changes then constitute something less than a full-fledged "evolutionary" phenomenon?[91] Again, what if multiple alleles exist for the expression of a gene, and the "creation" of the potential for giftedness merely requires the substitution of a *tandem duplicate* (which may not differ from the previously active copy except in its proximity to the DNA sequences that regulate its expression)?[92] In either event, the existing definition of the term *evolution* would seem in need of some refinement to specifically include or exclude the effects of such a "threshold penetration" of adaptive plasticity.

Nevertheless, with at least 20,000 different proteins being produced and used in the brain, and many genes having the capacity to produce a number of different proteins, it is likely

that the development of at least some types of intellectual giftedness have necessitated the expression of a preexisting but previously unexpressed capacity to produce a given protein (or to
produce it in an alternative manner in a particular brain region).[93] If some of the many changed "instructional messages"
needed to enlarge the neurons that perform a cognitive task (or
to "recruit" the assistance of cells that, in one's forefathers, performed different functions) have engendered a single instance
in which the creation of a "new" protein has occurred, then
evolution would be an appropriate term for this ***multigenerational
transmission of adaptive versatility***.

Technical Note One: The Extraordinary Adaptive Plasticity of Tadpoles in Desert Ponds

The term *plasticity* is used to denote the ability of an organism to adapt to
variability in its environment. When the environmental conditions faced by
that organism during its early development are highly variable, it is advantageous to have a high degree of adaptive plasticity, and such plasticity tends
to be present. For such plasticity to exist, it must have evolved, and there must
have been (and still be) considerable variability in the extent of plasticity
possessed by individual members of the population in question.

To explore these questions, this technical note presents findings from an
excellently conceived series of studies by Robert Newman concerning the
developmental plasticity of tadpoles in desert ponds (Newman, 1988a,
1988b).

In certain American Southwestern desert areas, toads breed in small rain-
filled depressions that are extremely variable in their duration.[94] Rapid
development (which results in a smaller size at metamorphosis) is particularly advantageous in short-duration "ponds," with slower development
advantageous in long-duration ponds. These studies have revealed the existence of a process by which heredity and environment have jointly effectuated a trade-off between a tadpole's "fitness" for survival in long- or short-
duration ponds and the extent to which its developmental timetable and/or
size is influenced by its early environment.[95] Specific findings include:

Pond duration did not affect all sibling groups in the same way, as
increased development time did not benefit all sibships equally in terms of
their size at metamorphosis. Of the five sibships studied (1) the two that
developed most rapidly in short-duration ponds were no larger at metamorphosis in the long-duration ponds; (2) one metamorphosed at a much
larger size in long-duration ponds, but in short-duration ponds its slow
development resulted in a high mortality rate; and (3) the two remaining
sibships evidenced an adaptive plasticity well suited for survival in ponds of
varying duration.

These results demonstrate that some tadpole sibships can alter their developmental trajectories in response to pond drying and that genetic factors determine whether this adaptive plasticity is present, with three disparate genotype/phenotype "interactive models" seen in five sibships.

A key question that further studies in this area might be able to address is, How many generations would it take for this adaptive plasticity to dissipate or disappear if future environmental conditions caused one of these "developmental tracks" to fall into disuse?[96]

Technical Note Two: Adaptive Plasticity in the Salience of Shapes

A facility in categorizing shapes represents an important survival element in solving certain types of problems found on IQ tests. Evidence that shape-categorization skills are a learned (as well as an innate) aptitude would provide part of the rationale for the extraordinarily rapid rise in nonverbal IQ scores during the present century, as well as suggest an important ingredient of early childhood education programs.

Experiments with animals demonstrate that exposure to particular kinds of environmental stimuli during specific stages of early postnatal development is essential to their becoming cognizant that these stimuli have a special significance. In a famous experiment with cats (Hubel and Wiesel, 1970), the ability to maneuver vertically (which enables cats to land properly when they jump) was shown to depend on an early exposure to "verticalness"—as evidenced by a permanent loss of cats' ability to perceive the importance of this dimension when they were raised in an environment devoid of such experiences until they were fourteen weeks old. Because cats' jumping and springing behavior is clearly innate, this experiment shows that *innate cognitive activities and abilities* requiring visual perception need early environmental reinforcement—or else the development of the cells that perform this function will be altered.

Similarly, it has been amply demonstrated that the human neonate is "preprogrammed" to give special significance to particular shapes—for example, the human face (in a zero-degree alignment). Because the neurons that compare incoming shapes with those previously given a special salience have analogous or identical responsibilities in humans and cats, these cells can be presumed to be—and indeed have been shown to be—extremely similar (structurally, biochemically, functionally, and locationally). Consequently, these results suggest that, in humans, preprogrammed visuospatial analytical mechanisms are responsive to early childhood stimulation and deprivation.

To examine this area empirically, Allport and Pettigrew (1957) combined a famous illusion—which is based on the ability to perceive what appears (to people familiar with rectangular-shaped objects) to be a window—and a population with virtually no environmental exposure to rectangles. This so-called Ames trapezoid illusion uses a rotating trapezoid-shaped window to create an illusion that (rather than rotating) the window sways back and forth at an arc of 90 to 180 degrees.[97] When a cube and a rod are added, the subjects' interest is heightened considerably, since the way in which these objects rotate conflicts sharply with the perceived swaying of the "window." The cube is then seen as detaching itself and swinging without support in front of the "window" in a ghostly fashion (during that period of time when the shorter edge is nearer to the subject), and the rod is seen to bend or to cut through the panels of the "window" to accommodate the window's oscillation.

The cultural upbringing of Zulu children living on the Nongoma reservation in the middle 1950s was exceptionally spherical. Zulu huts were invariably round or beehive shaped, had no windows, and their doors were round entrance holes. Further, the Zulu language has no word for window or for such concepts as square or rectangle. Because this illusion is predicated on the observer's conceiving of the trapezoid as a rectangle, which, in turn, is predicated on the assumption that straight lines and rectangles form the basis of the observer's object-recognition categories, the authors hypothesized that the lack of early familiarity with these shapes[98] would prevent most or all of the Nongoma children from being able to perceive the illusion. The results confirmed these expectations; only three of the twenty Nongoma boys aged ten to fourteen (who had never been off this reservation) were able to see the illusion,[99] compared with twenty-four of forty urban counterparts.[100] Similarly, in further studies, (1) only two of twenty-four children from another (deep) part of the reservation (Ceza) perceived the illusion, compared with fourteen of twenty-one urban controls; and (2) none of eleven expectant mothers (all of whom had never been off the reservation) could perceive it.

Thus, in humans, the salience of shapes, *although genetically preprogrammed*, is environmentally responsive, and this suggests that experience with toys that teach shape analysis during the so-called critical or sensitive period of brain development[101] can have a permanent effect on IQ scores.

Notes

1. Two-thirds, according to a recent estimate (Hahn, personal communication, 1988). As more organs have been examined, this proportion has tended to decline slightly (Hahn and Owens, forthcoming). Earlier estimates of 30,000 different brain-active genes (Sutcliffe, Milner, and Bloom, 1983) now appear to be somewhat overstated, because the complexity (sequence length) of "nonhousekeeping" brain-active genes is usually far beyond the norm. Because genes can be used in the "manufacture" of more than one protein, the number of proteins in the brain is far greater than the number of genes.

2. Approximately 19 percent of so-called single-copy DNA is transcribed into nuclear RNA. Because only one of the DNA strands tends to be a "sense" strand, and the other its inactive complement, this proportion (in terms of a "sense strand" equivalent) is likely to be almost double or 33 percent (Hahn, personal communication, 1988), with a higher proportion likely in the "most advanced" areas of the brain, such as the cerebral cortex and the hippocampus. The remaining DNA sequences, the so-called introns (or intervening sequences

that neither code for proteins nor govern gene function) are composed primarily of "random" arrangements of letters of the genetic alphabet, plus some repetitive noncoding sequences.

3. As indicated by findings that elsewhere in the body, whenever a DNA sequence is found in the ribosomes in adulthood, it is also found there at birth. These findings in rodents are thought to closely resemble what would be found in human beings (Chaudhari and Hahn, 1983).

4. Because postnatally activated DNA messages are much longer and more complex than those already present in the ribosomes at birth, only a small fraction of total brain protein is composed of these complex "rarer class" proteins. These have generally come to be known as "poly A⁻" sequences, because a marker for their message-ending point (called a tail) is not found in the usual position (Hahn and others, 1983).

5. A neuron's message-receiving connections (dendrites) have come to be called "dendritic trees." The so-called inner branches include the primary (first-order) branches that emanate from the cell body, plus its second and third orders of branching, with fourth and higher orders of branching called outer branches. A neuron's outer branches usually contain more receptors for excitatory neurotransmitters (which promote firing), and its inner branches more inhibitory receptors.

6. An event that can often be demarked by the formation of myelin sheaths around bundles of axons linking the neurons of relatively distant cell networks.

7. By age two, the nonwater content of the brain has reached approximately 72 percent of adult values; the gain from birth to age two constitutes two-thirds of the total postnatal increase (Dobbing and Sands, 1973; Dobbing, 1981). The consistent findings, from studies of rodents exposed to "enriched housing conditions" after weaning, of a significant increase in the number of outer branches (in large pyramidal and stellate neurons), without a corresponding increase in the number or length of their inner branches, distinguish the effects of early enrichment from those associated with the lifelong outer-branch plasticity of these neurons. The length and number (and possibly the thickness) of these inner branches determine a neuron's ability to support (or facility in supporting) outer-branch growth, as well as the number (and size) of its synaptic connections.

8. The dendritic development of some populations of neurons in the cerebral cortex occurs in stages, with the right hemisphere taking the lead during certain periods and the left during others. For some neuronal populations, the end of such critical periods can be marked by the formation of myelin sheaths around their axons; early deprivation can (for some functions but not others) considerably delay the end of such critical periods.

9. As well as the neurons of the hippocampus to which they are also connected. These are called pyramidal and stellate neurons (the latter generally having "spiny" synapses); neurons with spiny synapses apparently serve as rapidly constructable temporary informational

stores. Apparently, "retrieval cues" for (often geographically diverse) aspects of episodic and thematic memory are (after memory consolidation) stored in neurons with "nonspiny" synapses. In contrast to synaptic connections on dendritic branches, spiny synaptic connections are only weakly adhesive (Scheibel and Paul, 1985; Lund, 1984); they may be extremely dense (for example, 5,000 to a dendrite in the hippocampus not being unusual).

10.   During prenatal development, many other neuronal populations go through "cholinergic periods," during which NGF is used in the processes of dendritic growth and/or spiny-synapse formation; NGF receptor molecules are also found in the thalamus, even though no NGF effects are normally seen there (Taniuchi, Schweitzer, and Johnson, 1986). It might be speculated that the "self-repair" capabilities of the thalamus explain these receptors' presence after this cholinergic period ends.

11.   The excellent suitability of rodents as experimental animals stems from their relatively rapid gestation and sexual maturation, which (coupled with the size of their litters and the relatively small space needed for their maintenance) makes for a low cost per animal. Also, because inbreeding does not affect rodents adversely, it has been possible to "mass produce" genetically identical strains of rodents.

12.   The human cortex has six distinct layers; the rodent brain has three layers and no convolutions.

13.   Although other cortical areas are also affected, the occipital cortex shows the greatest changes. Maze training produces somewhat different effects, in terms of the nature of the dendritic growth produced and the magnitude of effects in different cortical areas (Greenough, 1976).

14.   Even when the enrichment is begun when rats are the human equivalent of seventy-five years of age (Diamond and others, 1985). The closer one gets to the midline of the brain, the greater the effect on cortical depth, particularly in the middle layer of the three-layer rodent cortex.

15.   The overall width of the cortex is likely to increase only if the enrichment is begun long before the end of weaning. When the overall findings (for example, an 8 percent increase in the thickness of the occipital cortex after 20 days of enrichment begun at 6 days of age and a 5 percent thickening after 138 days of exposure begun at 766 days) are applied to the middle cortical layer, the percentages are more than doubled. In one preweaning enrichment experiment (a large cage with three mothers and their litters, with a variety of toys), a 16 percent enlargement in the lateral occipital cortex was reported (Malkasian and Diamond, 1971), and, in another such study (Walsh, 1981), a 14 percent increase in the size of the lateral part of the frontal portion of the corpus callosum was reported ($p = .001$).

16.   In the "super-enriched" condition, the rats were housed in two large cages connected by tunnels and were provided with varied stimulus objects. They were made to shuttle back and forth between the cages (to get food in one and water in the other). Gradually, they were

made to solve problems and to climb ropes, or to jump from one platform to another to traverse the tunnels (Kuenzle and Knusel, 1974, summarized in Bennett, 1976). After three successive experiments gave similar results, the Berkeley and Urbana researchers further enhanced their "standard" enrichment condition by rotating animals among cages and providing more opportunities for climbing. This resulted in greater biological effects (including greater forebrain weight gains).

17. The increase in RNA synthesis reached significance within four days; similarly, cortical weight differences reached maximum levels fifteen to thirty days after enrichment was begun and then declined to a persisting, small difference. An increase also occurred in the number of a type of glial cell that provides structural support for these new and enlarged outer dendritic branches, with a slight increase in the amount of acetylcholine attributed to its presence in these glial cells (Walsh, 1981).

18. Mutations in their "structural" DNA sequences caused by single-letter transcription errors.

19. There was no diversity at twenty-three of the ninety-seven sites examined; three or four variants appeared at fifteen sites, including eleven of the thirty-three governing immune function, but at only four of the sixty-two protein-coding sites. Thus, viral infections were clearly not a primary cause of the (two-allele) findings.

20. 145 of 169 substitutions. Nearly half of these sequences constituted so-called parallel (or back) substitutions of one of the genetic sequences contained in the other half of these (145) variants.

21. Given their common ancestry, the number of intervening generations, and the relatively low frequency of loci with three or more alleles.

22. And, consequently, no greater rate of creation of unique DNA sequences. Point mutations consist of either single genetic "letter" (base-pair) mutations or single "letter" crossovers (translocations).

23. The giant panda is a case in point. This animal's chromosomal and morphological evolution has been immense. By examining this panda's chromosomes during prenatal development, however, researchers (O'Brien and others, 1985, p. 144) have concluded that its "evolutionary journey" has resulted primarily from positional changes in regulatory sequences rather than from mutations in structural genes. Using primary fibroblasts, the authors conclude that the ancestral history of this panda's chromosomes closely resembles that of a bear; then, as development progressed, these chromosomes underwent a massive rearrangement away from the primitive carnivore karyotype. The authors note, "Remarkably, nearly every large chromosome of the brown bear could be aligned with a giant panda chromosome arm." These chromosomes were "composed largely of bear chromosomes fused together in Robertsonian translocations." Smaller pandas are genetically unrelated to the giant panda.

24. Particularly if one accepts the proposition that modern birds are a "young" group, unrelated to those birds that were wiped out or all but

wiped out by a catastrophe sixty-five million years ago; point-mutation rates confirm this relatively short history. Birds were once thought to be more uniform anatomically than most classes of vertebrates.

25. By these measures, songbirds' relative brain size is about equal to that of hominoids (excluding man), twice that of other mammals, five times that of other birds, and a fifth that of man.

26. Although regulatory elements are tightly linked to the structural parts of a gene and in most cases act together (Klarenberg, 1988), regulatory genes may be distant (they may be located on the same chromosome or on other chromosomes). Such positional changes may include a transposition of the entire DNA sequence comprising an intron, in relation to the position of the other introns that compose the genes' protein-coding segments. Some types of regulatory genes have been given such functional names as "enhancers" and "promoters."

27. The importance of variation in these regulatory genes and elements has only recently been recognized, particularly with respect to these tissue-specific and life-stage-specific aspects (Klarenberg, 1988; MacIntyre, 1982).

28. Within a chromosome, and they will sometimes "hop" across chromosomal borders (usually as part of a "transposon" package containing protein-coding DNA segments). Functionally related genes do not need to be in close geographical proximity to one another.

29. The concept "one-gene/one-protein" has given way to an understanding that genes can be used in the "manufacture" of (for example) "families" of proteins and that movements of these regulatory sequences, by imbuing genes with different "instructional tags," may enable a single protein (such as calcitonin) to perform different functions in different environments (the brain and the body).

30. Which often results from an unequal crossing-over of chromosomes during cell division (leaving two copies of a DNA sequence on one cell and none on the other) or from a duplicative transposition of a DNA segment (such as an entire exon). This also occurs during the cell division that leads to the formation of the haploid germ cell (sperm or egg). "An unequal crossing-over occurring during the meiosis of a heterozygote can result in placing two former alleles of the same gene locus on the same chromosome" (Ohno, 1970, p. 92).

31. In evolutionary history, gene duplication is usually followed by accelerated amino acid substitutions; this has been demonstrated in the development of genes such as those that code for somatostatin and growth hormone (Li, 1985). Because this acceleration is limited to a relatively short period after duplication and because "no anomalies are observed in these amino acid substitutions," Ohta (1988, p. 375) argues that "positive selection" must (at least in large part) be responsible for this acceleration.

32. In mammals, most types of proteins are encoded by a series of related gene copies organized as multigene families. In some cases, the gene copies are identical to one another (the number of tandem duplicates

can be considerable and need not be under the control of a single regulatory gene locus).

33. Genes are the chemical substrates on which enzymes operate. There are at least twenty diverse enzymes capable of effecting an enormous variety of alterations in the structure of gene molecules (for a partial list, see Campbell, 1985, 1987), including transferring silent gene copies into special sites at which they can be expressed. Thus, these enzymes are indispensable to the expression and the evolution of complex multigene families; to achieve control and precision over these processes, multigene families have evolved elaborate control systems called "governors" (Campbell, 1982, 1983) to regulate their alteration by enzymes.

34. The developmental blueprint of any complex organism contains many crucial instructions for gene duplication, in particular for the duplication of regulatory genes (as this permits structural genes to have different uses in different tissue types at different developmental stages). Thus, the insertion of an additional copy of a regulatory DNA segment can alter the rate at which a gene's mRNA is transcribed, because it might be recognized by different types of transfer-RNA molecules, based on its proximity to them. The distinction is also made (Milkos and John, 1987) between efforts to study DNA sequences surrounding a gene's transcriptional parts (to learn about where, when, and how rapidly certain proteins are made, modified, and dispensed with) and to study the processes governing developmental regulation (for example, which "perfumes" in the growth environment say to a neuron's dendrite "come to me" or tell a migrating cell where to stop). Transgenes are now serving as probes for active chromosomal domains in development; one of those mapped developmentally is used for spatial and olfactory specificity in the developing and adult brain (Allen and others, 1988).

35. This is used to explain why, in multigene families undergoing rapid evolutionary change, little variation is found between members of a species, compared with interspecies variation.

36. A supplementary mechanism that induces exchanges of sequence information between chromosomes is suggested. This hypothesis is bolstered by such findings as that each of the five human chromosomes containing rDNA also contains every subfamily member (Krystal, Ruddle, and Arnheim, 1981); the extent of such exchanges would influence the extent to which members of a population evolve in unison.

37. Producing, for example, a three-to-one ratio of parental alleles at a given site rather than the normal two-to-two ratio. The frequency of gene conversion is locus specific and allele specific. A single gene-conversion event can involve more than one cistron; because it may also occur at meiosis and cause another "aberrant" event, post-meiotic segregation (Holliday, 1986), it could provide a means for the unfolding developmental blueprint to incorporate ancestral experience directly.

38. These sites are thought to have both promotor and recombinant

activity. This might enable an organism to "selectively" repress or remove nonbeneficial variants or undesirable methylation state defects (Holliday, 1986).

39. Transgenes are foreign genes that are introduced into zygotes or early embryos and become a permanent part of the genome; it appears that such genes are expressed only if the cytosine at adjacent sites is less than fully methylated. In all but one of the transgenic experiments where sex differences in methylation states have thus far been reported (Marx, 1988; Sapienza, forthcoming), the fully methylated version was transmitted by the female and the less-methylated version by the male; this exceptional line of transgenic mice, however, died out.

40. Moreover, alterations in the rate of transcriptional activity of transgenes during spermatogenesis have also been reported (Groudine and Conkin, 1985; Razin, Cidar, and Riggs, 1984), implying that movements in "regulatory sequences" of DNA were responsible for this change. In the human adult male, approximately 30 percent of testicular cells are in some stage of development (Hecht, 1987).

41. In one of these transgenic experiments, the expression of a gene was irreversibly repressed following its passage through the female germ line (Hadchouel and others, 1987).

42. A conclusion that the age of onset of Huntington's disease is primarily under genetic rather than environmental control emanates from findings that identical twins show far less variability in age of onset than do fraternal twins (Conneally, personal communication to Carmen Sapienza, 1988, summarized in Sapienza, forthcoming).

43. This review reported on 111 studies that furnished information on familial resemblances in cognitive ability; 140 studies were examined, but 29 were discarded through the application of explicit quality criteria (related to the populations studied and/or the cognitive measure employed), and all studies bearing the authorship of Sir Cyril Burt were also excluded (see notes to Chapter One). Because parents' IQ scores show only modest positive correlations with one another (+ .33), these results obviously cannot be attributed to the existence of a close correspondence between parental IQs.

44. The correlation between the IQs of children and their biological parents averaged + .42 (a weighted average based on thirty-two studies); both father-offspring and mother-offspring correlations averaged + .41 (based on twenty-two and twenty-five studies containing this information, respectively). Further, the gender of neither the parent nor the child had any appreciable impact on the findings, as (1) mother-son correlations averaged + .39 (twelve studies) and father-son correlations averaged + .38 (fourteen studies); (2) father-daughter correlations averaged + .39 (ten studies) and mother-daughter correlations averaged + .43 (in the same ten studies); and (3) same-sex parent-offspring correlations averaged + .40 (fourteen studies), compared with + .39 for opposite-sex pairings (twelve studies).

45. This possibility seems remote, given the enormous difference in time spent, the correlational patterns shown in Part Three (especially

Chapter Eight), and the preponderance of women teachers in pre-school and early elementary school. All these factors would seem to preclude a special paternal role as a "model for learning."

46.   Although adoptive mothers are likely to be more involved with their children than biological mothers, the incremental increase in parental involvement is apt to have been much greater among adoptive fathers. In the modern era, where sterility of the adoptive father is a more frequent impetus for adoption, some have argued that the "real" enthusiasm for an adoption is apt to emanate from the mother.

47.   Because (except for one chromosome) children obtain half of their genes from each parent.

48.   This concept (the isolation of the germ line from the soma) is known as Weissmann's Doctrine. In the 1880s, August Weissmann cut off the tails of twenty successive generations of mice and demonstrated that there was no effect on the twenty-first generation.

49.   This occurs in a variety of plants; some bacteria also have mechanisms for incorporating foreign genes (for example, erythromycin-resistant streptococcus bacteria).

50.   Meaning half of the offspring of the tolerant males acquired the tolerance, as did a fourth in the following generation—with no reacquisition (of tolerance) among the offspring of nontolerant second-generation mice. Females were not used in this experiment because such tolerance might be transmittable through the milk (and/or the placenta).

51.   The actual data from the experiments of some of the critics suggest that a more limited sort of transgenerational carryover tolerance may be possible (Steele, 1981; Brent, 1981). Recent investigations designed to foster the "routine" use of transgenes as probes for active chromosomal domains in mouse development (Allen and others, 1988) suggest a reason for such disparate findings.

52.   Campbell and Perkins (1988, p. 544) note, "Most neuroendocrines have multiple target tissues and functions Some are broadcast throughout the bloodstream as endocrines,. . . many are used simultaneously to regulate and coordinate the nervous system (as neurotransmitters and neuromodulators),. . . and development (as trophic and trophic agents)." Thus, they suggest that it is more meaningful to conceive of these chemical messengers as conveyors of information (or as so-called cybernins) rather than as hormones, neuroendocrines, or hormonelike growth factors to emphasize that some cybernins (Guillemin, 1978) are recognized by a variety of different cell types and may carry out several of these interwoven functional roles, depending on the environment in which they are activated (Campbell, 1982; Campbell and Zimmermann, 1982). Consequently, Campbell and Perkins (1988, p. 545) theorize that "[t]he inheritance of thyrostat settings would only require [that] the genes activated at the critical perinatal period in the thyrotroph cell also be expressed at that time in germ cell lines." Technical Note One provides an example of this.

53.   These findings in male rodents were serendipitous, since the experi-

ment (Bakke and others, 1975) was originally meant as a control for assessing the multigenerational effects of this procedure on the progeny of treated females; similar effects were then found after treatment with thyroxin.

54. Alloxan kills or injures "beta" cells in the pancreas (Spergel, Kahn, and Goldner, 1975).

55. In contrast to the RNA of genes active outside the brain, where all DNA species expressible in the adult are also expressible (that is, present in the ribosomes) prenatally.

56. Since, with the notable exception of the brain (and possibly the testes), the blueprint governing gene expression is apparently "hard wired" before birth.

57. The recent discovery that human mitochondria are transmitted exclusively through the female germ line (Caan, Stoneking, and Wilson, 1987) adds additional credence to the possibility of there being different roles for the sexes in other evolutionary phenomena. In accessing the human DNA storehouse, these rapidly evolving organisms (which long ago established a symbiotic residence in human cells) have the capacity to take up and utilize acetyltransferase, which joins the acetyl to the choline to produce acetylcholine (Boutry and others, 1987).

58. The so-called acidic form of fibroblast growth factor (FGF) is found in the brain, retina, and testes but not in a variety of other tissues examined (Bohlen, Esch, and Baird, 1985; Esch and others, 1985). This substance could be one of the factors whose inclusion in the "paternal contribution" to the fetus is necessary for fetal growth; consequently, FGF could serve as a "carrier" for some aspects of the "developmental message."

59. Accompanying this massive pubescent reduction in glucose use, considerable numbers of receptor sites for acetylcholine in, for example, the frontal cortex are lost (Huttenlocher, 1979), much episodic childhood memory fades, and the IQ scores of adoptive children tend to regress slightly (toward their biological parents' mean), as do the scores of children who experienced a substantial increase in IQ between the ages of four and eleven.

60. For a discussion of the *innate* salience of particular shapes, see Chapter Eleven; for a discussion of the lack of horizontal edge detectors, see Technical Note Two in this chapter; for the importance of critical-period exposure to the reinforcement of vertical edge detectors in cats, see Hubel and Wiesel, 1970; for a discussion of the utility of such redundancy, see Part Five.

61. If findings in toad oocytes are indicative, germ cells have receptors for purines (Lotan and others, 1982) and acetylcholine, the latter apparently being activated only by acetylcholine from outside the cell (Kusano, Miledi, and Stinnaker, 1977). Further, the mitochondria of sperm and Sertoli cells have the capacity to use ChAT. Purine metabolism (as reflected in uric-acid concentrations) shows positive correlations with intelligence.

62. The catechol*amines* are dopamine, epinephrine, and norepineph-

rine, the latter two having gone by the names of adrenaline and noradrenaline; norepinephrine is a breakdown product of dopamine.

63. For example, when neuroleptics are taken during the critical stage of prenatal dopamine-receptor development, the number of dopamine receptors is reduced (by about a fourth in rodents), and the usual dopamine-receptor effects of treating that offspring with a neuroleptic are not seen. Similar cross-placental transmission is seen from taking antidepressants or Valium, with the offspring (human as well as animal) tending to show increased difficulty in coping with stress and anxiety, as well as corresponding biological effects.

64. The cholinergic and aminergic systems are "counteracting" (for example, dopaminergic activity inhibits cholinergic activity); thus, inhibiting dopamine produces a marginal increase in muscarinic receptors and (in the striatum) ChAT activity (Miller and Friedhoff, 1988).

65. The lack of effects from (pharmacological) cholinergic intervention (Miller and Friedhoff, 1988) during the second half of pregnancy is unlikely to result from a prior development of cholinergic-muscarinic receptors. After appearing in the cortex at around sixteen to eighteen weeks of age, this development is followed by slow development until twenty weeks, a four- to six-week plateau, and then a period of rapid receptor formation covering the last trimester, during which 60 percent of the receptors found at term are generated (Ravikumar and Sastry, 1985).

66. Situated in the hippocampus, this area directly connects with the cells responsible for olfactory analysis (the entorhinal cortex), the "seat of working memory" (certain hippocampal areas), and the "seat of thinking and judgment" (the frontal cortex); it appears to be capable of producing neurons, glial cells, and so-called intermediates. In rodents, these cells primarily subserve the exceptionally important "smart-cell" network associated with encoding and retaining olfactory information. In humans, it is entirely possible that these cells have been deeded over to other cognitive purposes—a theory compatible with the high rate of allergy among extraordinarily gifted people.

67. This is not meant to imply that the processes governing the transmission of environmentally induced changes to the germ line are either this simplistic or specifically involve the transportation of NGF to the germ line (either as NGF or in an altered form).

68. Encoded together with a set of constraints respecting the biochemical nature of environments in which a gene's products may be active; these are specified at conception.

69. Sertoli cells stand like long narrow trees in an orchard; to accommodate the shape of a germ cell as it is pushed along its upward path, the Sertoli cells change shape. In the rat, there are fourteen "steps" (morphological stages) of spermatogenesis, each having a constant duration (Fawcett, 1975).

70. Meaning a small proportion of heterochromatin and a large proportion of euchromatin, a finding "consistent with its being synthetically active and highly versatile in its functions" (Fawcett, 1975, p. 23).

71. Mitochondria are organisms without a nucleus but with genetic material that long ago established a residence in human cells. The pace of their "evolution" has been exceedingly rapid, and inheritance of mitochondria is transmitted solely through the female germ line. Thus, mitochondria (as part of their symbiotic relationship with humans) **might serve to speed human evolution, possibly by providing a biological template for the encoding, storing, and passing on of certain aspects of the male's biological programming to his seed**. With respect to this hypothesis, it would be interesting to compare rates of evolution in mitochondria to extremely short-term culturally based advances in human cognitive development (for example, language development). The mitochondria found in the Sertoli cells' columnar portion tend to be long and slender, and a large proportion of those found near its base are cup-shaped (Fawcett, 1975).

72. Few would argue that a pubescent boy's predisposition to be strongly "right-brained" would be greater if his immediate male forebears' "rites of passage" into manhood involved mastering a harsh physical environment than if these rites consisted of memorizing a complex verbal liturgy to be sung before a religious congregation. The issue is whether "survival of the fittest" can account for the entirety of such differences or whether environment can, over the course of a few generations, affect the heritable aspects of cognitive function so dramatically.

73. Both this and transferrin (also produced by Sertoli cells and apparently "encoded" onto sperm during maturation) are found in large quantities in the brains of Alzheimer's and Scrapie victims (Duguid, personal communication to Richard Fine).

74. The human blood-brain barrier does not reach maturity until six months after birth, based on cerebrospinal fluid studies (Adinolfo, 1985). This suggests that the central nervous system is accessible to a variety of peptides during both the prenatal and the early postnatal periods (Handelmann, 1988). This barrier is "located in the capillary endothelium or more probably in the foot processes of the glial cells which invest them" (Setchell and Waites, 1975, p. 143). Since some glial cells subserving cholinergic neurons are NGF reactive (Shelton and Reichardt, 1986) and some glia can transverse cell walls, glia might serve as neuropeptide "transport vehicles." The continuing production of new neurons and glia in the dentate gyrus might also create special messengers to aid in or to perform this process.

75. Because Sertoli cell proliferation ceases at birth, these cells may be able to encode the biochemical accoutrements of environmentally generated changes that reach them through the blood-brain barrier prior to the closure of that part of the blood-testes barrier not under the control of these cells. Moreover, neuropeptide molecules are significantly smaller than their neurotransmitter "cousins," and the "coded instructions" for a peptide's expression need not be as large as the peptide itself.

76. Including a variety of connections to the association cortex from the thalamic and speech areas, as well as portions of the hippocampal commissure.

77. Including the inferior parietal lobule, the remaining portions of the hippocampal commissure, and parts of the reticular formation.

78. For example, among thirdborn children (in each of the three occupational-class families) the highest averages were registered by children born to mothers over forty years of age.

79. Except for very young mothers, among whom it is clear that inadequacies in maternal nurture, born of maternal immaturity, are the paramount reason for their offsprings' sharply lower IQ scores.

80. Ten-minute-old infants fixated more on facial designs than on simpler patterns and preferred normal facial features over scrambled features with the same level of complexity. Virtually all forty infants exhibited the same rank order of preference among the exemplars shown (Jirari, 1970, summarized in Freedman, 1974).

81. Such schema would seemingly contain formulations of abstract concepts, as well as rules governing their valuation. From a biological perspective, to build relatively precise constructs into the brain's screening and coding apparatus is less costly than not having such biases, given the metabolic cost of converting imprecision into repeatedly used directions and maintaining unused predispositions.

82. For a theoretical approach to distinguishing between "experience-expectant" and "experience-dependent" information-storage system plasticity, see Greenough, 1986.

83. In addition to citing several studies where, after environmental treatment made a preexisting trait expressible, genetic selection resulted in the spontaneous prevalence of the trait in environmentally untreated populations, Kovach demonstrated the existence and nature of the multigenerational genetic and environmental interplay of color preferences among Japanese quail that were "imprinted" in infancy with reds and/or blues.

84. The ability to digest lactose (an ingredient of milk) in adulthood is a case in point. Human populations who are descendants of cattle-raising cultures possess lactase (the lactose-splitting enzyme) in their intestines as adults, while the rest of the world's population does not. The biochemical ability to continue to be able to digest lactose is genetically based and is presumed to have begun developing and spreading in response to the domestication and routine consumption of cow's milk, which began roughly 10,000 years ago (Flatz and Rotthauwe, 1977). The "early" cessation of lactase production in Oriental children is also presumably predicated on the ancestral environment. The ability to process the lysine found in maize and to digest fava are comparable examples.

85. As demonstrated by the effects of lesions (or microelectrode implants), this domain is controlled by a specific area of the hippocampus; the cells governing this function have come to be called "place" cells.

86. This selective mating also produced a "maze-dull" strain; these strains were neither exceptionally bright nor exceptionally dull in other learning situations (Tyron, 1940; Searle, 1949).

87. A well-known example of this occurred when some members of a

species of British birds (tits) learned to open the wax-board tops of milk bottles left on doorsteps in the early morning, an act that, within twenty-five years, became a widespread habit among three species of tit and eight other bird species in many parts of the British Isles. Because these tits are resident (rarely migrating more than a few miles from their breeding grounds), an in-depth study of first and subsequent recorded instances revealed that individual tits had learned the habit *de novo* (insight learning) and that it had then spread within these populations by imitation or learning. In some districts the practice became relatively widespread, while in neighboring districts it was unknown (Fisher and Hinde, 1949). Thus, the biochemistry of the offspring of milk-drinking tits adapted rapidly to cope with the unusual chemicals found in it (Hardy, 1965).

88. The earliness with which the precursors to these extraordinary skills become manifest—coupled with clear findings that the entire bell-shaped curve of proficiency in the cognitive domain has risen markedly—strongly suggests that the multigenerational effects of training have engendered a *biological preparedness* that enables the patterns of cognitive abilities and inabilities evidenced in offspring to mimic those trained for in their ancestors.

89. The small proportion of Jewish people with below-average verbal skills and the small proportion of Japanese people with below-average block-design scores imply that the transition from "normalcy" to intellectual giftedness has been the culmination of a multistep, multigenerational process involving the interaction of genes that bestow greater fitness in combination than alone—not the result of a single-step process involving a single gene. Further, although intellectual giftedness may arise from seemingly unexceptional family backgrounds, it is much more likely to have been preceded by a family history that includes people of considerably above average cognitive ability. In addition, the early age at which the precursors to gifted performance tend to be evident (and, by force of circumstances, the even earlier age at which the biological *underpinnings* to that giftedness must have become established) suggests that an innate biological preparedness to "imprint" and assign special salience to specific environmental stimuli preceded the exposure to these stimuli.

90. That is, when the processes for determining which preexisting adaptive plasticity to use is separate from, and has no influence on, that involved in the development of new potentials.

91. For example, the functional nature of the **cognitive deficits** found in a large proportion of extremely gifted populations suggests that, in response to the ancestral stress placed on particular (cholinergic) neuronal networks, portions of *other biochemically related neuronal populations have been* **recruited** *to help perform these cognitive functions* or to provide support to neurons that do.

92. Some genes determine the fates of cells between alternative developmental pathways. For example, the so-called notch locus in fruit flies governs whether cells will become skin or neurons; a mutant variety (producing embryos with all brain and no skin) contains thirty-six *tandem repeats* of a DNA sequence.

93. Which may depend on instructions to gene-cleaving enzymes concerning alternative sites at which to cleave.

94. Couch's spadefoot toads on Tornillo Flat in the Big Bend National Park in Texas.

95. Tadpole larvae from a single egg cluster were placed in each of eight "desert ponds," each initially standardized as to depth (four deep ponds, four shallow), size, and food supply. There were thirty tadpoles per sibship per pond and four enclosures per pond (each containing a different sibship); subsequent rainfall then created additional pond-drying variability.

96. Conversely, would the progeny of tadpoles not possessing this adaptive plasticity develop it if the pond durations to which their forefathers were exposed had been manipulated to produce alternations between long-pond and short-pond durations — and if so, how many generations would it take for adaptive plasticity to begin to evolve?

97. It is proportioned in such a way that, as it rotates, the longer edge is always longer on the retina than is the shorter edge, even when the shorter edge is nearer. Observers who are familiar with windows perceive the longer edge as nearer, and the "window" is seen to sway back and forth instead of rotating.

98. The Zulus from the reservations had little or no exposure to straight lines of any kind in their native habitat and reputedly had to be taught how to plow a straight furrow.

99. At a distance of ten feet, using both eyes; at twenty feet, with one eye, almost everyone sees the illusion.

100. There was no difference between the proportions of urban European and urban Black African males ten to fourteen years old who were able to visualize the illusion; this rules out any racially based genetic difference.

101. For example, toys that require the insertion of plastic or wooden pieces of various shapes either through or part way into similarly shaped holes.

Contents

ℵ 20 ℵ

The Multigenerational Development of Intellectual Giftedness

20.0 Thesis

Many ethnogeographic populations display exceedingly high rates of domain-specific intellectual giftedness. Several factors combine to suggest that (1) such heightened ability can become manifest in quite large populations over the course of what the classical theory of population genetics would view as an impossibly small number of generations and that (2) multigenerational adaptation to cultural and/or other environmental imperatives has been the basic driving force behind the "evolution" of these proficiencies.

This chapter further suggests that heightened domain-specific intellectual ability can permeate a population with extreme rapidity when the culture possesses the following attributes: (1) its child-rearing and educational practices are nearly uniform and have a strong influence on behavior, (2) the society has been isolated reproductively, and (3) exceptional aptitude in the cognitive domain in question is highly valued and has been cultivated.

20.1 Introduction

The world literature contains many instances of ethnogeographic cultures whose members, considered as a group, display

495

domain-specific cognitive abilities that are far superior to those routinely found in society at large. In each case, a high degree of "population superiority"[1] is manifested, this superiority appears very early in children, and there are clear links between the abilities in question and specific aspects of the maternal behavior and educational training of past generations. All these factors suggest that a single generation of such environmental exposure could not have been sufficient to produce either the overall magnitude of the effects displayed or the relatively small difference in cognitive ability found between the sexes in those instances where substantial sex-related differences existed in cognitive training.

However, for us to establish unequivocally that *multigenerational* environmental adaptation has contributed heavily to the evolution of heightened intellectual ability, human models must satisfy a number of conditions:[2]

- There must be a clear demonstration of the existence of geocultural populations whose members possess, on the average, an exceptionally high level of competence in one or more cognitive domains.
- There must be a close correspondence between the domain(s) in which heightened intellectual competence is displayed and skills that have come to be held in exceptionally high esteem by the culture and have been taught as part of its traditional parenting techniques.
- The extent of intellectual proficiency displayed — as evidenced by either an exceedingly large proportion of gifted individuals and/ or an average level of ability far above the norm (as well as by the early age at which the precocious ability becomes evident) — must be sufficiently above that of society at large to imply that its attainment could not have been entirely the result of one generation of environmental exposure on the person tested (the phenotype).
- Evidence must exist that the performance of these same populations in intellectual domains that were not given significant ancestral priority is either far less advanced or not advanced at all.
- It must be possible to show that the "adaptive advantage" generated by the possession of these heightened abilities either does not confer a strong survival advantage or that its widespread manifestation in the population occurred far too rapidly for "survival of the fittest" to form the total (or even the primary) basis for its attainment, or both.
- There must be evidence that when the traditional values and child-

rearing practices associated with the attainment of heightened skills undergo radical changes, these abilities do not disappear in one or two generations. Rather, in the absence of a cognitively stimulating environment, performance tends to regress slowly toward the norm; or if a cognitively stimulating environment is provided without these traditional practices, performance tends not to decline.

The task of demonstrating the existence of cultures whose members, on the average, excel in one or more highly valued cognitive domains is not difficult. Neither is the task of establishing that (1) this performance is linked to ancestrally determined social traditions and/or geographical imperatives; that (2) the high level of competence displayed by these populations— rather than representing a *general* ability to perform well intellectually—is domain specific; or that (3) in those cognitive areas which utilize sensory systems that receive little nurture under the culture's child-rearing practices, performance tends to be near the norm for the population at large, or even slightly below.[3]

The principal difficulty in demonstrating the **hereditary transmission of newly utilized adaptive versatility** lies in being able to subdivide the heightened cognitive abilities displayed into (1) those that are likely to have been induced in the phenotype by a single generation of training, (2) those that could have become widespread in the genotype (the population's gene pool) by the application of survival-of-the-fittest principles,[4] and (3) those that seem to imply a purposeful adaptation of the developmental blueprint in directions that serve to strengthen the offspring's biological preparedness for ancestrally stressed experiences. The findings presented in this chapter, however, support the conclusion that a multigenerational stressing of a cognitive skill that confers *any cognitive advantage—not just one having a high survival value*—will enhance domain-specific abilities.

The cultures and specific abilities selected to demonstrate these points will be discussed in the following order:

- Populations exhibiting particularly strong performance on tasks that focus on the ability to analyze spatial information, such as rural Eskimos, the Murray Islanders, and the Puluwat.

- The aptitude of the Japanese people for the structurally based sciences and how this aptitude is linked with their traditional child-rearing and educational practices.
- The verbal-conceptual analytical ability of Jewish people from Western cultures and its relation to particular aspects of traditional "Jewish mothering" and the importance placed on adroitness in verbal reasoning; this will be contrasted with the cognitive performance of Jewish people whose ancestors lived in backward (Arab) lands for several hundred years.

This will be followed by a discussion of the role of culture in determining how quickly environmentally induced changes in the expression of genomic "preadaptive versatility" might be expected to spread through a population.

20.2 Populations That Demonstrate Adaptively Evolving Heightened Spatial Ability

An analysis of the world literature reveals many instances in which an exceptionally high level of spatial competence has appeared in response to a multigenerational stressing of the specific kinds of spatial skills dictated by cultural and/or other environmental imperatives.

Rural Eskimos, for example, often evidence a superlative ability to perceive, remember, and use detailed visual information. In *Frames of Mind*, for example, Howard Gardner (1985) indicates that it is not unusual to find Eskimos who are able to read as well upside down as right side up, who can carve complexly designed figures without having to orient them correctly, or who have a knack for being able to repair never-before-seen equipment "when none of its customary users can" (p. 202). Gardner notes that in the Arctic, in the face of the near uniformity of landscape, Eskimos must possess a keen spatial intellect to travel great distances and then return home safely and that they must also be able to detect and assess slight cracks in the ice, attend to the angle and shape of small drifts of snow, and judge weather conditions quite carefully. Thus, keen spatial ability is, even today, a necessary part of survival for the rural Eskimo. Gardner concludes, "This ability presumably calls for a union of spatial skills with other forms of intelligence" (p. 202).[5]

A rather large study of visual memory for shapes, which compared the abilities of rural and semirural Eskimo children with 500 like-aged Caucasian residents of Alaska's urban centers in 1970, found that by age nine or ten, the ability of the average rural child had already surpassed that of urban-reared Caucasian children aged fourteen to sixteen (Kleinfeld, 1971). In highlighting the areas in which this visual acuity is manifest, Kleinfeld (1973) indicates that their teachers frequently comment on rural Eskimo children's exceptional "ability to quickly learn the spelling of unfamiliar words (perhaps by memorizing the word's visual form)" (p. 137).[6]

Following are some of the other ethnogeographic populations that evidence extraordinary performance in spatially oriented cognitive skills:

- *The Murray Islanders.* The visual acuity of these inhabitants of remote islands in the Coral Sea is legendary. They are able to describe objects on the distant horizon, even though a nonnative sitting beside them in a boat might only be able to see the water and the sky. In addition, they can detect extremely well camouflaged fish resting motionless against virtually identical backgrounds (Lewis, 1979).
- *The Puluwat.* The navigational abilities of these canoe-sailing inhabitants of the Caroline Islands in the South Seas have often left Western-trained navigators filled with awe: "The student at his instructor's request can start with any island in the known ocean and rattle off the stars both going and returning between that island and all the others" (Gladwin, 1970, p. 131).[7]
- *The Gikwe Bushmen.* The ability to notice and evaluate fine details by these bushmen of the Kalahari (in Africa) is astonishing; for example, many Gikwe can deduce from the spoor of an antelope not only its size, sex, and build but also its mood. Moreover, even though their territory usually encompasses many hundreds of square miles, they may know "every bush and stone, every convolution of the ground, and have usually named every place in it where a certain kind of veldt food may grow (even if that place is only a few yards in diameter) or where there is only a patch of tall grass or a bee tree" (Twan, 1974, p. 78).[7]
- *The Kikuyu.* This African tribe (from Kenya) highly prizes a keen visual memory, and the feats of its members are sometimes astounding; for example, a child of a herdsman may be taught how to recognize all the many hundreds of head of livestock in his family's herd from their color, markings, and size and type of horns (Zaslavski, 1973, p. 225).[7] Testing may include removing several

animals from the herd and requiring the child to describe those
missing, or intermingling herds and requiring the child to discern
those belonging to his family.

20.3 The Perceptual Skills of the Japanese People

The exceptional performance of the Japanese people in the
spatial and structural aspects of perception and reasoning represent a well-documented instance of the development of
domain-specific areas of superior intellectual competence. First
of all, the extent of population superiority in these cognitive
areas is so considerable that it does not seem possible for an
increase of this magnitude to have been the result of a single
generation of training. Second, a clear relationship can be
shown to exist among the areas in which the Japanese display
excellence, the nature of the culturally based child-rearing and
educational practices employed, and the kinds of early brain
stimulation that would be likely to foster development in the
particular regions of the brain used to perform these skills.
Third, because of the Japanese people's relative geographical
and ethnic isolation for at least 1,500 years, a rapid rate of
"fixation" of any environmentally generated alterations in the
developmental blueprint governing brain activity would be expected to take place. And, finally, an abrupt disappearance of
these heightened abilities has not been occurring among (Japanese American) children not exposed to this strong early regimen of maternal nurture and traditional Japanese educational
practices.

Behavioral Imperatives of the Japanese: Historical Perspective

At the beginning of the twentieth century, "[t]he Japanese had
been ethnically united for 1,000 years and were a highly homogeneous population — racially, linguistically, and culturally"
(Caudill, 1973). For over 260 years (from about 1600 through
1867), they had been ruled over by a harsh centralized authority.
Along with their "virtually complete [isolation] from the outside
world, [the existence of this centralized authority] greatly as-

sisted further development of cultural homogeneity and led to a highly prescribed and predictable behavior in social interaction, much of which was nonverbal" (Morsbach, 1973). Demeanor was so elaborately regulated that, even thirty-five years after this rule ended, Lafcadio Hearn could describe it as follows: "Everyone was trained from infancy in this etiquette of expression and deportment. . . which extracted much more than impassiveness [requiring] not only that any sense of anger or pain should be denied all outward expression. . . ([for] to betray any natural feeling under such circumstances was a grave breach of decorum). . . but that the sufferer's face and manner should indicate a contrary feeling. The strange fact is that the old-fashioned manners appear natural rather than acquired, instinctive rather than made by training" (Hearn, 1904, summarized in Morsbach, 1973, p. 263).

These social imperatives in essence commanded the Japanese mother to teach her baby to be inwardly passive and outwardly impassive, to pay strict attention to the visually observable aspects of a situation, and to learn how to exercise strict control over its body behavior.

The rural nature of the population,[8] the high frequency with which three- and four-generation families shared the same household, and the preponderance of arranged marriages, all combined to produce a similarity of mind-set. In accordance with the concepts proposed in Chapter Nineteen, this mind-set would induce similar alterations in the *developmental blueprint* that governs gene expression in the brains of people exposed to such strong and uniform traditions. It would also heighten the potential for the widespread development and hereditary transmission of any newly utilized adaptive versatility.

Cognitive Ability of the Japanese People

The considerable record of achievement of the Japanese people in such areas as mathematics, computer science, and the physical sciences is well documented. This record appears to be an outgrowth of the exceptional acumen that Japanese children display on spatially oriented IQ questions in general, on questions that focus on three-dimensional transformations,[9] and on the ability to use structural reasoning approaches to problem solving in particular.

Even though a considerable increase occurred in the average IQ scores of Japanese children born after the turmoil following World War II had subsided,[10] it is nonetheless apparent that the spatial acumen of the Japanese people has been well above the norm for the observable past. In the early 1920s, for example, tests administered to Japanese American schoolchildren born in the United States show that they were able to "significantly exceed the norms of American children on tests involving visual perception, spatial orientation, and sustained attention," even though they scored below the norms on verbal tests (Darsie, 1926, p. 85). Moreover, recent data show a continuing verbal-spatial dichotomy; for example, the verbal IQ of young school-age children in Japan was, at best, average,[11] and their scores on the so-called verbal-comprehension primary were significantly below the norm (Lynn and Hampson, 1986d).

Relationship Between Intellectual Ability and Child-Rearing Practices

A clear relationship between (1) the areas of cognitive excellence displayed by Japanese children, (2) the kinds of culturally based traditional Japanese child-rearing and educational practices employed in their early upbringing, and (3) the types of early brain stimulation that would foster greater biological development in those brain regions "responsible" for these skills has been firmly established (see Chapter Thirteen). The common denominator seems to be that these child-rearing practices fostered the development and use of spatially oriented, externally focused, nonlinguistic approaches to integrating thinking and feeling, as well as a holistic approach to reading—all of which would seem to favor a "right-brained" approach to cognition and analysis.

If this construct is in large part correct, it might be expected that Japanese and American infants would respond somewhat differently to similar types of maternal behaviors because their *biological* needs would differ. Specifically, if the *innate preprogramming* for brain growth among American infants does favor a greater innervation of its language areas — in comparison with Japanese infants whose brains might be programmed to "expect" more visual and tactile stimulation — this would suggest that infants in each of these cultures will *respond more favorably to stimulation that is in accord with their ancestral experience* and less favorably to experiences that alter this "experience-expectant" programming.

The evidence supports this view. In Caudill's Japanese sample (see Chapter Thirteen), those babies who received more rocking, carrying, and lulling from their mothers were more active, playful, and happily vocal (Caudill and Schooler, 1973), whereas, in the American families studied, playfulness and happy vocalization were strongly correlated with the amount of "chatting" that the mother did with her infant. Thus, these Japanese and American infants **were expressing different needs** — which strongly suggests that ingrained "experience-expectant" behavior guided their responses.

One could argue that these maternal and infant behavioral differences might be an outgrowth of intrinsic and racially based biological differences and that they therefore evolved over a very long time period, rather than being a product of (perhaps) ten generations of training. However, Caudill's study of three-month-old infants from third-generation Japanese American families (Caudill and Frost, 1971, summarized in Morsbach, 1973) suggests otherwise. Since the distinctive patterns of maternal behavior observed in Japan were not present, this seems to demonstrate that these maternal behaviors are indeed culturally rather than racially generated.

These findings also indirectly support the conclusion that the effects of culture on cognitive ability are multigenerational. If the cognitive precocity displayed was generated solely by the effects of these child-rearing practices on the phenotype (and Caudill's Japanese American studies seem to indicate this), then the supplanting of these traditional practices by American child-rearing approaches should have been accompanied by a substantial decline in the mathematical and scientific proficiency of these children. Since there is no evidence that such a decline has occurred,[12] this strongly implies that a nearly total discontinuance of these behaviors does not lead to an *abrupt* disappearance of these abilities.

20.4 Verbal-Conceptual Reasoning and the Jewish Family

An entirely different type of cognitive ability is displayed by the Jewish people — one that centers on the left hemisphere's verbal and numerical ability and on skills that require an ability to integrate the right hemisphere's sensory-emotional perceptions into the left hemisphere's analytical mode.

Considerable evidence suggests that the development of these cognitive skills represents a case of multigenerational adaptation:

- The areas of cognitive strength evidenced by the Hebrew people correspond quite closely to specific aspects of maternal interactive behavior and educational practices prevalent over many hundreds of years in what was a culturally uniform, strongly traditional society.
- The *intellectual heights* attained by members of the Jewish sects that followed these child-rearing and educational practices — whether considered in terms of test scores (see section 14.2) or the frequency with which they have made important contributions to human progress in fields requiring exceptional ability in these domains (see section 14.3) — strongly suggest that this acumen could not have been induced in the phenotype by training since, if environment was that influential, studies relating IQ to heredity would show markedly lower correlations.
- The "loss" of these heightened abilities among members of Jewish geocultures that stopped instilling these environmentally enriching aspects of the traditional Jewish home life into their children *for several generations* — together with their partial recovery after a single generation of exposure to an environmentally enriching infancy and toddlerhood (see section 10.4) — suggests that neither heredity nor environmental factors alone are capable of explaining the observed pattern of changes in cognitive performance.

20.5 Cultural Uniformity Among Ashkenazi Jews and the Sephardic Contrast

Although widely dispersed across many foreign lands for nearly 2,000 years, the people of the Jewish faith, by and large, were able to maintain a uniform set of cultural values and behaviors. The Torah provided the basic laws that they were commanded to follow, and the Talmud—the massive compendium of biblical commentary—prescribed how they were to behave in religious and human affairs. Through the fifteenth century, both the Eastern European (Ashkenazi) and Spanish (Sephardic) cultures followed these Talmudic precepts closely. However, after the expulsion of the Sephardic Jews from Spain in 1492 and their dispersal to a variety of Muslim countries, their traditional child-rearing practices (see section 14.4) began to erode. By contrast, the far more numerous Ashkenazim[13] experienced a continuing cultural and behavioral traditionalism. For example, Herschel (1946) writes, "All Ashkenazic Jews in the areas bounded by the Rhine and the Dnieper, the Baltic and Black seas [that is, in virtually all of Eastern Europe] and in some neighboring states as well, comprised a culturally uniform group" (p. 86).[14] By the end of the nineteenth century, the primary spoken language of almost all Ashkenazi Jews was Yiddish,[15] even though Hebrew remained the language of prayer.

The Spanish expulsion of the Sephardic Jews ended some 800 years of exceptional scholarly and scientific accomplishment. Moreover, many of the North African and Middle Eastern Muslim countries to which the Sephardim migrated had very low rates of literacy and rather poor attitudes toward women, both of which eventually had profound effects on Jewish child-rearing practices. As delineated by Raphael Patai in *Tents of Jacob*: "The position of women in the Middle Eastern diaspora [was in some ways] largely identical among Jews and Muslims. . . after marriage, [a woman's] husband becomes her master. . . it was a woman's destiny to be practically a slave to one man or another, her father, husband, son, or brother according to circumstances" (Patai, 1971, p. 177). Further, in contrast to the joyfulness that accompanied the birth of Ashkenazi children of either sex, only the birth of a son was viewed as a joyous event among most of these descendants of the Sephardim. In contrast to the warmth and attention given to mother and child in the early days of an infant's life among the Ashkenazi, Patai notes that, for several weeks after childbirth, a woman was considered to be "impure," and it was believed that "her touch deviled."[16]

Consequently, four to five hundred years of living in countries where there was a dearth of educational and intellectual opportunities, coupled with the partial assimilation of Muslim attitudes toward family and child rearing, had taken a major toll on the overall level of general intelligence of a large segment of this Middle Eastern and North African Jewish population, and the toll had been especially heavy on their verbal abilities.

The Ashkenazi/Sephardic IQ Dichotomy

The IQ difference between Ashkenazi and Sephardic Jews in Israel in the mid 1960s, as derived from test scores of 18,000 Israeli children segregated as to parental heritage (Ortar, 1967), was slightly less than a full standard deviation (see section 14.2). Nevertheless, now that most Sephardic immigrants have lived in Israel for a number of years, the magnitude of this difference has apparently been narrowing, as evidenced by the fact that the younger offspring of Sephardic immigrants tend to outperform their older siblings academically (Davis, Cahan, and Bashi, 1977).[17] This is thought to be a consequence of the mandatory education provided to the older children, which enables them to assist in the education of their younger siblings.

If the considerable disparity between Ashkenazi Jews and other Caucasian people in verbal and/or symbolic analytical reasoning ability was entirely a function of heredity, little or no difference would be found between the scores of Israeli Ashkenazim and those Israelis whose ancestors resided in Middle Eastern and North African lands, for two reasons: First, it has been less than 500 years since the era of extraordinary Sephardic intellectual accomplishment ended—not 50,000 or 5 million years. Second, during this period, rates of intermarriage between Sephardim and Muslims were extremely low. Conversely, if the difference between Jewish and non-Jewish verbal ability was entirely a function of the effects of environment on the phenotype, how could one explain the continuing (albeit reduced) IQ difference between the offspring of Ashkenazi and the offspring of Jewish immigrants to Israel from Arab regions when, as detailed in section 10.4, these two groups were reared from infancy in virtually identical kibbutz environments?[18] It is only when environment — *considered over the course of several generations* — is able to engender changes in heritable biological underpinnings to intelligence that evolutionary theory can explain the pattern of Ashkenazi and Sephardic scores actually found.

This suggests the presence of an interaction between heredity and environment that becomes manifest over the course of a relatively few generations.[19]

Gender Not a Factor

In addition, IQ-score comparisons of males and females in Orthodox Jewish families limit the extent to which a single generation of environment can be thought of as accounting for the heightened IQ performance of the Ashkenazim. Because the roles of men and women in Orthodox Jewish households differed so greatly and the early childhood activities of and expectations for young boys and girls reflected these differences,[20] it might be expected that the cultural imperative for boys to achieve intellectually would lead to significant differences in the intelligence test scores of boys and girls. However, this is not the case; for example, among 770 Jewish children who were given the Stanford-Binet test as part of school-readiness evaluations prior to entry into the first grade of full-day Hebrew day schools (Levinson, 1957b),[21] scores averaged 112.8 for the boys and 113.6 for the girls. Thus, major differences in the cognitive roles of young boys and young girls had little or no impact on their IQ scores.

20.6 The Japanese-Jewish Intellectual Contrast

The cognitive skills displayed by the Japanese and Ashkenazi peoples present a considerable contrast. The Japanese are proficient in those forms of intelligence requiring a perceptual, structural, and spatially based aptitude, while the Ashkenazim excel in the linguistically oriented, conceptually integrated, and causality-related domains. *This suggests the extent to which a culturally uniform, strongly traditional regimen of early child-rearing and educational practices can shape and uplift specific aspects of human intelligence over the course of what, at most, appears to be several hundred years.*

In the face of such findings, to maintain support for the traditional view that "survival of the fittest" must be responsible for these observed differences, a defender of the Darwinian faith must be able to explain why, on the one hand, a strong "right-brained" survival advantage existed among the Japanese people while, on the other hand, a strong "left-brained" survival advantage existed among Jews. Further (as detailed in section 14.2), because verbal acumen among Jews tends to be accompanied by an average or slightly below-average capability in space conceptualization and in visual-motor integration under speeded conditions (faculties that would seem to have a strong survival value), one must explain why in those areas of the world where the Ashkenazim lived, survival strongly favored people with high verbal but average spatial abilities rather than spatially adroit but verbally average people.[22] By the same token, why was it that among the Japanese, spatially adroit but verbally average people outsurvived their verbally adroit but spatially average counterparts?

20.7 Effects of Culture on the Pace of Evolution

The origin of modern man has been a unique evolutionary event—in terms of both its rapidity and the extent of development that it has required. Moreover, the pace at which human intelligence has evolved has accelerated dramatically the closer one gets to the present era. The only obvious novel factor to account for this acceleration is human culture, the development of which has dramatically altered the genome of human populations in at least two ways: First, through its effects on the choice of mates, it has altered the rate at which mutations can become fixed in a population. Second, by taking care of the physically weak members of society, it has reduced the importance of physical strength as the prime survivability factor. As a result, social behavior has increasingly replaced the external environment as the primary determinant of procreation and survival.

This chapter has proposed and documented specific instances of adaptively generated enhancements in particular cognitive skills. Taken together, these models suggest that the rate at which domain-specific intellectual giftedness becomes manifest in ethnogeographic populations is strongly influenced by the strength and uniformity of the society's enculturation practices, as well as by the extent to which these practices have fostered the development of domain-related cognitive skills.

The Japanese and the Jewish cultures embodied strongly held and essentially uniform "values" and behaviors that were deeply ingrained through (1) early child-rearing and educational practices (strengthened by the involvement of the extended family in children's early upbringing); (2) social isolation (which ensured that the large majority of social contacts would be with people sharing similar modes of thinking and behavior); and (3) "reproductive isolation" (through a high frequency of arranged marriages and through a strong cultural bias for monogamy).[23] In combination, these factors have assured that the environment provided to children during their formative years has usually been similar to that experienced by their immediate ancestors and by other members of their culture.

The theory proposed in Chapter Nineteen of a multigenerational transmission of newly utilized preadaptive versatility is supported by findings in human populations. Just as *social isolation and a similarity of ancestral environment* are, in the animal kingdom, associated with a rapid rate of fixation of regulatory-sequence rearrangements,[24] so too do greatly heightened cognitive skills and a high incidence of intellectual giftedness emerge in human populations meeting these criteria — *with the types of exceptional acumen displayed reflecting the demands placed on the cognitive systems of the population's direct ancestors.*

A number of sociobiologists suggest that the social transmission of learned behavior can generate selection pressures that favor complementary anatomical evolution (see section 19.11).

Virtually none, however, have suggested that a substantial genetic evolution of cognitive traits in humans might occur over less than fifty generations (Lumsden and Wilson, 1981), since there are no *scientifically oriented* hypotheses predicated on the existence of a recently-evolving self-directed capacity for evolution by the human genome in response to environmental experience.[25]

Some simple organisms possess genes that are capable of promoting their own perpetuation,[26] and the question of whether complex organisms have also evolved special structures to promote their capacities to evolve — and have thereby attained some measure of control over their own evolutionary development — has recently become the focus of increasingly serious discussion. John Campbell, for one, is convinced that the answer to this question is yes. He proposes that the anatomical evolution of the brain has become an "autocatalytic" process. He holds that some genetic structures, rather than adapting an organism to their environment, have evolved for the purpose of promoting and directing the process of evolution. As such, they function to enhance the capacity of the species to evolve. He has dubbed one possible mechanism by which evolution could be speeded *evolutionary recruitment*. In this process, after a phenotypic trait develops through direct natural selection (because it helps the species to adapt to its environment), the trait then becomes modified so that it can serve as a preadaptation for an evolutionary function, with just one or two mutations necessary to "recruit a very complex preformed adaptation into an evolutionary role" (Campbell, 1985, p. 141). Campbell postulates that not only do species become specialized to evolve in certain ways[27] but they also use their evolutionary experience as a mechanism for understanding which evolutionary strategies and directions have been successful. Consequently, he views evolution as a progressive process that teaches a species how to evolve.[28] If this is true, the genes expressed in the cerebral cortex would seem to be prime candidates for such an evolutionary progression.

The development of complex speech and written language are very recent evolutionary phenomena. For example, the "pre-proto-Indo-European" language, which is thought to have evolved a mere 10,000 years ago, does not appear to contain any differentiated vowels (Kratz, 1989). The prevailing theory has been that prehistoric man did not possess a bone structure in the area of the larynx compatible with an ability to articulate the range of sounds that modern man is capable of uttering. However, a recent archeological finding—that the shape and position of the hyoid bone in a 60,000-year-old Neanderthal man is extremely similar to our own—strongly suggests that there has been very little change in the biological structures underlying speech (Arensburg and others, 1989; Marshall, 1989; Bower, 1989). This further suggests that evolutionary change in this area has been relatively conservative, leading to the possibility that the capability for human speech existed for long periods of time before it began to be used. Thus, it appears to have been the recent evolution of *the brain*, not of *the body*, that has fostered the development of speech.

20.8 Broader Implications

What if this theory of the multigenerational **transmission of adaptively generated plasticity** is essentially correct—and the kind of environmental stimulation provided to infants and toddlers is capable of shaping not only their biological development but that of their progeny as well? What would be the most important implications of this? If we can determine *the kinds of environmental experiences that have led to the creation of giftedness in those domain-specific cognitive abilities that society holds in exceptionally high esteem,*[29] *would we not have thereby imposed on ourselves the* **duty** *to use this knowledge to expand our educational efforts?* Would we not in fact have a *moral obligation*, for example, to fund and develop **very early** child education programs that focus on training parents how to be effective teachers, to develop **language-training programs and manuals** for use in day-care programs that serve infants and toddlers, and to assure that these programs offer a favorable enough caretaker-child ratio to provide children with a near-optimal level of stimulation?

Notes

1. This term is not meant to imply that (1) all members of an ethnic group are of above-average ability or (2) that a majority of its members are highly gifted in the domain referenced. Rather, it suggests that the geoculture's members are substantially overrepresented at the highest levels of competence and/or that the mean level of ability is well above the norm.
2. It is, of course, quite impossible (both ethically and practically) to undertake the kind of controlled studies on human beings that would enable researchers to isolate the multigenerational effects of changes in specific variables on intellectual performance. Consequently, *naturalistic* studies cannot hope to achieve the standards of "clear and convincing proof" that some critics seeking to impugn these findings are likely to demand.
3. Information concerning the nature of acquired cognitive specificity is suggested by a small human study, appended as Technical Note Two to Chapter Nineteen, which indicates that the tendency to attribute special significance to particular shapes has both an environmental and an inherited basis.
4. For example, some of the more extreme manifestations of spatial ability presented (such as the exceptional spatial acuity among rural Eskimos) might be entirely attributable to the evolutionary consequences of "survival of the fittest." But the link between survival and cognitive ability becomes increasingly tenuous in populations that demonstrate enhanced acumen in other intellectual areas, particularly in those populations that demonstrate exceptional verbal ability.
5. For additional information on this subject, see Carpenter (1955) and Briggs (1970).
6. See also Lantis, 1968.
7. Summarized in Gardner, 1985.
8. In 1889, 9 percent of the Japanese population lived in urban areas, a figure that rose to 18 percent in 1920, 38 percent in 1940, and 68 percent in 1965 (Caudill, 1973); by 1965, many members of rural families were commuting to urban jobs.
9. For example, when scaled against the U.S. norms, the scores on the block-design subtest of the WISC-R for the 1,100 children comprising the Japanese standardization sample averaged an astonishingly high 14.3, even though the last problem on the Japanese version was made more difficult (Lynn, 1982). The extent of divergence from the U.S. norm is so extreme (and so stable in an age-by-age analysis) that it seems inconceivable that American children could, by being adopted at birth into traditional Japanese households, achieve such proficiency (see Chapters Five and Thirteen).
10. Some of this postwar increase can be attributed to the extremely favorable caretaker ratio present in these children's early upbringing. This favorable ratio had several causes: (1) three- and four-generation households were the norm during this period; (2) the death of consider-

able numbers of Japanese men in the war had left many mature females available to serve as full-time caregivers to their grandchildren, nieces and nephews, and even their great-grandchildren; and (3) the homage paid to elders in the Japanese family. In addition, the IQ scores of children born in the 1930s and early 1940s are apt to have been slightly depressed (see Chapter Five).

11. The WISC verbal subtest scores of these Japanese children did not approach the norm until after the age of nine, this increase being fueled by their scores on the math subtest of this verbal portion of the WISC (Lynn and Hampson, 1986a). From ages three to eight, their verbal development (as measured by the McCarthy scales) was substantially below American norms (Lynn and Hampson, 1986b).

12. Here, absence of evidence may be presumed to be "evidence of absence." If the spatial ability of third-generation Japanese American children had undergone a substantial decline, reports of such a decline would by now have permeated the literature and prompted considerable media discussion. In fact, Japanese Americans tend to perform very well in school, especially in math and science.

13. In 1939, there were approximately 15 million Jews of Ashkenazi descent in the world and 1.5 million non-Ashkenazi Jews; in 1945, there were approximately 9.5 million Ashkenazi and 1.35 million non-Ashkenazi survivors of the Nazi holocaust. In the United States, a large majority of Jews are of Ashkenazi descent; approximately 40 percent of Israel's Jewish population is of Ashkenazi heritage.

14. This citation refers to conditions from the sixteenth century through the end of the eighteenth century.

15. In the 1897 Russian census, for example, 97 percent of the Jews in the czarist empire gave Yiddish as their mother tongue. Among Jewish immigrants from Russia to the United States between 1899 and 1910, the recorded rate of illiteracy was 26 percent (including a sixth of the men and a third of the women). Many of these "illiterates" could read well but could not write (Schulman, 1971).

16. Nevertheless, the position of women in the Jewish community was somewhat better than among the Muslims, as the negative traits attributed to women were counterbalanced by the attractive portraits of women in the Scriptures, by the commandment to honor one's father and mother, and by a Talmudic code of behavior that favored honoring one's wife over disciplining her physically. Moreover, as the Arab world entered the modern era and educational opportunities expanded, Jewish families were much more likely to let their daughters attend school than were Arab families.

17. Based on a study of 192,000 eighth-grade Israeli schoolchildren (born between 1952 and 1956) that provides comparisons on tests of computational skills and problem-solving ability in mathematics by birth order and family size for the offspring of these two geocultures.

18. In this study of 1,600 children from 125 kibbutzim, the matched pairs of (Ashkenazi and Sephardic) children were raised by the same primary caregivers, lived in the same infant and toddler huts, and spent only a very small portion of the day with their biological families after

the first few weeks of life. Moreover, paternal education (which was also "matched") would not have had a great impact on IQ.

19. The prevailing opinion in Orthodox Jewish folklore is four generations.

20. For example, in the traditional Orthodox home, only male children had the responsibility for knowing the prayers, for accompanying their fathers to the synagogue, for learning the Torah and the Talmud, and for preparing for the rite of passage into manhood (the bar mitzvah). Young girls' responsibilities included learning how to prepare the home for the Sabbath and holidays, learning a few simple prayers, and providing child care, but learning to read was (in an earlier era) less of an imperative.

21. In the middle 1950s, the New York City public school system was quite good (particularly in those communities where there were high concentrations of Jewish people), and a majority of its teachers were Jewish. Consequently, those Jewish families who opted to send their children to full-day Hebrew language schools did so because they had a strong interest in maintaining traditional values.

22. Surely not by doing a better job of *talking* a concentration-camp guard into letting them escape or a pogrom mob out of killing them. Some have argued that the most intelligent Jews achieved greater prosperity and had more children and that their children had a higher rate of survival. However, the poor were always cared for by the community, and rates of assimilation among the intelligentsia tended to be far higher than among Jews who were less well educated.

23. For example, for several millennia, the Hebrew people married almost exclusively within their faith and, in postmedieval Europe, generally tended to live in ghettos (sometimes by choice but often by force of law). Similarly, the Japanese capped off over a thousand years of nearly total geographical and cultural isolation with nearly three hundred years of strict adherence to a host of externally generated and rigorously enforced behavioral imperatives borne of Chinese Buddhist influence (introduced four hundred years earlier [Morsbach, 1973]).

24. As detailed in Chapter Eighteen, the relationship between social structure and the rates at which animals are evolving strongly suggests that social isolation engenders a rapid rate of fixation of the genetic changes that are induced by changes in the position of the DNA sequences that regulate protein-coding genes. Evidence for this includes the exceedingly high rate of instructional-sequence evolution among inbred laboratory mice, the near-general finding of two alleles at chromosomal sites where diversity is displayed rather than more than two alleles, and Diamond's multigenerational "enriched environment" study.

25. Some theologians would assert that God imbued his children with an evolutionary capacity. In this respect, it is interesting to note that the neurons involved in higher cognitive function possess the potential for "immortality," in that (in an otherwise healthy body) they neither die nor lose their youthful vigor (as witness the eighty-five-year-old symphony orchestra conductor's continuing abilities). This is in sharp

contrast to somatic cells, which die after going through a finite number of cell divisions.

26. For a discussion of these so-called selfish genes, see Doolittle (1981) and Doolittle and Sapienza (1980).

27. An erythromycin-resistance determinant *Streptococcus* (Tn917) is a case in point (Tomich, An, and Clewell, 1978). "It has a repression system so that the resistance gene is expressed only in the presence of erythromycin.... In addition, Tn917 transposes only when erythromycin is present. The repressor serves a second, evolutionary function of rendering the transposon mobile only when it is relevant to the phenotype" (Campbell, 1985, p. 141).

28. Campbell has also coined the term *evolutionary driver* for genetic structures that carry out such evolutionary functions, and he differentiates between those that provide the direct force for evolutionary change (see the discussion of molecular drive in section 19.6) and those that *steer* the direction in which evolution is moving without actually driving it (which he has dubbed *evolutionary directors*). Moreover, the processes that govern the *execution* of changes in the developmental program during embryonic development may be programmed differently from the processes that induce these changes.

29. For example, delineating some *common* aspects of maternal interactive behavior and educational practices indigenous to the Japanese and Ashkenazi cultures may prove instructive in designing effective infant, toddler, and preschool education programs. These common aspects include (1) an abundance of rocking and other soothing behaviors in early infancy (which promotes visual tracking and the encoding and imprinting of visual information); (2) an abundance of attention (aided by what is usually a very favorable caretaker ratio); (3) a promotion of feelings within the child that he or she is part of a familial and societal "we"; and (4) a requirement that specific material be learned perfectly, whether it be the verbal recitation of prayers (in the case of the Ashkenazi child) or the step-by-step components of procedural learning (in the case of the Japanese child). In both cultures, the child strives to become part of an elite group, and great importance is placed on the child's performance (and/or that of the group as a whole).

⚭ *Epilogue* ⚭

The nature-nurture controversy has not abated despite an out-pouring of studies designed to assess IQ correspondences among members of biological and adoptive families, as well as an abundance of studies that seek to elucidate the causal relationships between specific environmental features and IQ outcomes.

At one extreme, proponents argue that intelligence is so strongly governed by heredity that environment scarcely influences it, although they may acknowledge the ability of extremely deprived upbringings to stifle intellectual development. At the other extreme are people convinced that (with rare exceptions) a person's environment has far more to do with how well he or she performs on an IQ test than does his or her heredity. As a consequence, this group tends to view IQ tests as indicators of environmental deprivation rather than as measures of differences in innate ability.

The near-universal acceptance of the Darwinian proposition that the broad sweep of evolution stems from random genetic mutation and "survival of the fittest" has led most people to assume that intelligence, like most other traits, is primarily a hereditarily driven characteristic. Some people, however, have taken this hereditary perspective a step further and concluded that efforts to increase children's intelligence cannot have a substantial lasting impact. Unfortunately, this relatively extreme view has occasionally been used by members of privileged classes to justify their elite station in life, as well as by members of racist groups to justify their persecution of culturally backward or less powerful peoples (on the grounds that their "genetic inferiority" makes them subhuman). This misunderstanding and/or deliberate misuse of genetic theory does much to explain the tenacity and passion with which some proponents of the extreme environmentalist position express their opinions. Their views, in fact, sometimes reflect their political and economic philosophy — *egalitarianism* — rather than a dispassionate understanding of the data. This egalitarian philosophy:

- Is based on the principle of social justice and equal economic opportunity for all.
- Promotes a vigorous commitment to helping less fortunate members of society overcome their environmental deprivations.
- Houses a fear that societal acceptance of a strong genetic component to intelligence would undermine these goals and possibly open the door to a destruction of democratic ideals by racists or other self-styled elitists.

Proposed Resolution of This Controversy

This book suggests a four-part resolution to the nature-nurture controversy — a resolution that supports some aspects of both the hereditarian and the environmentalist perspectives. It proposes, first, that, on the average, 70 percent of an individual's IQ is determined by heredity and 30 percent by environment.

Second, to the question, Can early exposure to a very enriched cognitive environment engender a large, permanent increase in intelligence? — it replies that such an outcome is clearly attainable if age-appropriate stimulation is provided during the so-called sensitive or critical periods of postnatal brain development, most of which are limited to infancy and/or toddlerhood.

Thereafter, efforts to increase children's IQs tend to be less successful initially and are apt to dissipate markedly, but not entirely, during adolescence.

Third, the answer to the highly sensitive question—To what extent are racial differences in IQ scores a manifestation of innate differences and to what extent do they reflect environmental factors?—depends on what is meant by the words *genetic, innate,* or *inherited.* For example, if a person is born a low-birth-weight baby because his or her mother did not receive an adequate rate of nutrition during her growth years, then it may be said that the newborn child inherited *a nongenetic tendency* to have its IQ potential affected adversely. As shown in Chapter Six, at least half of the present IQ disparity between Blacks and Whites in the United States can be accounted for by nongenetic factors. Further, because a relatively steady and fairly rapid increase in measured IQ has occurred across the developed world throughout the twentieth century, the considerably below-average IQ scores registered by some economically disadvantaged ethnic groups today are nevertheless higher than those attained by society at large in earlier generations. This suggests that the present disparities in IQ are likely to be an indication of how long it might take for low-scoring groups to attain today's norms rather than a reflection of an insurmountable barrier.

Fourth, it is proposed that the nature-nurture controversy has proven so difficult to resolve because there is a multigenerational interplay between heredity and environment. On the one hand, a person's early cognitive environment can exert a profound impact on his or her lifetime cognitive ability. On the other hand, the early cognitive environment of an individual's *ancestors* can exert a profound impact on that individual's own heredity—not by altering the genes that the ancestors who experienced this environment then pass on to their descendants but by altering the "blueprint" for the developmental program that governs the expression of these genes.

This last proposition flies in the face of conventional thinking, which holds that—irrespective of the extent to which exposure to cognitive enrichments might be able to raise people's intelligence—environmentally induced changes in cell-network interconnections cannot alter what ancestors pass on to their descendants. However, recent knowledge about the processes that govern gene expression suggests that, in response to the stress placed on certain intellectual skill areas by (at least) several generations of ancestors, the developmental blueprint for the growth of those neuronal networks that govern the higher sensory or analytical functions associated with these skills generates an increased biological preparedness for similar types of stimulation at the same stage of their offspring's development. The developmental blueprint accomplishes this by diverting some growth energy from other biochemically related cell networks and/or by altering the length or strength of the right and left hemispheres' "growing seasons" in the affected brain regions. Thus, even without effecting any change in the internal structure of the genes inherited at conception, ancestral experience can alter the "shape" of human intelligence.

Future Trends in Human Intelligence

When combined with the abundant evidence that IQ has risen at a relatively steady rate throughout the twentieth century, the thesis that long-term improvements in children's early cognitive environments have engendered biological changes conducive to further IQ growth suggests a very optimistic future for the intelligence of the human race. And even if this thesis is not valid, it is still possible to ensure a continuing rapid growth in highly valued cognitive skills by applying our newfound knowledge about how to foster cognitive development during infancy and toddlerhood. Moreover, the large proportion of college-educated couples that have chosen to delay childbearing until they attain a certain measure of financial security would seem to imply that many of the children of our brightest people will be exposed to highly advantaged family configurations during their formative years.

Indeed, recent statistics developed by the National Center for Health Statistics (1989) indicate that between 1970 and 1986 a substantial change took place in the age at which most American mothers bore their first child:

- In 1970, more than 80 percent of first-time mothers were younger than twenty-five years of age, including nearly 36 percent who were still teenagers and 46 percent who were in their early twenties. By 1986, these proportions had fallen by almost a third, to 23 percent and 33 percent, respectively.
- Conversely, the proportion of first-time mothers aged twenty-five to twenty-nine almost doubled.
- During this same period, the proportion of first-time mothers older than thirty years of age quadrupled, increasing from 4 to 16 percent.

However, the enormous upsurge in full-time employment among the mothers of infants and toddlers—in combination with the declining role of extended-family members in children's early upbringing—now threatens to reverse some of these hard-won gains. Because much of the task of providing early nurture has fallen into the hands of paid caregivers, it becomes difficult, if not impossible, for many parents to provide the same quantity and quality of early nurturing to their children as they received from their own parents. This situation creates a pressing need that paid caregivers be supplied with an up-to-date understanding of the principles of early cognitive development, as well as with a working knowledge of those programs that have been effective in raising children's intelligence.

From an even broader perspective, we recognize that rising human intelligence leads to rising productivity, which in turn fuels economic progress. In a world of fierce international competition, the extent to which a country's standard of living will grow (or whether it will grow at all) may depend on how much that country is willing to invest in educating its children and on the nature of the educational investments that it selects. Given the extreme importance of the cognitive environment provided during infancy and toddlerhood it is appropriate that we commit ourselves to providing children with as good an educational environment during the first and second years of their lives as we now provide to young men and women during their third and fourth years of college.

Thus, this book should be viewed as a vehicle for filling what is one of society's most important needs—educating parents, grandparents, paid caregivers, and government policy makers about how, with a relatively modest investment in time and money, they can reshape and uplift the world's most precious resource: the human intellect.

҂ Appendix ҂

Intelligence and the Intrauterine Environment

This appendix presents data that relate inadequacies in the prenatal environment to children's measured intelligence — using birth weight, either singly or in conjunction with the length of the pregnancy and/or the baby's head circumference, as a mechanism for estimating the extent to which the fetal environment may have been less than optimal.

This analysis addresses the following issues:

- What is the relationship between birth weight and IQ, and does this relationship change with the length of the pregnancy and/or the baby's head circumference?
- Are some aspects of intelligence affected by birth weight to a greater extent than others, and if so, what biological rationale could explain these differences?
- What are the implications of these findings with respect to IQ differences between twin and single births?
- What kinds of postnatal intervention seem to ameliorate these deficits?

The findings in this appendix provide an especially useful adjunct to Chapters One, Six, and Eleven.

Principal Findings

A considerable number of studies clearly demonstrate that low birth weight (defined as 2,000 grams or less)—and especially very low birth weight (less than 1,500 grams)—sharply increases the risk of moderate to severe IQ deficits.

When low birth weight is due solely to prematurity (the baby's weight-for-date is itself average or above), the incidence and severity of cognitive deficits are far smaller than among low-weight-for-date babies.

Among very premature infants who are of normal weight-for-date, the best indicator of whether severe cognitive deficits will occur seems to be the rate of head growth during the first few postnatal weeks and months.

At birth weights between 2,000 and 2,500 grams (4.5 to 5.5 pounds), IQ effects are apt to be less severe but are still frequently evident. As birth weight increases, IQ deficits (on a group basis) continue decreasing steadily.

These data suggest that (in terms of IQ outcome) **the optimal gestational period may be longer than the traditional thirty-nine weeks** and that *inducing labor prematurely poses some risk of slightly reducing measured intelligence.*

The nature of the cognitive deficits experienced by low-birth-weight (LBW) and very low birth weight (VLBW) children are such that they are likely to affect so-called performance IQ to a much greater extent than verbal IQ. Even when the impact on a child's overall IQ score is small, deficiencies in spatial relations and/or visual-motor integrative skills are often displayed.

Specific Studies of Interest

From among the many studies that have found links between birth weight and IQ, the following have been selected to highlight the overall patterns and some specific features of this relationship:

Record, McKeown, and Edwards (1969b). This extremely large British study compared the performance of 47,000 eleven-year-old children on a test of verbal reasoning ability with their birth weight and length of gestational

Table 39. Verbal IQ Scores by Birth Weight: The Birmingham Study.

Verbal Reasoning Scores by Birth Weight	Average Score	Percent of Births
Under 2,000 grams	93.5	0.8
2,000–2,499 grams	95.9	4.2
2,500–2,999 grams	98.0	19.2
3,000–3,499 grams	100.1	39.2
3,500–3,999 grams	101.7	28.0
4,000–4,499 grams	102.5	7.2
4,500 grams or more	103.0	1.4
Average/Total	100.2	100.0

Note: Scores have been standardized by birth rank; the standard deviation is 15.

Source: Adapted from Record, McKeown, and Edwards, 1969b.

period. The report excluded twins and children not attending public schools.

As shown in Table 39, the principal finding is that verbal IQ rose steadily with increasing birth weight; the scores of children weighing under 2,000 grams (4.4 pounds) at birth averaged 9 points below those attained by children weighing 9 pounds or more at birth.

An analysis of the relationship between birth weight and duration of gestation revealed that for each birth-weight class there is an optimal gestational period, with longer or shorter gestational periods associated with lower IQs, even at normal birth weights (Table 40).

Later commentators on these findings have suggested that children whose birth weights are unduly heavy for their gestational period often represent instances in which bleeding early in pregnancy was mistaken for a period rather than instances of very rapid intrauterine growth.

At birth weights below 2,000 grams, IQ scores were slightly higher at a gestational period of thirty-four to thirty-seven weeks (94.5) than at longer gestational periods (91.3), or shorter gestational periods (93.1). At birth weights of 2,000 to 2,500 grams, a thirty-four- to thirty-nine-week gestational period was optimal (96.8), with progressively lower IQ scores found at progressively longer gestational periods.

Hunt, Tooley, and Harvin (1982). The IQs of VLBW children were compared with those of their same-sex non-LBW siblings on the same IQ tests (WISC-R or Stanford-Binet). The average IQ disadvantage of the VLBW child was 16.7 points (excluding the three sets of twins who averaged 3.4 points apart). Virtually all the nontwin VLBW children's scores were at least 10 points lower than those of their non-LBW siblings. Unfortunately, the sample size, thirty-eight, was relatively small. Other findings from this study are presented later in the appendix.

Table 40. Verbal IQ Scores by Birth Weight and Gestational Period:
The Birmingham Study.

	IQ by Birth Weight (grams)				
Length of Gestational Period	*2500–3000*	*3000–3500*	*3500–4000*	*4000–4500*	*4500+*
"Optimal" date-for weight[a]	99.1	100.4	102.0	102.8	103.4
Short gestation-for-weight[b]	97.7	98.3	97.6	101.5	100.7
Long gestation-for-weight[c]	97.5	98.1	98.5	NC[d]	NC
Very short date-for-weight[e]	93.8	93.9	95.5	95.2	NC

[a] Defined as 38–39 weeks for 2,500–3,000 grams; 38–41 weeks for 3,000–4,000 grams; 40–41 weeks for 4,000–4,500 grams; and 40 weeks or longer for more than 4,500 grams.

[b] 34–37 weeks, 36–37 weeks, 36–37 weeks, 38–39 weeks, and 38–39 weeks.

[c] 40 weeks or longer, 42 weeks or longer, and 44 weeks or longer.

[d] NC = not computed.

[e] 32–33 weeks, 34–35 weeks, 34–35 weeks, and 36–37 weeks.

Source: Adapted from Record, McKeown, and Edwards, 1969b.

Francis-Williams and Davies (1974). This study compared the IQs of small-for-date and appropriate-for-date VLBW British children. On the performance IQ portion of the WISC, the thirty-three small-for-date children averaged 89.6, or 8.8 points below that scored by the seventy-two appropriate-for-date premature infants. The average difference between the groups in the verbal IQ portion of the WISC, however, was only 3.4 points.

Sixty-five of these VLBW children were tested on the Bender Gestalt Test: slightly more than half scored at least one standard deviation below the norm applicable to the child's age and overall mental ability, with many scoring more than two standard deviations below this norm. A particularly poor performance was found on tasks involving the integration of patterns to form a whole.

Silva, McGee, and Williams (1984). The IQ scores of 71 small-for-gestational-age New Zealand children averaged 5 points below those of 748 full-term appropriate-weight-for-date children (across three separate testing periods: ages five, seven, and nine) on the Stanford-Binet and WISC, with these differences deepening slightly with increasing age. In contrast, 30 appropriate-weight-for-date premature children had IQs only slightly below (1.0 point) those of the full-term children of normal birth weight.

Ounsted, Moar, and Scott (1984). A low-weight-for-date birth, when combined with a relatively small head circumference in early childhood (defined as one standard deviation or more below the weight-for-date group average), resulted in severely delayed cognitive development. At four years of age, the developmental scores (for the residents of this upper-middle-class English community) were as follows:

- 39.1, for the 22 small-for-date, small-head-circumference infants.
- 43.6, for the 52 average/large-for-date, small-head-circumference infants.
- 45.5, for the 120 small-for-date, average/large-head-circumference infants.
- 50.7, for the 300 average/large-for-date, average/large-head-circumference infants.

The components of this Developmental Index most affected were: (1) visual-motor function (but not among the large-for-date infants), (2) comprehension, and (3) language. Gross-motor coordination and fine-motor coordination were also affected, but to a lesser degree.

Other studies cited in this article linking "small-for-datedness" with reductions in IQ include Douglas (1969), Neligan (1967), and Bazso, Karnaysin, and Gelec (1964).

Brennan, Funk, and Frothingham (1985). Among a large sample of children, a *relatively* small head circumference at birth—defined as a small head in relation to the rest of the body but not in the smallest 10 percent of the population (for that gestational age)—bore *no relationship* to intellectual development on the Stanford-Binet at age four or the WISC-R at age seven. By contrast, an *extremely* small head (microcephaly, or a head circumference less than the 10th percentile for gestational age)—if maintained at one year—posed a *nearly 100 percent risk of retardation* (O'Connell, Feldt, and Stickler, 1965) and a 50 percent overall risk of an IQ of less than 80 at four years of age (Nelson and Deutschberger, 1970).

Hack and Breslau (1986). The IQs of 139 appropriate-for-gestational-age VLBW infants at three years of age were shown to be highly dependent on head circumference at eight months (corrected) postnatal age. The sample (52 percent Black; 19 percent of the mothers with more than a high school education; gestational age averaging twenty-nine weeks; and birth weights averaging 1,194 grams) had an overall average IQ at age three of 93.

Nineteen of these children had subnormal head circumference at eight months, and *their IQ averaged only 79* (irrespective of whether their head circumference "normalized" at twenty months). In contrast, the children with normal head circumference at eight months had IQs averaging 95 (irrespective of whether their head circumference was subnormal at birth or even at twenty months). After adjustments were made for race and social class, a 10-point IQ disparity still remained.

Hack and others (1982) note that nearly half of the VLBW infants who had grown normally in utero failed to grow adequately during the neonatal period.

Table 41. Effects of Prematurity and Size for Date on IQ Scores
of Scottish Children by Social Class (mid 1950s).

Social Class and Prematurity Status	Small for Date	Normal for Date	Small-for-Date Deficit
Average and Poor Working Class			
Full-term ($n = 46$ and 30)	93.4	102.1	− 8.7
Premature ($n = 17$ and 26)	88.5	95.8	− 7.3
Prematurity effect	− 4.9	− 6.3	—
Above-Average Classes			
Full-term ($n = 21$ and 44)	110.9	110.6	Negl.
Premature ($n = 16$ and 16)	96.6	96.6	None
Prematurity effect	− 14.3	− 14.0	—

Source: Adapted from Drillien, 1970.

Gross, Oehler, and Eckerman (1983). Cognitive development at fifteen months among a sample of eighty-five VLBW infants was shown to depend both on whether the infant was microcephalic and on *the rate of head growth during the first six weeks of infancy* (more or less than 3.5 centimeters). The scores (on the Bayley Mental Index) averaged as follows:

- 74, for nine microcephalic, slow-postnatal-head-growth premature infants.
- 85, for thirty-two normocephalic, slow-growth premature infants.
- 98, for twelve microcephalic, good-growth premature infants.
- 102, for thirty-two normocephalic, good-growth premature infants.
- 104, for ninety-five full-term, normal-weight infants.

Drillien (1970). This study of premature and full-term small-for-date infants born in the mid 1950s in Scotland compared the IQs (at ten to twelve years of age) of the offspring of relatively affluent families with those of average and poor working-class homes. The principal findings were that prematurity impaired IQ development in both social classes but that "small-for-datedness" (irrespective of whether it was coupled with prematurity) led to a greater cognitive impairment only in the working-class families (Table 41).

In a later study of 261 Scottish children divided into four social grades (where two-thirds of the children weighed between 1,500 and 2,000 grams and one-third below 1,500 grams at birth), IQ scores at six and a half years were compared with those of children of the same social grades attending the same school, with these results: (1) the LBW children in the highest social grade again had the largest IQ deficit (10 points); (2) in the two middle social grades, deficits of 6 points in performance IQ and 3 points in verbal IQ

(WISC) were found; and (3) in the lowest social grade, a 3-point deficit was reported (Drillien, Thomson, and Burgoyne, 1980).

Gotlieb, Biasini, and Bray (1988). The "recognition memory" of twenty full-term infants who were very low weight-for-date was shown to be markedly poorer at seven months of age than that of twenty matched normal-birth-weight infants ($p < .002$); the correlation between birth weight and "novelty preference" was $+ .55$ (see Chapter Seven for an analysis of the predictive relationship between novelty preference in infancy and later IQ scores).

Klein, Hack, Gallagher, and Fanaroff (1985). In this recent study of spatial and motor skills, forty-six VLBW children of normal intelligence were compared with SES-matched full-term classmates of comparable IQ at age five (both groups having been enrolled in preschool programs). Administration of the Woodcock-Johnson Psycho-Educational Battery and the Beery Development Test of Visual-Motor Integration revealed the following:

- On the spatial relations subtest of the Woodcock-Johnson, the full-term classmates substantially outperformed their VLBW peers ($p < .001$).
- The full-termers also did substantially better ($p < .01$) on the test of visual-motor integration.
- On those subtests carrying a heavy auditory loading, there was no difference between the groups.

O'Connor (1980). On a test of auditory discrimination at four months of age (in which stimulus encoding and memory for auditory stimuli were measured by cardiac deceleration), there was no difference in performance when the premature and full-term infants were equated on conceptional age.

Wallace, Escalona, McCarton-Daum, and Vaughn (1982). In an ethnically mixed sample of thirty-three relatively LBW six-year-old children from New York City (average weight 1,700 grams; maximum weight 2,250 grams), visual-motor integration skills averaged somewhat below normal, even though the children were in the normal IQ range and most had above-average reading scores.

Hunt, Tooley, and Harvin (1982). Evidence suggests that the cognitive deficits experienced by VLBW children worsen in the early school years as greater intellectual demands are placed upon their cognitive information-processing networks.

This study examined twenty VLBW children who tended to have above-average IQs at school entry (their Stanford-Binet average was 112.4) and were also in the normal range for (1) visual-motor integration skills (tested by two separate clinical measures) and (2) such language skills as "use of language as a cognitive tool, language tracking and processing," and language comprehension. When reexamined at age eight, however, only nine were still in the normal range on both the visual-integrative and language measures, seven were in the "suspect" range, and four were clearly "abnormal" (adequate in rote skills but definitely lacking in abstract abilities). Their IQs (on the somewhat less verbally oriented WISC) had dropped an average of 7.3 points.

Among the larger group of fifty-three VLBW children (from which this subsample had been drawn), half were in the abnormal range at age eight, and only a fourth were clearly normal on both sets of (linguistic and visual-motor) measures.

These findings suggest that some VLBW children manage to compensate for cognitive deficits during early childhood but that when the "intellectual demands of school require more complex and fluid intellectual capacities" (p. 286), their compensatory mechanisms no longer suffice, and learning disabilities emerge.

Asher and Roberts (1949). This early British study compared the birth weights of a large number of children attending secondary grammar schools (where the Stanford-Binet IQs averaged about 120) with those of children attending secondary modern schools (where IQs averaged about 95), those of children attending special schools, and those of institutionalized mentally defective children. The results were as follows:

- Only 0.8 percent of the girls attending the grammar schools weighed under 4.5 pounds at birth, compared with 4.7 percent in the modern schools, 6.4 percent in the special schools, and 10.5 percent in the institutions.
- Only 1.4 percent of the boys attending the grammar schools weighed under 5.0 pounds at birth, compared with 4.8 percent in the special schools and 5.2 percent in the institutions.
- There was also a tendency for a substantially smaller proportion of the grammar-school population to have had very high birth weights (10 pounds for girls, and 10.5 pounds for boys), compared with the proportions reported in the other-school and institutional populations.

Overcoming Cognitive Deficits in Premature and/or Small-for-Date Infants

The finding that adequate postnatal growth during the first several weeks or months of life can reduce the incidence and/or severity of cognitive deficits among infants born into these at-risk groups has led to the exploration of various intervention strategies.

A priori, one would expect that those strategies that stress additional vestibular stimulation (rocking) and possibly visual stimulation would show greater success than those that have a primary or exclusive stress on auditory or tactile stimulation. There are several reason for this assumption:

- The cognitive deficits that are ultimately manifest in premature or otherwise underdeveloped infants affect primarily the spatial and the visual-motor integrative domains.
- The auditory system is well developed long before term, in contrast to the visual system, which undergoes a rapid development during the third trimester of pregnancy and beyond (see Chapter Eleven); the vestibular system, however, is still underdeveloped at birth and requires a great deal of postnatal stimulation for adequate visual and visual-motor development.
- Infants receive a great deal of "movement stimulation" in the womb, but preterm infants receive very little of this kind of stimulation when growing to term in incubators.

The following review of the literature supports this hypothesis.

Kramer and Pierpont (1976). Placing appropriate-weight-for-date premature infants (less than thirty-four weeks old) on waterbeds inside their incubators and mechanically rocking these waterbeds for one hour prior to each feeding caused significantly greater weekly weight gain ($p < .01$) and *doubled* the increase in (biparietal) *head circumference ($p < .001$)*, compared with premature infants given standard incubator nursing care. The rocking was coupled with the playing of a taped simulated heartbeat and was supplemented by insertions of a woman's voice at decibels near to that experienced in utero.

Neal (1968). Rocking twenty-eight- to thirty-two-week gestational-age infants in hammocks suspended in their incubators or cribs until thirty-six weeks of gestational age led to significantly greater weight gain and visual-motor development.

Barnard and Bee (1983). Fifteen minutes of rocking coupled with heartbeat sounds made a large difference in the early development of IQ (as measured by the Bayley MDI at twenty-four months). This study of seventy-two preterm children (average gestational age thirty-one weeks and average birth weight 1,355 grams) found a "mental level" averaging 112 for the fifty-nine stimulated infants—or 19 points above that of the controls. Replicating these findings in another population and retesting these children at later ages will determine the import of this finding.

Gregg, Haffner, and Korner (1976). Rocking is highly effective in evoking visual alertness in neonates, particularly after a feeding and bowel movement (Wolff, 1965). Undertaken when an infant is in a wakeful, noncrying, and bundled condition, rocking, either in an upright or vertical position, promotes visual alertness and the ability to orient to changing conditions, including the ability to track moving objects.

Korner, Schneider, and Forrest (1983). A group of twenty premature infants (twenty-two to thirty-two weeks old) who were on ventilators for severe respiratory distress were randomly assigned to an experimental group, which received waterbed flotation, or to a control group. At thirty-four to thirty-five weeks of postconceptional age, the infants in the experimental group (who were removed from the waterbeds forty-eight hours before testing) were in a visually alert, inactive state more than twice as often as the controls, performed significantly better in attending to and pursuing visual and auditory stimuli, were much less irritable, and demonstrated significantly more mature motor behavior.

Rose (1980). Extrasensory stimulation of preterm infants in the hospital—including twenty-minute sessions of rocking three times daily, together with exposure and habituation to sets of visual stimuli (photographs) containing patterns and faces—resulted in enhanced visual recognition abilities at six months of age compared with preterm controls. Performance, in fact, was restored to the level of full-term infants. The "habituation and novelty" test paradigms used have been demonstrated to be relatively strong predictors of IQ at an extremely early age—even as young as four months of age (see Chapter Seven).

The "untreated" preterm infants failed to differentiate the novel from the familiar stimuli (within the allotted looking times); they looked equally long at previously seen and newly shown faces, and at multidimensionally varied patterns. By contrast, both the full-term group and the preterm group that received the stimulation looked at the novel stimuli 50 percent longer than they did the familiar stimuli.

When the "untreated" preterm group was given substantially longer exposure times, they were able to habituate to the familiar stimuli (that is, to reduce the length of time they looked at them).

Thus, many preterm infants appear to register and/or process visual information much more slowly than full-term infants. Through a brief intervention program, however, it might be possible to ameliorate, if not totally eliminate, this deficit.

By contrast, intervention programs featuring other forms of stimulation produced less-favorable results.

Rice (1977). An intervention program that featured 120 fifteen-minute periods of stroking (with an emphasis on stroking of the head) produced absolutely no advantage in head circumference size at four months of age for the fifteen stimulated (minority-group) infants, compared with controls.

Powell (1974). When provided with a regimen of tactile stimulation through stroking, many of the infants who weighed less than 1,500 grams responded to the stroking as if it was quite noxious.

Malloy (1979). A large sample (127) of premature infants were (1) exposed to six daily five-minute recordings of their mothers' voices until their weight reached 2,000 grams, (2) exposed to a similar regimen of Brahms's "Lullaby," or (3) given no special regimen of auditory stimulation. At nine months of age there were no discernible differences in cognitive or physical development between the three groups.

A recent study of a three-month intervention program for LBW infants (under 2,200 grams) found that their thirty-six- and forty-eight-month IQs (McCarthy General Cognitive Index scores) could be restored to normal, that is, were equal to those of full-term normal-birth-weight controls (Rauh and others, 1988). However, even though this experimental group's average was 13 points above that of LBW infants not receiving this intervention, the "flip-a-coin" selection process that was used produced a (LBW) control sample with an SES and parental education average lower than that of the experimental group, so the direct comparison is subject to bias.

The program featured seven in-hospital sessions and four in-home follow-up (one-hour) sessions that focused on such areas as demonstrating the infant's potential for self-regulation and interaction, suggesting techniques for recognizing infant distress and infant readiness for interaction, and explaining mechanisms for inducing a state of quiet alertness. Sixteen of the twenty-five infants in the experimental group were firstborns, and the average maternal age was twenty-nine. At forty-eight months, the experimental group's McCarthy IQ scores averaged 111.6.

In a series of recent studies, Stern and Karraker (1988, 1989, forthcoming) have shown that (1) the mothers of premature neonates have a number of negative biases concerning these infants (demonstrated by showing them videotapes of two full-term nine-month-old infants playing with toys, telling them that one was premature and the other full term, and asking them to rate these infants in a variety of areas). Moreover, these biases negatively affect their perceptions of their own infants and do so in ways that are likely to affect their caregiving style adversely.

But when a brief description of the similarities between full-term and premature infants was read to them just prior to showing these videotapes, the mothers altered their biases (they no longer rated the infants they thought were premature as less cognitively competent and less sociable, and they liked them more than they did the infants they were told were full term). These mothers were Caucasian, averaged thirty years of age, and four-fifths of them had some college background.

Mothers of LBW infants were found to be "significantly behind mothers of normal-term babies in smiling at them and holding them close, both before discharge and four weeks after discharge" (Leifer, Leiderman, Barnett, and Williams, 1972). This was true whether or not these mothers had been allowed to have physical contact with them in the hospital.

Even though (at four, eight, and twelve months) the mothers of preterm infants were reported as having consistently worked harder at engaging their babies than did the mothers of full-term infants, their children smiled less, displayed less positive affect, and averted their gaze from their mothers more frequently than did the full-term infants studied (Crnic and others, 1983). In still another study, preterm infants were reported to have a tendency to be less responsive and less active than their full-term counterparts, even though the parents of the former tended to invest more effort in stimulating and interacting with them (Goldberg, 1979). Thus, it appears that mothers of preterm infants need to adapt their normal nurturing behavior to address the special stimulatory needs of these infants.

Effects of Historical Trends in Medical Technology

Over the past generation, medical technology has markedly increased the survival rates for LBW babies and has progressively lowered the weight threshold above which premature infants stand good survival chances. Although this would suggest that the number of premature infants who experience moderate-to-severe cognitive deficits has been increasing, there are indications that improvements in neonatal intensive care practices are reducing the severity of these deficits. For example, a decade-long study of the auditory and visual orienting responses of twenty-five to thirty-four-week gestational-age infants (assessed just prior to hospital discharge) found that the responses of the premature infants born between 1984 and 1987 were significantly better developed than those of the premature infants born in the same hospitals between 1977 and 1979 (Riese, 1989).

Nevertheless, the rate of cognitive deficits of moderate severity remains relatively high, and — because it appears that these can (in large part) be overcome if appropriate intervention strategies are initiated on a timely basis — there is a clear need to develop and fund programs designed to educate hospital staff and parents of LBW and microcephalic babies about their special needs, as well as recognizing and altering their preconceptions about premature infants. Further, the use of gently oscillating waterbeds would seem to be an especially important addition to neonatal intensive care units, because these provide compensatory vestibular stimulation to preterm infants, who normally experience a great deal of this type of stimulation prenatally but are largely deprived of it when growing to term in incubators (Korner, 1986).

The Medical Risks of Later Childbearing

Later childbearing has long been associated with increased medical risks. In addition to a markedly higher incidence of Down's syndrome, the medical literature often links midlife childbearing with increased risk of complicated delivery and higher rates of perinatal, infant, and maternal mortality. Given the strong secular trend toward postponing family formation and the positive correlation between maternal age and IQ, it is appropriate to provide an up-to-date assessment of these risks.

The prevalence of Down's syndrome increases with maternal age — from approximately 0.1 percent of live births to thirty-year-old women to 0.3 percent to thirty-five-year-old women, 0.9 percent to forty-year-old women, and 3.1 percent to forty-five-year-old women (Hook, 1976; Hook and Chambers, 1977). Amniocentesis and chorionic villi sampling represent two low-risk methods for detecting the presence of this condition (Brody, 1989).

A critical evaluation of the medical literature linking pregnancy outcome with maternal age has concluded that most of the 104 studies examined are biased in ways that significantly overstate the risks of age. For example, the fact that the number of previous pregnancies (and children) increases with age and a disproportionate number of midlife childbearers are of lower SES status and/or already have several children to care for contribute to these mothers' lowered ability and willingness to obtain appropriate prenatal care. As well, even after equating for birth order, midlife childbearers are more likely to have medical problems that interfered with earlier efforts to conceive or to carry a fetus to full term (Mansfield, 1986a, 1986b, 1988). When only high-quality studies were analyzed (for example, those that took into account social class and birth order), Mansfield found that the age-related incidence of certain birth complications (such as LBW or longer duration of labor) disappeared and that the influence of other age-related conditions could be attributed in large part to specific health problems (such as an increasing incidence of hypertension and diabetes with age) or to the markedly higher rate of cesarean sections performed on older women (which Mansfield concludes is, in the main, a response by the medical community to its perception that midlife pregnancies represent high-risk pregnancies). *Confirming this view is a recent study of 511 pregnancies to women over the age of forty, which indicates that healthy women of normal body weight* (below 150 pounds) *receiving modern medical care can expect a pregnancy outcome virtually identical with that of younger women* (Spellacy, Miller, and Winegar, 1986).

✖ References ✖

Achenbach, T. M. (1978). The Child Behavior Profile. *Journal of Consulting and Clinical Psychology, 46*, pp. 478–488.

Adevai, G. Silverman, A. J., and McGough, W. E. (1970). Ethnic Differences in Perceptual Testing. *International Journal of Social Psychology, 16*, pp. 237–239.

Adinolfo, M. (1985). The Development of the Human Blood-CSF-Brain Barrier. *Developmental Medicine and Child Neurology, 27*, pp. 532–537.

Aged Apes Show No Decline in Learning Ability. (1985). *New York Times*, June 11, p. C-3.

Ahern, S., and Beatty, J. (1979). Pupillary Responses During Information Processing Vary with Scholastic Aptitude Test Scores. *Science, 205*, pp. 1289–1292.

Allen, N. D., and others. (1988). Transgenes as Probes for Active Chromosomal Domains in Mouse Development. *Nature, 333*, pp. 852–855.

Allport, G. W., and Pettigrew, T. F. (1957). Cultural Influence on the Perception of Movement: The Trapezoidal Illusion Among Zulus. *Journal of Abnormal and Social Psychology, 66*, pp. 104–113.

Alvarez-Baylla, A. and Nottebohm, F. (1988). Migration of Young Neurons in Adult Avian Brain. *Nature, 335*, pp. 353–354.

American Society of Anesthesiology. (1974). Occupational Disease Among Operating Room Personnel. *Anesthesiology*, 41, pp. 131–180.

Anderson, A. M. (1982). The Great Japanese IQ Increase. *Nature*, 297, pp. 180–181.

Anderson, B. A., Vietze, P. M., and Dokecki, P. R. (1977). Reciprocity in Vocal Interactions of Mothers and Infants. *Child Development, 48*, pp. 195–203.

Aram, D. M., and Healy, J. M. (1988). Hyperlexia: A Review of Extraordinary Word Recognition. In L. K. Obler and D. Fein (Eds.), *The Exceptional Brain: Neuropsychology of Talent and Special Abilities.* New York: Guilford Press.

Arensburg, B., and others. (1989). A Middle Paleolithic Human Hyoid Bone. *Nature, 338*, pp. 758–760.

Arezzo, F. (1989). Sea Urchin Sperm as a Vector of Foreign Genetic Information. *Cell Biology International Reports, 13*, pp. 391–404.

Armitage, S. E., Baldwin, B. A., and Vince, M. A. (1980). The Fetal Sound Environment of Sheep. *Science, 208*, pp. 1173–1174.

Asher, C., and Roberts, J.A.F. (1949). A Study of Birth Weight on Intelligence. *Journal of the British Society of Medicine, 3*, pp. 56–68.

Aslin, R. N. (1986). Visual and Auditory Development in Infancy. In J. D. Osofsky (Ed.), *Handbook of Infant Development.* (2nd ed.) New York: Wiley.

Babson, G., and others. (1964). Growth and Development of Twins of Dissimilar Size at Birth. *Pediatrics, 33*, pp. 327–333.

Backman, M. E. (1972). Patterns of Mental Abilities: Ethnic, Socioeconomic, and Sex Differences. *American Educational Research Journal, 9*, pp. 1–12.

Badger, E. (1977). The Infant Stimulation/Mother Training Program. In B. M. Caldwell (Ed.), *Infant Education: A Guide for Helping Handicapped Children in the First Three Years.* New York: Walker.

Bahrick, H. (1984). Semantic Memory Content in Permastore: Fifty Years of Memory for Spanish Learned in School. *Journal of Experimental Psychology, 113*, pp. 1–29.

Bahrick, L. E. (1988). Intermodal Learning in Infancy: Learning on the Basis of Two Kinds of Invariant Relations in Audible and Visual Events. *Child Development, 59,* pp. 197–209.

Bahrick, L. E., and Pickens, J. N. (1989). *Infant Memory for Object Motion Across a One-Month Period as Indexed by a Familiarity Preference.* Paper presented at biennial meeting of the Society for Research in Child Development, Kansas City, Mo.

Bakke, J. L., and others. (1975). Endocrine Syndromes Produced by Neonatal Hyperthyroidism, Hypothyroidism, or Altered Nutrition and Effects in Untreated Progeny. In D. A. Fisher and G. N. Burrow (Eds.), *Perinatal Thyroid Physiology and Disease.* New York: Raven Press.

Ball, W. A., and Tronick, E. (1971). Infant Responses to Impending Collisions: Optical and Real. *Science, 171,* pp. 818–820.

Banks, M. S. (1980). The Development of Visual Accommodation During Early Infancy. *Child Development, 51,* pp. 646–666.

Banks, M. S., and Salapetek, P. (1981). Infant Pattern Vision: A New Approach Based on the Contrast Sensitivity Function. *Journal of Experimental Child Psychology, 31,* pp. 1–45.

Bardin, C. W., and others. (1988). The Sertoli Cell. In E. Knobil and J. Neil (Eds.), *The Physiology of Reproduction.* New York: Raven Press.

Barnard, K. E., and Bee, H. L. (1983). The Impact of Temporally Patterned Stimulation on the Development of Preterm Infants. *Child Development, 54,* pp. 1156–1167.

Barnard, K. E., Bee, H. L., and Hammond, M. A. (1984). Home Environment and Cognitive Development in a Healthy, Low-Risk Sample: The Seattle Study. In A. W. Gottfried (Ed.), *Home Environment and Early Cognitive Development.* Orlando, Fla: Academic Press.

Barrera, M. E., and Maurer, D. (1981). The Perception of Facial Expression by the Three-Month-Old. *Child Development, 52,* pp. 203–206.

Bayley, N. (1969). *Bayley Scales of Infant Development.* San Antonio, Tex.: Psychological Corporation.

Bayley, N., and Schaefer, E. (1964). Correlations of Maternal and Child Behaviors with the Development of Mental Abilities.

Monographs of the Society for Research in Child Development, serial no. 97.

Bazso, J., Karnaysin, L., and Gelec, K. (1964). Observations on the Physical and Mental Development in Newborn Infants of Intrauterine Growth Retardation. *Proceedings of the International Copenhagen Congress on the Scientific Study of Mental Retardation.*

Beale, I. L., and Corballis, M. C. (1983). *The Ambivalent Mind: The Neurophysiology of Left and Right.* Chicago: Nelson Hall.

Beckwith, L., and Cohen, S. E. (1984). Home Environment and Cognitive Competence in Preterm Children During the First 5 Years. In A. W. Gottfried (Ed.), *Home Environment and Early Cognitive Development.* Orlando, Fla.: Academic Press.

Beckwith, L., and Cohen, S. E. (1989). Maternal Responsiveness with Preterm Infants and Later Competency. In M. H. Bornstein (Ed.), *Maternal Responsiveness: Characteristics and Consequences.* New Directions for Child Development, no. 43. San Francisco: Jossey-Bass.

Belmont, L., and Marolla, F. A. (1973). Birth Order, Family Size, and Intelligence. *Science, 182*, pp. 1096–1101.

Belmont, L., Stein, Z., and Zybert, P. (1978). Intellectual Abilities in Two-Child Families. *Science, 202*, pp. 995–966.

Belmont, L., and others. (1981). Maternal Age and Children's Intelligence. In K. G. Scott, T. Field, and E. Robertson (Eds.), *Teenage Parents and Their Offspring.* New York: Grune & Stratton.

Benbow, C. P. (1985). Paper presented at the Foundation for Brain Research conference on Neurobiology of Extraordinary Intellectual Giftedness, New York, Apr.

Benbow, C. P. (1987). Possible Biological Correlates of Precocious Mathematical Reasoning Ability. *Trends in Neurosciences, 10*, pp. 17–20.

Benbow, C. P. (1988). Neuropsychological Perspectives on Mathematical Talent. In L. K. Obler and D. Fein (Eds.), *The Exceptional Brain.* New York: Guilford Press.

Benbow, C. P., and Benbow, R. M. (1984). Biological Correlates of High Mathematical Reasoning Ability. *Progress in Brain Research, 61*, pp. 469–490.

Benbow, C. P., and Benbow, R. M. (1986). Physiological Correlates of Extreme Intellectual Precocity. *Mensa Research Journal*, *21*, pp. 54–87.

Benbow, C. P., and Benbow, R. M. (1987). Extreme Mathematical Talent: A Hormonally Induced Ability? In D. O. Hossu (Ed.), *Duality and Unity of the Brain*. New York: Macmillan.

Benirschke, K., and Harper, V.D.R. (1977). The Acardiac Anomaly. *Teratology*, *15*, pp. 311–316.

Bennett, E. L. (1976). Experiential Influences on Brain Anatomy and Chemistry in Rodents. In M. R. Rosenzweig and E. L. Bennett (Eds.), *Neural Mechanisms of Learning and Memory*. Cambridge, Mass.: MIT Press.

Bennett, S. (1971). Infant-Caretaker Interactions. *Journal of the American Academy of Child Psychiatry*, *10*, pp. 321–335.

Benowitz, L. I., and others. (1983). Hemispheric Specialization in Nonverbal Communication. *Cortex*, *19*, pp. 5–11.

Berg, C., and Sternberg, R. (1985). Response to Novelty: Continuity Versus Discontinuity in the Developmental Course of Intelligence. *Advances in Child Development and Behavior*, *5*, pp. 143–158.

Berg, W. K., and Berg, K. M. (1979). Psychophysiological Development in Infancy: State, Sensory Function, and Attention. In J. D. Osofsky (Ed.), *Handbook of Infant Development*. New York: Wiley.

Bertoncini, J., and others. (1988). An Investigation of Young Infants' Perceptual Representation of Speech Sounds. *Journal of Experimental Psychology*, *117*, pp. 21–33.

Binet, A. (1966). Mnemonic Virtuosity: A Study of Chess Players. *Genetic Psychology Monographs*, *74*, pp. 127–162.

Birnstiel, M. L., and Busslinger, M. (1989). Dangerous Liaisons: Spermatozoa as Natural Vectors for Foreign DNA? *Cell*, *57*, pp. 708–709.

Birren, J. E., and Schaie, K. W. (1985). *Handbook of the Psychology of Aging*. New York: Van Nostrand Reinhold.

Blinkhorn, S., and Hendrickson, D. (1982). Average Evoked Responses and Psychometric Intelligence. *Nature*, *295*, pp. 596–597.

Bloch, A. (1966). The Kurdistani Cradle Story: A Modern Analysis of This Centuries-Old Infant-Swaddling Practice. *Clinical Pediatrics, 5*, pp. 641–645.

Block, J. (1986). *The Child-Rearing Practices Report (CRPR): A Set of Q Items for the Description of Parental Socialization Attitudes and Values.* Berkeley: University of California Press.

Bloom, B. S. (1982a). The Master Teachers. *Phi Beta Kappan*, pp. 664–668.

Bloom, B. S. (1982b). The Role of Gifts and Markers in the Development of Talent. *Exceptional Children, 48*, pp. 510–522.

Bloom, B. S., and Sosniak, L. A. (1981). Talent Development Versus Schooling. *Educational Leadership, 39*, pp. 86–94.

Bohlen, P., Esch, F., and Baird, J. (1985). Acidic Fibroblast Growth Factor (FGF) from Bovine Brain. *Embryology, 4*, pp. 1951–1956.

Bomba, P. C., and Siqueland, E. R. (1983). The Nature and Structure of Infant Form Categories. *Journal of Experimental Child Psychology, 35*, pp. 294–328.

Bornstein, M. H. (1984). *Infant Attention and Caregiver Stimulation: Two Contributions to Early Cognitive Development.* Paper presented at International Conference on Infant Studies, New York.

Bornstein, M. H. (1985). How Infant and Mother Jointly Contribute to Developing Cognitive Competence in the Child. *Proceedings of the National Academy of Sciences, 82*, pp. 7470–7473.

Bornstein, M. H., and Benasich, A. A. (1986). Infant Habituation: Assessments of Individual Differences and Short-Term Reliability at Five Months. *Child Development, 57*, pp. 87–99.

Bornstein, M. H., Ferdinandsen, K., and Gross, C. G. (1981). Perception of Symmetry in Infancy. *Developmental Psychology, 17*, pp. 82–86.

Bornstein, M. H., and Krinsky, S. (1985). Perception of Symmetry in Infancy: The Salience of Vertical Symmetry and the Perception of Pattern Wholes. *Journal of Experimental Child Psychology, 39*, pp. 1–19.

Bornstein, M. H., Krinsky, S., and Benasich, A. A. (1986). Fine Orientation Discrimination and Shape Constancy in Young Infants. *Journal of Experimental Child Psychology, 41*, pp. 49–60.

Bornstein, M. H., and Ruddy, M. G. (1984). Infant Attention and

Maternal Stimulation. Prediction of Cognitive and Linguistic Development in Singletons and Twins. In D. Bouma and D. Bouwhuis (Eds.), *Attention and Performance*. Vol. 10. Hillsdale, N. J.: Erlbaum.

Bornstein, M. H., and Sigman, M. D. (1986). Continuity in Mental Development from Infancy. *Child Development, 57*, pp. 251–274.

Bornstein, M. H., and Tamis, C. (1986). *Origins of Cognitive Skills in Infants*. Paper presented at the International Conference on Infant Studies, Los Angeles.

Bornstein, M. H., and Tamis-LeMonda, C. S. (1989). Maternal Responsiveness and Cognitive Development in Children. In M. H. Bornstein (Ed.), *Maternal Responsiveness: Characteristics and Consequences*. New Directions for Child Development, no. 43. San Francisco: Jossey-Bass.

Borton, R. W. (1979). *The Perception of Causality in Infants*. Paper presented at biennial meeting of the Society for Research in Child Development, San Francisco.

Bouchard, T. J., Jr. (1983). Do Environmental Similarities Explain the Similarity of Identical Twins Reared Together? *Intelligence, 7*, pp. 175–184.

Bouchard, T. J., Jr., and McGue, M. (1981). Familial Studies of Intelligence: A Review *Science, 212*, pp. 1055–1059.

Boutry, M., and others. (1987). Targeting of Bacterial Chloramphenicol Acetyltransferase to Mitochondria in Transgenic Plants. *Nature, 328*, pp. 340–342.

Bouvier, U. (1969). *Evolution des cotes à quelques tests* [Evolution of scores from several tests]. Brussels: Center of Research into Human Traits, Belgium Armed Forces.

Bower, B. (1989). Talk of Ages. *Science News, 136*, pp. 24–26.

Bower, T.G.R. (1971). The Object in the World of the Infant. *Scientific American, 225*, no. 5, pp. 38–47.

Bower, T.G.R. (1974). Repetition in Human Development. *Merrill-Palmer Quarterly, 20*, pp. 303–318.

Bower, T.G.R. (1979). *Human Development*. New York: W. H. Freeman.

Brackbill, Y. (1971). Cumulative Effects of Continuous Stimulation on Arousal Levels in Infants. *Child Development, 42,* pp. 17–26.

Brackbill, Y., and Nichols, P. L. (1982). A Test of the Confluence Model of Intellectual Development. *Developmental Psychology, 18,* pp. 192–198.

Brackett, B G., Baranska, W., Sawicki, W., and Koprowski, H. (1971). Uptake of Heterologous Genome by Mammalian Spermatozoa and Transfer to Ova Through Fertilization. *Proceedings of the National Academy of Sciences, 68,* pp. 353–357.

Braddick, O., and others. (1979). A Photorefractive Study of Infant Accommodation. *Vision Research, 19,* pp. 1319–1330.

Bradley, R. H., and Caldwell, B. M. (1984). 174 Children: A Study of the Relationship Between Home Environment and Cognitive Development During the First 5 Years. In W. Gottfried (Ed.), *Home Environment and Early Cognitive Development.* Orlando, Fla.: Academic Press.

Bradshaw, J. L., and Nettleton, N. C. (1981). The Nature of Hemispheric Specialization in Man. *Behavioral and Brain Sciences, 4,* pp. 51–91.

Bradshaw, J. L., and Nettleton, N. C. (1983). *Human Cerebral Asymmetry.* Englewood Cliffs, N. J.: Prentice-Hall.

Brand, C. R. (1984). Intelligence and Inspection Time: An Ontogenetic Relationship. In C. J. Turner and H. B. Miles (Eds.), *The Biology of Human Intelligence. Proceedings of the 20th Annual Symposium of the Eugenics Society.* Nafferton, England: Nafferton Books.

Brand, C. R. (1987). Bryter Still and Bryter. *Nature, 328,* p. 110.

Brazelton, T. B. (1973). Neonatal Behavioral Assessment Scale. Philadelphia: Lippincott.

Brazelton, T. B. (1974). The Origins of Reciprocity: The Early Mother-Infant Interaction. In M. Lewis and L. Rosenblum (Eds.), *The Origins of Behavior.* New York: Wiley.

Brazelton, T. B. (1986). Development of Newborn Behavior. In F. Farkner and J. M. Tanner (Eds.), *Human Growth: A Comprehensive Treatise.* Vol. 2. New York: Plenum.

Breland, H. M. (1974). Birth Order, Family Configuration, and Verbal Achievement. *Child Development, 45,* pp. 1011–1019.

Brennan, T. L., Funk, S. G., and Frothingham, T. E. (1985).

Disproportionate Intrauterine Head Growth and Developmental Outcome. *Developmental Medicine and Child Neurology, 27*, pp. 746–750.

Brent, L. (1981). Lamarck and Immunity: The Tables Unturned. *New Scientist, 90*, p. 493.

Briggs, J. L. (1970). *Never in Anger: Portrait of an Eskimo Family.* Cambridge, Mass.: Harvard University Press.

Brinker, R. P., and Lewis, M. (1982). Contingency Intervention in Infancy. In J. Anderson and J. Cox (Eds.), *Curriculum Materials for High Risk and Handicapped Infants.* Chapel Hill, N. C.: Technical Assistance and Development System.

Broadbent, D. E. (1984). The Maltese Cross. *Behavioral and Brain Sciences, 7*, 55–94.

Brody, J. E. (1989). Changing Times and Medical Advances Make Later Pregnancies More Common and Much Less Risky. *New York Times,* July 13, 1989, p. B5.

Broman, S. H., Nichols, P. L., and Kennedy, W. A. (1975). *Preschool IQ: Prenatal and Early Developmental Correlates.* Hillsdale, N. J. Erlbaum.

Bronson, G. (1974). The Postnatal Growth of Visual Capacity. *Child Development, 45*, pp. 873–890.

Bruner, J. S. (1977). Early Social Interaction and Language Acquisition. In H. R. Shaffer (Ed.), *Studies in Mother-Infant Interaction.* Orlando, Fla.: Academic Press.

Burks, B. S. (1928). The Relative Influence of Nature and Nurture upon Mental Development. *Twenty-Seventh Yearbook of the National Society for the Study of Education, 27* (1), pp. 219–316.

Burks, B. S. (1938). One the Relative Contributions of Nature and Nurture to Average Group Differences in Intelligence. *Proceedings of the National Academy of Sciences, 24*, pp. 276–282.

Burling, T. A., Sappington, J. T., and Mead, A. M. (1983). Lateral Specialization of a Perpetual Calendar Task in a Moderately Mentally Retarded Adult. *American Journal of Mental Deficiency, 88*, pp. 326–328.

Burnett, S. A., Lane, D. M., and Dratt, L. M. (1979). Shape Visualization and Sex Differences in Quantitative Ability. *Intelligence, 3*, pp. 345–354.

Bush, G. L., Case, S. M., Wilson, A. C., and Patton, J. L. (1977).

Rapid Speciation and Chromosomal Evolution in Mammals. *Proceedings of the National Academy of Sciences, 74* (9), pp. 3942–3946.

Bushnell, I.W.R. (1982). Discrimination of Faces by Young Infants. *Journal of Experimental Child Psychology, 33*, pp. 298–308.

Bushnell, I.W.R., Gerry, G., and Burt, K. (1983). The Externality Effect in Neonates. *Infant Behavior and Development, 6*, pp. 151–156.

Butterfield, E. C., and Cairns, G. F. (1974). Discussion Summary: Infant Reception Research. In R. L. Schiefelbusch and L. L. Lloyd (Eds.), *Language Perspectives: Acquisition, Retardation, and Intervention*. Baltimore: University Park Press.

Butterworth, G., and Cochran, E. (1980). Toward a Mechanism of Joint Visual Attention in Human Infancy. *International Journal of Behavioral Development, 3*, pp. 253–272.

Caan, R. L., Stoneking, M., and Wilson, A. C. (1987). Mitochondrial DNA and Human Evolution. *Nature, 325*, pp. 31–36.

Caldwell, B. M. (1967). *The Preschool Inventory*. Princeton, N. J.: Educational Testing Service.

Caldwell, B. M., and Bradley, R. H. (1978). *Home Observation for Measurement of the Environment*. Little Rock: University of Arkansas Press.

Caldwell, B. M., and Bradley, R. H. (1984). *Home Observation for Measurement of the Environment, Administrative Manual*. (Rev. ed.) Little Rock: University of Arkansas Press.

Campbell, J. H. (1982). Autonomy in Evolution. In R. Milkman (Ed.), *Perspectives on Evolution*. Sunderland, Mass.: Sinauer.

Campbell, J. H. (1983). Evolving Concepts of Multigene Families. *Isozymes, 10*, pp. 401–417.

Campbell, J. H. (1985). An Organizational Interpretation of Evolution. In D. J. Depew and B. H. Weber (Eds.), *Evolution at a Crossroads: The New Biology and the New Philosophy of Science*. Cambridge, Mass.: MIT Press.

Campbell, J. H. (1987). The New Gene and Its Evolution. In K.S.W. Campbell and M. F. Day (Eds.), *Rates of Evolution*. London: Allen & Unwin.

Campbell, J. H., and Perkins, P. (1988). Transgenerational Effects of Drug and Hormonal Treatments in Mammals. *Progress in Brain Research, 73,* pp. 535–553.

Campbell, J. H., and Zimmermann, E. G. (1982). Automodulation of Genes: A Proposed Mechanism for Persisting Effects of Drugs and Hormones in Mammals. *Neurobehavioral Toxicology and Teratology, 4,* pp. 435–439.

Campos, J. J., and Bertenthal, B. I. (1989). Locomotion and Psychological Development in Infancy. In F. Morrison, K. Lord, and D. Keating (Eds.), *Applied Developmental Psychology.* Orlando, Fla.: Academic Press.

Cantor, S. (1973). Some Aspects of Cognitive Function in Twins. In G. S. Claridge, S. Cantor, and W. I. Hume (Eds.), *Personality Differences and Biological Variation.* Elmsford, N. Y.: Pergamon Press.

Capron, C., and Duyme, M. (1989). Assessment of Effects of Socioeconomic Status on IQ in a Full Cross-Fostering Study. *Nature, 340,* pp. 552–553.

Carew, J. V. (1980). Experience and the Development of Intelligence in Young Children at Home and in Day Care. *Monographs of the Society for Research in Child Development,* serial no. 187.

Carmon, A. (1978). *Asymmetrical Function of the Brain.* Cambridge, England: Cambridge University Press.

Carmon, A. (1981). Temporal Processing and the Left Hemisphere. *Behavioral and Brain Sciences, 4,* pp. 66–67.

Caron, A. J., Caron, R. F., and Glass, P. (1983). Responsiveness to Relational Information as a Measure of Cognitive Functioning in Nonsuspect Infants. In T. Field and A. Sostic (Eds.), *Infants Born at Risk: Physiological, Perceptual, and Cognitive Processes.* Orlando, Fla.: Grune & Stratton.

Caron, A. J., Caron, R. F., and MacLean, D. J. (1988). Infant Discrimination of Naturalistic Emotional Expressions. *Child Development, 59,* pp. 604–616.

Carpenter, E. S. (1955). Space Concepts of the Aivilik Eskimos. *Explorations, 5,* pp. 131–145.

Carpenter, G. C. (1974). Visual Regard of Moving and Stationary Faces. *Merrill-Palmer Quarterly, 20,* pp. 181–194.

Carroll, J. B., Kjeldegaard, P. M., and Carton, A. S. (1962). Opposites versus Primaries in Free Association. *Journal of Verbal Learning and Verbal Behavior, 1*, pp. 22–30.

Castillo, M, and Butterworth, G. (1981). Neonatal Localization of Sound in Visual Space. *Perception, 10*, pp. 331–338.

Catherwood, D., Crassini, B., and Freiberg, K. (1989). Infant Response to Stimuli of Similar Hue and Dissimilar Shape: Tracing the Origins of the Categorization of Objects by Hue. *Child Development, 60*, pp. 752–762.

Cattell, J. M. (1903). A Statistical Study of Eminent Men. *Popular Science Monthly, 5*, pp. 359–377.

Cattell, J. M., and Brimhall, D. R. (1921). *American Men of Science.* New York: Science Press.

Cattell, R. B. (1950). The Fate of National Intelligence. *Eugenics Review, 42*, pp. 136–148.

Caudill, W. A. (1972). Tiny Dramas: Vocal Communication Between Mother and Infant in Japanese and American Families. In W. F. Lebra (Ed.), *Transcultural Research in Mental Health.* Vol. 2: *Mental Health and Research in Asia and the Pacific.* Honolulu: University Press of Hawaii.

Caudill, W. A. (1973). Social Structure and Culture in Japan and America. *Journal of Nervous and Mental Disease, 157*, pp. 240–257.

Caudill, W. A., and Frost, L. (1971). *A Comparison of Maternal Care and Infant Behavior in Japanese American, American, and Japanese Families.* Paper presented at the Stanford Conference on Mental Health and Anthropology, Palo Alto, Calif.

Caudill, W. A., and Schooler, C. (1973). Child Behavior and Child Rearing in Japan and in the United States: An Interim Report. *Journal of Nervous and Mental Disease, 157*, pp. 323–338.

Caudill, W. A., and Weinstein, H. (1969). Maternal Care and Infant Behavior in Japan and America. *Psychiatry, 32*, pp. 12–43.

Chang, H. W., and Trehub, S. E. (1977). Auditory Processing of Relational Information by Young Infants. *Journal of Experimental Child Psychology, 24*, pp. 324–331.

Charness, N., and Campbell, J.I.D. (1988). Acquiring Skill at

Mental Calculation in Adulthood: A Task Decomposition. *Journal of Experimental Psychology, 117*, pp. 115–129.

Chaudhari, N., and Hahn, W. E. (1983). Genetic Expression in the Developing Brain. *Science, 220*, p. 924.

Chugani, H. T., Phelps, M. E., and Mazziotta, J. C. (1987). Positron Emission Tomography Study of Human Brain Functional Development. *Annals of Neurology, 22*, pp. 487–497.

Cicirelli, V. G. (1976). Sibling Constellation, Creativity, IQ, and Academic Achievement. *Child Development, 12*, pp. 369–370.

Cicirelli, V. G. (1978). The Relation of Sibling Structure to Intellectual Abilities and Achievement. *Review of Educational Research, 48*, pp. 365–379.

Clarke, S.C.T., Nyberg, V., and Worth, W. H. (1978a). *Alberta Grade III Achievement Study*. Edmonton: University of Alberta Press.

Clarke, S.C.T., Nyberg, V., and Worth, W. H. (1978b). *Technical Report on Edmonton Grade III Achievement: 1956–1977 Comparisons*. Edmonton; University of Alberta Press.

Clarke-Stewart, K. A. (1973). Interactions Between Mothers and Their Young Children: Characteristics and Their Consequences. *Monographs of the Society for Research in Child Development*, serial no. 153.

Clarkson, M. G., Morrongiello, B. A., and Clifton, R. K. (1982). Stimulus Presentation Probability Influences Newborns' Head Orientation to Sound. *Perceptual and Motor Skills, 55*, pp. 1239–1246.

Clifton, R. K., and Nelson, M. N. (1976). Developmental Study of Habituation in Infants: The Importance of Paradigm, Response System, and State. In T. J. Tighe and R. N. Leaton (Eds.), *Habituation: Perspectives from Child Development, Animal Behavior, and Neurophysiology*. Hillsdale, N. J.: Erlbaum.

Coates, D. L., and Lewis, M. (1984). Early Mother-Infant Interaction and Infant Cognitive Status as Predictors of School Performance and Cognitive Behavior in Six-Year-Olds. *Child Development, 55*, pp. 1219–1230.

Cohen, L. B., and Younger, B. A. (1984). Infant Perception of Angular Relations. *Infant Behavior and Development, 7*, pp. 37–47.

Cohen, P., and others. (1980). The Effects of Teenaged Motherhood and Maternal Age on Offspring Intelligence. *Social Biology, 27*, pp. 138–154.

Cohn, J. F., and Tronick, E. Z. (1987). Mother-Infant Face-to-Face Interactions: The Sequencing of Dyadic States at Three, Six, and Nine Months. *Developmental Psychology, 23*, pp. 68–77.

Cohn, J. F., and Tronick, E. Z. (1988). Mother-Infant Face-to-Face Interactions: Influence Is Bidirectional and Unrelated to Periodic Cycles in Either Partner's Behavior. *Developmental Psychology, 24*, pp. 386–392.

Cohn, S. J., Carlson, J. S., and Jensen, A. R. (1985). Speed of Information Processing in Academically Gifted Youths. *Personality and Individual Differences, 6*, pp. 621–629.

Coker, R. E., and others. (1959). Public Health as Viewed by the Medical Student. *American Journal of Public Health, 49*, pp. 601–609.

Collis, G. M. (1977). Visual Co-Orientation of Maternal Speech. In H. R. Schaffer (Ed.), *Studies in Mother-Infant Interaction*. Orlando, Fla.: Academic Press, pp. 355–375.

Collis, G. M., and Schaffer, H. R. (1975). Synchronization of Visual Attention in Mother-Infant Pairs. *Journal of Child Psychology and Psychiatry, 16*, pp. 315–320.

Colombo, J., Mitchell, D. W., and Horowitz, F. D. (1988). Infant Visual Attention in the Paired-Comparison Paradigm. *Child Development, 59*, pp. 1198–1210.

Colombo, J., Mitchell, D. W., Horowitz, F. D., and Rash, S. (1989). *Infants' Detection of Frequency Modulation in Noise*. Paper presented at biennial meeting of the Society for Research in Child Development, Kansas City, Mo.

Comber, L. C., and Keeves, J. (1973). *Science Education in Nineteen Countries: An Empirical Study*. New York: Wiley.

Commons, M. L. (1985). Paper presented at the Foundation for Brain Research conference on Neurobiology of Extraordinary Intellectual Giftedness, New York, Apr.

Condon, W. S., and Sander, L. W. (1974). Synchrony Demonstrated Between Movements of the Neonate and Adult Speech. *Child Development, 45*, pp. 456–462.

Corballis, M. C., and Sergent, J. (1989). Hemispheric Specialization for Mental Rotation. *Cortex, 25,* pp. 15–26.

Cornell, E. H. (1979). Infant's Recognition Memory, Forgetting, and Savings. *Journal of Experimental Child Psychology, 28,* pp. 359–374.

Cox, C. M. (1926). The Early Mental Traits of Three Hundred Geniuses. *Genetic Studies of Genius.* Vol. 2. Stanford, Calif.: Stanford University Press.

Cranberg, L. D., and Albert, M. L. (1988). The Chess Mind. In L. K. Obler and D. Fein (Eds.), *The Exceptional Brain: Neuropsychology of Talent and Special Abilities.* New York: Guilford Press.

Crick, F., and Mitcheson, G. (1983). The Function of Dream Sleep. *Nature, 292,* pp. 186–188.

Crnic, K. A., and others. (1983). Effects of Stress and Social Support on Mothers and Premature and Full-Term Infants. *Child Development, 54,* pp. 209–217.

Culp, R. E. (1973). *Effect of Mothers' Voices on Infant Looking Behavior.* Paper presented at annual meeting of the American Psychological Association, Montreal.

Culp, R. E., Appelbaum, M. I., Osofsky, J. D., and Levy, J. A. (1988). Adolescent and Older Mothers: Comparison Between Prenatal Maternal Variables and Newborn Interaction Measures. *Infant Behavior and Development, 11,* pp. 353–362.

Darsie, M. L. (1926). Mental Capacity of American-Born Japanese Children. *Comparative Psychology Monographs, 3* (15).

Davies, M., and Hughes, A. G. (1927). An Investigation into Comparative Intelligence and Attainments of Jewish and Non-Jewish Children. *British Journal of Psychology, 28,* pp. 134–146.

Davis, D. J., Cahan, S., and Bashi, J. (1977). Birth Order and Intellectual Development: The Confluence Model in the Light of Cross-Cultural Evidence. *Science, 196,* pp. 1470–1472.

Davis, F. A., and DeCasper, A. J. (1989). *Intrauterine Heartbeat Sounds Are Reinforcing for Newborns Because of Active Right-Lateralized Processes.* Paper presented at the biennial meeting of the Society for Research in Child Development, Kansas City, Mo.

Davis, J. A. (1962). *Stipends and Spouses: The Finances of American*

Arts and Sciences Graduate Students. Chicago: University of Chicago Press.

Davis, J., and Rovee-Collier, C. K. (1985). Alleviating Forgetting of a Learned Contingency in 8-Week-Old Infants. *Developmental Psychology, 19*, pp. 353–365.

Deary, I. J., Caryl, P. G., Egan, V., and Wight, D. (1989). Visual and Auditory Inspection Time: Their Interrelationship and Correlations with IQ in High-Ability Subjects. *Personality and Individual Differences, 10*, pp. 525–533.

DeCasper, A. J., and Fifer, W. P. (1980). Of Human Bonding: Newborns Prefer Their Mothers' Voices. *Science, 208*, pp. 1174–1176.

DeCasper, A. J., and Spence, M. J. (1986). Prenatal Maternal Speech Influences Newborns' Perception of Speech Sounds. *Infant Behavior and Development, 9*, pp. 133–150.

DeFries, J. C., and Plomin, R. (1978). Behavior Genetics. *Annual Review of Psychology, 29*, pp. 473–515.

deGroot, A. D. (1978). *Thought and Choice in Chess.* (2nd ed.) The Hague: Mouton.

deLemos, M. M. (1984). A Note on the Australian Norms of the Standard Progressive Matrices. *ACER Bulletin for Psychologists, 36*, pp. 9–12.

Delis, D., and others. (1983). The Contribution of the Right Hemisphere to the Organization of Paragraphs. *Cortex, 19*, pp. 43–50.

Demany, L. (1982). Auditory Stream Segregation in Infancy. *Infant Behavior and Development, 5*, pp. 261–276.

Demany, L., MacKenzie, B., and Vurpillot, E. (1977). Rhythm Perception in Early Infancy. *Nature, 266*, pp. 718–719.

Depression Linked to Stroke Damage (1982). *Science '82, 3* (5), p. 8.

Dershowitz, Z. (1971). Jewish Subcultural Patterns and Psychological Differentiation. *International Journal of Psychology, 6*, pp. 223–231.

Dershowitz, Z., and Frankel, Y. (1975). Jewish Culture and the WISC and WAIS Patterns. *Journal of Consulting and Clinical Psychology, 43*, pp. 126–134.

Diamond, M. C. (1985). Paper presented at the Foundation for

Brain Research conference on the Neurobiology of Extraordinary Intellectual Giftedness, New York, Apr.

Diamond, M. C., and others. (1984). Increased Cortical Thickness in Male Progeny from Enriched Parents Before and During Gestation. *Proceedings: 16th Annual Meeting of the Society for Neuroscience*, sequence 287.8.

Diamond, M. C., and others. (1985). Plasticity in the 904-Day-Old Male Rat Cerebral Cortex. *Experimental Neurology, 87*, pp. 309–317.

Dobbing, J. (1981). The Later Development of the Brain and Its Vulnerability. In J. A. Davis and J. Dobbing (Eds.), *Scientific Foundation of Pediatrics*. London: Heinemann.

Dobbing, J., and Sands, J. (1973). Quantitative Growth and Development in the Human Brain. *Archives of Disease in Childhood, 48*, pp. 757–767.

Doolittle, R. F. (1981). Similar Amino Acid Sequences: Chance or Common Ancestry? *Science, 214*, pp. 149–159.

Doolittle, R. F., and Sapienza, C. (1980). Selfish Genes, the Phenotype Paradigm, and Genomic Evolution. *Nature, 284*, pp. 601–603.

Douglas, J.W.B. (1969). Effects of Early Environment on Later Development. *Journal of the Royal College of Physicians, 3*, p. 359.

Douglas, J.W.B., Ross, J. M., and Simpson, H. R. (1968). *All Our Future: A Longitudinal Study of Secondary Education*. London: Davies.

Dover, G. A. (1982). Molecular Drive: A Cohesive Model of Species Evolution. *Nature, 299*, 111–117.

Dover, G. A., and Flavell, R. B. (1984). Molecular Co-Evolution: rDNA Divergence and the Maintenance of Function. *Cell, 38*, pp. 622–623.

Drash, P. W., and Liebowitz, M. J. (1973). Operant Conditioning of Speech and Language in the Nonverbal Retarded Child. *Pediatric Clinics of North America, 20*, pp. 233–243.

Drash, P. W., and Stolberg, A. L. (1972). *Acceleration of Cognitive, Linguistic, and Social Development in the Normal Infant*. Tallahassee: Florida State Department of Health and Rehabilitation Services. (ED 145938)

Drash, P. W., and Stolberg, A. L. (1979). *Intellectual Acceleration in*

Normal and Down's Syndrome Children Through Infant Stimulation and Language Training. Paper presented at 25th annual conference of the Southeastern Psychological Association, New Orleans. (ED 176482)

Drash, P. W. , and Tutor, R. M. (forthcoming). Cognitive Development Therapy: A New Model for Treatment of an Overlooked Population, Developmentally Delayed Preschool Children. *Psychotherapy in Private Practice.*

Drillien, C. M. (1970). The Small-for-Date Infant: Etiology and Prognosis. *Pediatric Clinics of North America, 17,* pp. 9–23.

Drillien, C. M., Thomson, A.J.M., and Burgoyne, K. (1980). Low-Birth-Weight Children at Early School Age: A Longitudinal Study. *Developmental Medicine and Child Neurology, 22,* pp. 26–47.

Dunn, J. P., and others. (1963). Social-Class Gradient of Serum Uric-Acid Levels in Man. *Journal of the American Medical Association, 185,* pp. 431–436.

Dunn, L. M., and Dunn, L. N. (1981). *Peabody Picture Vocabulary Test — Revised.* Circle Pines, Minn.: American Guidance Service.

Durden-Smith, J., and DeSimone, D. (1984). Hidden Threads of Illness. *Science Digest,* Jan., p. 53.

Easley, J., and Easley, E. (1982). *Math Can Be Natural.* Urbana: University of Illinois Committee on Culture and Cognition.

Eilers, R., and Minifie, F. D. (1975). Fricative Discrimination in Early Infancy. *Journal of Speech and Hearing Research, 18,* pp. 158–169.

Eilers, R., and Oller, D. K. (1985). Infant Speech Perception: Environmental Contributions. In S. E. Trehub and B. Schneider (Eds.), *Auditory Development in Infancy.* Vol. 10: *Advances in the Study of Communication and Affect.* New York: Plenum.

Eimas, P. (1975). Speech Perception in Early Infancy. In L. B. Cohen and P. Salapatek (Eds.), *Infant Perception: From Sensation to Cognition.* Vol. 2. Orlando, Fla.: Academic Press.

Eimas, P., Siqueland, E., Jusczyk, P., and Vigorito, J. (1971). Speech Perception in Infants. *Science, 171,* pp. 303–306.

Einstein's Brain Abounds with Glia. (1985). *Gifted Children Monthly, 6* (6), p. 5.

Eisenberg, R. B. (1976). *Auditory Competence in Early Life: The Roots of Communicative Behavior*. Baltimore, Md.: University Park Press.

Eisenberg, R. B., Coursin, D. B., and Rupp, N. R. (1966). Habituation to an Acoustical Pattern as an Index of Differences Among Human Neonates. *Journal of Auditory Research, 6*, pp. 239–248.

Eisenman, R., and Schussel, N. C. (1970). Creativity, Birth Order, and Preference for Symmetry. *Journal of Consulting and Clinical Psychology, 34*, pp. 275–280.

Elley, W. B. (1969). Changes in Mental Ability in New Zealand Schoolchildren. *New Zealand Journal of Educational Studies, 4*, pp. 140–155.

Ellis, H. (1904). *A Study of British Genius*. London: Blackett.

Emmett, W. G. (1950). The Trend of Intelligence in Certain Districts of England. *Population Studies, 3*, pp. 324–371.

Erlenmeyer-Kimling, L., and Jarvik, L. F. (1963). Genetics and Intelligence: A Review. *Science, 142*, pp. 1477–1479.

Esch, F., and others. (1985). Primary Structure of Bovine Brain Acidic Fibroblast Growth Factor. *Biochem. Phys. Res. Comm.*, 1985, *133*, pp. 554–562.

Eysenck, H. J., and Kamin, L. J. (1981). *The Intelligence Controversy*. New York: Wiley.

Fagan, J. F., and McGrath, S. (1981). Infant Recognition Memory and Later Intelligence. *Intelligence, 5*, pp. 121–130.

Fagan, J. F., and Singer, L. T. (1983). Infant Recognition Memory as a Measure of Intelligence. In L. Lipsitt and C. Rovee-Collier (Eds.), *Advances In Infancy Research*. Vol. 2. Norwood, N. J.: Ablex.

Fagen, J. W., and others. (1987). *Infant Long-Term Memory for a Conditioned Response and Intelligence Test Performance at 2 Years of Age*. Paper presented at biannual meeting of the Society for Research in Child Development, Baltimore, Md., Apr.

Fantz, R. L., and Nevis, S. (1967a). Pattern Preferences and

Reciprocal-Cognitive Development in Early Infancy. *Merrill-Palmer Quarterly, 13*, pp. 77–108.

Fantz, R. L., and Nevis, S. (1967b). The Predictive Value of Changes in Visual Preferences in Early Infancy. In J. Helmuth (Ed.), *The Exceptional Infant.* Vol. 1. Seattle: Special Child Publications.

Farrer, L. A., and Conneally, P. M. (1985). A Genetic Model for Age of Onset in Huntington's Disease. *American Journal of Human Genetics, 37*, pp. 350–357.

Fawcett, D. W. (1975). Ultrastructure and Function of the Sertoli Cell. In *Handbook of Physiology.* Vol. 5, sec. 7: *The Male Reproductive System.*

Fenson, L., Vella, D., and Kennedy, M. (1989). Children's Knowledge of Thematic and Taxonomic Relations at Two Years of Age. *Child Development, 60*, pp. 911–919.

Fernald, A. (1987). Acoustic Determinants of Infant Preferences for Motherese Speech. *Infant Behavior and Development, 10*, pp. 279–294.

Field, T. M. (1977). The Effects of Early Separation, Interactive Deficits, and Experimental Manipulations on Infant-Mother Face-to-Face Interaction. *Child Development, 48*, pp. 763–771.

Field, T. M. (1981). Infant Arousal, Attention, and Affect During Early Interactions. In L. P. Lipsitt (Ed.), *Advances in Infancy Research.* Vol. 1. Norwood, N. J.: Ablex.

Field, T. M., Woodson, R., Greenburg, R., and Cohen, D. (1982). Discrimination and Imitation of Facial Expressions by Neonates. *Science, 218*, pp. 179–181.

Fischer, K. W. (1987). Relations Between Brain and Cognitive Development. *Child Development, 58*, pp. 623–632.

Fischer, K. W., and Silvern, L. (1985). Stages and Individual Differences in Cognitive Development. *Annual Review of Psychology, 36*, pp. 613–648.

Fisher, C. B., Ferdinandsen, K., and Bornstein, M. H. (1981). The Role of Symmetry in Infant Form Discrimination. *Child Development, 52*, pp. 457–462.

Fisher, J., and Hinde, R. A. (1949). The Opening of Milk Bottles by Birds. *British Birds, 42*, pp. 347–357.

Fishman, I. (1944). *Jewish Education in Central Europe (1600–1800)*. London: Goldstone.

Fiske, E. B. (1987). Comparing the U.S. and Japan. *New York Times*, Jan. 11, p. A-1.

Fitch, W. M., and Atchley, W. R. (1985). Evolution in Inbred Strains of Mice Appears Rapid. *Science*, 228, pp. 1169–1175.

Flatz, G., and Rotthauwe, H. W. (1977). The Human Lactase Polymorphism: Physiology and Genetics of Lactose Absorption and Malabsorption. *Progress in Medical Genetics*, 2, pp. 205–250.

Flemington, J. J., Dalton, R., and Standage, K. F. (1977). Age as a Factor in the Handedness of Adults. *Neuropsychologia*, 15, pp. 471–473.

Flynn, J. R. (1982). Lynn, the Japanese, and Environmentalism. *Bulletin of the British Psychological Society*, 35, pp. 409–413.

Flynn, J. R. (1983). Now the Great Augmentation of the American IQ. *Nature*, 301, p. 655.

Flynn, J. R. (1984a). IQ Gains and the Binet Decrements. *Journal of Educational Measurement*, 21, pp. 283–290.

Flynn, J. R. (1984b). The Mean IQ of Americans: Massive Gains 1932 to 1978. *Psychological Bulletin*, 95, pp. 29–51.

Flynn, J. R. (1987). Massive IQ Gains in 14 Nations: What IQ Tests Really Mean. *Psychological Bulletin*, 101, pp. 171–191.

Fodor, J. A., Garrett, M. F., and Brill, S. L. (1975). Pi Ka Pu: The Perception of Speech Sounds by Prelinguistic Infants. *Perception and Psychophysics*, 18, pp. 74–78.

Fogel, A. (1988). Cyclicity and Stability in Mother-Infant Face-to-Face Interactions: A Comment on Cohn and Tronick. *Developmental Psychology*, 24, pp. 393–397.

Fowler, W. (1971). Mental Prodigies. *Encyclopedia of Education*. Vol. 6. New York: Macmillan.

Fowler, W. (1972). A Developmental Learning Approach to Infant Care in a Group Setting. *Merrill-Palmer Quarterly*, 18, pp. 145–175.

Fowler, W. (1975). How Adult-Child Ratios Influence Infant Development. *Interchange*, 6, pp. 17–31.

Fowler, W. (1983). *Potentials of Childhood.* 2 vols. Lexington, Mass: Lexington Books.

Fowler, W. (forthcoming). *Talking in Infancy: How to Nurture and Cultivate Early Language Development.* Cambridge, Mass.: Brookline Books.

Fowler, W., and Swenson, A. (1979). The Influence of Early Language Stimulation on Development: Four Studies. *Genetic Psychology Monographs, 100*, pp. 73–109.

Fox, R., Aslin, R. N., Shea, S. L., and Dumais, S. T. (1980). Stereopsis in Human Infants. *Science, 218*, pp. 486–487.

Francis-Williams, J., and Davies, P. A. (1974). Very Low Birth Weight and Later Intelligence. *Developmental Medicine and Child Neurology, 16*, pp. 709–728.

Freedle, R., and Lewis, M. (1977). Prelinguistic Conversations. In *Interaction, Conversation, and the Development of Language.* New York: Wiley.

Freedman, D. G. (1974). *Human Infancy: An Evolutionary Perspective.* Hillsdale, N. J.: Erlbaum.

Freeman, J. (1983). Environment and High IQ: A Consideration of Fluid and Crystallized Intelligence. *Personality and Individual Differences, 4*, pp. 303–313.

Freeman, J. (1985). Emotional Aspects of Giftedness. In J. Freeman (Ed.), *The Psychology of Gifted Children.* New York: Wiley.

Fried, I., and others. (1982). Organization of Visuospatial Functions in Human Cortex: Evidence from Electrical Stimulation. *Brain, 105*, pp. 349–371.

Fried, P. A., and Charlebois, A. T. (1979). Cannabis Administration During Pregnancy: First-and-Second Generation Effects in Rats. *Physiological Psychology, 7*, pp. 307–310.

Friedler, G. (1974). Long-Term Effects of Opiates. In J. Dancis and J. E. Hwang (Eds.), *Perinatal Pharmacology: Problems and Priorities.* New York: Raven Press.

Friedman, S. (1972). Habituation and Recovery of Visual Response in the Alert Human Newborn. *Journal of Experimental Child Psychology, 13*, pp. 339–349.

Fujikura, T., and Froehlich, L. A. (1974). Mental and Motor Development in Monozygotic Co-Twins with Dissimilar Birth Weights. *Pediatrics, 53*, p. 8.

Furnham, A., and Rawles, R. (1988). Spatial Ability at Different Times of Day. *Personality and Individual Differences*, *9*, pp. 937–939.

Galbraith, R. C. (1983). Individual Differences in Intelligence: A Reappraisal of the Confluence Model. *Intelligence*, *7*, pp. 185–194.

Galper, R. E., and Costa, L. (1980). Hemispheric Differences for Recognizing Faces Depends on How They Are Learned. *Cortex*, *16*, pp. 21–38.

Galton, F. (1874). *English Men of Science: Their Nature and Nurture*. New York: Macmillan.

Galton, F. (1907). *Inquiries into the Human Faculty and Its Development*. London: Dent.

Ganon, E. C., and Swartz, K. B. (1980). Perception of Internal Elements of Compound Figures by One-Month-Old Infants. *Journal of Experimental Child Psychology*, *30*, pp. 159–170.

Garber, H. L., and Heber, R. (1973). *The Milwaukee Project: Early Intervention as a Technique to Prevent Mental Retardation*. Report to the Social and Rehabilitation Service, Department of Health, Education, and Welfare. (ED 080162)

Garber, H. L., and Heber, R. (1977). The Milwaukee Project. In P. Mittler (Ed.), *Research to Practice in Mental Retardation*. Vol. 1: *Care and Intervention*. The Hague: IASSMD.

Garber, H. L., and Heber, R. (1981). The Efficiency of Early Intervention with Family Rehabilitation. In M. J. Begab, H. C. Haywood, and H. L. Garber (Eds.), *Psychosocial Influences in Retarded Performance*. Vol. 2: *Strategies for Improving Competence*. Baltimore, Md.: University Park Press.

Gardner, H. (1985). *Frames of Mind: The Theory of Multiple Intelligences*. New York: Basic Books.

Gardner, J. W., and others. (1985). Residual Function Following Hemispherectomy for Tumor and for Infantile Hemiplegia. *Brain*, *79*, pp. 487–502.

Gardner, M. F. (1981). *Expressive One-Word Picture Vocabulary Test*. Novato, Calif.: Academic Therapy Publications.

Gates, A., and Bradshaw, J. L. (1977). Music Perception and Cerebral Asymmetries. *Cortex*, *13*, pp. 390–401.

Gazzaniga, M. S., and others. (1984). Profiles of Right-

Hemisphere Language and Speech Following Brain Bisection. *Brain and Language*, *22*, pp. 206–220.

Geschwind, N., and Behan, P. (1982). Left-Handedness: Association with Immune Disease, Migraine, and Developmental Learning Disorder. *Proceedings of the National Academy of Sciences*, *79*, pp. 5097–5100.

Geschwind, N., and Behan, P. (1984). Laterality, Hormones, and Immunity. In N. Geschwind and A. Galaburda (Eds.), *Cerebral Dominance: The Biological Foundations*. Cambridge, Mass.: Harvard University Press, pp. 211–224.

Giacoman, S. L. (1971). Hunger and Motor Restraint on Arousal and Visual Attention in the Infant. *Child Development*, *42*, pp. 605–614.

Gibson, E. J. (1987). Introductory Essay: What Does Infant Perception Tell Us About Theories of Perception. *Journal of Experimental Psychology: Human Perception and Performance*, *13*, pp. 515–523.

Gibson, E. J., and Walker, A. S. (1984). Development of Knowledge of Visual-Tactual Affordances of Substances. *Child Development*, *55*, pp. 453–460.

Gibson, E. J., and Walker-Andrews, A. S. (1986). What Develops in Bimodal Perception. In L. Lipsitt and C. Rovee-Collier (Eds.), *Advances in Infancy Research*. Vol. 4. Norwood, N.J.: Ablex.

Giray, E. F., and others. (1976). The Incidence of Eidetic Imagery as a Function of Age. *Child Development*, *47*, pp. 1207–1210.

Giray, E. F., and others. (1978). *Incidence of Eidetic Imagery in Adulthood and in Old Age*. Paper presented at annual convention of the American Psychological Association, Toronto.

Girod, M., and Allaume, G. (1976). L'evolution du niveau intellectuel de la population française pendent le dernier quart de siècle [The evolution of the intellectual level of the French population during the last quarter century]. *International Review of Applied Psychology*, *25*, pp. 121–123.

Gladwin, T. (1970). *East Is a Big Bird*. Cambridge, Mass.: Harvard University Press.

Goertzel, M. G., Goertzel, V., and Goertzel, T. G. (1978). *Three Hundred Eminent Personalities*. San Francisco: Jossey-Bass.

Goldberg, S. (1979). Premature Birth Consequences for the Parent-Infant Relationship. *American Scientist, 67*, p. 211.

Golinkoff, R. M., and others. (1986). The Infant's Perception of Causal Events: The Distinction Between Animate and Inanimate Objects. In L. Lipsitt and C. Rovee-Collier (Eds.), *Advances in Infancy Research.* (Vol. 3). Norwood, N.J.: Ablex.

Gorczynski, R. M., and Steele, E. J. (1981). Simultaneous Yet Independent Inheritance of Somatically Acquired Tolerance to Two Distinct H-2 Antigenic Haplotype Determinants in Mice. *Nature, 289*, pp. 678–681.

Gotlieb, S. J., Biasini, F. J., and Bray, N. W. (1988). Visual Recognition Memory in IUGR and Normal Birth-Weight Infants. *Infant Behavior and Development, 11*, pp. 223–228.

Gotlieb, S. J., and Sloane, M. E. (1989). *Memory in Human Neonates.* Paper presented at biennial meeting of the Society for Research in Child Development, Kansas City, Mo.

Gottfried, A. W., and Gottfried, A. E. (1984). Home Environment and Cognitive Development in Young Children of Middle-Socioeconomic-Status Families. In A. W. Gottfried (Ed.), *Home Environment and Early Cognitive Development.* Orlando, Fla.: Academic Press.

Gottfried, A. W., and Gottfried, A. E. (1986). Home Environment and Children's Development from Infancy Through School-Entry Years: Results of Contemporary Longitudinal Investigations in North America. *Children's Environments Quarterly, 3*, pp. 3–9.

Greenberg, D. J. (1971). Accelerating Visual Complexity Levels in the Human Infant. *Child Development, 42*, pp. 905–918.

Greenberg, D. J., Hillman, D., and Grice, D. (1975). Perceptual Incongruity and Social Interaction as Determinants of Infants' Reaction to Novel Persons. *Journal of Genetic Psychology, 127*, pp. 215–222.

Greenberg, D. J., and O'Donnell, W. J. (1972). Infancy and the Optimal Level of Stimulation. *Child Development, 43*, pp. 839–845.

Greenberg, D. J., Uzgiris, I. C., and Hunt, J. M. (1970). Attentional Preference and Experience: III. Visual Familiarity and Looking Time. *Journal of Genetic Psychology, 117*, pp. 123–135.

Greenough, W. T. (1976). Enduring Brain Effects of Differential Experience and Training. In M. R. Rosenzweig and E. L. Bennett (Eds.), *Neural Mechanisms of Learning and Memory*. Cambridge, Mass.: MIT Press.

Greenough, W. T. (1986). What's Special About Development? Thoughts on the Basis of Experience-Sensitive Synaptic Plasticity. In W. T. Greenough and J. N. Juraska (Eds.), *Developmental Neuropsychobiology*. Orlando, Fla.: Academic Press.

Gregg, C. L., Haffner, M. E., and Korner, A. F. (1976). The Relative Efficacy of Vestibular-Proprioceptive Stimulation and the Upright Position in Enhancing Visual Pursuit in Neonates. *Child Development, 47*, pp. 309–314.

Grieser, D., and Kuhl, P. K. (1989). Categorization of Speech by Infants: Support for Speech-Sound Prototypes. *Developmental Psychology, 25*, pp. 577–588.

Gross, S. J., Oehler, J. M., and Eckerman, C. O. (1983). Head Growth and Developmental Outcome in Very Low Birth Weight Infants. *Pediatrics, 71*, pp. 70–75.

Grosvenor, T. (1970). Refractive State, Intelligence Test Scores, and Academic Ability. *American Journal of Ophthalmology, 36*, pp. 355–361.

Groudine, M., and Conkin, K. F. (1985). Chromatin Structure and *de Novo* Methylation of Sperm DNA: Implications for Activation of the Paternal Genome. *Science, 228*, pp. 1061–1065.

Grubar, J.-C. (1985). Sleep and Mental Efficiency. In J. Freeman (Ed.), *The Psychology of Gifted Children*. New York: Wiley.

Gruber, H. E. (1986). The Self-Construction of the Extraordinary. In R. J. Sternberg and J. E. Davidson (Eds.), *Conceptions of Giftedness*. Cambridge, England: Cambridge University Press.

Guilford, J. P. (1967). *The Nature of Human Intelligence*. New York: McGraw-Hill.

Guilford, J. P. (1977). *Way Beyond the IQ: A Guide to Improving Intelligence and Creativity*. Buffalo, N.Y.: Creative Education Foundation.

Guilford, J. P. (1979). Intellect and the Gifted. In J. Gowan, J. Khatena, and E. Torrence (Eds.), *Educating the Ablest*. Itasca, Ill.: Peacock.

Guillemin, R. (1978). Peptides in the Brain: The New Endocrinology of the Neuron. *Science, 202,* pp. 390–402.

Guinagh, B. J., and Gordon, I. J. (1976). *School Performance as a Function of Early Stimulation.* Final Report to the Office of Child Development, Institute for Development of Human Resources, University of Florida, Gainesville. (ED 135469)

Gutman, A. B., and Yu, T. F. (1965). Uric-Acid Metabolism in Normal Man and in Primary Gout. *New England Journal of Medicine, 273,* p. 252.

Haber, R. N. (1979). Twenty Years of Haunting Eidetic Imagery: Where's the Ghost? *Behavioral and Brain Sciences, 2,* pp. 583–629.

Haber, R. N., and Haber, R. B. (1964). Eidetic Imagery: Frequency. *Perceptual and Motor Skills, 19,* pp. 131–138.

Hack, M., and Breslau, N. (1986). Very Low Birth Weight Infants: Effects of Brain Growth During Infancy on Intelligence Quotient at 3 Years of Age. *Pediatrics, 77,* pp. 196–201.

Hack, M., and others. (1982). The Prognostic Significance of Postnatal Growth in Very Low Birth Weight Infants. *American Journal of Obstetrics and Gynecology, 143,* pp. 693–699.

Hadchouel, M., and others. (1987). Maternal Inhibition of Hepatitis B Surface Antigen Gene Expression in Transgenic Mice Correlates with *de Novo* Methylation. *Nature, 329,* pp. 454–456.

Hahn, W. E., and Owens, G. P. (forthcoming). *Genes Expressed in the Brain: Evolutionary and Developmental Considerations.*

Hahn, W. E., and others. (1983). Genetic Expression and Postnatal Development of the Brain: Some Characteristics of Nonpolyadenylated mRNAs. *Cold Spring Harbor Symposium on Quantitative Biology, 48,* pp. 465–475.

Haier, R. J., and others. (1983). Electrical Potentials of the Cerebral Cortex and Psychometric Intelligence. *Personality and Individual Differences, 4,* pp. 591–599.

Haier, R. J., and others. (1988). Cortical Glucose Metabolic Rate Correlates of Abstract Reasoning and Attention Studied with Positron Emission Tomography. *Intelligence, 12,* pp. 199–217.

Haith, M. M. (1980). *Rules Babies Look by: The Organization of Newborn Visual Activity.* Hillsdale, N. J.: Erlbaum.

Haith, M. M., Bergman, T., and Moore, M. J. (1977). Eye Contact and Face Scanning in Infancy. *Science, 198*, pp. 853–855.

Handelmann, G. E. (1988). Neuropeptide Influences on the Development of Their Receptors. *Progress in Brain Research, 73*, pp. 523–533.

Hanet, J.-L. (1984–85). Étude comparative du WISC-R et des autres échelles de D. Wechsler pour enfants sur un échantillon de 150 sujets normaux âgés 6 à 10 ans [Comparative study of the WISC-R and the other scales of D. Wechsler for children on a sample of 150 normal subjects aged 6 to 10 years]. Unpublished mémoire de licencié, Université de Liège, Belgium.

Hang, H. (1987). *The German Tribune,* Oct. 25, 1987, p. 14.

Hardy, A. C. (1965). *The Living Stream.* London: Collins.

Hardy-Brown, K., Plomin, R., and DeFries, J. C. (1981). Genetic and Environmental Influences on the Rate of Communicative Development in the First Five Years of Life. *Developmental Psychology, 17*, pp. 704–717.

Hardyck, C., Petrinovich, L. F., and Goldman, R. F. (1976). Left-Handedness and Cognitive Deficits. *Cortex, 12*, pp. 266–279.

Harlow, H. F. (1950). Learning and Satiation of Response in Intrinsically Motivated Complex Puzzle Performance in Monkeys. *Journal of Comparative Physiological Psychology, 43*, pp. 289–294.

Harlow, H. F., Harlow, K., and Meyer, D. R. (1950). Learning Motivated by Manipulation Drive. *Journal of Experimental Psychology, 40*, pp. 228–234.

Haviland, J. M., and Lelwica, M. (1987). The Induced Affect Response: 10-Week-Old Infants' Responses to Three Emotional Expressions. *Developmental Psychology, 23*, p. 97–104.

Hayes, R. F., and Bronzaft, A. L. (1979). Birth Order and Related Variables in an Academically Elite Sample. *Journal of Individual Psychology, 35*, pp. 214–224.

Haynes, H., White, B. L., and Held, R. (1965). Visual Accommodation in Human Infants. *Science, 148*, pp. 528–530.

Hearn, L. (1904). *Japan: An Attempt at Interpretation.* New York: Macmillan.

Hebb, D. O. (1949). *The Organization of Behavior.* New York: Wiley.

Hecht, N. B. (1987). Regulation of Gene Expression During Mammalian Spermatogenesis. In J. Rossant and R. A. Pederson (Eds.), *Experimental Approaches to Mammalian Embryonic Development*. Cambridge, England: Cambridge University Press.

Heilman, K., and others. (1975). Auditory Affective Agnosia. *Journal of Neurology, Neurosurgery, and Psychiatry, 38*, pp. 69–72.

Heimer, L. (1983). *The Human Brain and Spinal Cord*. New York: Springer-Verlag.

Held, R., Birch, E. E., and Gwiazda, J. (1980). Stereoacuity of Human Infants. *Proceedings of the National Academy of Sciences, 77*, pp. 5572–5574.

Hellerstein, D. (1988). Plotting a Theory of the Brain. *New York Times Magazine*, May 22, 1988, p. 17.

Hendrickson, D. E. (1982). The Biological Basis of Intelligence. In H. J. Eysenck (Ed.), *A Model for Intelligence*. New York: Springer.

Heron, E., and Zytkoskee, A. (1981). Visual Performance and Test Performance. *American Journal of Ophthalmology, 58*, pp. 176–178.

Herschel, A. (1946). The Eastern European Era in Jewish History. *Yivo Annual of Jewish Social Science*. Vol. 1. New York: Yiddish Scientific Institute.

Hershenson, M. (1967). Development of the Perception of Form. *Psychological Bulletin, 67*, pp. 326–336.

Hertzog, C. (1989). Influences of Cognitive Slowing on Age Differences in Intelligence. *Developmental Psychology, 25*, pp. 636–651.

Hess, R., and Azuma, H. (1986). Mothering, East and West: What's the Difference. *Gifted Child Monthly, 4*, p. 4.

Hicks, R. A., and Dusek, C. M. (1980). The Handedness Distributions of Gifted and Non-Gifted Children. *Cortex, 16*, pp. 479–481.

Hill, A. L. (1978). Savants: Mentally Retarded Individuals with Special Skills. In N. Ellis (Ed.), *International Review of Research in Mental Retardation*. Orlando, Fla.: Academic Press.

Hirsch, M. J. (1959). The Relationship Between Refractive State of the Eye and Intelligence Test Scores. *American Journal of Ophthalmology, 36,* pp. 12–21.

Holland, B. A. (1986). MRI of Normal Brain Maturation. *American Journal of Neuroradiology, 7,* pp. 201–208.

Holliday, R. (1986). Gene Conversion. In H. Gershowitz, D. L. Rucknagel, and R. E Tashian (Eds.), *Evolutionary Perspectives and the New Genetics.* New York: Liss.

Hollingworth, L. S. (1942). *Children Above 180 IQ, Stanford-Binet.* Chicago: World Book.

Honzik, M. P. (1957). Developmental Studies of Parent-Child Resemblance in Intelligence. *Child Development, 28,* pp. 215–228.

Honzik, M. P., MacFarlane, J. W., and Allen, L. (1948). The Stability of Mental Test Performance Between Two and Eighteen Years. *Journal of Experimental Education, 17,* pp. 309–324.

Hood, L., Campbell, J. H., and Elgin, S.C.R. (1975). The Organization, Expression, and Evolution of Antibody Genes and Other Multigene Families. *Annual Review of Genetics, 9,* pp. 305–353.

Hook, E. B. (1976). Estimates of Age-Specific Risks of a Down's Syndrome Birth by Women Aged 34–41. *Lancet, 2,* pp. 33–34.

Hook, E. B., and Chambers, G. M. (1977). Estimated Rates of Down's Syndrome in Live Births by One Year Maternal Age Intervals for Mothers Aged 20–49 in a New York State Study. *Birth Defects: Original Article Series, 13,* pp. 123–141.

Hopfield, J. J., Feinstein, D. I., and Palmer, R. G. (1983). "Unlearning" Has a Stabilizing Effect in Collective Memories. *Nature, 304,* p. 158.

Horn, J. M., Loehlin, J. C., and Willerman, L. (1979). Intellectual Resemblance Among Adoptive and Biological Relatives: The Texas Adoption Project. *Behavior Genetics, 9,* pp. 177–207.

Horowitz, F. (1974). Visual Attention, Auditory Stimulation, and Language Discrimination in Young Infants. *Monographs of the Society for Research in Child Development, 39,* serial no. 158.

Howell, J. R. (1955). Changes in Wechsler Subtest Scores with Age. *Journal of Consulting Psychology, 19,* pp. 47–50.

Hubel, D. H., and Wiesel, T. N. (1970). The Period of Susceptibility to the Physiological Effects of Unilateral Eye Closure in Kittens. *Journal of Physiology, 206*, pp. 419–436.

Hughes, A. G. (1928). Jews and Gentiles. *Eugenics Review, 20*, pp. 89–94.

Humphrey, G. K., Humphrey, B. E., Muir, D. W., and Dodwell, P. C. (1986). Pattern Perception in Infants: Effects of Structure and Transformation. *Journal of Experimental Child Psychology, 41*, pp. 128–148.

Hunt, J. McV. (1981). Experiential Roots of Intention, Initiative, and Trust. In H. I. Day (Ed.), *Advances in Intrinsic Motivation and Esthetics*. New York: Plenum.

Hunt, J. McV. (1986). The Effects of Variations in Quality and Type of Early Child Care on Development. In W. Fowler (Ed.), *Early Experience and the Development of Competence*. New Directions for Child Development, no. 32. San Francisco: Jossey-Bass.

Hunt, J. McV., Mohandessi, K., Ghodssi, M., and Akiyama, M. (1976). The Psychological Development of Orphanage-Reared Infants: Interventions with Outcomes (Tehran). *Genetic Psychology Monographs, 94*, pp. 177–226.

Hunt, J. V., Tooley, W. H., and Harvin, D. (1982). Learning Disabilities in Children with Birth Weights Below 1,500 Grams. *Seminars in Perinatology, 6*, pp. 280–287.

Hunter, J. E. (1986). Cognitive Ability, Cognitive Aptitudes, Job Knowledge, and Job Performance. *Journal of Vocational Behavior, 29*, pp. 340–362.

Hunter, J. E., and Hunter, R. F. (1984). Validity and Utility of Alternative Predictions of Job Performance. *Psychological Bulletin, 96*, p. 110.

Huron, J. (1981). Electrophysiological Analysis of Sleep Cycles in Normal and "Gifted" Adults. *Journal of Electroencephalography and Clinical Neurophysiology*, 1981, *52*, p. 128.

Husen, T. (1960). Abilities of Twins. *Scandinavian Journal of Psychology, 1*, pp. 125–135.

Husen, T. (Ed.) (1967). *International Study of Achievement in Mathematics: A Comparison of Twelve Countries*. New York: Wiley.

Huttenlocher, P. R. (1979). Synaptic Density in Human Frontal

Cortex: Developmental Changes and Effects of Aging. *Brain Research, 163*, pp. 195–205.

Huxley, A. (1970). *The Doors of Perception.* New York: Harper & Row.

Inouye, E., Park, K. S., and Asaka, A. (1984). Blood Uric Acid Level and IQ: A Study in Twin Families. *Acta Genet. Med. Gemellol., 33*, pp. 237–242.

Jacobs, B. S., and Moss, H. A. (1976). Birth Order and Sex of Sibling as Determinants of Mother and Infant Interaction. *Child Development, 47*, pp. 315–322.

Jacobson, S. W. (1979). Matching Behavior in the Young Infant. *Child Development, 50*, pp. 425–430.

Jencks, C., and others. (1972). *Inequality: A Reassessment of the Effect of Family and Schooling in America.* New York: Harper & Row.

Jensen, A. R. (1985). The Nature of the Black-White Differences on Various Psychometric Tests: Spearman's Hypothesis. *Behavioral and Brain Sciences, 8*, pp. 193–263.

Jensen, A. R., Cohn, S. J., and Cohn, C.M.G. (1989). Speed of Information Processing in Academically Gifted Youths and Their Siblings. *Personality and Individual Differences, 10*, pp. 29–33.

Jirari, C. C. (1970). *Form Perception, Innate Form Preference, and Visually Mediated Head-Turning in the Human Neonate.* Unpublished doctoral dissertation, Department of Psychology, University of Chicago.

Joffe, J. M. (1979). Influence of Drug Exposure of the Father on Perinatal Outcome. *Clinics in Perinatology, 6*, pp. 21–36.

Johnson, F. M., and others. (1981). The Detection of Mutants in Mice by Electrophoresis: Results of a Model Induction Experiment with Procarbazine. *Genetics, 97*, p. 113.

Jones, H. E., and Conrad, H. S. (1933). The Growth and Decline of Intelligence: A Study of a Homogeneous Group Between the Ages of Ten and Sixty. *Genetic Psychology Monographs, 13*, pp. 223–298.

Joseph, R. (1982). The Neuropsychology of Development: Hemispheric Laterality, Limbic Language, and the Origin of Thought. *Journal of Clinical Psychology, 13*, pp. 527–544.

Joseph, R., and others. (1984). Two Brains, One Child: Interhemispheric Information Transfer Deficits and Confabulatory Responding in Children Aged 4, 7, and 10. *Cortex, 20*, pp. 317–321.

Juel-Nielson, N. (1980). *Individual and Environment: Monozygotic Twins Reared Apart*. New York: International Universities Press.

Jusczyk, P. W., and Thompson, E. (1978). Perception of a Phonemic Contrast in Multisyllabic Utterances by 2-Month-Old Infants. *Perception and Psychophysics, 23*, pp. 105–109.

Jusczyk, P. W., and others. (1977). Categorical Perception of Non-Speech Sounds by 2-Month-Old Infants. *Perception and Psychophysics, 21*, pp. 50–54.

Kaelber, C. T., and Pugh, T. F. (1969). Influence of Intrauterine Relations on the Intelligence of Twins. *New England Journal of Medicine*, Aug. 5, pp. 1030–1034.

Kamin, L. J. (1978). Transfusion Syndrome and the Heritability of IQ. *Annals of Human Genetics, 42*, pp. 161–171.

Kanarfogel, E. (1985). Attitudes Toward Childhood and Children in Medieval Jewish Society. In D. R. Blumenthal (Ed.), *Approaches to Judaism in Medieval Times*. Vol. 2. Chico, Calif.: Scholars Press.

Kaneko, S. (1970). Changes in Intelligence Test Performance. *Bulletin of Niigata University, 15*, pp. 11–20.

Karlsson, J. L. (1973). Genetic Relationship Between Giftedness and Myopia. *Hereditas, 73*, pp. 85–86.

Karlsson, J. L. (1975). Influence of the Myopia Gene on Brain Development. *Clinical Genetics, 8*, pp. 314–318.

Kaufman, A. S. (1976). Verbal-Performance IQ Discrepancies on the WISC-R. *Journal of Consulting and Clinical Psychology, 44*, pp. 739–744.

Kaufman, A. S., and Doppelt, J. E. (1976). Analysis of WISC-R Standardization Data in Terms of the Stratification Variables. *Child Development, 47*, pp. 165–171.

Kaufman, A. S., and Kaufman, N. L. (1977). *Clinical Evaluation of Young Children with the McCarthy Scales*. Orlando, Fla.: Grune & Stratton.

Kaufman, A. S., and Kaufman, N. L. (1983). *KABC Interpretative Manual*. Circle Pines, Minn.: American Guidance Service.

Kellman, P. J., Gleitman, H., and Spelke, E. S. (1987). Object and

Observer Motion in the Perception of Objects by Infants. *Journal of Experimental Psychology: Human Perception and Performance, 13*, pp. 586–593.

Kellman, P. J., and Short, K. R. (1987). Development of Three-Dimensional Form Perception. *Journal of Experimental Psychology: Human Perception and Performance, 13*, pp. 545–557.

Kessen, W., Levine, J., and Wendrich, A. (1979). The Imitation of Pitch in Infancy. *Infant Behavior and Development, 2*, pp. 93–99.

Kinney, D. K., and Kagan, J. (1976). Infant Attention to Auditory Discrepancy. *Child Development, 47*, pp. 155–164.

Kinsbourne, M. (1981, May). Sad Hemisphere, Happy Hemisphere. *Psychology Today*, p. 1235.

Kirk, S. A., McCarthy, J. J., and Kirk, W. D. (1968). *Illinois Test of Psycholinguistic Abilities*. Urbana: University of Illinois Press.

Kirkwood, T.B.L. (1982). IQ Jump or Trend? *Nature, 299*, p. 8.

Kitano, M. K., and DeLeon, J. (1988). Use of the Stanford Binet Fourth Edition in Identifying Young Gifted Children. *Roeper Review, 10*, pp. 156–159.

Klarenberg, A. J. (1988). The Functional Significance of Regulatory Gene Variation. In G. de Jong (Ed.), *Population Genetics and Evolution*. Berlin: Springer-Verlag.

Klein, N., Hack, M., Gallagher, J., and Fanaroff, A. A. (1985). Preschool Performance of Children with Normal Intelligence Who Were Very Low Birth Weight Infants. *Pediatrics, 75*, pp. 531–537.

Kleiner, K. A., and Banks, M. S. (1987). Stimulus Energy Does Not Account for Two-Month-Olds' Face Preferences. *Journal of Experimental Psychology: Human Perception and Performance, 13*, pp. 594–600.

Kleinfeld, J. S. (1971). Visual Memory in Village Eskimo and Urban Caucasian Children. *Arctic, 24*, pp. 132–138.

Kleinfeld, J. S. (1973). Intellectual Strengths in Culturally Different Groups. *Review of Educational Research, 43*, pp. 341–359.

Kleinman, J. C., and Kessel, S. S. (1987). Racial Differences in Low Birth Weight: Trends and Risk Factors. *New England Journal of Medicine, 317*, pp. 749–753.

Knobloch, W. H., and others. (1985). Eye Findings in Twins

Reared Apart. *Ophthalmology and Paediatric Genetics, 5,* pp. 59–66.

Koppman, L., and Postal, B. (1979). *Guess Who's Jewish in American History?* New York: Shapolsky Books.

Korner, A. F. (1986). The Use of Waterbeds in the Care of Preterm Infants. *Journal of Perinatology, 6,* pp. 142–147.

Korner, A. F., Schneider, P., and Forrest, T. (1983). Effects of Vestibular-Proprioceptive Stimulation on the Neurobehavioral Development of Preterm Infants: A Pilot Study. *Neuropediatrics, 14,* pp. 170–182.

Korner, A. F., and Thoman, E. B. (1970). Visual Alertness in Neonates as Evoked by Maternal Care. *Journal of Experimental Child Psychology, 10,* pp. 67–78.

Kosslyn, S. M. (1980). *Image and Mind.* Cambridge, Mass.: Harvard University Press.

Kosslyn, S. M. (1988). Aspects of a Cognitive Neuroscience of Mental Imagery. *Science, 240,* pp. 1621–1626.

Kosslyn, S. M., and others. (1985). A Computational Analysis of Mental Image-Generation: Evidence from Functional Deassociation in Split-Brain Patients. *Journal of Experimental Psychology, 114,* pp. 311-341.

Kovach, J. K. (1983). Perceptual Imprinting: Genetic Influences and Genotype-Environment Interactions. *Developmental Psychobiology, 16,* pp. 413–422.

Kovach, J. K. (1985). Constitutional Biases in Early Perceptual Learning. *Journal of Comparative Psychology, 99,* pp. 35–46.

Kovach, J. K. (1986). Toward the Genetics of an Engram: The Role of Heredity in Visual Preferences and Perceptual Imprinting. In J. L. Fuller and E. C. Simmel (Eds.), *Perspectives in Behavior Genetics.* Hillsdale, N.J.: Erlbaum.

Kramer, L. I., and Pierpont, M. E. (1976). Rocking Waterbeds and Auditory Stimuli to Enhance Growth of Preterm Infants. *Journal of Pediatrics, 88,* pp. 297–299.

Kratz, G. S. (1989). Voice-Speech-Language. In M. E. Landesberg (Ed.), *The Genesis of Language.* Berlin: de Gruyter.

Krugman, J. (1951). Pupil Functioning on the Stanford-Binet

and the WISC. *Journal of Consulting and Clinical Psychology, 15*, pp. 475–483.

Krystal, M., Ruddle, F. H., and Arnheim, N. (1981). Human Nucleolus Organizers on Nonhomologous Chromosomes Can Share the Same Ribosomal Gene Variants. *Proceedings of the National Academy of Sciences, 78*, pp. 5744–5748.

Kuczynski, L., and Kochanska, G. (1987). *Developmental Change in Parental Control Strategies During the Second and Third Years of Life.* Paper presented at biennial meeting of Society for Research in Child Development, Baltimore, Md., Apr.

Kuenzle, C. C., and Knusel, A. (1974). Mass Training of Rats in a Super-Enriched Environment. *Physiology and Behavior*, 1974, *13*, pp. 205–210.

Kuhl, P. K. (1976). Speech Perception in Early Infancy: The Acquisition of Speech-Sound Categories. In S. K. Hirsh and others (Eds.), *Hearing and Davis: Essays Honoring Halowell Davis.* St. Louis, Mo.: Washington University Press.

Kuhl, P. K., and Meltzoff, A. N. (1982). The Bimodal Perception of Speech in Infancy. *Science, 218*, p. 1138.

Kuhl, P. K., and Meltzoff, A. N. (1988). Speech as an Intermodal Object of Perception. In A. Yonas (Ed.), *Perceptual Development in Infancy: Minnesota Symposium on Child Psychology.* Hillsdale, N.J.: Erlbaum.

Kuhl, P. K., and Miller, J. D. (1975). Speech Perception by the Chinchilla. *Science, 190*, pp. 69–72.

Kusano, K., Miledi, R., and Stinnaker, J. (1977). Acetylcholine Receptors in the Oocyte Membrane. *Nature, 270*, pp. 739–741.

Lally, J. R. (1973). *The Family Development Research Program.* Progress Report, College of Human Development, Syracuse University.

Lancer, J., and Rim, Y. (1984). Intelligence, Family Size, and Sibling Age Spacing. *Personality and Individual Differences, 5*, pp. 151–157.

Lantis, M. (1968). A Teacher's View of Culture. In *A Positive Image for the Alaska Native Learner.* Anchorage: Bureau of Indian Affairs, pp. 17–61.

Lavitrano, M., and others. (1989). Sperm Cells as Vectors for

Introducing Foreign DNA into Eggs: Genetic Transformation of Mice. *Cell, 57*, pp. 717–723.

Lazar, I., and Darlington, R. (1982). Lasting Effects of Early Education: A Report from the Consortium for Longitudinal Studies. *Monographs of the Society for Research in Child Development*, Serial no. 195.

Leahy, A. M. (1935). Nature-Nurture and Intelligence. *Genetic Psychological Monographs, 17*, pp. 237–308.

Leeuw, J. de, and Meester, A. C. (1984). Over het intelligente — onderzoek bij de militaire keuringen vanaf 1925 tot heden [Intelligence — as tested at selections for the military service from 1925 to the present]. *Mens en Maatschappij, 59*, pp. 5–26.

Leifer, A. D., Leiderman, P. H., Barnett, C. R., and Williams, J. A. (1972). Effects of Mother-Infant Separation on Maternal Attachment Behavior. *Child Development, 43*, pp.1203–1215.

Lesser, G. S., Fifer, G., and Clark, D. H. (1965). Mental Abilities of Children from Different Social-Class and Cultural Groups. *Monographs of the Society for Research in Child Development*, serial no. 102.

Levinson, B. M. (1957a). A Comparative Study of the Intelligence of Jewish Preschool Boys and Girls of Orthodox Parentage. *Journal of Genetic Psychology, 90*, pp. 17–22.

Levinson, B. M. (1957b). The Intelligence of Applicants to Jewish Day Schools. *Jewish Social Studies, 19*, pp. 129–140.

Levinson, B. M. (1958). Culture, Pressure, and WAIS Scatter in a Traditional Jewish Setting. *Journal of Genetic Psychology, 93*, pp. 277–286.

Levinson, B. M. (1959). A Comparison of the Performance of Monolingual and Bilingual Native-Born Jewish Children of Traditional Parentage on Four Intelligence Tests. *Journal of Clinical Psychology, 15*, pp. 74–76.

Levinson, B. M. (1960). A Comparative Study of the Verbal and Performance Ability of Monolingual and Bilingual Native-Born Jewish Preschool Children of Traditional Parentage. *Journal of Genetic Psychology, 97*, pp. 93–112.

Levinson, B. M. (1962). Subcultural Values and IQ Stability. *Journal of Genetic Psychology, 98*, pp. 69–82.

Levinson, B. M. (1963). Some Research Findings with Jewish Subjects of Traditional Backgrounds. *Mental Hygiene, 47*, pp. 129–134.

Levinson, B. M. (1977). Cognitive Styles of Eastern European Jewish Males. *Perceptual and Motor Skills, 45*, pp. 279–283.

Levinson, B. M., and Block, Z. (1977). Goodenough-Harris Drawings of Jewish Children of Orthodox Background. *Psychological Reports, 41*, pp. 155–158.

Levitt, A., and others. (1988). The Perception of Place of Articulation Contrasts in Voiced and Voiceless Fricatives by 2-Month-Old Infants. *Journal of Experimental Psychology: Human Perception and Performance, 14*, pp. 361–368.

Levy, J. (1969). Possible Basis for the Evolution of Lateral Specialization of the Human Brain. *Nature, 224*, pp. 614–615.

Lewis, D. (1979). *How to Be a Gifted Parent.* New York: Norton.

Lewis, J., and others. (1975). *Family Developmental Center: A Demonstration Project.* Final Report to the Office of Child Development. (ED 121412)

Lewis, M., and Coates, D. L. (1980). Mother-Infant Interaction and Cognitive Development in Twelve-Week-Old Infants. *Infant Behavior and Development, 3*, pp. 95–105.

Lewis, M., and Goldberg, S. (1969). Perceptual-Cognitive Development in Infancy: A Generalized Expectancy Model as a Function of the Mother-Infant Interaction. *Merrill-Palmer Quarterly, 15*, pp. 81–100.

Lewis, M., and Kreitzberg, V. S. (1979). Effects of Birth Order and Spacing on Mother-Infant Interactions. *Developmental Psychology, 15*, pp. 617–625.

Lewis, M., Sullivan, M., and Brooks-Gunn, J. (1985). Emotional Behavior During the Learning of a Contingency in Early Infancy. *British Journal of Experimental Psychology, 3*, pp. 307–316.

Lewis, N. A. (1989). Fifty-one Percent of Pupils Score Poorly in Reading. *New York Times,* June 30, 1989, p. B1.

Lewkowicz, D. J. (1988a). Sensory Dominance in Infants: Vol. 1. Six-Month-Old Infants' Response to Auditory-Visual Compounds. *Developmental Psychology, 24*, pp. 155–171.

Lewkowicz, D. J. (1988b). Sensory Dominance in Infants: 2. Ten-Month-Old Infants' Response to Auditory-Visual Compounds. *Developmental Psychology, 24*, pp. 172–182.

Lewy, A. J. (1983). The Effects of Light on Human Melatonin Production and the Human Circadian System. *Progress in Biological Psychiatry, 7*, pp. 551–556.

Lewy, A. J., and others. (1980). Light Suppresses Melatonin Secretion in Humans. *Science, 210*, pp. 1267–1269.

Li, W.-H. (1985). Accelerated Evolution Following Gene Duplication and Its Implications for the Neutralist-Selectionist Controversy. In T. Ohta and K. Aosi (Eds.), *Population Genetics and Molecular Evolution.* Tokyo: Japanese Science Society.

Lieberman, E., and others. (1987). Risk Factors Accounting for Racial Differences in the Rate of Premature Birth. *New England Journal of Medicine, 317*, pp. 743–748.

Liederman, J., Merola, J., and Hoffman, C. (1986). Interhemispheric Inhibition Increases During Early Adolescence. *Proceedings: 16th Annual Meeting of the Society for Neuroscience,* 194.7.

Light, L. L., and Singh, A. (1987). Implicit and Explicit Memory in Young and Older Adults. *Journal of Experimental Psychology: Learning, Memory, and Cognition, 13*, pp. 531–541.

Lin, C.-Y.C., and Fu, V. R. (1989). *A Comparison of Child-Rearing Practices Among Chinese, Immigrant Chinese, and Non-Asian American Parents.* Paper presented at biennial meeting of the Society for Research in Child Development, Kansas City, Mo.

Lin, L.L.K., and Chen, C. J. (1988). A Twin Study of Myopia in Chinese School Children, 1986. *Acta Ophthalmology, 66*, suppl. 105, pp. 51–53.

Ling, D., and Ling, A. A. (1974). Communication Development in the First Three Years of Life. *Journal of Speech and Hearing Research, 17*, pp. 146–159.

Linn, R., Pagliari, C., and Chan, J. (1988). Intelligence in Hong Kong Measured for Spearman's *g* and the Visuospatial and Verbal Primaries. *Intelligence, 12*, pp. 423–433.

Linn, S. J., Reznick, J. S., Kagan, J., and Hans, S. (1982) Salience of Visual Patterns in the Human Infant. *Developmental Psychology, 18*, pp. 651–657.

Lipton, E. L., Steinschneider, A., and Richmond, J. B. (1965). Swaddling, a Child-Care Practice: Historical, Cultural, and Experimental Observations. *Pediatrics*, Mar., suppl., pt. 2, pp. 521–567.

Loehlin, J. C., Horn, J. M., and Willerman, L. (1989). Modeling IQ Change: Evidence from the Texas Adoption Project. *Child Development, 60*, pp. 993–1004.

Loehlin, J. C., and Nichols, R. C. (1976). *Heredity, Environment, and Personality*. Austin: University of Texas Press.

Lohman, D. F. (1987). Spatial Abilities as Traits, Processes, and Knowledge. In R. J. Sternberg (Ed.), *Advances in the Psychology of Human Intelligence*. Vol. 4. Hillsdale, N.J.: Erlbaum.

Lohman, D. F., and Kyllonen, P. C. (1983). Individual Differences in Solution Strategy on Visual Tasks. In R. F. Dillon and R. R. Schmeck (Eds.), *Individual Differences in Cognition*. Vol. 1. Orlando, Fla.: Academic Press.

Lotan, I., and others. (1982). Adenosine-Induced Slow Ionic Currents in the *Xenopus* Oocyte. *Nature, 298*, pp. 572–574.

Lovell, K. (1986). Some Recent Studies in Cognitive and Language Development. *Merrill-Palmer Quarterly, 14*, pp. 123–128.

Lumsden, C. J., and Wilson, E. O. (1981). *Genes, Mind, and Culture: The Coevolutionary Process*. Cambridge, Mass.: Harvard University Press.

Lund, J. S. (1984). Spiny Stellate Neurons. In A. Peters and E. C. Jones (Eds.), *Cerebral Cortex*. Vol. 1. New York: Plenum.

Lutwak-Mann, C. (1964). Observations on Progeny of Thalidomide-Treated Male Rabbits. *British Medical Journal, 1*, pp. 1090–1091.

Lynn, R. (1982). IQ in Japan and the United States Shows a Growing Disparity. *Nature, 297*, pp. 222–223.

Lynn, R., and Hampson, S. L. (1986a). Further Evidence of the Cognitive Abilities of the Japanese: Data from the WPPSI. *International Journal of Behavioral Development, 10*, pp. 233–260.

Lynn, R., and Hampson, S. L. (1986b). Intellectual Abilities of Japanese Children: An Assessment of 2½–8½-Year-Olds Derived from the McCarthy Scales of Children's Abilities. *Intelligence, 10*, pp. 41–58.

Lynn, R., and Hampson, S. L. (1986c). The Rise of National

Intelligence: Evidence from Britain, Japan, and the U.S.A. *Personality and Individual Differences*, 7, pp. 23–32.

Lynn, R., and Hampson, S. L. (1986d). The Structure of Japanese Abilities: An Analysis in Terms of the Hierarchical Model of Intelligence. *Current Psychological Research Review*, 4, pp. 302–322.

Lynn, R., Hampson, S. L., and Mullineux, J. C. (1987). A Long-Term Increase in the Fluid Intelligence of English Children. *Nature*, 328, p. 797.

Maazel, M. (1950). What to Do About the Child Prodigy. *Etude*, 68 (8), p. 12.

McCall, R. B., Appelbaum, M. I., and Hogarty, P. S. (1973). Developmental Changes in Mental Performance. *Monographs of the Society for Research in Child Development*, 38, serial no. 150.

McCall, R. B., and Kagan, J. (1967). Attention to the Infant: Effects of Complexity, Contour, Perimeter, and Familiarity. *Child Development*, 38, pp. 939–952.

McCarthy, D. (1972). *McCarthy Scales of Children's Abilities*. San Antonio, Tex.: Psychological Corporation.

McCartney, K., Robeson, W., Jordan, E., and Mouradin, V. (1989). *Mothers' Language with First and Secondborn Children: A Within-Family Study*. Paper presented at biennial meeting of the Society for Research in Child Development, Kansas City, Mo.

Maccoby, E. E., and others. (1979). Concentrations of Sex Hormones in Umbilical-Cord Blood: Their Relation to Sex and Birth Order of Infants. *Child Development*, 50, pp. 632–642.

McCurdy, H. G. (1957). The Childhood Patterns of Genius. *Journal of the Elisha Mitchell Society*, 73, pp. 448–462.

McDowd, J. M., and Craik, F.I.M. (1988). Effects of Aging and Task Difficulty on Divided Attention Performance. *Journal of Experimental Psychology: Human Perception and Performance*, 14, pp. 267–280.

McGee, M. G. (1979). Human Spatial Abilities: Psychometric Studies and Environmental, Genetic, Hormonal, and Neurological Influences. *Psychological Bulletin*, 86, pp. 889–918.

McGrath, J., and Solter, D. (1984). Completion of Mouse Embryogenesis Requires Both the Maternal and Paternal Genomes. *Cell*, 37, pp. 179–183.

MacIntyre, R. J. (1982). Regulatory Genes and Adaptation: Past, Present, and Future. *Evolutionary Biology, 15*, pp. 247–285.

McKenna, V. V., Null, C. B., and Ventis, I. (1979). *Marital Age and the Spacing of Children.* Washington, D.C.: National Institute for Child Development, Center for Population Research.

McKenzie, B., and Day, R. H. (1971). Operant Learning of Visual Pattern Discrimination in Young Infants. *Journal of Experimental Child Psychology, 11*, pp. 45–53.

McKim, R. H. (1972). *Experiences in Visual Thinking.* Monterey, Calif.: Brooks/Cole.

McManus, I. C. (1979). *Human Laterality.* Unpublished doctoral dissertation, Department of Psychology, Cambridge University.

McNewar, Q. (1942). *The Revision of the Stanford-Binet Scale: An Analysis of Standardization Data.* Boston: Houghton Mifflin.

Malkasian, D., and Diamond, M. C. (1971). The Effect of Environmental Manipulation on the Morphology of the Neonatal Brain. *International Journal of Neuroscience, 2*, pp. 161–170.

Malloy, G. B. (1979). The Relationship Between Maternal and Musical Auditory Stimulation and the Developmental Behavior of Premature Infants. *Birth Defects: Original Article Series, 15*, pp. 81–89.

Mansfield, P. K. (1986a). *Pregnancy for Older Women.* New York: Praeger.

Mansfield, P. K. (1986b). Re-Evaluating the Medical Risks of Late Childbearing. *Women and Health, 11*, pp. 37–60.

Mansfield, P. K. (1988). Midlife Childbearing. *Psychology of Women Quarterly, 12*, pp. 445–460.

Marjoram, D.T.E., and Nelson, R. D. (1985). Mathematical Gifts. In J. Freeman (Ed.), *The Psychology of Gifted Children.* New York: Wiley.

Marjoribanks, K. (1972). Ethnic and Environmental Influences on Mental Abilities. *American Journal of Sociology, 78*, pp. 323–337.

Marshall, J. C. (1989). The Descent of the Larynx? *Nature, 338*, pp. 702–703.

Martin, M. (1984). Memory and Mood. *Behavioral and Brain Sciences, 7*, p. 75.

Martinez, M. (1982). Myelin Lipids in the Developing Cerebrum, Cerebellum, and Brain Stem of Normal and Undernourished Children. *Journal of Neurochemistry, 39*, pp. 1684–1692.

Marx, J. L. (1982). Autoimmunity in Left-Handers. *Science, 217*, p. 141.

Marx, J. L. (1988). A Parent's Sex May Affect Gene Expression. *Science, 239*, pp. 352–353.

Meeker, M. N. (1969). *The Structure of Intellect.* Westerville, Ohio: Merrill.

Mehler, J., and others. (1978). Infant Recognition of Mother's Voice. *Perception, 7*, pp. 491–497.

Melnechuk, T. (1983). The Dream Machine. *Psychology Today,* Nov., p. 22.

Meltzoff, A. N. (1988a). Imitation, Objects, Tools, and the Rudiments of Language in Human Ontogeny. *Human Evolution, 3*, pp. 47–66.

Meltzoff, A. N. (1988b). Infant Imitation and Memory: Nine-Month-Olds in Immediate and Deferred Tasks. *Child Development, 59*, pp. 217–225.

Meltzoff, A. N., and Moore, M. J. (1983). Newborn Infants Imitate Adult Facial Gestures. *Child Development, 54*, pp. 702–709.

Mendelson, M. J. (1979). Acoustical-Optical Correspondences and Auditory-Visual Coordination in Infancy. *Canadian Journal of Psychology, 33*, pp. 334–346.

Messer, D. J. (1978). The Integration of Mothers' Referential Speech with Joint Play. *Child Development, 49*, pp. 781–787.

Metzl, M. N. (1980). Teaching Parents a Strategy for Enhancing Infant Development. *Child Development, 51*, pp. 583–586.

Meyerhoff, M. K., and White, B. L. (1986). Making the Grade as Parents. *Psychology Today,* Sept., p. 38.

Miles, C. C., and Miles, W. R. (1932). The Correlation of Intelligence Scores and Chronological Age from Early to Late Maturity. *American Journal of Psychology, 44*, pp. 44–78.

Milewski, A. E. (1976). Infants' Discrimination of Internal and

External Pattern Elements. *Journal of Experimental Child Psychology, 22*, pp. 229–246.

Milewski, A. E. (1978). Young Infants' Visual Processing of Internal and Adjacent Shapes. *Infant Behavior and Development, 1*, pp. 359–371.

Milewski, A. E. (1979). Visual Discrimination and Detection of Configurational Invariance in 3-Month Infants. *Developmental Psychology, 15*, pp. 357–363.

Milkos, G.L.G., and John, B. (1987). From Genome to Phenotype. In K.S.W. Campbell and M. F. Day (Eds.), *Rates of Evolution*. London: Allen & Unwin.

Miller, J. C., and Friedhoff, A. J. (1988). Prenatal Neurotransmitter Programming of Postnatal Receptor Function. *Progress in Brain Research, 73*, pp. 509–522.

Mitchell, S. K., and Gray, C. A. (1981). Developmental Generalizability of the Inventory. *Educational and Psychological Measurement, 41*, pp. 1001–1010.

Miyawaki, K., and others. (1975). An Effect of Linguistic Experience: The Discrimination of [r] and [l] by Native Speakers of English and Japanese. *Perceptual Psychophysiology, 18*, pp. 331–340.

Monk, M., Boubelik, M., and Lehnert, S. (1987). Temporal and Regional Changes in DNA Methylation in the Embryonic, Extraembryonic, and Germ Cell Lineages During Mouse Embryo Development. *Development, 99*, pp. 371–382.

Montague, A. (1983). The Lambskin Connection. *Science Digest*, Aug., p. 22.

Moore, J. M., Wilson, W. R., and Thompson, G. (1977). Visual Reinforcement of Headturn Responses in Infants Under Twelve Months of Age. *Journal of Speech and Hearing Disorders, 43*, pp. 328–334.

Moos, R. H., and Moos, B. S. (1981). *Family Environment Scale Manual*. Palo Alto, Calif.: Consulting Psychologists Press.

Moran, G., Krupka, A., Tutton, A., and Symons, D. (1987). Patterns of Maternal and Infant Imitation During Play. *Infant Behavior and Development, 10*, pp. 477–491.

Morrongiello, B. A., Kulig, J. W., and Clifton, R. K. (1984).

Developmental Changes in Auditory Temporal Perception. *Child Development, 55*, pp. 461–471.

Morsbach, H. (1973). Aspects of Nonverbal Communication in Japan. *Journal of Nervous and Mental Disease, 157*, pp. 262–277.

Morse, P. A. (1972). The Discrimination of Speech and Nonspeech Stimuli in Early Infancy. *Journal of Experimental Child Psychology, 14*, pp. 477–492.

Morse, P. A. (1985). Infant Speech Perception: Nature's Contribution. In S. E. Trehub and B. Schneider (Eds.), *Auditory Development in Infancy*. Vol. 10: *Advances in the Study of Communication and Affect*. New York: Plenum.

Morse, P. A., and Suomi, K. (1979). *Probing Perceptual Constancy for Consonants with the Non-Nutritive Sucking Paradigm*. Infant Development Laboratory Research Status Report no. 3. University of Wisconsin.

Moss, H. A., and Robeson, K. S. (1967). Maternal Influences in Early Visual Behavior. *American Journal of Orthopsychology, 37*, pp. 394–395.

Moss, J., and Solomons, H. C. (1979). Swaddling, Then, There, and Now: Historical, Anthropological, and Current Practices. *Maternal-Child Nursing Journal, 8*, pp. 137–151.

Muir, D. S. (1985). The Development of Infants' Auditory Spatial Sensitivity. In S. E. Trehub and B. Schneider (Eds.), *Auditory Development in Infancy*. Vol. 10: *Advances in the Study of Communication and Affect*. New York: Plenum.

Muir, D. S., and Field, J. (1979). Newborn Infants Orient to Sounds. *Child Development, 50*, pp. 431–436.

Muir, D. S., and others. (1979). The Ontogenesis of an Auditory Localization Response from Birth to Four Months of Age. *Canadian Journal of Psychology, 33*, pp. 320–333.

Muir, J., and Bjorklund, D. F. (forthcoming). Developmental and Individual Differences in Children's Memory Strategies: The Role of Knowledge. In W. Schneider and W. E. Weinert (Eds.), *Interactions Among Strategies, Knowledge, and Aptitude in Cognitive Performance*. New York: Springer-Verlag.

Muir, J., and others. (1989). *Training and Transfer of an Organizational Strategy in Gifted and High-Average Nongifted Children*. Paper presented at biennial meeting of the Society for Research in Child Development, Kansas City, Mo.

Mullbacher, A., Ashman, R. B., and Blanden, R. V. (1983). Induction of T-Cell Hyporesponsiveness to Bebaru in Mice, and Abnormalities in the Immune Response of Progeny in Hyporesponsive Males. *Australian Journal of Experimental Biology and Medical Science, 61*, pp. 187–191.

Munsinger, H. (1977). The Identical-Twin Transfusion Syndrome: A Source of Error in Estimating IQ Resemblance and Heritability. *Annals of Human Genetics, 40*, pp. 307–321.

Munsinger, H., and Douglass, A. (1976). The Syntactic Abilities of Identical Twins, Fraternal Twins, and Their Siblings. *Child Development, 47*, pp. 40–50.

Murphy, C. M. (1978). Pointing in the Context of Shared Activity. *Child Development, 49*, pp. 371–380.

Murphy, C. M., and Messer, D. J. (1977). Mothers, Infants, and Pointing: A Study of a Gesture. In H. R. Schaffer (Ed.), *Studies in Mother-Infant Interaction*. Orlando, Fla.: Academic Press.

Murray, A. D., Johnson, J., and Peters, J. (1989). *Motherese to Preverbal Infants: Effects on Later Language Development*. Paper presented at biennial meeting of the Society for Research in Child Development, Kansas City, Mo.

Murray, J. L., and Bernfield, M. (1988). The Differential Effects of Prenatal Care on the Incidence of Low Birth Weight Among Blacks and Whites in a Prepaid Health Care Plan. *New England Journal of Medicine, 319*, pp. 1385–1391.

Nardi, N. (1948). Studies in Intelligence of Jewish Children. *Jewish Education, 19*, pp. 41–45.

National Center for Health Statistics. (1989). Trends and Variations in First Births to Older Women, 1970–1986. *Vital Health Statistics Series*, Series 21, No. 47.

Naylor, S. L., and others. (1987). Loss of Heterozygosity of Chromosome 3p Markers in Small-Cell Lung Cancer. *Nature, 329*, pp. 451–454.

Neal, M. V. (1968). Vestibular Stimulation and Developmental Behavior of the Small Premature Infant. *Nursing Research, 3*, pp. 2–5.

Nei, M. (1987). *Molecular Evolutionary Genetics*. New York: Columbia University Press.

Neligan, G. A. (1967). The Clinical Effect of Being "Light for Date." *Proceedings of the Royal Society of Medicine, 60,* p. 877.

Neligan, G. A., and Prudham, D. (1976). Family Factors Affecting Child Development. *Archives of Disease in Childhood, 51,* pp. 853–858.

Nelson, K. E., and Deutschberger, J. (1970). Head Size at One Year as a Predictor of Four-Year IQ. *Developmental Medicine and Child Neurology, 12,* pp. 487–495.

Newman, H. H., Freeman, F. N., and Holzinger, K. J. (1937). *Twins: A Study of Heredity and Environment.* Chicago: University of Chicago Press.

Newman, R. A. (1988a). Adaptive Plasticity in Development of *Scaphiopus Couchii* Tadpoles in Desert Ponds. *Evolution, 42,* pp. 774–783.

Newman, R. A. (1988b). Genetic Variation for Adaptive Plasticity in Development of *Scaphiopus Couchii* Tadpoles in Desert Ponds. *Evolution, 42,* pp. 763–773.

Nichols, R. C. (1965). The National Merit Twin Study. In S. Vandenberg (Ed.), *Methods and Goals in Human Behavior Genetics.* Orlando, Fla.: Academic Press.

Nistal, M., Abaurrea, M. A., and Paniagua, R. (1982). Morphological and Histometric Study on the Human Sertoli Cell from Birth to the Onset of Puberty. *Journal of Anatomy, 134,* pp. 351–363.

Niswander, K. R., and Gordon, M. (1972). *Women and Their Pregnancies.* Philadelphia: Saunders.

Norton, D. (1980). Interrelationships Among Music Aptitude, IQ, and Auditory Conservation. *Journal of Research in Music Education, 28,* p. 207.

Nottebohm, F. (1981). A Brain for All Seasons. *Science, 214,* pp. 1368–1370.

Nye, F., Carlson, J., and Garrett, G. (1970). Family Size, Interaction, Affect, and Stress. *Journal of Marriage and Family, 32,* pp. 216–226.

O'Brien, S. J., and others. (1985). A Molecular Solution to the

Riddle of the Giant Panda's Phylogeny. *Nature, 317,* pp. 140–144.

O'Connell, E. J., Feldt, R. H., and Stickler, G. B. (1965). Head Circumference, Mental Retardation, and Growth Failure. *Pediatrics, 36,* pp. 62–66.

O'Connor, M. J. (1980). A Comparison of Preterm and Full-Term Infants on Auditory Discrimination at Four Months and on Bayley Scales of Infant Development at 18 Months. *Child Development, 51,* p. 81.

O'Connor, M. J., Cohen, S., and Parmelee, A. (1984). Infant Auditory Discrimination in Preterm and Full-Term Infants as a Predictor of 5-Year Intelligence. *Developmental Psychology, 20,* pp. 159–165.

Oden, M. H. (1968). The Fulfillment of Promise: Forty-Year Follow-Up of the Terman Gifted Group. *Genetic Psychology Monographs,* no. 77.

Ohno, S. (1970). *Evolution by Gene Duplication.* Berlin: Springer-Verlag.

Ohta, T. (1983). On the Evolution of Multigene Families. *Theoretical Population Biology, 23,* p. 216.

Ohta, T. (1987). A Model of Evolution for Accumulating Genetic Information. *Journal of Theoretical Biology, 124,* pp. 199–211.

Ohta, T. (1988). Further Simulation Studies on Evolution by Gene Duplication. *Evolution, 42,* pp. 375–386.

Ojemann, G. (1983). Brain Organization for Language from the Perspective of Electrical Stimulation Mapping. *Behavioral and Brain Sciences, 6,* pp. 189–230.

O'Keefe, J., and Nadel, L. (1978). *The Hippocampus as a Cognitive Map.* Oxford, England: Oxford University Press.

O'Keefe, J., and Nadel, L. (1979). Precis of *The Hippocampus as a Cognitive Map. Behavioral and Brain Sciences, 2,* pp. 487–533.

Oldfield, R. C. (1971). The Assessment and Analysis of Handedness: The Edinburgh Inventory. *Neurophysiologica, 9,* pp. 97–113.

Olson, G. M. (1979). Infant Recognition Memory for Briefly Presented Visual Stimuli. *Infant Behavior and Development, 2,* pp. 123–134.

Olson, G. M. (1981). The Recognition of Specific Persons. In

M. E. Lamb and L. R. Sherrod (Eds.), *Infant Social Cognition: Empirical and Theoretical Considerations.* Hillsdale, N.J.: Erlbaum.

Olson, G. M., and Sherman, T. (1983). Attention, Learning, and Memory in Infants. In P. H. Mussen (Ed.), *The Handbook of Child Psychology.* Vol. 2. New York: Wiley.

Olson, M. B. (1984). What Do You Mean by Spatial? *Roeper Review, 6,* pp. 240–244.

Olson, M. B. (1985). *Profiles of Three Subtypes of Giftedness.* Paper presented at the Foundation for Brain Research conference on Neurobiology of Extraordinary Intellectual Giftedness, New York, Apr.

Olson, S. L., Bates, J. E., and Bayles, K. (1984). Mother-Infant Interaction and the Development of Individual Differences in Children's Cognitive Competence. *Developmental Psychology, 20,* pp. 166–179.

Olson, S. L., Bayles, K., and Bates, J. E. (1986). *Predicting Social and Cognitive Competence at Age Six from Early Mother-Child Interactions.* Paper presented at the International Conference on Infant Studies, Los Angeles.

Olton, D. S., Becker, J. T., and Handelmann, G. E. (1979). Hippocampus, Space, and Memory. *Behavioral and Brain Sciences, 2,* pp. 313–365.

Orowan, F. (1955). The Origin of Man. *Nature, 175,* pp. 683–684.

Ortar, G. (1967). Educational Achievements of Primary School Graduates in Israel as Related to Their Socio-Cultural Background. *Comparative Education, 4,* pp. 23–35.

Osofsky, J. D., and Commons, K. (1979). Mother-Infant Interaction. In J. Osofsky (Ed.), *Handbook of Infant Development.* New York: Wiley.

Ounsted, M. K., Moar, V. A., and Scott, A. (1984). Associations Between Size and Development at Four Years. *Early Human Development, 9,* pp. 259–268.

Owen, L. (1983). Swaddling and CDH. *Pediatric Nursing,* Mar./Apr., p. 143.

Owsley, C. (1983). The Role of Motion in Infants' Perception of Solid Shape. *Perception, 12,* pp. 707–717.

Page, E. B., and Grandon, G. M. (1979). Family Configuration and Mental Ability: Two Theories Contrasted with U.S. Data. *American Educational Research Journal, 16*, pp. 257–272.

Painter, G. (1969). The Effect of a Structured Tutorial Program on the Cognitive and Language Development of Culturally Disadvantaged Infants. *Merrill-Palmer Quarterly, 15*, pp. 279–294.

Panneton, R. K., and DeCasper, A. J. (1986). *Newborns' Postnatal Preference for a Prenatally Experienced Melody.* Paper presented at the International Conference on Infant Studies, Beverly Hills, Calif., Mar.

Papousek, M., and Papousek, H. (1981). Musical Elements in the Infant's Vocalization: The Significance for Communication, Cognition, and Creativity. In L. P. Lipsitt (Ed.), *Advances in Infancy Research.* Vol. 1. Norwood, N.J.: Ablex.

Papousek, M., and Papousek, H. (1982). Vocal Imitation in Mother-Infant Dialogues. *Infant Behavior and Development, 5*, p. 176.

Papousek, M., Papousek, H., and Bornstein, M. H. (1985). The Naturalistic Vocal Environment of Young Infants: On the Significance of Homogeneity and Variability in Parental Speech. In T. M. Field and N. A. Fox (Eds.), *Social Perception in Infants.* Norwood, N.J.: Ablex.

Parker, K.C.H. (1986). Changes with Age, Year-of-Birth Cohort, Age by Year-of-Birth Cohort Interaction, and Standardization of the Wechsler Adult Intelligence Tests. *Human Development, 29*, pp. 209–222.

Patai, R. (1971). *Tents of Jacob.* Englewood Cliffs, N.J.: Prentice-Hall.

Patai, R. (1977). *Journey into the Jewish Mind.* New York: Scribner's.

Paul, S. M. (1985). The Raven's Advanced Progressive Matrices: Normative Data for an American University Population and an Examination of the Relationship with Spearman's *g. Journal of Experimental Education, 54*, pp. 95–100.

Pawlby, S. J. (1977). Imitative Interaction. In H. R. Schaffer (Ed.), *Studies in Mother-Infant Interaction.* Orlando, Fla.: Academic Press.

Peak, L. (1986). Training Learning Skills and Attitudes in Japanese Early Educational Settings. In W. Fowler (Ed.), *Early*

Experience and the Development of Competence. New Directions for Child Development, no. 32. San Francisco: Jossey-Bass.

Pearson, J. S., and Amacher, P. L. (1956). Intelligence Test Results and Observations of Personality Disorder Among 3,594 Unwed Mothers in Minnesota. *Journal of Clinical Psychology, 12,* pp. 16–21.

Pederson, D. R. (1975). The Soothing Effect of Rocking as Determined by the Direction and Frequency of Movement. *Canadian Journal of Behavioral Science, 7,* pp. 237–243.

Pederson, D. R., and Ter Vrugt, D. (1973). The Influence of Amplitude and Frequency of Vestibular Stimulation on the Activity of Two-Month-Old Infants. *Child Development, 44,* pp. 122–128.

Peeples, D. R., and Teller, D. Y. (1975). Color Vision and Brightness Discrimination in Two-Month-Old Human Infants. *Science, 189,* pp. 1102–1103.

Perl, D. P., and Good, P. F. (1987). Uptake of Aluminum into Central Nervous System Along Nasal-Olfactory Pathways. *Lancet,* May 2, p. 1028.

Pilliner, A. G. E., Sutherland, J., and Taylor, E. G. (1960). Zero Error in Moray House Verbal Reasoning Tests. *British Journal of Educational Psychology, 30,* pp. 53–62.

Plomin, R., and DeFries, J. C. (1980). Genetics and Intelligence: Recent Data. *Intelligence, 4,* pp. 15–24.

Plomin, R., and DeFries, J. C. (1985). A Parent-Offspring Adoption Study of Cognitive Abilities in Early Childhood. *Intelligence, 9,* pp. 341–356.

Plomin, R., and DeFries, J. C. (1986). *Origins of Individual Differences in Infancy.* Orlando, Fla.: Academic Press.

Poltrock, S. E., and Agnoli, F. (1986). Are Spatial Visualization Ability and Visual Imagery Ability Equivalent? In R. J. Sternberg (Ed.), *Advances in the Psychology of Human Intelligence.* Vol. 3. Hillsdale, N.J.: Erlbaum.

Porac, C., Coren, S., and Duncan, P. (1980). Life-Span Age Trends in Laterality. *Journal of Gerontology, 35,* pp. 715–721.

Poulson, C. L., and others. (1989). *Generalized Vocal Imitation in Infants.* Paper presented at 15th annual convention of the Association for Behavioral Analysis, Milwaukee, Wis.

Powell, L. F. (1974). The Effect of Extra Stimulation and Maternal Involvement on the Development of Low-Birth-Weight Infants and on Maternal Behavior. *Child Development, 45*, pp. 106–113.

Powell, P. M. (1987). Genius. *Roeper Review, 10*, pp. 96–100.

Prescott, P., and DeCasper, A. J. (forthcoming). *Human Perception of Speech and Nonspeech Is Functionally Lateralized at Birth.*

Priester, H.-J. (1958). *Die Standardisierung des Hamburg-Wechsler-Intelligenztests für Kinder (HAWIK) [The Standardization of the Hamburg Wechsler Intelligence Test for Children (HAWIK)]* Berne, Switzerland: Huber.

Pulvino, C. J., and Lupton, P. E. (1978). Superior Students: Family Size, Birth Order, and Intellectual Ability. *Gifted Child Quarterly, 22*, pp. 212–216.

Pylyshyn, Z. W. (1973). What the Mind's Eye Tells Us About the Mind's Brain: A Critique of Mental Imagery. *Psychological Bulletin, 80*, pp. 1–24.

Pylyshyn, Z. W. (1980). Computation and Cognition: Issues in the Foundations of Cognitive Science. *Behavioral and Brain Sciences, 3*, pp. 111–116.

Racine, R. R., and Langley, C. H. (1980). Genetic Heterozygocity in a Natural Population of *Mus Musculus* Assessed Using Two-Dimensional Electrophoresis. *Nature, 283*, p. 855.

Ramey, C. T., Farran, D. C., and Campbell, F. A. (1979). Predicting IQ from Mother-Infant Interactions. *Child Development, 50*, pp. 808–814.

Ramey, C. T., and others. (1984). A Biosocial Systems Perspective on Environmental Interventions for Low-Birth-Weight Infants. *Clinical Obstetrics and Gynecology, 27*, pp. 672–694.

Randhawa, B. S. (1980). *Change in Intelligence and Academic Skills of Grades Four and Seven Pupils over a Twenty-Year Period.* Paper presented at the 22nd International Congress of Psychology, Leipzig, East Germany. (ED 194580).

Rasmussen, T., and Milner, B. (1977). The Role of Early Left-Brain Injury in Determining Lateralization of the Cerebral Speech Functions. *Annals of the New York Academy of Sciences, 299*, pp. 355–369.

Rauh, V. A., and others. (1988). Minimizing Adverse Effects of

Low Birth-Weight: Four-Year Results of an Early Intervention Program. *Child Development, 59,* pp. 544–553.

Raven, J. (1981). *Standard Progressive Matrices: Research Supplement, no. 1.* London: Lewis.

Ravikumar, B. V., and Sastry, P. S. (1985). Muscarinic Cholinergic Receptors in Human Fetal Brain: Characterization and Ontogeny of [3H] Quinuclidinyl Benzilate Binding Sites in Frontal Cortex. *Journal of Neurochemistry, 44,* pp. 240–246.

Razin, A., Cidar, H., and Riggs, A. D. (1984). *DNA Methylation: Biochemistry and Biological Significance.* New York: Springer-Verlag.

Rebelsky, F., and Hanks, C. (1971). Fathers' Vocal Interaction with Infants in the First Three Months of Life. *Child Development, 42,* pp. 63–68.

Record, R. G., McKeown, T., and Edwards, J. H. (1969a). The Relation of Measured Intelligence to Birth Order and Maternal Age. *Annals of Human Genetics* (London), *33,* pp. 61–69.

Record, R. G., McKeown, T., and Edwards, J. H. (1969b). The Relation of Measured Intelligence to Birth Weight and Duration of Gestation. *Annals of Human Genetics* (London), *33,* pp. 70–79.

Record, R. G., McKeown, T., and Edwards, J. H. (1970). An Investigation of the Difference in Measured Intelligence Between Twins and Single Births. *Annals of Human Genetics* (London), *34,* pp. 11–20.

Reik, W., and others. (1987). Genomic Imprinting Determines Methylation of Parental Alleles in Transgenic Mice. *Nature, 328,* pp. 248–252.

Restak, R. (1984). *The Brain: The Last Frontier.* New York: Bantam Books.

Reynell, L. (1981). *Developmental Language Scales.* (Rev. ed.) Windsor, England: NFER-Nelson.

Reynolds, C. R., and Gutkin, T. B. (1981). Multivariate Comparison of the Intellectual Performance of Blacks and Whites Matched on Four Demographic Variables. *Personality and Individual Differences, 2,* pp. 175–181.

Rheingold, H. L. (1961). The Effect of Environmental Stimulation upon Social and Exploratory Behavior in the Human Infant. In B. M. Foss (Ed.), *Determinants of Infant Behavior*. Vol. 1. London: Methuen.

Rheingold, H. L., Gewirtz, J. L., and Ross, H. W. (1959). Social Conditions of Vocalization in the Infant. *Journal of Comparative and Physiological Psychology, 52*, pp. 68–73.

Riccillo, S. C., and Watterson, T. (1984). The Suppression of Crying in the Human Neonate: Response to Human Vocal Tract Stimuli. *Brain and Language, 23*, pp. 34–42.

Rice, R. D. (1977). Neurophysiological Development in Premature Infants Following Stimulation. *Developmental Psychology, 13*, pp. 69–76.

Richards, M. P. M. (1971). A Comment on the Social Context of Mother-Infant Interaction. In H. R. Schaffer (Ed.), *The Origins of Human Social Relations*. Orlando, Fla.: Academic Press, pp. 187–193.

Riese, M. L. (1989). *Preterm Infants' Orienting Responses: Improvements Over Time*. Paper presented at biennial meeting of the Society for Research in Child Development, Kansas City, Mo.

Rimland, B. (1978). Savant Capabilities of Autistic Children and Their Cognitive Implications. In G. Serban (Ed.), *Cognitive Defects in the Development of Mental Illness*. New York: Brunner/Mazel.

Rist, T. (1982). Det intellektuelle prestasjonsnivaet I befolkninger sett I lys av den samfunns-messige utviklinga [The level of the intellectual performance of the population seen in the light of developments in the community]. Oslo: Norwegian Armed Forces Psychology Service.

Roberson, E. W. (1988). *An Investigation of the Concurrent Validity of the Kaufman Assessment Battery for Children as a Measure of Preschool Giftedness*. Unpublished doctoral dissertation, Department of Education, Southern Illinois University.

Roberts, J., and Engel, A. (1974). *Family Background, Early Development, and the Intelligence of Children 6–11 Years*. Hyattville, Md., National Center for Health Statistics, U.S. Department of Health, Education, and Welfare. (75–1624)

Roberts, K. (1987). *Representation and Structure of a Basic-Level Category in 9-Month-Old Infants*. Paper presented at biennial meeting of the Society for Research in Child Development, Baltimore, Md.

Roberts, K. (1988). Retrieval of a Basic-Level Category in Prelinguistic Infants. *Developmental Psychology, 24*, pp. 21–27.

Robeson, W. W. (1989). *Are Mothers' Interrogatives Fine-Tuned?* Paper presented at biennial meeting of the Society for Research in Child Development, Kansas City, Mo.

Robinson, H. B. (1969). From Infancy Through School. *Children, 16*, pp. 61–62.

Robinson, H. B., and Robinson, N. M. (1971). Longitudinal Development of Very Young Children in a Comprehensive Day-Care Program: The First Two Years. *Child Development, 42*, pp. 1673–1683.

Roe, A. (1953). A Psychological Study of Eminent Psychologists and Anthropologists and a Comparison with Biologists and Physical Scientists. *Psychological Monographs, 67* (352), entire monograph.

Roe, K. V. (1978). Infants' Mother-Stranger Discrimination at 3 Months as a Predictor of Cognitive Development at 3 and 5 Years. *Developmental Psychology, 14*, pp. 191–192.

Roe, K. V. (1987). *Planned vs. Unplanned Status of Infant and Vocal Interaction with Mother and Stranger.* Paper presented at biennial meeting of the Society for Research in Child Development, Baltimore, Md., Apr.

Roe, K. V. (forthcoming). Vocal Stimulation and Cognitive Processing. *Infant Behavior and Development.*

Roe, K. V., and Bornstein, R. (forthcoming). Maternal Education and Infant Cognitive Processing. *International Journal of Behavioral Development.*

Roe, K. V., McClure, A., and Roe, A. (1982). Vocal Interaction at Three Months and Cognitive Skills at Age 12 Years. *Developmental Psychology, 18*, pp. 15–16.

Roe, K. V., and others. (1985). Vocal Interaction at Three Months and Cognitive Skills at Age 12 Years. *Developmental Psychology, 21*, pp. 372–384.

Rolls, E., and others. (1982). Neuronal Responses Related to Visual Recognition. *Brain, 105*, pp. 611–646.

Romanko, M. V., and Brost, B. A. (1982). Swaddling: An Effective

Intervention for Pacifying Infants. *Pediatric Nursing*, July/Aug., pp. 259–261.

Romanoff, J. S. (1976). *Birth Order, Family Size, and Sibling Spacing as Influences on Intelligence and Academic Abilities of Jewish Adolescents.* Unpublished doctoral dissertation, Department of Psychology, Temple University.

Root, W. T. (1921). A Socio-Psychological Study of Fifty-Three Supernormal Children. *Psychological Monographs*, no. 29.

Rose, D., Slater, A., and Perry, H. (1986). Prediction of Childhood Intelligence from Habituation in Early Infancy. *Intelligence, 10*, pp. 251–263.

Rose, S. A. (1980). Enhancing Visual Recognition Memory in Preterm Infants. *Developmental Psychology, 16*, pp. 85–92.

Rose, S. A. (1981). Developmental Changes in Infant's Retention of Visual Stimuli. *Child Development, 52*, pp. 227–233.

Rose, S. A., Feldman, J. F., and Wallace, I. F. (1988). Individual Differences in Infants' Information Processing: Reliability, Stability, and Prediction. *Child Development, 59*, pp. 1177–1197.

Rose, S. A., Feldman, J. F., Wallace, I. F., and McCarton, C. (1989). Infant Visual Attention: Relation to Birth Status and Developmental Outcome During the First Five Years. *Developmental Psychology, 25*, pp. 560–576.

Rose, S. A., and Wallace, I. F. (1985). Visual Recognition Memory: A Predictor of Later Cognitive Functioning in Preterms. *Child Development, 56*, pp. 843–852.

Rosenthal, M. (1982). Vocal Dialogues in the Neonatal Period. *Developmental Psychology, 18*, pp. 17–21.

Roskies, D., and Roskies, D. (1975). *The Shtetl Book.* New York: Ktav Publishing House.

Rosner, M., and Belkin, M. (1987). Intelligence, Education, and Myopia in Males. *Archives of Ophthalmology, 105*, pp. 1508–1511.

Rothenberg, A. (1979). Einstein's Creative Thinking and the General Theory of Relativity: A Documented Report. *American Journal of Psychiatry, 136*, pp. 38–43.

Rothenberg, A. (1982). Janusian Thinking and Nobel Prize Laureates. *American Journal of Psychiatry, 139*, p. 122.

Rovee-Collier, C. K., and Fagen, J. W. (1981). The Retrieval of Memory in Early Infancy. In L. P. Lipsitt (Ed.), *Advances in Infancy Research*. Vol. 1. Norwood, N.J.: Ablex.

Rovee-Collier, C. K., and Lipsitt, L. P. (1980). Learning, Adaptation, and Memory in the Newborn. In P. M. Stratton (Ed.), *Psychology of the Human Newborn*. New York: Wiley.

Rovee-Collier, C. K., and others. (1980). Reactivation of Infant Memory. *Science, 208*, pp. 1159–1161.

Ruddy, M. G., and Bornstein, M. H. (1982). Cognitive Correlates of Infant Attention and Maternal Stimulation over the First Year of Life. *Child Development, 53*, pp. 183–188.

Ruff, H. A. (1987). Preference for Rotating Objects in 5-Month-Old Infants. *Infant Behavior and Development, 10*, pp. 365–369.

Sachs, O. (1985). *The Man Who Mistook His Wife for a Hat*. New York: Simon & Schuster.

St. Lis, A. J-K. (1974). Development of Premature Twins with Dissimilar Birth Weight. *Acta Genet. Med. Gemellol., 27*, suppl. 1, pp. 125–128.

Salkind, N. J., Kojima, H., and Zelniker, T. (1978). Cognitive Tempo in American, Japanese, and Israeli Children. *Child Development, 49*, pp. 1024–1027.

Salthouse, T. A. (forthcoming). Aging and Skilled Performance. In A. Colby and J. Beech (Eds.), *The Acquisition of Cognitive Skills*. New York: Wiley.

Salthouse, T. A., and Somberg, B. L. (1982). Skilled Performance: Effects of Adult Age and Experience on Elementary Processes. *Journal of Experimental Psychology, 111*, pp. 176–207.

Sano, T. (1974). Differences over Time in Intellectual Ability. *Japanese Journal of Educational Psychology, 22*, pp. 110–114.

Sapienza, C. (forthcoming). Genome Imprinting and Dominance Modification. *Annals of the New York Academy of Science*.

Sapienza, C., and others. (1987). Degree of Methylation of Transgenes Is Dependent on Gamete of Origin. *Nature, 328*, pp. 251–254.

Sarton, G. (1927–1948). *Introduction to the History of Science*. 5 vols. Washington, D.C.: Carnegie Institute of Washington, D.C.

Scaife, M., and Bruner, J. S. (1975). The Capacity for Joint Visual Attention in the Infant. *Nature, 253,* pp. 265–266.

Scarr, S. (1982). Effects of Birth Weight on Later Intelligence. *Social Biology, 29,* pp. 230–239.

Scarr, S., and Carter-Saltzman, L. (1982). Genetics and Intelligence. In R. J. Sternberg (Ed.), *Handbook of Human Intelligence.* Cambridge, England: Cambridge University Press.

Scarr, S., and Weinberg, R. A. (1977). Intellectual Similarities Within Families of Both Adopted and Biological Children. *Intelligence, 1,* pp. 170–191.

Scarr, S., and Weinberg, R. A. (1978). The Influence of "Family Background" on Intellectual Attainment. *American Sociological Review, 43* (5), pp. 674–692.

Scarr, S., and Weinberg, R. A. (1983). The Minnesota Adoption Studies: Genetic Differences and Malleability. *Child Development, 54,* pp. 260–268.

Schacter, S. (1963). Birth Order, Eminence, and Higher Education. *American Sociological Review, 28,* pp. 757–768.

Schaffer, R. (1977). *Mothering.* Cambridge, Mass.: Harvard University Press.

Schaie, K. W. (1983). The Seattle Longitudinal Study: A 21-Year Exploration of Psychometric Intelligence in Adulthood. In K. W. Schaie (Ed.), *Longitudinal Studies of Adult Psychological Development.* New York: Guilford Press.

Schaie, K. W. (1988). Variability in Cognitive Function in the Elderly: Implications for Social Participation. In A. Woodhead, M. Bender, and R. Leonard (Eds.), *Phenotypic Variation in Populations: Relevance to Risk Management.* New York: Plenum.

Schaie, K. W., Labouvie, G. V., and Buech, B. U. (1973). Generational and Cohort-Specific Differences in Adult Cognitive Functioning: A Fourteen-Year Study of Independent Samples. *Developmental Psychology, 9,* pp. 151–166.

Schallberger, U. (1985). HAWIK und HAWIK-R: Ein empirischer vergleich [HAWIK and HAWIK-R: An empirical comparison]. Zurich: Psycholisches Institut der Universität.

Scheibel, A. B. (1985). Paper presented at the Foundation for Brain Research conference on Neurobiology of Extraordinary Intellectual Giftedness, New York, Apr.

Scheibel, A. B., and Paul, L. (1985). On the Apparent Non-adhesive Nature of Axospinous Dendritic Synapses. *Experimental Neurology, 89,* pp. 279–283.

Scheibel, A. B., and others. (1985). Differentiating Characteristics of the Human Speech Cortex: A Quantitative Golgi Study. In D. F. Benson and E. Zaidel (Eds.), *The Dual Brain.* New York: Guilford Press.

Schiff, M., and others. (1978). Intellectual Status of Working-Class Children Adopted into Upper Middle-Class Families. *Science, 200,* pp. 1503–1504.

Schneiderman, E. I., and Desmarais, C. (1988). A Neuropsychological Substrate for Talent in Second-Language Acquisition. In L. K. Obler and D. Fein (Eds.), *The Exceptional Brain.* New York: Guilford Press.

Schroeder, W. T. (1987). Nonrandom Loss of Maternal Chromosome 11 in Wilms' Tumors. *American Journal of Human Genetics, 40,* pp. 413–420.

Schulman, E. (1971). *A History of Jewish Education in the Soviet Union.* Hoboken, N.J.: Ktav Publishing House.

Schwartz, J., and Tallal, P. (1980). Rate of Acoustic Change May Underlie Hemispheric Specialization for Speech Perception. *Science, 207,* pp. 1380–1381.

Schwartz, M., and Day, R. H. (1979). Visual Shape Discrimination in Early Infancy. *Monographs of the Society for Research in Child Development, 44* (7).

Scottish Council for Research in Education. (1949). *The Trend in Scottish Intelligence.* London: University of London Press.

Scottish Council for Research in Education. (1961). *The Level and Trend of National Intelligence.* London: University of London Press.

Searle, L. V. (1949). The Organization of Hereditary Maze-Brightness and Maze-Dullness. *Genetic Psychology Monographs, 39,* pp. 279–325.

Seashore, H. A. (1950). The Standardization of the Wechsler Intelligence Scale for Children. *Journal of Consulting Psychology, 14,* pp. 99–110.

Segal, N. L. (1985). Monozygotic and Dizygotic Twins: A Comparative Analysis of Mental Ability Profiles. *Child Development,* *56,* pp. 1051–1058.

Sergent, J. (1984). Processing of Visually Presented Vowels in the Cerebral Hemispheres. *Brain and Language, 21,* pp. 136–148.

Setchell, B. P., and Waites, G.M.H. (1975). The Blood-Testes Barrier. In *Handbook of Physiology.* Vol. 5, sec. 7: *The Male Reproductive System.*

Sheldon, P. M. (1954). The Families of Highly Gifted Children. *Marriage and Family Living, 16,* pp. 59–61.

Shelton, D. L., and Reichardt, L. F. (1986). Studies on the Expression of the Beta Nerve Growth Factor (NGF) Gene in the Central Nervous System. *Proceedings of the National Academy of Sciences, 83,* pp. 2714–2716.

Shields, J. (1962). *Monozygotic Twins Brought Up Apart and Brought Up Together.* Oxford, England: Oxford University Press.

Shiono, P. H., and others. (1986). Birth Weight Among Women of Different Ethnic Groups. *Journal of the American Medical Association, 255,* pp. 48–52.

Sigman, M., Cohen, S. E., Beckwith, L., and Topinka, C. (1986). *Task Persistence in Two-Year-Olds in Relation to Subsequent Attentiveness and Intelligence.* Paper presented at International Conference on Infant Studies, Los Angeles.

Silva, P. A., McGee, R., and Williams, S. (1984). A Longitudinal Study of the Intelligence and Behavior of Preterm and Small-for-Gestational-Age Children. *Developmental and Behavioral Pediatrics, 5,* pp. 1–5.

Simonds, R. J., and Scheibel, A. B. (forthcoming). *The Postnatal Development of the Motor Speech Area: A Preliminary Study.*

Simonton, D. K. (1976). Biographical Determinants of Achieved Eminence: A Multivariate Approach to the Cox Data. *Journal of Personality and Social Psychology, 33,* pp. 218–226.

Sincoff, J. B., and Sternberg, R. J. (1987). The Two Faces of Verbal Ability. *Intelligence, 11,* pp. 263–276.

Skeels, H. M. (1966). Adult Status of Children with Contrasting Early Life Experiences: A Follow-Up Study. *Monographs of the Society for Research in Child Development,* serial no. 105.

Skodak, M., and Skeels, H. M. (1949). A Final Follow-Up Study of

One Hundred Adopted Children. *Journal of Genetic Psychology*, 75, pp. 85–125.

Slater, A., Cooper, R., Rose, D., and Perry, H. (1985). *The Relationship Between Infant Attention and Learning, and Linguistic and Cognitive Abilities at 18 Months and at 4½ Years.* Tours, France: International Society for the Study of Behavioral Development.

Slater, A., Earle, D. C., Morison, V., and Rose, D. (1985). Pattern Preferences at Birth and Their Interaction with Habituation-Induced Novelty Preferences. *Journal of Experimental Child Psychology*, 39, pp. 37–54.

Smilansky, M., and Smilansky, S. (1968). *The Intellectual Development of Kibbutz-Born Children of "Oriental" (Middle Eastern and North African) Origin.* Research Report no. 120, Publication no. 465. Jerusalem: Ruth Bressler Center for Education Research, Henrietta Szold Institute.

Smilansky, S. (1964). *A Demonstration Program of Preschool Activities to Promote Scholastic Success for Culturally Disadvantaged Children.* Jerusalem: Henrietta Szold Institute.

Smith, S. B. (1988). Calculating Prodigies. In L. K. Obler and D. Fein (Eds.), *The Exceptional Brain: Neuropsychology of Talent and Special Abilities.* New York: Guilford Press.

Snow, C. E. (1976). The Development of Conversation Between Mothers and Babies. *Journal of Child Language*, 13, pp. 1–22.

Snow, C. E. (1981). The Uses of Imitation. *Journal of Child Language*, 8, pp. 205–212.

Sofaer, J. A., and Emery, A. H. (1981). Genes for Super-Intelligence. *Journal of Medical Genetics*, 18, pp. 410–413.

Solomon, E. R., and others. (1987). Chromosome 5 Allele Loss in Human Colorectal Carcinomas. *Nature*, 328, pp. 616–619.

Solter, D. (1988). Differential Imprinting and Expression of Maternal and Paternal Genomes. *Annual Review of Genetics*, 22, pp. 127–146.

Sonderegger, T., O'Shea, S., and Zimmermann, E. (1979). Progeny of Male Rats Addicted Neonatally to Morphine. *Proceedings: Western Pharmaceutical Society*, 22, pp. 137–139.

Sophian, C. (1980). Habituation Is Not Enough: Novelty Preferences, Search, and Memory in Infancy. *Merrill-Palmer Quarterly, 26,* pp. 237–259.

Sorsby, A., and Fraser, G. R. (1964). Statistical Note on the Components of Ocular Refraction in Twins. *Journal of Medical Genetics, 1,* pp. 47–49.

Soyka, L. F., and Joffe, J. M. (1980). Male-Mediated Drug Effects on Offspring. In R. H. Schwartz and S. J. Yaffe (Eds.), *Drug and Chemical Risks to the Fetus and New Born.* New York: Liss.

Spearman, C. (1904). General Intelligence, Objectively Determined and Measured. *American Journal of Psychology, 15,* pp. 201–293.

Speidel, G. E., and Nelson, K. E. (1989). *The Many Faces of Imitation in Language Learning.* New York: Springer-Verlag.

Spelke, E. S. (1979). Perceiving Bimodally Specified Events in Infancy. *Developmental Psychology, 15,* pp. 626–636.

Spelke, E. S., and Cortelyou, A. (1981). Perceptual Aspects of Social Knowing: Looking and Listening in Infancy. In M. E. Lamb and L. R. Sherrod (Eds.), *Infant Social Cognition: Empirical and Theoretical Considerations.* Hillsdale, N.J.: Erlbaum.

Spellacy, W. N., Miller, S. J., and Winegar, A. (1986). Pregnancy After 40 Years of Age. *Obstetrics and Gynecology, 68,* pp. 452–454.

Spergel, G., Kahn, F., and Goldner, M. G. (1975). Emergence of Overt Diabetes in Offspring of Rats with Induced Latent Diabetes. *Metabolic Clinical Experiments, 24,* pp. 1311–1319.

Steele, E. J. (1981). Lamarck and Immunity: A Conflict Resolved. *New Scientist, 90,* pp. 360–361.

Stern, D. N. (1974). *The Origins of Behavior: The Effect of the Infant on Its Caregiver.* New York: Wiley.

Stern, D. N. (1985). *The Interpersonal World of the Infant.* New York: Basic Books.

Stern, D. N., Beebe, B., Jaffee, S., and Bennett, S. L. (1975). Vocalizing in Unison and in Alternation: Two Modes of Communication Within the Mother-Infant Dyad. *Annals of the New York Academy of Science, 263,* pp. 89–100.

Stern, D. N., Jaffee, S., Beebe, B., and Bennett, S. L. (1977). The Infant's Stimulus World During Social Interaction: A Study of Caregiver Behaviors with Particular Reference to Repetition and Timing. In H. R. Shaffer (Ed.), *Studies in Mother-Infant Interaction.* Orlando, Fla.: Academic Press.

Stern, D. N., Spieker, S., and MacKain, K. (1982). Intonation Contours as Symbols in Maternal Speech to Prelinguistic Infants. *Developmental Psychology, 18,* pp. 727–735.

Stern, M., and Karraker, K. (1988). Premature Stereotyping by Mothers of Premature Infants. *Journal of Pediatric Psychology, 13,* pp. 255–263.

Stern, M., and Karraker, K. (1989). *Modifying the Prematurity Stereotype: The Impact of Individual Difference Factors.* Paper presented at biennial meeting of the Society for Research in Child Development, Kansas City, Mo.

Stern, M., and Karraker, K. (forthcoming). Modifying the Prematurity Stereotype: The Effects of Information on Negative Perceptions of Infants. *Journal of Social and Clinical Psychology.*

Sternberg, R. J. (1985). *Beyond IQ: A Triarchic Theory of Human Intelligence.* New York: Cambridge University Press.

Sternberg, R. J. (1986). A Triarchic Theory of Intellectual Giftedness. In R. J. Sternberg and J. E. Davidson (Eds.), *Conceptions of Giftedness.* Cambridge, England: Cambridge University Press.

Sternberg, R. J., and Davidson, J. E. (1982). The Mind of the Puzzler. *Psychology Today,* June, pp. 37–44.

Sternberg, R. J., and Powell, J. S. (1983). Comprehending Verbal Comprehension. *Educational Psychologist, 38,* pp. 878–893.

Stetton, D., Jr. (1958). Intellectual Level Measured by Army Classification Battery and Serum Uric Acid Concentrations. *Scientific American, 198,* p. 73.

Stevens, J. H., and Bakeman, R. (1985). A Factor Analytic Study of the HOME Scales for Infants. *Developmental Psychology, 21,* pp. 1196–1203.

Stigler, J. W., and others. (1982). Curriculum and Achievement in Mathematics: A Study of Elementary School Children in Japan, Taiwan, and the United States. *Journal of Educational Psychology, 74,* pp. 315–322.

Stites, D. P., and others. (1982). *Basic and Clinical Immunology.* (4th ed.) Los Altos, Calif.: Lange Medical Publications.

Stratton, P., and Connolly, K. (1973). Discrimination by Newborns of the Intensity, Frequency, and Temporal Characteristics of Auditory Stimuli. *British Journal of Psychology, 64,* pp. 219–232.

Suchindran, C. M., and Lingner, J. M. (1977). On Comparison of Birth Interval Distribution. *Journal of Biosocial Science, 9,* pp. 25–31.

Sullivan, J. W., and Horowitz, F. D. (1983a). Intermodal Perception in Infancy and Its Implications for Language Development. In L. Lipsitt (Ed.), *Advances in Infancy Research.* Vol. 2. Norwood, N.J.: Ablex.

Sullivan, J. W., and Horowitz, F. D. (1983b). The Effects of Intonation on Infant Attention: The Role of Rising Intonation Contour. *Journal of Child Language, 10,* pp. 521–534.

Sullivan, J. W., Rovee-Collier, C. K., and Tynes, D. M. (1979). A Conditioning Analysis of Infant Long-Term Memory. *Child Development, 50,* pp. 152–162.

Surani, M. A., and others. (1988). Influence of Chromosomal Determinants on Development of Androgenetic and Parthenogenetic Cells. *Development, 103,* pp. 171–178.

Sutcliffe, J., Milner, R., and Bloom, F. (1983). Cellular Localization and Function of the Proteins Coded by Brain-Specific mRNAs. *Cold Spring Harbor Symposium on Molecular Neurobiology, 48,* pp. 477–484.

Suzuki, S. (1969). *Nurtured by Love.* New York: Exposition Press.

Swain, I. U., Clifton, R. K., and Clarkson, M. G. (1989). *Change in Stimulus Location Influences Newborns' Head Orientation to Sounds.* Paper presented at biennial meeting of the Society for Research in Child Development, Kansas City, Mo.

Swain, J. L., Stewart, T. L., and Leder, P. (1987). Parental Legacy Determines Methylation and Expression of an Autosomal Transgene: A Molecular Mechanism for Parental Imprinting. *Cell, 50,* pp. 719–727.

Swoboda, P., Kass, J., Morse, P., and Leavitt, L. (1978). Memory Factors in Vowel Discrimination of Normal and At-Risk Infants. *Child Development, 49,* pp. 332–339.

Tamis-LeMonda, C. S., and Bornstein, M. H. (1989). Habituation and Maternal Encouragement of Attention in Infancy as Predictors of Toddler Language, Play, and Representational Competence. *Child Development, 60,* pp. 738–751.

Tan, L. (1983). Handedness in Two Generations. *Perceptual and Motor Skills, 56,* pp. 867–874.

Taniuchi, M., Schweitzer, J. B., and Johnson, E. M., Jr. (1986). Nerve Growth Factor Receptor Molecules in Rat Brain. *Proceedings of the National Academy of Sciences, 83,* pp. 1950–1954.

Taylor, H. F. (1980). *The IQ Game: A Methodological Inquiry into the Heredity-Environment Controversy.* New Brunswick, N.J.: Rutgers University Press.

Teasdale, T. W., Fuchs, J., and Goldschmidt, E. (1988). Degree of Myopia in Relation to Intelligence and Educational Level. *Lancet,* Dec. 10, pp. 1351–1354.

Ter Vrugt, D., and Pederson, D. R. (1973). Rocking Effectiveness: Frequency, Displacement, and Direction. *Child Development, 44,* pp. 205–209.

Terman, L. M. (1916). *The Measurement of Intelligence.* Boston: Houghton Mifflin.

Terman, L. M. (1919). *The Intelligence of Schoolchildren.* Boston: Houghton Mifflin.

Terman, L. M. (1925). Mental and Physical Traits of a Thousand Gifted Children. *Genetic Studies of Genius.* Vol. 1. Stanford, Calif.: Stanford University Press.

Terman, L. M., and Merrill, M. A. (1973). *Stanford-Binet Intelligence Scale.* (1972 Norms ed.) Boston: Houghton Mifflin.

Terman, L. M., and Oden, M. H. (1947). The Gifted Child Grows Up. *Genetic Studies of Genius.* Vol. 4. Stanford, Calif.: Stanford University Press.

Thomas, D. G., and others. (1981). Semantic Comprehension in Infancy: A Signal Detection Analysis. *Child Development, 52,* pp. 798–803.

Thomas, J. O., and Thompson, R. J. (1977). Variation in Chromatin Structure in Two Cell Types in the Same Tissue: A Short DNA Repeat Length in Cerebral Cortex. *Cell, 10,* p. 633.

Thorndike, R. L., Hagen, E. P., and Sattler, J. M. (1986). *Stanford-Binet Intelligence Scale: Technical Manual.* (4th ed.) Chicago: Riverside Press.

Thurstone, L. L., and Thurstone, T. G. (1949). *Examiner Manual for the SRA Primary Mental Abilities Test*. Chicago: Science Research Associates.

Timmons, R. (forthcoming).

Tizard, B., Cooperman, O., Joseph, A., and Tizard, J. (1972). Environmental Effects on Language Development: A Study of Young Children in Long-Stay Residential Nurseries. *Child Development, 43*, pp. 337–358.

Toguchida, J., and others. (1989). Preferential Mutation of Paternally Derived RB Gene as the Initial Event in Sporadic Osteosarcoma. *Nature, 338*, pp. 156–158.

Tomich, P. K., An, F. Y., and Clewell, D. B. (1978). A Transposon (Tn917) of *Streptococcus Faecalis* That Exhibits Enhanced Transposition During Induction of Drug Resistance. *Cold Spring Harbor Symposium on Quantitative Biology, 43*, pp. 1217–1221.

Trehub, S. (1985). Auditory Pattern Perception in Infancy. In S. E. Trehub and B. Schneider (Eds.), *Auditory Development in Infancy*. Vol. 10: *Advances in the Study of Communication and Affect*. New York: Plenum.

Treiber, F., and Wilcox, S. (1980). Perception of a "Subjective" Contour in Infants. *Child Development, 51*, pp. 915–917.

Trevarthen, C. (1974). Conversations with a Two-Month-Old. *New Scientist*, May 2, pp. 230–233.

Trevarthen, C. (1977). Descriptive Analyses of Infant Communicative Behavior. In H. R. Schaffer (Ed.), *Studies in Mother-Infant Interactions*. Orlando, Fla.: Academic Press.

Tuddenham, R. D. (1948). Soldier Intelligence in World Wars I and II. *American Psychologist, 3*, pp. 54–56.

Twan, Y.-F. (1974). *Topophilia*. Englewood Cliffs, N. J.: Prentice-Hall.

Tyron, R. C. (1940). Genetic Differences in Maze-Learning Ability in Rats. *Thirty-Ninth Yearbook of the National Society for the Study of Education*. Bloomington, Ill.

Ushijima, Y. (1961). Changes in IQ Level. *Jido Shinri, 15*, pp. 629–635.

Uzgiris, I. C. (1972). Patterns of Vocal and Gestural Imitation in Infants. In F. J. Monks and others (Eds.), *Determinants of Behavior Development*. Orlando, Fla.: Academic Press.

Uzgiris, I. C. (1981). Two Functions of Imitation During Infancy. *International Journal of Behavioral Development*, *4*, pp. 1–12.

Vandenberg, S. C., and Johnson, R. C. (1968). Further Evidence of the Relation Between Age of Separation and Similarity in IQ Among Pairs of Separated Identical Twins. In S. G. Vandenberg (Ed.), *Progress in Human Behavior Genetics*. Baltimore, Md.: Johns Hopkins University Press.

Vandenberg, S. J., and Kuse, A. R. (1978). Mental Rotations, a Group Test of Three-Dimensional Spatial Visualization. *Perceptual and Motor Skills*, *47*, pp. 599–604.

Van Giffen, K., and Haith, M. M. (1984). Infant Visual Response to Gestalt Geometric Forms. *Infant Behavior and Development*, *7*, pp. 335–346.

Vince, M. A., and Billing, A. E. (1986). Infancy in the Sheep: The Part Played by Sensory Stimulation in Bonding Between the Ewe and the Lamb. In L. Lipsitt and C. Rovee-Collier (Eds.), *Advances in Infancy Research*. Vol. 4. Norwood, N.J.: Ablex.

Vining, D. R., Jr. (1983). Mean IQ Differences in Japan and the United States. *Nature*, *301*, p. 738.

Vinogradova, O. S. (1970). Registration of Information and the Limbic System. In G. Horn and E. Hinde (Eds.), *Short-Term Changes in Neural Activity and Behavior*. Cambridge, England: Cambridge University Press.

Visher, S. S. (1948). Environmental Backgrounds of Leading American Scientists. *American Sociological Review*, *13*, pp. 65–72.

Vogel, F., and Matulsky, A. G. (1979). *Human Genetics*. Berlin: Springer-Verlag.

Wagner, M. E., Schubert, H. J., and Schubert, D. S. (1985). Effects of Sibling Spacing on Intelligence, Interfamilial Relations, Psychosocial Characteristics, and Mental and Physical Health. *Advances in Child Development and Behavior*, *19*, pp. 149–206.

Walden, T. A., and Ogan, T. A. (1988). The Development of Social Referencing. *Child Development*, *59*, pp. 1230–1240.

Wallace, B. (1978). Restoration of Eidetic Imagery via Hypnotic Age Regression: More Evidence. *Journal of Abnormal Psychology*, *87*, pp. 673–675.

Wallace, I. F., Escalona, S. K., McCarton-Daum, C., and Vaughn, H. G., Jr. (1982). Neonatal Precursors of Cognitive Development in Low-Birth-Weight Children. *Seminars in Perinatology, 6,* pp. 327–333.

Walsh, R. (1981). *Toward an Ecology of the Brain.* New York: Spectrum.

Wapner, S., Hamby, S., and Gardner, H. (1981). The Role of the Right Hemisphere in the Apprehension of Complex Linguistic Materials. *Brain and Language, 14,* pp. 15–33.

Watson, J. S. (1972). Smiling, Cooing, and the Game. *Merrill-Palmer Quarterly, 18,* pp. 324–339.

Watson, M. W., and Fischer, K. W. (1977). A Developmental Sequence of Agent Use in Late Infancy. *Child Development, 48,* pp. 828–835.

Wechsler, D. (1939). *The Measurement of Adult Intelligence.* Baltimore, Md.: Williams & Wilkins.

Wechsler, D. (1955). *Manual for the Wechsler Adult Intelligence Scale.* San Antonio, Tex.: Psychological Corporation.

Wechsler, D. (1967). *A Manual for the Preschool and Primary Scale of Intelligence.* San Antonio, Tex.: Psychological Corporation.

Wechsler, D. (1981). *Manual for the Wechsler Adult Intelligence Scale — Revised.* San Antonio, Tex.: Psychological Corporation.

Weingartner, H., and others. (1983). Forms of Memory Failure. *Science, 221,* p. 380.

Weissmann, A. (1893). *The Germ-Plasm: A Theory of Heredity.* New York: Scribner's.

Weizmann, F., Cohen, L. B., and Pratt, R. J. (1971). Novelty, Familiarity, and the Development of Infant Attention. *Developmental Psychology, 4,* pp. 149–154.

Wendt, R. A., and Burwell, E. (1964). Test Performance of Jewish Day Students. *Journal of Genetic Psychology, 105,* pp. 99–103.

Werker, J. F., and Tees, R. C. (1983). Developmental Changes Across Childhood in the Perception of Non-Native Speech Sounds. *Canadian Journal of Psychology, 37,* pp. 278–286.

Werker, J. F., and Tees, R. C. (1984). Cross-Language Speech Perception: Evidence for Perceptual Reorganization During the First Year of Life. *Infant Behavior and Development, 7,* pp. 49–63.

White, B. L. (1967). An Experimental Approach to the Effects of Experience on Early Human Development. *Minnesota Symposium on Child Psychology, 1*, pp. 201–226.

White, B. L. (1977). Early Stimulation and Behavioral Development. In A. Oliverio (Ed.), *Genetics, Environment, and Intelligence*. Elsevier/North-Holland.

White, B. L. (1981). Education for Parenthood 1981. *Journal of Education, 163*, pp. 205–218.

White, B. L. (1985). New Parents as Teachers Project. Evaluation Report, Missouri Department of Elementary and Secondary Education, Jefferson City, Mo.

White, B. L., Kaban, B. T., and Attanucci, J. (1979). *The Origins of Human Competence*. Lexington, Mass.: Lexington Books.

Whitehurst, G. J., and others. (1988). Accelerating Language Development Through Picture Book Reading. *Developmental Psychology, 24*, pp. 552–559.

Whitehurst, G. J., and others. (1989). *Intervening in Early Shared Book Reading: Scripts Versus Direct Training*. Paper presented at biennial meeting of the Society for Research in Child Development, Kansas City, Mo.

Whiting, J. (1981). Environmental Constraints on Infant Care Practices. In R. H. Munroe, R. L. Munroe, and B. Whiting (Eds.), *Handbook of Cross-Cultural Human Development*. New York: Garland.

Wiener, G. (1970). The Relationship of Birth Weight and Length of Gestation to Intellectual Development at Ages 8 to 10 Years. *Journal of Pediatrics, 76*, pp. 694–699.

Wiener, G., and others. (1965). Correlates of Low Birth Weight: Psychological Status at Six to Seven Years of Age. *Pediatrics, 35*, pp. 434–444.

Wilkins, R. J. (1988). Genomic Imprinting and Carcinogenesis. *Lancet*, Feb. 13, pp. 329–331.

Willerman, L. (1987). *What Adoption Studies Tell Us About Environmental Effects on Development*. Paper presented at biennial meeting of the Society for Research in Child Development, Baltimore, Md., Apr.

Willerman, L., and Churchill, J. A. (1967). Intelligence and Birth Weight in Identical Twins. *Child Development, 38*, pp. 623–632.

Willhoughby, R. R. (1927). Family Similarities in Mental-Test Development. *Genetic Psychology Monographs*, *2*, pp. 235–278.

Wilson, A. C., Bush, G. L., Case, S. M., and King, M.-C. (1975). Social Structuring of Mammalian Populations and Rate of Chromosomal Evolution. *Proceedings of the National Academy of Sciences*, *72*, pp. 5061–5065.

Wilson, A. C., Carlson, S. S., and White, T. J. (1977). Biochemical Evolution. *Annual Review of Biochemistry*, *46*, pp. 573–639.

Wilson, D. M., and others. (1986). Growth and Intellectual Development. *Pediatrics*, *78*, pp. 646–650.

Wilson, E. O. (1975). *Sociobiology: The New Synthesis*. Cambridge, Mass.: Harvard University Press.

Wilson, R. S. (1978a). In F. Minifie and L. Lloyd, (Eds.), *Communicative and Cognitive Abilities: Early Behavioral Assessment*. Baltimore, Md.: University Park Press.

Wilson, R. S. (1978b). Synchronies in Mental Development: An Epigenetic Perspective. *Science*, 1978, *202*, p. 939.

Wilson, R. S. (1983). The Louisville Twin Study: Developmental Synchronies in Behavior. *Child Development*, *54*, pp. 298–316.

Wilson, R. S. (1986). Growth and Development of Human Twins. In F. Farkner and J. M. Tanner (Eds.), *Human Growth: A Comprehensive Treatise*. Vol. 3. New York: Plenum.

Wirtz, W. (1977). *Report of the Advisory Panel on the Scholastic Aptitude Test Score Decline*. Princeton, N.J.: College Entrance Examination Board.

Witkin, H. A. (1962). *Psychological Differentiation*. New York: Wiley.

Wolff, P. (1965). The Development of Attention in Young Infants. *Annals of the New York Academy of Sciences*, *118*, pp. 815–830.

Wolff, P. (1966). The Causes, Controls, and Organization of Behavior in the Neonate. *Psychological Issues*, *5* (17).

Wolff, P. (1969). Observations on the Early Development of Smiling. In B. M. Foss (Ed.), *Determinants of Infant Behavior*. Vol. 4. London: Methuen.

Wood, F. (1983). Cortical and Thalamic Representation of the Episodic and Semantic Memory Systems: Converging Evidence from Brain Stimulation, Local Metabolic Indicators, and Human Neuropsychology. *Behavioral and Brain Sciences*, *6*, pp. 220–221.

Wyles, J. S., Kunkel, J. G., and Wilson, A. C. (1983). Birds, Behavior, and Anatomical Evolution. *Proceedings of the National Academy of Sciences, 80,* pp. 4394–4397.

Yakolev, P. I., and Lecours, A. R. (1967). The Myelogenetic Cycles of Regional Maturation in the Brain. In A. Minkowski (Ed.), *Regional Development of the Brain in Early Life.* Oxford, England: Blackwell.

Yoder, G. E. (1897). A Study of the Boyhood of Great Men. *Pedagogical Seminary, 3,* pp. 134–156.

Young, A., Ellis, A., and Bion, P. (1984). Left-Hemisphere Superiority for Pronounceable Nonwords, but Not for Unpronounceable Letter Strings. *Brain and Language, 22,* pp. 14–25.

Young, J. Z. (1971). *An Introduction to the Study of Man.* Oxford, England: Oxford University Press.

Younger, B., and Gotlieb, S. (1988). Development of Categorization Skills: Changes in the Nature and Structure of Infant Form Categories. *Developmental Psychology, 24,* pp. 611–619.

Zaidel, E. (1983). Advances and Retreats in Laterality Research. *Behavioral and Brain Sciences, 6,* pp. 523–528.

Zaidel, E., Zaidel, D., and Sperry, R. W. (1981). Left and Right Intelligence: Case Studies of Raven's Progressive Matrices Following Bisection and Hemidecortication. *Cortex, 17,* pp. 167–186.

Zajonc, R. B. (1976). Family Configuration and Intelligence. *Science, 192,* pp. 227–236.

Zaslavski, C. (1973). *Africa Counts: The Number and Pattern of African Cultures.* Boston, Mass.: Prindle, Weber, and Smith.

Zborowski, M. (1949). The Place of Book Learning in Traditional Jewish Culture. *Harvard Educational Review, 19,* pp. 87–109.

Zborowski, M., and Herzog, E. (1952). *Life Is with People.* New York: International Universities Press.

Zimmerman, I. L., Steiner, V. G., and Pond, R. E. (1979). *The Preschool Language Scale.* San Antonio, Tex.: Psychological Corporation.

Zweig, C. (1985). The Secret of Einstein Area 39. *OMNI,* July, p. 32.

Zybert, P., Stein, Z., and Belmont, L. (1978). Maternal Age and Children's Ability. *Perceptual and Motor Skills, 47,* pp. 815–818.

✗ *Name Index* ✗

↧ *Subject Index* ↧